FROM THE DOMESDAY BOOK TO SHAKESPEARE'S GLOBE

WARWICK STUDIES IN RENAISSANCE THOUGHT AND CULTURE

VOLUME 1

From the Domesday Book to Shakespeare's Globe

The Legal and Political Heritage of Elizabethan Drama

DOMINIQUE GOY-BLANQUET

BREPOLS

D/2023/0095/62
ISBN 978-2-503-60131-1
eISBN 978-2-503-60132-8
DOI 10.1484/M.WSRTC-EB.5.130699

Printed in the EU on acid-free paper.

Table of Contents

Editorial Note

Quotations from Shakespeare's works are taken from the bilingual *Œuvres complètes*, ed. by Jean-Michel Déprats and Gisèle Venet, 8 vols (Paris: Gallimard Pléiade, 2002–2021).

To avoid confusions of Philips, Williams, Charleses, and Henrys, I use the original names of foreign rulers.

All translations mine, unless otherwise stated.

Plate I. Frontispiece of *Des cas des nobles hommes et femmes*, Premierfait's translation of Boccaccio's *De casibus*, held in Munich, Bayerische Staatsbibliothek, Cod. Gallicus, 6, fol. 2v. Reproduced with permission.

Introduction: Law or Liberty?

To no one will we sell, to no one deny or delay, right or justice.

Magna Carta, 1215

Britain is an island, of determined yet imperfect insularity. The development of law is a European construction, in which England shared before it grew entire of itself, eager to advertise the uniqueness and antiquity of its legal system. No matter how strongly English lawyers and writers asserted their independence from all continental authorities, they had been nurtured by European works, engaged in a long European disputation on the best form of government, exchanging theories, books, ideas, and scholars who circulated them, a point long overlooked in studies of the relationship between literature and law in early modern England. While papacy, empire, and monarchies fought for supremacy, they devised models of government to deal with the main points of tension between *regnum* and *sacerdotium*.[1] Like the Germanic emperors, the kings of France and England employed scores of lawyers to establish their claims to supreme authority against the very model they were aping, Roman *potestas*. In this ongoing contest, memorable figures like Kaiser Friedrich II, Henry II Plantagenet, John Lackland, Saint Louis, Philippe le Bel, Henry VIII, who all resisted papal authority, created precedents and offered models of judicial innovation to their successors.

A significant number of legal exchanges took place across the Channel. Before their ways parted under the pressure of competing ideologies, French and English monarchies were originally one family, with all the love affairs and rivalries Aristotle could have wished for in a good tragedy. The Norman Conquest, still resented by Tudor polemicists like Thomas Starkey as an embarrassment for English culture, or simply denied by the famed jurist Edward Coke, marked a sensitive turning point. France, where the law was 'what pleases the Prince', headed steadily towards absolutism, whereas medieval English legists advocated a form of mixed monarchy. John of Salisbury, Henry de Bracton, John Fortescue, and their successors all firmly placed royal authority under the rule of law. Who made the laws remained a moot point, as the power to legislate gradually moved from the Church to the Prince, then to the people as represented in Parliament, against a background of unwritten laws inherited from a legendary past.

1 Kantorowicz, 'Mysteries of State'.

'The great transformation of medieval ideas took place during the Tudor period', one legal historian claims, and 'the smithy was the Inns of Court'.[2] The term 'smithy', with its modest note of craftsmanship, is appropriate, but the actual transformation had begun much earlier, and in a much larger smithy than the Inns, a point which deserves further study, as we shall see in Chapters 1–3. In fact, several invasions contributed to the development of legal practices. Each wave of foreign immigrants provided a variant opening to the lawyers' epic tale of origins: Danelaw, the Domesday Book, Geoffrey of Monmouth's *Historia*, Magna Carta, or nearer to the Tudors, the exemplary afterlife of Sir John Fortescue, Chief Justice of the King's Bench, who survived the Wars of the Roses and wrote an essay of lasting influence praising the laws of England and their nursery, the Inns of Court.

'How precisely did law "find its way" into literature at the Inns, and what, if anything, did it do there?', Jessica Winston asks — a question, she notes, usually sidestepped by literary critics and historians of the Inns. What was it, to continue her list of queries, that made the Elizabethan theatre unique of its kind in Renaissance Europe and beyond? The legal professional changes no doubt played a part in motivating literary production, but it is other aspects of their interplay, political and artistic, that I mean to study while examining 'these foundational features of the legal, intellectual, and literary life of the Inns'.[3] Where she focuses on the 1560s, I will follow the shaping of legal thought, judicial institutions, and professional theatre in England, both along and at odds with their developments on the continent, from their earliest emergence to the end of Shakespeare's career. Outside the world of jurists, the Inns of Court are famous as the birthplace of Elizabethan drama.[4] Rather than set their productions apart from those of professional playwrights as a distinct literary domain, my own question would be: Why did the Elizabethan theatre begin at the Inns?

The Inns' main contribution to the Elizabethan theatre was less as law instructors than as pioneers in the structuring of the dramatic *agon* and of its rhetorical patterns. It is plain from the records that they also played a major part in the evolution of law under the Tudors, that they both supported and challenged the central government through a corpus of ideas fashioned out of antique, medieval, and contemporary foreign literature (Chapters 4–6). When the playwrights took up issues of sovereignty, counsel, dynastic succession, matrimony, tyrannicide, ancient liberties, providential punishment, or more prosaic matters like usury, inheritance, land property, and taxation, they were participating in debates that had been threshed out for centuries, in and outside England (Chapter 7). Dialogue had a long tradition of educative virtues which the Inns lawyers, trained to defend opposite points of view, practised *ad libitum*, sometimes *ad nauseam*. The *pro et contra* debate remained predominant in the intellectual equipment of the

---

2 Schoeck, 'Aspects of the Inns of Court', p. 41, with reference to Kantorowicz's *The King's Two Bodies*.

3 Winston, *Lawyers at Play*, pp. 10, 20.

4 A phenomenon first examined by Finkelpearl in *John Marston of the Middle Temple* (1969), which I explored in *Côté cour, côté justice*.

English Renaissance, a habit, as Joel Altman has shown, which permeated virtually all areas of intellectual life.[5] The ingrained belief that from a confrontation of opposite ideas truth will out ensured the durability of this mode in political, legal, parliamentary, or dramatic debates. If Shakespeare, the lawyers, and so many of their contemporaries have faith in the power of the theatre to edify, educate, convince by a play of 'seems', it is largely inherited from the practice of the dialectical argument over cases *in utramque partem,* whether in Parliament, on stage, or in a trial court.

The French theatre originally had similar links with lawyers. Before the fraternity of the Inns came into existence, the Parlement de Paris had a society of clerks ruled by a *roi de la Basoche* and his court of officials, who performed mock pleadings, moralities, and satirical plays, until the Valois monarchs that they aimed to instruct found their stage-shows critically irksome and banned them ('Mock Kings and Trials' in Chapter 7). Not so in England, where it is vain to disengage literary from legal practices at the Inns. The programmes of festive occasions on royal visits to the Inns or the universities show no clear distinction between the students' teaching exercises, the scholarly pleadings, and the performance of plays, nor between the authors who wrote both educative texts and entertainment. The rhetoric developed in moots, performed by students discussing an imaginary legal case, the arguments *pro et contra* brought fuel to staged oral jousts. Works authored by lawyers at the crossroads of Mary's and Elizabeth's reigns — *The Mirror for Magistrates* (1555), translations from Seneca (1560), and the first Elizabethan tragedy, *Gorboduc* (1561) — aimed to provide lessons in government. In 1566, *Jocasta,* authored by two inmates of Gray's Inn, gave evidence of their enduring concern for the evils of an unsettled succession. Sovereignty, mixed polity, and the need for counsel remained crucial issues in and out of the Inns throughout Elizabeth's reign. In the prologue to *The Misfortunes of Arthur* (1587), the gentlemen of Gray's Inn are presented as 'politically sophisticated citizen-subjects offering service and admonitory advice to the queen', Curtis Perry observes.[6] As a number of recent studies have shown, they and members of other Inns were far more attuned to Renaissance humanism than has long been claimed and made significant contributions to the literary, legal, and political productions of the 1560s (examined in Chapter 8). In this large intellectual network, Winston identifies over thirty major and minor writers who used writing to argue for the special role of the magistracy in the commonwealth.[7] Some thirty years after *Gorboduc, Misfortunes* shows similar didactic aims, a similar blend of British history and Senecan themes, but, as she convincingly argues, the play appears at a transitional moment in the status of the law and governance. It was a show of resistance to what John Guy has called Elizabeth's 'second reign', marked by an increasing use of her royal prerogative, in contrast with the idealized mixed polity

5 Altman, *The Tudor Play of Mind*, pp. 390–91.
6 Perry, 'British Empire on the Eve of the Armada', pp. 534–35.
7 Winston, *Lawyers at Play*, ch. 2.

of the early years.[8] In Winston's view, even if individually loyal to the monarchy, members of the legal profession imagined it as an alternative polity devoted to the safety of the commonwealth. Whether they did form the nest of parliamentary rebels that would defeat the Stuarts' absolutist leanings remains undecided. Most historians today deny them a leading role in the political thought of the English revolution.[9] However, on the eve of the Civil War, the Inns members made up over half of Parliament, had important links with both Commons and court, and were divided equally between the two camps on the battlefields, up to the point when Parliament upstaged all actors in the commonwealth by crowning itself king a century and half before the French Revolution.[10]

Stage, rehearsal, and other theatrical metaphors came naturally to the main actors of public life. Government members, often themselves former alumni like William Cecil or Nicholas Bacon, were regular visitors to the Inns and watched plays which built arguments over current affairs in attempts to guide State policy. Dramatic productions played an active part in the political agenda, urging the queen to marry, pointing to the best candidate, staging exemplary dialogues that revived heroic or rebellious figures of the past, warning all in high places against the perils of ambition. Along with support and advice, criticism was lavishly delivered, creating tensions that worked both ways: the rising opposition in Parliament to the queen's authority drove her also to the role of a resistant, fighting to maintain her prerogative (Chapter 9).

The Inns' early Elizabethan productions lit the way to the building of permanent theatres in London. The public theatre had not yet given its full measure when Sir Philip Sidney expressed contempt for the barbarity of the English stage and its ignorance of the neoclassical rules established by French and Italian theoreticians.[11] He was right in observing that the Elizabethan theatre turned its back on continental models. This most brilliant offshoot of the legal tradition is an English specificity, the one Tudor production, unlike England's law code, where claims of national independence are fully justified. There is no early modern equivalent on the continent of its unique dramaturgy: free from the constraints of the neoclassical unities, it allowed room for an active participation in matters of legal and political governance.

The British legal doxa is remarkable for a persistent demand from concurrent, often conflicting voices, for both rule of law and ideals of freedom. Royal prerogatives were met by firm requests that kings obey the law, while the Commons petitioned for free speech as the only way to provide 'good counsel'; corporations clung to their 'ancient liberties'; scholars searched foreign sources to free history from political fetters; poets and playwrights searched consciences. Requests for

8 Introduction to Guy, ed., *The Reign of Elizabeth I*, pp. 10–11.

9 Norbrook, *Writing the English Republic*, traces the suppression of the republican element in English cultural history to the 1660 Act of Indemnity and Oblivion.

10 Prest, *The Inns of Court*, pp. 221–24.

11 Sidney, *An Apologie for Poetrie*, written *c.* 1580, published posthumously in 1595.

freedom of speech see-sawed between the theatre and Parliament in the Tudor period, when the theatre grew more adventurous while the sovereigns worked to repress their outspoken Commons. In this mosaic of individual or collective bids for liberty, no one thought yet of fighting for the independence of justice, a lack that appears at its direst in the workings of the Tudor legal machine. Even if fair trial by jury had marked a definite advance on arbitrary procedures, justices and jurymen would seldom dare to exercise their power when matters came to a State trial. Athens in the fifth century BC had seen the simultaneous emergence of public trials, tragedy, and democracy. Another such 'historical moment' took place in Elizabethan England, with democracy still a long way away.[12]

A complex knot of causes concurred to make law, politics, and drama complicit, a long process stretching, I aim to show, from the Domesday Book to Shakespeare's Globe. Among these causes was a need for the government, at various points in history, to advertise or legitimize royal policy, both at home and abroad. One crucial instance under the Tudors was Henry VIII's triple divorce from his Spanish wife, Roman Catholicism, and the European tribe, which occasioned a considerable production of legal quiddities, archival research, and hostile pamphlets. Apart from disrupting the international diplomatic network, the severance of ties with the continent put an end to the traditional forms of theatre connected with religious activities, while encouraging propagandist playwrights like John Bale to advertise the king's good deeds. Another major crisis occurred when the presence of two rival queens on English soil presented a renewed threat of civil discord after the murderous Wars of the Roses. The events leading up to the trial and execution of Mary, Queen of Scots, followed by the victory over the formidable Armada, encouraged a large resourcing of the dramatic repertory in the chronicles of the last Plantagenet reigns.

In the next decade, when the arenas of public policy were kept under strict control, the theatre provided a safer outlet for debate than pamphlets or sermons. Elizabethan historians like John Hayward, the unhappy author of *The Life and Reign of Henry IV*, dedicated to the Earl of Essex and suspected of drawing treasonous parallels with the present, soon learnt as Walter Ralegh would that following truth 'too near the heels' was a perilous exercise. But playwrights could find ways of coding controversial ideological matters to circumvent censorship or retreat behind the subversive, apparently eccentric views of their characters, so that words spoken *in situ* could still pass muster.[13] Even while exercising a great deal of self-censorship, theatre never stopped discussing politics. As did Parliament members: the queen's repeated orders to avoid issues touching *arcana imperii*, 'mysteries of State', are evidence enough that her prohibitions were disregarded.

Miming the contemporary language of orators in courts, Parliament, pulpit, print, the Elizabethan stage drew on layers of political, legal, and religious theories

12 Vernant, 'The Historical Moment of Tragedy', in Vernant and Vidal-Naquet, *Myth and Tragedy*.
13 See Clare, *'Art made tongue-tied by authority'*.

to hold its part in the national debate over the rights and duties of each component. However commercial its origin and targets, the public theatre performs the concerns developed, at rather immoderate length, in the Commons. Seneca, Plautus, Euripides travelled between Parliament and stage via the Inns of Court that moulded William Cecil, Nicholas Bacon, their fellow councillors, and a large portion of the Lower House. The political debate, with its arguments *pro et contra*, its strong moral vein spiced with strong common sense, posturings, and dramatic turns of the wheel, its range of interests from the price of corn to a royal wedding or a royal execution, its language, ruled by architectural symmetry, corporal metaphors, learned quotes, wise saws, and modern instances, has all the makings of the Elizabethan stage repertory. All it needed was an answer to the queen's requests, more matter with less words, and a muse of fire for true artists to shape the material into sparkling blank verse (Chapter 10).

Shakespeare is not the central object of the present study, but he is central to its argument, and references to his plays will be made where relevant. No other writer addressed with such insight the difference between the letter and the spirit of the law, none absorbed so much extratheatrical matter in his thought process. His interest in political representation was 'unparalleled among Elizabethan and Jacobean literary artists'.[14] Going one step further than his contemporaries, Shakespeare unravels the contradictions between appeals to rule of law and ancient liberties, the fallacies of commonly held 'truths', the tensions of conflicting desires. His babes in the wood who seek to escape constraining authorities soon discover that they cannot live up to nature's lawlessness and must return to civilized boundaries. Unlike a revenge tragedy hero, Hamlet refuses to imitate Pyrrhus by acting in hot or cold blood. Isabella, in her plea for Angelo whom she believes guilty of her brother's murder, gives new strength to the value of forgiveness which had degraded into laxity at the onset of *Measure for Measure*, and which staunch Calvinists condemned as 'renegade tolerance'. Cymbeline and his sons reject the narrow insularity and the archaic nostalgias of die-hard Britishers in agreeing to pay tribute to continental culture. The popular crowds of *Coriolanus*, even though manipulated by wily tribunes, show a mature will to exercise their civic duties when called upon to vote: they have evolved a long way, perhaps after much inner debate on the playwright's part, since the depiction of Cade's brutal troops or the Roman mob who tear a poet to pieces.

Significant distinctions have been made between law as literature and law in literature. Law as literature seeks to apply techniques of literary criticism to legal texts, Ian Ward explains, whereas law in literature examines the possible relevance of literary texts as appropriate for study by legal scholars. He extends the field to include law *in* theatre or law *as* theatre, with a special focus on Shakespeare.[15] But this working distinction of today's research in law and humanities does

---

14 Arnold, *The Third Citizen*, p. 10.

15 Ward, *Law and Literature*, ch. 1. His ch. 4, 'Shakespeare Revisited', explores constitutional issues in three history plays.

not properly operate in early modern England. English law made the English stage. Their joint development over the centuries — the subject explored here — owes nothing to 'the voodoo of resemblance' that stigmatizes the new historicists' efforts when they attempt to make 'difficult connections between historical phenomena'.[16] The whole business of law was self-consciously theatrical, and its conflicting demands, under the Tudors' political reversals, potentially tragic.[17] Elizabethan drama is one episode of a long resistance to absolutism, theatre pursuing the war of rival ideologies by other means. As chapters in this book discuss, the growth of this alliance extends from Anglo-Saxon or Norman to Elizabethan England, when lines of exchange run most visibly around 'this tight-knit community of Inns of Court men, Members of Parliament and writers of dramatic poetry'.[18]

Among recent scholars working at the interfaces of law and literature, Jessica Winston has argued that it was the pervasive influence of Inns culture in the 1560s that shaped legal drama. According to Lorna Hutson and Bradin Cormack, the involvement of an increasing number of individuals in the legal machinery had taught Elizabethan audiences to weigh evidence, evaluate intents, and form their own judgement of stage villains or innocent victims. It was this 'evidential awareness' of the public at large that led the dramatists of the 1590s to cultivate a taste for the workings of judicial inquiry: tearing apart Michel Foucault's transition from spectacular to disciplinary power, Hutson advances 'the possibility that the detection of criminality and the right to judge it may have figured in popular English consciousness as, at least in part, the responsibility of the people'.[19] Cormack similarly argues, although along a rather convoluted path, that law found its way into literature through popular engagement with the law, rather than via the Inns.[20] Both have chapters on Thomas More and Shakespeare, as I do, but they tend to leave aside the strong connections tying both these authors with the Inns. However little Greek Shakespeare may have had, the cultural background of his plays is far more extended than a popular 'evidential awareness', and much closer to the intellectual equipment of the Inns inmates.

Rhetoric, which played a prominent part in this equipment, has been fruitfully explored by various scholars. Colin Burrow points out that 'there were many layers to the concept of "antiquity" in Shakespeare's period' and 'a whole range of classical writers' at the source of his structural and stylistic devices.[21] Quentin Skinner concentrates on judicial rhetoric, arguing that Shakespeare's knowledge of classical and Renaissance treatises is extensive enough to qualify some of his

16 Wilson, *Theatres of Intention*, pp. 25–26, quoting Alan Liu's phrase in *Local Transcendence: Essays on Postmodern Historicism and the Database* (Chicago: Chicago University Press, 2008), p. 48.

17 See Biet, 'Law, Literature, Theatre'.

18 Hutson, *The Invention of Suspicion*, p. 8.

19 Hutson, *The Invention of Suspicion*, p. 67.

20 Cormack, *A Power to Do Justice*.

21 Burrow, *Shakespeare and Classical Antiquity*, pp. 241, 247.

works as forensic plays. Shakespeare could quote directly from *Ad Herennium* or from Cicero's *De inventione*, as well as make direct reference to Thomas Wilson's *Arte of Rhetorique*. His protagonists use a large palette of rhetorical utterances, but being principally concerned with judicial rhetoric, and thus 'with the question of how to develop an argument in accusation or defence before a judge', Skinner privileges text over the larger context and legal background explored here.[22]

Elizabethan playwrights who used 'cant legalese' in their dialogues no doubt expected their audience to understand it: 'the currency of the legal language suggests the symbiotic nature of law and the Renaissance theatrical world in which Shakespeare wrote'. Brian Corrigan's aim is to set right 'a history of misconception in the criticism of early modern drama, which cries out for correction and clarification', by selecting just two legal concepts out of hundreds, use and clandestine marriage.[23] A number of other legal concepts will be discussed here, with due attention paid to the origins and history of this symbiosis. What Shakespeare knew of law when he appeared on the London stage was what the collective memory had stored from centuries past, in layers that deserve a closer analysis. Along with this common heritage, as Hutson points out, the participatory structures of English criminal justice, the growth of popular litigiousness, and the bureaucratic entanglements of everyday life ensured that a large variety of legal concepts were familiar to a large section of society, thus leading dramatists to exploit forensic models of narrative.[24] In the wake of her *Invention of Suspicion*, many recent studies stress the growth of participatory justice and the role played by the community in the evolution of the law during the sixteenth century.[25] Not without a touch of demagogy sometimes, for instance when Katherine Attié declares that 'of course, well-educated early moderns routinely denied that uneducated people could judge anything intelligently'. More convincingly, Attié shows that Shakespeare's wooing of his popular audience is 'no mere flattery': he transforms, if momentarily, the 'fool multitude' into a judging audience.[26] To Penelope Geng, English playwrights, including Shakespeare, used the participatory nature of drama to deepen the understanding of and respect for communal justice.[27] Still, one would hardly think of Justice Shallow as a model to imitate.

Shakespeare humanizes the law, through a teeming world of clerks, notaries, scriveners, and their paraphernalia who stand in the margins of his stage. These are dramatic characters first rather than exponents of the law. Only on rare occasions do they come to the forefront to expose a distortion of justice, as does the Scrivener of *Richard III*, or the Lord Chief Justice who confronts Falstaff. What

---

22 Skinner, *Forensic Shakespeare*, p. 48.

23 Corrigan, *Playhouse Law*, pp. 22, 24–25.

24 Hutson, *The Invention of Suspicion*, pp. 11, 45–50, 67.

25 See the essays collected in Curran, ed., *Shakespeare and Judgment*; Geng, *Communal Justice in Shakespeare's England*.

26 Katherine Attié, 'Minds at War in *Henry V*', in Curran, ed., *Shakespeare and Judgment*, pp. 99–100.

27 Geng, *Communal Justice in Shakespeare's England*, p. 98.

they do reflect, like Jack Cade's declared will to 'kill all the lawyers' or Justice Shallow's flexible conscience, is the widespread unpopularity of the judicial personnel, which went at least as far back as Chaucer's corrupt 'Manciple of a Temple'. Equally widespread was the appeal to a superior or alternative form of justice, evidenced among other clues by the success of revenge plays modelled on *The Spanish Tragedy*, in which even the mighty who believed they stood above the law could not escape the righteous avenger. Like Hamlet, Massinger's Roman actor, or Sidney, a majority of playwrights and their audiences believed in the power of the stage to expose hidden crime and cure the realm of its ulcers by unmasking the culprits.

At various points in the canon, the trial court functions as a mirror image of the theatre, exposing at once in conflicting modes its mendacious shows, actors' tricks, denials of justice, along with a rather desperate quest for truth. The first trial staged by Shakespeare, Eleanor of Gloucester's in *Henry VI Part II*, is a mockery of justice, for its actual target is her husband Humphrey, the Lord Protector. Other trials will follow throughout the playwright's career, figuring in a variety of genres, developing complex combinations of motives before plots are unravelled and verdicts reached. Those staged in *The Comedy of Errors, King John, Richard II, The Merchant of Venice, Julius Caesar, Othello, Hamlet, Measure for Measure, King Lear, Henry VIII, The Winter's Tale, Cymbeline* have already received close attention from legal historians and Shakespeare scholars.[28] Yet Hutson diagnoses a lack of interest among them after the 1970s for the mimetic development of English Renaissance drama. Another element that has 'dropped somewhere below the current critical radar',[29] to use her phrase, is its long history of legal mimesis. Elizabethan drama does emerge like a thing new-born, but its legal fabric is woven from ancient shreds and patches. The dialogue form of polemical or didactic pamphlets, the judicial rhetoric, serve to examine age-old concerns, taking up the part of Good Counsel in a healthy body politic.

The Inns playwrights who initiated the Elizabethan legal trend of dramatization had concerns other than private litigation and a larger range of models than has been allowed. We shall see, for instance, that manuals designed for law students could offer more than rhetorical patterns: some of Shakespeare's plots show great similarities with real or hypothetical cases collected in moot books.[30] There is an underlying unity of the Inns' intellectual contributions in varied areas of public life, government, diplomacy, parliamentary legislation, religious oratory, poetry, drama, translation, antiquarian studies which have been thoroughly but separately researched. Thomas Norton's biographer, for one, expresses an interest

28 Apart from those already cited, Richard Weisberg, Daniela Carpi, Anton Schütz, Armelle Sabatier, James Funk, Martha Nussbaum, Eric Spencer, Brian Lockey, Donna Hamilton, Peter Goodrich, François Ost, Richard McAdams, Eric Heinze, Thomas Regnier, Derek Dunne, Richard Helmholz, Kimberly West, Daniel Kornstein, B. J. and Mary Sokol, to name a few.

29 Hutson, *The Invention of Suspicion*, p. 108.

30 See *Readings and Moots at the Inns of Court*, ed. by Thorne and Baker, vol. II: *Moots and Readers' Cases.*

in the lawyer's literary works 'only insofar as they throw light on his political career'.[31] But Norton and his fellows would not have endorsed this division of literature and politics. Evidence of their intersections can be traced in political treatises, parliamentary debates, historical and theatrical texts, and significant contributions at the sources of the legal/historical progress towards England's specific brand of mixed monarchy.

An investigation of this progress calls for a study of exchanges between various modes of addressing public opinion.[32] Current scholarship offers invaluable insights, to which I will return as they intersect with mine. I do not mean to rewrite the well-documented relation of law and theatre but to follow some salient threads in the long history of theatrical dialectics. Among the topics addressed are the formal and rhetorical similarities of dramatic and legal expression; the successive recyclings of polemical pamphlets; the evolution of matrimonial or land law; the political debates over dynastic rights, constitutional theories, and parliamentary privileges. Examining the origins and transmission of legal materials that found their way to the stage will reposition the lawyers and playwrights of early modern England in relation to their broader European heritage. Where a number of valuable essays concentrate on a specific area in a restricted time and space, my own area of study is the legal hinterland of early modern theatre and the traffic between its various modes of delivery, its continuities. They should help restore what the English doxa has studiously ignored or denied for centuries, the successive stages of England's long debate with its European sources, those seeds of the Elizabethan theatrical dialectics which lie buried in the past. 'There is a history in all men's lives | Figuring the nature of the times deceased.'

As Hutson puts it, 'objections to a trans-historical interdisciplinary illusion should not apply to the rich conversations between literature, history and law that have been emerging, for the last twenty years, as each of the disciplines in the triad has refined and rethought the texts, archives, and institutions of early modern England as its object of study'.[33] It is time to repair some of those 'missed opportunities' deplored by Christopher Brooks, 'to consider legal, political and social change over a longer period' than the actual scope of his own volume, 1485–1642.[34] My work owes much to medieval and early modern historians, to researchers of law and literature studies, and in a lesser degree to those Shakespeare scholars who are not guided by a wish to reverse the majority view or 'alter common opinion'.[35] I concur with Subha Mukherji who wisely advises 'close attention to literary texts' engagement with legal facts and perceptions without

31 Graves, *Thomas Norton*, p. 4.

32 Hutson, *The Invention of Suspicion*, p. 2.

33 Introduction to Hutson, ed., *The Oxford Handbook of English Law and Literature*, p. 3. For a concise history of these interdisciplinary developments, see pp. 3–11.

34 Brooks, *Law, Politics and Society*, p. vii. The first chapters offer a clear overview of the political background to the role of law.

35 Patterson, *Shakespeare and the Popular Voice*, p. 1.

occluding the diversity of this relation, or trying to make it fit into an overarching theory about any one aspect of law'.[36]

Most books in this area of study explore in depth a concise corpus over a limited period. Some have offered valuable contributions on the daily business of Elizabethan private law which permeates Shakespeare's plays. Hutson concentrates on the late sixteenth century, Winston on the 1560s, Virginia Lee Strain on the turn of the seventeenth century, whereas Cormack travels through time focusing on one particular theme, the recurrent pattern of invasions on English soil.[37] Quentin Skinner studies Shakespeare's engagement with the '*genus judiciale*' in his Jacobean plays. Luke Wilson and Jeffrey Knapp offer localized readings through specific case studies. I agree with Wilson's view of the theatre as conceptually indebted to the law, but doubt its rather flimsy evidence when he dedicates pages to the meanings of some portentous monosyllable.[38] Similarly Knapp detects numerous messages in the knot of 'seeming contradictions' encoded in *King John,* which 'appears' to follow the Protestant polemical tradition of resistance to popery but also strongly criticizes John.[39] Dermot Cavanagh thinks it was Shakespeare's interest in rumour that shaped his histories and is so focused on the 'challenges presented by turbulent language' that he pays little attention to other main issues of *King John* or *Henry V*.[40] These critics tend to read plays as essays at the expense of their theatrical dimension. Shakespeare may well have infused in one phrase as many layers of thought and intent as various scholars credit him with these days, but one wonders how an unprepared audience, however alert, could possibly have caught, let alone decoded, so many innuendoes in the fleeting moment of a performance. Lukas Erne's answer to this problem is that Shakespeare wrote primarily for readers, then cut his plays for performance before unliterary audiences.[41] Yet it seems unlikely that he wrote plays for lawyers to read and then cut the legal elements on stage. Russ Leo firmly shoves drama, performance, and the spectacular away from his history of tragedy, because their 'deleterious distortions' are prejudicial to tragedy's philosophical precision. Early modern poetics of tragedy were 'preoccupied with questions of causality, freedom, and necessity, that traversed boundaries between art and life'.[42] One can only agree.

Studies which do address theatrical representation as a channel of ideological communications mark a welcome development. Oliver Arnold's masterly *Third Citizen* asks the reader to consider a large number of Renaissance plays as questions and not statements — about love, justice, sovereignty, nature, imagination

36 Mukherji, *Law and Representation*, p. 16.
37 Cormack, *A Power to Do Justice*, ch. 4.
38 Wilson, *Theatres of Intention*, pp. 31–34.
39 Knapp, *Shakespeare's Tribe*, pp. 62, 95–96.
40 Cavanagh, *Language and Politics*, chs 4 and 6.
41 Erne, *Shakespeare as Literary Dramatist*; Erne, *Shakespeare and the Book Trade*.
42 Leo, *Tragedy as Philosophy*, p. 9.

— far exceeding the didactic programmes long advanced by historical critics.[43] Under a title that recalls the subtle scene of the Plebeians' votes in *Coriolanus*, he defines political representation as an effective ideology. However, he pays only scant attention to a parliamentary stance against autocracy built through centuries of actual and theoretical conflict. Similarly, the rhetoric of arguments *in utramque partem* also focused on by Joel Altman in *The Tudor Play of Mind* did not operate in a political vacuum. If the representational ideal was a fallacy, as Arnold vividly argues, it was still no mean prowess, but the outcome of dogged resistance to tyrannical impulses. Shakespeare's Third Citizen plays the necessary link with the audience in perhaps a more active fashion than is usually stressed. In the echo chamber of the theatre, the lawyer-scholar Paul Raffield claims, 'Shakespeare understood and expressed law not as the formal expression of rules but rather as the symbolic representation of *societas*': his plays demonstrate that the ideal constitution for the governance of England 'was predicated on the classical principle of the *pactum*: the equitable social contract between magistrate and citizen'.[44]

A number of deconstructive fashions have come and gone since Roland Barthes proclaimed the death of the author, the latest being Shakespeare as part writer of serials, 'play-patcher', or, in Tiffany Stern's more attractive phrase, 'company wordsmith'.[45] Recent scholarship has produced numerous terms and concepts to analyse the evolution of legal thought and practice in sixteenth-century England — collaborative justice, alternative polity, community building, inclusive public space, invasive bureaucracy, self-serving strategies, agency, whiggish tales, topical politics — all laudably aiming to shift the angle of view. In the shift, the old authorities of French theory — Michel Foucault, Roland Barthes, Jacques Lacan, Jacques Derrida — have been replaced by Carl Schmitt, Jürgen Habermas, Theodore Adorno, Hannah Arendt, Giorgio Agamben, and their followers. I have no major quarrel with their works or those of law and literature scholars. Any specific point of disagreement will be raised as I go.

However historical my own approach, it is important to recognize how the legal and political-theological issues explored in this book have engaged twentieth-century writers. Controversial thinkers like Carl Schmitt, Walter Benjamin, Ernst Kantorowicz, Ernst Cassirer traced the roots of modern contradictions on the nature of sovereignty to medieval theory-making. Arendt herself has exposed our contradictory demands for a national authority both guaranteeing rule of law and ruling above it.[46] To Eric Santner, the immaterial body of the king did not disappear with his execution but continues to haunt us. The logic of sovereignty still administers the fluctuations our flesh is heir to. Those remains owe their second life to the age-old ideal of the body politic: the transition from royal to popular sovereignty records a history of striving towards the establishment of a

43 Arnold, *The Third Citizen*, chs 1 and 5.
44 Raffield, *Shakespeare's Imaginary Constitution*, p. 9.
45 Stern, *Documents of Performance*, p. 111.
46 Arendt, *The Origins of Totalitarianism* (Cleveland: World Pub. Co., 1958), II, p. 230.

viable human community, *politeia,* and from community to State as the institution best designed to guarantee the good life. Its variants — rule of law, mixed polity, commonwealth, or Lupton's *death into citizenship,* that is, the renunciation of claims to distinction — are all opposites to sovereign exception.[47] It is Shakespeare, without recourse to the subtleties of legal speech, who has externalized the metaphor of the king's two bodies, Santner argues. Like Julia Lupton, he hopes to discover in theatrical fictions some truth about our inner lives, 'a glimpse of the substance that sustains their uncanny vitality'.[48] As Jonathan Bate observed in reviewing Lupton's *Thinking with Shakespeare,* every new technique of analysis throughout the twentieth century 'has been tested against Shakespeare. And the test nearly always works. Such is the suppleness of Shakespeare's movement of mind and word that he always proves to be an invaluable tool for thinking with'.[49] This suppleness, I want to show, incorporates the subtleties of legal speech as very much part of the 'externalizing' process. Closer to my object than the Schmittian and anti-Schmittian rereadings of *Hamlet* which have been going strong in recent years (for a full account, see Lupton and Santner), the transition from royal to popular sovereignty, the movement from subject to citizen, does have its roots in medieval theories. Closer to *Hamlet* than the Stuart family plot, the debate on succession both precedes and surrounds its creation.

Delving deeper into the notion of citizenship, the philosopher Paul Ricœur makes the '*citoyen*' the 'ultimate arbiter' as third party between the judge and the historian, one whose gaze is 'diversely educated by judicial verdict and historical inquiry'. 'It is the citizen who militantly carries the "liberal" values of constitutional democracy.'[50] An enlightened public opinion will free the meditation on evil from the awful dilemma between infinite lamentation and disarming melancholy, or worse still between inculpation and exculpation, by placing it under the aegis of promise. The retrospective judgement of the singular event will thus be transformed into a solemn oath to avoid its return. Ricœur put special stress on reception: 'The issues at stake concern memory, no longer as a mere matrix of history but as the reappropriation of the historical past by a memory taught by history and often wounded by history.'[51] A reappropriation shared by Shakespeare's audience when they vibrated with Nashe at the ordeal of 'brave Talbot' or the ravages of civil war in peasant families.

Successive generations of scholars have inferred Shakespeare's ideological stance from his plays, making him move over the whole range of political opinions. Would Shakespeare the common man adhere to an anti-popular myth, Annabel Patterson rhetorically asks, and answers no, refuting the widespread opinion that his attitude to common people ranged from amusement to

---

47 Lupton, *Citizen-Saints,* pp. 121–38.
48 Santner, *Royal Remains,* p. 45.
49 Bate, 'The Playwright's Prescriptions', *Times Higher Education,* 16 June 2011.
50 Ricœur, *Memory, History, Forgetting,* p. 332.
51 Ricœur, 'Memory, History, Oblivion', lecture of March 2003.

contempt.[52] Could Shakespeare the King's Man write as a staunch republican? Yes, in Patrick Collinson's view of Elizabethan England as a collection of village-sized republics.[53] On this topic, I occasionally cross references with their works, without sharing Andrew Hadfield's periodization, nor his belief in a global anti-Caesarism. Shakespeare's political culture has been seriously misrepresented, Hadfield argues. His early plays and poetry suggest that he wanted to present himself as a republican author.[54] This particular brand of republicanism is definitely not an early modern phenomenon but the slow growth of perhaps the oldest seeds of British polity, as will appear from a survey of the law's past history. Most of the ingredients imputed to *Pharsalia*, for instance, Shakespeare could have read in Hall's *Chronicle* or Plutarch's *Lives*. However strong the republican spirit, admiration for the imperial model was equally strong among the humanists, who nostalgically extolled the golden age of Augustus and its dreams of universal *pax romana*.

Shakespeare's dialogues do not necessarily reflect his own private opinions, yet they are certainly true to the range of ideas circulating in his time, ideas refigured and reallocated to antagonists in the theatre. Rather than isolate one voice, popular, republican, regal, tribal, or Shakespeare's own unfathomable views, we need to follow the pattern of thoughts that innervate the Elizabethan *agon*, its steady stream of debates over the issues spanning the Tudor reigns: supremacy, succession, ecclesiastical courts, treason, privileges, and liberties. The points of law and politics discussed here all have resonances in the Elizabethan theatre. Its multitude of opinions is a creative rehearsal as well as a reassessment of discourses held in all areas of public speech, reaching for at least some temporary release to political tensions in the commonwealth, when secular rulers strive to keep the monopoly of law-making with the support of old or new founding myths. The texts quoted to illustrate this process will of necessity be selective, focused primarily on political issues argued in parliamentary debates, polemical pamphlets, staged dialogues, school exercises, and on the trials presided over by State authorities.

The aim of this volume is threefold: to resituate England's struggles for national independence in the larger European context, to study at the national level the judicial conflicts between this native spirit of liberty and the authorities, and to trace their dialectical expression in a variety of dramatic forms prior to the appearance of the Elizabethan theatre. The question of resistance to tyrants runs like a red thread, or red threat, through successive constitutional theories. Justifications for the depositions of Plantagenet kings resurface with the trial of Mary, Queen of Scots, when Parliament members are repeatedly harangued with biblical and historical precedents. Following the evolution of legal and dramatic thought processes as they transit from texts to performances in court, pulpit, or

---

52 Patterson, *Shakespeare and the Popular Voice*.
53 Collinson, 'The Monarchical Republic'.
54 Hadfield, *Shakespeare and Republicanism*.

stage will highlight the elements that set England apart from the rest of Europe and made the Elizabethan theatre unique. Theories significant enough to have been tossed back and forth around the continent will be examined in relation with facts that were common knowledge to Shakespeare and his contemporaries,[55] so common that their origin is all but forgotten. They should help us recover what the playwrights did know, what inherited line of reasoning, what turns of speech and images stood behind their protagonists' arguments, what Shakespeareans like myself have always wanted to know about the Elizabethan cult and culture of law.

The interaction of facts, texts, debates relevant to the Shakespeare canon is narrated in three parts, centred around government, justice, and public discourse. Part I of the book, '*Jus* Uncommon: Freedom of the State', introduces the long history in England and France of legal theories that will continue to exercise the minds of lawyers, governors, and playwrights in the sixteenth century. At the centre of this discussion are the conflicts between *regnum* and *sacerdotium* and their variant treatment across the Channel. Relevant texts and events from Domesday Book to the end of the Plantagenets illustrate how French and English monarchies recycled each other's political, legal, and constitutional theories in their centuries-long struggle with Rome; how early English legists set down the basic principles of mixed monarchy, often using the dialogue form to develop their arguments, and how they dealt with the conflicts of common law and jurisdiction with rival law codes; how European controversies, internal quarrels, legal texts, discourses, and social practices helped fashion the legal system, legal education, and the authority of Parliament, while constructing a pervasive intellectual culture from which Elizabethan drama arose.

Part II, 'Fair Trial: Freedom of Magistrates', reviews the spectacular trials and reversals of the first Tudor reigns; the lawyers' rise to prominence in State business; the battles of books and the precedents invoked in Henry VIII's conservative revolution; the political controversies up to the execution of Mary Stuart; the tragic falls that lent models to playwrights; the circulation of ideas, themes, and figures of speech between Commons, pulpit, Inns of Court, and the stage coinciding with those momentous events. I offer detailed descriptions of the various ways that involved members of the Inns in the Tudor debates over 'imperial monarchy', 'mixed polity', and revisionist histories of civil and common law. These will show how issues, characters, themes, theories, metaphors dramatized by the Elizabethan playwrights follow paths opened at the Inns of Court. Emblematic figures of lawyers-writers and their Senecan patterns pave the way to *Gorboduc* and to Shakespeare's histories.

---

55 Quite a few have already received legal attention, especially around Cardozo School, Birkbeck College, Warwick's *Law and Humanities*, the CERSA of Université Paris-II Panthéon-Assas, and the research team on 'Arts du Spectacle' at Nanterre University, whose main focus, 'Law in Literature or Law as Literature', has evinced fruitful essays on Shakespeare's plays. See the dossier in Presses de Sciences Po, 'La démocratie peut-elle se passer de fictions?', special issue, *Raisons politiques*, 27.3 (2007).

Part III, 'The Conscience of England: Freedom of Speech', moves from the stage's models of legal language, political philosophy, and narrative structures to the enrolment of the theatre under religious/political causes, before radical Protestants who had been pioneers in using the stage as a forum rejected it as an enticement to vice. This section reviews links between early modern English political and legal culture and the representations of new models of commonwealth on the Elizabethan stage, the parallel rise of Parliament where Inns members held a large number of seats and began to cut down the monarch's privileges. I examine their contributions to the establishment of a *via media* between papists and Puritans, to the parliamentary debates on matters ideological, legal, or practical up to James I, with special focus on their intellectual involvement in a wide range of areas, from John Selden's historical research to John Donne's theological meditations, from Nicholas Bacon's navigation guides on a sea of political trouble to his son Francis's and Edward Coke's legal wars. The final chapter, dedicated to Shakespeare's Parliament of voices, will show how the histories and the Roman plays chronicle the emergence of a politically audible popular voice.

Part I

Jus Uncommon

Freedom of the State

CHAPTER 1

Dreams of Empire

Although the victor, we submit to Caesar,
And to the Roman empire; promising
To pay our wonted tribute, from the which
We were dissuaded by our wicked queen.

Cymbeline, V.v

While engaged in the European struggle for autonomy from papal or imperial authority, the medieval English lawyers were busy establishing full independence for a law system no less derivative than their monarchs' agenda. A number of British historians claim that common law shares little or nothing with the *jus commune*, a false friend if there ever was one, that became 'the common coin of European law'.[1] A heated debate revolves today around this coin, which some Italian and German historians would like to erect into a model for developments of European law, and the mythical singularity of the English law system.[2] Britain remains true to itself: at the opening of Parliament 2022, the queen's speech promised that 'a bill will enable law inherited from the European Union to be more easily amended'.

The name 'common law' is ambiguous, attached as it is to a set of rules that stood apart from the European *jus*, the common law of Christendom. Whatever its earliest supporters liked to claim, however original among European law systems, British common law did not spring fully armed from the native soil. It was the mongrel product of a long thought-process in and outside England, which collected material on the way from Sicily, Rome, Bologna, Florence, Paris.... The myth-making industry took a large share in the forging of British independence, and in its revisions of the tale. Medieval and early modern writers worked hard to integrate the fact of the Norman Conquest, with its unpleasant note of submission, into the literary imagination. Geoffrey of Monmouth turned the Roman soldier Arthur into a Briton and avoided mentioning Caesar's invasions of

1 Pennington, 'Learned Law, Droit Savant, Geltes Recht', p. 206.

2 For instance Bellomo, *The Common Legal Past of Europe*. Reinhard Zimmerman, 'Roman Law and the Harmonization of Private Law in Europe', in *Towards a European Civil Code*, ed. by A. S. Hartkamp, 4th rev. edn (Alphen: Kluwer Law International, 2011), pp. 27–54, stresses the vital connection that ties present to past. See also Jean-Louis Halpérin's more sober 'Jus commune: Histoire et Problématique', *Revue internationale de droit comparé*, 52.4 (2000), 717–31.

England. Four centuries later, Sir John Fortescue acknowledged a debt to Roman law but chose to ignore the Conquest and its muscular enforcement of rules, thus strengthening the myth of a common law born and bred on English soil: since Brutus and his band of Trojans, 'the realm has been continuously ruled by the same customs as it is now'.[3] Edward Coke, the champion of this 'ancient constitution', denied that the Normans introduced a foreign legal system in Britain and reversed the proposition by claiming that William the Conqueror, 'finding the excellencie and equitie of the Lawes of England, did transport some of them to Normandy'. In return, 'So taught hee Englishmen the Norman tearmes of hunting, hawking, and in effect of all other playes and pastimes, which continue to this day'.[4]

Early Steps to Singularity

Such founding political legends grew on both sides of the Channel, to find a new life in the nineteenth-century rereadings of the Middle Ages. Augustin Thierry, a renowned historian of the communes, played no mean part in the myth of ancient Anglo-Saxon liberty fighting the Norman barbarians and reviving in parliamentary monarchy. His *Histoire de la Conquête de l'Angleterre par les Normands* treated the confrontation of two peoples as a long dramatic history of violence until both sets of customs and races merged into one nation. In the wake of his favourite guides, the philosopher Saint-Simon and Walter Scott, Thierry wrote from the point of view of the serf: rich Normans and poor Saxons inhabit two countries 'entwined one on the other' yet 'more distinct than if the sea rolled between them. Each has its separate idiom'.[5] As Scott's Wamba complained, we raise the swine, they eat the pork: 'Mynheer Calve, too, becomes Monsieur de Veau in the like manner; he is Saxon when he requires tendance, and takes a Norman name when he becomes matter of enjoyment.'[6] The Romantic rewritings of the Middle Ages revived the spirit of ancient freedom: to young Victor Hugo and his friends, England was the blessed land of *habeas corpus*, and Shakespeare's 'free' genius the incarnation of its resistance to all forms of oppression.

Today, a majority of historians consider the Norman law codes as the true origin of the English legal system, yet some of them remain as nostalgically attached to an idealized vision of the old Anglo-Saxon liberties as Wamba. Like the English language, English law carries traces of its double inheritance, Saxon and Norman. Old England had law courts, a criminal law, and ordeals like *judicium Dei* that the Norman conquerors added to their more sophisticated legal system. According to

---

3 Fortescue, *On the Laws and Governance of England*, ed. by Lockwood, p. 26.

4 Coke, 'To the Reader', in *The Reports*, Pt III, pp. xxi–xxii. All further references to Coke's *Reports* will be to this 1738 edition, part of the George Whyte Collection at the Wolf Law Library.

5 Thierry, *History of the Conquest of England*, trans. by Hazlitt, I, p. xxii (Introd.), and Book VI, p. 324.

6 Walter Scott, *Ivanhoe: A Romance* (Edinburgh: Archibald Constable, 1820), p. 17.

a legend recorded in the annals, William the Conqueror met the men of Kent, led by Stigand, archbishop of Canterbury, at Swanscombe Down and agreed to preserve their ancient laws and customs:[7] these continued along with the Norman feudal system, and through the Gregorian reform.[8] The legend would resurface under the Tudors in William Lambarde's *Perambulation of Kent*, which makes special mention of gavelkind, its ancient system of land tenure, and still inspired the historians Raphael Holinshed and John Speed or the poet Samuel Daniel.[9] As we shall see (in Chapters 5, 9, 10), these as well as Lambarde's *Archeion*, the Antiquarians', and other Elizabethan works would show a lasting interest for both Anglo-Saxon and other early legal systems to serve claims that the religious changes were but a restoration of the primitive Christianity that ruled England before Romish usurpations, or to discuss dynastic rights and various political issues.

Rather than punishing wrong, the first object of early justice was to stop or at least restrain blood feuds. The whole principle of Danelaw, itself a mixture of Old English and Old Norse, was the price to pay for the settling of a grievance, by *wite, wer, bot,* various forms of financial compensation.[10] Among the earliest documents written in the English language, King Aethelbert's ninety Dooms, dated around 600, dealt almost exclusively with monetary compensation payable to victims, the Church being head of the list: 'Theft of God's property and the Church shall be compensated twelve fold; a bishop's property eleven fold'.[11] Its hierarchy is eloquent: compensation for theft of the king's property was a modest ninefold, equivalent to an ordinary priest's. Penalties for physical harm varied with the grievousness of the wound and the quality of the victim: freeman, servant, or slave. A specific price was set for each bodily part: broken tooth, cracked skull, ear torn off, hurt thumb or finger. Personal guilt was not a primary concern; the family of the culprit was collectively responsible for payment of the blood debt to the family of the victim.[12] Nor was intent. It will be centuries before Edward Coke bases his distinction between manslaughter and murder on the notion of *malicia praecogitata*, premeditated malice, in law French, *malice prépensée*. The malicious intent becomes crucial in Elizabethan revenge tragedies, when the arrow, dagger, or poison of the murderer misses its intended target and kills an innocent victim.

Aethelbert's laws, the oldest surviving example of Anglo-Saxon law codes, were part of a body of continental juridic traditions brought over by Augustine,

7 'Statutes of William the Conqueror', in *Select Historical Documents of the Middle Ages*, ed. and trans. by Henderson, from Stubbs's *Charters*, articles 7 and 8, p. 8.

8 Gregory VII's decree against lay investitures and the twenty-seven propositions of the *Dictatus papae* of 1075 establish a papal theocracy based on the Petrine commission.

9 See Holt, 'The Ancient Constitution in Medieval England', pp. 71–72.

10 *The Laws of the Earliest English Kings*, ed. and trans. by Attenborough, pp. 4–17. *Bot*, compensation, *wite*, fine, *wer*, *wergeld*, the price paid to the deceased's kin.

11 *Ancient Laws and Institutes of England*, ed. and trans. by Thorpe, Item 1, p. 3. The *Textus Roffensis*, the only surviving manuscript, dates from the twelfth century.

12 Berman, 'The Background of the Western Legal Tradition', pp. 556–58.

first archbishop of Canterbury, whose mission was to convert the kingdom of Kent to Christianity. Aethelbert's wife Bertha was a Christian, and the great-granddaughter of the Frank Clovis, who had issued the *lex salica* shortly after his own conversion in 496. The Venerable Bede, in his funeral eulogy of Aethelbert, writes that 'among other benefits which he conferred upon the nation, he also, by the advice of wise persons, introduced judicial decrees, after the Roman model; which, being written in English, are still kept and observed by them.'[13] The law books were a Roman gift, marking the new convert's entrance in the family of Catholic kings.[14] As for the Dooms of King Alfred, often considered the source of English common law, they were largely a recollection of older Saxon codes:

> If any one break the king's 'borh', let him make 'bot' for the plaint, as the law shall direct him; and for the 'borhbryce' with five pounds of 'maerra' pence. For an archbishop's 'borhbryce', or his 'mundbyrd', let him make 'bot' with three pounds: for any other bishop's or an ealdorman's 'borhbryce', or 'mundbyrd', let him make 'bot' with two pounds.[15]

In other words, if anyone should violate the king's dwelling, let him make compensation for breaking and entering with five pounds of pure sterling pence, for an archbishop's dwelling, three pounds, etc. Dooms were the judgements rendered by tribal assemblies in the separate realms of England. The *witenagemot*, a group of senior clergy, ealdormen, and leading thegns, met on 5 January 1066 after the death of Edward the Confessor to approve the succession of Harold Godwinson. This would help Edward Coke deny the fact of the Conquest: William had not won the throne with his sword but by election of this assembly. The term 'Doomsmen' survived to designate the *iudices regis*, judgement-finders declaring the royal law, until the establishment of the writ procedure in the twelfth century.[16] A hierarchy of reeves (sheriffs), aldermen, and magnates exercised justice over manors, hundreds, boroughs, counties, and so on.[17]

The collection of *Leges Henrici Primi* around 1115 still specifies the payment of Danegeld, compensations for assaults on the king's highway, ordeals, and fines for the family of an escaped murderer, if the victim is French or Norman (art. 91).[18] The *Dialogus de Scaccario* (*Dialogue of the Exchequer*), written under the reign of Henry II Plantagenet, explains at length why killing 'an Englishman is not regarded or paid for as murder, but only a Frenchman':

---

13 Bede, *Ecclesiastical History of the English Nation*, trans. by Jane, Bk II, ch. 5.

14 Wallace-Hadrill, *Early Germanic Kingship*, refutes the theories of Richardson and Sayles, *Law and Legislation*, who aim to demonstrate that English laws owed little to foreign influence and were promulgated before Aethelbert's conversion. The correspondence with Pope Gregory proves the contrary.

15 *Ancient Laws and Institutes of England*, Doom no. 3, p. 63.

16 Berman, 'The Background of the Western Legal Tradition', pp. 571–72.

17 *Sources of English Constitutional History*, ed. and trans. by Stephenson and Marcham.

18 *Leges Henrici Primi*, ed. and trans. by Downer.

> 'murdrum' means the same as 'hidden' or 'occult'. Now in the primitive state of the kingdom after the Conquest those who were left of the Anglo-Saxon subjects secretly laid ambushes for the suspected and hated race of the Normans, and, here and there, when opportunity offered, killed them secretly in the woods and in remote places.[19]

But one can hardly tell today 'who is of English and who of Norman race', the Master notes: all must be punished equally, excepting of course the bondsmen, *villani*. The Master likewise explains Danegeld, Doomsday, 'What is a Hide, what a Hundred, what a County', the fine mechanisms of fiscus, summonses, writs, escheats, pleas, and covenants, thus making the *Dialogus* a precious adjunct to the *Leges*, and recording the progress made since the Conquest towards centralization and uniformity of the law.

Forest Laws: Royal Violence

> O world, thou wast the forest to this hart,
> And this indeed, O world, the heart of thee.
> How like a deer, stroken by many princes,
> Dost thou here lie!
>
> *Julius Caesar, III.i*

The Norman Conquest had brought few immediate changes in everyday life, John Baker writes, apart from racial discrimination, trial by battle, and 'an alien and oppressive "forest law" to protect the royal hunt'.[20] The lectures collected in Anne Barton's posthumous book, *The Shakespearean Forest*, examine the ancient difference between woods, the untamed wilderness, 'unromantic and harsh', and forests in which law is imposed since the Conqueror, set aside for hunting and juridically delineated.[21] This most arrogant expression of royal prerogative operated outside of common law. That it was much resented at the time appears in a poem, 'The Rime of King William' written in 1087, the year of the Conqueror's death. Portraying the king as a better father to his deer than to his people, it expressed the English indignation against this Norman law and its injustice, the first in a long line of literary protests.[22]

A century later, the *Dialogus de Scaccario* points out that forest laws did not derive from the common law of the kingdom and that whatever decisions were made according to them was not just in the absolute but just only under those

---

19 Fitz Nigel, *The Dialogue concerning the Exchequer*, Book 1, x, in *Select Historical Documents of the Middle Ages*, ed. and trans. by Henderson, pp. 20–134.
20 Baker, *An Introduction to English Legal History*, p. 14.
21 Barton, *The Shakespearean Forest*, ch. 3.
22 Stefan Jurasinski, 'The Rime of King William and its Analogues', *Neophilologus*, 88.1 (2004), 131–44. *The Anglo-Saxon Chronicle*, modern trans. by G. N. Garmonsway (London: Dent, 1953).

laws. At about the same time, around 1184, these rules were codified by the Assize of the Forest. Henry II had knights appointed in each county 'to guard his vert and venison' and placed large tracts of land under forest law.[23] Five articles in Magna Carta aim to restrict the king's right by forest law. A long hierarchy of stewards or bailiffs, foresters, agisters, woodwards, rangers, serjeants-in-fee, surveyors, regarders, purley-men watched over the forest and its purlieus under the authority of the Warden, the chief royal officer. A court of attachment, Woodmote, was held every forty days, presided over by the Warden or his deputy and the verderers, to examine cases and forward them if need be to the Swainmote, held three times a year, or to the court of justice-seat. This, the highest of the forest courts, was held every three years by justices in eyre (circuit of the court between the different royal forests) to inquire into the state of the forest and punish offenders with penalties that ranged from blinding to hanging.[24]

The royal forest, the king's liberty, was not restricted to wooded areas: it extended to any land where deer or other game could dwell and soon grew to include a good third of England. At its peak, Henry III was compelled to grant the Charter of the Forest, restoring a right of access for free men and some protection against aristocratic abuses, which earned it a place among Coke's Charters of English Liberties. In *A Brefe Collection of the Lawes of the Forest* (1592), John Manwood, a barrister of Lincoln's Inn, gamekeeper, and justice in eyre, quotes the *Dialogus de Scaccario*, '*viz. Quia in forestis penetralia Regum sunt, & eorem maxima deliciae*', in defence of the king's right as parallel to the wild beasts' right of sanctuary, in places 'privileged for wild Beasts and Fowls of Forest, Chase, and Warren, to rest and abide there in the safe Protection of the King, for his Delight and Pleasure'.[25] He also frequently refers to Guillaume Budé's treatise on venery, *De philologia libri II* (1532). The copy of this printed work owned by the Bibliothèque nationale has the name 'Lumley' written on the frontispiece. It is set as a dialogue with King Francois Ier, in which the erudite Budé plays the part of the instructor. He explains the technicalities of venery, while persistently extolling the virtues of the Latin idiom, although he admits that French offers a greater wealth of hunting vocabulary.[26] François, like Saint Louis before him, and like Henry V, was an active supporter of the national vernacular (see below, 'Won in Translation' in Chapter 7).

Away from the civilized turmoils of the court, the medieval forest is a privileged retreat where the king inhales the fresh air of natural liberty. At the same time, a number of other claimants enjoy its gifts. Visions of the forest bring up conflicting dreams of freedom. Many sorts of inmates take refuge there from a despotic rule: the oppressed peasants and the king of the wild, errant knights,

---

23 Assize of the Forest, in *Select Pleas of the Forest*, ed. by Turner, pp. cxxxv–cxxxvii.

24 In 1236, they were formally divided between north and south of the River Trent.

25 Manwood, *Treatise of the Forest Laws*, ed. by Elton, I, pp. 206 and 143.

26 Budé's *Traitté de la vènerie* was translated into French from *De philologia libri II* by order of King Charles IX.

poachers, magicians, hermits, fairies, Herne's hunt.... This 'free' space restores energies, awakens man's animal nature, revives his wilder instincts. Its place in Elizabethan drama, from the Robin Hood plays to Shakespeare's Arden and 'hart' puns, would need volumes, none so far having surpassed Richard Marienstras's groundbreaking study of Manwood's treatise.[27] Like other pastoral spaces, the forest reflects the ambivalence of nature and functions like a microcosm of society. Shakespeare's dukes in exile are reminded by sour observers that they do but usurp, that their ideal court away from court is doomed to be short-lived. Justice Shallow who wants to 'make a Star Chamber matter' of Falstaff's poaching awakens little sympathy around him. But runaway lovers who hope to escape rigid laws encounter madness, wood in the wood, before they return with renewed vitality to civilization. *Titus Andronicus* operates the other way round: after the rape and mutilation of Lavinia, the savagery of unrepressed desire in the forest overtakes the Roman city, where it initiates the reign of lawlessness.

The ambivalence of the royal figure appears fully exposed in Manwood's portrayal of the king's 'nature', on the edge of civility. When Shakespeare's kings turn to the forest as a road of escape, their disguise plays up their 'outlawed' status and the savage side of the monarch's double nature.[28] The term 'outlaw' could apply to anyone who rejected the rules of the community, but in practice it meant expulsion beyond the protection of the law. With the process of hue and cry, the Anglo-Norman *hu e cri,* made compulsory in 1285 by the Statute of Winchester, common law suspended its own rules by making the chased thieves or poachers common quarry and did not require any evidence of guilt. After the proclamation of outlawry, Bracton wrote, 'henceforth they bear the wolf's head and in consequence perish without judicial inquiry; they carry their judgment with them and they deservedly perish without law who have refused to live according to law'.[29] Justice suspended itself. A criminal's right to a defence counsel and the adage 'innocent until proven guilty' would have to wait centuries to be adopted.

The trilogy of *Henry VI* unfolds a rich network of hunting images to illustrate the progress of anarchy leading up to the Wars of the Roses. In *Part I,* Talbot was trapped with his troops, 'A little herd of England's timorous deer' assaulted by 'a yelping kennel of French curs', and ended his life with a glorious pun:

> Sell every man his life as dear as mine,
> And they shall find dear deer of us, my friends.
>
> *(IV.ii.53–54)*

In *Part II,* selfless heroism is a thing of the past, the kennel of curs now English in the fierce political games of the court. A chronicled episode of 'Hawking and

27 Marienstras, *New Perspectives on the Shakespearean World,* chs 1 and 2.

28 Goy-Blanquet, *Shakespeare's Early History Plays,* pp. 80–81, 146.

29 Bracton, *On the Laws and Customs of England,* trans. by Woodbine, ed. by Thorne, II, p. 354.

Huntynge' is used on stage to set a trap for Good Duke Humphrey, now labelled by his enemies deceitful fox, raven decked in the plumes of the dove, wolf in a lamb's skin.[30] In both source and play, the hunters pursue human game instead of the wildlife that served as pretext for the chase: denounced as eagle, vulture, hungry kite, Humphrey must be destroyed 'by gins, by snares'. In *Part III*, the realm having lost its strongest pillars, hunter and prey are made to exchange roles in the course of two successive hunting parties. Henry VI is captured by game-keepers — 'Ay, here's a deer whose skin's a keeper's fee!' — Edward IV escapes his guards. In these parallel scenes where the pretenders to the throne exchange places, the king is identified as the game. In Henry's case, the hunt initiates his role as sacrificial victim, whereas Edward regains his freedom and his crown.

Incidentally, this and other elements of progression make it difficult to believe that *Part I* was written after two far more sophisticated plays, even if Shakespeare was only a part author: it shows an artistic will in the masterly selection of material scattered over Hall's chronicle, its main source, but also an unquestioning acceptance of its simplistic moral and political rule — all would be well if England were united against a common peril — which the next parts of the first Henriad will blow to smithereens.

Domesday Book: Royal Government

Law in England, we saw, originally had little to do with right or wrong; it dealt primarily with property. By right of conquest, everything above, on, or under ground belonged to William of Normandy: private occupation of the land was exclusively through a gift of his. The rise of lawyers to prominence, most of them ecclesiastics from the continent, goes back at least to the Domesday Book, a distant ancestor of the *cadastre* (land registry), which required their competence to establish the extent, value, and ownership of landed property. The Conqueror launched this survey to end all quarrels over land while saving the lion's share for the Crown. The result is a map of all landed property, specifying the size, prize, owner, rent value, and easements of every land in the realm, designed to settle any kind of conflict between the king's vassals. A survey so detailed and precise it can specify the presence of 'an eyrie of hawks' on the grounds of Leominster, the number of pigs owned by its villeins, and calculate the total revenue 'except the eels' to a penny.[31] The name 'Domesday Book', the Book of Judgement, only came into use a century later.[32] Its state of the nation is revealing: fewer than 250 people, most of them Normans, possessed the bulk of the wealth. King William and his

30 2 *Henry VI*, III.i, based on Hall, *The union of the two noble and illustre famelies of Lancastre and Yorke* (1548), ed. by Ellis (hereafter, *Hall's Chronicle*), p. 206.

31 The manor of Leominster, which returned to the king at the death of Edward the Confessor's widow, Queen Edith.

32 *Domesday Book*, ed. by Williams and Martin.

family owned around 17 percent of the land, while the Church held over a quarter and the tenants-in-chief 54 percent.[33]

Before common law distanced itself from the medieval *jus commune*, England was very much part of a European pattern. William's conquest shared many features with that of an earlier Norman venture, the conquest of Sicily in 1059.[34] In both cases, the enterprise was approved by the pope, as part of a general policy to win support against imperial domination. Like Alexander II to William the Norman, Pope Nicholas II had given his blessing to the Hauteville brothers' raid on Sicily in exchange for their support, only too happy to see them spend their energy some distance away from the Papal States. Their official mission in Sicily, like William's in England, was to reform their conquered domains, establish justice, and protect the Church. William's knights were proclaimed 'soldiers of Christ'.[35] As bearers of the true faith, they were sent to reform the corrupt churches of England. However, William helped their Christian spirit with more material promises before the Battle of Hastings: 'Fight your best, and put every one to death; for if we conquer, we shall all be rich. What I gain, you gain; if I conquer, you conquer; if I take the land, you will share it.'[36]

The arrangement with the papacy was the germ of endless struggles. From his mission, William I retained the right to appoint bishops, and replaced a majority of those in exercise by Normans, not all of whom had received the pope's blessing. With his chief advisor Lanfranc du Bec, he confirmed the pattern for collaboration with clergymen jurists. The son of an Italian jurisconsult, Lanfranc was reputed an expert in civil law. His lifelong amity with the Conqueror began before the Conquest, by a conflict over a marriage suit. As prior of Bec-Helluin, a renowned abbey in Normandy, Lanfranc had opposed the union of William to Matilda of Flanders on grounds of consanguinity, and been sentenced to exile for his pains, but the quarrel was mended just before he left. Eventually he managed to obtain the needed dispensation to the marriage from Pope Alexander II, who happened to be one of his former pupils, and had the interdict over Normandy removed. Lanfranc was soon rewarded by William with the seat of Canterbury, acting as vice-regent in the king's absence. And it was Lanfranc who organized William's peaceful succession by his son William Rufus (1087–1100).[37]

The union of Church and law became proverbial under Rufus: *nullus clericus nisi causidicus*. The cooperation between prelates and sovereigns continued in England with great efficiency through the Middle Ages, down to Wolsey's chancellorship and his dismissal. Bishops versed in law regularly took part in the royal governments. Their competence ignored frontiers, meaningless by definition in

33 Poole, *Domesday Book to Magna Carta*, vol. III.

34 See Douglas, *The Norman Achievement*.

35 See Berman, *Law and Revolution*, pp. 435–36.

36 Thierry, *History of the Conquest of England*, III, p. 175.

37 Orderic Vitalis, *Historiae ecclesiasticae*, VII, XVI, ed. by Le Prévost, III, pp. 244–56. See Barlow's modern biography, *William Rufus*.

a unified Christendom. However, parallel with this collaboration, there begins a long history of conflicts between English monarchs and their leading prelate, the Archbishop of Canterbury, who officially represented an alien power in the realm. The dispute between Henry II and Thomas Becket was but a continuation of the perennial tussle between monarchy and papacy. Under the Tudors, John Bale, author of a lost play on Becket in 1538, the year of the official process against the martyr,[38] would launch a fierce attack on Lanfranc and his successor Anselm of Canterbury for having brought into England the novelties of Popes Sylvester and Gregory VII: the 'relygyon of the clergy was none other in those dates, than a very treason or utter betrayeng of the worldly governors'.[39] The same Sylvester would repeatedly pop up in Tudor controversies for his alleged role in the Constantine Donation (see below, 'Clashes of Jurisdictions').

After Lanfranc's death, the Lombard Anselm, then prior of Bec, was considered his natural successor to the see of Canterbury, but Rufus left it vacant for four years, adding the revenues to his treasury with the help of 'a most cruel extortioner', Ranulf Flambard, who wrung the kingdom even to the drawing of blood: while Anselm dragged 'a weary existence in exile beyond sea, mercy and truth with him had taken to flight from out of the land, and justice and peace had been banished therefrom'.[40] *Terras Astrea reliquit*. Rufus was set on retaining full control over ecclesiastical affairs, not to mention Church lands, while Anselm supported the Gregorian reforms and their guiding motto, freedom of the Church. The Investiture Controversy was in full swing on the continent. Chancellor Lanfranc had stood fast by his sovereign, resisting all papal attempts to scare or seduce him. When Anselm went to Rome in 1097, Rufus forbade him to return to England and kept him in exile to the end of his reign.

After Rufus's unpopular rule, Henry I Beauclerc (1100–1135), fourth son of the Conqueror, earned praise from contemporary chroniclers as an inflexible administrator of justice. The *Leges Henrici Primi*, an anonymous compilation composed in the eighteenth year of his reign, was the first book written in the West to describe a secular legal order. It followed the tradition of Penitentials in emphasizing the fact that English law prefers *amicitia*, friendly settlement, to *judicium*, litigation, its main concern being to preserve the peace. It reappears for instance in the practice of 'love-days', evoked by Chaucer's Friar, when disputes were submitted to friendly arbitration rather than expensive lawsuits:

38 See W. T. Davies, 'A Bibliography of John Bale', *Proceeedings and Papers*, 5 (1940), 209–11.

39 Bale, *The First Two Partes of the Actes of the Englyshe Votaries*, II, fol. [H.vi^{v}], in Levy, *Tudor Historical Thought*, p. 91.

40 Peter of Blois, in *Ingulf's Chronicle*, trans. by Riley, p. 229.

In love-dayes ther koude he muchel helpe,
For ther he was nat lyk a cloisterer,
With a thredbare cope, as is a poore scoler,
But he was lyk a maister or a pope.

(Prologue, 258–61)

Where Henry Beauclerc had worked towards centralization, his successor Stephen of Blois (1135–1154) languidly gave in to opposition, much of his energy being spent in fights with Beauclerc's daughter, Matilda, who claimed the throne as hers by right of inheritance. Despite constant warfare, Stephen managed to keep his crown to the end by designating Matilda's son Henry as his heir, but he allowed the Church much judicial latitude, at the cost of his own authority, and signally failed to impose order on his barons. Nor did he escape conflicts with the papacy, particularly over the appointment to the see of York. When Pope Eugene III summoned the bishops to a council at Reims in 1148, Stephen forbade them to go and had all the ports closed. Theobald, the archbishop of Canterbury, managed to slip through with his clerk, Thomas Becket, and was banished in retaliation. After many ups and downs he was back in office to negotiate the Treaty of Wallingford which secured the succession of Henry of Anjou, and the appointment of Becket as chancellor. This, and the new king's personality, would have long-term consequences.

After Stephen's 'Anarchy', a number of major changes were made under Henry II's reign (1154–1189). The Constitutions of Clarendon (1164) were presented as a revival of old customs, franchises, and privileges collected by his grandfather Beauclerc, approved at the time by both nobility and clergy, and lost in the ensuing disorders of Stephen's misrule. Trial by jury became the norm at the Assize of Clarendon, against the trial by ordeal or wager of battle. This is where French and English judicial systems took different ways, Hutson points out, the French extending the Roman canon law system of inquisition to extract confessions from suspected criminals, the English relying on evidence and testimony in an open, participatory, adversarial trial.[41] Actually, despite the unpleasant later associations of the word, 'inquisitorial' procedures, which involved judicial enquiry to determine the facts of a case, were an improvement on hearsay or dubious reports.[42]

To Frederick Maitland's school, Henry II's legislative reforms were resolutely anti-feudal and anti-baronial. But to Milsom's, their aim was to make the law courts more efficient: the end results, the undermining of the lords' authorities over their tenants, were unlooked for,[43] a variant of today's major issue in historical disputes, functionality versus intentionality. Whether a royal monopoly

41 Hutson, 'Rethinking Foucault', in *The Invention of Suspicion*, pp. 70–73.
42 Kelly clarifies the procedure in 'Thomas More on Inquisitorial Due Process', pp. 853–62.
43 Milsom, *The Legal Framework of English Feudalism*, pp. 175–87.

introduced by the Normans or an Old English custom they adopted, Henry II's innovations thoroughly upset the feudal structure.[44] A similar judicial evolution takes place between Acts I and IV of Shakespeare's *Richard II*. Richard interrupts the trial by combat from a fear that God's judgement will reveal his own responsibility in the murder of Woodstock. The usurping Bolingbroke, even before he is duly crowned, presides over a brisk, wholly secular, trial of his cousin's supporters.

Likewise, the ordeal of an armourer's servant plays a pivotal role in 2 *Henry VI*: from Holinshed's account, it is an obsolete, inefficient form of justice, for the armourer, hampered by an excess of drink, 'was slaine without guilt. As for the false seruant, he liued not long vnpunished; for being conuict of felonie in court of assise, he was iudged to be hanged'. A marginal note sums up the lesson: 'Drunkenese the ouerthrow of right and manhood'.[45] Hutson misreads me when she states that I believe it 'intended to prove the immanence of God in human affairs', and misses the point of Shakespeare's rewriting: the play reverses the chronicles' 'overthrow of right', instead of exposing, as she claims, the inadequacy of the trial by combat system or lending plausibility to the charges against Humphrey.[46] On stage, wine takes sides with divine justice: the Armourer is truly guilty and confesses his treason. The dialogue offers two explanations of this unexpected dénouement. For the pious Henry VI it shows the workings of Providence:

> Go, take hence that traitor from our sight,
> For by his death we do perceive his guilt,
> And God in justice hath reveal'd to us
> The truth and innocence of this poor fellow.
>
> *(II.iii.95–98)*

As for York, he advises the servant to 'thank God, and the good wine in thy master's way'. Despite Hutson's partiality to civic modes of justice, Warwick's 'positioning of the commons as a kind of jury' does not yet promise greater equanimity when they burst in to the cries of 'An answer from the king or we will all break in', a prologue to Jack Cade's attacks against the legal system.[47]

---

44 H. Brunner, *The Sources of the Law of England: An Historical Introduction to the History of English Law*, trans. by W. Hastie (Edinburgh: T. & T. Clark, 1888), II.2, pp. 16–31. Douglas, *William the Conqueror*, p. 309. To Sutherland, *The Assize of Novel Disseizin*, pp. 20–21, Roman law, canon law, and English administrative practice all played a part in the sources of the assize.

45 *Hall's Chronicle*, pp. 207–08. *Holinshed's Chronicles*, ed. by Ellis (citations throughout are to this edition), III, p. 210.

46 Hutson, *The Invention of Suspicion*, pp. 248–49.

47 Hutson, *The Invention of Suspicion*, p. 245. 2 *Henry VI*, III.ii.

Recording Demons: Clerical Teachings

Tutivillus, the devil of hell,
He writhes har names, sothe to tell
Ad missam garulantes.

Anonymous poem, fifteenth century

Anselm of Canterbury, sometimes hailed as the Scholastic Doctor, has another claim to our interest as a forerunner of legal education and his use of the dialogue form as best suited to his purpose. Most of his treatises adopt the Socratic method of question and answer that would be standard practice in the forthcoming schools of law and theology down to Aquinas. The model came from Alcuin (Albinus), who wrote several educational books set as dialogues, two of them between himself and his pupil Charlemagne. In *Cur Deus Homo*, Anselm answers the questions of his student Boso about the wages of sin, stressing the symmetry required between fault and reparation.[48] The student, rather a timid antagonist, does argue that God could have forgiven man out of his mercy. No, the master answers, evil cannot be allowed to triumph, nor God's charity to overwhelm his justice. Man cannot repay the debt of his sin; he needs to be redeemed. Only Christ's voluntary death can bring atonement. Since men have continued to sin under the new contract, human law is necessary to judge them.[49] Anselm's legalist attitude was abundantly echoed in the secular sanctions provided by the penitentials of his time.[50] Traces of their symmetries will remain in the morality plays, with their rituals of confession, penance, and absolution, which Robert Potter sums up as a kind of penitential theatre.[51] After the Reformation, they would also inspire Christopher Saint-German's dialogue on the Church's jurisdiction, *Doctor and Student*, between a university doctor of canon law and an Inns of Court student of common law, as we shall see below ('King's Printer' in Chapter 5).[52]

Most historians of early English drama place at the source of morality plays a lost Pater Noster play, possibly designed like a *psychomachia*, which is mentioned in the vernacular version of Wycliff's *De officio pastorali* (*c.* 1398): 'herefore freris han tauȝt in englond þe Pater Noster in engliȝsch tunge, as men seyen in þe pley of ȝork' (friars have taught in England the Pater Noster in English tongue, as they say in the play of York).[53] From other records, it condemns in turn the

48 Anselm of Canterbury, *The Major Works*, ed. by Davies and Evans, pp. 260–356.

49 Anselm, *Cur Deus Homo*, I, ch. 3, trans. by Fairweather as *Why God Became Man*, in *The Major Works*, pp. 268–69.

50 Berman, 'The Background of the Western Legal Tradition', p. 584.

51 Potter, *The English Morality Play*, p. 16.

52 Hutson, *The Invention of Suspicion*, pp. 21–22.

53 Anna E. Gotschall, 'The *Pater Noster* and the Laity in England, *c.* 700–1500' (PhD diss., University of Birmingham, 2014), ch. 6, p. 137.

Seven Deadly Sins, each cured by a corresponding petition in the Lord's Prayer.[54] In illustrations of vernacular texts, and allegorical paintings in churches, a Tree of Vice, its trunk or crown Pride, each branch one of the Deadly Sins, stood opposed to a Tree of Virtue loaded with good fruit. This tree showed to unlearned people the symmetries of the penitentials. Tutivillus the recording demon first appears around 1285 in John of Wales's *Tractatus de poenitentia*. In the Towneley play *Judgment* he claims to have 'Yit of the synnes seven | Somthyng special', and names four:

> Of ire and envy
> Fynde I herto,
> Of covetyse and glotony
> And many other mo.[55]

Lorna Hutson has a rich chapter on the coincidences of 'so-called morality plays' with the Church's penitential jurisdiction: for instance, 'Both *Mankind* and *Jacob's Well* imagine the criminal procedures of the mid-fifteenth-century common law as just such a devilishly inflexible machinery of condemnation, a path to "Myscheff" as opposed to the "Mercy" of the sacrament of penance.' Some 150 years later, 'a seismic shift in the relative powers of the spiritual and temporal jurisdictions had taken place'.[56] Potter notes the same fusion of didactic and penitential aims in a French *Moralité des Sept Péchés Mortels et des Sept Vertus* which he identifies as the missing link with fifteenth-century morality plays in England: Lucifer, '*Li Maistre Dyable*', has a clerk record the evidence to be used in the Last Judgement against the Sins.[57] The imagery will continue to inform Edmund Dudley's *Tree of Common Wealth* and Dekker's *Seven Deadly Sinns of London*, while Greedy-gut in *The Trial of Treasure* may well be a distant ancestor of Falstaff.[58] The tensions of Justice and Mercy, dramatic combats between vices and virtues, as well as trial scenes, were a frequent feature of moralities and of Tudor interludes. As for Lucifer, 'son of the morning', 'fallen angel', he would give birth to the ambiguities of the free spirit on the Elizabethan stage and beyond.

In laying the bases of ecclesiastical justice, churchmen put a new emphasis on the sacraments of confession, eucharist, and extreme unction, which opened new hopes of atonement.[59] It is no coincidence if the doctrine of purgatory developed in the course of the twelfth century: until then, the Last Judgement had allowed no way of escape between salvation and damnation, no extenuating circumstances

---

54 See Johnston, 'The Plays of the Religious Guilds of York'.

55 *Judgment*, no. 27 in *The Towneley Plays*, ed. by Epp, ll. 443–44, 482–85.

56 Hutson, *The Invention of Suspicion*, pp. 34, 43.

57 Potter, *The English Morality Play*, pp. 25–29.

58 Anderson, *Drama and Imagery in English Medieval Churches*, p. 69.

59 Peter Lombard, *Sententiarum Libri Quatuor*, ed. by J.-P. Migne, *Patrologiae cursus completus, series Latina*, 192 (Paris: Garnier, 1855), cols 1089–1111, listed seven sacraments, the three above plus baptism, confirmation, marriage, and ordination.

or possibilities of expiation on earth; the debt must be paid in full in the world beyond. Purgatory, or to quote Jacques Le Goff, 'the projection into the afterlife of a highly sophisticated legal and penal system', offered a new way to settle debts incurred on earth through the frailty of the flesh.[60] Personal responsibility and intention to do harm became important factors in establishing the degree of guilt, not just the victim's prejudice. Since the world was so much in the devil's power, there was little hope of living a flawless life: even holy Bernard de Clairvaux was expected to spend some time of penance in the middle place. The ghost of Hamlet's father may be held there, but Stephen Greenblatt feels that Purgatory must seem 'a vast piece of poetry' to the Protestant Hamlet when he directs the King's messenger to seek dead Polonius 'i' the other place' if he cannot be found in heaven.[61]

Following the invention of purgatory, models for sermons appeared in the thirteenth century, using a large variety of sources. Some three thousand *exempla* are collected in the *Tractatus* (*c.* 1250) of the Dominican Étienne de Bourbon. His warning against the pains of Purgatory, 'timenda est pena purgatorii propter paucitatem subeuenientium', introduces the story of King Leyr's three daughters which he read in *Historia Brittonum*. The moral of it is that men are loved and feasted when their hands are full of riches. 'Cum non habent res, cessat amor.'[62]

The apocalyptic hymn *Dies irae*, also written in the thirteenth century, dramatized the conflict of justice and forgiveness, which would be reconciled at the end of times in the divine judgement:

> Judex ergo cum sedebit,
> quidquid latet apparebit:
> nil inultum remanebit.
>
> > (When the Judge his seat attaineth,
> > and each hidden deed arraigneth,
> > nothing unavenged remaineth.)[63]

New theories of redemption brought about a progressive shift from transcendence to immanence, from the almighty power of God the Creator to the humanity of Christ the Son, from the Church as a community of saints in heaven to a community of sinners on earth. It was Lanfranc who defended the theory later known as transubstantiation,[64] the real presence of Christ's body in the Host,

---

60 Le Goff, *The Birth of Purgatory*, p. 5.

61 Greenblatt, *Hamlet in Purgatory*, ch. 1.

62 Étienne de Bourbon, *Tractatus*, I, CXXIV, *Capitulum* 6, pp. 163, 166, *exemplum* procured by Françoise Gomez, 'Une source retrouvée de la légende du roi Lear', Ministère de l'éducation nationale et de la jeunesse, 14 November 2021,<https://odysseum.eduscol.education.fr/une-source-retrouvee-de-la-legende-du-roi-lear>.

63 This English version, translated by William Josiah Irons in 1849, appears in the English Missal.

64 Lanfranc's view of the Eucharist, expressed in his *De corpore et sanguini Domini* (1079), received the name transubstantiation at the Lateran Council of 1215.

against the abbot Bérenger de Tours (Berengar), for whom there was no miracle of the Eucharist: bread was bread and remained so after the elevation. The question would hold a central place in early modern Protestant debates. To Anselm, Christ's incarnation was the only rational way to redeem man from his debt of sin. This was the main point of division between East and West: the Eastern Church never accepted the addition to the Christian creed of the *filioque* clause that made the Holy Spirit proceed from the Father through the Son, where the original text of the Nicene Creed said 'ex Patre procedit'.[65] Byzantine liturgy and iconography celebrated Christ's resurrection and victory over death; Western theology stressed his crucifixion and victory over sin, placing his vulnerable humanity at centre stage.[66]

Clashes of Jurisdictions

> Anon as *Constantine* left *Rome*, for *Greece*, to *Sylvester*,
> (So cal'd of liuing in the Woods, whence earst he durst not ster)
> For consecrating after. Popes they golden Rites prefer,
> And, hansling *Rome* with Heresies, in factious Schismes did erre.
>
> *William Warner, Albions England, Book XII, Chapter 75*

In the struggles for national independence, the fight for supremacy raged between spiritual and temporal governors. Debates revolved around the central issue: Who made kings or emperors? Who made priests and bishops? There were kings before there were priests, the saying went, and emperors before popes.[67] For a while, a decree of William the Conqueror having asserted the king's right to make canonical laws himself, England escaped the quarrel of investitures that inflamed all Europe.[68] In 1106, Henry I Beauclerc renounced the privilege to choose bishops but retained his right to *hominium*, the homage paid by the prelates. On the continent, the Concordat of Worms reached a similar compromise, dividing temporal from spiritual goods, and laid the basis of a *regnum teutonicum* by establishing the imperial bishoprics as elective fiefs of the empire.

The struggle for power between papacy and empire, the great serial story of the Middle Ages, shows a resolute progress towards papal supremacy, while monarchies strove to liberate themselves from both these authorities. The quarrel over temporal jurisdiction would be frequently rekindled, down to John Donne's

65 Charlemagne altered the Nicaean Creed in 809 by adding to the phrase the clause '*filioque*' at the Masses celebrated in his chapel. Its inclusion in the liturgy of Rome caused the schism between Eastern and Western Church. See Berman, *Law and Revolution*, pp. 105, 581 n. 26, 596 n. 28.

66 Berman, *Law and Revolution*, pp. 168–72.

67 John of Paris's view in *De regia potestate et papali*, written during the conflict between Bonifacio VIII and Philippe le Bel.

68 See Honoré, *Emperors and Lawyers*. Cheney, *The Papacy and England*.

arguments against the Jesuit Bellarmine under James's reign (see below, Chapter 10). The medieval legend of Empire begins with Charlemagne, emperor of the Franks, whom his biographer Eginhard presented as the thirteenth Caesar after Suetonius's twelve.[69] In the high Middle Ages, as God's representative, the emperor was the spiritual leader of all Christendom, while the pope was only Saint Peter's substitute. Aquinas reasserted the theory of two distinct powers, *regnum* and *sacerdotium*, both held from God, but made no clearer division between their areas of authority, leaving food for endless arguments to medieval political theorists. Most subsequent works refer to Aquinas's definition of the four laws — eternal, divine, natural, human — in his *Summa theologica* (Question 91), and his views of *aequitas* in his commentaries on *The Nicomachean Ethics*. His greatest admirer, Dante, praised him for having reconciled Aristotelian philosophy with Christian faith and placed him with the souls of the wise in the fourth sphere of *Paradiso*.[70]

Popes were designated by the emperor, and could be similarly deposed, until the election of Hildebrand as Gregory VII by popular acclaim in 1073. Within two years of his election his *Dictatus papae* ruled that only the pope could make new laws, he alone had the right to depose bishops and, if need be, kings and emperors.[71] His declaration of authority over the community of Christians, allegedly a return to the legitimacy of Saint Peter's rule, was in fact a complete break from tradition. Heinrich IV had the Council of Worms depose him and was excommunicated in retaliation. The next step was Canossa, where his subjects were relieved from their allegiance, and the penitent emperor was kept standing barefoot in the snow for three days to await his pardon. Five hundred years later, Pius V's bull would call Elizabeth's subjects to open rebellion in hopes of reviving this precedent. Reviewing the full history of the struggles over papal authority in *Pseudo-Martyr*, the poet John Donne recalls the submission of Friedrich Barbarossa, when Pope Alexander III had said, 'treading upon Fredericke, *Super aspidem & Basiliscum ambulabis*', an act which a servile bishop commended as 'lawfully and worthily done'.[72]

In all Western countries including England, Church jurisdiction over land was subordinated to secular jurisdiction.[73] But the Church, as one of the main landowners in Christendom, still had a say in all questions of rights and duties touching property. Bernard de Clairvaux's 'mirror for popes', *De consideratione ad Eugenium papam*, set them an overall spiritual mission and recommended that they leave the cares of the world to reigning monarchs. Popes should not spend time judging squabbles over contemptible goods: 'Why should they not scorn to

69 Durand-Le Guern and Ribémont, *Charlemagne, empereur et mythe d'Occident*, p. 23.

70 In Canto x, ll. 94–99, Aquinas meets his two masters, Saint Dominic, the founder of the order, and Albert the Great. Aquinas answers Dante's questions, xiii, ll. 1–51.

71 *Dictatus papae*, in *Select Historical Documents of the Middle Ages*, Dictate 12.

72 Donne, *Pseudo-Martyr*, ed. by Raspa, p. 82.

73 Berman, *Law and Revolution*, pp. 237–40.

give judgement concerning men's poor earthly possessions, seeing that they shall judge heavenly things, and angels too? Your jurisdiction, therefore, is over criminal cases, not over property.'[74] But Gregory VII's successors, with instruments devised to assert papal authority, generally managed to bow recalcitrant monarchs to their superior will.

With papacy on the ascendant, several emperors were deposed and realms kept for years under interdicts. Philippe Auguste in France, Henry II and John in England all had to surrender. But the pope's rebellious children did not submit without fight; indeed they used his very models of authority against him. Kantorowicz agrees with Maitland that eventually 'the nation stepped into the shoes of the Prince', yet he adds one qualification: 'Not before the Prince himself had stepped into the pontifical shoes of Pope and Bishop.'[75] Ironically enough, the popes' construction of *plenitudo potestatis* provided models of sovereignty and emancipation to the emerging nation-states. The *curia regis* and its governing branches were replicas of the Roman Curia.

Medieval controversies between empire, Church, and monarchies revolved around the Donation of Constantine. According to a document long believed authentic, on leaving Rome for his new capital Byzantium, Constantine transferred his authority over Italy and the Western provinces to Pope Sylvester, who had cured him of leprosy, and to his successors. Charlemagne confirmed the Donation, augmenting it with the Patrimony of Saint Peter, lands reconquered from the Lombards. The forged document got included in decretals of the ninth century, forming the basis for all the papacy's future territorial and jurisdictional claims. Its validity in law was soon questioned by theologians who denied the emperor a right to give away what was in his trust. Discussions over which lands were part of the Donation involved genealogies as long-winded and spurious as the archbishops' in *Henry V*. Philippe le Bel's jurists claimed that France had never been part of the Donation, and thus stood outside the pope's authority anyway. Dante believed Constantine's Donation was genuine but considered it invalid: the emperor cannot divide the empire, since his office is to hold humankind under one rule. The popes were committed to the third circle of hell as guilty of simony, causing the poet to exclaim: 'Ah Constantine! of how much ill was mother | Not thy conversion, but that marriage dower | Which the first wealthy Father took from thee!'[76]

Various imperial propagandists after Dante questioned the legitimacy of the Donation. William of Ockham openly doubted its authenticity. The philological examination of Lorenzo Valla would establish the document was a fake, written in clumsy medieval Latin some four hundred years after Constantine's death. The

---

74 Bernard de Clairvaux, *On Consideration*, trans. by Lewis, I, vi, 7, 25. *De consideratione*, written between 1149 and 1152, is a piece of advice addressed to Pope Eugene III.

75 Kantorowicz, 'Mysteries of State', p. 67.

76 *Inferno*, xix, ll. 115–17, in Dante, *The Divine Comedy*, trans. by Longfellow. Bonifacio is also satirized in Boccaccio's *Decameron*, Day i, tale 1 and Day x, tale 2.

De falso credita et ementita Constantini donatione declamatio (1440) was printed in 1506 and made widely known by the editions of Ulrich von Hutten in 1517–1518, the year of Luther's ninety-five theses. It was first translated into English under Henry VIII, several years before he had any thought of divorce, and later included in Cranmer's *Collectanea satis copiosa* to prove the pope's usurpation of his sovereignty.[77] The forged Donation features in Thomas Kirchmeyer's *Pammachius* (1538) to signify the original corruption of the papacy and the empire under Julian the Apostate. The play would raise a fierce controversy when performed at Christ's College, Cambridge in 1545 (see below, Chapter 7).

Stupor mundi: *Kaiser Friedrich II* v. *Innocent III*

The conflict between *regnum* and *sacerdotium* raged around Europe for centuries. Gregory VII had declared that only the pope could make new laws, 'appropriate to the needs of the times':[78] the *jus antiquum* must be integrated into the *jus novum*, the living body of decretals. In the wake of this revolution, a large work of canonical collections was taking place on the continent, in Rome, and in the workshops of Yves de Chartres. On a similar model, Lanfranc constituted his own collection of canons,[79] which became the code of reformation in England, and launched another innovation that William of Normandy's successors would bitterly regret, the creation of independent ecclesiastical law courts.[80] The Church courts claimed subject-matter jurisdiction in cases touching the administration of the sacraments, testaments and wills, benefices and Church property, oaths and pledges of faith, and sins incurring ecclesiastical censures. They claimed personal jurisdiction over clergy and their household, students, crusaders, *miserabiles* ('the wretched', which included the poor, widows, and orphans), Jews in cases against Christians, and travellers. In practice, anyone could bring a suit in an ecclesiastical court by arguing a 'default of secular justice'.[81]

Despite their earlier concord, Gregory VII signally failed to rally the Norman kings to his cause. In both countries, relations with the papacy soon soured, as the conquerors' first move was to assume leadership of the Church. Instead of eradicating Islam, the Hautevilles' Sicily became famous as a bridge between Europe and the East, enjoying the riches of Greek, Arabic, Jewish, and Norman cultures, building Byzantine and Roman churches alongside mosques and synagogues. Three generations later, Friedrich II Hohenstaufen, heir to the Hauteville

77 BL, Cotton MS Cleopatra E. vi, fols 16–135. See Ullmann, 'This Realm of England Is an Empire'.

78 *Dictatus papae*, Dictate 7, in *Select Historical Documents of the Middle Ages*, p. 366.

79 Lanfranc, *De corpore et sanguine Domini*, ed. by J.-P. Migne, *Patrologiae cursus completus, series Latina*, 150 (Paris: Garnier, 1854), cols 407–42.

80 'Ordinance of William I, separating the Spiritual and Temporal Courts', Latin text, *Select Charters*, ed. by Stubbs, pp. 81–82.

81 Berman's lists, in *Law and Revolution*, pp. 221–23.

brothers, would incur the ire of the papacy, and two excommunications, for pursuing the same policy of intercultural exchanges and religious tolerance.

Pope Innocent had invented the *plenitudo potestatis*. Kaiser Friedrich retaliated with the divinity of Justice, and a secular order, the chivalry of justiciars.[82] Hailed as '*stupor mundi*' by the Benedictine chronicler Matthew Paris, he was to his own time a terrifying wonder, whose innovations served as models to lesser monarchs. Historians, even those who criticize Kantorowicz's romantic idealization of the man, generally nominate Friedrich as one of the three dominant figures of the thirteenth century, with Saint Louis and Francesco d'Assisi. Political necessity guided his every move, the *imminens necessitas imperii* whose ultimate goal must be *Pax* and *Justitia*. Instead of going on crusade as the pope commanded, he negotiated a treaty with the Soldan of Egypt, thus raising fierce opposition in both Christian and Muslim camps who resented his practical pacifism.

To his most eminent biographer, Friedrich (1215–1250) was the inventor of the modern State. The realm of Sicily was to be a laboratory for the universal monarchy he strove to establish, an object of envy for princes, a norm for kingdoms.[83] With this aim, he recruited an international team of jurists to collect and update all previous Norman, Arab, and Byzantine laws, and produce a unified code of Sicilian laws emulating Justinian's.[84] The Melfi Constitutions of 1231, compiled by 'maître Pierre de la Vigne, de Capoue, juge à notre grande cour', who had studied in Bologna, included much material borrowed from the Assizes of Ariano promulgated by his maternal grandfather, Roger II of Sicily, and were soon famous around Europe as the *Liber Augustalis*.[85] Friedrich's titles on the frontispiece express his image of himself as a combination of Caesar, Augustus, and Justinian, conqueror, governor, and law-giver, an example Henry VIII would aim to surpass on the title page of the Great Bible (see below, Chapter 4). The mysterious Castel del Monte, in Apulia, still testifies to Friedrich's fusion of classical Antiquity and Arabic philosophy. His model of centralized bureaucracy was imitated by the neighbouring Romance kingdoms, France especially where it proved most enduring. Holy Louis IX, a declared champion of Gallicanism, shared Friedrich's concern for justice and adopted some of his reforms.[86] Henry III of England submitted without argument when Friedrich told him to stop all payments of the tribute to Rome and gave the widowed emperor his sister Isabella in marriage.

The Sicilian laboratory produced another lasting model for the rest of Europe: the sonnet, which exercised the inventive talents of the Sicilian jurists.[87] Along with Friedrich's sonneteers, a long line of poets, from Virgil to Dante and Petrarch,

82 Kantorowicz, *Frederick the Second*, pp. 272–79; on Justitia, pp. 224–61.
83 Kantorowicz, *Frederick the Second*, p. 255.
84 Pennington, 'The Birth of the "Ius commune"'. Houben, *Roger II of Sicily*, pp. 135–47.
85 An edition of parallel texts shows that over half of Roger's legislation was repeated in the *Liber Augustalis*. Pier delle Vigne is saluted by Dante in Canto XIII of *Inferno*, ll. 58–78.
86 LaBarge, *Saint Louis*, pp. 169–87. Le Goff, *Saint Louis* (1996), repr. in *Héros du Moyen Âge*, p. 771.
87 Anne Robin, 'Une innovation sicilienne', in Darras, ed., *Les Métamorphoses du Sonnet*, pp. 5–12.

shared glorious visions of Empire and dreams of universal peace at least as potent as republican ones. Defined by the medievalist Alain Boureau as 'the last of the Ghibellines', Kantorowicz recognized the nature of his own fascination for the Hohenstaufens: the stemma of 'Ein Volk, ein Reich, ein Führer' went back via Barbarossa to 'Unus Deus, unus Papa, unus Imperator'.[88] After his ambiguous *Kaiser Friedrich*, he ends *The King's Two Bodies* with a splendid chapter on Dante and his centring on man of political sovereignty.[89] Dante, a White Guelf only by an accident of Florentine politics, believed in the virtue of universal monarchy and undertook to demonstrate its benefits in *De monarchia*.[90]

Under the aegis of Virgil, the imperial poet, Dante invests Caesar with a sacred mission. Christ chose to be born under the reign of Augustus, the only time when the world was at peace: 'sub divo Augusto monarcha, existente Monarchia perfecta, mundum undique fuisse quietum'. He who has charge of the world must ensure that in this little court of mortals one may live freely in peace, 'ut scilicet in areola ista mortalium libere cum pace vivetur'. The best condition for humankind is the maximum possible liberty under a monarch, who is least exposed to greed. Rome's election at the head of the world appears in the many miracles that saved this most noble of people from destruction. They were naturally ordained to command and, in subjecting the whole earth, came by right to world dominion, 'ergo romanus populus subiciendo sibi orbem de iure Imperium venit'.[91] Augustus's decree of a worldwide census quoted by Saint Luke (2. 1) proves that the Romans exercised universal jurisdiction.

Dante's mode of reasoning will reappear in many ulterior arguments. In the philosopher Claude Lefort's view, supporters and detractors of universal monarchy, from Elizabeth's transfiguration into Astrea, or La Boétie's radical criticism of solitary power, to Michelet's designation of France for world leadership, all drank from the same source, Dante.[92] Michelet writes: 'As early as the year 1300, I behold the great Ghibelin poet, who, in opposition to the pope, strengthens and exalts to heaven the Colossus of Caesar. Unity is salvation; one monarch, one for the whole earth.' The more omnipotent he is, the less he will abuse his power: having all, he desires nought. 'He is perfect, and perfectly, sovereignly just; he governs infallibly, like the justice of God.'[93] Michelet sets the '*simple*' folk against the '*habiles*', the clever ones who at heart despise the people, and he names three illustrious ancestors to those simple men, Dante, Luther, Shakespeare.[94]

---

88 Kantorowicz, *'Laudes regiae'*. Boureau, *Histoires d'un historien*, p. 1228, detects the source of this fascination in Kantorowicz's *'Laudes regiae'*, pp. 129–46.

89 Kantorowicz, *The King's Two Bodies*, ch. 8. Critics have read his *Kaiser Friedrich* in opposite ways, as a Ghibelline praise of its hero, or an expiatory monument.

90 Dante's party, the White Guelfs, temporarily allied themselves with the Ghibellines, who supported the emperor against the Black Guelfs.

91 Dante, *La Monarchie*, trans. by Gally, bk I, p. 120, bk III, p. 238, bk II, p. 154.

92 Lefort, 'La modernité de Dante', Preface to *La Monarchie*, p. 20.

93 Michelet, *History of the French Revolution*, Part II, I, 35.

94 Michelet, *Histoire de la Révolution française* (Paris: Librairie Internationale, 1868), I, p. 32.

The author of the *De monarchia* found great favour among English reformists. He was soon recruited as a proto-Protestant by the likes of John Bale and John Foxe.[95] A distant echo of the imperial theme is still audible in the revels of Gray's Inn due to be performed on 28 December 1594 before a guest of honour, the ambassador of the Inner Temple's emperor, Frederick Templarius, 'who was then busied in his Wars against the Turk', but he left in anger at the 'disordered Tumult and Crowd upon the Stage' before the play.[96] After his departure, since the sports intended were especially for the Templarians, 'nothing of account was offered' save dancing and revelling, 'and a Comedy of Errors (like to Plautus his Menechmus)'. The next night, a Commission of Oyer and Terminer was set up to enquire into the cause of the disorders committed, 'especially by sorceries and enchantments', which linked up the unscheduled confusions with those performed in the play. It is impossible to tell if this Frederick, who fights against 'the known enemies to all Christendom', has more than a distant connection in the lawyers' mind with the *stupor mundi*: his host the Prince of Purpoole's court with its long list of 'Officers and Attendants' was patently an ideal projection of the King-in-Parliament model. As for *The Comedy of Errors* (discussed below, in Chapter 9), though the play is dismissed as 'nothing of account', it does refer at the start to a similar constitution in Ephesus where laws have been decreed 'in solemn synods', Raffield points out.[97]

It is plain that the young Shakespeare did not share Dante's faith in the imperial model. His only depiction of the empire, in *Titus Andronicus*, shows its decline into barbarian tyranny as Astrea forsakes the earth, a flight that initiates the Iron Age in Ovid's *Metamorphoses*. When Titus and his family send arrows to heaven with messages begging her to return, Saturninus, officially your supreme law-maker, meets their effort with a double-edged irony: 'A goodly humour, is it not, my lords? | As who would say, in Rome no justice were.' The later Roman plays will retrace the steps of the republic's fall and the tragic deaths of its heroic figures leading to an absolutist imperial order. The dismemberment of the commonwealth is visibly exercised on the mutilated bodies of the Andronici, on those cut hands and heads that litter the stage, on raped and muted Lavinia. The continuity with Troynovant, present-day London, is stressed by the Roman Lord who denounces the fatal engine 'That gives our Troy, our Rome, the civil wound'.[98] An Elizabethan audience might not have agreed with Muriel Bradbrook that in *Titus Andronicus* 'the horrors are classical and quite unfelt'.[99] Pig's blood was but a substitute for the human blood of other popular public shows, the executions

95 On Dante's popularity with early modern English writers, see Boswell, *Dante's Fame in England*.

96 *Gesta Grayorum*, ed. by Bland, pp. 31–32. See Strain's analysis of these revels in her *Legal Reform in English Renaissance Literature*, pp. 66–68, 76–78.

97 Raffield, '*The Comedy of Errors* and the Meaning of Contract', *Law and Humanities*, 3.2 (2009), 227. *The Comedy of Errors*, I.i.13.

98 *Titus Andronicus*, IV.iv.19–20; V.iii.86.

99 Bradbrook, *Themes and Conventions of Elizabethan Tragedy* (Cambridge: Cambridge University Press, 1969), p. 98.

of 'traitors' cut open and disembowelled in front of the crowd. According to a witness, three strokes of the axe were needed to cut the hand of John Stubbs, of Lincoln's Inn, guilty of having written a pamphlet against Queen Elizabeth's matrimonial plans.[100]

Tables of Affinity: Gratian v. *Pierre Lombard*

> I might ask you for your commission. But I do take thee Orlando for my husband: there's a girl goes before the priest, and certainly a woman's thought runs before her actions.
>
> *As You Like It, IV.i*

The Great Matter of Henry VIII's break with Rome on an issue of matrimony also had a long legal ancestry. Among other points of interest, the *Liber Augustalis* is the first European code that makes the presence of a priest a requisite for the validity of a marriage.[101] With the Council of Trent's canon *Tametsi dubitandum non est*, it became an obligation.[102] The Church had worked for ages to bring matrimony under ecclesiastical control. After investitures, it was the next important area of conflict between medieval monarchs and the papacy. In the two decades before 1100, the historian Georges Duby notes, 'the church finally won the exclusive jurisdiction over all matters pertaining to marriage that it had long claimed as its right'.[103]

Plays like *The Merchant of Venice*, *As You Like It*, or *King Lear* show how the last will of an autocratic father can defy elementary justice, Gary Watt points out.[104] It was generally agreed that a father's oath could not compel his daughter to marry the man of his choice, a rule seldom observed in royal families. The dispute would lead to a great debate between Gratian and Pierre Lombard in the twelfth century. In Gratian's view, the contract concluded *per verba de presenti*, words spoken in the present, was the efficient cause of matrimony: 'Consent makes marriage'. But the contract could be dissolved if there was no consummation: 'Marriage, which is begun by agreement, is completed by intercourse.'[105] To Lombard, consummation did not matter, since no one could doubt the validity of the Virgin Mary's marriage. The promises exchanged with or without a priest were all that was needed. By a papal rescript of 1143, in the case of Richard de Anesty, 'a marriage solemnly celebrated in church, a marriage of which a child had been born, was set

---

100 *John Stubbs's 'Gaping Gulf'*, ed. by Berry, p. xxiv.

101 Constitution 26, BAV, MS Vat. lat. 8782, fols 92ra–93rb, in Pennington, 'The Birth of the "Ius commune"'.

102 *Conciliorum oecumenicorum decreta*, ed. by G. Alberigo and others, 3rd edn (Bologna: Istituto per le scienze religiose, 1973), p. 756, ll. 4–5. See Reynolds, *Marriage in the Western Church*, pp. 401–12.

103 Duby, *Medieval Marriage*, p. 20.

104 Watt, *Shakespeare's Acts of Will*, ch. 6.

105 *Decretum*, Case 27, Question II, Part I, § 1, and Part III, C. 37.

aside as null in favour of an earlier marriage constituted by a mere exchange of consenting words'.[106] Similarly, in the statute *Titulus Regius* adopted by Parliament in 1484 and echoed in *Richard III*, Edward IV's children are declared bastards and barred from the succession, owing to their father's earlier promise of marriage to Lady Eleanor Butler. Henry VII's first move on ascending the throne would be to repeal *Titulus Regius* which made his wife Elizabeth of York an illegitimate daughter of Edward instead of a legitimate Plantagenet heiress.

Unlawful unions and the connected problems of inheritance kept ecclesiastical courts busy long before they severed England from Catholic Europe. A problem quoted in the Digest had perplexed the Roman jurists: whether an error of identity touching one of a couple made the marriage null. The medieval canonists found a way out by reformulating it: Would the mistaken party agree to be married or not if the truth were known? In *As You Like It* the mistaken Orlando would no doubt have answered yes regardless. So his rustic marriage to Rosalind, even disguised as Ganymede, must be valid. Their exchange of vows under the aegis of a dubious minister does bind them, though Orlando could have pleaded that his bride's disguise made the vows null had he wished to be set free. What made a marriage, consent or consummation, is all the matter of *All's Well That Ends Well*, in which a desperate Helena uses a bed trick to tie up her husband to his reluctant word, 'I take her hand', and confirm her married status.[107] With two incomplete and symmetrically opposite engagements, *Measure for Measure* gives precedence to the exchange of vows: Claudio's affair is punishable by death, Angelo's is legitimized by an earlier promise to wed Mariana, although he too was deluded by a false identity when he consummated their union. In the three plays, as in all Shakespeare's comedies, a working compromise must be found if the world is to be peopled. In each case, the goal is achieved through deviousness and disguise, a lesson on the virtues of theatrical delusions.

What unmade a marriage was an even larger source of conflict. Not only blood ties but spiritual kinship was a cause of impediment, which explains the frequent choice of godparents among grandparents, to avoid extending the network of relatives. Sexual intercourse, licit or illicit, created an affinity between relatives of the two parties exactly equivalent to a blood relation. By the end of the twelfth century, it was standard practice to illustrate the 'Matrimony' section of Gratian's *Decretals* with two tables of affinity and consanguinity designed like a family tree.[108] In 1059, a canon of the Council of Rome had extended the impediments to the seventh degree, a count of seven generations from an individual up to the common ancestor. At the Council of the Lateran, Innocent III brought them

106 Pollock and Maitland, *The History of English Law*, II, p. 367. On the uncertainties of marriage law, see Mukherji, *Law and Representation*, ch. 1.

107 See Lupton's illuminating study of the play in *Thinking with Shakespeare*, pp. 97–126, and Mukherji's *Law and Representation*, pp. 28–50.

108 A French manuscript dated *c*. 1170–1180, MS Ludwig XIV 2, fol. 228, at the Paul Getty Museum has one illuminated in gold leaf showing Adam and Eve, identified as *primum genus*, first degree.

down to four, perhaps to limit the kind of clash he had just been through with Philippe Auguste. In Philippe's case, the problem was not consanguinity, a frequent flaw, but repudiation, no novelty either. Several Capetian kings before him had pleaded consanguinity to obtain an annulment, most recently Louis VII who let Alienor and her duchy of Aquitaine escape to England's welcoming arms. With these precedents, and the support of an ecclesiastical court led by his own uncle, Philippe II Auguste repudiated his lawfully wedded wife Ingeburge to marry Agnès de Méranie. But instead of returning to Denmark as told, Ingeburge appealed to Rome. Philippe refused to dismiss Agnès, was excommunicated, and remained unbent. So the pope placed the whole realm under interdict in January 1200, condemning his people to live and die in sin until he submitted.

Even with a relaxation of rules, finding an eligible spouse remained a tricky business at all levels of society: 'Cruel indeed was the social system of those days. Authority bade men marry, but rendered marriage nearly impossible, at once by the excessive misery of most, and the senseless cruelty of the canonical prohibitions.'[109] At a monarch's level, the dynastic urge to marry within a restricted number of powerful families inevitably led to endogamy, and ensuing annulments.[110] Hence the dilemma of Henri Ier, allied by blood to all French ladies of suitable rank.[111] Sending helpless princesses far from home was an ordinary feature of royal policy in both countries. Of all the princely brides thus sacrificed on Shakespeare's stage, Blanche is the only one who briefly stirs pity in one of the witnesses, the Bastard of Faulconbridge, who is revolted by the bridegroom's rhetoric:

> He doth espy
> Himself love's traitor: this is pity now,
> That hang'd and drawn and quartered, there should be
> In such a love so vile a lout as he.
>
> (*King John*, II.i.506–09)

Blanche herself unprotestingly bows to her fate: 'My uncle's will in this respect is mine'. As for Henry VI's wife Margaret of Anjou, any sympathy that might have been spent on her as the victim of an equally cynical selling off is soon dispelled by her own wiles. It is very likely, as John Watkins argues, that the Henriad reflected a popular hostility to foreign marriages that had dragged England into endless wars. In his view, Shakespeare's treatment of both Joan of Arc and Margaret 'brings together misogyny, xenophobia, and nationalist paranoia as the basis of a new theory of diplomacy'.[112] And yet, however hostile the treatment, Shakespeare proves far more temperate than Stubbs's vociferations in

---

109 Michelet, *La Sorcière*, p. 162, and pp. 159–61 on the prohibition of incest.
110 See Lewis, *Royal Succession*, pp. 21–24, 54.
111 Lewis, *Royal Succession*, p. 45.
112 Levin and Watkins, *Shakespeare's Foreign Worlds*, p. 73.

The Discouerie of a Gaping Gulf Whereinto England is like to be swallowed by another French marriage, who quotes the precedent of Henry VI's disastrous French bride to stigmatize Elizabeth's marriage plans to her 'little frog', François d'Alençon.[113]

Bellowing Legists: Thomas Becket v. *Henry II*

Have I no friend will rid me of this living fear?

Richard II, V.iv

Along with matrimony, last wills and testaments were another area where canon law ruled, as part of a ritual during which the dying man was shriven and given viaticum once he had made his peace with God. This was but the emerged tip of the iceberg. By creating a distinct State, the Vatican, the papal revolution at the end of the eleventh century invested the clergy with a form of political power, while the monarchs, Capetian or Plantagenet, increasingly thought of themselves as reformers and law-givers, in spiritual as well as temporal affairs. Clashes of authority began in England when King Henry II asked the clergy to acknowledge the equality of all subjects before the law and renounce their exemption from civil jurisdiction.[114] The Assize of Clarendon in 1166 created the Grand Jury and ruled that criminals were to be tried before the king's court. This unifying process did much to transfer power from local barons to the royal judges. It also came against the canonical courts. Eight of the nine articles affecting the Church conflicted with canon law. To all these articles, Becket expressed radical opposition.[115] When summoned to appear before a great council at Northampton to answer charges of malfeasance in his office, he denied their right to judge him and appealed to the pope. According to Matthew Paris, Becket's refusal to accept the ancient customs and dignities of the realm made the king 'burn with fierce anger'. Henry used every legal weapon to force him into submission, to no avail. His legal advisers were romanists and canonists unskilled in English law, Matthew repeatedly complains.[116]

As long as there was no clear division between clerical and secular courts, the problem of bringing criminal clerks to justice did not arise, but it became crucial with the establishment of a new ecclesiastical jurisdiction. The dividing line remained hazy, bringing more appeals from England to the Roman Curia than from any other country. Becket did not mince words when he put his case to Pope Alexander: 'if in many things we must obey the king, we must not obey him on

113 *John Stubbs's 'Gaping Gulf'*, pp. 53–54.

114 See Mary Cheney, 'The Litigation between John Marshal and Becket in 1164: A Pointer to the Origin of Novel Disseizin', in Guy and Beale, eds, *Law and Social Change in British History*, pp. 9–26.

115 See Smalley, *The Becket Conflict*.

116 'Ira vehementi incanduit', in Matthew Paris, *Chronica Majora*, ed. by Luard, II, pp. 229, iii. Pollock and Maitland, *The History of English Law*, I, p. 215 n. 176.

those points, the result of which would be, that he would not be a king. To do thus would be to make him not Caesar, but a tyrant'. Though he too disapproves of the Constitutions, Pope Alexander writes in a much milder tone. His policy, he explains to Gilbert, bishop of London, is to give the king gentle advice and, if he continues dutifully to pay Peter's pence, repay him with sincere affection: 'We prefer to outdo him in patience and long-suffering, so long as we can possibly endure so to do, rather than cause him vexation in any way.' To a man of Becket's stubborn integrity, this was no better than compounding sin. He threatened to excommunicate Henry himself 'if he does not speedily recover his senses, and submit to discipline for what he has done'. His shocked suffragans advocated patience and humility. In their opinion, the wished-for end, peace, might have been attained 'if the asperity of our father, the lord archbishop of Canterbury, had not kindled afresh the anger that was now subdued and almost extinguished'.[117]

In the end it was not the threat to ecclesiastical courts that caused the tragedy, but the coronation of Henry's son, performed in Becket's absence by the Archbishop of York. Becket secured letters from the pope ordering the suspension of all the prelates involved in the ceremony and returned 'burning with zeal for justice' to England.[118] In Voragine's *Golden Legend*, 'the king was much wroth and said: If he had men in his land that loved him they would not suffer such a traitor in his land alive'.[119] Interpreted as a royal command, it set the standard for ulterior stories of angry monarchs asking for blood. The murder of the proud prelate washed away all criticisms of his obduracy. For centuries, the horror of the transgression, stressed by vivid accounts of the scene, would feed anger and veneration: 'in the whiteness of the brains was shown the purity of his innocence, while the purple colour of the blood bespoke his martyrdom'.[120] The repentant Henry swore to abolish all customs prejudicial to the Church. He also engaged to take the cross and go to Jerusalem, if he found the time between other battles.[121] In 1220, Becket's remains were conveyed to a shrine in the newly built Trinity Chapel of Canterbury. Archbishop Langton, freshly returned to England after King John's death, supervised the transfer of the relics, and 7 July became St Thomas of Canterbury's Day.[122] For a while.

Despite his heroic stance, Becket never became a republican icon: the insular spirit proved stronger. Henry VIII paid back the Plantagenets' humiliation to the full. The last pilgrimage to the shrine took place in 1538: on 24 April, the

117 Becket's address to King Henry, letters to Alexander and to his suffragan bishops (1165), are reproduced in Roger de Hoveden, *The Annals*, trans. by Riley, I, pp. 270–79.

118 William of Newburgh, 'Of the Coronation of Henry the Third, and the Murder of St Thomas', in *The Church Historians of England*, trans. by Joseph Stevenson (London: Seeley's, 1856), IV, II, 478–81.

119 Jacques de Voragine, *The Golden Legend*, trans. by Caxton, ed. by O'Neill, p. 201.

120 Roger de Hoveden, *The Annals*, I, p. 337, under the year 1171.

121 Roger de Hoveden, 'The Purgation of King Henry for the Death of the blessed Thomas', *The Annals*, I, pp. 355–57; 'The Charter of Absolution of our Lord the King', pp. 357–58.

122 Cheney, *From Becket to Langton*. Langton's *Tractatus de translatione Beati Thomae* is probably the text of the sermon he preached then.

dead Becket was summoned by writ 'within thirty days to answer to a charge of treason, contumacy, and rebellion against his sovereign lord, King Henry II' and, having failed to appear, sentenced on 10 June to have his bones burnt, his shrine forfeited to the Crown, his name and sainthood wiped out of memory.[123] A royal proclamation declared that Becket was 'really a rebel who fled to France and to the bishop of Rome to procure the abrogation of wholesome laws': his pictures 'are to be plucked down and his festivals shall no longer be kept, and the services in his name shall be razed out of all books'.[124] Foxe's *Monuments of Martyrs* declares that this example should 'teach all Romishe prelates not to be so stubberne in such matters not pertayning to them against their prince, vnto whom God had subiected them'.[125] But Becket's heroic memory lived on: in a play at the Jesuit College of Saint-Omer in 1599, militant seminarians complain that through the divisions over the calendar, St Thomas's Day has been doubly displaced.[126]

Magna Carta: Stephen Langton v. *King John*

Thou canst not, cardinal, devise a name
So slight, unworthy and ridiculous,
To charge me to an answer, as the pope.

King John, III.i

When Henry II tried to restrict the jurisdiction of ecclesiastical courts, Chancellor Becket took the opposite way to Lanfranc's, posthumously making the monarch bow to the Roman pontiff. Henry's son John was similarly humiliated, forced to accept papal interference and declare himself Rome's vassal. When the monks of Canterbury made irregular attempts to elect their own archbishop, Stephen Langton was elected in Rome, but King John denied him entrance to the realm. His entreaties being unheeded, Innocent III's delegates, Pandulph and Durand, laid the interdict on England. Shakespeare stages this momentous episode, yet never mentions the other major event of John's reign, the drafting of Magna Carta.

King John opens on a double issue of inheritance, with two mothers casting doubts on the legitimacy of their sons' claims. Lady Faulconbridge confesses her firstborn is a bastard. Queen Elinor tells John he owes his title to 'Your strong possession much more than your right'. According to the order of primogeniture, her grandson Prince Arthur was undeniably heir to the throne, but the case

---

123 Victor Houliston, 'St Thomas Becket in the Propaganda of the English Counter-Reformation', *Renaissance Studies*, 7.1 (1993), 43.

124 *Letters and Papers, Henry VIII*, ed. by Brewer, Brodie, and Gairdner, XIII.2, p. 848.

125 Foxe, *Actes and Monuments*, Bk IV, p. 279. Unless otherwise stated, all references are to the 1570 edition.

126 *Brevis dialogismus exhibitus in festo sancti Thomae Cantuariensis Anglorum patroni anno 1599*, in Victor Houliston, '*Brevis Dialogismus*: An Anonymous Becket Play from the Jesuit Seminary at St Omer', *English Literary Renaissance*, 23 (1993), 382–427. The play was found among the Cecil Papers.

was not so clear-cut in John's time, when King Richard's brother seemed to the assembly of barons a sounder choice than this child born and raised abroad. This, however, is only a side issue in a play primarily concerned with the European power games: 'Mad world! mad kings! mad composition!' When ordered to let Langton occupy his see, John denounces the pope's 'usurped authority', causing King Philip to admonish him, 'Brother of England, you blaspheme in this', and Pandulph to threaten excommunication: 'blessed shall he be that doth revolt | From his allegiance to an heretic'.[127] The unholy alliance of rebellious barons, foreign kings, and popish legates is denounced as endangering England's loyalty to its true self, but faced with their coalition, the defiant John must submit to the pope's will.

On a mounting scale of sanctions designed to bring a rebellious monarch to obedience, interdict improved on personal excommunication by inciting his subjects to dissociate themselves from the rebel. Along with John, three kings were under ban of the Church in 1212–1213.[128] In England, the churches stayed closed for over six years: no Masses, marriages, or burials were celebrated, no church service of any kind allowed except baptism and viaticum. Far from being bowed by the interdict, John hit back with instructions to officers of the Crown to take custody of all the clergy's properties, leaving them only estovers, 'what is necessary' for reasonable maintenance. But his show of strength proved futile. The proud tale of England's resistance told in schoolbooks was recently invalidated, as well as the tale that Pope Innocent deposed John and invited Philippe to take possession of his realm. Its main source is Roger de Wendover's lively but unreliable account, from which all other versions derive.[129] The pope's letters tell a different story: *Auditis verbis nuntiorum tuorum*, dated 27 February 1213, held a veiled threat of deposition if John did not submit by 1 June, but John did, well before the deadline.[130] Philippe's preparations for invasion, along with threats of rebellion at home, left him no alternative. In July, he welcomed Langton with a great show of joy and was absolved from excommunication. John had to give the clergy eighty thousand marks by way of amend, receive his realm in vassalage from Rome, and engage to pay an annual tribute of a thousand marks, a contract that would be honoured until 1343.[131] Its echo still reverberates in *Cymbeline*: thanks to a brilliant anachronism, modern corrupt Italy in the guise of the villain Iachimo is defeated by Celtic Britain, whose victorious king freely agrees to pay tribute to Augustan Rome, a neat way to acknowledge cultural, as distinct from political, debts.[132]

---

127 *King John*, I.i.40; II.i.561; III.i.85, 87, 100–101.

128 Otto IV, who was eventually deposed, Alfonso II of Portugal, and Leo II of Armenia.

129 Roger de Wendover, *Flores historiarum*, ed. by Coxe, pp. 235–57.

130 Cheney, *The Papacy and England*, XII, pp. 100–117. See *Selected Letters of Pope Innocent III*, ed. by Cheney and Semple.

131 This feudal census, sometimes confused with the much older Peter's Pence or Romescot, was formally repudiated in 1366 and abolished by Parliament.

132 See Hadfield, *Shakespeare and Republicanism*, pp. 165–66.

John's vassalage to the Apostolic See had direct bearings on the next sequence of events. Langton, now the undisputed spiritual leader of the nation, took an important part in its legal development. At a council held in Saint Albans, he brought a copy of Henry I Beauclerc's laws and asked King John to ratify them, in vain. In January 1215, the northern barons came to the king's council with a demand that he confirm their ancient liberties, according to the 'old laws and customs of the realm', else they would resort to force. Civil war broke out in the first days of May. When London fell to the rebels a fortnight later, Langton urged the barons to treat of peace at Staines, near Runnymede. Because no one was as learned as he, Langton is generally credited with a large share in the writing of Magna Carta. He was undoubtedly responsible for the preamble and the first clause guaranteeing the liberty of the Church.[133] Clause 39 promised to every man legal trial by his peers, and Clause 40 guaranteed that justice should not be sold, denied, or delayed to anyone. The last one, Clause 61, provided a security, a standing committee of twenty-five, to supervise the executive government.

The principle implicit in the Charter was that the king is under the law. But the security clause was a denial of normal kingly rights. This, from the point of view of the Church, was a fatal flaw. Pope Innocent declared Magna Carta null and void, since it had been extorted from the king, his vassal and would-be crusader, by violent pressure. As for Langton, he was suspended by the pope's legates for refusing to excommunicate the rebels. When the Dauphin Louis made his claim to the throne of England, the regency council removed the offensive security clause to make it more compatible with traditional views of royal authority. Thus purged, Magna Carta was sanctioned by the papal legate, renewed with minor alterations in 1217, and confirmed again with a few alterations by Langton himself in 1225. In this version, it stands as Statute I of English law.[134] There would be no reversing of a constitutional trend now a century old: 'Magna Carta had come to stay, and the English hierarchy was committed to safeguarding it.'[135] Which did not mean that it was written in stone. Fifteenth-century judges, for instance, were aware that the law had changed several times in the recent past. In their readings, statutes (i.e. positive law) were made to remedy defects within the common law.[136] What remained intact was the value of its safeguard in public opinion. Francis Ashley's lectures on Magna Carta at the Middle Temple in 1616 still insisted that the law included 'liberties' and 'freedoms' inherited by all the freemen of England.

A conflict of vassalage between John and his liege lord Philippe Auguste created another significant precedent: the ruling of the case by Innocent III, who was well versed in canon law. There is no sure basis to the story that he had

---

133 Cheney, *The Papacy and England*, XV, pp. 266–72.

134 Its eventful history was recorded in the exhibition of 2015 at the British Library on its eight-hundredth anniversary, 'Magna Carta: Law, Liberty, Legacy'.

135 Cheney, *The Papacy and England*, XV, p. 272.

136 See Brooks, *Lawyers, Litigation*, ch. 8.

been a pupil of the jurist Uguccio da Pisa in Bologna, but he did consult Uguccio repeatedly when elected to the papacy. His Decretal *Novit* (1204) justified his intervention in a secular matter *ratione peccati*, by reason of sin, which in this case took the form of oath breaking. The *ratione peccati* principle offered almost unlimited possibilities of interference and would be made to serve many turns. Another of Innocent's bulls would have equally momentous long-term effects in England: *Deus qui Ecclesiam* declared valid marriage to the widow of a brother deceased *sine prole*, without offspring. It would provide the ground of dispensation for young Henry Tudor to marry Catherine of Aragon, the widow of his brother Arthur (see below, 'King's Conscience' in Chapter 5).

Fulminating Bulls: Philippe le Bel v. *Boniface VIII*

The various points of tension between *regnum* and *sacerdotium* — investitures, matrimony, inheritance, fees — generally led to larger issues and argumentative theories. There were numerous complaints from clergy and kings throughout Europe in the twelfth century, reaching a peak in the thirteenth, against excessive papal demands. French monarchy marked a decisive triumph over papal authority, providing models and texts that would serve in successive monarchic fights for autonomy. Quarrels over taxation would lead to a major crisis between Philippe le Bel and Pope Boniface VIII. Several points were at stake in the conflict: the king's right to try criminous clerks in his own courts, which had opposed Becket to Henry II, and the king's right to tax the clergy, which Henry VIII would use with a vengeance. The issue behind these specific points, on which Boniface capitulated, was the temporal authority of the pope.

The fight began with a papal bull of 1296, *Clericis laicos*, threatening excommunication to all who attempted to appropriate Church revenue or tax the clergy without the pope's permission. Philippe IV's *légistes* retaliated with an axiom they found in the archives, 'Li roi n'a point de souverains es choses temporeix' (the king has no sovereign in matters temporal), which laid the basis for a doctrine of national sovereignty.[137] Among the answers to the bull, the anonymous *Disputatio inter clericum et militem* argues that the kingdom of France has equal dignity with the empire. Other tracts followed, augmenting the argument with new material. One among them, probably dating from 1302, was known later as the *Quaestio in utramque partem pro et contra Pontificiam Potestatem* because it puts both cases impartially, the king's and the pope's, after the manner used in law courts. It concludes unequivocally against the pope's temporal authority: there is no basis in scripture, historical precedent, or any other source for plenitude of power.

Boniface was emulating Gregory VII and the great canonist popes when he aimed to raise spiritual over earthly power. Philippe le Bel, then at war with England, was severely taxing the French Church. The bull *Clericis laicos* infuriated

---

137 Soulier, *L'Europe*, p. 48.

him. All attempts to placate him, even the canonization of his grandfather Louis, failed to restore peace: in 1300, he had the bull *Unam sanctam* publicly burnt. His *légistes*' arguments were endlessly rehearsed up to the sixteenth century, especially the limits of the Constantine Donation, the status of *regnum Franciae* in Charlemagne's empire, and its Trojan origins.[138] In their long history of independence, the submission to Rome was only temporary and illegitimate: the Roman Empire was born from murder, but force cannot create right.[139] Boniface, though reputed the most clever canonist of his time, did not have the fulminating stamina of Innocent III, and the fight soon left the legal ground. France after all was 'the Church's eldest daughter', an alliance of politics with religion on which its monarchs were steadily building absolutism.

The bulls *Ausculta fili* (1301) and *Unam sanctam* (1302), rehearsing the full thesis of *plenitudo potestatis*, marked the height of papal theocracy. The French jurists and their thugs brought it down with one blow at Anagni. Dante, who cannot be suspected of undue sympathy for popes, reports the shocking scene in *Purgatorio* (xx, l. 86): 'I see the flower-de-luce Alagna enter, and Christ in his own Vicar captive made'. But he does not confuse the man with the dignity: in *Inferno*, Boniface is committed to the third circle of hell, with the popes guilty of simony.[140] With the backing of the three estates, Philippe could proclaim himself 'emperor in his kingdom' without need for a more radical break. Instead of consigning Rome to exile, Coriolanus-like, he found it more judicious to bring Rome closer to home and keep the pope under scrutiny. The removal of the papacy to Avignon under control of the French kings sparked off the political fights of the Great Schism. The theory of *plenitudo potestatis* now gave rise to opposition everywhere, including inside: the conciliarists attacked it with the view that spiritual authority resided with the whole corporation of Christians represented by the general councils of the Church, not the person of the pope. Conciliarism had strong advocates around Europe: William of Ockham, Marsiglio da Padova, and followers of Dante generally. Thomas More would still suggest it to Henry VIII as a way out of his matrimonial difficulties.

As for the *Disputatio*, its afterlife is a telling instance of the ways texts travelled through time and space in revised forms to suit varying causes. Through its avatars, it provides a significant landmark in the transfer of a legal practice, the *pro et contra* argument, to the larger political arena and of the nice sharp quillets of the law to the dialogue mode that would invest the public stage. The pamphlet reappeared in a collection of Gallican propaganda compiled at the request of King Charles V the Wise (1364–1380). Around 1380, John Trevisa, vicar of Berkeley, Gloucestershire, wrote an English translation entitled *Disputation between a Clerk and a Knight*. Wycliff, Chaucer, and Jack Straw were just about to rise. In the

138 See Goy-Blanquet, '"This Realm Is an Empire"'.

139 A theme developed by Évrart de Trémaugon in *Le Songe du vergier* (1376), ed. by Schnerb-Lièvre, I, pp. 53–57, which borrows from the *Disputatio* and other texts.

140 *Purgatorio*, xx, ll. 86–87; *Inferno*, xix, ll. 112–17.

argument over the notion of imperium, Trevisa's knight points out to the clerk that bishops' laws 'may wel be lawe to thou but nought to us', for the pope has no lordship, therefore no power, over temporalities. The Old Testament teaches 'that kynges ordeynede who schulde be prestes; and prestes ordeynede nought who schulde be kynges'.[141] Many early printed versions attest to its enduring services in various causes of national emancipation. Henry VIII's printer, Thomas Berthelet, published *A Dialogue betwene a Knyght and a Clerke* in 1531, at the turning point of the king's relations with Rome. It was one of the pamphlets that the Council of Trent put on the Index of Prohibited Books.

Sacred Monarchy

With few occasional drawbacks, the Capetians worked successfully hand in hand with their churchmen to establish their authority, up to their crowning success, the canonization of Louis IX, which rewarded some two centuries of ecclesiastical lobbying. The founding couple of sacred monarchy, the Gaul Clovis and Bishop Rémi who christened him and his kingdom, made Reims the first cardinal point of French regalia. According to Hincmar, Rémi's Carolingian biographer, among miracles that occurred during the baptism ceremony, elevating it to a full '*sacre*', a dove appeared carrying the ampulla filled with chrism that would serve in all royal coronations henceforth.[142] Before he became bishop of Reims himself, Hincmar was a monk of Saint-Denis, where the historiographical work begun by the Benedictine monks for King Robert the Pious (987–1031) was taken over by Abbot Suger. It was Suger who undertook to transform the old Carolingian building with the luminous Gothic architecture that made Saint-Denis one of the most prestigious abbeys of the realm. Nicknamed 'Vulcan's workshop' of the dynasty by Bernard de Clairvaux, its chronicles provided ideological basis to the claims of the Capetian monarchs, advertising their descent from Charlemagne in support of their fights against the rival Plantagenets or the empire.

In England, on the contrary, the attempts at absolutism met constant checks, perhaps because the models of insubordination were within the royal family. Henry II made shares between his sons like the Capetians, to ensure concord, and reaped war.[143] King John's barons cannot have felt sacrilegious when they followed the example set by Henry's mutinous relatives. The chaplain of Henry II, Gerald of Wales, laments the quarrels that prevented this talented family from making a major mark in history.[144] His diagnosis is that they came from corrupt sources on both sides: Alienor's father, the Count of Poitou, and Henry's mother, the Empress Matilda, combined adultery with incest and other carnal horrors which

---

141 Trevisa, *Dialogus inter Militem et Clericum*, ed. by Perry, p. 18.
142 Hincmar, *Vita Remigii*, in Le Goff, *Héros du Moyen Âge*, pp. 993–97.
143 Lewis, *Royal Succession*, pp. 69–72.
144 Gerald of Wales, *The Topography of Ireland*, ch. 50, in *The Historical Works*, trans. by Forester, p. 164.

he meticulously catalogues. Another chronicler records that Richard the Lion Heart wept when he saw the corpse of his father, 'immediately on which the blood flowed in streams from the nostrils of the body at the approach of his son'.[145] Shakespeare found a similar tale of cruentation about the corpse of Henry VI in Holinshed, and imputed it to Richard of Gloucester's presence. He could also have read its legendary source in Chrétien de Troyes' *Yvain*.[146] In *A Warning for Fair Women* the fifteen wounds inflicted on the victim are 'fifteene mouthes that doe accuse me, | In ev'ry wounde there is a bloudy tongue', the murderer confesses, echoing the thousand several tongues who cry all 'Guilty! guilty!' in Richard's nightmare.[147]

Priam's Sons: Plantagenets **v.** ***Capetians***

There is no bar
To make against your highness' claim to France,
But this, which they produce from Pharamond:
In terram Salicam mulieres non succedant.

Henry V, I.ii

The emblems and legends surrounding Capetian monarchs created emulation. Tales of their healing gifts were organized into a consistent cycle by Charles V's apologists, in the turmoils of the Hundred Years' War. Their most prestigious feature, the Holy Ampulla, made the chronicler Matthew Paris grant precedence to the French monarchy over other earthly monarchs. So prestigious that the Plantagenets devised their own miraculous balm, the oil of Thomas Becket, and subsequently tapped its legitimizing power at various hard times.[148] Edward II, who was desperately trying to strengthen his insecure position, begged permission to be crowned anew with this holy oil. Pope John XXII refused the reanointment but allowed the king to hold a second coronation if he so wished, on the ground that this ceremony printed nothing in the soul.[149] The first to be crowned with Becket's oil was Henry IV, who badly needed supernatural support after the deposition of an anointed king. The legend was further embellished for the occasion: the vessel had been found by John of Gaunt, given by him to his elder brother the Black Prince, lost at the prince's death, and recovered again long after Richard II's own

145 Roger de Hoveden, in 1189, *The Annals*, II, p. 111. The story is in several accounts, including Gerald of Wales.

146 'Le sang vermeil jaillissait tout chaud de la plaie du mort! C'était la preuve évidente que le meurtrier se trouvait là, présent dans la pièce.' Chrétien de Troyes, *Yvain, le Chevalier au lion*, ed. by Anne-Marie Cadot-Collin (Paris: Hachette, 2006), ch. 3. *Holinshed's Chronicles*, III, p. 324. Cf. *Richard III*, I.ii.

147 *A Warning for Fair Women*, IV.ii.84–85. *Richard III*, V.iii.196–202. See Mukherji's discussion of *A Warning* in *Law and Representation*, p. 112.

148 Bloch, *The Royal Touch*, pp. 37–43.

149 Goy-Blanquet, 'Images de la monarchie'.

coronation. The story is such a medley of genuine and mendacious details that Marc Bloch himself gave up trying to sort them out.[150] The successive kings, be they Lancaster, York, or Tudor, held onto this legend, without notable profit, up to Henry VIII who, after using the vial like his predecessors, had Becket's name erased from the calendar.

French and English monarchs vied with each other through writers who enrolled popular legends in their support: Walter Map for the Plantagenets, Hélinand de Froidmont for the Capetians tell the story of the Mesnie Hellequin, the wild hunt of King Herle, an incarnation of the Celtic god Herne, from whom the kings of France and England inherit the power to heal scrofula.[151] All these tales built up competing national myths, exhibiting the features listed by Colette Beaune: a famous ancestor, warlike feats, link to a territory, continuity, and purity of blood.[152] Just as Geoffrey of Monmouth had traced the origin of British kings to Aeneas's grandson Brutus, the French claimed descent from Hector's son, Francion, ancestor of the mythical Pharamond. According to Jean Juvénal des Ursins, 'When the Trojans came to France, there they made the Salic law'.[153] In France, the myth was invoked to prove that the English were a mongrel inferior race.[154] Allegedly promulgated by Pharamond, the Salic law would serve Charles V retroactively against English claims to his throne, and again under Charles VII to attack the Treaty of Troyes.

The French chroniclers summoned up all the available millenarist and messianic themes to support their monarchs' claims. Rigord, a monk of Saint-Denis, was the first to decorate Philippe II with the name *semper Augustus*, a title used by the Carolingian and Hohenstaufen emperors.[155] The theme of *reditus*, Charlemagne's return and the return of the kingdom to his race, is revived by Guillaume le Breton in the *Philippide*, a royal command after the Bouvines victory.[156] Long before Shakespeare's archbishops, this lengthy epic unfolds the tale of the Franks, from Francio Priamida, Francion, and Pharamond, down to 'our carolide' Philippe. His successors adapted the idea of French royal eschatology to their own reign. In the *Grandes Chroniques* illustrated by Jean Fouquet for Charles VII (1422–1461), fifty-one miniatures represent the kings of France from Pharamond to Charles VI. In other works, the family tree grows from the mouth of dead Priam.

The claims on Priam's sons were legion. Aenea Silvio Piccolomini, Pope Pius II, who had at first accepted the Trojan origin of the Franks, was much

150 Bloch, *The Royal Touch*, p. 139.

151 Lombard-Jourdan, *Aux origines de Carnaval*, pp. 261–67.

152 Beaune, *Naissance de la nation France*, pp. 20–82.

153 Juvénal des Ursins, *Écrits politiques*, ed. by Lewis, I, p. 156. Beaune, *Naissance de la nation France*, pp. 269–73.

154 See A. Bossuat, 'Les origines troyennes: Leur rôle dans la littérature historique du XVe siècle', *Annales de Normandie*, 8 (1958), 187–97.

155 'The "Karolinus" of Egidius Parisiensis', ed. by M. L. Colker, *Traditio*, 29 (1973), 199–326.

156 A continuation of Rigord. See Lewis, *Royal Succession*, p. 121.

incensed by the Turks' similar claims. His *Cosmographia* limits this ascendancy to the Romans and criticizes the pretensions of those in search of glorious ancient origins.[157] The humanist Robert Gaguin was the first in France or England to express even louder scepticism in his *Compendium*, to the great irritation of chroniclers in both countries.[158] The legend of Trojan origins still makes the core of Ronsard's *Franciade*, while across the Channel, Geoffrey's history of Arthur was revived by the Welsh Tudors up to the demise of the Faerie Queene. *Albion's England*, a verse history stretching from Noah to the beheading of Mary Stuart, by William Warner, attorney of the Common Pleas, proved so popular that it superseded *The Mirror for Magistrates*. Under James I, John Selden still hoped to find evidence for the cognate myth of Brutus, while Edward Coke thought that law originated in Troy, preceding the Greeks and Romans. Those two scholars would make significant contributions to the history of law in their respective fields (see below, Chapters 9 and 10).[159]

As for Charlemagne, it is predominantly as a patron of education and learning that he reappears under the reign of Charles V, hailed as the king's ancestor to support Charles's claim as heir to the *translatio studii et imperii*.[160] The University of Paris, undeterred by the fact that he could not write, made him its founding father.[161] He figures with Arthur among the medieval Nine Worthies, 'the best that ever were' in Caxton's Preface to his edition of Malory's *Morte Darthur*.[162] In *Love's Labour's Lost*, the grotesque show of the Nine Worthies is interrupted before Charlemagne delivers his speech, but he did have a monologue in Richard Lloyd's verse composition of 1584 which inspired Shakespeare's parade. By then, *Orlando furioso* had already begun to turn him into a fragile figure, the better to praise the new emperor whom Ariosto connects directly with the Roman Empire. François Ier had claimed Charlemagne's inheritance and failed, bitterly wondering what clause in Adam's will had excluded him from a share of the earth: it was Carlos de Habsburgo, another Carolingian heir, who won the imperial crown. In France the hagiography continued, down to Robert Garnier's *Bradamante* (1582), where Charlemagne embodies the link between Roman and Christian virtues, and rules over all Europe:

---

157 Piccolomini, *Cosmographia*, in *Opera omnia*, xxxv (p. 433), lxvii (p. 349). See Meserve, *Empires of Islam*.

158 See Charrier, *Recherches sur l'œuvre latine en prose de Robert Gaguin*, pp. 454, 517.

159 See Ziskind, 'John Selden'.

160 In Philippe de Mézières, *Le Songe du Vieil Pèlerin*, ed. by Coopland, and John of Salisbury, *Le Policratique*, trans. by Foulechat.

161 Jacques Verger, 'Charlemagne fondateur de l'université de Paris', in *Famille, violence et christianisation au Moyen Âge*, ed. by M. Aurell and T. Deswarte (Paris: Presses de l'Université Paris-Sorbonne, 2005), pp. 493–504.

162 They are first described in Jacques de Longuyon's *Vœux du Paon* in 1312.

L'Italie m'obeit, la superbe Alemagne,
Et les Rois reculez de l'ondeuse Bretagne.
(I.i.13–14)

(Italy obeys me, as does proud Germany,
And the distant kings of watery Brittany.)

Engraving Myths and Crusades

Henry the Fifth, thy ghost I invocate:
Prosper this realm, keep it from civil broils,
Combat with adverse planets in the heavens.

1 Henry VI, I.i

If martial ancestors were an asset in the fights for supremacy or autonomy, other founding virtues were required as well. The French dynasty could boast a long record of pious kings. Too pious sometimes, in the view of their consorts. Of Louis VII, ape-led by Bernard de Clairvaux, Alienor is reported to have complained, as would Shakespeare's Queen Margaret: 'This is not a man, but a monk I married'. French monarchy made its most decisive advances under Saint Louis (1226–1270) and his biographers.[163] Louis' moral prestige was such that Emperor Friedrich II referred his conflict with Pope Innocent at the Lyon council to the arbitration of the French king 'qui prud'homme était'.[164]

In a way, Louis' greatest defeat was his greatest victory. His major contribution to the legend of sacred monarchy was the cult of the dead monarch, crowned by his own self-sacrificial death in the crusade. He died, the records say, with the word 'Jerusalem' on his lips. Louis was the ideal *paterfamilias* at home and to the whole realm. His family meekly followed him on crusade, and not one but five royal coffins returned from the Holy Land. Richard the Lion Heart had been to the crusade before him, making an equally sad botch of the whole trip, but won little praise for it and failed to get himself killed, no doubt his worst political error. He was the last English king who did go to the Holy Land, yet down to Henry VIII, his successors would still harp on Jerusalem. Both King John and his son Henry III took crusading vows, as would Richard II, and Henry IV, who had to be content with a bathetic death in a room called Jerusalem.[165]

The link to a territory extends to the last one, burial in doubly hallowed grounds, Saint-Denis or Westminster. In France, it seems Saint Louis was the

163 Le Goff, *Saint Louis*, in *Héros du Moyen Âge*, p. 357.
164 Le Goff, *Saint Louis*, in *Héros du Moyen Âge*, pp. 398, 726.
165 The Jerusalem chamber at Westminster Abbey, transferred in the play to the royal palace. *2 Henry IV*, IV.ii.361–67, from *Holinshed's Chronicles*, III, p. 541.

first to stress this continuity.[166] Not content with engraving the royal history in the archives of the abbey, Louis reorganized the necropolis in magnificent style and expelled all non-royal corpses from the nave. Tombs of Merovingian and Carolingian kings were laid by pairs in chronological order on the right side of the choir, facing eight symmetrical Capetian tombs on the left, decorated with sixteen statues of *gisants*, effigies. In the centre, exalted graves of gold and silver were built two and a half feet above the ground for his forebears and himself.[167] In the prologue of his chronicle, Guillaume de Nangis informs visitors to the abbey that those who have no Latin can now read on the ground the French kings' genealogy. In a similar visual display of dynastic succession, Richard II commissioned thirteen statues of kings, from the Confessor to himself, for the freshly rebuilt Westminster Hall, though only six were actually set on its south wall. He also had a golden monument built in Edward the Confessor's chapel where he was to lie with his first wife. Each dynastic change after him caused jockeying for eminent positions in the central line and rearrangements of the chapel in Westminster, most notably by James I.[168] Richard's own plans for burial were thwarted by Henry IV, who chose to ignore his last will. But in 1413, Henry V had Richard rehearsed in his golden tomb, a good deed he recalls to God's memory in Shakespeare's play, on the eve of Agincourt.

A significant turning point in burial rites occurred at the height of the Hundred Years' War, with the demise in quick succession of the two competing monarchs. In this case, it was English practice that set the example. Henry V, having died in Vincennes, must take a long journey home. An effigy made of boiled leather wearing royal dress was laid on his coffin. When the French king Charles VI died two months later, the disinherited Dauphin claimed the crown on the strength of a royal ordinance taken in 1407 asserting his right of primogeniture. A letter from the regent Bedford bid the royal council acknowledge Henry VI as their sovereign, but after a reading of the ordinance they decided to defer until he arrived and ordered an effigy of the French king for his funeral.[169] Narratives of its journey from Amboise to Paris show a vivid contrast between the signs of sorrow and the signs of passage from death to life. An atmosphere of mourning dominated until the entrance to the capital, when the centre of attention moved from the coffin to the effigy: as in a Joyous Entry, it was carried in majesty under an azure blue canopy, followed by the unfurled banner, with the honours due to a king.

The presence of the Parlement de Paris around the coffin in the furred red robes of their function is one of the oldest features of the ritual:[170] as Martial

---

166 In the epitaph of Philippe I[er], 'this king belonged to the family of great Priam' implies a claim to be descended from the Carolingians.

167 Lewis, *Royal Succession*, pp. 116–17, 132–33.

168 Walker, 'Reading the Tombs of Elizabeth I'.

169 See Giesey, *The Royal Funeral Ceremony*, ch. 8, pp. 126–35, and appendix II, pp. 197–201.

170 Giesey, *The Royal Funeral Ceremony*, Appendix II, 'Cérémonial de l'inhumation de Charles VI'.

d'Auvergne explains in his *Vigiles de Charles VII*, the red cloak signifies that 'Justice jamais ne bouge' (justice is immovable).[171] After its fortuitous entrance, the effigy figures with increasing prominence in the ritual, while the two levels of symbolism, constitutional and personal, begin to draw apart, as do the body and image of the monarch. In his study of royal burials, Ralph Giesey reports an undignified quarrel at the obsequies of Henri IV (1589–1610), the first Bourbon, when the red magistrates jostled with the bishops for position, not around the coffin of the dead king but around the effigy representing the new one at some distance from the hearse. In England, at the death of Edward IV in 1485, the heralds threw their old coats of arms in the grave, put on new ones, and shouted 'Le roy est vif' (the king lives) three times.[172] In 1509, the cry became 'The Noble Kynge Henry the Seaventh is deade — Vive Le noble Roy Henry le VIIIth', the Franglish equivalent of the traditional formula that saluted the accession of the last Angevin, 'Mort est le roi Charles, vive le roi Louis'.[173] It was meant to express the distinction between person and dignity, whereas in France, the distinction is lost when *regia majestas non moritur* is translated as *le roi ne meurt jamais*. Both realms borrowed from the same source, the medieval *dignitas non moritur*.[174] Like numerous concepts of government, it was first formulated by the Church to define the permanence of dignities.[175] From its original object, the *dignitas* of an abbot, it was soon applied to all manners of *dignitas* — papacy, empire, monarchy — then to corporations and collective bodies.[176] In France, by successive drifts, it became attached to the king himself.

Constitutional Theories

> This land of such dear souls, this dear dear land,
> Dear for her reputation through the world,
> Is now leas'd out, I die pronouncing it,
> Like to a tenement or pelting farm
>
> *Richard II, II.i*

The major drawback in the French monarchy's progress towards full power was an accident of history, which again initiated a long line of flexible political theorizing. Philippe le Bel left three sons who died without male heirs. The death in 1316

171 'Les Vigilles de la mort du Roy Charles VII', in Martial d'Auvergne, *Les Poésies*, II, p. 170.

172 *Letters and Papers of Richard III and Henry VII*, ed. by Gairdner, I, pp. 3–10.

173 See Kantorowicz, 'Dignitas Non Moritur', *The King's Two Bodies*, pp. 383–450. For a critique of his theory, and errors, see Raffield, *Shakespeare's Imaginary Constitution*, pp. 89–101; Lorna Hutson, 'Not the King's Two Bodies', in Kahn and Hutson, eds, *Rhetoric and Law in Early Modern Europe*, pp. 166–98.

174 See Kantorowicz, 'Dignitas Non Moritur', pp. 316, 401–36.

175 Decretals of Gregory IX, X. I.29.14, in *Corpus Juris Canonici*, ed. by Friedberg, II, p. 162.

176 Kantorowicz, 'Dignitas Non Moritur', pp. 398–406.

of the eldest, Louis X, opened a succession crisis, the first in three centuries. His daughter's right to the crown was successfully usurped by his brother, Philippe V, who drew on the fact that no woman had ever ruled the realm to make it a law, 'Femme ne succède pas au royaume de France', though he agreed she could rule her kingdom of Navarre.[177] The argument backfired on his own daughter when he died six years later and was succeeded by his brother Charles, Philippe le Bel's last surviving son. Charles IV's demise without heir ended the line of 'Capétiens directs' and eventually launched the Hundred Years' War. Misogyny had played no direct part in the exclusion of women from the French throne, but it was a common theme in the circle of intellectuals under Charles V and would take far more prominence in the next phase of historiography.[178]

French *légistes* were hard at work again in the reign of Charles VI (1380–1422), whose mental instability brought France to a state of civil war between his powerful relatives. The humanist Robert Gaguin reports the quarrel for precedence that erupted at the coronation banquet of the twelve-year-old king between his uncles, Anjou and Burgundy, and their rivalry when he fell 'sick'. His grandson Henry VI would inherit his mental disease and endure the same surfeit of ambitious uncles. The hatred between brothers tore the realm apart between their Armagnac and Bourguignon supporters, reaching a peak with the murder of the king's brother Louis d'Orléans by the hired assassins of his cousin Jean sans Peur (John the Fearless), duke of Burgundy.[179] Jean Gerson, Chancellor of the University of Paris and renowned theologian, tried to obtain an indictment of the murderer at the Council of Constance, but the duke escaped scot free thanks to the efforts of his advocates, the theologian monk Jean Petit and Pierre Cauchon, the same clergyman who would convict Joan of Arc.[180] The Dauphin was less fortunate when John was murdered in his presence at Montereau: Parlement declared him 'indigne de succession' (unworthy of succeeding), for his alleged complicity.[181] The English entered France, so the saying went, through the hole in Duke John's skull: as direct heir through the female line, Henry V claimed the crown, though the terms agreed upon in the Treaty of Brétigny by his grandfather Edward III limited claims to restitution of the 'Plantagenet empire'.[182] The Parlement de Paris had rejected earlier English requests on the ground that the king could not alienate his demesne, which he swore at his coronation to keep.[183] The Treaty of Troyes confirming Henry V as heir to the French crown made no mention of his lineal rights: he was Charles VI's son by virtue of his marriage

177 Giesey, *Le Rôle méconnu de la loi salique*, ch. 2, pp. 27–47.
178 Giesey, *Le Rôle méconnu de la loi salique*, p. 78 and p. 298 n. 44.
179 Gaguin, *Grandes chroniques*, IX, pp. 120–120vo, 139, 140.
180 See Turchetti, *Tyrannie et tyrannicide*, ch. 13.
181 Paul Bonenfant, *Du meurtre de Montereau au traité de Troyes* (Brussels: Palais des Académies, 1958), p. 155.
182 The term used in *Dialogus de Scaccario* and after for the territories under Henry II's control.
183 Barbey, *La Fonction royale*, pp. 80, 305–14.

to Catherine.[184] The Dauphin's supporters, led by Juvénal des Ursins, denied its validity, borrowing arguments from the jurist Jean de Terrevermeille,[185] while Gerson and Christine de Pizan wrote treatises for the Armagnac party supporting Joan the Pucelle.[186] What happened next is told in *Henry VI*.

Terrevermeille's *Tractatus de jure futuri successoris legitimi in regiis hereditatis*, written two years before the Treaty of Troyes, was indebted to papal ideas on at least two points: the inalienability of the royal demesne, and the perpetuity of *dignitas*. Following earlier religious debates, he argues that the French crown is a *dignitas*, existing by itself independently of its successive holders.[187] The royal succession is neither hereditary nor patrimonial but statutory, and thus cannot be altered from its customary course by any will, testament, or treaty. With the support of Aristotle and Aquinas, Terrevermeille drew on both civil and canon law to systematize a growing current of thought.[188] From the eleventh century onwards, bishops had to swear on their consecration that they would not alienate the property of their dioceses. Likewise, the king did not own the royal demesne — he had the *usus* and *fructus*, not the *abusus* — so he could not alienate it nor the right of his natural heir. Thus Charles V and his successors would invoke the *promesse du sacre*, their coronation oath, to renege on agreements conceded in treaties of the Hundred Years' War.[189] This valuable tool would be turned against them by the Monarchomachs in the 1580s, at the height of the religious wars. It had found large echoes in England when the Protestant bishop John Ponet used it against Mary's attempt to restore Church property at the expense of the Crown, and would again when François Hotman, the militant Calvinist lawyer, re-edited the *Tractatus* in 1585 as a cornerstone in his constitutionalist theory (see below, Chapter 7).[190]

Monarchy is a function, not a property of the king, Terrevermeille argues. The rules regulating its transmission are all of customary nature, which is stronger than any positive law.[191] This does not justify other limitations to royal authority, which Terrevermeille fervently supports, exhorting the loyal people of the south to rally around the Dauphin. Once safely enthroned, Charles VII neutralized the Estates of the realm by gaining a permanent right to levy the *taille*: the great fiscal reform of 1439 made him sole master of taxation and enabled him to keep

---

184 Eugène Cosneau, *Les Grands Traités de la Guerre de Cent Ans* (Paris: Picard, 1889), pp. 100–115. See Valérie Toureille, ed., *Troyes 1420: Un roi pour deux couronnes* (Ghent: Snoeck, 2020).

185 Lewis, 'War Propaganda and Historiography'.

186 Goy-Blanquet, 'Shakespeare and Voltaire Set Fire to History'.

187 Jean de Terrevermeille, *Tractatus*, ed. by Hotman, I, art. I, concl. 3, 28.

188 Jean de Terrevermeille, *Tractatus*, I, art. II, concl. 1, from Aristotle, *On the Generation of Animals*, trans. by Platt, I, XIX, p. 27. Thomas Aquinas, *Summa theologica*, Qu. 119 art. 2, trans. by Roguet, I, pp. 939–43.

189 Jackson, *Vive le Roi!*, pp. 68–93.

190 Giesey, *Le Rôle méconnu de la loi salique*, pp. 134–35, 149, 321 n. 58.

191 Jean de Terrevermeille, *Tractatus*, I, art. I, concl. 24.

a standing army.[192] Here the course of history changed radically, sending France and England further on their separate ways. France would remain French, and the Estates General seldom meet again until 1789.[193] In England, kings would still need Parliament's consent to taxation. As Shakespeare rightly diagnoses at the opening of *Henry VI,* not evil stars but 'want of men and money' caused them to lose the conquests of Henry V.

Another principle, the instantaneity of the succession, had come into practice *de facto* when Louis IX died in Tunis in 1270. His son who had followed him on crusade could not be crowned for months but was allowed by the assembly of barons to issue documents in his own name. In legal terms, the king is never a minor: he holds full sovereignty from the moment of his father's demise.[194] Dynastic succession followed the *saisine,* the old medieval rule of inheritance: 'le mort saisit le vif, son hoir le plus proche et habile à lui succéder'. The reigns of all French kings after Louis IX were dated from the day of death of their predecessors, though their sovereignty was felt imperfect until blessed by the *sacre.* In popular opinion, as expressed by Joan of Arc's determination to take the Dauphin to Reims, the coronation ceremony made the king.

In France, as we saw earlier, crowned kings do not die. Giesey traces the first use of the phrase to Jean Bodin's *Six Livres de la République* (1576): 'For it is an old prouerbe with vs, That the king doth neuer die, but that so soone as he is dead, the next male of his stocke is seised of the kingdome, and in possession thereof before he be crowned'. In Bodin's definition of sovereignty as 'the most high, absolute, and perpetuall power ouer the citisens and subiects in a Commonweale: which the Latines cal *Maiestatem*', the term *République* has nothing to do with democracy. It stands for the State, as it does for Sir Thomas Elyot, but to Bodin this power is unequivocally embodied in the king: the sovereign cannot be subject to the commands of another, for his office

> is to giue laws vnto his subiects, to abrogat laws vnprofitable, and in their stead to establish other: which hee cannot do that is himselfe subiect vnto lawes, or to others which haue commaund ouer him. And that is it for which the law saith, That the prince is acquitted from the power of the lawes: and this word the Law, in the Latine importeth the commaundement of him which hath the soueraigntie.

Yet when Bodin comes to consider the English mode of government, it is clear that this power has limits, and not just in England, where no extraordinary taxes or subsidies can be imposed without the consent of Parliament:

---

192 Ordonnance (royal edict) of 2 November 1439, promulgated in Orleans, to create a standing army.

193 They were not summoned once between 1614 and June 1789.

194 On 26 April 1403 was promulgated the ordonnance organizing the succession, and a regency during the king's 'absences', his periods of mental incapacity.

> for so it is prouided by an auntient law of *Edward* the first, king of England, wherewith the people as with a buckler hath bene oftentimes seene to defend it selfe against the prince. Whereunto mine aunswere is, That other kings haue in this point no more power than the kings of England: for that it is not in the power of any prince in the world, at his pleasure to rayse taxes vpon the people, no more than to take another mans goods from him.[195]

Bodin had accompanied Elizabeth's suitor François d'Alençon to England in 1581, and been privileged to hear a Latin translation of his work by Cambridge scholars. Between his redefinition of sovereignty and the Bourbons' accession to power in 1589 after the religious civil wars, Giesey observes, a decisive step was taken, betraying the slant of French political progress towards absolutism.[196] James VI who owned a copy of *Les Six Livres de la République* would find in it ample food for thought.[197]

Had these two principles, inalienability of the crown and instantaneity of the succession, been adopted in England, Shakespeare's *Henry VI* and *Richard II*, Marlowe's *Edward II* would have taken a different course. All three monarchs were forced to abdicate in favour of an heir, with legal arrangements discussed below. That this heir was not the next of blood in Henry's and Richard's cases made material for the two Henriads. Richard II, whose original was so deeply impressed by French models, expresses the sacrilegious, sheer impossibility of being thus 'unkinged': 'With mine own tears I wash away my balm', 'My acts, decrees, and statutes I deny'. When Richard is ordered in Parliament to read

> These accusations and these grievous crimes
> Committed by your person and your followers
> Against the state and profit of this land:
> That, by confessing them, the soul of men
> May deem that you are worthily depos'd
>
> (IV.i.21–25)

only the Bishop of Carlisle protests:

> Would God that any in this noble presence
> Were enough noble to be upright judge
> Of noble Richard!
>
> (ll. 117–19)

But Bolingbroke has already taken justice in his own hands, before he is even crowned Henry IV, by presiding over the trial of Richard's followers: in thirty lines

195 Bodin, *The six bookes of a common-weale*, trans. by Knolles, I, VIII, pp. 113, 85, 92, 98.
196 Giesey, *The Royal Funeral Ceremony*, ch. 10, 'The King Never Dies', pp. 177–92.
197 Evrigenis, 'Sovereignty, Mercy, and Natural Law'.

he pronounces their indictment, verdict, and death sentence and has them led straight to the execution. Essex no doubt cast himself in this role of great justiciar when he ordered a revival of the play in 1601 on the eve of his own rebellion.

Holy Conversions

> Consideration like an angel came
> And whipp'd th'offending Adam out of him.
>
> *Henry V, I.i*

Far from turning their backs on the continent, English medieval chroniclers repeatedly urged their kings to reap the material rewards of virtue by modelling themselves on holy Louis or wise Charles V. Richard II, an admirer of both, consciously used some of their recipes in his last years to restore a sacred aura that had been seriously damaged by his brush with the Appellant Lords. In the Wilton Diptych, a striking example of his syncretic view of kingship, Richard kneels between two Saxon kings who came to be revered as saints: Edward the Confessor, founder of Westminster, hailed in *Macbeth* as healer of the realm, and Edmund, the last king of East Anglia. Beside these Anglo-Saxon tutelaries, Richard and the angels wear collars made from *planta genista*, pods of the broom plant, the emblem of his ancestor Geoffroy d'Anjou, but also the emblem of a mythical order, Ordre de la Cosse de Genêt, allegedly founded by Saint Louis. On the banner above the cross, a tiny orb shows a white castle standing on an island, a perfect miniature of Gaunt's 'sceptered isle'. His choice of patrons was carefully designed to combine several titles. Bury St Edmunds, which harbours various episodes in Shakespeare's histories, had many claims to historic significance. The motto of the Benedictine abbey, *sacrarium regis, cunabula legis*, records both the burial place of King Edmund, 'Shrine of the King', and the origin of Magna Carta, 'Cradle of the Law'.

Towards the end of 1214, according to the chronicler Wendover, a group of barons, disguised as pilgrims, took an oath before the High Altar in the abbey at Bury, that they would make King John put his seal to the Great Charter, a scene recorded in *King John* (V.vi), though without any mention of Magna Carta. The choice of the place was itself a gesture of protest. Edmund, the patron saint of England for over a thousand years, had been progressively eclipsed by saints of Norman pedigree. Edward the Confessor was canonized at the request of Henry II, who promoted him as England's second patron saint. Edmund's decline continued under Edward III, who dedicated his Order of the Garter to Our Lady and Saint George. Just as Chaucer and Langland were celebrating the culture of old England, Richard's diptych was politically rallying both Norman and Saxon cult figures.

But the best English parallel to Louis' masterly achievements must be that of Henry V. A direct heir of the holy king, as he loudly reminded everyone at the time of his claim to the French crown, he deliberately modelled himself on his ancestor. If he hadn't read Joinville's *Vie de Saint Louis,* he could have found plenty of material in the *Chronica Majora* of Matthew Paris, an admirer of both Louis IX and Friedrich II. Matthew often praises Louis the better to disparage Louis's brother-in-law, the English king Henry III, whom he finds too weak in front of the pope's legates, those insatiable leeches thirsting for English money.[198] God works in mysterious ways, but success at war was generally considered a sure sign of his favour, which Shakespeare's Henry V advertises when he has 'Non nobis' sung after his victory at Agincourt, God's victory.

Henry V, who unlike Louis had a pressing need to mend any trace of usurpation in his lineage, was equally aware of the need to present a faultless façade. He too showed great political wisdom behind a front of heroic and Christian virtues. Like Louis's, his charisma was made of hard work, genuine valliance, and exemplary virtue. Both French and English kings placed their footsteps in those of a victorious grandfather, Philippe Auguste in Louis's case, Edward III in Henry's, neither of them scrupling to use the somewhat cynical advice of their forebears. Both neatly divided rigorous public rule from private charity. Both aimed to lead Christian kings to the crusade and fought their just wars with the blessing of the Church, all the while dreaming of universal peace. Acts of mercy related by Louis's biographers read like the blueprints of Henry's show of magnanimity in Shakespeare's play. Lastly, both in some degree extended the sacredness of the kingly person to the State.[199]

Shakespeare scholars will have noted these and other familiar strains. *King John* stages the Tudor nightmare, when the Pope's legate sides with the nobility against their monarch. The sequence from *Henry VI* to *Henry V* upsets chronology but develops a continuous reflection on kingly power. Shakespeare's scrutiny of political institutions shows thinly veiled references to the Tudor resolution of the dilemma. Richmond, who arrives at the end of *Richard III* like a posthumous child, is the unknown quantity in the play. His 'miraculous' entrance, heralded by holy Henry's prophecy, is expected to found an ideal society, the pattern of which is left ideally unclear. Henry VI's imitation of Christ has proved a political disaster, when neither military heroism nor judicial talents could stem the mounting anarchy. Richard of Gloucester, who anachronistically claimed he could 'set the murderous Machiavel to school', fared no better. How Richmond will reconcile Christian charity with the rigour of statesmanship, how virtue can hope to triumph when the trinity of brave Talbot, wise Humphrey of Gloucester, holy Henry VI so signally failed, no one tries to explain. 'Whosoever shall follow truth too near the heels', Walter Ralegh warned all would-be historians, 'it may happily strike out his teeth.'[200] Any sequel to *Richard III* showing Richmond's

198 Matthew Paris, *Chronica Majora,* III, pp. 328, 374; IV, pp. 84, 137, 284–85. See Vaughan, *Matthew Paris,* pp. 140–41.

199 Le Goff, *Saint Louis,* in *Héros du Moyen Âge,* pp. 752, 846, 841.

200 Ralegh, *The History of the World,* Preface, p. lxiii.

management of the State would have come dangerously close to the Tudors' heels. *Richard II* returns to the crucial event, killing the anointed king, to face this tricky question. The point of the second sequence is not so much to study the inception of the Wars of the Roses as Edward Hall read it, but to pursue a line of inquiry blocked by Richmond's providential appearance in the plot.

Shakespeare's Lancastrian Henriad is definitely a sequel, not a prequel, to the first histories. After the unthinkable regicide, in *Henry IV* we see Prince Hal come to terms with his prickly inheritance and undergo a series of trials to regain effective mastery of the realm. *Parts I* and *II* deal with two phases of his education, first on the battlefield where he must prove his valliance and superior lucidity against the heroic Hotspur, then in the government of the realm, where he stands between Falstaff and the Lord Chief Justice. Falstaff's first reaction on hearing the king's demise must have damned him in the Elizabethans' eyes: 'Let us take any man's horses; the laws of England are at my commandment. Blessed are they that have been my friends; and woe to my lord chief-justice!'. In one devastating sentence, the Chief Justice exposes the seductive Falstaff as pernicious to the moral health of the commonweal: 'You speak as having power to do wrong'.[201]

With calculated measures of compensation, the reformed Hal recreates something of the mythical aura that remains essential to legitimacy in men's eyes, first twisting the churchmen's arms to make sure of their support. The Archbishop's sceptical reading of the Salic law allows the new king to claim Edward III's inheritance 'with right and conscience', thus placing himself in a line of heroes that bypasses the embarrassing usurpation. Henry IV disappears behind exalted memories of the Black Prince, the victor of Crécy, and Edward III. Now identified as 'a stem | of that victorious stock', Henry V adds a glorious episode to their high deeds, and for better safety, initiates the telling of it himself on the day of Crispin Crispian: 'This story shall the good man teach his son', his own heroic legend, amplified by 'a muse of fire'. His successful claim to the throne of France, 'this best garden of the world', makes up for the lost Eden of old Gaunt, Richard II's wasted garden. The wounds of civil wars are healed by the creation of a national army, 'we band of brothers', burying a past of endless fighting on the marches of England with those same Welsh, Scottish, and Irish captains: a thorough rewriting of facts, quite at odds with Hardyng's, Hall's, and Holinshed's accounts of Anglo-Scots relations.[202] An anonymous poet had opened the way to this revision in *The Mirror for Magistrates* (see below, Chapter 8) with a 'Tragedie' designed to 'quicken up spirites' entitled 'How King Iames the first for breaking his othes and bondes was by gods suffrauns miserably murdred of his owne subiectes', denouncing the Scots' role in the collapse of the later sixteenth-century plan for

---

201 2 *Henry IV*, V.iii.122–25; II.i.125.

202 *Henry V*, I.ii.96; II.iv.62–63; IV.iii.55; Prologue, 1; V.ii.36; IV.iii.59. See Hutson, ed., *The Oxford Handbook of English Law and Literature*, ch. 35, pp. 699–707.

Anglo-Scottish union, while the leaders of Lancastrian England are models of civility and order.[203]

In Shakespeare's play, the command Henry has won over himself further legitimates his accession:

> We are no tyrant, but a Christian king,
> Unto whose grace our passion is as subject
> As is our wretches fetter'd in our prisons
>
> (*Henry V, I.ii.241–43*)

— a grisly image of virtue, in the guise of a gaoler. Hal's reformation at his father's death is confirmed by the reaffected Church, a variant of the healing powers of the coronation. Henry V thus reconciles the opposite imperatives of morals and power by drawing an official line, a 'secret curtain' recalling Saint Louis's *secret*, between his own and the body politic. Virtue, like the soldier's soul, is a personal responsibility, with no place in the direction of public affairs. If the king shows magnanimity in forgiving private offences, royal dignity is an unforgiving, dehumanized machine. This audibly echoes the arguments around the trial and execution of Mary Stuart, when Parliament members warned Queen Elizabeth against the perils of excessive leniency (see below, Chapter 6). Now it is the threat to State security that is held sacrilegious. Rebellion may be still labelled 'another fall of man', but the religious overtones colour a civil doctrine of obedience, supported by a Church seriously concerned with its material goods. Shakespeare's plays re-enact the slow death of medieval monarchy and its laboured resurrection. The king who dies in the long agony of the Plantagenets is the divine king of stained-glass windows, whose doom critical observers of monarchy like John of Salisbury, or Shakespeare, foresaw long before it became fact. Henry V's exertions to reconcile virtue and practical demands briefly revive sacred monarchy, but it is ostensibly a myth in another sense of the word, Lévi-Strauss's logical construct to solve a contradiction.

---

203 Lucas, *'A Mirror for Magistrates' and the Politics of the English Reformation*, pp. 148–57.

CHAPTER 2

England's Mixed Polity

English Democrats

Compared with medieval French fashionings of the royal cult, the English kings stepped down from hallowed to mixed monarchy. Perhaps the unruly Plantagenets were too ill-fitted for hagiography, or too careless in omitting to enrol personal biographers, a fault the Tudors would strive to mend. They did manage to antagonize clergymen, who were never drawn to sing their praise as their colleagues did for French monarchs. Whereas in France the crowned head begins to devour the body, checks to absolutist leanings and lessons to rulers begin early in England, both through major political essays and in legal textbooks like Bracton's that shaped common law. Four resonant voices above many others laid the groundwork of alternative political theories, providing images and arguments that would continue to nourish Elizabethan debates.

The Body of the Realm: John of Salisbury (c. 1115–1180)

so work the honey-bees,
Creatures that by a rule in nature teach
The act of order to a peopled kingdom.

Henry V, I.ii

A former student of Abélard and Gilbert de la Porrée, John of Salisbury was a close friend of Becket, to whom he dedicated his work. While secretary to the former archbishop of Canterbury, Theobald, he had already incurred the king's displeasure by defending the rights of the Church and was thought responsible for the conversion of Becket from worldly warrior to militant priest, following him to France in his exile, returning with him in 1170. The story that he witnessed the murder in the cathedral and was wounded himself during the assault is probably a legend, for he makes no such claim in his own account of the event.

John's *Policraticus* is a mirror for wise princes, supported by lists of exempla and by some fanciful authorities of his own making, like Plutarch's 'Instruction of Trajan'. He undertook like many canonists and civilians to reconcile various continental currents of thought into a consistent theory, applying to politics the method applied by Irnerio to Roman law, by Abélard to theology, by Gratian to canon law. *Policraticus* remained the authoritative work of political science in all Europe until the *De regimine principum* that Gilles de Rome would write for the instruction of young Philippe le Bel, one in a long line of mirrors for princes.[1] Salisbury's metaphor of the State is probably drawn from the fable of the belly and limbs told in Livy by Menenius Agrippa, thanks to which 'he turned quite the peoples hearts'.[2] It is one of many variants of an old Egyptian fable, 'The dispute between the body and the head'.[3] Shakespeare read one version in Plutarch's 'Life of Coriolanus', but he could also have found it translated from *Policraticus* in Camden's *Remaines*.

The Prince, *potestas publica*, stands for all secular and spiritual leaders. His subjects are the *res publica*, the community. He is the head of this body, governors and judges act as his eyes and mouth, the senate as the heart, and the Church as the soul. His wealth is the wealth of his subjects. *Fiscus*, the stomach, occupies the middle level with the administrators who form the interior organs, while the soldiers, sheriffs, tax collectors are the arms and hands of the State. Salisbury does not expect virtue from this level; they have to be held to their duties by rewards and punishments. The courtiers who make the flanks, the gates of justice and power, are the part most exposed to corruption, and the object of his harshest criticism. The faults and frivolities of actual court life make up the 'nuggets' of his title, *Policratici sive de nugis curialium et vestigiis philosophorum*. The peasants, craftsmen, and tradesmen, who form the feet, are the basis of society; it is the rulers' first responsibility to protect and look after them. All parts are unified in working for the good of its members, a good defined as both happiness on earth and happiness in salvation. To Salisbury, there are two types of princes: those who rule by law and equity for the common good; those who rule by coercion for their own ends and reduce their subjects to servitude. How they accede to power, by heredity or election, is one of the first contradictions that must be solved. Both factors are important; neither is absolute. Ideally, the community of men elect the firstborn son of the preceding ruler. The question had immediate relevance in England, when Henry II considered having his eldest son crowned to ensure his succession, but Salisbury makes no topical allusions. His examples are taken from the Bible and Greek or Roman literature.

Salisbury thought of England as a sovereign State under a sovereign king, but there was no ambiguity as to the limit of this sovereignty: a law superior to all governors, which a righteous king respects, whereas a tyrant will break and destroy it. Last but not least, the *Policraticus* is not only the first known theory of the modern State, it is the first in a long line of radical writings to consider and dedicate several chapters to 'the most disconcerting theory of tyrannicide in

---

1 Berman, *Law and Revolution*, pp. 279–88, shows that the treatise draws on both Aristotle and Salisbury.

2 Livy, *Ab Urbe Condita*, II, 32.9–11, in *The Romane Historie written by T. Livius of Padua*, trans. by Philemon Holland (London: W. Hunt, 1659), p. 54.

3 F. R. Adrados, *History of the Graeco-Latin Fable*, trans. by Leslie A. Ray (Leiden: Brill, 1999), I, p. 329.

perhaps the whole Middle Ages'.[4] Book VIII also mentions his *De exitu tyrannorum* (Of the death of tyrants), which has not survived. Tyranny is the sick root which poisons the tree and must be cut with an axe; the tyrant must in most cases be killed (*occidendus*; VIII, 17). Whether Salisbury recommends execution as a moral duty or simply makes the point that violent death is a likely end for tyrants, confirmed by numerous exempla, is still undecided among scholars. After him the idea of tyrannicide becomes part of a common cultural equipment, in theory at least. More and Erasmus debate it while translating Lucian of Samosate's *Tyrannicida*. When confronted with reality, for instance under the rule of 'bloody Mary', or the threat of 'the Scottish Queen' (see below, Chapter 6), and again under the first Stuarts, most political experts would recommend deposition rather than such an extreme solution, even those who advocate civil disobedience.[5]

Salisbury's distinctions between lawful government and tyranny will be repeated in political treatises and poems down to the Renaissance and after. In France, Charles V had the *Policraticus* translated for his own library in 1372 by the Minorite Denis Foulechat. Its 'Nuggets' on courtiers will inspire Walter Map's *De nugis curialium* and feed popular hostility to these or other caterpillars of the State. In his admonitions to Richard II, the poet John Gower uses the old organic metaphor 'Quo caput infirmum, nichil est de corpore firmum, | Plebs neque firmatur, ubi virtus non dominatur' (when the head is infirm, nothing is firm about the body, and the people are infirm when virtue does not rule).[6] Anticipating Shakespeare's Gaunt, in the *Cronica tripertita* Gower condemns Richard's arrogant young ministers and the vices of his court. Salisbury's comment on the role of the Senate, drawn from Roman history, reappears in Fortescue's lessons to his prince, as it will in Lodge's *Wounds of Civill War*: the decay of the Roman Empire began with the expulsion of the Senators. James Morice's reading of 1579 at the Middle Temple still harps on the various forms of government and their perils: democracy tends to anarchy, ochlocracy to faction, monarchy to tyranny. A better kind of monarchy 'hathe byne by common Assent ordayned and established', wherein the Prince is ruled by law, while 'the People in due obedience saeflie lyve and quyetly enioye their owne'.[7]

The image of the body politic continues to inform the national debate, endlessly rehearsed by Elizabeth's Speakers in Parliament who urge the need for solidarity. In his accession speech, James I declares it unthinkable 'that I, being the Head, should have a divided and monstrous Body', the primary aim being to gather all the people in his two kingdoms, his 'natural Vassals', as one under his rule, while proclaiming the creed of his *True Lawe of free Monarchies*, 'the Head is ordained for the body, and not the body for the Head'. This brings an ominous

4 Turchetti, *Tyrannie et tyrannicide*, p. 251. See his ch. 12 on the important production of treatises on tyranny in the fourteenth century.

5 Turchetti, *Tyrannie et tyrannicide*, ch. 16.

6 Gower, 'O Deus immense', in *The Minor Latin Works*, ed. and trans. by Yeager, no. 4, ll. 85–86.

7 BL, MS Add. 36081, fol. 231, in Brooks, *Lawyers, Litigation*, pp. 212–13.

reminder from the Speaker that the body politic of His Majesty's commonwealth is 'figured and drawn out of the Rules of Law', and as the natural body cannot breathe without the soul, 'no more can the Politick Head of the other (although the supreme and commanding Part) stand secure without his Subjects, being the Politick Body, nor the Politick Body without his Laws, being his Politick Life, nor his Politick Life without his Politick Soul, being Execution'.[8] The image will become fact at Charles I's beheading.

Cure of the Church: Robert Grosseteste (c. 1175–1253)

Our next politologist is Robert Grosseteste. There are disagreements among scholars as to where he began his career, Oxford or Paris, but by 1230, he was teaching theology to the Franciscan friars of Oxford. As bishop of Lincoln, he went in 1245 to the First Council of Lyon, where the Roman Curia was then in exile, after the capture of many council fathers by Friedrich II's forces. In the midst of the conflicts tearing up Europe and the Holy Land, the English delegation distinguished themselves by asking to put on the agenda the canonization of the late archbishop of Canterbury, Edmund Rich of Abingdon, formerly Grosseteste's colleague at Oxford. Pope Innocent IV tartly answered that they had more pressing matters to deal with; nonetheless he agreed to start an enquiry into Rich's case and proclaimed him a saint at the end of the session.

The main business of the council was reform of the Church and the pope's struggle with the emperor. At the third session, when the resolutions were read, Matthew Paris reports that the English team protested against the report of King John Lackland's surrender of his kingdom to the vassalage of Rome, which had never been agreed on by the nobility. Their protests included specific points like the recent papal taxation. Grosseteste must have had a decisive influence on these, his biographer believes, for they fit the views he expounded five years later, when he pointed out that under the provision system, seventy thousand marks were paid yearly to alien nominees in Rome. The pope delegated the matter again, this time to the Curia, and returned to his main point, the rights of Saint Peter's successors over the Papal States through the Constantine Donation, and the bull of deposition against Friedrich II.[9]

Among the English grievances voiced at the council, one is directed against the see of Canterbury, its abusive authority and excessive power of visitation, which restricted episcopal initiative. Grosseteste's main concern is the need to appoint good pastors who will tend over their sheep with sound doctrine and justice: it is the duty of papacy to cure negligences and support bishops who aim to remedy the Church's evils. On the basis of Aristotle's *Nichomachean Ethics* and the *Hierarchies* of Pseudo-Denys, both of which he translated into Latin, Grosseteste

8 'Mr Speaker's Speech to the King', 22 March 1604, *Journal of the House of Commons*, 1, p. 147.
9 McEvoy, *Robert Grosseteste*, pp. 33–37.

contrasts tyrannical with legitimate rule and pleads for a rigorous hierarchical government of the Church, arguments that will return persistently in the ensuing controversies. According to Matthew Paris, Grosseteste was revolted to see the Curia wallow in money. He rebuked them vehemently and was overheard by the pope who retorted that English bishops were even greedier than they in pressuring the poor monks. Actually, in the reports, Grosseteste expressed great love and respect for the Roman see. It was later, in his final epistle, that he grew truly angry, when told to confer a benefice in the Lincoln diocese on the pope's nephew. The letter of confirmation threatened excommunication to those who rebelled against its command. Grosseteste then extolled the duty of disobedience, like a dutiful son against erring parents: 'as a Catholic, a proper son, and one who owes obedience, I disobey, I oppose, and I rebel against the things contained in that letter, chiefly because they so clearly verge upon the sin I mentioned'.[10] A similar claim makes the basis of the Protestant resistance theory that would be developed by Melanchthon and his friends: the Schmalkaldic League of Lutheran princes was looking for legal arguments to justify the use of force against Emperor Carlos V, although Luther forbade recourse to violence, even in defence of the Gospel, as he had condemned the Peasants' War.[11]

Matthew Paris lends Grosseteste a dying speech in which he calls the pope a heretic and the Antichrist: it was his ghost's appearance, predicting to Innocent he would soon lie in hell, that caused the pope's death the following night. In this colourful account, Grosseteste appears an early champion of the English Church against the proud Roman pontiff, a legend that persisted in the national historiography. To James McEvoy, the myth of the heroic bishop grew by gradual but traceable accretion. Ockham in his *Dialogus* took up the story of Grosseteste's encounter with the malicious pope: though denied the support of an attorney in pleading his case, he answered the canonists with the higher resources of theology and philosophy, which are 'the principles, roots and causes of all laws and canons'.[12] The chronicler Ranulf Higden reports his 'noisy' letter to the pope and adds to it an excommunication, which he appealed to the tribunal of Christ.[13] Wycliff invoked him to support his own attacks against papacy and repeated the story that he had died excommunicate. Foxe in his *Book of Martyrs* reproduced 'the Pope's unreasonable Letter' and 'The Answer of Bishop Grosthead', with a

---

10 McEvoy, 'The Final Letter (1253)', in *Robert Grosseteste*, pp. 48–49.

11 See Lazarus, 'Tragedy at Wittenberg', pp. 38–39. On Luther's position, see Turchetti, *Tyrannie et tyrannicide*, pp. 377–80.

12 Ockham, *Dialogus*, Part I, Book I, ch. 9. An edition of the Latin text and translation by John Kilcullen and others, commissioned by the British Academy, is available at <http://publications.thebritishacademy.ac.uk/pubs/dialogus/ockdial.html>. It is McEvoy, *Robert Grosseteste*, p. 67, who identified the anonymous 'commentator on blessed Dionysius'.

13 Ranulf Higden, *Polychronicon*, trans. by John Trevisa [1387], ed. by J. R. Lumby (London: Longman, 1876).

lengthy account of his resistance to the corrupt papacy. Others followed suit, until the nineteenth-century rewriting of the Middle Ages made him a proto-Protestant, despite his strong belief in *plenitudo potestatis*.

Franciscan Rebels: William of Ockham (c. 1288–1348)

Apart from his famous razor ('Entia non sunt multiplicanda sine necessitate', do not multiply entities where unnecessary), William of Ockham is best remembered for philosophical essays that made him the epitome, if not the caricature, of scholastic disputation, 'ad primam [...] ad secundam', rather than his political works. That his name still evokes inept scholasticism may be due to the lasting influence of Rabelais: 'Then was it that men began to tie their breeches to their doublets, and not their doublets to their breeches: for it is against nature, as hath most amply been showed by Ockham upon the exponibles of Master Haultechaussade.'[14] Ockham had studied at Oxford, perhaps at Paris, perhaps with the Franciscan Duns Scotus in both places, and may just have met Roger Bacon if he was indeed thirteen years old on entering the order. Whether or not he was directly influenced by these two staunch resistants, he breathed in at an early age an air rebellious to intellectual dogmas. Wycliff, Jan Hus, Luther, Melanchthon are often cited as his disciples.

The 'Testament' of Francesco d'Assisi had recalled his brethren to the original rule of the order: the imitation of the poverty of Christ. The most zealous of them, the Observants or Spirituals, did not tolerate any possession of property, while the Dominicans were opposed to the theory itself, raising fierce quarrels of the kind zestfully revisited in Umberto Eco's *Name of the Rose*. Matthew Paris, who is very critical of the new orders, notes in 1259 that the University of Paris, like Oxford and Cambridge, is 'not a little disturbed by the Preachers and Minorites' (see below, Chapter 3).[15] In the long run, the Dominicans conquered Paris, the Franciscans took Oxford. Ockham, who had friends in both mendicant orders, did not agree with an absolute renunciation that included study, provided that learning be put to the service of preaching. But Pope John XXII favoured the less rigorous conventual party and sided with the Dominicans. The Spiritualists who openly defied papal authority were delivered to the Inquisition. In 1322 the Franciscan doctrine of the poverty of Christ was pronounced heretical, and the chancellor of Oxford denounced Ockham for criticizing established theology. Ockham, with the Franciscans Michele da Cesena and Bonagrazia of Bergamo, was detained for years in Avignon while the Inquisition examined their works. Emperor Ludwig IV of Bavaria, who was also engaged in a fight with the papacy, helped the suspects flee to his court, where Marsiglio da Padova soon joined

---

14 Rabelais, *Premier Livre*, I, VIII, ch. 6, in *Gargantua and his Son Pantagruel*, trans. by Urquhart. See for instance Ockham, *Dialogus*, pars 3, tr. 2, lib. 1, cap. 7.

15 *English Historical Documents*, ed. by Rothwell, III, p. 151.

them. From their exile, they pursued the fight in writing against papal power and Dominican theories.

The *Dialogus*, 'A Dialogue between Master and Student concerning matters disputed among Christians', is thought to have strongly influenced the conciliar reform movement during the Great Schism and contributed to the emergence of liberal democratic ideologies.[16] The protagonists of *Dialogus* discuss learned opinions on the matters disputed between the pope and the dissident Franciscans, thus keeping a safe distance from those matters. The Master disagrees with Marsiglio's radical views in *Defensor Pacis* (1324) on the limitations of papal authority, so radical that Henry VIII's brain trust would commission an English translation to support his claim to supremacy (see below, Chapter 5). Marsiglio goes further than Dante in putting the Church under State control, while denying all churchmen any jurisdiction in temporal matters.[17] According to the *Defensor*, sovereignty resides in a select (*valientior*) body of citizens who make the laws and choose the mode of government, delegating their authority to the Prince.

To Ockham's Magister, the pope can do anything allowed by natural law or divine positive law, but from his authority 'there must be excepted the legitimate rights of emperors, kings and the rest, believers or non-believers, which do not conflict with good morals, God's honour and the observance of the gospel law'. The power of the emperor comes from God, not through the pope but through the people, for the empire was established by the Roman people. Neither he nor the pope has 'fullness of power'. Nor is it true, the Master argues, that he is 'released from the laws' (*a legibus solutus*), because he is bound also by the law of nations. 'What pleases the Prince has the force of law' only when it is something reasonable and just, for the sake of the common good.[18] If Ockham disagreed with Aquinas's division of the intellect, he shared his view of good government as the mixed product of three main forms: monarchy, aristocracy, democracy.

Like the Franciscan Spirituals, Ockham was incensed by the abuses of John XXII's controversial reign, which proved particularly inventive and greedy in fiscal matters. The treatise *An princeps pro suo succursu* integrates the arguments of Philippe le Bel's jurists to show that the king needs no papal authorization to tax his clergy. Church goods were conceded by the king under feudal law, they are the common wealth of the realm, and must serve primarily to preserve it from peril or poverty.[19] Ockham is also the author of *A short discourse on the tyrannical government over things divine and human, but especially over the Empire and those subject to the Empire, usurped by some who are called Highest Pontiffs*.[20] Yet at the

---

16 O'Donovan, *Theology of Law and Authority*.

17 Marsilius of Padua, *The Defender of the Peace*, trans. by Brett, I, XV, 10, 95; II, II, 7, 150; II, XVII, 1–19, 335–51.

18 Ockham, *Dialogus*, Part III, Book I, ch. 4. See George D. Knysh, *Political Ockhamism* (Winnipeg: WCU Council of Learned Societies, 1996). Kilcullen, 'Ockham's Political Writings'.

19 C. J. Nederman, 'Royal Taxation and the English Church: The Origins of William of Ockham's *An princeps*', *Journal of Ecclesiastical History*, 37.3 (1986), 377–88.

20 Also known as *Breviloquium*.

end of his life, a short treatise *On the Power of Emperors and Pontiffs* seems to repent his earlier anti-papal stance. In some stories, he made his submission to the pope shortly before his death. In others, he died excommunicate.[21] Though he is often saluted as a forerunner of Luther, recent scholarship tends to see him as less of a radical than was long thought. Brian Tierney interprets his variability as 'a tangle of self-contradictions', though to John Kilcullen, the apparent tangle is due to Ockham's method of exposition, which reflects the variety of current views without committing him to any.[22] Brother Franciscans had recently died at the stake. Evasion and ambiguity were needed to survive suspicions of heresy.

The basic principles of Ockham's earlier treatises will reappear under various guises in the polemics between secular and spiritual powers. The Master of *Dialogus* claims the liberty to criticize papal and conciliar views, even in defence of erroneous opinions, since no part of the Church is infallible: heresy begins with the obstinate belief in an opinion proved contrary to the faith. No secular ruler, king or emperor, is absolute, but their powers are independent from the Church. All rulers, lay or religious, must respect the civil laws, rights, and liberties of their subjects, so long as these are consistent with natural or positive Divine law, else they deserve to be deposed as tyrants.

Popular Grievances: John Wycliff (c. 1330–1384)

> Well, I say it was never merry world in England till gentlemen came up.
>
> *2 Henry VI, IV.ii*

John Wycliff certainly owed much to the political views of Ockham, though he professed a divergent Realism in philosophical matters. It has long been assumed that his *Determinatio quaedam de dominio*, in which, after Grosseteste and Ockham, he denounced the heavy sums levied in England for the crusades, was written in answer to demands for the English tribute. After several decades of non-observance, Pope Urban V had asked its payment in 1366 and met with a firm denial from Parliament, who declared England was subject to no foreign power. But Wycliff's tract, it seems, was written several years later. That he was granted a papal licence to keep his Westbury prebend in 1374 and sent abroad on a negotiatory mission with papal envoys shows he had not yet made himself obnoxious to the Curia.

In 1376, Wycliff read to his Oxford students his *Tractatus de civili dominio*, parts of which were integrated in the 'long bill' of grievances against the Curia at the Good Parliament. Pope Gregory IX condemned his theses the following year, attributing their source to Marsiglio, while Wycliff's fierce attack on the corrupt

---

21 G. Gal, 'William of Ockham Died Impenitent in April, 1347', *Franciscan Studies*, 43 (1983), 90–96, asserts he died excommunicate.

22 Tierney, *Origins of Papal Infallibility*, p. 227. Kilcullen, 'Ockham and Infallibility'.

Avignon papacy, his stance against the temporal rule of the clergy, his suggestion to secularize English Church property and impose reforms under the authority of the king, all found sympathetic echoes in both aristocratic and intellectual circles. These views must have found favour in Parliament, for he was consulted on the lawfulness of refusing to satisfy the pope's financial demands. How far they influenced the Peasants' Revolt is difficult to assess, but they were fully adopted by Jan Hus and had a direct bearing on the revolution in Bohemia.[23] Wycliff went on writing ever more radical works against the papacy and all levels of Church hierarchy. His arguments are summed up in the *Trialogus*, a dispute on doctrine and philosophy between three characters, Alithia (*solidus philosophus*), Pseustis (*infidelis captiosus*), and Phronesis (*subtilis theologus et matures*) 'who leads the discussion to the truth'.[24] It had its first printing in 1525.

The *De officio regis* asserts that the king is God's vicar, second to none on earth, and that the bishops derive their jurisdiction from him. In matters of faith, Wycliff's main target as a Realist philosopher was the doctrine of transubstantiation, to him a folly that led to idolatry, philosophically untenable since it involved a cessation of being. On this point he reopened a theological debate over the centuries with Lanfranc's 'artificial invective' against Berengar about the Eucharist. In the Great Schism, Wycliff chose as the true pope the one whom he thought best followed Christ's example, but his hopes that Urban VI would prove a reforming priest were soon disappointed and confirmed his view that God's Church could well live without a leader. The popes' vengeance was posthumous: by decree of the Council of Constance in 1415 Wycliff's books were destroyed, his remains exhumed and burned.[25] His most faithful disciple Jan Hus refused to recant and died at the stake, 'handing on from Wycliffe to Martin Luther the torch which kindled the Reformation'.[26]

How far Wycliff took part in the translation of the Vulgate is not exactly known. The initiative, prompted by a wish to bring Scripture, the one and only religious authority, to the mass of English Christians was certainly his, and he is thought to be the translator of the New Testament. The idea itself was an old one, close to the roots of English poetry: Bede had translated the first chapters of John's Gospel in Old English prose. The shepherd Caedmon's dream included versified extracts from the Bible. Wycliff's Bible and his Lollard movement coincide with the egalitarian visions of *Piers Plowman*, so vivid that the rebels borrowed phrases

23 Jan Hus vainly appealed to Pope Alexander V after a bull in December 1409 ordering the abjuration of Wycliff's teachings and the surrender of his books.

24 Wycliff's Latin Treatise, *Trialogus*, trans. by Lahey, Introd. p. 38. See Mark Thakkar's brilliant criticism of Lahey's translation in '*Duces caecorum*: On Two Recent Translations of Wyclif', *Vivarium*, 58.4 (2020), 357–83.

25 See Herbert B. Workman, *John Wyclif: A Study of the English Medieval Church* (Oxford: Clarendon Press, 1926).

26 'Jan Hus', *Notable Names Data Base*, Soylent Communications, <https://www.nndb.com/people/556/000094274/>.

and imagery from the poem.[27] When the Peasants' Revolt erupted in Kent, Wycliff was busy with plans to create an order of Poor Preachers. Even if he publicly condemned the uprising, blaming it on the mendicant friars, its themes had much in common with his theses. Parliament must have thought so too, for they banned the Lollards and repressed both types of rebel leaders equally without distinction.

The Suppression of Heresy Act of 1414 in the reign of Henry V specified 'that whoever should read the Scriptures in English, which was then called "Wiclifes learning" should forfeit land, cattle, goods, and life, and be condemned as heretics to God, enemies to the crown, and traitors to the kingdom'. John Ball, the outlawed priest of 1381, declared at his trial that he had learnt his lesson from Wycliff, though in fact he had begun to preach his revolutionary programme long before Wycliff defied traditional beliefs. The programme would travel through centuries from Jack Straw to Jack Cade and their reincarnation in *Henry VI*: take degree away, put all property in common, and live happily in the reformed commonwealth of merry old England. To the rioters, Parson Ball's rhyme 'When Adam delved and Eve span, | Who was then a gentleman?' evoked a happy state prior to all written laws, which were only devised to rob poor unlearned men.

Shakespeare's Cade likewise claims to create a new commonwealth when he anachronistically raids the Inns of Court, returns parchment to the original innocent lamb's skin, or absorbs Parliament in his Gargantuan mouth. In *Henry VI Part II*, public anger goes through degrees of discontent, from unheeded petitioners to angry commons to popular rebellion, but there is no suspicion that the playwright endorsed their communistic views. Cade is made even more of a cynical villain than in the chronicles, set on destroying the emblems of law and order, while the characters in the histories are generally as indignant as Edward Hall against 'the unruly commons'.

Good Counsel

The questioning of royal authority could erupt even nearer home, within the inner circle of counsellors, Becket's critical stance being but the first of many to have such resonant echoes. The tradition of religious advisers was plainly broken in England when, on his return from the failed campaign of Tournai in 1340, an irate Edward III ordered the arrest of the 'false guardians in England' and declared that he would no longer appoint clerics to great offices but only men whom, if convicted of treason, 'he could cause to be drawn, hanged, and beheaded'.[28] Several decades of mutual annoyance stood behind his fit of anger. Its chief target, Archbishop Stratford, when summoned to the king's presence to hear a long list of accusations,[29] denied the validity of any secular jurisdiction against him. He no

27 See Hudson, '*Piers Plowman* and the Peasants' Revolt', pp. 95–106.

28 *The French Chronicle of London*, ed. by Riley, pp. 82–87.

29 The *Libellus famosus*, or infamous pamphlet, issued on 10 February 1341, accuses him of treason.

doubt had Becket in mind when, being refused entrance at the Easter Parliament of 1341, he offered his body for sacrifice on the steps of Westminster. But once admitted in, instead of courting martyrdom he attracted many to his side and urged them to resist the king's encroachments on their liberties. The clergy, lords, and commons petitioned for a parliamentary control of justices and ministers, and audits for all accounts, foreign or domestic. Edward was forced to accept their demands as the price for a grant of thirty thousand sacks of wool, only to repeal the new statutes six months later, arguing they were contrary to the laws and customs of the realm and to the royal prerogative.[30] However, parliamentary recordings of the petitions and statutes still made it an important precedent. So did the Commons' reminder in 1343 that they had granted the levy of a ninth in exchange for the king's concessions, implying they could well withhold supplies if need be.

Attempts to define the conceptual basis of Parliament long hesitated as to its nature, whether it should be termed *concilium* or *curia* or both. *Concilium* was the name used for councils, the assembly of the religious authorities of the Church, inspired by the same ideology: shared responsibility. The debate about the role and composition of a council was not restricted to England; it coincided with debates within the Church over conciliar as opposed to papal authority, in which Ockham and Marsiglio both took part. Gratian and his successors considered a pope should be deposed if he violated *jus*, but there was no one in authority above him to decree it. English jurists like Bracton answered the same contradiction with the notion 'rule of law'. The limits to monarchic power were a shadowy area. The king is morally bound to obey his own laws, but there is no legal obligation for him to do so, nor judge above him to criticize his own rule if he will not.[31]

There were long-established precedents to the king's counsel or council, before the two meanings of *concilium* were clearly distinguished. Its oldest root, the tribal *witenagemot*, was an assembly appointed by the king, which suggests an institution submitted to his authority rather than the prototype of today's Parliament. Oliver Arnold voices scepticism about the representational ideology of Elizabethan and Jacobean MPs, without giving time or thought to the centuries of theoretical and armed conflict that established it. Undeniably, Shakespeare's interest in political representation is unique, and invaluable, but its alleged pessimism needs to be qualified. Though Arnold is right in reminding 'Whiggish critics' that Shakespeare is not our liberal contemporary, we do not just 'briefly glimpse the English Parliament' in the second tetralogy. It has at least one crucial scene that Arnold does not discuss:[32] the deposition of Richard II is moved from the secret of the Tower, where the chroniclers placed it, to the open stage of Parliament, to be performed in full view of the public as an effective transmission of power.

30 Ormrod, *The Reign of Edward III*.
31 See Kantorowicz, *The King's Two Bodies*, pp. 143–92.
32 Arnold, *The Third Citizen*, p. 10.

Parliament or Parlement

The oldest known use of the term 'parliament' in an official document appears in 1236 during Henry III's reign, in the records of a court of law.[33] The assembly could not write their own agenda, but the main purpose of the meeting, to raise funds for the king's wars, still offered opportunity for grievances and criticism of government policy. Edward I in his writ of summons insists that a most righteous law of the emperors 'ordains that what touches all should be approved by all' and that 'common dangers should be met by measures agreed upon in common'. What the king enacts with the consent of the whole body of representatives from all estates of the realm is a statute, a disposition which, even before their establishment as a separate house, conferred on the commons elected to the assembly some part of its legislative power. Most of the early rolls of Parliament, in which petitions were enrolled, date from the latter part of Edward I's reign: 'they are almost entirely taken up with the problems of common people in their everyday lives' and show why Parliament had such high value in popular opinion.[34]

The Parlement de Paris, an offshoot of the medieval *curia* like the English parliaments, took a different course, unconnected with today's Assemblée nationale which is a creation of the French Revolution. Apart from its judicial work, Parlement stood for the king in his absence but could not easily stand against him. According to the adage *Adveniente principe, cessat magistratus* (when the prince arrives, the magistrate is suspended), the royal presence turned judges back into simple counsellors. They could refuse to record a decision judged contrary to the law, in which case the king could force them to comply by holding a *lit de justice*.[35] This method, a meeting of Parlement in the presence of the king, became the quickest way to overpass recalcitrant judges. In the seventeenth century Louis XIV would suppress even their modest *droit de remontrance* by having his decisions recorded before Parlement was given a chance to remonstrate.

It was through the steady taxation caused by the Hundred Years' War that the English Commons began to acquire political influence.[36] The opinion in both countries since the early days of monarchy was that the king must live of his own, *vivre du sien*.[37] Matthew Paris generally praises Saint Louis above Henry III but for one fault, the excessive taxation of his realm to fund his crusades and a long list of extortions, for which God punished him.[38] Admittedly the revenues of the royal demesne were insufficient for a military campaign, but taxation must remain exceptional. This principle was repeatedly confirmed in England after the Model

33 Turner, 'The Origins of Common Pleas and King's Bench', in *Judges, Administrators and the Common Law*, p. 18.

34 *Parliament Rolls*, ed. by Given-Wilson. See Richardson and Sayles, *The English Parliament*, II, p. 749.

35 See Plate I, p. 8, Jean Fouquet, 'Le lit de justice de Vendôme', treason trial in 1458 of Jean II d'Alençon, Joan of Arc's comrade in arms who appears in *Henry VI Part I*.

36 McKenna, 'The Myth of Parliamentary Sovereignty'.

37 Wolffe, *The Royal Demesne in English History*, pp. 40–65.

38 Matthew Paris, *Chronica Majora*, V, pp. 171–72.

Parliament of 1295 that no tax should be levied without consent of the realm as a whole, represented by Parliament. In France, the Estates General were summoned likewise to meet urgent needs of money until 1439, when they very imprudently voted Charles VII a permanent right to levy the *taille* every year. Henceforth they would be allowed little say on the running of the realm until the summons of 1789. Not so in England. On this point, Shakespeare's Bagot voices a common feeling when he says that Richard II's excessive levies is the surest way to alienate his subjects, 'for their love | Lies in their purses'.[39]

From Curia regalis *to Privy Council*

Money was a powerful factor in the evolution of the law. When Henry III begged for help out of his financial straits, Simon de Montfort and a group of barons replied with the Provisions of Oxford. Their programme of reform placed power in the hands of a council of fifteen, elected by a parliament. There were to be three parliaments a year in which the councillors would 'treat of the common business of the kingdom and of the king likewise'. Four law-worthy knights in each county would 'hear all complaints of trespasses and injuries whatsoever inflicted upon any persons whatsoever by any sheriffs, bailiffs or whatsoever others'. These complaints would be enrolled for each hundred separately and submitted to the justiciar at his next coming.[40] Henry III swore to observe the Provisions, had them solemnly proclaimed in Latin, French, and English around the realm, and on being released from his oath by a papal bull of 1261, instantly overthrew them.

After resisting the Provisions in his father's time, Edward I adopted this innovation thirty years later:[41] the Parliament of 1295 made the practice regular, providing for ulterior ones a pattern of composition which earned it the retroactive name of 'Model Parliament', and Edward the title of 'Lawgiver' or 'the English Justinian'. It was under his reign (1272–1307) that Parliament began to meet regularly, with forty-six summonses in his thirty-five years of rule, and that the limit of 'time immemorial', that is, beyond legal memory, was fixed by the First Statute of Westminster as the accession date of Richard I, 6 July 1189.

The voice of the Commons begins to make itself clearly heard near the end of Edward III's reign, in a burst of outspokenness against the king's corrupt ministers.[42] The Good Parliament of 1376 insisted that they were representing the Crown when they took the initiative to designate a Speaker, impeach members of

---

39 *Richard II*, II.ii.128–29. *Holinshed's Chronicles*, III, pp. 844, 849–50. Blank charters and other exactions play a significant part in *Woodstock*. Walsingham reports that in 1397, Richard 'began to tyrannize' his subjects. On his evolution, see Saul, *Richard II*, pp. 366–68, 388–91.

40 'The So-Called Provisions of Oxford, 1258', trans. in *English Historical Documents*, III, no. 37, pp. 361–67.

41 Huw Ridgeway, 'The Lord Edward and the Provisions of Oxford (1258): A Study in Faction', in Coss and Lloyd, eds, *Thirteenth Century England*, V, pp. 89–99.

42 Roskell, *The Commons and their Speakers*, pp. 119–20.

the government, and name new ones. For the first time in history, the Commons were acting as a court for State trials. The king had urgently demanded a subsidy, but they were determined to obtain reforms in exchange.[43] As they anxiously wondered whom they should send to the king, 'God lifted up the spirit of a certain knight of their company whose name was Peter de la Mare,' pouring into him eloquence and wisdom: 'He stood with his colleagues before the Lords, of whom the greatest was John Duke of Lancaster, whose deeds always stood out in discord with his name' — deeds that Shakespeare would clear him of in *Richard II*.[44] The original John of Gaunt planned to terrify them into submission, but his men-at-arms remonstrated with him that the protesters had the support of the Lords and of the Prince of Wales his elder brother, not to mention God's manifest will.[45]

Again, Parliament was no sooner dissolved than Gaunt set to undoing its work. The new councillors assigned to the king were refused admission. The corrupt ministers were released, and Peter de la Mare thrown into jail. The Bad Parliament sat from January to March 1377, made a generous grant of taxation, introducing the first poll tax, and had the Good Parliament declared unconstitutional and its acts removed from the books. On 19 February, Gaunt offered to place the city under the jurisdiction of the marshal, his ally Henry Percy. On the twentieth, his palace of the Savoy was assaulted by angry citizens.[46] The plot of *Richard II*, which takes place some twenty years after the assault, shows no trace of these specific grievances and little sympathy for popular uprisings. Shakespeare, whose first concern is not historical accuracy, gives the expression of England's woes to 'time-honoured' Gaunt. The Savoy had anachronistically been destroyed in *2 Henry VI* by his senseless mobs, 'Rebellious hinds, the filth and scum of Kent'. Jack Cade claims to embody 'ancient freedom', but he is monitored by a discontented nobleman, and his rule represents the acme of the anarchy imputed by the chronicler Edward Hall to the 'rage' of 'the mutable commons'.[47]

The people's disappointment is most audibly voiced by Langland's council of rats in *Piers Plowman*. Before the barons and the wealthy burgesses, the lawyers are the first target of their resentment, having 'Pleden for pons and poundes the lawe | Not for love of ur lord unloseth heore lippes ones.'[48] Various analysts of the Peasants' Revolt consider the uprising as a symptom of popular frustration in the face of Parliament's inability to redress abuses. The levying of a poll tax, which triggers the rebellion in the anonymous *Life and Death of Jack Straw*, was

43 The debates of April–May 1376 are reported in the *Chronicon Angliae*.

44 In later revisions, Walsingham's attacks against Gaunt were suppressed. Stow, 'Richard II in Thomas Walsingham's Chronicles'. *Richard II*, I.i.

45 *Chronicon Angliae*, ed. and trans. by Thompson, pp. 68–85. For a more recent translation of Walsingham's continuation, see Walsingham, *The Saint Albans Chronicle*, ed. by Taylor, Childs, and Watkiss, vol. I, *1376–1394*.

46 *Chronicon Angliae*, p. 126.

47 *2 Henry VI*, IV.ii.113, IV.viii.26. *Hall's Chronicle*, pp. 207–08, 217–19.

48 Prologue, ll. 213–14, B-Text (*c*. 1379), printed in 1550. See Dodd, 'A Parliament Full of Rats?'.

just one of many grievances. Perennial issues like the problems of aristocratic livery and maintenance, which threaten the king's justice, corruption in the legal profession, evil counsellors remained unsolved. But the proceedings, with the Commons' petitions covering larger areas of discontent, were duly recorded in Parliament Rolls and in contemporary chronicles. The Commons' Speaker Sir Richard Waldegrave repeated many of the rebels' complaints in his warnings to the government in 1381.[49] Gaunt paid no heed to the knights' petitions, but the seeds sown by the discontented people would slowly mature.

Model Parliaments

> Now call we our high court of Parliament,
> And let us choose such limbs of noble Counsel
> That the great body of our state may go
> In equal rank with the best govern'd nation.

2 Henry IV, V.ii

A succession of 'Good', 'Bad', 'Model', 'Wonderful', 'Merciless' Parliaments who kept asking to be heard in their requests for reformation were instrumental in the deposition of three kings. In 1460, when Richard of York claimed the throne as descendant of Edward III's third son, his oration left the Lords speechless, Hall reports, 'as though their mouthes had been sowed up'.[50] After long arguments, it was agreed in Commons that Henry VI would reign to the end of his natural life and York be designated as his heir instead of young Edward. But Margaret summoned her supporters to fight for her son's inheritance. Armies then took the lead, reversing Cicero's 'Cedant arma togae'. In the throes of civil war, York like Cicero met a violent death. The crown was tossed several times between its rival claimants, leaving Parliament with little say in the matter. But constitutional issues had played an active role in two earlier succession crises.

Depositions

> For God's sake, let us sit upon the ground
> And tell sad stories of the deaths of kings:
> How some have been depos'd, some slain in war,
> Some haunted by the ghosts they have depos'd.

Richard II, III.ii

---

49 John Taylor, 'The Good Parliament and its Sources', in Taylor and Childs, eds, *Politics and Crisis in Fourteenth-Century England*, pp. 81–96. *Rotuli Parliamentorum*, ed. by Strachey, II, pp. 337–60. Dodd, 'A Parliament Full of Rats?', p. 47.

50 *Hall's Chronicle*, p. 248. See Kelly's commentary on his oration, *Divine Providence*, pp. 121–25.

At the Lincoln Parliament of 1301 Edward the Lawgiver's son was formally made Prince of Wales, the first in English history. His deposition twenty-five years later combined old themes and new ideas. How far Parliament was involved in the proceedings is not clear. A deputation sent to Kenilworth confronted Edward II with a choice of resigning in favour of his son or being forcefully deposed without guarantee of his son's succession. He agreed to resign, and William Trussell, the Speaker of Parliament, withdrew homage on behalf of all those listed in his proxy. Although the decision was taken by the magnates, in their speeches to the assembly they insist it must be done by unanimous consent. Any dissenting voices were wiped out from the records.[51] As to the validity of such an abdication, no one questioned it at the time. The decision was justified by a list of articles recording Edward's faults, mostly due to 'mavois consailiers' (evil counsellers).[52] It is echoed in a contemporary poem, 'The Lament of Edward II', in which the king deplores the betrayal in Parliament of his familiars, 'Lour faus foy en parlement | de heut en bas me descendi', but nonetheless confesses he deserved his downfall because he used his power to advance private friends. If he has done wrong it was in heeding their counsel.[53] In *Edward II*, it is the Speaker Trussel who confronts the king, 'My lord, the parliament must have present news, | And therefore say, will you resign or no?' (V.i.84–85), but Marlowe wastes no time on parliamentary procedures. Edward being warned that if he refuses 'the prince shall lose his right', he bows to the inevitable. The Bishop of Winchester announces that 'the king hath willingly resigned the crown'. Prince Edward is crowned two scenes later without further ado.[54]

In the case of Edward II, Parliament had only anticipated the natural succession of the king's eldest son, but it still made a significant precedent to the deposition of a king via parliamentary proceedings. Henry Knighton's *Chronicon* reports that the terms of this 'old statute' were invoked in 1386 by the Appellants who claimed the right to depose Edward's great-grandson Richard II for misgovernance, *malignum concilium, inepta contumacia,* and refusal to be guided by *salubri concilio,* the healthy advice of the nobles.[55] When Richard counter-attacked in 1397, he accused them of having searched the royal treasury for the articles of Edward II's deposition.[56] According to the reports, both kings resigned, then

51 *Forma depositionis Regis Edwardi* in Fryde, *The Tyranny and Fall of Edward II*, pp. 233–34. Valente, 'The Deposition and Abdication of Edward II', p. 871 n. 3, points out that Fryde's presentation of the manuscript is misleading: it is a biased record, monitored by Queen Isabella's circle, of the proceedings.

52 'The "Articles of Accusation against Edward II" according to Adam of Orleton', in Valente, 'The Deposition and Abdication of Edward II', p. 880. As to her query about 'deguerpist' (p. 879), the verb *déguerpir*, still in use, means 'to leave fast'.

53 'The Lament of Edward II', ed. by Smallwood, ll. 19–20, 25–30.

54 Marlowe, *The Complete Plays*, ed. by Romany and Lindsey.

55 *Chronicon Henrici Knighton*, ed. by Lumby, Rolls Series, 1889–95, II, p. 219, in Valente, 'The Deposition and Abdication of Edward II', p. 857.

56 Valente, 'The Deposition and Abdication of Edward II', p. 857 n. 4.

were deposed, and had homage withdrawn. Constitutional historians still discuss whether Edward was deposed in or by Parliament, and whether the assembly called at Westminster was a Parliament at all. Clare Valente finds the distinction anachronistic, since 'Parliament was still as much an event as an institution': the process stands at the crossroads between 'the old tradition of magnate oligarchy, new ideas of representation and popular or parliamentary authority, and an enduring ideal of the community of the realm'.[57] It was a deposition, she concludes, whitewashed as a voluntary resignation, despite the articles which were clearly an indictment, as in a trial. The *Modus tenendi parliamentum*, long read as a political tract on the deposition, seems more concerned with the way parliaments were run: it validates the idea of participation by subjects and points out that on taxation two knights in parliament carry more weight than the greatest earl of England.[58] It will resurface under Elizabeth to nourish debates on the authority of the Commons (see below, Chapter 9).

A doctrine of parliamentary authority, latent since the crisis of 1340, developed by steps in the following decades: deposition had been within the range of practical politics 'ever since the parliament of 1386 threatened Richard with the fate of Edward II'.[59] Once Richard had won the upper hand against the Appellants, his reallocation of titles and lands soon alienated most of the realm. In the poem 'O Deus Immense', Gower asks that he pay attention to his subjects instead of forbidding them to speak up,

Rex qui plus aurum populi quam corda thesaurum
Computat a mente populi cadit ipse repente.
Os ubi vulgare non audet verba sonare,
Stat magis obscura sub murmure mens loqutura.

(A king who treasures gold more than his people's hearts
Straightaway must fall from the people's mind.
Where the people's voice dare not speak aloud,
Their mind speaks more darkly in whispers.)[60]

He goes even further, 'Nomen regale populi vox dat tibi' (l. 61, the voice of the people gives you the royal title). A wise king will have ears for them if he wishes to be secure. At that point, Gower had 'not yet given up hope for Richard'.[61] Increasingly disgusted with Richard's rule, he would go over to the Lancastrians and write a poem praising Henry IV for a blessed act of war that rid the country of

57 Valente, 'The Deposition and Abdication of Edward II', p. 868.
58 *Parliamentary Texts*, ed. by Pronay and Taylor, p. 168. On problems connected with this text, see Prestwich's appendix, 'The Modus Tenendi Parliamentum', in *Plantagenet England*, pp. 224–26.
59 Gaillard T. Lapsley, 'The Parliamentary Title of Henry IV, Part II', *English Historical Review*, 49.196 (1934), 585.
60 Gower, 'O Deus Immense', 4, ll. 21–24, in *The Minor Latin Works*.
61 Introduction to Gower, *The Major Latin Works*, ed. by Stockton, p. 36.

a tyrant and drove the legitimate heir to the throne, 'So stant thi regne of God and man confermed'.[62] He quotes Bracton's statement that if *rex sapiens* loses his mind, corruption of the head descends to the members:[63]

> Ordine quo regnant Reges, sua nomina pregnant.
> Quo caput infirmum, nichil est de corpore firmum,
> Plebs neque firmatur, ubi virtus non dominatur
>
> (The kings who reign in good order, their names are fruitful.
> When the head is infirm, nothing is firm about the body
> And the people are infirm when virtue does not rule.)[64]

Gower seems untroubled by the fact that Edmund Mortimer, fifth Earl of March, the nearest heir to the crown, was bypassed, despite a family tree that would be rehearsed at length in Shakespeare's early histories.

The Merciless Parliament dominated by the Lords Appellant had convicted Richard's courtiers of treason and executed several of his favourites. In July 1397 three of the Appellants were arrested and declared guilty by the Revenge Parliament of September. Richard Fitzalan, Earl of Arundel, was tried and executed. His younger brother the Archbishop of Canterbury was exiled. Woodstock was imprisoned and murdered in Calais. The quarrel between Hereford and Mowbray, which launches the action of *Richard II*, erupted the following year, during the Parliament session of Shrewsbury. To Froissart, Richard made a grievous mistake in allowing their duel, as his counsellors told him: 'if ye suffre these two erles to come into the place to do batayle, ye shal nat be lorde of the felde, but the Londoners and suche lordes of their parte wyll rule the felde'.[65] On stage, the fall of medieval monarchy begins then.

Legal Process

The deposition of Richard II and Henry IV's contentious 'parliamentary' title partly repeated the transfer of power from Edward II to his son. The official report, the Lancastrian 'Record and Process of the renunciation of King Richard the Second after the Conquest', from which most English accounts derive, is full of inconsistencies.[66] The French *Chronicque de la Traïson et Mort de Richart Deux Roy Dengleterre*, Jean Créton's versified *Histoire du Roy d'Angleterre Richard II*, and Froissart's chronicle, which all support Richard, cannot be wholly trusted

62 Gower, 'In Praise of Peace', 2. 14, *English Works*, in *The Complete Works*, ed. by Macaulay, II, p. 481. Marginal notes stress the role of Parliament in the procedure.

63 Bracton, *On the Laws and Customs of England*, trans. by Woodbine, II, p. 306.

64 Gower, 'O Deus Immense', ll. 84–86.

65 Froissart, *Chronicles*, trans. by Lord Berners, XII, pp. 153–58.

66 *An Exact Account of the Proceedings and Articles against King Richard II*, in *English Historical Documents*, IV, pp. 401–08.

either. Before the meeting of the parliament, according to Adam of Usk, doctor in canon law, the estates set up a committee of learned doctors, jurists, and bishops who were instructed to find a way by which the king could be legally deposed. Again, the model came from abroad: the commission followed the procedure used against Friedrich II in 1245 at the Council of Lyon, where he was deposed for his crimes and dissolute behaviour in a document signed by 150 bishops.

Parliament was summoned by writs on 19 August for 30 September 1399. When it convened, the king was unrepresented, there was no presiding officer, no opening speech to explain the business to be done. It is not recorded as a parliament at all, neither as the last of Richard nor the first of Henry, and some reporters call it a convention of estates.[67] Even a staunch Lancastrian like Walsingham betrays doubt as to the validity of the procedure. On the eve of the meeting a self-appointed committee of lords spiritual and temporal, doctors of law and other notable persons representing the estates of the realm went to the Tower and obtained the king's abdication. Adam of Usk, who was part of the Tower committee, writes in his *Chronicon* that the abdication was read 'in pleno parliamento'. In the official account, the assembly concluded that the king had broken his coronation oath and deserved to be deposed.

The 'Record and Process' notes like Adam that no royal commissioner was there to open the meeting at Westminster and never calls it a 'parliament'. This document, monitored by the managers of the revolution and inserted in the roll of Henry IV's first parliament, betrays a complex state of irregularities. The sanction of the estates was the only one invoked throughout the proceedings: they were on one side *status*, the estates of the realm summoned by writ, on the other *populus*, the anonymous crowd of Londoners, to whose acceptance each step of the procedure was duly submitted. In the rewriting of facts, Richard gently resigns, confessing his faults, and designates his cousin as successor, a well-organized ambiguity left to be sorted out through the ironies of Shakespeare's dialogue, in the famously censored deposition scene.

The *gravamina*, the list of faults recorded against Richard II, gave this assembly the aspect of a tribunal.[68] They include practices depriving his subjects of rights guaranteed by Magna Carta, like arrests on suspicion, infringing on the 'potestas et status parliamenti', appealing to the pope for confirmation of statutes 'contra coronam et dignitatem regiam' and against the statutes and liberties of the realm. He is also charged with having alienated the property of the Crown without leave of the estates of the kingdom. The interests of the nation must be protected by Parliament against his arbitrary personal interference. The distinction between

67 Lapsley considers the 'Record and Process' a piece of Lancastrian propaganda. His three articles, 'The Parliamentary Title of Henry IV, Part I' and 'Part II, 'Richard II's "Last Parliament"', *English Historical Review*, 49.195 (1934), 423–49; 49.196 (1934) 577–606; 53.209 (1938), 53–78, are reprinted in *Crown, Community and Parliament*, pp. 272–340.

68 The *gravamina* are listed in *Rotuli Parliamentorum*, III, pp. 417–22, nos 18–51.

the royal person and the office is palpable here, opening the split that will leave Shakespeare's 'unkinged' Richard naked, and divine monarchy an empty effigy.

In Archbishop Arundel's view, brutally delivered to Richard at Flint Castle then repeated in his sermon to Parliament, the king's persecuted noblemen have a duty to restrain him, as the statutes give them power, and peril to the reign obligation.[69] This is the crux of the constitutional problem: Who may judge the king? To Bracton, if the king persists in doing wrong, only God's justice can punish him, the doctrine firmly adhered to by Shakespeare's Gaunt, drawn from Paul's reminder, 'Vengeance is mine saith the Lord'.[70] This double bind is still heavily pondered under the Tudor reigns. Arguably, one should not wait for divine justice to set things right if the king is a tyrant. In that case, as John of Salisbury allowed, it might be wise to take action before the whole country becomes lawless. Bracton himself admits a need to discuss this possibility. Yet all are aware that violent action in bringing down the tyrant will call down God's wrath upon the afflicted people. The growing political importance of Parliament and its progress in public opinion seem to designate it as the proper instrument to enforce the nation's will without illegitimate violence.

But Henry Bolingbroke had other plans. Once the throne was visibly vacant, he claimed it in right of descent vindicated by conquest, which the estates, *status regni et vulgus*, accepted. The lords gave their answers severally, and the people agreed by *acclamatio*. Henry showed them the signet given by Richard, as pledge of his cousin's will he should succeed, and had writs issued in his own name summoning a Parliament for the following Monday. Since there was no time for elections, the Commons resumed their authority without mandate from their constituencies, 'thereby creating an undesirable precedent'.[71] From the accounts, despite the care displayed in the 'Process' to distinguish it clearly from the earlier meeting, it was held in contemporary opinion as a continuation of it. The same people, under a different designation.

The commission's suggestions of legal or acceptable ways to make Henry king have not survived. The reports agree on the three modes of accession he chose to present, those summed up in Gower's marginal note to the poem known as 'In Praise of Peace' — 'primo successione : secundo eleccione : tertio conquestu sine sanguinis effusione' — as well as in Froissart, where Richard formally resigns the kingdom.[72] Chaucer's envoy in his 'Compleint to his Empty Purse' strikes a different note, through a different order which puts conquest first:

69 Lapsley, 'The Parliamentary Title of Henry IV, Part II', notes that similar charges were made at Flint by Arundel.

70 Romans 12. 19, quoting Deuteronomy 32. 35.

71 Lapsley, 'The Parliamentary Title of Henry IV, Part I', p. 428.

72 Gower, *The English Works*, in *The Complete Works*, III, pp. 481–94. Froissart, *Chronicles*, XII, xxvi, p. 156.

O conquerour of Brutes Albioun,
Which that by lyne and free eleccioun
Ben verray king, this song to yow I sende.[73]

Henry IV was received as king by Parliament on 30 September 1399, and on 3 October he gave Chaucer an added yearly grant of forty marks.

Right of Conquest

With such a set of motifs, Bolingbroke owed nothing to Parliament, contrary to the original doctrine of the Lancastrian party, who had encouraged public opinion to expect a parliamentary treatment of the matter. The case was trickier than in 1327, when the function had continued without dynastic break. Henry took advantage of the legal impasse created by the vacancy of the throne to dictate his terms to his allies and stated his claim to succeed by conquest of his inheritance. The presence of a disorderly mob, interpreted as a form of *acclamatio* in the 'Process', no doubt exercised some influence on the events. Troops in black armour darkly fill half the miniature of Henry's coronation in Jean de Wavrin's *Chroniques*, adding shades to his statement that it was done 'du consentement du commun dangleterre'.[74] All Parliament was asked to do was to secure Richard's resignation and declare Henry his successor, then incorporate the transaction in the official record.

Once crowned, Henry IV summoned a new Parliament, where he heard the challenges between rival factions, ordered a new enquiry into Woodstock's murder, and had the Bishop of Carlisle arrested, all episodes which *Richard II* stages before the actual deposition.[75] Shakespeare thoroughly upsets the proceedings by altering the sequence of events and by restoring the invisible Richard to centre stage. The duke is trapped in Richard's masterly performance when he puts his hand on the crown tantalizingly held before him, for instead of graciously resigning as expected, Richard taunts him:

Here, cousin, seize the crown.
Here, cousin, on this side my hand, on that side thine.

(*IV.i.180–81*)

Bolingbroke loses the benefit of the carefully designed show: 'I thought you had been willing to resign', and rather clumsily insists, 'Are you contented to resign the crown?', with no better success: 'Ay, no; no, ay'. Now the ritual uncrowning

---

73 Chaucer, *Minor Poems*, in *The Complete Works*, ed. by Skeat, I, no. XIX, p. 406, and note pp. 562–64. B. W. Lindeboom, 'Chaucer's Complaint to his Purse: Sounding a Subversive Note?', *Neophilologus*, 92 (2008), 745–51, thinks it may have been originally dedicated to Richard.

74 Jean de Wawrin, *Anchiennes Chroniques d'Engleterre*, fol. 262.

75 *Holinshed's Chronicles*, III, pp. 4–6. *Richard II*, IV.i.

empties each gesture to be performed at his ensuing coronation of their symbolic charge. The anointment, the regalia, the oaths will all appear meaningless parodies. Richard and sacred medieval monarchy hold the stage for one last tragic scene.[76] The sound of footsteps on his grave will echo through the next plays, under showers of English blood: 'sad stories of the death of kings' told at the fireside will still draw tears from the hearers before the common weal begins to move away from the warlike court to a world of taverns, rural towns, and prosaic trade.

There is still much argument among scholars about the presence or absence in the play of the deposition scene, which appeared in print for the first time in Q4. To Cyndia Clegg, it was censored in the earlier texts because the notion that Parliament had the authority to make or unmake kings must have been anathema in 1597, when Elizabeth had no declared successor, yet far less subversive in 1608.[77] But Richard Dutton thinks it equally possible that it was genuinely a new addition for the Jacobean era.[78] Too late, then, to inflame Essex's London troops. Even more significantly, Shakespeare departs from his sources to highlight the role of Parliament by transferring the deposition scene from the Tower to Westminster. François-Victor Hugo, a staunch republican, was the first to stress the significance of this revolutionary move: 'In front of the wretched Westminster that divinizes tyranny, Shakespeare erects the formidable Westminster where it is unthroned'. What, Richard calls on God for help? He deserves no sympathy, and will get none. To the French progressivist, Elizabeth, who chose to identify herself with Richard, deserved no better fate, exercising as she did 'the double supremacy of pope and emperor, mistress of all consciences as of all destinies, arbiter of faith, arbiter of law'. That the prince should behave as 'le droit vivant', law incarnate, is but another phrase for tyranny: 'he is subject, as we all are, to the universal laws of equity'. The poet, like a justiciar (here Shakespeare stands for François-Victor's father, Victor Hugo, champion of liberty, exiled by an arbitrary power), did not alter the work of Providence, he was just God's stage director. He dared to stand up against 'la sultane toute puissante de l'Angleterre', the almighty sultana of England, 'and summon before the people's bar this imperial monarchy that claims to hold a mandate from above'. His play will 'establish by a famous and revealing example that law is the supreme force'.[79]

The similarity between Richard and Elizabeth has often been discussed, though seldom with such passion. Any doubts as to the authenticity of her conversation with Keeper of the Records William Lambarde — 'I am Richard II. Know ye not that? — have recently been cleared by Jason Scott-Warren's thorough investigation. She read the volume Lambarde presented her with, a digest of rolls

76 *Richard II*, III.ii.145–47, 155–56.

77 Cyndia Clegg, '"By the Choice and Inuitation of Al the Realm": *Richard II* and Elizabethan Press Censorhip', *Shakespeare Quarterly*, 48 (1997), 432–48.

78 Dutton, *Shakespeare, Court Dramatist*, pp. 262–63.

79 Hugo, 'La Patrie, I', pp. 25–30.

running from King John to Richard III, 'not just as a catalogue of documents, but as a list of monarchs, something akin to the portrait gallery at Westminster', where she had inserted a newly discovered picture of Richard II.[80] Her position at the time may have been imperilled by the Essex uprising, but Shakespeare's play did not inspire a spirit of rebellion in the Londoners. The Tudors made abundant use of the royal prerogative, yet were wise enough not to advertise absolutist views. However, the young James VI, who had suffered from the Ruthven Raiders an oppression as humiliating as Richard's by the Appellants, did not share their caution. When urged by Elizabeth's minister Walsingham to follow the advice of his Parliament if he did not want to end like Edward II, he declared his will to be 'an absolute king'.[81]

In James's view, Parliament holds its authority from the king, who holds his from God: 'And so it followes of necessitie, that the Kinges were the authors & makers of the lawes, and not the lawes of the Kings.'[82] He finds a legal basis to his claim that 'Monarchie is the true paterne of Diuinitie' in Jean Bodin's recently published theory of the State. To Bodin, as we saw above, 'the subiect oweth his obedience to his soueraigne prince, towards and against all, the maiestie of God excepted, who is the absolute soueraigne of all the princes in the world', but the power of the State is unambiguously embodied in royal power. The king, like the pope, cannot tie himself with his own hands: 'Wee see also in the end of all edicts and lawes, these words, *Quia sic nobis placuit*, Because it hath so pleased vs: to giue vs to vnderstand, that the lawes of a soueraigne prince, although they be grounded vpon good and liuely reasons, depend neuerthelesse vpon nothing but his meere and franke good will.'[83] The doctrine would lead James's son to the scaffold, while French kings would enjoy another century and a half of absolutism before they met the doom promised to tyrants by the poets.

80 Scott-Warren, 'Was Elizabeth I Richard II?', p. 226, confirms the report of their meeting.
81 From Walsingham's notes on their interview, in Read, *Mr Secretary Walsingham*, II, pp. 213–18.
82 James VI & I, *The True Lawe of free Monarchies*, ed. by Craigie, pp. 57–82.
83 Bodin, *The six bookes of a common-weale*, I, VIII, 106, 92.

CHAPTER 3

Rival Law Codes

England's great war of independence from foreign powers focused around its law system, with early attempts to sever it from its European roots. Geoffrey of Monmouth's *Historia* unfolded a tale of its immemorial ancienty: his British kings all build cities and make laws when they find a moment to spare from their endless wars. In the 1470s, Fortescue's colleagues claimed that common law went back to the creation of the world.[1] William Blackstone in his *Commentaries on the Laws of England* defines it as the equivalent of *jus non scriptum* in Aulus Gellius, 'tacito et illiterato hominum consensu et moribus expressum' (existing by the tacit consent and practices of illiterate men) — unwritten rules observed throughout the kingdom and made binding by immemorial usage.[2] He does not say how common law singularly grew apart from the European *jus commune*, a point that deserves further exploration. Outside England, *jus commune* meant the jurisprudence of Roman, canon, and feudal law taught from the eleventh to the sixteenth century in the universities of Europe, whose network of alumni played major roles in both the circulation of a legal doxa and the administrative growth of chanceries. The term 'common law' was taken over from the canonists by English lawyers, who reinterpreted the original *jus commune*, a system common to Europe, to distinguish the general law of England from local English practices.

Roman Law

> *Suum cuique* is our Roman justice.
> This prince in justice seizeth but his own.
>
> *Titus Andronicus, I.i*

The teaching of law, and the creation of universities with which it is intimately connected, has a troubled history. It was a major issue in the strife for the imperial rule of Christendom. The question of *jus*, both 'right' and 'law', occupies a central place in the politics of princes learned in law themselves, or who employed jurists formed in the leading schools of Europe. Innocent III built his theory of theocracy

1 Baker, *The Oxford History of the Laws of England*, VI, p. 18.

2 Blackstone, *Commentaries on the Laws of England*, ed. by William Carey Jones (San Francisco: Bancroft-Whitney, 1915), § 75, p. 108.

with the help of his friend Uguccio da Pisa, who taught at Bologna.[3] A long line of jurist popes ruled almost uninterrupted through the high Middle Ages. Twelve of those elected between 1187 and 1389 had studied law at Bologna, Paris, or Orleans. Simultaneously, many lawyers nurtured in the Roman Curia emigrated to other European courts. By the first half of the twelfth century, *jus commune* had significantly penetrated into other legal systems. Jurists around Europe used it to build the norms that governed medieval society but felt no obligation to adopt each and every rule like gospel truth, in England especially, where Roman law made a delayed entrance.[4]

In the turmoils of the dying Roman Empire, the main secular source of Roman law was the *lex romana Visigothorum*, later known as Alaric's *Breviarum*, which the Frank Clovis had declared applicable to all the Gallo-Romans. The Justinian code, recovered around 1080 in northern Italy,[5] helped to validate the role of the emperor as legislator of the divine will. When the Byzantine emperors lost the power to enforce this domination, popes took over the charge of *pontifex maximus* which had been the imperial prerogative since Constantine. After years of struggle, Friedrich I Barbarossa recognized the pope's sovereignty over the Papal States, while the pope acknowledged his overlordship of the imperial Church. Having thus made his peace with his old enemy, Barbarossa went on the Third Crusade with Philippe Auguste and Richard the Lion Heart, but died in Cilicia before he had a chance to confront Saladin. His grandson Friedrich II would still have to deal with crusading demands and conflicts with successive popes.

Bologna

Politics was a dominant factor in the creation of universities, spiritual and temporal powers again competing to promote or control them. When the Diet of Roncaglia was called in 1158 to determine the rights of the rebellious cities assembled in the Lombard League and those of their feudal sovereign, the case was put to four jurists from Bologna, the famed Four Doctors, who argued that the Roman law entrusted to the empire was the only valid one and ruled in favour of the emperor. Barbarossa thanked them with a *privilegium scolasticum* that made Bologna a precursor of medieval universities in Europe, as its motto *Alma mater studiorum* legitimately claims. Until then public instruction everywhere had been mostly confined to monasteries. However, this *Habita* was not a foundation charter, and he betrayed little further interest in the Bolognese *studium*.[6] For more than a century, the Bologna law school was free from any ecclesiastical control,

3 Two of Innocent's letters to Uguccio were inserted in the decretals of Gregory IX.

4 Pennington, 'The "Big Bang"'.

5 It had disappeared after the empire's loss of the Exarchate of Ravenna in the eighth century.

6 David Lines, who kindly allowed me to read sections of his forthcoming *Dynamics of Learning* on the University of Bologna, shows that the students owed more to papal than to imperial support and points out various fabrications in the historiography of the Bolognese *studium*.

run by the students, who negotiated with the town authorities a charter enabling them to recruit, pay, or dismiss their teachers and to decide on the contents of the teaching.[7]

The papacy was striving to keep schools within the ecclesiastical institution and occasionally forbade clerks to study lucrative profane disciplines like law or medicine. In 1291, Pope Nicholas IV granted Bologna's graduates the privilege to teach anywhere in Christendom.[8] The teaching of civil law was prohibited in Paris, because it drew students away from theology, then the great specialty of the Sorbonne, but allowed ten years later in Toulouse by Gregory IX, after the Albigensian crusade, to pursue the fight against heresy. Friedrich II tried to dissolve the *studium* of Bologna to promote the University of Naples he had just founded, with the express mission of training his civil servants. Aquinas studied at Naples for six years before he entered the Dominican order, moving on to Cologne and Paris. Laymen trained in Bologna or Orleans came to occupy posts in chanceries and administrations which had until then been filled by ecclesiastics.

It was in Bologna that teachers operated fundamental developments in civil and canon law in the first half of the twelfth century, David Lines shows. There and in other European cities, the curriculum opened up during the second half to include the *Decretum Gratiani*, the canon law of the Catholic Church. This helped the pope grow from bishop of Rome to universal leader of Christendom, uniting the whole corpus of written codes in the archive of his body. Bernard de Clairvaux, a leader of the Cistercian reformation, soon foresaw perils in this domination of jurists over the administrative wheels of papacy. In 1139, he complained that the pope had paid no heed to his advice in a religious arbitration: 'Who will do me justice against you? If I had a judge before whom I could take you, I would quickly show you what you deserve.'[9] The papacy's will to legislate for the whole of Christendom resulted in a number of decretals and their glosses which Accursius undertook to arrange into one body. His *Glossa magistralis*, one hundred thousand glosses written in mediocre Latin, made him the idol of contemporary jurisconsults, and the target of Rabelais' scorn for his gloss, 'so scurvy, vile, base, and unsavoury' that the books of civil law are like 'a wonderfully precious, royal and triumphant robe of cloth of gold edged with dirt'.[10] His son Francesco d'Accorso was invited to lecture on law at Oxford by King Edward I, 'the English Justinian', but consigned to the seventh circle of hell by Dante with a bunch of scholars who failed to perform the duties of their profession.[11]

After the Avignon interim, the Bolognese jurists regained their position in Rome and rose in full strength with Gregory XIII, doctor *in utroque jure* (canon

---

7 Rashdall, *The Universities of Europe*, I, pp. 87–267.
8 Lines, *The Dynamics of Learning*, introduction.
9 Bernard de Clairvaux, Letter CCXIII, in *Life and Works*, ed. by Mabillon, trans. by Heales, II, p. 623.
10 Rabelais, *Gargantua and his Son Pantagruel*, Bk II, ch. 2.v.
11 *Inferno*, Canto XV, l. 110A. Richard Kay, 'Dante's Unnatural Lawyer: Francesco d'Accorso in Inferno XV', *Studia Gratiana* 15 (1972), 147–200.

and civil law) of Bologna where he had taught for eight years. Under his pontificate they made a tight group in the Curia, organizing, among momentous reforms, the suppression of ten days from the Christian calendar, 4–15 October 1582, to bring it in agreement with the moon. The commission that recommended this solution to the gap between tropical and civil years included several curialists, and scholars from all parts of Europe. When this decision was made, most Protestant countries rejected it. In England, the astrologer John Dee and the various scientists consulted by the Privy Council were on the whole favourable to the reform, but the bishops were unanimously against it, and the Parliament of 1584, whose main concern was the safety of the queen, buried the bill. In Robert Poole's opinion, the dividing line on the issue 'lay not between England and Rome, but within England, between church and state'.[12] The Old Style would remain in use until 1752, when the leap from September 2 to 14 caused popular riots and banners demanding 'Give Us Our Eleven Days'.

Paris and Orleans

The University of Paris, with privileges officially granted by Philippe Auguste in a charter of 1200, claimed Charlemagne's École du Palais in its origins, though there is no evidence that this school was settled in France. It began as a guild of teachers, who professed in separate faculties: unlike Bologna, where the students took the initiative in structuring their own university, in Paris the masters ruled the schools.[13] The faculty of arts was the first, obligatory level of studies, before a move on to the higher faculties of law, medicine, and theology. The art of dialectics took its full measure there, through the argumentation *pro et contra* and *disputatio* which increasingly took the place of the traditional textual commentary. The disputations, often held over several days, made high drama of the dialogue mode and gave star status to figures like the monk Abélard. Aristotle's treatises, which had resurfaced at the end of the twelfth and through the thirteenth century via Latin translations, held the centre of controversies. Aquinas's attempt to accommodate Aristotelian physics to the dogmas of Christian faith and the precepts of natural law raised fierce disputes long after him between defenders and supporters of his theories. The doctrinal censures of Aristotle's works, as reread by the Andalusian jurist Averroes, culminated with the condemnation by the bishop of Paris, Etienne Tempier, of over two hundred theses in 1277, but failed to close the argument.[14]

Roman law at first was not well received in France, where it was felt to be the law of Empire, the enemy power. Pope Honorius III (the same one who gave his support to the mendicant orders) had prohibited it at the University of Paris to

---

12 Poole, *Time's Alteration*, chs 2–4.

13 Baldwin, *Paris, 1200*, pp. 211–12.

14 For a summary of the events and of the scholarship on these verdicts, see König-Pralon, *Avènement de l'aristotélisme*, pp. 15–23, 63–66.

protect the teaching of theology, threatened by its mercantile appeal. Masters and students then moved with their Roman texts to Orleans, where law studies were formally allowed by a bull of 1235. Its schools of law and *litterae*, famed since the ninth century for their *ars dictaminis*, the writing of letters and drafting of official documents, were raised to the status of university in 1306 by Clement V, a former student of theirs. Now established as the French centre of Roman law, Orleans produced most of the *légistes* who perfected French Gallicanism under Philippe le Bel, as well as government officials and authors of *coutumiers* (collections of provincial customs) like Philippe de Beaumanoir.[15] Professors travelled back and forth with enviable ease. King Philippe's chancellor Pierre de Belleperche, a former Orleans student, had taught the Post-Glossators in Bologna. Accursius's three sons lectured for a while in Orleans before they returned to Bologna, where Francesco taught Cino da Pistoia, whose most illustrious pupil was Bartole, who taught Balde....[16] As in the Sicilian court, law sometimes mixed well with poetry. Cino the jurist was also an admired poet, one of the first to use the *dolce stil nuovo*, and a friend of Dante who praises his poetry in *De vulgari eloquentia*.[17]

Orleans's connection with Naples was kept up by the Anjou claims. Pope Innocent IV had invited Saint Louis' brother Charles of Anjou to a share of Italy, hoping by this move to withdraw it from the imperial obedience. After many reversals of alliances, and upheavals like the Sicilian Vespers, the Angevin domination was finally defeated in 1412, leaving the last Anjou heir, 'poor King Reignier, whose large style, | Agrees not with the leanness of his purse', to be the butt of Shakespeare's irony.[18] The University of Orleans reached a peak in the late fourteenth century, shut down after Agincourt, and only resumed its teaching when the siege of the city was raised. It grew into an important centre of Renaissance humanism, drawing in its ranks Erasmus, Rabelais, Guillaume Budé, Calvin, and an active centre of Reformation, until seriously weakened by the religious divisions.

Oxford and Cambridge

There were many channels through which Roman law travelled to England. Culture and science were transnational: students learnt in one place and brought their knowledge to another. Itinerant clerics, like *condottiere*, offered their trade and served masters in different countries. The poet Henri d'Avranches moved from Germany to England, with spells in Rome and the Netherlands. Diplomatic events provided more opportunities for cultural exchanges with the continent.

---

15 On the teachers of the Orleans *studium*, see Feenstra, 'L'École de droit d'Orléans'.

16 Soetermeer, *Livres et juristes au Moyen Âge*, pp. 51–60. Kees Bezemer, 'Word for Word (or Not): On the Track of the Orleans Sources of Cinus' Lecture on the Code', *Legal History Review*, 68.4 (2000), 433–55.

17 *Rime di messer Cino da Pistoja jureconsulto e poeta celebratissimo* (Rome, 1559).

18 *2 Henry VI*, I.i.108–09.

Chaucer attended the marriage of Galeazzo Visconti's daughter Violante in Milan where he could commune with other famous guests, Froissart and Petrarch, or infamous ones like the renowned mercenary John Hawkwood.

Lanfranc, Anselm, Vacarius, John of Salisbury had all studied and taught in continental schools or universities before they came to England. Stephen Langton and Thomas of Chobham, like Hildebrand, were students of Pierre le Chantre before they returned home. John of Bologna, Italian secretary of Archbishop John Peckham of Canterbury, wrote a dictaminal treatise based on his experience in the Roman Curia, to teach English clerks how to frame official letters. The diplomatic correspondence of kings of England thus borrowed their elegant preambles from papal models. It was common practice for English bishops to send young clerics to Bologna. Becket was there when Vacarius was thought to study law with the Four Doctors. The French diplomat Pierre de Blois, who was chancellor of Sicily before he served Henry II, Alienor, and several archbishops of Canterbury as Latin secretary, had studied law in Bologna and theology in Paris.[19] The English kings found no difficulty in recruiting Norman or Sicilian servants.[20] The office of justiciar itself was imported from Sicily, where at least a third of all the students and masters were English. The English administration, both royal and ecclesiastical, offered more jobs than France at the time. The Capetian government would take half a century to catch up, during the bureaucratic growth led by Saint Louis.[21] Around 1200, the only teacher known to lecture on Roman law in Paris was Roger le Normand, who had publicly debated the case of Thomas Becket with Pierre le Chantre.[22]

It was during the years of 'Anarchy' under Stephen's reign that Roman law began to spread through more conventional channels. Archbishop Theobald of Canterbury, who needed expert legal advice in his struggle for primacy with the Bishop of Winchester, returned to England with Vacarius. The Italian canonist gave lectures on the *Corpus juris*, either at Oxford or at Theobald's law school.[23] His *Liber pauperum*, a compendium of the *Codex Justinianus*, was devised for the poorer students who could not afford the complete texts, since the law should not belong by monopoly to the wealthy. In one important section dealing with the relation between civil law and custom (1, 8), the original authority of the *Codex* is interpreted as 'the emperor, or custom', which Vacarius considers derived from consent of the people, 'consuetudo populi tollit legem', a wide step away from his Bolognese masters.

The teaching of Roman law raised fierce insular opposition. The lay baronage 'stood up for the Teutonic feudal law of the Anglo-Normans against the decrees of

19 Baldwin, '*Studium et Regnum*', pp. 199–211.
20 Haskins, 'England and Sicily', pp. 433–47.
21 Hollister and Baldwin, 'The Rise of Administrative Kingship'.
22 Baldwin, *Paris, 1200*, pp. 189, 276 n. 74.
23 Southern, 'Master Vacarius', denies the theory that Oxford was a centre of Roman law in the twelfth century and doubts Vacarius actually taught there.

Roman popes and emperors',[24] and Salisbury's *Policraticus* reports that by an edict of Stephen prohibiting civil law, 'our Vacarius was silenced'.[25] But the 'silencing' did not last. By the next generation, Oxford was famous for its study of civil law. As it spread to other parts of the realm, in 1234 Henry III forbade its teaching in London, again under pressure from the barons. Two years later the parliament of Merton issued a proclamation that they would admit no change to the used and approved laws of England, 'nolumus Angliae leges mutare, quae huiusque usitatae sunt et approbatae'.[26] It was too late. The fame of Azo, saluted as 'Master of all the Masters of the laws' at the head of the Bolognese school was such that in 1205 Thomas of Marlborough, future abbot of Evesham, spent six months at Bologna attending his daily lectures. Two of Azo's works, a *Summa* of the first nine books of the Justinian Code and a *Summa* of the *Institutes*, would be Bracton's main source.

The Common Law of the Realm

Despite claims of a home-made law, there is strong evidence that Roman *jus* was studied in many English centres of learning.[27] The first school of law opened at Oxford, using Vacarius's *Liber pauperum* as a textbook, at about the time when Ranulf de Glanville's treatise was composed. Whether it was influenced by Roman law is tied up with a larger question, its influence on the shaping of Henry II's reforms, which a fair number of British scholars tend to minimize. John of Salisbury records the circulation of Roman legal doctrines at Henry's court, while Becket complained that the king was using learned men from Bologna in his cause.[28] Still, common law grew into a settled system before the Commentators offered an alternative in the late thirteenth century by harmonizing customary law with Roman law. The Norman Conquest had unified England earlier than other European countries and left no strong provincial custom to survive as it did in a France split between north and south, *droit coutumier* and *droit romain*. Local customs did not need Roman law to be harmonized; they could simply be ignored.[29]

---

24 Lieberman, 'Magister Vacarius', p. 311.

25 'Vacario nostro indictum silentium'. Charles Casassa, 'Magister Vacarius "hic in oxonefordia legem docuit": An Analysis of the Dissemination of Roman Law in the Middle Ages', 26 November 1991, <https://web.archive.org/web/20060212234625/http://history.eserver.org/dissemination-of-law.txt>.

26 In a debate on the legitimation and rights of children born before or out of wedlock. Statute of Merton, 20 Henry III.

27 Zulueta and Stein, *The Teaching of Roman Law in England*, p. xxx.

28 John of Salisbury, *Policraticus*, VII, 20. See *Materials for the History of Thomas Becket*, ed. J. C. Robertson (1875–85, VII, 26 n. 358), in Watson, *Legal Origins and Legal Change*, p. 85.

29 Theodore F. T. Plucknett, 'Roman and English Law', *University of Toronto Law Journal*, 3.1 (1939), 47–50.

Textbooks and Sources: Ranulf de Glanville (c. 1112–1190)

When did the writing of common law begin? In Maitland's vibrant homage,

> If we must fix a date at which English law becomes articulate, begins to speak to us clearly and continuously, on 3 September 1189 is perhaps the best date that we can choose. The writer whom we call Glanvill had just finished the first text-book that would become a permanent classic for English lawyers.[30]

The *Tractatus de legibus et consuetudinibus regni Angliae*, the first known treatise on English jurisprudence, commonly called the Glanvill, was commissioned by Henry II.[31] Roger of Hoveden in his *Chronica* imputes it to the wisdom of the justiciar Ranulf de Glanville, but Maitland, who found this attribution too 'obscure', suggested it was the work of Hubert Walter, Glanville's nephew and secretary. Walter had gone on the Third Crusade, acting there as intermediary with Saladin, and imposed heavy taxes to raise the Lion Heart's ransom. On Richard's return, Walter was elected to the archbishopric of Canterbury and made justiciar the same year, serving efficiently in both capacities to the end of his life. He appears on a list of contributors to a chapel in Bologna commemorating Becket.[32] Since he lacked professional training, other authors have been suggested, or a weaving together of several shorter treatises by all these candidates, helped by members of the justiciar's staff at Westminster, in the same way that 'Bracton' grew out of small tractates on particular topics.[33]

The Glanvill's practical approach suggests that it was meant as a handbook for the personnel of Westminster, in the wake of the great legal reforms of 1166–1176, when the administration of justice was being organized into more permanent shape. Among the possible influences listed by scholars were early decretal collections, especially as the author argues that English unwritten customs are equal to the *jus scriptum* of Rome and the Church. Glanville had some knowledge of Roman law, but little use for it since the main object of his work was feudal tenures and relationships between owners and tenants. What he owed to Roman law was more a general spirit of order that he applied in attempting to extract a rational system from the mass of royal writs, rather than specific debts over legal cruxes.

Whoever wrote the Glanvill adhered to the Constitutions of Clarendon in putting the royal court above ecclesiastical ones. A Prologue praises Henry II's military valour, love of peace, and high standards of justice and asserts that the

---

30 Maitland, 'Why the History of English Law Is Not Written', in *The Collected Papers*, I, p. 488.

31 Pollock and Maitland, *The History of English Law*, I, p. 164.

32 Cheney, *Hubert Walter*, p. 18, and 'Hubert Walter and Bologna', *Bulletin of Medieval Canon Law*, 2 (1972), 81–84, thinks he studied in Bologna.

33 Turner, *Judges, Administrators and the Common Law*, pp. 72–74, 93–101. See his introductory essay, pp. ix–xxiv, for a critical survey of the divisions between schools of thought over the origins of English law.

laws of England had their origin in reason. The Roman maxim 'What pleases the prince' is qualified with a note that the king 'does not scorn to be guided by the laws and customs of the realm' and that he takes the advice of his magnates to make laws. Yet much depends on his mercy. The grand assize is a royal favour emanating from his clemency to the people, an alternative to the establishment of proof by combat.[34] The *Dialogus de Scaccario* and the Glanvill, both written by faithful servants of monarchy, both speak in support of royal supremacy.

Law Makes the King: Henry de Bracton (c. 1210–1268)

Rex non debet esse sub homine sed sub Deo et sub lege, quia lex facit regem.

De legibus et consuetudinibus Angliae, I, 39

Born shortly before the Great Charter of English liberty, the first great English juridical writer, Henry de Bracton, served King John's son, Henry III, as a judge of the court then known as *coram rege*. Like a majority of professional judges at the time, he was also a clergyman. The legal historian Samuel Thorne stresses the European character of his *De legibus et consuetudinibus Angliae*, a detailed and accurate statement of English law:[35] Bracton drew both on native materials and on works by continental jurists and canonists. He was engaged in writing his *De legibus* at the time of Friedrich II's death, and Kantorowicz finds many similarities of expression with the *Liber Augustalis*, though no evidence that Bracton was familiar with it. The analogies may well be due to common sources of Roman law, Azo for one.[36] The jurist's understanding of *rex legia* is radically different from Friedrich's, and even from his master Azo's gloss, which transfers all its power and authority to the prince: 'The king will be the minister of him whose work he performs. Therefore as long as he does justice he is the vicar of the Eternal King, but the devil's minister when he deviates into injustice.'[37] This endows him with more duties than exceptional powers.

'Though in almost all lands use is made of the *leges* and the *jus scriptum*, England alone uses unwritten law and custom',[38] Bracton begins, laying the foundations of British creative originality. They still deserve to be called laws, since whatever has the consent of the whole *res publica* and the authority of the king has the force of law. In describing the *jus commune* that was then taught at the universities, he uses principles of Roman law to rationalize results reached in English courts, which makes his manual 'the last English law book' to take its

34 Glanville, *The Treatise on the Laws and Customs*, ed. by G. D. G. Hall, Prologue, 12.23, 14.8, 2.7.

35 Written before 1259, first printed in 1569 in folio, and reprinted in quarto in 1640. Maitland gives an account of Bracton's life in his edition of *Bracton's Note Book*, I, *Apparatus*.

36 Kantorowicz, *The King's Two Bodies*, pp. 187–88.

37 Bracton, *On the Laws and Customs of England*, trans. by Woodbine, II, p. 305.

38 Bracton, *On the Laws and Customs of England*, II, p. 33.

place in the mainstream of European development, 'the first heroic attempt to show the coherence and essential rationality of English law'.[39] He too held that 'the king must not be under man but under God and under the law, because law makes the king', an opinion in agreement with contemporary theories of national independence. Archbishop Arundel in his sermon at the opening of Henry IV's first Parliament will repeat Bracton almost verbatim in stressing three requisites of every government: justice, the observance of the laws of the kingdom, the maintenance of every man in his estate and degree. The law is supreme, whether formulated in statutes or judgements, and the king is its agent.[40] Yet, by arguing that law makes the king, Bracton heralded Fortescue's notion of mixed polity and furnished Edward Coke's ulterior legal arguments against James I.

Like all the authors of major treatises, Bracton was confronted with the problem of defining *jus naturale*. It is 'what natural reason has established among men': 'In one way, what is always equitable and just is called *ius*, as is *ius naturale*'. To the civilians, its meanings included a state prior to the existence of human laws, an instinctive mode of behaviour, or rules of equity common to all men, inspired by Providence before the enactment of civil codes that vary between countries. In the last meaning, *jus naturale* and *jus gentium* can be reconciled (II, 26–27). More generally, natural law is understood as the law that governed God's people before Moses gave them his commandments, preceding and surpassing human positive laws. The phrase 'Natura, id est Deus' (Nature, that is, God), which occurs in both Azo's *Summa* and in the *Gloss* of Accursius, shows the complex interplay of classical and Christian ideas in the thought of the glossators.

An exploration of *natura* and its theological background is outside the scope of this book, as it was beyond some of the jurists' who had to cope with its varied meanings. To Brian Tierney, Accursius, for one, did not have the philosophical equipment needed to solve the contradictions between varying interpretations of the term, but his gloss perfectly fits the theologians' distinction between *natura naturans*, God's creative 'nature', and *natura naturata*, the created world. Thus God is equated with *natura naturans*, interpreted by the Dominican Vincent de Beauvais as the 'supreme law of nature': 'natura naturans, id est ipsa summa lex naturae quae Deus est'.[41] The interchangeability for the fifteenth-century jurists of divine with natural law developed from this equation, down to the debate between Perdita and Polixenes over the powers of 'great creating nature' in *The Winter's Tale*: 'Yet nature is made better by no mean | But nature makes that mean'. The point here is its impact on the discussion of equity, which will become a major issue in the early sixteenth century with the extension of the 'courts of conscience' under the chancellor's authority (see below, Chapter 4).

---

39 Thorne, *Essays in English Legal History*, p. 78.

40 *Rotuli Parliamentorum*, III, p. 415. See Lapsley, 'The Parliamentary Title of Henry IV, Part II', p. 577.

41 Tierney, 'Natura Id Est Deus: A Case of Juristic Pantheism?', *Journal of the History of Ideas*, 24.3 (1963), 315–17.

Bracton applied to English law Aristotle's principle of *epieikeia* (fairness, equity) in *The Nicomachean Ethics*: the *dikastes* (juror/judge) must judge according to *dikè* (justice), but the *diaitetes* (arbitrator) should make his decision according to *epieikeia*, which takes into account the presumed intention of the lawgiver. Bracton argues that this principle serves to unify practices, because it 'desires like right in like cases and puts all things on an equality'. Aristotle's discussion of natural law in *Rhetoric* is augmented with Aquinas's comprehensive discussion in the *Summa theologica*.[42] Is *epieikeia* a virtue or not? asks Aquinas. Is it part of justice or not? Within the law or outside the law?[43] To Bracton, because they were 'made and chosen' to exercise equity, English kings have a large discretionary power, which for practical reasons they delegate to judges. Through the judges' decisions, equity is part and parcel of the common law. Yet the Statute of Northampton in 1328 would set them at odds by ruling that no royal command 'shall disturb the course of common law, and that if such a command is issued, the judges shall ignore it'.[44] By denying themselves the right to use this delegation of royal power, the judges were outlawing equity.

Edmund Plowden would still quote Aristotle when he argued that no lawmaker can foresee all that can happen, hence the need to interpret the reason of a law instead of sticking to its letter and to imagine what the lawmaker would answer 'touching the Equity' if he were present, for then 'you do not act contrary to the Law, but in Conformity to it'.[45] In Constance Jordan's words, here 'Plowden makes the interpreter of a statute its quasi-author'.[46] Nonetheless, common lawyers would grow increasingly hostile to the arbitrariness of equity, up to the point when John Selden declared 'equity is a roguish thing'. To some, it was an evasion from common law, even if its supporters argued after Aquinas that equity stood within the law and served to mend its imperfections. The very suggestion that common law could be imperfect was blasphemy to its staunch advocates, not to mention the danger to their practice when faced with competing equity courts (see below, Chapter 4). As for the nature of natural law, it involved so many contradictions between types and levels of authorities, what were or were not precepts grounded in 'the reason of natural law', that it would take centuries before the jurists agreed on its contents. To Kenneth Pennington, 'Bracton's discussion of natural law did not bear fruit in English legal thought until the fifteenth and sixteenth century, but the seeds of a natural law tradition in the common law were planted early.'[47]

42 Aristotle, *Ethics*, v. 2–4, 10, 25–26. Aquinas, *Summa theologica*, I, pt II, questions 91 and 94.

43 Aquinas, *Summa theologica*, question 120.

44 Plucknett, *A Concise History of the Common Law* (London: Butterworth, 1940), p. 145.

45 Plowden, 'Eyston v. Studd, Easter Term, 16 Elizabeth', in *The Commentaries, or Reports*, Pt II, pp. 466–67.

46 Jordan, 'Shakespeare's Law and Plowden's Authority', in Curran, ed., *Shakespeare and Judgment*, p. 86.

47 Pennington's 'History of Natural Law' is no longer available online. For his views on Bracton's 'heady broth' of Roman law doctrines, see his *The Prince and the Law, 1200–1600* (Berkeley: University of California Press, 1993), pp. 91–94, and ch. 4 on positive and natural law.

In Praise of England: John Fortescue (c. 1394–1476)

Elected to Parliament during the minority of Henry VI, Sir John Fortescue of Lincoln's Inn went up the steps of the legal cursus to the post of Chief Justice of the King's Bench in 1442, the position he was occupying at the outbreak of the Wars of the Roses. He fought at Towton on the king's side, fled with him to Scotland, then spent seven years in exile at the French court. There he probably grew acquainted with Jean de Terrevermeille's statutory theory and wrote various tracts himself on the succession, including a memoir for King Louis XI refuting Edward IV's claim to both English and French crowns. His argument that the Yorkist title was invalid because it rested on descent through women drew on Juvénal des Ursins' *Tres chretien, tres hault, tres puissant roy* (1444). In *De natura legis naturae et eius censura in regnorum suprema* Fortescue discusses at length all the weaknesses that make women naturally unfit to govern or act as judges, largely based on Aristotle's view of them as imperfect males. John Knox would heartily concur in *The First Blast of the Trumpet against the monstrous regiment of women*, leaving Aylmer to reopen the case at Elizabeth I's accession, in *An Harborowe for Faithfull and Trewe Subiectes*.

Fortescue's works did not alter French custom, but they had echoes on the continent. Craig Taylor notes extensive parallels with Guillaume Cousinot's *Pour ce que plusieurs*, which likewise countered Edward IV's claims and was included in a large number of manuscript collections, generally hostile to the English.[48] Either Cousinot read the pamphlets of Fortescue, whom he may have met in Scotland, or he drew on their common source, Juvénal des Ursins. *Pour ce que plusieurs* is the first Valois treatise to assert that the Salic law had ruled the succession in France ever since Pharamond enacted it. 'Salic' came from *sal*, salt, Cousinot argued, which meant that the law would conserve the kingdom for all times. Nor did he scruple to fabricate precedents in his effort to exclude all cognates from the line of succession. This drew him into intricate reviews of Philippa Mortimer's place on the Plantagenet genealogical tree, an element later rehearsed at length by the Duke of York in *Henry VI*.

Fortescue's didactic dialogue *In Praise of the Laws of England* warns Prince Edward that the prime duty of a king is justice. The prince need not explore the mysteries of law, only learn its principles and causes: the people's will formed a body that grew its own head, the king, and from them the kingdom blossomed. It 'issued from the people', *ex populo erupit*, and 'exists as a body mystical'. Thus the English kingship is both 'political and royal' because it exists by common assent, and because a king leads the community, whereas the French kingship of civil law is 'only royal'.[49] In *The Governance of England*, originally called 'Of the difference between an absolute and a limited monarchy', Fortescue returns to the main issue,

---

48 *Debating the Hundred Years War*, ed. by Taylor, pp. 24–28. See also Taylor's 'Sir John Fortescue'.

49 Fortescue, *On the Laws and Governance of England*, pp. xii–xiv, 17–24. The volume includes both dialogues, *In Praise of the Laws*, pp. 1–80, and *The Governance of England*, pp. 81–124.

royal or mixed dominion, and the resulting differences in taxation modes. The great danger to be avoided is poverty of the monarch, for it leads inevitably to greed and tyrannical exactions, a point that will be stressed in *Richard II*. Since the Crown has many needs, its stability requires the recovery and inalienability of Crown lands, to provide revenue for yearly maintenance, and a reformed council to prevent dilapidation. The king's counsellors should be chosen for their wisdom and competency. Fortescue's readers are reminded that the Romans prospered as long as they had a great council. Their decline began when ill-disposed emperors like Nero slew senators. The chronicles are full of examples showing that those who were ill-advised fell into non-power, like Athens, which is now but a poor village.

A comparison with the civil law systems shows a clear advantage to the English people in specific matters like taxation, freedom from servitude, the preference for proof over confessions extracted by torture, and the pride of the system, its trial by jury: if laws are defective, they can be amended in Parliament, so 'it can rightly be concluded that all the laws of this realm are the best in fact or potentiality'.[50] This unique body of customary law is taught in a special academy, the Inns of Court, where learning and amity rule. Some of these views draw on Bracton's synthesis between Roman civil law *princeps* and English *rex*. Fortescue's interpretation of polity is an ambivalent pun on *polis* and *hoi polloi*, supported by fanciful etymology: '*Policia* is so called from *poles*, that is many, and *ycos*, that is, wisdom'.[51] English 'political and royal kingship' is the best insurance against tyranny, its governance being based on free consent of the realm, given through Parliament. Fortescue's attempt to find a way out of this contradiction is artfully resolved by Shakespeare's Henry V, whose 'band of brothers' plays up this construction of comrade solidarity under the leadership of a natural guide.

In both *De laudibus* and *De natura legis naturae*, the equitable adjustment of law is synonymous with royal prerogative. Natural law ruled mankind before the Fall of man. Positive laws were added later, by custom or statute, in answer to what men felt necessary. Equity was needed 'lest the strictness of the words of the law, confounding its intent, should hurt the common good'.[52] However, the good prince should not enact new laws without consulting the chief men of his kingdom, nor bring in foreign ones. The danger may have seemed remote then, but it would come close under Henry VIII, when Christopher Saint-German stated that the Law of Reason is an unalterable principle, 'and therefore against this law, prescription, statute nor custom may not prevail'.[53]

This depiction of the English law system is an idealized one, perhaps made brighter through the tears of exile. After returning from France with Queen Margaret's army, Fortescue was captured at Tewkesbury. The price of his

---

50 Fortescue, *In Praise of the Laws*, p. 78.

51 Fortescue, *The Governance of England*, p. 86.

52 *De natura legis naturae*, trans. by C. Fortescue, in *The Works of Sir John Fortescue*, pp. 194, 215.

53 Young, 'Christopher Saint-German's *Doctor and Student*', pp. 52–53.

reconciliation with the Yorkist winners was to renege on his earlier theories. At this advanced stage in his career, the Chief Justice was submitted to an exercise of the kind usually performed by apprentices at law: a plea *in utramque partem*. Edward IV would pardon him on condition that he write a new treatise refuting his memoir and arguing for the Yorks' hereditary right. Edward's claim being through the female line, this led him to contradict his earlier assertions that women could neither reign nor transmit a right to the crown. 'He had argued well and ingeniously', his biographer comments, 'as a lawyer for his client'.[54] 'The two treatises appear in his works', John Maxcy Zane notes, 'and each of them constitutes the best argument for the respective opposing claims'.[55] Edward must have been satisfied too, for he gave the old judge a place in his council. As a lawyer for his client, so the playwright for his audience, a sound recipe for theatrical debate.

After his forced exercise *in utramque partem*, Fortescue himself was subject to endless posthumous revisionism. The *De laudibus* remained a focal standpoint throughout the Tudor period, when it was mobilized, again, to support the claims of the then reigning dynasty: it was first printed under Henry VIII, and translated under Elizabeth, all in a fine nationalist spirit. The claims of the 1537 Latin address to the 'pio lectori' are advertised in the title of the translation, according to which the laws of England 'are plainelye proued farre to excell, as well the ciuil lawes of the Empire, as also all other lawes of the world, with a large discourse of the difference betwene the two gouernments of kingdomes, whereof the one is onely regall, and the other consisteth of regall and politique administration conioyned', the government 'onely regall' being of course France, the permanent rival brother.[56] It served with other authorities as basis for Henry VIII's fight against the papacy. Enthusiastic teams of lawyers worked to establish its claims and advertise the superiority of common over canon law. Yet they were equally sensitive to other aspects of Fortescue's thesis: his plea for mixed polity was drawn from the bitter lessons of civil war and his own divided allegiance, a complex connection of facts, records, and theory that Shakespeare's histories would memorably illuminate. It would be Henry VIII's remarkable achievement to turn Fortescue's plea for shared power into a claim for absolute *imperium* (see below, 'King's Conscience' in Chapter 5).

54 Lord Clermont's 'Life of Sir John Fortescue', in John Fortescue, *De Laudibus Legum Angliae: A Treatise in Commendation of the Laws of England* (Union, NJ: The Law Book Exchange, 1999), p. xxxix. 'Of the Title of the House of York', of which only fragments have survived, and 'A Defense of the House of Lancaster', nos 5 and 6 on Clermont's list of works, p. liii, were first printed in Clermont's *Works of Sir John Fortescue*.

55 Zane, 'The Bronze Age of the Common Law', in *The Story of Law*, Bk III, p. 321.

56 Fortescue, *A Learned Commendation of the Politike Laws of England*.

Lords and Tenants: Thomas de Littleton (c. *1407–1481*)

Few changes had been made in the courts during Fortescue's exile. They continued to operate through the civil wars, while most of the personnel who had practised with him kept their posts. Thomas de Littleton was one of the judges who remained in office under Lancaster and York regimes and was appointed to the court of Common Pleas in 1466.[57] *Tenures*, his treatise on English property law, was probably written after his appointment to the bench, during the restoration of Henry VI. Unlike his predecessors, Littleton borrows nothing from the sources of Roman law but undertakes to classify the variety of rights over land under a dozen different types of tenure, from the mass of materials recorded since Henry II in the rolls of the various courts and the reports of important cases published in the Year Books. The popularity of his work, originally designed for law students, is attested by an impressive number of over ninety re-editions.

The constitutionalist François Hotman (1524–1590) would express scorn for Littleton's work, yet it played a significant role in the theories of England's 'ancient constitution'. A later Inner Templar, Edward Coke, who translated the law French of Littleton's *Tenures* into English, praised the treatise in even warmer terms than the *De laudibus*, describing it as 'the most perfect and absolute work that ever was written in any human science', and deploring the loss of the 'ancient lectures or readings upon statutes', for the new ones had lost their authority, being now full of 'conceits', 'riddles', 'evasions', and were susceptible to a variety of interpretations. He developed Littleton's principle, 'a tempore cujus contraria memoria hominum non existit', that a rule was established by common law when a custom or usage had existed so long that human memory did not remember anything contrary to it.[58]

The exercise of law evolved radically in the course of the sixteenth century, with a gradual shift from legal learning to jurisprudence. The *Tenures* had relied almost exclusively on doctrine; now they were practically superseded by 'judge-made law'.[59] Today the Littleton building is the home of the Inner Temple's archives.

Emergence of the Inns

'The early centralization of justice gives to our history a wonderful unity', Maitland declared; 'we have not to compare the customs of divers provinces, or the

57 'James Gresham to John Paston', 16 October 1456, *The Paston Letters*, ed. by Gairdner, III, Letter 348, p. 107.

58 Coke, *The First Part of the Institutes of the Laws of England or A Commentary on Littleton* [1628], ed. by F. Hargrave and C. Butler, 2 vols (London: Selden Society, 1823), I, Preface, p. xxxvi; I, lib. II, cap. 10, section 170, p. l.

59 Baker, *Readers and Readings*, p. 237.

jurisprudences of rival schools; our system is a single system and revolves round Westminster Hall'.[60] As soon as the building was finished, in the reign of Rufus, Westminster Hall harboured the first court of justice. Long before Saint Louis under his legendary oak, the English king sat in this room with his council, to treat all affairs of the realm. It would be centuries yet before the executive and the judiciary became separate powers. The court remained mobile, and justice moved with it, until the King's Bench settled at Westminster, in the mid-fourteenth century. This is when the Inns begin to appear on record, yet Coke in his *Institutes* gives them a much earlier birth, 'after the making of *Magna Charta,* and *Charta de Foresta*', in the nineteenth year of Henry III's reign, when 'divers learned men in the laws, that I may use the words of the record, kept schooles of the law in the city of London, and taught such as resorted to them, the laws of the realme'.[61] Thus were the Inns made part of the glorious history of common law.

Settlement

> Within the Temple-hall we were too loud;
> The garden here is more convenient.

1 Henry VI, II.iv

The professional organization of secular lawyers emerges in England with an ordinance of Edward I in 1292, the oldest known regulation of admission of attorneys as a professional class.[62] The Inns had no foundation comparable to that of the university colleges, no royal charters or benefactors. They were formed as a society of lawyers in the last quarter of the fourteenth century but may have begun in the 1340s, 'in the crisis years between Halidon Hill and Crécy',[63] when the settlement of the royal law courts in Westminster drew professional counsels to find lodgings nearby, on the slope of Holborn. Various forms of fellowship constituted at the time may have suggested models: chivalric fraternities like the Order of the Garter in 1348, academic associations, craft guilds like the Fraternity of Saint Nicolas formed about then by the Parisian advocates, or the *clercs de la Basoche* (see below, Chapter 7). Richard II undertook huge works of enlargement and embellishment at Westminster, after the model of Philippe le Bel's Palais de Justice in île de la Cité.[64] What happened next is partly conjecture, for most of the records were destroyed in Wat Tyler's uprising.

---

60 Maitland, 'Why the History of English Law Is Not Written', in *The Collected Papers*, I, p. 6.

61 Edward Coke, 'A Proeme', in *The Second Part of the Institutes of the Laws of England: Containing the Exposition of Many Ancient and Other Statutes* (London: Thomas Basset, 1681), (s.n.)

62 *Parliament Rolls*, ed. by Given-Wilson, 20 Edw. I, no. 22, p. 84.

63 Baker, *The Third University of England*, p. 21.

64 In 1599, Thomas Platter counted fifty-eight statues there, 'Description de Paris par Thomas Platter le jeune de Bâle', in *Mémoires de la Société de l'Histoire de Paris et de l'île de France*, vol. XXIII (Paris: Champion, 1896), p. 180.

The positive image of the Inns is one largely of their own making, initiated by Fortescue's *Praise* which presents them as the perfect place of education for young gentlemen of the nobility. In rehearsing the distinctive features of the English legal system, he offers the first extended portrait of the Inns of Court, a place unique in Europe, where England's good laws are taught. None of the French universities except Paris has so many students. The idealization of both common law and Inns, their ancient origin, and excellent modes of education certainly owes much to its actual context, the Wars of the Roses. In the midst of destructive disorder, his Inns stand for a model commonweal, united by a love of justice, regulated by courtly manners and strict rules.

The portraits pictured in literature were not so glamorous. In his catalogue of detested professions, Gower's *Mirour de l'Omme* damns lawyers for their failure to live up to their God-given duties: 'Throughout the country everyone is complaining about them. They are the people called men of law, but the name they bear is an empty one', for law should include justice, and 'I bear witness to these people that right gets but little if wrong pays generously'.[65] Chaucer's corrupt 'Manciple of a Temple' is probably drawn from experience. His Serjeant-at-Law is a man of fame, learning, and high position, yet 'al was fee symple to hym in effect'.[66] The Elizabethan recorder Fleetwood observes in discussing precedents 'That Chawcer, sometimes a Speaker in this parliament howse, said well, "*Elecet nos per implere omnem iustitiam*"'.[67] Chaucer was appointed justice of the peace for Kent in 1385, when the memory of Wat Tyler's raid on the Temple was still fresh. This episode of the Peasants' Revolt is recycled in *Henry VI Part II*, allied with Cade's plan to pull down the Inns of Court. Down to Shakespeare's 'mad' Shallow, a self-proclaimed fellow of infinite jest, the literary image of the common lawyer, his greed, barbarity, and dullness, was an unflattering one.[68] As for the students, they were notorious for violent behaviour and excessive spending, encouraged by London's endless temptations. They too inspired a long line of dissipated stage characters who would rather watch plays than read statutes (see below, Chapter 8).

Shakespeare's choice of Temple Garden as the nursery of the Civil War is uncannily apt. Apart from a fine dramatic instinct, it suggests some knowledge of legal sources and a shrewd understanding of the values at stake, as does his fashioning of Duke Humphrey into an exemplary judicial figure. The death of this wise Protector means the fall of the last rampart against anarchy. The following act, with its anachronistic use of events from the 1381 Peasants' Revolt, makes the Inns and lawyers specific targets of Cade's vindictiveness. Fortescue's images of the body politic and its sinews, *nervi*, the law binding it together, are echoed

---

65 Gower, *Mirour de l'Omme, French Works*, in *The Complete Works*, I, p. 274.
66 Chaucer, *The Canterbury Tales*, Prologue, l. 319.
67 On 16 May 1572, *Proceedings in the Parliaments of Elizabeth I*, ed. by Hartley (hereafter *Proceedings*), I, p. 358.
68 On the degradation of the Renaissance lawyers' image, see Raffield, *The Art of Law in Shakespeare*.

in Talbot's 'substance, sinews, arms, and strength' of soldiers led by a charismatic captain, contrasting with the wrecks of this vulnerable construction:

> As fester'd members rot but by degree,
> Till bones and flesh and sinews fall away,
> So will this base and envious discord breed.
>
> (*1 Henry VI, III.i.192–94*)

New concepts of common weal, and the English phrase itself, appeared during the crisis of 1449–1450 in the Commons' allegations against the Earl of Suffolk, and according to *Gregory's Chronicle*, in the mouth of Jack Cade, to culminate with the Yorkist magnates' claim to the throne in 1460.

The negative image of lawyers, accused by the rebels of causing people's misery, is also historically sound. Fortescue is occasionally mentioned in the Paston letters, mostly in hostile tones, especially during Cade's rebellion: 'The Chief Yistice hath waited to be assauted all this sevenyght nightly in hes hous, but nothing come as yett, the more pitie, &c.'[69] He may well have been one of those 'insatiable, covetous, malicious' persons around the king who 'daily inform him that good is evil and evil is good' according to a contemporary 'Complaint' of Jack Cade. This sums up the worst mode of inversion, anticipating the witches' charm, 'Fair is foul and foul is fair'.[70] Cade's charge on stage that Lord Saye had hanged poor men because they could not read is a direct reference to benefit of clergy, which enabled literate offenders to escape the death penalty. His outrageous ruling on measurements — 'There shall be in England seven halfpenny loaves sold for a penny: the three-hooped pot shall have ten hoops' — parodies Article 35 of Magna Carta: 'There shall be one measure of wine throughout our whole realm, and one measure of ale and one measure of corn — namely, the London quart'. Cade the lawmaker's promise to 'apparel them all in one livery, that they may agree like brothers and worship me their lord' confronts Fortescue's happy community with a mirrored bloodthirsty distortion.[71]

Tuition

Bracton's treatise, *De legibus et consuetudinibus Angliae*, gives an accurate picture of the advancement of judiciary learning in mid-thirteenth-century England. Edward I's ordinance of 1292 'De attornatis et apprenticiis' notes a superabundance of law students and instructs judges to pick the most promising ones: 'those so chosen only, and no other, should follow his court and transact the affairs therein',

69 'John Bockyng to William Wayte', 2 January 1451, *The Paston Letters*, II, Letter 169, p. 205.
70 'Complaint' of Jack Cade quoted by Harvey in *Jack Cade's Rebellion*, p. 189. *Macbeth*, I.i.10.
71 Cf. *2 Henry VI*, IV.ii.60–63, 65–67.

their number being left to the judges' discretion.[72] Gower in his *Vox clamantis*, written during the Peasants' Revolt, confirms the degrees of the legal profession: 'Et apprenticius, sergandus post et adultus, | Judicis officium fine notabat eum.' The hierarchy of authority — benchers, barristers, apprentices — was defined by the learning exercises, according to the cursus later detailed in Coke's *Third Part of the Reports*:

> Of Mootemen after eight years study or thereabouts, are chosen Utter-barristers; of these are chosen Readers in Inns of Chancery. Of Utter-barristers after they have been of that degree twelve years at least, are chosen Benchers or Antients; of which one, that is of the puisne sort, reads yearly in summer vacation, and is called a single Reader; and one of the Antients, that had formerly read, reads in Lent vacat. and is called a double Reader, and commonly it is between his first and second reading, about nine or ten years. And out of these the King makes choice of his Attorney, and Solicitor General, his Attorney of the Court of Wards and Liveries, and Attorney of the Duchy. And of these Readers are Serjeants elected by the King, and are, by the King's writ, called *ad statum et gradum servientis ad legem*.[73]

The Inns may have been educational houses from their earliest days,[74] though no trace is found of compulsory exercises before the 1440s, and no clear set of qualifications for professional practice until the last quarter of Elizabeth's reign. By then, it was necessary to perform in moots and deliver a set of lectures to be recognized as advocate. No one could be made a serjeant unless he had read, and only serjeants became judges of the King's Bench or Common Pleas. Maitland's hypothesis, confirmed by the research of John Baker, was that 'law schools made the law'. To Maitland, the main difference between England and other countries is that for a long time English law had been 'systematically and academically taught' by a fellowship of lawyers, which saved it from the 'danger' of Roman law. Only professors could become leaders of the bar and judges. The most formal tuition was dispensed through the readings, which took place twice a year, in Lent and August. They were practised at least as early as the 1420s and followed a chronological cycle of statutory texts.[75] A system of lecturing on statutes can be traced even further back, to the time of Richard II. The Readers were expected to do little more than repeat the work of their predecessors, continuing the chapters of statutes they had begun, generally old ones. Under Henry VIII, the reading of 'new' statutes became possible: 'new', as in a reading at Lent 1523, Middle Temple, meant the reign of Richard III. The readings, like the moot books,

72 20 Edw. I, Latin text and translation in W. F. Willcocks, 'Devonshire Men at the Inner Temple, 1547–1660', in *Reports and Transactions of the Devonshire Association for the Advancement of Science, Literature, and Art* (Plymouth: Brendon & Son, 1885), XVII, pp. 246–47.

73 Coke, 'To the Reader', in *The Reports*, Pt III, p. xix.

74 Baker, *The Legal Profession and the Common Law*, pp. 1–24.

75 Thorne, *Essays in English Legal History*, ch. 10, pp. 137–54.

seem to have generally avoided open reference to contemporary events or biting statutes. Edward Hall's reading at Gray's in 1541 dealt with the liberties of the Church … under Henry IV!

In medieval practice all over Europe, the teacher read the text, *lectio*, explaining words or ideas, while students kept silent until *disputatio*, when they were set questions and discussed the proposition. An *opponens* raised objections to the thesis proposed, and a *respondens* presented counter-arguments to these objections, as in the *sic et non* method initiated by Abélard, which juxtaposed apparently contradictory quotations from the Church Fathers on theological topics. Unlike the didactic dialogue's progress towards the truth by an exploration of principles, the *quaestio* determined a solution by way of a concrete and contingent case. In the 'discussed questions', the problems would be argued by two groups acting like defendant and plaintiff at a trial, ranged in two lines of battle facing each other, as they would, entering from two doors at the back of the stage, in the Elizabethan theatres. According to the German jurist Hermann Kantorowicz, it was the style first established in real litigation, then imitated in the classroom and in dramatic literature.[76] These *quaestiones* have often been compared with the moot courts of common law, but the subject debated was a point of juridical principle, not a real or imagined case. The *quodlibet*, a form of *disputatio* that appeared in Paris around 1230, was organized twice a year, before Christmas and before Easter, in the faculties of arts, medicine, and law. As its name indicates, questions could be put to the masters on any subject. After discussing the two theses in dispute, the master would give his solution, *determinatio*, at a second public meeting.[77]

Similarly at the Inns, the vital part of exercises was the contradictory debate that made a trial the stage of duelling eloquence. Such an education encouraged a pluralistic consciousness that would fully express itself in the theatre.[78] Court proceedings were mimicked in moots where students performed pleas for opposite parties, while manuals recreated the atmosphere of the classroom through exchanges between master and pupil. The pedagogical value of this mode had revered authorities behind it. Cicero explains in *De amicitia* why he chose it: Laelius's views on friendship are the report of a report that he has wrought up, 'after my own manner, in the following essay. But that I might not encumber the dialogue with perpetually interposing *said I* and *said he*, I have introduced the speakers themselves to the reader; by which means he may consider himself as a sort of party in the conference.'[79]

---

76 Hermann Kantorowicz, 'The Quaestiones disputatae of the Glossators', *Revue d'Histoire du Droit*, 16.1 (1937/1938), 1–67. And his *Studies in the Glossators of the Roman Law*.

77 The discussed questions of Aquinas's *De anima* are considered by various scholars the 'archetype of *disputatio*', König-Pralon, *Avènement de l'aristotélisme*, p. 25.

78 Altman, *The Tudor Play of Mind*, pp. 48–53.

79 Cicero, *Laelius or an Essay on Friendship*, trans. by Melmoth, p. 4.

Rhetorical Models

in her eye I find
A wonder, or a wondrous miracle,
The shadow of myself form'd in her eye,
Which being but the shadow of your son,
Becomes a sun and makes your son a shadow.

King John, II.i

In our age of suspicion, fed by many an eloquent fascistic leader, the rhetorical flourishes of politicians inevitably sound mendacious and manipulative, at best dusty and ridiculous like Polonius's. Not so in the Middle Ages, and still not in the Renaissance. Dante's figures of speech, for instance, were not 'merely antiquated rhetorical devices, but serious and practical means of making the spiritual visible', T. S. Eliot points out.[80] 'Across England grammar schools shared the aim of making their pupils wise, pious and eloquent', while the humanist educational theorists generally agreed that the best training to produce these qualities was a study of classical languages and literature, an education that 'created the Elizabethan audience'.[81] On the Elizabethan stage, a young dramatist could display his talent in well-made speeches for the innocent pleasure of audiences, so much so that asides were needed like marginal notes, warning them that this particular orator should not be trusted. Thus the hyperboles of Lear's daughters must be weighed against Cordelia's motto: 'Love, and be silent.' The Dauphin's vows to Blanche are not basically different from the Elizabethan sonneteers': the Bastard of Faulconbridge must expose his insincere technique, probably because the hint was felt necessary.

As Ricœur observes, political rhetoric seeks to convince, through arguments or through seduction: 'Set between two limits exterior to it — logic and violence — rhetoric oscillates between its two constitutive poles — proof and persuasion. When persuasion frees itself from the concern of proof, it is carried away by the desire to seduce and to please'.[82] It is this polarity that has made rhetoric since Plato simultaneously praised and despised, unjustly so, Brian Vickers amply argued.[83] But rhetoric came into its own under the humanists' impetus. Their hunts for manuscripts had unearthed complete texts of Quintilian and Cicero to replace the mutilated versions that circulated in the Middle Ages. In Vickers's calculation, based on James Murphy's bibliography, several million Europeans must have had a working knowledge of rhetoric. In sixteenth-century England, it reached 'a greater status than ever before' and became a strong basis of the

80 Eliot, 'Dante', in *Selected Essays*, p. 267.
81 Mack, *Elizabethan Rhetoric*, pp. 11, 47.
82 Ricœur, *The Rule of Metaphor*, p. 32.
83 Vickers, *In Defence of Rhetoric*, ch. 2. On the power and manipulative uses of rhetoric in the European tradition, see Rebhorn, *The Emperor of Men's Minds*.

secondary schools' tuition.[84] It also played an active part in shaping characters and motives on the Elizabethan stage.

Benet Brandreth, who trained the actors of the Royal Shakespeare Company in basic rhetoric, deplores its diminished status, a difficulty many a director of Shakespeare today must confront.[85] Peter Stein was trying to overcome this general distrust of rhetorical speech, at its strongest in his own country, Germany, when he went to Italy in 1990 to direct a *Tito Andronico*, hoping to find there a love of language and figures that might defeat the catastrophic records of eloquence in twentieth-century Europe. The young Shakespeare who wrote *Titus* was 'peacocking', Stein thought, displaying his skill.[86] As a result, unwarned audiences may well misunderstand the significance of much oratory in his early plays. As the years passed, the poet would grow more adept at *sprezzatura*. Thus, the wily Henry V disclaims any talent for eloquence, Hamlet affects to be 'ill at these numbers', and Polonius answers the Queen's request, 'More matter with less art', with the assurance, 'Madam, I swear I use no art at all', humility topoi all. In the meantime, each part of the first Henriad experiments with varied rhetorical tools to illustrate the conflict between cultural values and the progress of anarchy. *Henry VI Part III* takes an innovative step by using tropes to shape brute reality. The whole play is an ordered representation of disorder. Insults follow the score, murders observe a ritual, battles are fought according to a strict choreography, figures of speech and ballet figures fill the dramatic space. The curses over Clifford's dead body, the entrance of four armies before Coventry, the assassination of Prince Edward follow rigidly stylized patterns. Symmetry, as a wishful expression of world order, is descanted by King Henry, stressed by a double sequence of anaphora, while the battle rages: 'How many hours brings about the day', 'So many hours must I tend my flock'. His vision of a simple shepherd's life is shattered by the intrusion of violence, no less symmetrical, in the family of anonymous peasants: '*Enter a Sonne that hath kill'd his Father, at one doore: and a Father that hath kill'd his Sonne at another doore*' (II.v). Witnessed by the King, the scene achieves a maximum tension between the formality of the design and the emotions released.

The duplicity of language is perceptible in the ambiguous prophecies of *Part II*, but only in *Part III* and henceforth is the art of eloquence directly impeached as the art of lying. York's *vituperatio* (I.iv) still observed a formal protocol in denouncing Margaret's unsuitability to the kingly role she usurped, as foreigner, woman, of shabby rank, deprived of beauty or virtues. Literally pleaders before the court of Lewis XI, Warwick and Margaret both attempt to win the support of France for their party, Warwick wooing the king's sister by proxy. When Warwick stands surety for Edward IV — 'Thereon I pawn my credit and mine honour'

---

84 Vickers, *In Defence of Rhetoric*, p. 256. James J. Murphy and Laurence D. Green, *Renaissance Rhetoric: Short-Title Catalogue, 1460–1700* (1981; repr. Aldershot: Ashgate, 2006).

85 Brandreth, *Shakespearean Rhetoric*.

86 Goy-Blanquet, 'Titus Resartus'.

(III.iii) — Margaret is quick in accusing him of deceit, but her counter-rhetoric is ineffective against the material benefits of a union with the House of York. It takes the news that Edward is already married to discredit Warwick's courting.

The seduction of language as opposed to the truth revealed in actions becomes a dominant theme in the next play. Richard of Gloucester speaks very little in Thomas More's *History*; the task of gulling audiences is usually left to his accomplices. On stage More's own *ars rhetorica* is transferred to the witty hunchback. Young Richard first practises it in *3 Henry VI* by 'demonstrating' how his father can legally break his oath, then confides in a soliloquy that he masters all the rules of the art. After his wooing of Lady Anne, the seducer takes audible pleasure in showing off his abilities with a perfect isocolon:

> Was ever woman in this humour woo'd?
> Was ever woman in this humour won?
>
> (*Richard III, I.ii.231–32*)

He then straightaway mocks its symmetry with a terse 'I'll have her, but I will not keep her long.' No less ironically, his confidences to the public parody a set pattern — a character's origin, education, physical and moral qualities, gifts of fortune — when he lists the 'virtues' that mark him for the throne, an exact counterportrait of the ideal sovereign.

The rhetorical manuals had a protocol for each mode of enunciation. Whether they revile, curse, or implore, Shakespeare's villains and victims fall back on established procedures to voice their passions in style. Cicero and Quintilian are quoted verbatim by his characters, who also prove familiar with neo-Ciceronian treatises like Thomas Wilson's *Arte of Rhetorique* or George Puttenham's *Arte of English Poesie*.[87] The authors of these manuals were lawyers themselves, or judges like Wilson, Brandreth points out; their 'focus is on the topics as they arise in judicial speeches'.[88] Such protocols formed an important part of the skills taught in grammar schools and at the Inns.[89] During term time, the Inns apprentices learnt their trade by attending court sessions at Westminster Hall. Originally this was all the tuition they received.

As the tuition system formally developed, the students took part in various learning exercises. Books being scarce, these were mainly oral, especially the moots, mock trials modelled on the procedure of Common Pleas. The matter taught, both in content and shape, was consistently theatrical, as numerous essays have shown since Finkelpearl's groundbreaking study of Marston.[90] Some cases recorded refer to actual court cases; others were purely hypothetical. The intricacy

---

87 See Skinner, *Forensic Shakespeare*. Vickers, *In Defence of Rhetoric*, pp. 335–39, gives examples of *aposiopesis* in Shakespeare and, pp. 491–98, a quotation from Shakespeare for each figure or trope.

88 Brandreth, *Shakespearean Rhetoric*, ch. 6.

89 See Skinner, *Forensic Shakespeare*, pp. 25–33.

90 Finkelpearl, *John Marston of the Middle Temple*.

of the family romances thus designed could rival with the writers' most complex fictions. The 'Case called *the little rose*, or *FitzJohn*' discusses a Lear-like share of inheritance between three daughters, in which 'the younger daughter is ousted, the youngest gets possession of the whole rent'. Others oppose bastard and legitimate sons, twins, children in their nonage and maternal uncles, ravished wards, uncles marrying their nieces, villains, monks, women kept like minors under the authority of an abbot or a husband, clerks between two jurisdictions.[91] Incidentally, they provide unexpected viewpoints on the status and rights of women:

> In an appeal of rape it is a good plea to abate the writ that she is pregnant by the same rape, because that proves her consent. It was said by the counsel of Bishop Nevil of York that although the body consents nevertheless the mind does not; to which the justices said that their authority extended only to the body and not the mind. That occurred in the Lady Butler's case in the time of Edw. IV.[92]

The said lady, Eleanor Butler, was involved in the case of Edward IV, when rumours of a pre-marital contract with her served as motive to denounce the bastardy of his children and have them excluded from the succession in the *Titulus Regius*. Yet on the whole, the records tend to stay clear of politics. They list few criminal cases: felony is of interest not so much in itself as in its consequences for the heirs involved. All the intricacies of divorce, dowries, waste, disseisin, wills, tenancies, leases, chattels real and personal, gambling and dice playing, widowers, bailiffs, expulsions, property of denizens, aliens, and foreigners are deployed, mostly in the strange mixture of Norman and English known as law French, which was still used in the report of proceedings and in legal treatises (see below, 'Won in Translation' in Chapter 7).

The most popular handbooks, as Quentin Skinner shows, judging by the number of reprints, were the *Rhetorica ad Herennium* long attributed to Cicero, and his *De inventione*, followed by Quintilian's more demanding *De institutione oratoria*, books all available at the printing house of Shakespeare's schoolfellow Richard Field. Another strong influence was the philosopher Pierre de la Ramée (Petrus Ramus, one of the Protestant victims in Marlowe's *Massacre*), who produced 'a vernacular digest of his logic, the *Dialectique*, in 1555'.[93] One of the best known English Ramists, Abraham Fraunce, would train as a lawyer at Gray's Inn, then publish *The Lawiers Logike* for the use of younger trainees, which did not manage to evince Wilson's pre-Ramist *Arte of Rhetorique* (1560) and its stress on invention as the most important part of this art.

---

91 *Moots*, in *Readings and Moots at the Inns of Court*, II, p. 29 no. 42, p. 49 no. 4, p. 242 no. 56, p. 18 no. 5b, p. 145 no. 33, p. 251 no. 68, p. 54 no. 5, p. 293 no. 139, p. 279 no. 110.

92 *Moots*, case no. 101, from MS Hargrave 87, *Readings and Moots at the Inns of Court*, II, p. 275.

93 Skinner, *Forensic Shakespeare*, pp. 29, 37, 52.

Exercises *in utramque partem* also used guides like Aphthonios whom Erasmus recommends in his list of teaching authorities along with Pliny and Cicero.[94] *Progymnasmata* offered a wealth of fables classified as moral, ethical, or mixed, anecdotes as logical, practical, or mixed, maxims as hortatory, dissuasive or declarative, simple or compound, plausible, true, or hyperbolical, questions argued *pro et contra*, models of division and development under the headings of encomium, paraphrase, cause, converse, analogy, example, testimony of ancients, brief epilogue. The 'Common topic', for instance, amplifies evil attributes with those recipes rehearsed by the wailing queens of *Richard III*: expose the facts to provoke the audience, discredit the intent of the agent, abuse his earlier life, and finally reject pity. 'Think that thy babes were sweeter than they were, | And he that slew them fouler than he is': Margaret's lesson on amplification was one of the basic skills taught to law students and in secondary schools through exercises of the kind listed by Erasmus in his *De verborum ac rerum copia*. The chosen example of common topic is a plea against a tyrant. All the heads argued show he must be punished:

> Will anyone then try to win his release by emotional appeal? Probably his children will. But when they come into court weeping, think that the laws stand before you; surely it is much more righteous to cast a vote for them than for the children of this man: for (if you pity him) this man's tyranny will have been secured by means of his children, but it is through the laws that you have acquired the right to make judgment.[95]

The model for invective borrows from Demosthenes, a precedent that Thomas Norton would follow in his *Oration, of Arsanes agaynst Philip the trecherous kyng of Macedone*. In pathetic characterizations, the student must imagine what Hecuba would say after the sack of Troy, or tearful Niobe on the death of her children, as does Hamlet when ruing his own lack of emotional reaction.

'Should one marry?', one of the set questions asks. To the list of blessings conferred by marriage, a contradicting voice raises a number of objections, the final one being '"Yes," he says, "but marriage is tiresome."' If not the arguments themselves, William Cecil used the same mode of *pro et contra* reasoning when he compiled a list of reasons for or against the Anjou marriage:[96] 'The Queen wanted an answer, but all she got was a disputation', Joel Altman comments.[97] Aphthonios's comparison of Achilles and Hector notes that 'both born of a land worthy of praise, both were equal in kindred'. No doubt there were salmons in both lands, as in the rivers of Macedonia and Monmouth. It is easy to see what

---

94 Erasmus, in his letter 'De ratione studii' to Petrus Viterius, in *La Correspondance*, ed. by Gerlo, pp. 131, 159.

95 Schools used the Latin translation of Rudolf Agricola. *Progymnasmata*, trans. by Kennedy, p. 107.

96 Cecil, 2 October 1579, 'Questions moved concerning the Quene's Mariadge with Monsieur d'Anjow, "Perils" and "Remedies"', in *State Papers, Elizabeth*, ed. by Murdin, pp. 322–23.

97 Altman, *The Tudor Play of Mind*, p. 40.

protocols for prosopopoeia, arguments *pro et contra*, characterization, or slanging match not only training lawyers, but chroniclers like Edward Hall, parliamentarians, half of whom came from the Inns, or budding playwrights like Norton and Sackville would draw from such models. As would Hamlet, Beatrice and Benedick, Clarence's children, Queen Margaret, Lear's daughters, or good Captain Fluellen. As for pieces of political rhetoric in *Henry V*, the Archbishop's speech on Salic law, his analogy of the beehive to justify social hierarchy, or Burgundy's mourning over the woes of devastated France, they may have been *margaritas ante porcos*, or in Hamlet's words, 'caviary to the general'. Specifically designed for 'the wiser sort', Shakespeare's audience at court, to Dutton, 'the very institution which allowed Shakespeare's theatre to flourish specifically as it did', and to Lukas Erne 'purple patches' he wrote for his learned readers, safe 'in the knowledge that they might well be omitted on stage'. Where Erne concludes that Burgundy's speech, for one, would hardly have been appropriate on stage, Dutton retorts that 'on the contrary, this is classic rhetorical fare for the *courtly* stage'.[98]

The practice of mooting, more directly connected with the structure of the dramatic *agon*, seems to go as far back as the Inns themselves. The essence of the medieval moot was not abstract legal argument like modern ones, Baker explains, but oral pleading, sufficiently intricate to raise all points in each complex case.[99] Bolts, in-house disputes, were argued by students, whereas in the more formal moots (derived from the Saxon *gemot*, public meeting) they merely recited the pleadings argued by barristers and judged by benchers. A mooter could not choose his side; he had to defend the party entrusted to him, like a barrister his client, or an actor his part. To Thomas Elyot, 'the pleadynge used in courte and Chauncery called motes' is 'a maner, a shadow, or figure of the auncient rhetorike'. And though lawyers use a barbarous tongue 'in arguynge their cases, in myn opinion, they very litle do lacke of the hole arte'.[100]

Elizabethan mootmen could find help in the collection of 376 moot points put together by Edmund Plowden, which circulated in manuscript long before its publication.[101] For centuries, lawyers had used notes of cases and arguments collected in the Year Books of the Inns. These were almost continuous from the reign of Edward I to Richard III, but subsisted only intermittently after.[102] The earliest surviving records, the Black Books of Lincoln's Inn, date from 1422. It is to Maitland an 'ominous event' that in 1535, the year in which More was done to death, the Year Books come to an end: 'the stream of law reports which has been flowing ever since the time of Edward I, seems to be on the very point of running

98 Dutton, *Shakespeare, Court Dramatist*, pp. 192, 194. Erne, *Shakespeare as Literary Dramatist*, p. 227.
99 Baker, *The Third University of England*, p. 13, stresses the complexity of these exercises.
100 Elyot, *The Boke named the Gouernour*, ed. by Croft, I, ch. XIV, p. 148.
101 Plowden's *The Commentaries, or Reports* were published in October 1571 by Richard Tottel. *Les Quaeres del Mounsieur Plowden* was printed only in 1620.
102 Parmiter, *Edmund Plowden*, p. 110. The last printed Year Book is for Trinity Term, 27 Henry VIII, in 1535.

dry'.[103] At least Henry VIII did not follow his 'project for the reformation of the Inns of Court, which happily were not rich enough to deserve dissolution'.[104]

Mootings may have sounded gloomier notes as they 'ritualized and emphasized the issue of proprietorship', stressing the unreliability of property rights: these unstable performances provided 'an important model for analyzing the volatile discursive relations among the Crown, English subjects, and those who wrote for the theater in early modern England'.[105] Karen Cunningham exposes the myth of a feudal culture in which landholdings were secure, and the social relationships that they symbolized equally stable. This instability reaches tragic heights in *King Lear*, where the Fool's allusion to the pirating cuckoo — 'They took from me the use of mine own house' — heralds the violations of all rules of ownership and hospitality, when no dwelling is safe and former landlords are turned into homeless outcasts. The imbrication of public and domestic anxieties echoes very practical concerns about the nature of land law itself, challenged by resilient local practices, manorial customs, varying modes of inheritance, transfers of property or tenure, which led to a series of new statutes in the 1530s, and the most epoch-making, the Statute of Uses, of which more later (see below, Chapter 5).

Upward Mobility

Historians of the law generally observe a spectacular increase of litigation between 1560 and 1640, with lawsuits brought before the King's Bench and the court of Common Pleas by a large spectrum of society, although they differ on the causes of this influx: social change, inadequacy of the common law, or increase of wealth after the dissolution of monasteries. Predictably, it was accompanied by a no less spectacular increase in the number of lawyers, far superior to increases in population, and a steep rise in the number of entrants to the Inns. In contemporary opinion, it was the swarm of attorneys that created a multitude of suits, as well as covetousness and lack of charity between neighbours. Much of the work of these lawyers, their training and their business, was concentrated in London. Given those circumstances, Christopher Brooks notes, the Inns of Court and Inns of Chancery 'both expanded in size and grew in stature'.[106]

103 Maitland, 'Records of the Honourable Society of Lincoln's Inn', in *The Collected Papers*, III, pp. 78–79.
104 Maitland, *English Law and the Renaissance*, pp. 20–22.
105 Cunningham, 'So Many Books, So Many Rolls of Ancient Times', in Kezar, ed., *Solon and Thespis*, p. 198. On the pedagogical and literary aspects of mooting, see her 'Fugitive Forms' in *Imaginary Betrayals*, pp. 21–39.
106 Brooks, *Lawyers, Litigation*, ch. 2, and ch. 5 p. 130.

Encomium

At the onset of the Tudor dynasty, the Inns had acquired most of their enduring features. Still, they were not quite the nursery of nobility, the Athens of the law, or the Third University praised by Fortescue's followers. Many records suggest, and a former alumnus like William Cecil still acknowledges, the lack of student guidance and supervision. The study of common law did not have a classic pedigree like Roman or canon law and was not taught at the universities. No educational prerequisites were needed for admission at the Inns. To the first generation of humanists, lawyers were a barbarous set armed with crude Latin and no Greek. Scholars like Thomas Smith or Richard Mulcaster thought the exercise of law should not be entrusted to professional jurists but to gentlemen well versed in legal science and eager to serve the common weal without expectations of personal profit. The humanists' ideal lawyer is a gentleman of independent means, accomplished in the liberal arts, who employs his learning to counsel the prince and serve the public good. With this chip on the shoulder, as Prest calls it, the Inns were all the more eager to advertise the scientific status of their teachings. The manuals of common law were constant in asserting its supremacy over all other codes, especially the canon and civil law taught in the universities.

The Inns of Shakespeare's days compensated for their alleged lack of classical learning with an enviable position at the heart of the realm's activities. Holborn was still a quiet suburban village, but its proximity to Westminster enabled the Inns to play up the ambivalence of their name, as closely related with the royal court and the law courts. All the more glamorous accounts from Fortescue to Selden stress the point that the youth of the nobility and gentry study there. Elyot's *Boke named the Gouernour* recommended the study of law as the best possible education for young gentlemen. Gerard Legh, recording the famous revels of 1561 at Inner Temple, calls the Inns 'a place priviliged by the most excellent princes wherein are the store of gentlemen of the whole realm, that repair thither to learn to rule, and obey by law'.[107] Jasper Heywood salutes them in the preface to his translation of *Thyestes*. William Harrison insists that 'out of these also come many scholars of great fame', although he deplores that the younger ones cannot be bridled by any good order, a fault 'that was wont also greatly to reign in Cambridge and Oxford, between the students and the burgesses'.[108] Ben Jonson, whose plots abundantly exploit popular law-mindedness and forensic rhetoric, dedicates *Every Man Out of his Humour* to 'the Noblest Nurseries of Humanity, and Liberty, in the Kingdom; the Inns of Court', giving 'liberty' a more flattering note than it used to have in medieval comments on their students' misbehaviour.[109] Coke confirms that they 'altogether do make the most famous

107 Legh, *Accedens of Armorie*, fols 118^{v}–119^{v}.

108 Harrison, *The Description of England*, ed. by Edelen, Bk II, ch. 6, pp. 65–66.

109 Jonson, *Every Man Out of his Humour*, ed. by Ostovich, Appendix C, Dedication, p. 383. On its forensic rhetoric, see Hutson, *The Invention of Suspicion*, ch. 7.

Universitie for profession of law only, or of any one human Science, that is in the world, and advanceth itself above all others'.[110] Clarendon's *Discourse Concerning Education* (1666), written on his return from exile, still calls the Inns 'the suburbs of the Court'.

The study of law, offering as it did both practical and spiritual benefits, acquired an ennobling quality of itself. Apart from readings and moots, students could learn the courtly *trivium*, fencing, dancing, music, if they were prepared to pay for extra tuition, and practise courtly manners at the revels held every Saturday night from All Saints' Day to Candlemas, or at occasional masques and feasts offered by the Societies of Inns members. In the course of the sixteenth century, an increasing number of low-born aspirants came to the Inns in hopes of social promotion. To Wilfrid Prest, it was probably the continuing decline in prestige and authority of the Church, the first learned profession, that gave lawyers their great chance and made the Inns the most promising gateway to upward mobility in early modern England.[111]

Rules and Reports

The admissions boom began around 1550 and reached a summit of popularity under Elizabeth when Gray's Inn especially, thanks to its aristocratic image, attracted a large share of entrants. A 1586 census shows a total of 356 members for Gray's against 200 for each of the other three Inns, much less altogether than the estimated 3,000 of Oxford plus Cambridge at the time.[112] Hardly any domestic records exist of the Inns of Chancery. Fortescue's *De laudibus* mentions ten, of which nine are listed under Henry VIII, and only eight left in Coke's *Reports*. For a long while they functioned as junior or preparatory Inns for the Inn of Court to which they were attached, without obligation to the students. It was the threat that Middle Temple might gain control over Lyon's Inn that would send the Inner Templars running for help to Robert Dudley, Earl of Leicester.

Confirming their claims to dispense a liberal education, the Year Books show that a large portion of the students were there not to train for a legal career but to acquire some principles of law that might prove useful to them as future landowners and magistrates. The government's close interest in their running appears in enquiries ordered by the Privy Council. First of its kind, a report of 1540 to Henry VIII gives an elaborate description of their parts and degrees.[113] A survey in 1574 points to a severe shortage of accommodation, forcing some to find lodgings outside.[114] Another survey ordered by the Privy Council from

110 Coke, 'To the Reader', in *The Reports*, Pt III, p. xx.
111 Prest, *The Rise of the Barristers*, p. 323.
112 Prest, *The Inns of Court*, pp. 12–35.
113 Bacon, Denton, and Carey, 'Henry VIII's Royal Commission on the Inns of Court', pp. 183–94.
114 'A survey of the Chambers and societies of all the Innes of Courte', in *Calendar of State Papers, Domestic*, ed. by Lemon and Green, XCV, art. 91.

the Lord Keeper Nicholas Bacon in 1577, hard on the heels of the first Jesuit missions, examines the religious conformity of the Inns, which were thought to be 'greatlie infected with poperie'.[115] Bacon's eight surveyors listed 180 Catholics, approximately one member in five. The highest proportion was found in Gray's Inn and Inner Temple, around 13 and 16 per cent of their resident membership, while the other two houses had less than 5 per cent. The Privy Council ordered a large search for recusants at Gray's in November 1585, with unknown effects. Cecil, whose sons Robert and Thomas were studying at Gray's as he had, kept by him a complete list of its members and an active interest in the administration of the Inns.

The Inns were ruled by 'benchers' or 'governors' with most 'ancienty'. How efficiently remains dubious. Their sumptuary edicts were frequently repeated, in both house rules and royal proclamations. In 1557, under Mary's reign, the Inns issued an order forbidding 'the Companions, except Knights, or Benchers, to wear in their Doublets or Hoses any light colours, except Scarlets or Crimsons', velvet hats, scarves, 'velvet shooes, double cuffs on their shirts, feathers or ribbens in their caps, upon pain to forfeit, for the first default'.[116] Visibly these 'companions' were thought of as a higher sort of apprentices rather than students. Under Elizabeth it was 'the superfluitie of unnecessary forreyne wares' that was particularly reproved.[117] The students were supposed not to bear weapons or wear long beards. They must be in their houses by six o'clock and keep commons, both the meal they ate and the dining hall where it was served, holding up Fortescue's corporate spirit.[118] The exercises continued after meals through mooting or putting of cases. These, Henry's reporters explain, were argued by utter or outer barristers — advanced students, ranked next to the benchers, who sat just outside the bar to take part in the moots — since the younger men 'for lack of learning, and continuance, are not able to argue and reason in these Motes', but two of them sit with the utter barristers on the 'formes which they call the barr' in the midst of the hall, and recite by heart in law French the pleading of the moot case, 'the one of them taking the part of the plaintiff, and the other the part of the defendant'.

Denton's report for Henry VIII confirms that reading was a prerequisite before a call to the bar. However, the small number of opportunities to deliver a reading made this rule impractical, and the distinction grew blurred as other honours or offices ensured promotion. At the onset of Edward VI's reign, a proclamation allowed lawyers who had been fellows for eight years to plead and be counsellors in any court of the realm except Common Pleas, which was the exclusive right of

115 *Acts of the Privy Council*, ed. by Dasent, x, pp. 94–95. See Prest, *The Inns of Court*, ch. 8.

116 Dugdale, *The History and Antiquity of the Inns*, ed. by Cunningham, pp. 310–11.

117 *Tudor Royal Proclamations*, ed. by Hughes and Larkin, vol. II, 16 Eliz.1, 15 June 1574. Similar orders are repeated in 24 Eliz. and 42 Eliz.

118 On the community of the Inns and its symbolic associations, see Raffield, *Images and Cultures of Law*, pp. 9–48.

serjeants-at-law.[119] The Reader was warned half a year in advance he must prepare for his mission. Having selected an act or a statute for the basis of his lectures, he would read it, point out its difficulties, the doubts it raised, and declare his own judgement. A younger utter barrister would try to prove it against the law, then the other utter barristers, judges, and serjeants would speak in order of seniority and declare their objections, which the Reader would set out to confute. His set of lectures went on for two or three weeks, rounded up by a dinner he offered to his audience at the end of the vacation. It was to fulfil this expensive tradition that the chronicler Edward Hall begged his friend Thomas Cromwell to 'ask the King to grant me some venison at my reading the week after Lammas'. A note in Cromwell's own hand appears after a list of instructions to an ambassador in France, 'to remember Edward Hall for a buck and a stag'.[120]

Politic Revels

That debates were not confined to the Inns' classrooms, nor to the trivialities of land law, appears from testimonies like the Earl of Leicester's, riding from London to Windsor with Sackville and Fleetwood in 1575, when among other themes they discussed the royal dignity of a king: 'Leicester enthused, put a proposition to them — why the prerogatives of the queen be as great as those of "her most noble progenitors being kings" — and insisted on riding between them and interjecting whilst they debated the matter. And so they continued until he exclaimed that "we be come to Windsor and truely methinkes that the way is made shorter than it was wonte to be, by reason of our disputations. And I thanke you both".'[121]

The dividing line between work and entertainment was a thin one. Moots and bolts were reproduced in ironical or inverted mode in the masques performed on feast days, many of which end with the burlesque trial of a fanciful case. Various Inns events were festive occasions. The creation of serjeants was marked by a feast lasting seven days, and a distribution of gold rings by the new-made serjeants. Feasts were costly events, and occasionally rowdy ones, which sometimes led benchers to suspend or suppress them. The liberties of Christmas could easily cause offence. According to Dugdale's *Origines Juridiciales*, the doors were broken in 1517 by the intrusion of a 'Jake Stray', 'apparently a popular anti-king or pretender' — an impersonation of Wat Tyler's partner in the Peasants' Uprising — which resulted in an order concluding, 'Item, that Jack Strawe and all his adherentes be from hensforth uttrely banyshed and no more to be used in

119 *Tudor Royal Proclamations*, vol. I, 28 Nov 1547, pp. 408–09. See Parmiter, *Edmund Plowden*, pp. 18–20.

120 'Henry VIII: June 1533, 26–30', in *Letters and Papers, Henry VIII*, VI, pp. 313, 334.

121 J. Bruce, 'Particulars Respecting Thomas Sackville, Lord Buckhurst, with a Fragment of the "Itinerarium ad Windsor" Written by Mr Serjeant Fleetwood, Recorder of London', *Archaeologia*, 1.37 (1856), 351–62.

Lincolles Inne', upon pain of a £5 fine.[122] Hall reports how John Roo's play at Gray's Inn on Christmas 1526 was praised by everybody except Cardinal Wolsey who thought he recognized himself under the guise of its Lord Governance, 'by whose misgouernace and euil order, lady Publike wele was put from gouernance', till a great multitude rose to expel them.[123] Roo was deprived of his coif and sent to the Fleet prison until he was delivered by the means of friends.

In theory, the presence at commons also required the solemn keeping of Christmas; in practice it was irregularly applied. The oldest records of Christmas revels come from the Black Books of Lincoln's Inn.[124] They are mentioned in the Paston letters of 1451, and in Fortescue's account. Some festivities were solemn affairs, designed as a compulsory part of the students' education. At the first benchers' meeting of November, special officers were appointed, who 'for the most part are such as are exercised in the King's Highness's house, and other noblemen, and this is done only to the intent that they should in time come to know how to use themselves'.[125] When Middle Temple kept Christmas, a steward, marshal, butler, master of the revels, constable of the Tower, and marshal's constable were designated, practices inspired by the French *Basoche*. All these offices, save the steward's, were filled by junior members. The steward was a barrister, often the Reader designated for the next vacation, which further points to the Christmas revels as a sort of dress rehearsal for later practice. These rituals may have been disliked by many young men fined for non-attendance. The records of Lincoln's show that some were disbarred for not dancing on Candlemas day in the presence of judges, 'according to the antient Order of this Society'. The poet John Donne would have to pay the customary fine of 26s. 8d. in 1593 for having declined to act as steward of Christmas, shortly after his brother's death.[126]

Both Inns and universities followed the court's practice of electing a Lord of Misrule. The affair developed on a grand scale, with marked emulation, in the early reign of Henry VIII. The splendours of Christmas somewhat abated under the Protestant guardians of Edward VI, but in 1551, as he worried over the condemnation of his uncle the Duke of Somerset, it was thought a good idea to cheer him up with some entertainments. Those were devised by the lawyer poet George Ferrers 'of Lincolnes Inne, being Lord of the merry Disports all the 12 dayes, who so pleasantly and wisely behaved himselfe, that the King had great delight in his pastimes'.[127] In Holinshed's account, the feast went with a swing, enjoyed by everybody and 'best of all by the yoong king himselfe', at the end of which, 'Christmas being thus passed with much mirth and pastime', wherewith

---

122 Dawson, *Christmas*, p. 113.

123 *Hall's Chronicle*, p. 719.

124 *Records of the Honorable Society of Lincoln's Inn*, ed. by Baildon, I, p. 1. The first nine volumes of the Black Books, 1422–1691, are now digitized and accessible at <https://archives.lincolnsinn.org.uk>.

125 Bacon, Denton, and Carey, 'Henry VIII's Royal Commission on the Inns of Court', p. 188.

126 I. A. Shapiro, 'John Donne and Lincoln's Inn', *Times Literary Supplement*, 16 and 23 October 1930, pp. 833, 861.

127 Stow, *Annals*, quoted in Dawson, *Christmas*, pp. 117–18.

the minds of murmurers were appeased, 'it was thought now good to proceed to the execution of the iudgment given against the duke of Summerset'.[128] Holinshed does not say that Ferrers would fight for the queen in the Wyatt rebellion and write part of *The Mirror for Magistrates*, nor that he had translated Magna Carta into English and been the hero of a case for Parliamentary privilege, one more instance of a Tudor lawyer's infinite versatility.

'One need only examine a map of theatrical London between 1567 and 1639 to see the movement of theatres toward the Inns of Court', Corrigan confidently asserts, stressing 'the clearly pronounced effect of law student patronage' on the new constructions. 'When James Burbage lost his lease in Shoreditch, he purchased Blackfriars with the intention of presenting his plays within walking distance of the Temple.'[129] The influence was not just a matter of patronage. Materials and rare precedents to Shakespeare's treatment of national issues came from Parliament debates and Inns models, not just from *Gorboduc*. As we shall see now, they provided a large store of phrases, commonplaces, images, and beliefs the poets would transform into telling metaphors. Where common law suits must concentrate on hard facts, Shakespeare's stage soliloquies could explore intentions and subtler levels of responsibilities. His mastery of legal terms did not require special training; he could have found them with suitable definitions in John Rastell's *Expositiones terminorum legum anglorum*, or any similar lexicon in circulation.[130] But his understanding of the issues required a higher degree of intellect, which the Tudor execution of justice and its gory sights in the streets of London must have sharpened to a point. Shakespeare's 'education' in law had a variety of sources ancient and modern, none probably so educative as the spectacular turns of events that made Tudor history. Books exalted the law. State trials performed and distorted it, leaving the theatre to problematize the gaps between theory, principles, and practice.

---

128 *Holinshed's Chronicles*, III, p. 1032. Somerset was executed on 22 January 1552.

129 Corrigan, *Playhouse Law*, p. 47.

130 See Ian Lancashire, 'Law and Early Modern English Lexicons', in *Selected Proceedings of the 2005 Symposium on New Approaches in English Historical Lexis (HEL-LEX)*, ed. by R. W. McConchie and others (Somerville, MA: Cascadilla Proceedings Project, 2006), pp. 8–23.

Part II

Fair Trial

Freedom of Magistrates

CHAPTER 4

Learned Counsel

No doubt sensitive to a continuing background discourse on counsel, good government, and the deposition of tyrannical rulers, the Tudor monarchs strove to keep on the right side of the law and lawyers, monitoring their public image with the help of their biographers or propagandists. Medieval chroniclers reporting the Wars of the Roses were occasionally driven to repent earlier choices when their king elect fell from power. Walsingham, Hardyng, Capgrave, like the lawyer Fortescue, had revised their works in favour of their new patrons after the fall of the Lancasters.[1] They were far outdone by the rewriters of Plantagenet history, from hagiographers like Cardinal Morton or Edward Hall, to the subtly critical Shakespeare. Stephen Greenblatt has overviewed 'the fundamental energies of a political authority that was itself already committed to histrionic display and hence was ripe for appropriation' by Elizabethan theatrical companies.[2] In the case of the first Tudor, one is tempted to accept Greenblatt's view of monarchy as ruled by his virtuous posturing. The circulation of energies between Renaissance theatre and society was indeed a dynamic exchange rather than a simple matter of reflection, but the theatricality of Tudor representations had far deeper significance than the manipulative deceit *Shakespearean Negotiations* concentrates on.

A Display of Legalism

> There is a law in each well-order'd nation
> To curb those raging appetites that are
> Most disobedient and refractory.
>
> *Troilus and Cressida, II.ii*

The Tudors all advertised themselves as defenders of law and right, yet each has a poor record of State trials, most of them connected with the successive religious turnovers. To the legal antiquary David Jardine, of Middle Temple, the proceedings against persons accused of State offences 'do not deserve the name of trials: they were a mere mockery of justice, being, in fact, only employed by the government as a means of destroying obnoxious individuals, with sufficient

1 See Kelly's comparison of their successive versions in *Divine Providence*, pp. 39–48.
2 Greenblatt, *Shakespearean Negotiations*, p. 40.

pomp and circumstance to hold the multitude in awe'.[3] How the legal machinery worked, and made Tudor lawyers accessories to this 'mockery of justice', we will now explore.

Tudor New Style

Like an actor, Henry VII, formerly Earl of Richmond, had many facets to his righteous soul. In Hall's chronicle, the first Tudor begins like Geoffrey of Monmouth's Welsh kings by establishing profitable laws. His descendants would maintain, like him, a close relation with the Inns, show ostensible respect for the law, and advertise their good behaviour. Only Mary ever dismissed a judge because of his private views.[4] Henry VII recognized his obligations to lawyers, who guided the first steps of his accession, and his generally harmonious relations with Parliament. He sometimes visited the Inns and attended festivities there.[5] Within days of his arrival in London after his victory at Bosworth, he issued writs of summons for a parliament, whose members dutifully agreed he had come to the throne by just title of inheritance and God's judgement in battle. The attainders against the Lancasters were cancelled or reversed, the most fervent surviving Yorkists attainted, and the statute *Titulus Regius* that had made his future wife illegitimate repealed.[6]

After the late Plantagenet turmoils, the first Tudor is reputed to have put the country back on its tracks and 'made the old machinery work'.[7] He did not attempt to replace the judges of his predecessors, though he sold some of the appointments at high price.[8] William Hussey, the Yorks' Lord Chief Justice of the King's Bench, was renewed in his post. Robert Rede, appointed to the King's Bench at Hussey's demise, bought the chiefship of the Common Pleas in 1506 for four thousand marks. Their first mission was to restore royal authority. Henry's 'over-mighty' subjects were prevented by laws against livery and maintenance from setting up private armies. The numbers and the authority of justices of the peace were considerably increased, but so were the instructions they received from his council, while royal proclamations told the public where to apply for redress in case of abuses, placing justice more firmly under the king's power.

The 'legalism' of Henry VII, who sought to increase royal revenue by what Fortescue had called 'exquisite means', is well known. Among other paying gestures was the confiscation of his mother-in-law's lands in 1487, on belated suspicions of conspiracy, because she had 'delivered her daughters out of sanctuary into

---

3 Jardine, *Criminal Trials*, I, p. 8.

4 Elton, *Policy and Police*, pp. 35–36.

5 *Calendar of the Inner Temple Records*, ed. by Inderwick, pp. xxxvii–xl.

6 Henry VII ordered all copies destroyed. Only one survived, in the Croyland Chronicle, where George Buc, one of Richard's early vindicators, found it a century later.

7 Mackie, *The Earlier Tudors*, p. 190.

8 See Ives, *The Common Lawyers*, pp. 85–86. Gunn, 'The Courtiers of Henry VII', pp. 45–46.

King Richard's hands', Francis Bacon reports in his history of the reign, marvelling that 'she should, upon a sudden mutability or disclosure of the King's mind, be so severely handled'. A more likely suspicion, drawn from Edward Hall, is that she had a hand in the recent Lambert Simnel rebellion, for 'none could hold the book so well to prompt and instruct this stage-play, as she could'.[9] Yet one fails to see what profit it would have brought even the 'shallow, changing woman' depicted by Shakespeare's Richard. Perhaps simple greed moved Henry, who gave to his beloved wife rather less than half of her mother's lands.[10] Whatever the true cause, the end result was the same: after a brief struggle with the king's lawyers Elizabeth Woodville was deprived of her dowry and spent the rest of her life on a meagre pension at Bermondsey Abbey.

It seems from contemporary testimonies that Henry VII sincerely grieved over the deaths of his wife and of his son Arthur, but scarcely months after their demise he was on the marriage path again, with plans ever wilder and greedier. He offered his own hand to all the available ladies in Europe, sent his sister off to France, his daughter to Scotland, and all the while kept his widowed daughter-in-law Catherine of Aragon dancing on a rope between remarriage and rejection, while the state of her virginity was discussed in all the chanceries of Christendom (see below, 'King's Conscience' in Chapter 5). His best-laid schemes brought short benefit and long trouble, as James IV and Louis XII both died his enemies, Catherine's and Mary's marriages both failed to provide male heirs, while Margaret's Scottish descent would live to burden the life of his own granddaughter Elizabeth.

The Lawyers' Common Wealth

Only a few common lawyers gained influence on the Privy Council or at court under the Tudors, to rise and fall from high places, but many became prominent in local government, as county justices of the peace or town recorders. When royal charters gave towns the right to appoint a recorder, the grant usually prescribed that the office must go to a man 'learned in the laws'. Recent studies also tend to qualify the theory that malcontents filled the seats of Elizabethan Parliaments and unseated the Stuart king, but generally agree that they played a major role in the Tudor revolutions. In Prest's view, the bar included some of the Crown's most valuable servants, as well as vigilant critics of government policies, roles that were not mutually exclusive. Their proximity to the law courts and to Westminster Hall made the Inns attractive hosts for committee meetings and formal or informal debates. Virtually every major development in Tudor and early Stuart England made work for the lawyers: they 'played an essential role in the consolidation of centralized monarchical rule, advising both government and their subjects, whose

---

9 Bacon, *History of the Reign of King Henry VII*, ed. by Lumby, pp. 27–28, 24.

10 Laynesmith, *The Last Medieval Queens*, pp. 236–37.

lives were increasingly regulated by judicial tribunals, old and new, and by an ever-expanding body of statutory legislation.'[11]

Legal expertise was needed in numerous areas besides administration. As the first landowner of the realm, the Crown was frequently involved in fights for land, leases, property forfeited by attainders, royal prerogatives on goods, underground mining, forests, and waters up to boundaries of the British seas, all of which required the services of lawyers. On a less lofty plane, lawyers' practice offered various profitable sidelines, from money lending to acquisition of landed property. Erasmus thought it was knowledge of common law, despite the lack of true learning, that secured their promotion at the court of Henry VIII: those 'who have made themselves authorities in the subject are in the first rank for eminence and distinction.'[12] Indeed, 'The law precipitated social mobility. It was the safest and most convenient way for a family to acquire free capital for investment in land or on the marriage market.'[13]

The fate of the Dudley family is a good index to the great expectations Tudor lawyers could entertain under the successive reigns. Three generations of Dudleys climbed from the Inns to a position at court and down. A theatrical image, Fortune's wheel, strove to make sense of spectacular falls like theirs, inspiring fear and awe. Their rise began in the unglamorous reign of Henry VII with the unglamorous task of filling the king's coffers. Edmund Dudley, a barrister of Gray's Inn, was under-sheriff of London for over six years before he went to court and rose so fast in the king's favour that he was soon made president of the Privy Council. He and his colleague Richard Empson were prominent in setting up the Council Learned in the Law, to collect debts owed to the Crown. Bacon's *History* charges them with having used their expertise to distort every article of law, and 'as the corruption of the best things is the worst, turned law and justice into wormwood rapine.' Their exactions made them so fiercely hated that one of Henry VIII's first measures on his accession was to have them executed, and their vast wealth confiscated. Although the real culprit was the late king who carried 'his affections and thoughts unto the gathering and heaping of treasure',[14] they were accused of exceeding their mission and condemned for high treason, upon fabricated charges according to Stow, Holinshed, or Lord Herbert.

While in prison, awaiting his sentence, Dudley wrote a book entitled *The Tree of Common Wealth*, an uncouth mixture of political and moral commonplaces, which was dedicated to Henry VIII but probably never reached him.[15] In this recycling of earlier medieval allegories, the Common Wealth is a mighty tree

11 Prest, *The Rise of the Barristers*, p. 49.

12 Erasmus, *The Correspondence: Letters 993 to 1121 (1519–1520)*, trans. by R. A. B. Mynors, in *Collected Works*, ed. by Vredeveld, VII, p. 19.

13 Ives, *The Common Lawyers*, p. 418, and 'The Will of Thomas Kebell', 25 June 1500, appendix A, p. 425.

14 Bacon, *History of the Reign of King Henry VII*, p. 190.

15 Stow writes he gave a fair copy of this treatise to Leicester, reserving the original for himself. See Gunn, 'Dudley, Edmund', *ODNB*, 2010, <https://doi.org/10.1093/ref:odnb/8147>.

with five roots, each bearing different fruits. Its chief root is the Love of God; the other four are justice, truth, concord, and peace. They are all rooted in the king himself, who must protect his poorer subjects from oppressive lords.[16] For the fruits have dangerous cores — pointed references to the vices of each class of men, including prelates, privy councillors, and lawyers, which Dudley exposes with practised knowledge. His pleas for virtuous education have practical motives: the children of the nobility and gentry of England are the worst brought up of any realm in Christendom; the children of poor folk should be promoted to positions of authority in their place. This daring programme is counterbalanced by an advice against Arrogancy to 'ye good Commoners, for yor owne ease, deale not wth this false core, but be contented wth the fruite of tranquillity'. They must order themselves, and be rewarded by God after this transitory life: 'Therefore mynde you not this purpose or intente, that is the equallitie of the mouldes betwene the nobles and you, nor the cognisaunce of the petegree from Adam'.[17] The book ends with a piece of *laudando praecipere*, God's own words in praise of Henry on his day of judgement, a paean to the rule of good ancient laws, and his administration of justice.

The Tree, for all its political correctness, did not save Edmund from the axe. His son John entered Inner Temple a year later, steadily restored the family fortune, was created Duke of Northumberland under Edward VI, but aspired too high and fell with his son Guilford, while his surviving children were sent to the Tower. Robert found refuge at Gray's Inn, and rose again to such favour that he could believe himself 'the king that is to be'. This is the title Ambassador De Quadra gives him in his dispatches of 1560, when various clients, including the authors of *Gorboduc*, supported his hopes to marry Elizabeth (see below, Chapter 8).[18] Some twenty years later, a Catholic pamphlet still declared that throughout all England 'my Lord of Leicester is taken for *Dominus factotum*', and though his will 'be seldom law, yet always is his power above law, and therefore we lawyers in all cases brought unto us have as great regard to his inclination as astronomers have to the planet dominant, or as seamen have to the North Pole'.[19] Despite his many blunders, Robert Dudley never lost the queen's favour nor its perquisites and eventually succeeded where his forebears had signally failed: he died in his bed.

---

16 Dudley, *The Tree of Common Wealth*, pp. 10, 24–26, 52.

17 Dudley, *The Tree of Common Wealth*, pp. 19, 51–52, 61. See Liedl's introduction to her modernized edition of the text.

18 See Graves, *Thomas Norton*, pp. 91–99.

19 *Leicester's Commonwealth*, ed. by Peck, p. 107.

Tudor Law Courts

> Thou robed man of justice, take thy place,
> And thou, his yoke-fellow of equity,
> Bench by his side.
>
> *King Lear, III.vi*

Parliament in Henry VII's reign 'was still a function of the royal council; it was still a high court; but it was already taking on the status of a grand jury of all England'.[20] The Westminster courts grew and multiplied from the medieval three, King's Bench, Common Pleas, and Exchequer, to the specialized Tudor courts. Where Henry VII had preserved the legal system he found after Bosworth, his son undertook various innovations, roughly ending centuries of quarrels, and opening a new one. By the Act for the Submission of the Clergy, the canons not repugnant to the royal prerogative, laws, and customs of the realm were allowed to remain provisionally. After the abrogation by Henry VIII of the teaching of canon law at Oxford or Cambridge, the 'civilians' took over what remained of the ecclesiastical courts, under the authority of the Crown. Several ineffectual projects to revise canon law followed. In Edward VI's reign, a committee led by Thomas Cranmer was set up to devise a comprehensive *Reformatio legum ecclesiasticarum*, but it failed in Parliament. Mary repealed the religious acts of her father and revived the old heresy laws, which were overturned again by her sister. Again, the 1559 Act of Unity and Supremacy ruled that canon law was valid only where not repugnant to the laws of the realm.

The growth of administration under the Tudors caused a large increase of justices of the peace in the shires, where they were supposed to enforce the directives of central government, often with only a slight legal education.[21] Their involvement in complex local networks of affinities was almost a necessity since they were virtually unpaid. The Gloucestershire scenes of *Henry IV*, like rural Windsor or not so exotic Messina in *Much Ado About Nothing*, show how early modern England was governed by Shallows and Dogberries on a daily basis, at fairly safe distance from the royal court. Major procedural changes in the mid-sixteenth century increased the active role of the community in the investigation and judgement of crime, Hutson points out, unlike continental practice in which the presiding judge played the main role: the development of such 'forensic' or 'detective' habits of mind among ordinary people would flourish in the murder enquiries and trial scenes of the Elizabethan theatre.[22] Or, to take her point further, be mocked, as when Jack Cade's lieutenants use inanimate objects as proof

20 Mackie, *The Earlier Tudors*, p. 197.

21 Lambarde lists their functions in *Eirenarcha*.

22 Changes discussed in Lorna Hutson, 'Noises Off: Participatory Justice in 2 *Henry VI*', in Jordan and Cunningham, eds, *The Law in Shakespeare*, pp. 143–66, and in her *The Invention of Suspicion*.

of his noble origin: 'the bricks are alive at this day to testify it'. More perversely still when Desdemona's handkerchief 'speaks against her with the other proofs'. If the violence of Shakespeare's commons in *2 Henry VI* 'seems shaped to avenge the all too evident judicial corruption of the governing classes',[23] they sound closer to mob rule than to justice. Barbara Shapiro detects in Cicero and Quintilian traces of Aristotle's distinction between artificial and inartificial proofs, and their influence on the legal evidentiary tradition. Artificial proofs were constructed, like Iago's, by the orator's art, in a narrative where probability mattered more than actual pieces of evidence. 'Witnesses and hearsay could be used pro and con.' In Roman rhetorical training, as in a detective novel, orators would build a case arguing the probable cause of the action, the character of the person involved, and the nature of the act. Their methods would be adopted 'by medieval canonists seeking alternatives to trial by ordeal and other "irrational proofs"'.[24]

In the common law courts, the practice was an adversarial representation of a case by advocates before a judge or a jury. According to some historians, the adversarial system, pitting prosecution against defence, might be an heir of the trial by combat, or wager of battle as it was called in England.[25] It set the mode for the Elizabethan dramatic *agon*, as well as setting common law courts against all others. The courts Christian, or courts spiritual, were governed by the code of canon law, itself based on Roman civil law, that ruled the medieval Church in all European realms. They followed an inquisitorial procedure, with the judges themselves leading the enquiry. At the top of the judicial hierarchy was the Archbishop of Canterbury, under whose authority several levels of tribunals operated. They had jurisdiction in spiritual and religious matters, with constant frictions over the limits of the religious sphere.[26] The Consistory Courts, presided over by a bishop's chancellor, were established to settle matters of clergy discipline in each diocese of the Church of England.

To the main courts must be added provincial jurisdictions like the Council of the North, the Council in the Marches of Wales, and various regional, occasional, or special jurisdictions. The Palatinates of Chester and Durham, the Duchy of Lancaster, originally erected to defend the Scottish and Welsh borders, had their own administration. Since Edward I, the mythical Brutus's division of Britain between his three sons, and Locrine's lordship over Albanact, had served to justify invasions of Scotland, an independent realm that English kings strove to bring under their authority, eventually subjected by a Scottish one (see below, Chapter 9).[27] Wales was administered with variable success by the Council in the Marches.

---

23 Hutson, 'Noises Off', p. 162.

24 Barbara Shapiro, 'Classical Rhetoric and the English Law of Evidence', in Kahn and Hutson, eds, *Rhetoric and Law in Early Modern Europe*, pp. 57, 59.

25 See for instance Kristen De Barba, 'Maintaining the Adversarial System: The Practice of Allowing Jurors to Question Witnesses during Trial', *Vanderbilt Law Review*, 55.5 (2002), 1521–48.

26 Outhwaite, *The Rise and Fall of the Ecclesiastical Courts*, pp. 5–14, 64–77.

27 See Hutson, 'On the Knees of the Body Politic'.

The Statute of Rhuddlan in 1284 after the defeat of Prince Llywelin by Edward I had transferred 'entirely to the king's dominion the land of Wales', dividing it into counties and lordships under Marcher Lords, each with its own courts. The counties were subject to English criminal law, but still used Welsh laws in civil cases, and were gradually annexed to England by the Laws in Wales Acts of Henry VIII. The first section of the act abolishing the lordships observed that the Welsh used a speech 'nothing like ne consonant to the naturall mother tongue' of the said realm, and set out to extirpate all their sinister usages and customs, the strange songs echoing still in the voices of Shakespeare's Welsh women. His superstitious Owen Glendower, the Percies' ally against Henry IV, was historically Owain Glyndwr ab Gruffyd, the last nationalist leader who claimed the title of an independent prince of Wales. In 1543 an *Act for certaine Ordinaunces in the Principalitie of Wales* established the court of great session, a system of four circuits based on the English model. The aim of these measures was not political union but uniformity.[28]

As for Ireland, its history is one of repeated ineffective conquests. When Ireland became Norman, its laws were partially superseded by English law, but they survived with eclipses until the seventeenth century. The first conquest was done by a party of Norman barons, who soon allied themselves with Irish families. Then, as in the good old days of William the Conqueror, Henry II was armed with a papal bull to invade Ireland in order to remedy its religious corruption. He landed there in 1171, recovered large portions of the land, created the Lordship of Ireland which he gave to his younger son John, and made legal reforms in the conquered parts. The Irish law system, the Brehon law, continued in areas outside his barons' control, while the Normans' territory soon shrank to a pale around Dublin.[29] Irish customs and the use of the Irish language were outlawed by the Statutes of Kilkenny in 1367. In vain, mostly, for the authority of the lord deputy of Ireland did not extend much beyond the pale. Henry VIII's policy of 'surrender and regrant', by which landowners were to receive their own lands back under the protection of a royal charter, still brought little change to their practices, till a statute of the Irish Parliament in 1541 converted the lordship into a kingdom, and proclaimed Henry VIII king of Ireland and head of the Church in Ireland. Rebellions continued to flare regularly under his successors. Those most sensitive to cultural differences, like Spenser, thought the English law system was ill suited to a reformation of Ireland, but still agreed that its barbarous customs must be reformed, and advised forceful colonization.[30] One English custom in particular that ran contrary to Irish ones, the right of primogeniture, caused

28 27 Hen. VIII c. 26. 34 and 35 Hen. VIII c. 26. It was the Welsh historian Owen Edwards who referred to them as 'Act of Union'.

29 From *palus*, the stakes surrounding a jurisdiction under a given authority.

30 Spenser, *A View of the Present State of Ireland* (1596). To Nicholas Canny, *Making Ireland British, 1580–1650* (Oxford: Oxford University Press, 2001), pp. 1–58, Spenser 'sets the agenda' for all subsequent approaches to Ireland.

endless disputes. Tradition has it that the last trial by combat under English law was fought in Ireland during the reign of Elizabeth, among members of the O'Connor clan, at Dublin Castle where the lord deputy's administration had its seat.[31]

The legal profession had begun a steep decline during the Wars of the Roses. From John Guy's figures, the King's Bench and Common Pleas at the end of the fifteenth century did only half the business they attained fifty years earlier, 'for the common-law courts had failed to move with the times'.[32] Separate tribunals were created to supplement them under the first Tudors. The Star Chamber was so named, according to John Stow's *Survey of London*, because its roof was decked with images of gilded stars. A court of original jurisdiction, it began as an extension of the king's council. The Act Pro Camera Stellata of 1487 empowered it to control abuses of the justice system.[33] To Chancellor Morton, its first concern was the offender's soul: 'I know that an executor who fraudulently misapplies the goods and does not make restitution will be damned in Hell, and to remedy this is in accordance with conscience as I understand it.'[34] Neither he nor Henry VII foresaw how deeply common lawyers would come to resent this 'court of conscience', and not just on matters of principles. The product of an age of force rather than cunning, common law was not well armed against devious practices like fraud and perjury, corruption, or dilatory tactics. Common law courts could not prevent nor remedy unlawful seizure of property, for instance, only fine the offenders and in limited cases send them to jail. As a result, the bulk of profitable litigation, on real property, went to equity courts. Chancery and the Star Chamber were better armed in commercial law and able by writs of subpoena to deal more rapidly with cases of property settlement, titles to land, mercantile debts, or undue imprisonment.[35] The bills brought before the Star Chamber rose to such a large number under Wolsey's chancellorship that he set up the court of Whitehall, 'the forerunner of the later court of Requests, to relieve the pressure', and 'apparently earned the general antipathy of the legal profession'. After his fall from the chancellorship, except under Mary's brief reign, 'the common lawyers dominated the post for the remainder of the sixteenth century'.[36]

The equity courts developed under the royal prerogative to provide equitable relief in areas that common law could not touch.[37] Since most chancellors before Thomas More had no legal training, their decisions were not guided by precedents and could vary significantly from one case to the next, one of the reasons that

---

31 On 7 September 1583. See the account of the proceedings by an Irish Privy Councillor in the *Calendar of State Papers, Ireland*, ed. by Hamilton, SP 63/104/69.

32 Guy, 'Law, Lawyers and the English Reformation', p. 17.

33 3. Hen.7 c.1. See *Select Cases before the King's Council*, ed. by Leadam, XVI.1, pp. ix–x.

34 Plucknett, *Studies in English Legal History*, pp. 613–14.

35 See Watt's chapter on 'Equity Captured in Chancery' in his *Equity Stirring*, pp. 48–54.

36 Brooks, *Law, Politics and Society*, pp. 37, 39, 40.

37 See Fortier's study of Shakespeare's use of the notion, *The Culture of Equity*, pp. 122–30.

made equity 'a Roguish thing' in the eyes of common lawyers.[38] Young barristers had no qualms about pleading before equity courts, but the older ones watched with a jaundiced eye these encroachments on their practice. Wolsey's extension of the equity principle caused Thomas Audley in his reading of 1526 at Inner Temple to argue that Chancery was a potential threat to common law.

Should chancellors continue to remedy the whole gamut of defects in the legal system? The problem was argued with due reference to Aristotle and Aquinas, still audible in Portia's remonstrances to Shylock on justice and mercy.[39] In the *Summa*, Aquinas had put the case for equity in most lawyerly form, a *pro et contra* dispute, later repeated in endless debates: Is equity a vice or a virtue? Is it a part of justice? The *pro* invoked *epieikeia*, the need to interpret the mind of the legislator and protect the rights of individuals within, or against, the commonweal. The *contra* stressed the risks of arbitrariness, subjectivity, and inroads into common law. All the shades of meaning given to 'equity', to mitigate or amend the law, implied a judgement on justice as inadequate, too harsh, unfair. There were hesitations over the meaning of 'equity': Morton's 'conscience as I understand it', a very flexible one in his own case, or a sort of consensus, broadly based on principles of English law? The notion continued to evolve while the growth of equity courts under the Tudor reigns gradually shoved 'conscience' from the offender's to the judge's place, till Selden dismissed the notion in his *Table Talk*: 'For Law we have a measure, know what to trust to. Equity is according to the conscience of him that is Chancellor, and as that is larger or narrower, so is Equity.'[40] As the length of a chancellor's foot varies, so his conscience.

The Courtly Muses of Europe

After a long sequence of rebellions and repressions, the early sixteenth century seemed to augur happier times for England. The accession of three learned young princes to the first thrones of Europe was expected to open up a new horizon of enlightenment. Pre-Reformation England was firmly anchored to the continent, sharing in the humanists' political and educative programmes. London, under a prince reputed to love letters, would be a haven of *pietas literata*, a new Athens, or better still an Augustan Rome.[41] Erasmus's hyperbolic eulogy of Henry VIII may be tinted with flattery, but he is obviously sincere when he describes the court of England in glowing terms to a Spanish correspondent: scholars are invited to the table of the king, where they debate over literary points. 'In one word, the

38 Selden, 'Equity', in *The Table Talk*, ed. by Reynolds, no. XXXVII, p. 61.

39 See discussions of *The Merchant* in Weisberg, *Poethics*, pp. 94–104; Lupton, *Citizen-Saints*, pp. 75–99; Hutson, *The Usurer's Daughter*.

40 Selden, *The Table Talk*, p. 61.

41 England and its young king are repeatedly praised by Erasmus, *La Correspondance*, I, nos 79, 204, 215; II, no. 333; III, nos 821, 834, 855, 917, 964, 965, 966, 967.

society of the court is such that no University could stand the comparison.' There is no doubt in his mind that *bonae litterae*, good letters, only strive by 'the favour and generosity of princes'. The sovereigns of Europe all receive praise; to each he prophesies a golden century in a world pacified by their means.[42] Thanks to their patronage, 'all the liberal arts revive, allowed by peace to bloom just as Zephyr makes all flowers grow'.[43]

Pacifism and New Learning

Erasmus, Juan Vives, and other humanists preached pacifism to their kings, confident that their own friendship would serve as model to a new amity between European nations. It did, as things turned out: peace deteriorated as fast as the relations soured within their group. When a meeting was arranged at Cambrai in 1516, Erasmus urged the leading princes to universal peace: quoting Plato's *Republic*, his *Querela Pacis* denounces militarism and begs them all to follow François, Carlos, Maximilian, Henry in their peaceful endeavours — again a fine instance of *laudando praecipere*, teaching by praise. 'Princes' kingdoms will be carefully amplified if they conscientiously rule their subjects by laws rather than by arms', Erasmus concludes.[44] Machiavelli was currently expressing contrary advice: ideally, city states should live peacefully side by side, neither too small to tempt their neighbours, nor too large to scare them, but 'since, however, all human affairs are ever in a state of flux and cannot stand still', they must either expand or face ruin.[45] By the time *Querela Pacis* appeared, the peace treaty was already nought, Erasmus would bitterly recall: 'Things turned out so that we ought to have prepared the epitaph of peace, for no hope remains to see it revive.'[46] The same year, the name of an unknown theologian appears in the humanists' correspondence: Martin Luther, who is said to be troubled by Erasmus's exegesis of Paul's Epistle to the Romans.[47] From then on both pro- and anti-Reformation parties begin to hurl Saint Paul's teachings at each other. Jeffrey Knapp notes Paul's adaptiveness and the stress on theatricality in 1 Corinthians, the text at the source of Christ-centred kingship translated by Tyndale, 'In all things I fashioned myself to all men'. Erasmus's *Ratio verae theologiae* observes how artfully Paul could 'play the chameleon' and defer truth so that 'he might bring some gain to Christ'. Far from sinful his deceit is judged, like Hamlet's, 'a sort of holy cunning'.[48]

---

42 Erasmus, Letters 333, 335, 966, 1005, 2211.

43 Erasmus, Letter 542.

44 Erasmus, *The Complaint of Peace*, ed. and trans. by Dolan, pp. 179, 189, 190, 203, 204.

45 Machiavelli, *The Discourses*, ed. by Crick, trans. by Walker, Book I.6, p. 123.

46 In a letter of 30 January 1523 to Johann Botzheim. *Querela Pacis* was published in 1517 in Basel, by Froben. See Erasmus, *Dulce bellum inexpertis*, 'war is sweet to those who have no experience of it'.

47 Letter 49 to Erasmus from a Saxon humanist, George Spalatin.

48 Knapp, *Shakespeare's Tribe*, pp. 34–35. Cf. *Hamlet*, III.ii, the Mousetrap scene.

Before Luther's name was even heard of around humanist circles, demands for reforms came from all sides: Brothers of the Common Life or anti-humanists like Girolamo Savonarola deplored the abuses of the Church, the sloth of monasteries, the illiteracy of clergymen. Ironically enough, it was through the armies of the Italian wars that the new learning conquered Europe with its combination of classical studies, courtly manners, and vestiges of chivalric exploits. The French court established at Milan from 1498 to 1512 multiplied the exchanges between scholars and artists. The new learning spread through the Netherlands and Germany via the Hieronymians, an order founded at Deventer who provided teachers of Greek, Hebrew, and Latin to the surrounding countries. Under the impulsion of their pupil Erasmus, a trilingual college was founded at Leuven in 1517. On this model, Guillaume Budé led François Ier to create the Collège de France. Johann Sturm, a graduate from Leuven, would teach there before founding his gymnasium at Strasbourg. There was still for a while a remarkable degree of unity in European education.

As in Germany, it was through secondary schools that the new learning circulated in England. Erasmus's educational programme, detailed in *De ratione studii*, was more successful there than his plans for peace.[49] With his support, after studying Greek at Florence, Grocyn, Linacre, and Colet had introduced the new learning at Oxford. Several younger Oxford men, William Latimer, Richard Pace, Cuthbert Tunstall, went to study Greek in Padua, while William Lily, Grocyn's godson, spent several years in Rhodes, learning Greek among exiles from Constantinople. As Micha Lazarus argues, Greek literacy, not exactly a synonym of Greek scholarship, was far more widespread than is usually acknowledged. But, he admits, if we know so much about these eminent early Greek scholars, it is because they were so few.[50] In the academic world, the humanist return to Greek sources inspired as much enthusiasm as hostility, and Corpus Christi College, Richard Fox's foundation, became a centre of resistance with the formation of a 'Trojan' faction against Greek studies, though Fox had established its statutes in 1517 with the express aim to develop the new humanist learning. Thomas More and Erasmus in their correspondence repeatedly warn each other to prepare for attacks from the Oxford 'Trojans' or the 'Sorbonagres', Sorbonne asses, in other words the tenants of old scholasticism. Kicking back, More praised the reception of Greek studies at Cambridge, where Erasmus had taught at the invitation of the then chancellor John Fisher, for 'even those who are not learning Greek are each moved by a common devotion to their school'.[51] The best reason to study Greek, Erasmus pleaded, was 'to be able to spend more time with more profit and more sure judgement on the Scriptures', an argument frequently repeated by supporters

49 Erasmus, *De ratione studii*, first published in 1511, revised and re-edited with the *De copia* in 1512.
50 Lazarus, 'Greek Literacy'.
51 More, 'Letter to the University of Oxford', Spring 1518, in *The Complete Works*, ed. by Sylvester and others, XV, p. 145.

of Greek studies.[52] His translation of the New Testament would cause the first fracture in the European community of *bonae litterae*, with fierce polemics over half a dozen words, beginning with the translation of *agape*, love or charity.

When Colet undertook the refounding of the cathedral school of St Paul's in 1510, Erasmus urged him to introduce a new educational programme along their principles, pure Latin and Greek, classical authors, Christian discipline. When William Lily, a pioneer of Greek learning, was appointed first high master there in 1512, more university graduates were available, and Greek became a regular part of the teaching programmes of the best grammar schools. Drama held a central place in the curriculum. Erasmus not only recommended the reading and performing of Greek and Roman drama, he translated several plays himself, a precedent that would inspire both university and Inns of Court students.[53] Among his texts of lasting influence was the publication of Seneca's works, in 1521, and an improved edition of 1529 (see below, Chapters 7 and 8). By the end of the century, most grammar schools in England, including King Edward VI School in Stratford-upon-Avon, had adopted Colet's model. The most renowned, Merchant Taylors' under Richard Mulcaster, drew its statutes literally from St Paul's, educating Kyd, Lodge, Spenser, Webster, and James Shirley among others.

Ideal Cities

The humanists' images of polity stood on layers of ancient and increasingly pessimistic wisdom.[54] Mixed polity, a kingship both 'political and royal' unified by the common law, the leitmotiv of Fortescue, would continue to inspire his successors until it became the actual regime of Great Britain. In his praise of English laws, Fortescue quotes Augustine, quoting Cicero quoting Aristotle, who defined *communitas* as 'a numerous gathering united in fellowship by a common sense of right and a community of interest'.[55] The ideal communality of the Inns looked back to Brutus and his Trojan band of brothers, who brought fellowship to England: not only law is taught there, but 'a cultivation of virtues and a banishment of vice'.[56] Shakespeare was nearer the mark when he placed the first quarrel of the Roses in their Edenic garden at Temple. Their amity, with its tragic context of civil war, carries as infinite a nostalgia as Plato's *Laws*, where the reliance on law sounds far more desperate than in the *Republic*. In *The Laws*, the Cretan city of Magnesia is only second-best, *deuterôs*, to Plato's ideal community of friends.[57] The constitution which the debaters undertake to write will be third best. Men are like puppets on strings to the gods. The first string they must grasp

52 Erasmus, Letter 540 to Latimer, February 1517, in Erasmus, *La Correspondance*, II, p. 618.
53 His Latin translations of Euripides, first printed in Paris, were republished by Manutius in 1507.
54 See Raffield, *Images and Cultures of Law*, pp. 59–60, on parallels in *Utopia*.
55 Augustine, *De civitate Dei*, XIX, xxi; Cicero, *De re publica*, I, xxv.
56 Fortescue, *In Praise of the Laws of England*, p. 69.
57 Plato, *The Laws*, trans. by Jowett, V. 739, p. 258.

and cling to is 'the sacred and golden cord of reason, called by us the common law of the State'.[58] To Aristotle, a city needs not only righteousness but *philia*, amity among the citizens: 'For in every community there is thought to be some form of justice, and friendship too'. In his view 'the proverb "what friends have is common property" expresses the truth; for friendship depends on community. Now brothers and comrades have all things in common'.[59] The same phrase is quoted in *The Republic* (there applied to the sharing of women and children), where the guardians 'all follow the general principle that friends have all things in common, as the proverb says'.[60]

These layers of pagan thought informed the Church Fathers' philosophy. Plato's and Aristotle's citizenship grows fiercely antagonistic in Paul's Christianized *politeuma*: Christians are surrounded by enemies who 'glory in their shame, with minds set on earthly things. But our commonwealth is in heaven'.[61] His citizens are distinguished by righteousness, *dikaiosunè*, not a righteousness of their own, 'based on law, but that which is through faith in Christ'.[62] Paul further claims that Christ has made all the Christians one 'by abolishing in his flesh the law of commandments and ordinances', though elsewhere he advises obedience to 'the powers that be'.[63] In either case, law seems a commodity that true Christians may dispense with. 'I through the law died to the law, that I might live to God': it was this sentence that made Luther crown Paul 'the most heretical of heretics' and declare death to the law on the basis of his Epistles. 'For the whole law is fulfilled in one word, "You shall love your neighbour as yourself"', Paul insists, giving a new twist to an old commonplace.[64] In their conflicts of interpretation, both supporters and enemies of the Reformation would brandish the Epistles. To Tyndale, 'the love of God and of his neighbour [...] is the spirit and the life of all laws'. His claim that 'the elect, having the law written in their breasts, and loving it in their spirits, sin there never' would cause More to describe Luther's sect as a 'secret unknowen sort of folk that do not sin'.[65]

Augustine gives human law an even worse record than Paul. There is no such thing as 'natural' or God-given law in the earthly city, only relative righteousness, which depends on *dominium*, the power of the State, to enforce order on sin. Ideally, all things should be common, as they were among the first Christians. But

---

58 Plato, *The Laws*, I. 628 p. 149; I. 645 p. 166.

59 Aristotle, *The Nichomachean Ethics*, trans. by Ross, VIII, p. 9.

60 Plato, *The Republic*, trans. by Lindsay, IV, 424a (subst. repeated in *Laws*, III).

61 Paul, Philippians 3. 19–20, in *The Writings*, ed. by Meeks, p. 100. On the Pauline common weal, see Lupton, *Citizen-Saints*, pp. 28–50, and her revision in *Thinking with Shakespeare*, pp. 221–41.

62 Paul, Philippians 3. 9; 'if righteousness were through the law, then Christ died to no purpose', Galatians 2. 21.

63 Paul, Galatians 2. 19. See also Ephesians 2. 14, Romans 3. 3, Romans 7. 12.

64 See Paul, *The Writings*, p. 20, n. 3.

65 Tyndale, *An Answer to Sir Thomas More's Dialogue*, ed. by Walter, pp. 8, 114. More, *The Dialogue Concerning Tyndale* (also known as *Dialogue Concerning Heresies and Matters of Religion*), II, ch. 4, in *The English Works*, ed. by Campbell, p. 142.

human greed requires control by laws and institutions. Augustine's faithful, as in Paul's *politeuma*, are pilgrims on earth, for whom all laws are equal. The powers that be are just the lesser of two evils, relative injustice imposing order on anarchy: 'Justice being taken away, then, what are kingdoms but great robberies?' The band of brothers, a band of thieves, 'is knit together by the pact of the confederacy; the booty is divided by the law agreed on'. If they grow enough to possess cities, then their government is no longer called thievish, but graced with the name of kingdom, 'not by the removal of covetousness, but by the addition of impunity'.[66] Between two tales of the city's origin, rather than the irenic *Aeneid*, Augustine retains the violent one, the legend of the Wolf's twins: 'Thus the founder of the earthly city was a fratricide. Overcome with envy, he slew his own brother, a citizen of the eternal city, and a sojourner on earth'. Romulus's archetypal crime sets the pattern for all ensuing civil wars, summed up in the image of father against son like gladiators in the arena. Here Augustine is as loud as Plato in his condemnation of poets and of stage plays, vile spectacles for the Roman gods who laugh at the miserably comic human show.[67]

Half way between Plato and Augustine, the first apostles formed a community that would feed the dreams of medieval and later egalitarian pamphlets: 'all that believed were together, and had all things common; / And sold their possessions and goods, and parted them to all *men*, as every man had need.'[68] Images of this fraternal community, sharing of goods, absence of hierarchy will have a double descent, one aristocratic, one popular. On the one hand the egalitarian utopias of rebel preachers, from Wycliff to Parson Ball; on the other the peaceful retreat and learned delights of some 'Palace of Pleasure' — Thélème, *Decameron* Tuscany, Inns of Court, or *Love's Labour's Lost* Navarre. The Platonist Utopians hold everything in common, wives, children, and goods, a practice repeatedly denounced in the Tudor chronicles as the extreme of outlawry. In *Utopia* Morus, who finds the State communism described by Hythlodaeus impractical, confronts it with the voluntary communism of the early Christians, and notes with the now familiar note of nostalgia 'that among the truest groups of Christians, the practice still prevails'.[69]

More himself is a good abstract of this layered culture. While teaching common law at Furnival's Inn, he attended Colet's exegeses of Paul's Epistles, and as utter barrister, 'he read for a good space a public lecture of St Augustine, *De civitate Dei*, in the church of St Laurence in the Old Jewry', attended by the most learned men in London.[70] These talks, combined with Plato's *Republic* which, unlike Augustine, More was able to read in the original, are often thought to have

66 Augustine, *The City of God*, trans. by Dods, XIX.xviii, IV.iv.

67 Augustine, *The City of God*, I.xxxi, II.viii–xiv, pp. 36, 47–53, III.xiv, p. 89. Plato's rejection of the theatre, *The Laws*, II. 658–70.

68 Acts of the Apostles 2. 44–45 and 4. 32–36, in *The Bible*, ed. by Carroll and Prickett.

69 More, *Utopia*, trans. by Adams, II, p. 79.

70 Roper, *The Lyfe of Sir Thomas Moore*, ed. by Hitchcock, p. 6.

suggested the composition of *Utopia*. According to Erasmus, 'while still a youth, he attempted a dialogue, in which he carried the defence of Plato's community even to the matter of wives!' He published it, Erasmus goes on, for the purpose of showing what things 'occasion mischief in commonwealths; having the English constitution especially in view, which he so thoroughly knows and understands'.[71]

Seen from the shores of another island, the laws of England deserve little praise. *Utopia* mentions a whole store of them 'not made according to equity'. Reporting a discussion at the house of Cardinal Morton, More's first mentor, the narrator Hythlodaeus stigmatizes the inequity of a system that allows the abuses of landlords and creates poverty with enclosures. It is absurd and harmful to punish theft and murder alike with hanging. Thefts are often the result of dire misery, committed by men wounded in the service of their country, starved by cupid landlords or sheep that eat them out of house and land: 'If you do not find a cure for these evils, it is futile to boast of your severity in punishing theft. Your policy may look superficially like justice, but in reality it is neither just nor practical.'[72]

Taking each topic in turn — community of goods, education, advice to princes, war and peace — *Utopia* throws a sceptical light on current practices and old theories, while pointing out potential conflicts of interest between ruler and commonweal.[73] Plato's *Laws* was written after his failure in educating his princely pupil and his flight from a city that he, the philosopher, had proved unable to mend: 'Plato certainly had this experience with Dionysius of Syracuse', Hythlodaeus recalls, of having his advice unheeded. Hovering behind Henry VIII stood the ghosts of Tacitus's tyrants and, closer to memory, Richard III. When advising His Grace, More would say to Thomas Cromwell, 'ever tell him what he owght to doe, but never what he is able to doe. For if a Lion knewe his owne strength, harde were it for any man to rule him'.[74] An adage he would soon himself verify (see below, 'King's Games' in Chapter 5).

Advice to the Prince

Resisting the temptations of an elegant retreat among chosen friends, Cicero had urged an engagement of wise men in public life. A number of humanists agreed that advice to the prince was their first natural destination, and law studies the best preparation to service of the State.[75] In England more lastingly than in France, the medieval ideal of 'good counsel' permeated political thought, resounding still in the Tudor Parliaments and theatres. John of Salisbury's considerations on the role of the Senate in Roman history reappear in Fortescue's lessons to his prince,

---

71 Erasmus, Letter 999 to Ulrich von Hutten.

72 More, *Utopia*, I, pp. 11–16.

73 A translation of *Utopia* was made in 1551 by Ralph Robynson, with a dedication to William Cecil.

74 Roper, *The Lyfe of Sir Thomas Moore*, pp. 56–57.

75 Guy, *Politics, Law and Counsel*, XIV, pp. 292–311.

in Elyot's *Gouernour*, and again in *Gorboduc*'s warnings to Elizabeth. Augustus and his successors owed their success to the fact that they regularly consulted the Senate, whereas Domitian and Nero slew the Senators, promoted 'private' counsellors, and led the empire into decay. From this precedent, Fortescue concludes that the king should not be counselled 'by menn of his Chambre', private chosen ones, but by a representative group of *conciliarii nati*, competent, not necessarily aristocratic advisors, working in a public assembly.

To a majority of humanists, it is good counsel that makes the exercise of power legitimate: a conjugal relationship with *concilium* mitigates the rigour of *imperium* just as equity tempers the rigour of common law. Thomas Starkey, who studied at Padua, was much attracted to the 'myth of Venice', where the combination of *doge* plus *concilio maggiore* guaranteed liberty and justice. However, most were aware that good counsel has its limitations. Erasmus, Colet, Elyot all had doubts about the ideal of the active citizen: Was it advisable for them to step on stage? Hythlodaeus criticizes Cicero's civil philosophy and repeats Plato's view that intellectuals should not serve princes, who will disregard their guidance unless they are philosophers themselves. But Morus suggests a mix of theatrical flexibility with adequate timing, a direct echo of Plato's *kairós*: what is needed is not the scholastics' but 'another philosophy that is better suited for political action' and will 'adapt itself to the drama in hand'.[76] The connection of stage and State service draws again on Cicero, who uses the phrase *scaenae servire*, to go through with the performance of a public duty, in the interim between Caesar's death and the conjurers' defeat at Philippi: 'I, Brutus, was at the time under no obligation save to the social code and the law of Nature; but *you* must now play up to the public and the stage you hold', for 'the gaze of your soldiers but not only of them, of all citizens, and of almost the entire world is centred upon you'.[77]

The English writings on education up to Ascham all derive from the humanists' pattern. Thomas Elyot's added law to their curriculum. Where the Latin *Utopia* was addressed to the international humanist community, a generation later *The Boke named the Gouernour* was written directly in English and had eight editions in England, but no known translation.[78] The son of a justice of the Common Pleas, Elyot studied law at Middle Temple.[79] According to Stapleton's *Life*, his wife Margaret Barrow was a student in the family 'school' of Thomas More. Yet in his correspondence More never mentions Elyot, who would take pains to defend himself in letters to Cromwell from close association with the fallen chancellor: 'I therefore beseech your good lordship now to lay apart the remembrance of the amity between me and sir Thomas More, which was but *Usque ad aras*', up

---

76 See M. S. Lane, *Method and Politics in Plato's 'Statesman'* (Cambridge: Cambridge University Press, 1998). More, *Utopia*, I, p. 28.

77 Cicero, in 'Epistulae ad Brutum', on the death of Portia, *The Letters to Brutus*, trans. by Cary, I. 9, pp. 690–91.

78 Norland, 'More's and Elyot's Perspectives', p. 140.

79 Elyot, *The Dictionary of syr Thomas Elyot knight* (London: Thomas Berthelet, 1538).

to the altar, for he was less addicted to More than he was to truth and fidelity to his sovereign.[80] This was not cowardice or equivocation, Greg Walker pleads: Elyot accepted the royal supremacy as a means to bring about necessary reform in the Church and forestall more radical innovations.[81] His position was quite compatible with the anticlericalism of Erasmus or the younger More. According to his biographer, he was walking a fine line in those letters, 'hoping to remain a conservative, but sound like a radical'.[82]

The Boke named the Gouernour was written rapidly after Wolsey's fall, which caused Elyot's dismissal from the clerkship of the council. Henry VIII must have appreciated its dedication to him, for it was barely out of the press when he entrusted Elyot with the task of representing him at the chapter of the Golden Fleece and using this opportunity to sound Emperor Carlos about his plans of divorce from Carlos's aunt. Actually the correspondence of Ambassador Chapuys, Capucius in *Henry VIII*, shows that Elyot's sympathies were on the side of Queen Catherine, who probably lent features to his later *Defence of Good Women*.[83] On his return in June 1532, he had a long interview with the king and plied him with warnings that he would repeat through the next decade, to mend his policy.[84]

In the context of the king's Great Matter, the *Gouernour* can be read as a set of pointed reflections on the present crisis: Elyot may genuinely have believed that Henry was seeking all good men's opinions on the best cure of evils. His own recipe combined the humanists' models with Fortescue's glorification of English laws. The best governance is the rule by one prince who exercises it for the weal of his people, assisted by those 'inferiour gouernours' who in Latin are named 'Magistratus. And herafter I intende to call them Magistratis, lackynge a more conuenient worde in englisshe.'[85] The word 'Weal' means profit, he explains, pointing out the distinction between public and common weal: profit for all the people but not property held in common, a notion he rejects with horror. God has put degree in all his creatures; the basis of public weal is order: 'take away ordre from all thynges what shulde than remayne? Certes nothynge finally, except some man wolde imagine eftsones Chaos'.[86] A veritable Ulysses.

The model of this order is the beehive, with 'one principal Bee for their governor, who excelleth all other in greatness, yet hath no prick nor sting'.[87] An admirer of Rome, Elyot disapproved of the Athenian commonalty: democracy was 'a monstre with many heedes', as repugnant to him as it would be to Shakespeare's

---

80 Elyot, *The Letters of Sir Thomas Elyot*, ed. by K. J. Wilson, *Studies in Philology*, 735 (1976), 30–33.

81 Walker, *Writing under Tyranny*, pp. 129–31.

82 Hogrefe, *The Life and Times of Sir Thomas Elyot*, p. 31.

83 See Norland, 'More's and Elyot's Perspectives', p. 126.

84 Walker, *Writing under Tyranny*, pp. 125–27.

85 Elyot, *The Gouernour*, ed. by Croft, 'The first Boke', ch. 1, p. 25. In the *OED*, the earliest recorded use of this word is in 1384: 'A civil officer charged with the administration of the law'.

86 Elyot, *The Gouernour*, I, 1, p. 3.

87 His immediate source for the beehive, drawn from Virgil's *Georgics*, is Erasmus, *The Education of a Christian Prince*, p. 29. Cf. *Henry V*, I.ii.332–50.

Coriolanus. A class of subordinates must overlook each part of the realm, as in the old organic metaphor: 'Aristotell in his politykes exorteth gouernours to haue their frendes for a great numbre of eyen, earis, handes, and legges; considering that no one man may see or here all thinge that many men may see and here, ne can be in all places'. Like Fortescue, Elyot believes that Rome prospered as long as the Senate did. He does not advise greater powers for Parliament, though, but a delicate balance of the king's authority by a select group of sober councillors, good counsel being 'the end of all doctrine and studie'.[88]

In its advocacy of learning, the *Gouernour* provides a good instance of the humanist reading lists. The education of a noble child destined to a role of public authority should begin from infancy. Aesop's fables, Lucian, Aristophanes, Homer would be good starting points for the study of Greek. Later, tragedies will teach him to execrate tyrants and contemn the folly of lascivious poets. At seventeen, a thorough learning of the sciences is needed, philosophy first, to bridle courage with reason. Aristotle's *Ethica*, Cicero's *De officiis*, and above all Plato's works are almost all that is needed to make an excellent governor. The mature man will read the Proverbs of Solomon and Erasmus's *Institutio Principis Christiani*, written for young Carlos, who is now emperor. Any talents for the arts should be cultivated, as well as sports. Shooting in the long bow has unhappily declined since 'crosse bowes and hand gunnes were brought into this realme, by the sleighte of our enemies'. Football should be 'put in perpetuall silence', for 'therein is nothing but beastly furie and external violence'. As long as it is not idolatrous, dancing is an excellent introduction to the concord of dualities, marriage, and all the branches of prudence, circumspection, modesty....[89]

This Gargantuan list is only the first phase. Those who have diligently read in their early years will be ready for phase II, the study of law. When brought to this 'moste difficulte and graue lernyng', unless kept to the task by 'lucre', many abandon the laws, vanquished by tediousness. The best pleaders combine the qualities of the Roman jurist and the English common lawyer. The 'exposition of maiestie' shown by the glorious figures of Antiquity has a match at home, 'our owne kynges of Englande', especially Henry V, whose most admirable trait was his humble submission to the Chief Justice who dared reprove his disrespect of the law[90] — a key episode in Shakespeare's conversion of Prince Hal when he must choose between two counsellors, the austere upright Chief Justice or the revelling, witty, lawless Falstaff. In Christopher Brooks's opinion, Elyot's *Gouernour* played a major role in fashioning the ideal of the humanist lawyer, one largely adopted by the English legal profession, including Sir Edward Coke, who would, like Elyot,

88 Elyot, *The Gouernour*, II, XIV, p. 157. Walker, *Writing under Tyranny*, pp. 161–63.

89 Elyot, *The Gouernour*, I, XXVII, p. 303; XXVII, 295. On dancing, I, ch. XIX; ch. XXI, pp. 237–38; and ch. XXII.

90 Elyot, *The Gouernour*, I, XIV, p. 136, 145; II, VI, pp. 60–72.

garnish his works with quotations from Cicero.[91] Some of Elyot's axioms would be reused in Thomas Baldwin's *Treatise of Moral Philosophy*.[92]

Lacking employment, Elyot continued to advise Henry in book after book to guide himself and the realm on these models of ideal kingship. In *Of the Knowledge which Maketh a Wise Man* a beggarly Plato explains to Aristippus that he has just escaped the tyranny of Dionysius and a death sentence for plain-speaking. Was it wise, Aristippus wonders, considering the results, to try and advise him? Elyot was not the only one to try. *Pasquil the Plain*, a dialogue published anonymously in 1533, just as the Act of Appeals was going through Parliament, portrays a well-meaning, wilful, not very wise prince liable to fall under the sway of flatterers who set him on his way to tyranny. When John Heywood wrote *The Play of the Weather*, drawn from Lucian's dialogues, in 1533, Henry's court was torn between conflicting advisors. In this comic plea for temperance, composed shortly after the resignation of Heywood's kinsman More from the chancellorship, the disputing gods have surrendered 'The full of theyr powrs for terme everlastynge' into Jupiter's hands, so it behoves him to avoid sectarian controversy.[93] As Altman shows, this pleasant interlude and Elyot's dialogues may have marked the last moment when open if oblique criticism could still vent itself in print.[94] In the same decade John Bale's *Kynge Johan* (see below, Chapter 7) celebrates the break with Rome through the voice of a character named Imperial Majesty, while Veritas reminds the audience that kings are near to God and have no other judge above them:

> All subjectes offendynge are undre the kynges judgement:
> A kynge is reserved to the Lorde Omnypotent.
>
> (*ll.* 2354–55)

Henry VIII's agenda needed no further prompting, though not along the Protestant lines that Bale had sketched for him. Between the Coverdale Bible (1535) and the Great Bible (1539), Peter Happé observes, he has moved from bottom to top of the frontispiece featuring him as inheritor of Solomon and David. To John Guy, it was Holbein who best caught the gist of Henry's message to the world, in 'Solomon Receiving the Homage of the Queen of Sheba', actually a portrait of the English monarch receiving homage from the Church of England.[95]

---

91 Brooks, *Lawyers, Litigation*, pp. 205–08.

92 See Peter Mack, 'Informal Ethics in the Renaissance', in Lines and Ebbersmeyer, eds, *Rethinking Virtue, Reforming Society*, pp. 201–02.

93 John Heywood, *The Play of the wether*, l. 74. Peter Happé, 'Dramatic Images of Kingship in Heywood and Bale', *Studies in English Literature, 1500–1900*, 39.2 (1999), 239–53, lists occurrences of Henry VIII in the role of Jupiter.

94 Altman, *The Tudor Play of Mind*, pp. 123–24.

95 John Guy, *Henry VIII: The Quest for Fame* (London: Allen Lane, 2014), ch. 5. Susan Foister, ed., *Holbein and the Court of Henry VIII* (London: Buckingham Palace, the Queen's Gallery, 1978), pp. 129–30.

Like Elyot, Thomas Starkey was all in favour of conciliarism. In the crucial years of Henry's break with Rome, *A Dialogue between Pole and Lupset*, later known as *Starkey's England*, advised a combination of executive council on the Venetian model and Parliament in the English baronial tradition. The council should be composed of four of the greatest lords, two bishops, four judges, and four of the wisest citizens of London, a distant echo of the Model Parliament. Its role was 'to see unto the liberty of the whole body of the realm, and to resist all tyranny which by any manner may grow upon the whole commonalty'.[96] In the *Dialogue* Reginald Pole, to whom Starkey was secretary, utters a violent attack on common law, adding that all defects might be cured if the heads of the State received the civil law of the Romans as the common law of England. Though it was presented to Henry VIII, the piece remained unpublished and had no more visible impact on the political situation than Dudley's *Tree of Common Wealth*. Pole himself remained prudently out of reach, leaving his family to face the king's reaction to good counsel.

Courtly Plays

When these suns
(For so they phrase 'em) by their heralds challeng'd
The noble spirits to arms, they did perform
Beyond thought's compass.

Henry VIII, I.i

Since time immemorial the king 'kept his Christmas' with varied entertainments, their standards raised by Burgundian examples under the last Plantagenets. In Edward IV's reign, during the negotiations for the marriage of his sister Margaret to Charles the Bold, each Inn supplied armed men for the king's guard and contributed to the cost of scaffoldings for a tournament between Anthony Woodville and Antoine, Grand Bastard of Burgundy: once the king was seated in his throne, 'the mayor of London, with the aldermen and men of law, entered the lists, the sword held before him'.[97] The London chroniclers were awed by the splendid Burgundian delegation, which fostered Caxton's taste for chivalry and romance. Edward IV was an exile in Flanders when he saw the manuscripts of his host, Louis de Gruuthuse, and started his own library, the first material of Caxton's print.[98] The London event was a paltry affair in comparison with the bride's Joyous Entry at Bruges, nine days of luxurious feasts and banquets enlivened among other amusements by an elaborate allegory in her honour, the Pas d'armes

96 Starkey, *A Dialogue between Reginald Pole and Thomas Lupset*, ed. by Burton, p. 167.

97 Olivier de la Marche, *Les Mémoires*, ed. by Petitot, I, XXXVII, 261. See also his hour-by-hour account of the marriage (II, IV, 299–391), which is still re-enacted at Bruges every five years for the tourists.

98 Edward's sister Margaret and Anthony Woodville were two of the printer's patrons.

de l'Arbre d'or, the pageant of Hercules' Labours, fireworks, a mobile whale harbouring sirens, a tower full of wild animals with music pouring forth from their mouths.…

The feasts offered by the Inns under the Tudors followed these earlier practices. Their plays and masques were modelled on courtly events. Sydney Anglo is in no doubt that Burgundian fashions had taken hold of England, and that 'life at the court of Henry VII may not have been as sober as the character of this monarch makes it appear'.[99] Sobriety had no place in the court of his son, who was made a knight of the Burgundian Golden Fleece while Prince of Wales. Nor was England closed yet to foreign fashions: on Twelfth Night 1512, Hall reports, the king and his companions had appeared in disguise 'after the manner of Italie, called a maske, a thyng not seen afore in England'.[100] Plays too had their part in the revels: an entertainment at Greenwich in March 1519 included a 'goodly commedy by Plautus'.[101] Tournaments, set in dramatic mode, preceded by challenges and debates, were Henry VIII's favourite sport. He was often the chief challenger of such jousts, until the court revels of May 1527 where he was asked instead to arbitrate a debate introduced by Jupiter and Mercury between Love and Riches. Emulation again plays a major part in the many-splendoured Field of the Cloth of Gold. Even though its ostensible programme is European concord and universal peace, by words, swords or lance, mock combats, the duel is the thing. In *Henry VIII*, Norfolk devastatingly compares this 'earthly glory' to a futile masque, where

To-day the French,
All clinquant, all in gold, like heathen gods,
Shone down the English; and to-morrow, they
Made Britain India.

(*I.i.18–21*)

It was around the time of its composition, after the revels for Princess Elizabeth's wedding where his plays figured prominently, that Shakespeare quit the stage (see below, 'A Parliament of Voices' in Chapter 10). To Richard Dutton, his career at the court of Elizabeth was as important as when he was made to wear the livery of James I. Edmund Tilney's commission on being made master of the revels in 1579 included two roles: act as licensor of the public theatre, and provide entertainment at court without excessive cost, which made him privilege plays over masques. This is Philostrate's role in *A Midsummer Night's Dream*, Shakespeare possibly 'offering a humorous version of his company's overseer even as he offers a travesty of himself and the Chamberlain's Men' in the parts of the

99 Anglo, *Spectacle, Pageantry, and Early Tudor Policy*, p. 109.
100 *Hall's Chronicle*, p. 515. See his account of the Field of the Cloth of Gold, pp. 592–97.
101 *Hall's Chronicle*, p. 585.

'rude mechanicals'.[102] There is a risk, though, in such topical readings: Dutton is less convincing when he argues, following Andrew Gurr, that King James must have appreciated *King Lear* as a justification of his plan to unite Britain, because his own sons were respectively Dukes of Cornwall and Albany — in *Lear*, an arch villain and a hen-pecked weakling.

A polite request made by the Lord Mayor to Archbishop Whitgift in 1592, that the queen might be entertained privately by her own players in a convenient place, thus saving the City from continual disorders, had no result. From 1594 to the end of Elizabeth's reign, the Chamberlain's Men performed every year at court on Saint Stephen's Day, 26 December, also at Candlemas, at Shrovetide, in a total of thirty-three over the period. The different versions of Shakespeare's plays that went to print during her reign may reflect his revisions for court performances. There the length of a play raised no objection, and entertainments could last quite late in the night. In support of this theory, Dutton quotes Thomas Heywood's reference in *An Apology for Actors* (1612) to the Office of the Revels 'where our court plays have been in late days rehearsed, perfected, and corrected before they come to the public view of the prince and the nobility'.[103] His hypothesis does explain rather more problematic examples of revision than the other scenarios. Still, Heywood writes under the Stuart regime, and 'in late days' may equally well suggest that the practice was a recent one, which does not necessarily apply to Shakespeare's Elizabethan variants.

That a number of revised versions have survived is a fact; the reason why they were revised remains speculation. Tiffany Stern, for instance, suggests that not just the plays written after 1608, but a number of earlier ones 'seem to have been reshaped with Blackfriars performance in mind'. *Measure for Measure*, written in 1604, which survives only in the Folio version, staging a novice and a friar (Duke Vincentio in disguise) must have been especially startling and 'made more, rather than less, ambiguous by location', with its questions about the competing claims of holy orders and secular life in a space 'that had (forcibly) given over the one for the other'.[104] Dutton does not discuss Inns of Court productions, while *Moving Shakespeare Indoors* concentrates on Blackfriars, with only brief mentions of the Inns, except to note that performances there would already have given the Chamberlain's Men 'a taste of the unique indoor aesthetic' that they would emulate.[105] And yet the Inns were the first, long before the Globe, to make the transition from their halls to the royal court, with two performances of *Gorboduc*, at the Inner Temple during the Christmas revels and three weeks later at Whitehall.

---

102 Or Egeus, in the F version. Dutton, *Shakespeare, Court Dramatist*, p. 62.

103 Dutton, *Shakespeare, Court Dramatist*, pp. 22–23, 26, 46–47, 108.

104 Stern, '"A Ruinous Monastery"', pp. 99, 104.

105 Farah Karim-Cooper, 'To Glisten in a Playhouse: Cosmetic Beauty Indoors', in Gurr and Karim-Cooper, eds. *Moving Shakespeare Indoors*, p. 184.

Under Edward VI's reign, for two successive years, it was George Ferrers, of Lincoln's Inn, who organized the exceptionally lavish festivities of the Christmas season as Lord of Misrule. The lawyers' taste for and share in royal entertainments, the presence of the theatre in political ceremonies, the double plots, moral saws, and versification of their revels, developed under the Plantagenets, continued through the Tudor reigns, along with a fitfully ambivalent attitude towards their foreign sources. The genre of courtly satire went back as far as John of Salisbury's *Nuggets* or Skelton's poems. Some Inns members would carry it to the stage, like Marston of the Middle Temple, whose *Parasitaster, or the Fawn*, performed the same year as Shakespeare's *Measure for Measure*, has many references to internal matters at the Inns.[106] Its hero Duke Hercules, disguised as a flattering courtier, the Fawn, enters the court of Duke Gonzago to observe his son's behaviour. Under the protection of his alias, he witnesses the lechery of the courtiers and the vanity of their master. At the play's conclusion, Hercules holds a symbolic Court of Cupid, in which all the more foolish ones are arrested for their crime against love and good sense.

The early Tudor plays and dialogues use the stage as a privileged sanctuary where heterodoxy may be expressed, but they lack the *mythos*, Altman rightly observes. To these models, the intellectual community will add Terencian comedies, where the protagonists test their strategies on each other, hold miniature trials and rhetorical debates, but also expose the limitations of rhetoric: rather than debate, unartificial proof, be it ring, oracle, or belated recognition, will save the day, most movingly in Shakespeare's comedies, where 'the desired unity of opposites' achieved in the final vision 'is a consummation not easily attainable by ordinary human means'.[107]

106 Finkelpearl, *John Marston of the Middle Temple*, pp. 30–32.
107 Altman, *The Tudor Play of Mind*, pp. 132–44.

CHAPTER 5

Divorcing Rome

A certain convocation of politic worms are e'en at him.
Your worm is your only emperor for diet.

Hamlet, IV.iii

We saw above that annulments, repudiations, and resulting conflicts with the papacy were no new events, the reason why Henry VIII's counsellors spent so much time studying legal precedents of royal divorces. A fortuitous cause, the king's wish for a male heir, set fire to deeply ingrained brands of discord. Royal quarrels with the pope over issues of regality and jurisdiction had often happened in the past, and divorces been granted time and again. But never before had matrimonial suits led to such a brutal and eventually final break away from Rome, with irreversible consequences for the country. The Diet of Worms, ironically evoked by Hamlet over Polonius's corpse, had condemned Luther's theses in 1521. *Cujus regio, ejus religio*: the principle if not the phrase, which would only be coined decades later by a Lutheran legist, was beginning to establish itself across the Holy Roman Empire in the 1530s, a continuation of the ancient debate between civil and spiritual powers, and would be confirmed at the Peace of Augsburg. The English people repeatedly experienced it under the successive Tudor reigns, when religious dissent caused so many spectacular tragic falls and executions (see below 'Common Prayers' and 'Heretics on Trial' in Chapter 6).

King's Conscience

Europe was engaged in peace conferences when a private concern began to trouble Henry VIII. This secret worry, soon transferred to the public sphere, would bring to a crisis the age-old conflict between *regnum* and *sacerdotium*, and severely tax the lawyers' legal erudition. The king is in great scruple of conscience, Edward Hall writes, for learned divines have told him secretly that he lives in adultery, but the people utter foolish words to the effect that the king wants for his pleasure another wife.[1] An opinion pithily summed up by Shakespeare's courtiers:

1 *Hall's Chronicle*, p. 782. Parmiter, *The King's Great Matter*, p. 16 n. 3, quoting Wolsey's letter of 5 July 1527 to Henry, thinks the story was concocted between them.

Chamberlain. It seems the marriage with his brother's wife
Has crept too near his conscience.
Suffolk. No, his conscience
Has crept too near another lady.

(*Henry VIII, II.ii.15–17*)

There are alternative versions to the origins of Henry's pangs, doubts on Princess Mary's legitimacy, his claim to have been troubled by Leviticus, or Reginald Pole's that he was troubled by his passion for a girl: 'The modest woman would not be your mistress; no, but she would be your wife.'[2] The very words that Henry's grandmother Elizabeth Woodville speaks in More's *History of Richard III* and in *3 Henry VI* when cavalierly courted by Edward IV. To Pole, Henry's fiercest opponent, the king concealed his cruel and sacrilegious deeds beneath a pretence of religion, taking a leaf from *Il Principe*, a book written by the finger of Satan.[3] Unlike his humanist friends' advice, Pole's strictures on the vagaries of the king's conscience were penned at safe distance from his mounting wrath. Henry was rejecting the papal dispensation, Pole further insists, but busy at the same time trying to procure the pope's permission to marry the sister of his former concubine. More bitterly ironic still, as it would turn out, the argument of Mary Boleyn's affair with Henry would serve against her sister when Anne's own marriage was declared invalid a few years later.

Reinvention of Imperium

Henry VIII's advisors worked four years in vain to procure a canonical annulment of his marriage to Catherine of Aragon. The original plan was that Wolsey, as legate, would summon the king to answer charges that he was living in sin with his brother's widow, examine the case, and pronounce the annulment, but just as Wolsey's court convened, news arrived that the imperial armies had mutinied and captured Rome. Since Catherine denied his jurisdiction, Wolsey needed the pope's written consent confirming his full power. Pope Clement VII, a prisoner for seven months, was in no position to sacrifice the emperor's aunt to please Henry.

Having called a conference at Hampton Court in October 1530, Henry asked the assembled clergy and lawyers whether Parliament 'could and would' enact a divorce granted by the Archbishop of Canterbury. In Hall's version, he unburdens his conscience, expressing his anxieties — lack of heir, doubts on his daughter's birth, memories of past mischief between York and Lancaster — but indeed he will be most happy if the queen is proved to be his lawful wife. After debating a

2 Pole, *Pro Ecclesiasticae Unitatis Defensione*, lib. Ill, fol. Ixxvi, Ixxvii, trans. in Thomas E. Bridgett, *Life of Blessed John Fisher, Bishop of Rochester* (London: Burns & Oates, 1888), p. 148.

3 See Anglo, *Machiavelli, the First Century*, ch. 4, on Cromwell and Henry VIII as disciples of Machiavelli, and Reginald Pole as their arch-opponent.

week, they returned a majority verdict that they were powerless: Hall glosses over their actual answer, that the divorce could be settled only in Rome.[4] The next step was a consultation of the main English and foreign universities.[5] The idea came from a Cambridge circle led by Edward Fox and Stephen Gardiner, later joined by Cranmer, who worked to exempt Henry from citation to a Roman court.

The first dramatic scene, the Legatine court trial, took place in the 'Parliament Chamber' of Blackfriars, the very room where it would be re-enacted in *Henry VIII* along with its twin mirror, the Queen's unfair trial in *The Winter's Tale*. This, Tiffany Stern points out, raises fascinating questions about Shakespeare's metatheatre. Performed in the very space where the trial was held gave added frisson to the claim 'All is true', possibly the initial reason why the poet chose this subject for a play. At the Globe, the very mention of the name in the dialogue — 'such receipt of earning is Blackfriars' — would recall both the historical site of the action and the company's alternate theatre, 'combining metatheatre with something more knowing: advertising'.[6] Even more striking is Shakespeare's remarkable tact in leaving out of his last history play most of what actually happened. Some of it is audible in the parallel plot of *The Winter's Tale*, which stages the trial of a great foreign princess and the exile of her 'bastard' daughter to 'some remote and desert place', uncanny echoes of the treatment dealt by Henry to his own family.[7] Catherine appeared on 8 June 1528 to contest the jurisdiction of the legates and appealed to the pope. A blueprint for Queen Hermione, she knelt before Henry's chair, saying she was a poor stranger in the king's dominions where she had neither assured friends, unbiased advice, nor indifferent judges. She would not submit to a court before which her lawyers, being the king's subjects, were afraid to speak freely. After this speech she left, and ignored all ulterior summonses. One of her counsel, John Fisher, defended the validity of the marriage, vowing he was prepared to die for his opinion, of a death as unjust as John the Baptist's. His allusion to Herod's lust for Salome raised great anger. Wolsey's then secretary, Gardiner, doctor of civil and canon law, fellow of Gray's Inn, was instructed to write a sharp retort.[8]

Meanwhile news from the continent lay heavily on the proceedings. The last thing Henry wanted was a separate peace between France and the emperor that would free Carlos V to take up arms for his aunt Catherine.[9] Tunstall and More were sent to reinforce the English embassy at Cambrai. The king was hoping for a quick judgement at Blackfriars, but Campeggio, the pope's legate, would not take such a momentous decision without reporting first to Rome, where Catherine's

4 *Calendar of State Papers, Spain*, 1529–30, ed. by Gayangos, IV, p. 460. See Guy, *Politics, Law and Counsel*, VII, p. 487.

5 *Hall's Chronicle*, pp. 754–68.

6 Stern, '"A Ruinous Monastery"', p. 105.

7 Pollard, *Greek Tragic Women*, ch. 5, stresses the Greek sources of Hermione's grief and relation with her daughter Perdita.

8 Gardiner, *Obedience in Church and State*, ed. by Janelle, pp. xvii–xx.

9 Parmiter, *The King's Great Matter*, pp. 98–110.

appeal was being examined.[10] The emperor's victory at Landriano put an end to diplomatic dalliance, and the Paix des Dames was signed on 5 August. Although More's embassy had achieved little, he was made Lord Chancellor in Wolsey's place on his return, an appointment that caused the French ambassador, Bishop Jean du Bellay, to predict that the great seal would never go again to a priest, and terrible alarms were to be expected in the forthcoming Parliament.[11]

The real cause of Wolsey's disgrace, everyone was aware, was his failure to free the king. His fall was signed by a writ of *praemunire*, for his 'power legantyne' proved him in the employ of a foreign prince, and Henry's lawyers set to work again. Cranmer suggested submitting the question of validity to theologians, six from Oxford and six from Cambridge, who all except one agreed after some dallying that the marriage was unlawful.[12] By September 1530, his team of researchers had put together the *Collectanea satis copiosa*, 'sufficiently large collections' of precedents establishing that the English Crown had no obligation whatever to any foreign authority. Henry's agents travelled around Europe to collect opinions from universities. Here, Hall slightly bends facts when he asserts 'that the saied vniuersities wer agreed and had clerly concluded, that the one brother to marry the other brothers wife, carnally knowne was directlie against Gods lawe, and that the pope nor the court of Rome could in no wise dispence with the same'.[13] The French and Italians did agree that the pope had no power to dispense in the first place, but the German Lutherans, and Tyndale, all pronounced against the divorce.[14] The consultation of universities brought into public controversy an issue that had so far only been hinted at.[15]

Henry's approach to the problem of validity went through extraordinary shifts: first the Leviticus prohibiting marriage with a brother's widow, then legal defects in the dispensation, and now the pope's power to grant it. Henry himself in his *Assertio* against Luther's theses had written that 'the whole church, not only is subject to Christ, but, for Christ's sake, to Christ's only vicar the pope of Rome'. Thomas More, a supporter of conciliar power over the pope's, had advised him against the insertion of this clause but was unheeded. Legal arguments over the validity of Julius II's brief allowing Catherine's remarriage were tossed back and forth from England to Rome, along with the conflicting texts in the Bible, Leviticus 20. 21 and Deuteronomy 25. 5. Affinity created links as potent as blood ties and fell under the same interdict, as Hamlet would remind his mother. In Gertrude's case, the presence of a male heir to the throne left her with no excuse to stand on.

---

10 Wolsey to Henry VIII, 5 July 1527, *Letters and Papers, Henry VIII*, I, pp. 196, 200. *Hall's Chronicle*, pp. 758–60.

11 Jean du Bellay, letter of 22 October 1529, quoted in Parmiter, *The King's Great Matter*, pp. 113–14.

12 Parmiter, *The King's Great Matter*, pp. 120–23.

13 *Hall's Chronicle*, p. 768.

14 *Letters and Papers, Henry VIII*, V, p. 83.

15 Parmiter, *The King's Great Matter*, pp. 125–29.

In a recapitulative letter to Cromwell, More advises him to wait for the General Council of the Church, by whom this pope might be deposed. For his own part he felt he would put his conscience in great peril if he denied the primacy and begged to be excused from further debates, which was granted, but kept him away from the inner circle of councillors who devised the king's policy.[16] On 3 November, the Reformation Parliament met, again in Blackfriars' hall, and continued with eight sessions from 1529 to 1536. The Commons were packed, Parmiter points out, not so much with the king's supporters as with a strongly anti-clerical laity, who had proved hostile to ecclesiastical courts long before the divorce issue. While few dared oppose, many actively assisted England's break with Rome. They welcomed its benefits, the expropriation of Church land and the reduction of privileges.

The first necessary step was to force the submission of the clergy. As Hall simply explains, all who had supported Wolsey's power legatine fell under the charge of *praemunire*, and the spiritual lords were duly called by process into the King's Bench. Before their day of appearance, the Convocation offered their humble submission and a gift of £100,000, which were accepted. Actually the clergy, led by Gardiner, had tried to resist, with a petition demanding the confirmation of the Church's ancient jurisdictional powers, guaranteed by Magna Carta, and a clear definition of *praemunire*.[17] Henry answered with five threatening articles claiming he had the cure of souls, and confirmed those privileges only that did not conflict with his authority or the laws of the realm.[18] On 11 May 1532, he told the Commons he had just discovered that the clergy of England were but half his subjects and exhibited the oaths they swore to the pope on their consecration. On 15 May, after vain attempts to mitigate the formula, the clergy finally agreed to the king's demand that they acknowledge him as 'sole protector and supreme head of the church and clergy'.[19] Thomas More resigned the following day.

It was at that point that Elyot had his interview with Henry, begging him to change his policy. Warham, who had protested against all acts of Parliament derogatory to the pope's authority, wrote a strong speech in defence of the liberties of the Church, quoting the Clarendon articles, Becket's letters, and Magna Carta, but he died in August without delivering it and was soon replaced by a more compliant archbishop. A special statute of Parliament authorized the king to be supreme head of the Church of England, 'by the which the Pope with all his College of Cardinalles with all their Pardons and Indulgences was utterly abolished out of this realm'. Cromwell sent instructions for a preaching programme to the clergy and organized the taking over of the public pulpit at Paul's Cross by sermons on the royal supremacy for six successive Sundays.[20] Commissions

16 More, letter to Cromwell, 5 March 1534, in *The Correspondence*, ed. by Rogers, no. 199, pp. 491–501.

17 Lehmberg, *The Reformation Parliament*, p. 150.

18 *Hall's Chronicle*, p. 774. Guy, 'Henry VIII and the *Praemunire* Manoeuvres of 1530–1531'.

19 Title confirmed in the First Act of Supremacy, passed by Parliament on 3 November 1534.

20 Elton, *Policy and Police*, pp. 206–14.

were sent all over England to take the oaths to the Act of Succession. Only three denied, Fisher, More, and Nicholas Wilson, a London parson who dissembled and escaped, 'But the other twayne stode against all the realme in their opinion.' The pope had sent Fisher a cardinal's hat that arrived just too late; the head to wear it was high on London bridge. Thomas More's head fell shortly after.[21]

Revision of Praemunire

> Lord cardinal, the king's further pleasure is,
> Because all those things you have done of late,
> By your power legantine, within this kingdom,
> Fall into the compass of a praemunire,
> That therefore such a writ be sued against you.
>
> *Henry VIII, III.ii*

In matters of faith Henry VIII was at heart a conservative, with no sympathy for Protestant radicals. Nor did he question ecclesiastical hierarchy; he only put himself at the top. The political theory developed in the preamble to the Act in Restraint of Appeals, in April 1533, borrows from Marsiglio da Padova's doctrines the view that the authority of the Church derives from the State:[22]

> Where by divers sundry old authentic histories and chronicles it is manifestly declared and expressed that this realm of England is an empire, and so hath been accepted in the world, governed by one supreme head and king having the dignity and royal estate of the imperial crown of the same, unto whom a body politic, compact of all sorts and degrees of people divided in terms and by names of spiritualty and temporalty, be bounden and owe to bear next to God a natural and humble obedience.[23]

Cromwell had helped pay for the publication in English of the *Defensor Pacis* in 1534. His 'preamble' is to Parmiter 'a remarkable essay in conservative revolution': it abolishes papal jurisdiction in one sweep and presents this move as a logical development of earlier statutes. Those had been devised in the past to prevent encroachments by the see of Rome or any foreign power, like the act made by 'the king's most noble progenitor, King Richard II'. The Statute of Praemunire of 1393 had done little service so far, and only to limit the pope's jurisdiction, never to deny it. Henry VIII turned it into a lethal weapon against his own clergy. *Praemunire* is a law that 'no one in England can understand', Chapuys wrote to

---

21 *Hall's Chronicle*, pp. 774, 815–17.

22 See Gaines Post, 'Medieval and Renaissance Ideas of Nation', in *Dictionary of the History of Ideas*, ed. by Philip P. Wiener (London: Macmillan, 1973), III, p. 320.

23 1533. 24 Henry VIII. c. 12. 3 S. R. 427, repr. in *Documents Illustrative of English Church History*, ed. and trans. by Gee and Hardy, pp. 187–95.

Emperor Carlos; 'its interpretation lies solely in the king's head, who amplifies it and declares it at his pleasure, making it apply to any cases he pleases'.[24]

A theory of monarchic spiritual authority existed in embryo long before there was any thought of divorce. John Guy notes the presence since 1485 of a 'vocal lobby at the Inns of Court' demanding the subordination of canon and papal law to common law.[25] It erupted in 1512 on the occasion of a private quarrel, when a London merchant-tailor, Richard Hunne, refused to pay his mortuary fee to the priest who had buried his son and was cited before the spiritual court at Lambeth. In an attempt to escape charges of heresy, Hunne and his attorney searched for arguments in the civil laws of England and answered with a writ of *praemunire*, which took the case to the King's Bench, but Hunne was arrested regardless, then found dead in his cell at Saint Paul's. John Hales took up the argument in his reading of 1514 at Gray's Inn, focusing on the parallel jurisdictions of Church and State, which could bring different conclusions in different courts.[26] When Parliament met in 1515, Wolsey begged that the case be sent to Rome, and Henry VIII refused, claiming twenty years before the Act of Supremacy that 'the kings of England in time past have never had any superior but God alone'.[27] When the next conflict occurred, over the privilege of sanctuary, Henry denied it quite as ingeniously as would Shakespeare's Buckingham in *Richard III*: he could not think that the kings and holy fathers who made it 'ever intended the sanctuary to serve for voluntary murder and larceny done outside the sanctuary'.[28]

A heated debate between Church and State continued in the aftermath of Hunne's *praemunire*. Discussing the case in *A Supplycacion for the Beggars*, Simon Fish of Gray's Inn accused the clergy of pillaging the realm and urged the king to whip these 'idle drones'. His argument that money spent on the dead would more profitably be devoted to the living caused More's indignant answer in a *Supplication of Souls* that heretics sought to plunder the Church, not to relieve poor beggars.[29] A short book entitled *The enquirie and verdite of the quest panneld of the death of Richard Hunne wich was founde hanged in Lolars tower*, printed around 1536, was included by Hall in his chronicle, and again by Foxe who made Hunne an eminent Protestant martyr of his *Monuments*.[30] Whether or not it was Hunne who first showed its virtues to Henry, *praemunire* certainly served its turn in

24 In Parmiter, *The King's Great Matter*, p. 155.

25 Guy, *Politics, Law and Counsel*, XII, pp. 13–46.

26 Spelman, *The Reports*, II, p. 65.

27 Ellesmere MS 1609, cited in Guy, 'Henry VIII and the *Praemunire* Manoeuvres of 1530–1531', p. 497. See W. R. Cooper, 'Richard Hunne', *Reformation*, 1.1 (1996), 221–51, <http://www.tyndale.org/reformj01/cooper.html>.

28 Spelman, *The Reports* II, pp. 342–43. *Richard III*, III.i.

29 Fish, *A Supplicacyon for the Beggars*, ed. by Furnivall, pp. 8–12. More, *The supplycacyon of soulys, agaynst the supplycacion of beggars*, in *The Complete Works*, VII, pp. 107–228.

30 *The Enquirie and verdite*, on microfilm in STC no. 13970, reel 53, item 12. *Hall's Chronicle*, pp. 573–80. Foxe, *Actes and Monuments*, Bk VII, pp. 969–78

subordinating the clergy, although it was found inadequate in the various attempts to set the king free.

The debate did not end with the divorce. In his 1579 reading at the Middle Temple, addressed to William Cecil and directed against the *ex officio* procedures (see below, Chapter 9), James Morice would reassert the royal supremacy with similar precedents. The continuity evidenced in the history of the common law, from the early Britons and through the Norman Conquest to the present, showed that English kings had always had authority over the Church except during the interval opened by the heathenish Becket. The liberties of the English Church, temporarily lost under Henry II, were reconquered through the Statute of Provisors under Edward III and the Statute of Praemunire under Richard II, which to Morice were precursors of the Act in Restraint of Appeals.[31] To many a common lawyer after him, down to Edward Coke, it was the common law, prior to the Reformation, that had protected the realm against popish encroachments.[32] The argument would serve again in the quarrels with civil lawyers over the payment of tithes (see below, Chapter 10).

King's Printer

> Here is such patchery, such juggling and such knavery! All the argument is a whore and a cuckold: a good quarrel to draw emulous factions and bleed to death upon.
>
> *Troilus and Cressida, II.iii*

Lawyers and the law took unprecedented importance in public affairs when required to shape a new political theory best suited to Henry's love life. They were greatly helped by a strong current of animosity against clerical privileges, which were only due to the goodness of kings, the argument ran, for their power was antecedent to the pope's. John Hales's reading of 1514 on the problems of dual authority was exhumed and frequently quoted in the discussions of the 1530s, which argued the king's right to monitor canon law. Lawyers in and out of Parliament worked with Cromwell to establish Henry's imperial kingship, yet those who shared his anti-clerical objectives did not all agree with views that his *imperium* was divinely ordained, nor with the absolutist leanings of the Acts of Appeals and of Supremacy. The Inns, Raffield argues, behaved as custodians of common law against mounting claims of divine kingship, using old models of limited authority and republican virtue: beside the lawyers' printed pamphlets,

---

31 Brooks, *Law, Politics and Society*, pp. 100–109.

32 On the expansion of *praemunire*, see David Chan Smith, 'Remembering Usurpation: The Common Lawyers, Reformation Narratives and the Prerogative, 1578–1616', *Historical Research*, 86.234 (2013), 619–37.

lobbying, think tanks and committees, the Inns' entertainments made serious legal and political statements in the guise of courtly masques. In their views, the prerogatives of the Crown were common law rights, granted to the king by English law. *Imperium* was limited by the assent of the kingdom in Parliament. Against Henry's propagandists who argued that 'the king makes the law', they replied with Bracton that law makes the king.

Glasses of Truth

> So all my best is dressing old words new,
> Spending again what is already spent.
>
> *Sonnet LXXVI*

In November 1531, the king's printer Thomas Berthelet had published *The Determination of the most famous and excellent Universities of Italy and France, that it is unlawful for a man to marry his brother's wife and that the pope hath no power to dispense therewith*, prefaced by the favourable opinions of eight foreign universities, and promptly answered from abroad by Catherine's chaplain, Thomas Abell, in *Invicta Veritas*. This in turn inspired *A Glasse of the Truthe* (1532), a dialogue between a divine and a lawyer, whose author is thought to be Henry himself: it includes Arthur's report on his wedding night, consummation being again deemed crucial to the validity of a marriage. According to Hall, the prince required a drink the following day because 'I haue this nyght bene in the middest of Spayne, whiche is a hote region.'[33] It also prepared the ground for what was brewing: if Parliament would but exert its 'wits and good will', it would soon find a way out of the dilemma.[34] An offshoot of all this activity was the official launching of Antiquarian studies in 1533, when Henry VIII appointed John Leland as King's Antiquary, with a mission to search the libraries of all cathedrals, abbeys, priories, and colleges for England's antiquities. Part at least of this antiquarian interest was directly inspired by the political agenda. While the king's scouts collected foreign opinions, searches were made at the University of Paris for the 'original' constitution of the Gallican Church.

One of the earliest propagandist moves was to republish old antipapal pamphlets. In 1531 Berthelet printed a revised edition of Trevisa's *Dialogue betwene a Knyght and a Clerke*, itself a translation of the *Disputatio* composed by French civil lawyers during Philippe le Bel's clash with Boniface. At the point where they discuss the freedom of the clergy, Berthelet restores a sentence omitted by Trevisa: the clerk claims that 'The emperours and not the kynges haue establisshed thos thynges', but he is told that 'this answer is blasphemous, you are ignorant of

---

33 *Hall's Chronicle*, p. 494.

34 Printed in *Records of the Reformation*, ed. by Pocock, pp. 385–421. See J. C. Warner, 'No Humanist Fiction: Henry VIII's Prose Dialogue *A Glass of Truth*', *Prose Studies*, 18.2 (1995), 123–34.

the beginnings of a kingdom'. As in the first text, the knight concludes from this origin that the French king may change or repeal the emperor's laws if he list, 'therfore syr clerke refrayne your tongue, and aknowlege the kynge by his royall power to be aboue your lawes, customes, priuileges, and liberties'.[35] Foxe, who thought the *Disputatio* was written by Ockham, relates the trials of Boniface with this marginal note: 'Here may all kings by the French king learne how to handle the pope.'[36] Other translations of anti-papal tracts came out from the London presses: *The Declamation of Lou. Valla against the vntruly forged falsely beleued donation of Constantine*, and the first English edition of Marsiglio's *Defensor Pacis* subsidized by Cromwell, *The Defence of Peace*, 'lately translated out of laten in to englysshe. with the kynges moste gracyous priuilege'.[37] Paradoxically, it was the conservative Gardiner who produced a full-fledged defence of royal supremacy in *De vera obedientia* (1535). To his dismay, his treatise became an instrument of Protestantism under Edward VI. He retracted it when made Lord Chancellor by Mary, but even she refused any infringement on *privilegium Angliae*.

Several methods were tried, and many books written, between 1527 and 1532, before the strategy decided upon finally was to make imperial kingship a reality through Parliament. The term 'imperial' no longer meant what it did originally, reigning over several kingdoms, but asserted total independence from 'the authority of any foreign potentates'.[38] The *Libellus* presented to Wolsey's legatine court rested Henry's case on the Levitical prohibitions, with a slight twist: where Leviticus states that if couples break the rules, 'children they shall have never', his translators altered *puer* into *filius* to argue that Henry's marriage, which produced a daughter but no son, fell under the curse that proved it illicit: the pope had no power of dispensation in such a case. Again, recycling ruled the day. Cranmer's *Collectanea satis copiosa* set out to prove the pope's usurpation of his sovereignty by appealing to legal and historical authorities, Scripture, English chronicles, Roman and Anglo-Saxon laws, the Donation of Constantine…, some of which had already served several turns.[39] The *Leges Anglorum* were exhumed to help free the king from popish rule: according to this text Lucius I, the mythical ruler of Britain, wrote to Pope Eleutherius after his conversion to Christianity in AD 187, asking him to transmit the Roman law, and was answered that he did not need it, since he already had the Old and New Testaments from which he might himself 'take a law' for his kingdom. Eleutherius's epistle, a forgery made in the time of King John,[40] relayed by Foxe's *Monuments*,[41] will be repeatedly invoked

35 *Trevisa's Dialogus*, pp. 36–37.
36 Foxe, *Actes and Monuments*, Bk IV, p. 458 [437]. In a printed volume of 1540 found in the Cambridge University Library, the tract is entitled *Dialogus* and attributed to Ockham.
37 Both are in the Cambridge University Library.
38 Preamble to Act in Restraint of Appeals.
39 BL, Cotton MS Cleopatra E. vi, fols 16–135. See Ullmann, 'This Realm of England Is an Empire', pp. 192–203. And below, 'Liberty of Research', in Chapter 10.
40 Ullmann, *Principles of Government and Politics*, pp. 161–62.
41 Foxe, *Actes and Monuments*, Bk I, pp. 33, 36, Bk II, 159–60.

to assert the independence of English common law from any foreign legal code. The decisive words, 'Vos estis vicarius Dei in terra vestra',[42] are still quoted in Elizabeth's last Parliament against the present 'Beliall or beast of Rome'.[43]

Thomas More's proclamations had initiated an inquisitorial campaign against works prohibited.[44] The term 'censure', originally 'a disciplinary measure taken by the Church against one of its offending members', first enters the English language in 1534. Very aptly, the opening of *Henry VIII* applies it to the encounter of the monarchs in Calais, where 'no discerner | Durst wag his tongue in censure.' The same year, the Treason Act (26 Hen.8 c. 13) augments the traditional definition, to wish or attempt the death of the king, with the notion of treason by words, the worst being to call the king heretic, schismatic, tyrant, infidel, or usurper, a fair index of ongoing public murmurs. Reginald Pole's friends and relatives, including his mother the old Countess of Salisbury, were all charged with treasonable words, expressing hatred of the king or questioning his supremacy. Worse still, the countess was found to have papal bulls in her possession.[45] Geoffrey Elton admits to a general feeling among historians that the act contained at least the potential of tyranny. Still, he argues, treason by words only was not so unprecedented nor outrageous as an indignant opinion maintains: Henry and Cromwell had good cause to feel that excitement to violence could harm State and public order. Since Henry could not lay his hands on Reginald Pole, he had the 'far from harmless' old countess beheaded.[46]

The fierce debates of the early 1530s grew increasingly one-sided in the course of the decade. From April 1535 onwards, a series of letters were addressed to bishops and lay officers, with strict instructions to enforce the law and detect suspected opponents. A letter of 9 June to sheriffs and justices of the peace reverses the traditional roles in setting them as watchdogs over bishops. Another letter, two weeks later, informs the justices of assizes of 'the treasons traitorously committed against us and our laws by the late bishop of Rochester and Sir Thomas More', although More has not been tried yet.[47] When the deed is done, Cromwell entrusts Richard Morison, freshly back from Padua, with the delicate mission of explaining to the world the policy of the past eight years and refuting all charges of tyranny. Morison, 'the first adequately documented English student of Machiavelli',[48] delivers the official version in *Apomaxis Calumniarum Convitiorumque*, which claims that all true scholars vindicate the king: More, a poor busy lawyer, could not compete with the learning of Gardiner, Foxe, or Tunstall.

42 On this quote from the *Collectanea*, see Fox and Guy, eds, *Reassessing the Henrician Age*, p. 159.
43 Speaker's opening speech, 30 October 1601, *Proceedings*, III, p. 260.
44 *Tudor Royal Proclamations*, I, no. 122, pp. 181–85; no. 129, pp. 193–97.
45 'Select Views of London and its Environs', Samuel Denne's Addenda to *History of Lambeth*, in *Cobbett's State Trials*, pp. 480–82.
46 Elton, *Policy and Police*, pp. 286–88.
47 *Letters and Papers, Henry VIII*, VIII, p. 921 [1].
48 See Anglo, *Machiavelli, the First Century*, pp. 98–101. *Apomaxis* quotes 'Nicholao Macchavallo' against papacy.

All the propagandists' resources are summoned to counteract the threats at home or abroad of pens like Morison's former patron Reginald Pole. Starkey, once the advocate of a *via media*, revises his position to fit the government's scheme in *An Exhortation to the people instructing them to Unity and Obedience*. Rebellions in Lincolnshire and Yorkshire are met with official *Answers to the Petitions of the Rebels* denouncing the sacrilegious offence to an anointed head. A proclamation of 1536 orders the surrender of all illicit books to Chancellor Audley, More's successor, and to Cromwell. A further proclamation in 1538 rules that all books must be licensed before printing by the Privy Council 'or other royal nominees'. It augments the list of forbidden works, prohibits the importing of foreign books in English, condemns Anabaptists to exile, and removes Thomas Becket from the calendar.[49] On a more material level, the destruction of Becket's shrine, with its two large chests of jewels, raised a protest from the pope. Henry not only ignored him but had Becket indicted as a rebel.[50] With the suppression of the Canterbury pilgrimage, Chaucer's immortal book became a substitute monument, a gospel for vernacular writers, and King John, at best a dubious hero, a protomartyr to popish wiles.

Battle of Books

Among the anti-clerical lawyers recruited in the service of Henry VIII's cause, Christopher Saint-German, utter barrister of Middle Temple, was one of the loudest.[51] So loud that in 1536 he was one of those whose heresies the 'northern rebels' wanted destroyed.[52] His *Dialogus de fundamentis legum Angliae et de conscientia* discussed common and Chancery law from a theoretical point of view, quite a novelty at the time for a system largely shaped by precedent and custom. Occasionally he compared them with civil and canon law, of which he had but mediocre knowledge, as Henry Kelly has shown.[53] His two *Dialogues in English, betweene a Doctor of Divinity and a Student in the Laws of England* were designed so that all men in the realm could know 'many things of the law of England'.[54] His use of the vernacular infuriated Thomas More, who demurely thought that abuse of the clergy should be confined to Latin. After his resignation More officially kept silence about the king's religious policy, but the argument with Saint-German provided a way of circumventing this restriction. *The Apologye of Syr Thomas More, Knyght*, and the *Debellation of Salem and Bizance*, under colour of answers to Saint-German, vigorously criticized Protestant theology. Since Saint-German's

49 *Tudor Royal Proclamations*, I, 16 November 1538, no. 186, pp. 270–76.
50 *Letters and Papers, Henry VIII*, XIII.2, p. 354.
51 Pearl Hogrefe, 'The Life of Christopher Saint German', *Review of English Studies*, 13.52 (1937), 402–04.
52 *Letters and Papers, Henry VIII*, XI, p. 1246.
53 Kelly, 'Thomas More on Inquisitorial Due Process'.
54 Young, 'Christopher Saint-German's *Doctor and Student*', pp. 64–68.

pamphlets were published anonymously, More pretended he had no idea who the author was and referred to him ironically as 'the pacifier'.

Saint-German was not directly involved in the divorce. His first concern was the harmonization of law systems and jurisdictions; the coincidence of his anticlericalism with the royal team's objective was only temporary.[55] If the lawyer placed the religious structure under the royal authority, he never entrusted absolute sovereignty to the king alone, but to a mixed monarchy inherited from Jean Gerson and Fortescue. His stress on the King-in-Parliament, based on the precedent of Richard II, his view that both royal and Church courts should reach similar decisions in similar cases, and that canon law should defer to the common law of the realm, could not but find favour at the Inns. In creating the impression that common law was a homogeneous *corpus*, his theory considerably enhanced its status. This was a large step on the way to denying Roman or canon law any significant part at its roots. *Doctor and Student* argued that the universal laws of God and nature preceded and coexisted with English common law, leaving the Doctor to establish 'how the law of England is grounded upon the law of reason, the law of God, the general customs of the realm', as well as statutes 'made in divers parliaments by our sovereign lord the king, and his progenitors, and by the lords spiritual and temporal, and all the commons of the realm'.[56]

Saint-German's first treatises aimed to codify the areas of conflict between Chancery and common law courts. The central issue of his *Second Dialogue*, the royal prerogative exercised by the chancellor through subpoenas or injunctions, drew 'reactionary' attacks from common lawyers.[57] What principles guided chancellors, apart from conscience as Morton understood it, remained vague. Saint-German's concept of equity was largely based on the works of the conciliarist Jean Gerson. Like More, he thought that equity was not against common law but part of it, or should be. Where they disagreed was over the legal independence of the Church. More insisted that canon law, the common law of Christendom, stood above any local code in Europe, while Saint-German wanted uniform civil principles, stressing the incompatibility between common law and spiritual courts. The Commons' Supplication against the Ordinaries in 1532, that 'canon law itself was inimical to the common law of England and that the independence of the church courts was insupportable', were in full sympathy with his latest treatises. The King-in-Parliament, he wrote in *Newe Addicions*, was 'the high sovereign ouer the people, which hath not only charge on the bodies but also on the souls of his subiects'. Quoting Gerson's view that all goods are temporal, he suggested the King-in-Parliament should control all that passed into Church hands,[58] and

---

55 Guy, 'Thomas More and Christopher St German: The Battle of the Books', in *Politics, Law and Counsel*, VIII, pp. 95–120.

56 Saint-German, *Doctor and Student*, ed. by Muchall, Dialogue I, ch. 32, p. 94.

57 Guy, *Christopher St German on Chancery and Statute*, pp. 56–57.

58 Saint-German, *Doctor and Student*, Dialogue I, ch. 4. Among Gerson's works that Saint-German relied upon is *Regulae Morales* IX, 94.

Parliament supervise various areas of religious life, such as prayers, holy days, pilgrimages, 'though it judge not upon the right of things that be mere spiritual'.[59]

Saint-German was especially critical of the inquisitorial *ex officio* procedure in cases of suspected heresy. More defended its principle in the *Debellation*, and the argument raged between the two experts on common law. According to Hutson, they were 'matched in lawyerly expertise and spiritual integrity',[60] but Kelly shows that Saint-German failed to understand the inquisitorial procedure to a degree More could not even imagine, and gives More the victory in the contest, though he agrees that pressure was indeed put on suspects to incriminate themselves. A suspect was required to swear that he would answer truthfully all questions, without knowing the charges against him nor his accusers. Conscientious people could only escape by refusing to take the oath: this is the main theme of Foxe's Martyrs, who die asserting their right 'to maintain ones silence', with virulent attacks against Chancellor More who caused several of these deaths. At his own trial, in refusing to incriminate himself, More claimed the right first argued by his old enemy Tyndale in 1528: *The Obedience of a Christian Man* accuses tyrants of breaking into the heart and conscience of men and asserts their right to silence against judges who try to make them forswear or incriminate themselves. The debate would erupt again when Archbishop Whitgift and the Elizabethan High Court of Commission used *ex officio* prosecutions in their fight against the Puritans ('"Shall Cassandra Bee Punished?"' in Chapter 9).

King's Games

The English Reformation caused revisions and upheavals in all areas of society. Rebellions against the break with Rome were fiercely repressed, forcing a majority of fearful subjects into submissiveness. Part of the new measures, especially those reducing ecclesiastical privileges, met with large support, while the instability of the times, the falls of Wolsey, Fisher, More, Anne Boleyn, Cromwell, Aske and his pilgrims, the rigged State trials (see below, Chapter 6), discouraged many adverse comments. They also set friend against friend, pupil against master or patron. Elyot distanced himself from More. Suffolk turned against his benefactor Wolsey. Morison hurled insults at Reginald Pole to whom he had earlier expressed gratitude for rescuing him from 'hunger, cold, and poverty'.[61] Families, as they had in the civil wars, would be split by divided loyalties that would long haunt the stage: 'though the wisdom of nature can reason it thus and thus, yet nature finds itself scourg'd by the sequent effects. Love cools, friendship falls off, brothers divide. In cities, mutinies; in countries, discord; in palaces, treason; and the bond crack'd 'twixt son and father' (*King Lear*, I.ii.96–101).

---

59 Saint-German, *Doctor and Student*, Additions to the Second Dialogue, ch. 8, p. 319, ch. 10, p. 328.
60 Hutson, *The Invention of Suspicion*, p. 49.
61 Morison, in a letter of August 1535 to Starkey, *Letters and Papers, Henry VIII*, IX, p. 102.

Scholars largely agree on the momentous transition that occurred in dramatic writing during the second half of the sixteenth century, and on the varied strands that brought it about. Most significant was the common experience of so many tragic falls, caused by legal and religious turns of the government's wheel, as witnessed at street level through the century. Just how guilty were the mighty who fell? The theatre put audiences in the position of popular juries:[62] at the end of the play the actors who have performed *in utramque partem* require them to judge for themselves now that they know the circumstances that led Titus, Othello, Hamlet, Brutus, and other unwilling murderers, or would-be assassins like Shylock, on their tragic path in search of justice:

> Now judge what cause had Titus to revenge
> These wrongs unspeakable, past patience,
> Or more than any living man could bear.
> Now you have heard the truth: what say you, Romans?
>
> (*Titus Andronicus*, V.iii.124–27)

Even a proven culprit like Vittoria Corombana advises the judge at her trial that 'all this assembly | Shall hear what you charge me with.' The jury she appeals to 'corresponds to the new common-law model of impartial, independent evaluators of testimony presented in court', Mukherji insists, as opposed to the earlier one of neighbours or peers.[63] To Kevin Curran, these rituals of evaluation applied to the play itself, pleading for approval by the audience: 'public-theater epilogues bore a striking resemblance to the procedures of law courts', unsurprisingly so since a fair portion of the theatregoers and a number of playwrights were affiliated with the Inns.[64] Still, this offered poor compensation for the known fact that popular juries or great judges alike had little say in the matter when justice became involved in State policy. In the major treason trials that punctuated the Tudor reigns, the object was less to establish the guilt or innocence of the defendant than to provide a stage upon which the narrative of the betrayal might be re-enacted.[65] When heads of dukes, priests, or chancellors could be seen rotting on Tower Bridge, and bodies torn alive or burnt in Smithfield, it must have struck Shakespeare's audiences that suspects were given a much fairer hearing on stage than did so many 'State pleaders' who fell victim to Tudor *realPolitik*.

62 See Hutson, *The Invention of Suspicion*, p. 70, on the suspicious deaths of Duke Humphrey and Ophelia, quoting Altman on Hieronymo, *The Tudor Play of Mind*, pp. 281–82.

63 Webster, *The White Devil*, III.ii.19–20, discussed in Mukherji, *Law and Representation*, ch. 4. See Daniela Carpi, 'The Trial in John Webster's *The White Devil*: Italy in the Reenactment of a Renaissance English Drama', *Forum Italicum*, 53.2 (2019), 363–74.

64 Kevin Curran, 'Prospero's Plea', in Curran, ed., *Shakespeare and Judgment*, p. 160.

65 Raffield, *Shakespeare's Imaginary Constitution*, p. 109.

The More Part

Thus fools oft times do help to mar the play.

Sir Thomas More, III.ii

The most eminent of these 'State pleaders' used the full strength of his legal knowledge in a losing battle against the Reformation. At the onset of his progress, while his friends were eagerly offering their services to Kings Carlos, François, or Henry, Thomas More was busy writing the *History of Richard III*. In this portraiture of tyranny, a butcher plays the lead, first subverting laws with the support of a flexible council who defer to his wishes.[66] Butchers also perform metaphoric roles in *Henry VI*: Duke Humphrey is dragged to the slaughterhouse, while Dick the Butcher becomes chief executioner of Cade's commonwealth. In More's *History*, Richard's farcical election, staged by his accomplice Buckingham, introduces the comment that if a spectator disturbs the performance, declaring that the king's part is performed by a 'sowter' (shoemaker), he will have his head broken: 'And so they said that these matters be kings' games, as it were, stage plays, and for the more part played upon scaffolds. In which poor men be but the lookers on. And they that wise be, will meddle no farther.'[67] 'The "More part" indeed', James Wood notes, stressing the irony of this unwitting pun.[68] More's first patron, Cardinal Morton, had survived through several Lancastrian and Yorkist regimes before he became chancellor to the first Tudor. Yet in the last paragraphs of the *History of Richard III*, he tells the same Buckingham that he has 'alredy medled to muche with the world, and would fro that day medle with his boke and his beedes and no farther'. Why the narrative stops in the middle of their conspiracy to get rid of the tyrant can only be guessed at. Young Henry was fast giving signs of despotism. By the time More engaged on his history, he knew that he was treading dangerous ground. A *lapsus calami* betrays the slant of his thoughts: Buckingham is misnamed Edward like the then living duke, instead of the correct Henry his ancestor — enough to suggest More was indeed concerned with present matters and living monarchs.

More's involvement with the theatre began even before his impromptu roles as a page in Morton's house. His circle of intimates was closely connected with early Tudor drama[69] — the Heywoods who wrote plays, the Rastells who printed them — and with the law: Sir John More, Roper, Christopher Stubbes, Rastell, the Heywoods all had connections with Lincoln's Inn. Drama also stood high in More's double education. Oxford and the Inns both included the study of plays,

66 This analysis is repeated in Roper's *Lyfe of Sir Thomas Moore*, p. 240. *Richard III*, III.iv. *2 Henry VI*, IV.ii.

67 More, *History of Richard III*, in *The Complete Works*, II, p. 83.

68 Wood, 'Sir Thomas More: A Man for One Season', in *The Broken Estate*, pp. 3–15, discussing Peter Ackroyd's *Life of Thomas More*.

69 See Reed, *Early Tudor Drama*.

as recommended by Erasmus, and use of the dialogue form, in manuals of the master/student type. Plato apart, one of the most popular models was the Roman counsellor Boethius, whose *Consolatio Philosophiae* summed up tragedy as a turn of Fortune's wheel. The ancient image of *theatrum mundi* appears first in More's Latin translation of Lucian's *Menippus*, a summary of all commonplaces about Fortune.

Henry VIII's unfortunate chancellor seems the perfect embodiment of all the Inns' most subtle combinations of law and theatricals, politics, polemics, and self-management.[70] He was 'muche geuen to mockinge, whiche was to his grauitie a great blemishe', and still joking on his way to the scaffold, so the chronicler cannot tell if he was 'a foolish wiseman or a wise foolish man'.[71] A walking oxymoron, as it were. Drama supplies him with models of realistic wisdom:

> When a comedy of Plautus is being played you propose to come on stage in the garb of a philosopher, and repeat Seneca's speech to Nero from the *Octavia*. Wouldn't it be better to take a silent role than to say something inappropriate, and thus turn the play into a tragi-comedy?
>
> (*Utopia, Book I, p. 29*)

Erasmus, whose joy at Henry's accession had begun to pale, observed with anxiety that his friend was now 'totus aulicus', wholly a court man, but excused him as the only man worthy of exercising power: 'You never saw anyone show more ambition to be admitted at court than he took care to avoid it'.[72] More, he claims, was forced into the legal profession, for which he had no liking though 'it is difficult to find any readier way to acquire fortune and honour'. Actually, More had steadily worked towards his goal, doing jobs for the government.[73] Famously portrayed as 'having always a hatred of tyranny and a great fancy for equality',[74] he was probably quicker than his friends to distrust princes, having seen another Duke of Buckingham summarily tried and executed. Yet unlike Erasmus, who soon left Prince Carlos to his own devices, he walked into Henry's court with open eyes, only to find he lacked Morton's flexibility. Against his will, he would be dragged away from Plautus into a Senecan tragedy by his own Nero.

The need for masks came early in More's political career.[75] As Speaker for the Commons, in 1523 he had presented the first petition in the history of Parliament for liberty of speech: 'if in communicacion and reasonyng any man in the common house should speake more largely then of dutie he ought to do,

70 See Goy-Blanquet, 'The More Part'.

71 *Hall's Chronicle*, p. 761.

72 Letter 999 to Ulrich von Hutten, 23 July 1519, More was *pertractus*, pressured, Erasmus repeatedly writes, to enter the king's service, letters 829, 832, 999.

73 Guy, *The Public Career of Sir Thomas More*, pp. 12–14.

74 In the portrait Erasmus draws for Von Hutten, letter 999.

75 Roper, *The Lyfe of Sir Thomas Moore*, p. 7. See Greenblatt, *Renaissance Self-Fashioning*, ch. 1.

that all such offences should be pardoned, and that to be entred of recorde'.[76] Far from being entitled to speak freely, as Lord Keeper he was the government's mouthpiece. On 30 March 1531, he had to read the opinions collected from European universities on the validity of the king's marriage; though he disagreed both as Christian and as lawyer, yet he stayed on. Like Elyot, Starkey, or Pole, he hoped to the last that Henry would come to his senses.

The contradictions between More's rules for Utopia and his own rule as chancellor have often been stressed. The Utopians have no illusions about the chances of peace. They fight wars with a clear conscience, collect tribute from many conquered countries, and never bother with treaties, since 'No treaty can be made so strong and explicit that a government will not be able to worm out of it'.[77] Among other unorthodox practices, and unlike his own monarch, Utopians are allowed to divorce. They hold everything in common, a horror repeatedly denounced in the Tudor chronicles as the extreme of outlawry.[78] Worse still, they claim 'it should be lawful for every man to follow the religion of his choice', because religious differences breed discord. This did not prevent More later from writing virulent attacks against Tyndale and his increasingly popular views. Their sparring began over points of translation. Both were impartially destroyed by imperial majesty, but England went the way of Tyndale, who is largely present in the wording of the King James Bible.

As Lord Chancellor, More was responsible for minors, a point stressed in *Henry VIII* by Wolsey's ominous parting wish, that More 'May have a tomb of orphans' tears wept on him'. His other duties included the punishment of heretics. The *Apologye* vows he did not do it gladly: 'I hate that vice of theirs and not their persons, and very fain would I that the one were destroyed and the other saved.' That one could kill Caesar's spirit and not dismember Caesar! Yet he fully approved the executions: those who threaten to rip the tissue of the 'holy common church' are 'well and worthely burned'. Antichrist was at hand; it was too late for tolerance, if More ever inclined to it. Bodies must be destroyed to save souls. Give heretics a fair trial and they will swarm the streets.[79] The same logic drove him to advocate the burning of books: he would destroy his own or Erasmus's with his own hands 'rather than folk would [...] take any harm of them'.[80] How could these contrarieties agree?

The new religion created a split between written and unwritten law that would reverberate through the whole realm,[81] and break down More's persona when he suffered the same tragic reversal as those kings made beggars by Fortune in

76 The draft of this petition, in 1523, reported in Roper's *Lyfe*, p. 16, was for the right to oppose bills. It did not include a right of initiative, which Commons won progressively.

77 More, *Utopia*, II, pp. 45, 46, 71–78; quotation at p. 70.

78 Since the Peasants' War and the preachings of John Ball in Froissart.

79 More, *Apology*, in *The Complete Works*, IX, p. 113. *The Debellation of Salem and Bizance*, ed. by Guy, *The Complete Works*, X, p. 104.

80 More, *The Confutation of Tyndale's Answer*, II, 1532, in More, *The Complete Works*, VIII.1, pp. 143, 179.

81 See Raffield's discussion of textual versus institutional authority, *Images and Cultures of Law*, p. 16.

Menippus. He who had fought sects of 'few brethren' was now accused of being 'alone' in refusing the oath of supremacy, a sect of one pitted against the whole realm.[82] He loathed Luther's 'secret sect' of people who never sin, and anticipated Shakespeare's 'mingled yarn' with a preference for 'the comen knowen multitude of Christian men, good and bad together'. Above all, as James Wood puts it, 'he turned his eyes from the awful challenge of Luther, which was to move God back from the visible'.[83] This challenge became official a year after More's death when it was ordained that religious images were 'only to represent things absent'.[84] It would reach a climax with the Puritan revolution and the closure of theatres.

More's defence of images fully agrees with his dramatic view of political philosophy, and his reading of the human condition in the world's theatre. His aim now in confinement is to make his own public image 'so nere to the quycke and to ye trouth' that it shall represent, as close as can humanly be, the imitation of Christ.[85] His faith in the theatre's search for truth had by then taken a wholly different shape. The debaters of *Utopia* defended opposite principles so well that today's scholars still argue as to which truly represent More's opinion. His English dialogues have no such ambiguities. Sharing the narrative voice is now purely formal; his arguments leave no place for rival viewpoints. The dialogue in his prison letter forbids his family all attempts to sway his conscience. The *Supplication of Souls* dramatizes voices in purgatory, two decades before ghosts of English statesmen return to confess their faults in *The Mirror for Magistrates* (see below, 'Dramatic Justice' in Chapter 8).

Having failed to reform the commonwealth, More retires to Plato's inner city of personal righteousness as preparation for the heavenly one, but still with an eye on his audience. In *A Dialogue of Comfort against Tribulations*, Leland Miles notes, few Tudors reading its description of the Turk would have failed to perceive the obvious parallels with Henry's more reprehensible activities.[86] But however polemical, it is first and foremost a rehearsal for martyrdom. The *De tristitia* shows Christ in his last role at Gethsemani, a weak man suffering all the anguish of his human body and soul to offer himself as a model to fearful martyrs. Pilate's soldiers mocked him with the title 'king of the Jews', which in truth he was. The dissembling show is not in the Catholic Mass, but with those who pretend to revere Christ while denying his real presence in the Host, with similar derision: 'Verily all these, whom I have here rehearsed you, do, in their salutation and

82 On More's faith in the authority of the law, see Goodrich, *Oedipus Lex*, pp. 93, 232.

83 Wood, 'Sir Thomas More: A Man for One Season'.

84 Rev. Hugh Latimer, 'Sermon Made to the Convocation of the Clergy', 9 June 1536, *Sermons on the Card and Other Discourses*, The Anglican Library, 2011, <http://www.anglicanlibrary.org/latimer/card/sermon04.htm>.

85 More, *Dialogue Concerning Heresies*, I.ii, II.viii, in *The Complete Works*, VI, pp. 231/30, 232/37.

86 More, *A Dialogue of Comfort against Tribulation*, ed. by Leland Miles (Bloomington: Indiana University Press, 1966), pp. xliii–xliv. Guy, *The Public Career of Sir Thomas More*, p. 203.

false traitorous kiss, plainly play us the traitor Judas's part.'[87] The fallen chancellor strains for the perfection of mimesis, for the coincidence of outward and inward show, making theatre true, making the truth of theatre Catholic. Forced into the martyr's part, More stoically prepared to die for his faith, but not till he had used all his lawyer's skill to avoid it. His prison letters show him still performing for an audience, still straining for a perfect adequacy of his public image and a true Christian's life. His literary image, one largely of his own making, amplified by a succession of biographers, has been thoroughly revised by various and varying historians, and thoroughly torn to pieces in Hilary Mantel's *Wolf Hall*.

Accounts of the trial were circulated around Europe.[88] More's execution raised protests abroad, with little political impact but loud enough to embarrass Henry VIII, who did not like to appear unfair, and led Cromwell to commission a defence of the government's legal position. His ambassador to Germany received clear instructions: 'If the Duke or any of the Princes express displeasure at the execution of the bishop of Rochester and Sir Thomas More, he shall say they were found traitors by due course of law [...]. For their better satisfaction he may point out that they were of such traitorous hearts, as even when in prison, to plan an insurrection within the realm, as proved by a great number of honest men.'[89]

The authors of the anonymous play *Sir Thomas More* found little to add to More's self-made portrait; they took his own stage directions and speeches verbatim. The witty humanist is pictured stepping on stage while the Lord Cardinal's players perform *The Marriage of Wit and Wisdom* and improvises the part of Good Counsel, which requires little acting from the man who was Good Counsel incarnate. But he can neither mend the show nor continue it to the end, for he is summoned 'in haste to council'.[90] What 'error' exactly he committed that could justify the king's anger is restricted to one question — 'Subscribe these articles? Stay, let us pause: | Our conscience first shall parley with our laws' (IV.i.73–74) — and one comment: 'This is no age for poets.' The play never reached the Elizabethan stage: the censor objected to the scenes of popular rebellion, but not to the glaring injustice that sends this paragon to the scaffold. The content of 'these articles' More is required to endorse is never revealed in the dialogues. He remains equally silent about the exact dictates of his conscience and goes

87 More, *De tristitia, tedio, pavore et oratione Christi ante captionem eius*, in More, *The Complete Works*, XIV, p. 4.

88 *Discours sur le procès et exécution de Thomas Morus, chancelier d'Angleterre*, BnF, MS fr. 2981, printed on 4 August 1535, reported in Latin by Morison to Cromwell on 27 August, *Letters and Papers, Henry VIII*, IX, p. 198. *Expositio fidelis de morte D. Thomae Mori et quorundam aliorum insignium uirorum in Anglia* (Basel: Froben, 1535), attributed to Erasmus, Gilbert Cousin, and Philippe Dumont, includes the deaths of Fisher and the Carthusians. See 'The *Expositio Fidelis*: Winter 1535–1536', in *Acta Thomae Mori: History of the Reports of his Trial and Death*, ed. by Henri de Vocht (Louvain: Leuwen University Press, 1947), VII, pp. 53–96.

89 Instructions to Edward Foxe, bishop of Hereford, *Letters and Papers, Henry VIII*, IX, no. 213, 31 August. Morison's *Apomaxis* aims to justify the executions of More and Fisher.

90 *Sir Thomas More*, III.ii.255–306.

to the Tower 'with all submissive willingness' (IV.iv.152).[91] So did the historical character, who did not condemn the supremacy, but 'merely kept silence for conscience's sake', according to his biographers.[92]

The witty More is allowed only a mute part in *Henry VIII*. The dominant tone is resolutely pathetic: despite the number of deaths, tragedy is eschewed; the successive falls cause pity but little awe, and no thunderous emotions, inspiring more remorse than rancour in the fallen. The spectacular events — masque, trial, coronation earthly and heavenly, christening — make abundant use of the pageantry so fiercely decried in the opening scene, and of the facilities offered by Blackfriars.[93] On being informed 'that Sir Thomas More is chosen | Lord Chancellor in your place', Wolsey answers with a eulogy of this 'learned man':

> May he continue
> Long in his highness' favour, and do justice
> For truth's sake and his conscience.
>
> (*III.ii.395–97*)

In the next scene, the Coronation of Anne Boleyn, the Lord Chancellor takes his place in the order of the ceremony, but the play omits to specify that this was no longer More, who had already resigned his office. His conscience is silenced before he even utters a word; he leaves his office and the stage world without attracting notice.

The king represented in *Henry VIII* is ill advised, or ill served, but once freed from Wolsey's pernicious influence, his justice and wisdom appear flawless. Apart from the gentlemen's brief allusion to his promiscuous conscience, no voice is raised to question his behaviour or its dire political effects, as if no sour note must be allowed to trouble the harmony of the picture. The play ends at the christening of the new-born Elizabeth, with a vision of her blissful reign. The rest is silence, for this commonwealth and its 'merry songs of peace', like More's, exist only in heaven: as the audience well knew, Anne, Cromwell, Cranmer, More's walking shadow must all be executed before the realm enjoys this happy end. Cranmer is miraculously saved from his enemies, but the good king's favour has only won him a reprieve: his final prophecy that the baby princess will enjoy a long and prosperous reign skips over the years of the Marian bonfires and his own approaching martyrdom. The alternative title of the play, *All Is True*, calls for a highly willing suspension of disbelief.

---

91 See Goy-Blanquet, 'The Silences of Sir Thomas More'.

92 Stapleton, *The Life and Illustrious Martyrdom of Sir Thomas More*, trans. by Hallett, p. 227.

93 As reconstructed in the various essays of *Moving Shakespeare Indoors*, ed. by Gurr and Karim-Cooper..

Cromwell's State Machines

It is still disputed among scholars whether the architect of national sovereignty was Cromwell or Cranmer, or Henry VIII alone. The reinvention of imperial kingship was largely Cranmer's idea, the collection of foreign opinions very much his good work. Yet he did not ask nor expect the archbishopric of Canterbury, having secretly married while in Germany. The pallium symbolizing his archiepiscopal authority was delivered to his proctors in exchange for an oath of spiritual allegiance to the pope. At his consecration, Cranmer swore before four witnesses that he would not bind himself to anything prejudicial to the rights of the king or prohibitory of such reforms useful to the Church of England, an oath he would be taxed with at his own trial, when he too got caught in Fortune's wheels (see below, Chapter 6). In early April, the Convocation sat at Dunstable under his guidance to examine Catherine's matrimonial cause.

After years of procrastination, Henry's Great Matter was settled at high speed. The Act in Restraint of Appeals drafted by Cromwell was passed on 7 April 1533, prohibiting any appeal from the archbishop's court. On 23 May, the marriage to Catherine was formally declared invalid *ab initio*. On the twenty-eighth, Cranmer validated Henry's secret marriage to Anne Boleyn. Anne's coronation, which More refused to attend despite his friends' urgings, was already scheduled for 1 June. Elizabeth was christened at Greenwich by Cranmer on 10 September. In December, the king's council determined that the pope's authority, usurped by the sufferance of princes, was no more than that of any bishop. Leaving no stone unturned, Henry, who stood under threat of excommunication, appealed to the next General Council against the pope and had transumpts of the legal documents stuck on church doors at home and abroad, 'to the intent the falshood, iniquity, malice, and injustice of the bishop of Rome may thereby appear to all the world'.[94] In January, Parliament met over a new set of bills to confirm the clergy's dependence on the Crown and Henry's new matrimonial state, settle the succession, pass bills of attainder against the Nun of Kent and her alleged accomplices, Fisher and More. The first Succession Act regularized the marriage and its consequences. A second act in 1536 revised the first according to the changes in Henry's family.

This swift mode of action, ending years of legal quiddities, the constitutional revision that made it possible, and its efficient propaganda were largely the result of Cromwell's efforts. The new doctrine was that Parliament could change all existing laws by statute. Canon law, considered until then separate and equal to statute, was now subordinate to it, and deemed invalid if it contradicted English customs. Whether or not the new rules made a revolution in government has been hotly debated since Elton formulated the theory that it laid the foundation

94 *Letters and Papers, Henry VIII*, in *England under the Tudors* (London: Methuen, 1955), I, p. 411. Parmiter, *The King's Great Matter*, points out similarities in phrasing with *A Glass of the Truth*.

of British stability and success.[95] His view of Cromwell's years in office is that there was a real revolution, but revolution under the law, neither holocaust nor reign of terror. It was well established through the religious settlements that the King-in-Parliament reigned supreme. How far the king's power could extend out of Parliament was a grey area left for the next dynasty to explore.

The positive aspect, in Elton's view, is that the common law had triumphed: one must forget the 'very special case' of Thomas More, pursued by a vengeful king. Unspecial trials for treason required solid proofs. Offenders would suffer the fate of traitors, provided they were 'lawfully convicted according to the laws and customs of this realm'. Unless condemned by an act of attainder, the traitors were dealt with by formal processes of law, judge, and jury, in common law courts.[96] There were no executions before 1534, but a marked increase after the Treason Act, with a peak in 1537, followed by a sharp decline. Yet the peak of 1536–1537 caused only a third of the deaths following the far less dangerous rising of 1569. Where Elizabeth's government made free use of martial law, Henry's generally preferred common law, with an exception for the Pilgrims of Grace. What Theodore Plucknett wrote of the 1388 Appellants could still apply to Henry VIII: 'their manipulations of procedure impressed upon all beholders the simple fact that legality was part of the nation's traditions'.[97] However recklessly vindictive their acts, they had felt the need of clothing them in ancient vestments of law, an homage that vice renders to virtue.

Historians are on the whole very tolerant towards Henry's 'rule of law'. Baker insists that the Tudors were from the first a limited monarchy, though he admits that in some cases the government acted despotically, 'in the sense that, although the outward forms of law were strictly observed, both judges and legislature were in practice amenable to the king's will'. Yet in his opinion, 'it was more a case of putting the clock back to an earlier period, and regaining the seignorial and prerogative rights which the common law itself gave to the Crown. That is a far cry from despotism as generally understood.' Moreover, he goes on, Henry's determination always to act within legal forms encouraged the general view that everyone, king included, was subject to the law.[98] No doubt it also encouraged the view that every abuse of justice could be glossed over with words — including despotism as generally understood, which by any other name could sound softer.

---

95 In Elton, *The Tudor Revolution in Government*, a thesis Elton developed in *England under the Tudors*.

96 Elton, *Policy and Police*, pp. 270–95.

97 Plucknett, 'State Trials under Richard II', in *Studies in English Legal History*, ch. IX, p. 171.

98 Baker, 'Human Rights and the Rule of Law in Renaissance England', *Northwestern University Journal of International Human Rights*, 2.1 (April 2004), article 3.

Biting Statutes

> We have strict statutes and most biting laws
> (The needful bits and curbs to headstrong steeds)
> Which for this fourteen years, we have let slip.
>
> *Measure for Measure, I.iv*

Considering the violence of Henry's revolution, it met with very few protesters of More's stature. Possibly because the Reformation policy not only affected the religious sphere, it also satisfied more material demands. Among the legal changes operated by Henry's revolution, the birth pangs of the Statute of Uses, which thoroughly upset the regime of landed property, is most revealing of the legal profession's ambivalent relation with the Crown. Undoubtedly it 'was forced upon an extremely unwilling Parliament by an extremely strong-willed King',[99] but on the other hand 'the evidence shows that this strong-willed King was obliged first to frighten and then to conciliate the common lawyers in order to get the statute through the House of Commons'.[100] Strong-willed but not tyrannical, mind you. Henry took the opportunity of their Supplication against the Ordinaries to warn Commons he would not suffer opposition and threatened to 'search out the extremity of the law' if they put obstacles to his wishes. Increasingly important fields of litigation in which common law could not or would not operate had been abandoned to Chancery. The Court of Chancery distinguished the seisin, or legal estate, from the use, or beneficial estate. Contrary to this doctrine, the Statute of Uses converted all equitable estates created through 'use' into legal estates, 'an invasion of private right by parliament almost, if not entirely, without precedent', that would lead in time to 'the constitutional doctrine of the omnipotence of parliament'.[101]

Most of the land in England was held by use. As a result, land litigation was the lawyers' chief business. Medieval landholders had to pay a fee to the king as legal owner of all their land, and additional fees when it went to an heir, but they could transfer their leasehold in the name of an individual for the benefit of another, *cestui que use*, a type of landownership recognized by English courts. Thanks to this custom, an owner could divest himself of the legal right in a property to one or more feoffees, and thus escape payment of debts, taxes, forfeiture, and other inconveniences. At common law the feoffees possessed the full legal estate, but at equity the rights of the user were enforceable. They offered many ways to cheat the Crown of its revenues. To Plucknett, the struggle over the Statute of Uses shows the critical, even desperate, position of common law. The final plan, passed with strong support from the legal profession, satisfied common lawyers in

---

99 Maitland, *Equity*, p. 35.
100 Holdsworth, *A History of English Law*, IV, p. 461.
101 McIlwain, *Constitutionalism Ancient and Modern*, pp. 137, 145.

transferring uses from equity to common law courts.[102] The legal title to a large portion of ecclesiastical land was held by feoffees for the use of monasteries: now, the king being head of the Church, it could be reverted from the new legal owners to the Crown. From a third of the property of feudal tenants in 1529, it secured rights over the whole in 1536. The lawyers benefitted materially as well. When the dissolution of monasteries released a flood of new wealth, their specialized knowledge gave them privileged access to the market. 'Why may not that be the skull of a lawyer?' Hamlet ironizes over Yorick's grave. 'This fellow might be in's time a great buyer of land, with his statutes, his recognizances, his fines, his double vouchers, his recoveries.' Many a lawyer had been made rich by the acquisition of church and churchyard property.

The Act of Supremacy had given Henry the authority to disband monasteries and confiscate their properties.[103] Cromwell's campaign against superstition, pilgrimages, and relics opened the way to looting and breaking of church valuables throughout the realm. This is when Leland was commissioned to rescue priceless antiquities. The First Suppression Act of 1536 dissolved over three hundred small houses and reverted their property to the Crown. Many of their members sided with the rebels when the Pilgrims of Grace rose, in the autumn of 1536. This gave the government lawyers a legal pretext for confiscation: if the prior were convicted of treason, the whole property of the abbey would legally revert to the Crown. In April 1539, a new law legalized 'voluntary' surrenders, in exchange for rights to life pensions, paid by the new Court of Augmentations where all Church money went. Three abbots who resisted the law were hanged for treason. The monastic lands represented around two million acres, over 16 per cent of the whole realm. The increased income for the Crown, approximately £150,000 per year, was supposed to free the realm from taxation, but Henry needed money for his military plans, so a large bulk of the property, and the advowsons that went with it, was sold off indifferently to Catholic or Protestant gentry. The redistribution of wealth was larger than anything since the land settlement of the Norman Conquest. The purchasers were peers and commoners, country esquires, lawyers and physicians, London merchants, civil servants. Against such a wide range of interests, Mary would find it impossible to reorganize religious life on its former basis.

The Pilgrims of Grace, led by Robert Aske, a London barrister of Gray's Inn, placed the Statute of Uses high on their list of grievances: 'It was at once seen that it would deprive men of that testamentary power, that power of purchasing the repose of their souls, which they had long enjoyed.'[104] After the rebels' defeat, a Statute of Wills in 1540 repealed part of it, keeping uses a legal estate, in charge

102 Ives, 'The Genesis of the Statute of Uses', *English Historical Review*, 82.325 (1967), 673–97, refutes Holdsworth's theory that a bargain was passed between the king and the common lawyers. See also J. L. Barton, 'The Medieval Use', *Law Quarterly Review*, 81 (1965), 562–77.

103 Twenty-two volumes and three folders have survived, kept at the Public Record Office in Kew.

104 Maitland, *Equity*, p. 35.

of common law judges, but allowing again the devise of land by will: Aske the common lawyer and his Pilgrims had not protested entirely without effect. If the legal profession did not yet represent a powerful lobby in Parliament, as Ives claims, it was fast rising in prestige and efficiency. Petitions and angry murmurs against lawyers adversely confirmed the place they had gained in Tudor society.[105]

The theme of good counsel resurfaced, with Cromwell in the role of evil counsellor. The pilgrims complained that Henry VIII was surrounded by 'persons as be of low byrth and small reputation which hath procuryed the proffits most especially for theyr own advantage, the which we suspect to be the lord cromwell and Sir Richard Riche Chanceler of the augmentations'.[106] They further deplored that against the old custom, most in the House of Commons were the king's servants. In the version served to the foreign ambassadors, the rebels were chiefly boys and beggars, deceived by the false rumours of traitors that new taxes would be levied.[107] Actually the pilgrimage received abundant support from the northern gentry and priests, united in hatred of the heretical upstart who raided monasteries, taxed goods, raised rents, and enclosed commons. Their eagerness to rescue the king from his sway shows how well Henry had managed to shift the responsibility of unpopular measures onto Cromwell in the public opinion.

Traditionally, the middle class of country gentlemen, burgesses, and lawyers were the monarchy's best allies against both arrogant nobility and unruly commons: in exchange for their support they were allowed a share in the executive government at central or local levels. Various historians consider that the Pilgrims' platform was proleptic of Charles I's opponents in 1642.[108] Yet their uprising still has all the features of a medieval *jacquerie* as defined in Leroy-Ladurie's typology: calls on the nobility as their natural leaders, and appeals to the king for redress of evil practices, no revolutionary challenging of his authority.[109] It was at best an uneasy alliance, covering a large range of antagonistic interests. A meeting at Lincoln had ended in great confusion, with a commoner in the audience crying it was time to kill some of the justices: even if they were to hang for it they would not leave a gentleman alive — an echo of the Peasants' War later revived by Shakespeare's Jack Cade.[110] The leaders met again at Pontefract castle to work on what would become the Twenty-Four Articles, a mixture of regional and larger political grievances.[111] They required the summons of a free parliament, respect

---

105 A petition of 1534 to the king and the lords complained of the misdeeds of lawyers, *Letters and Papers, Henry VIII*, VII.1611 (3). Ives, 'The Genesis of the Statute of Uses', p. 692, notes an inordinate number of complaints in the years 1534 to 1536.

106 Aske's programme, Item 4, *Letters and Papers, Henry VIII*, XI, 705 (1), in Fletcher, *Tudor Rebellions*, pp. 105–06.

107 *Letters and Papers, Henry VIII*, XI, p. 656. Dodds and Dodds, *The Pilgrimage of Grace*, I, p. 132.

108 Dodds and Dodds, *The Pilgrimage of Grace*, II, pp. 332–33. Guy, *Politics, Law and Counsel*, XIV, pp. 292–311.

109 Leroy-Ladurie, *Le Carnaval de Romans*, pp. 360–75.

110 *Letters and Papers, Henry VIII*, XI, p. 975. 2 *Henry VI*, IV.ii–viii.

111 Bush, *A Study of the Rebel Armies*.

for the customs of the lords, free speech, and free elections to Commons who could 'reason for the wealth' of their communities, instead of the king's 'private lucre'.[112] As to the supremacy, the pilgrims agreed to a limitation of the pope's authority on English affairs, but the cure of souls must be reserved to Rome.

Like their grievances and demands, the conclusion followed a repetitive pattern. In Shakespeare's *Henry VI*, Cade urges his men not to put any faith in the promises of the king's emissary, and judging by the usual fate of rebels in chronicles, he was right. Although the Tudor pilgrims were guaranteed 'a general pardon vnto all the offendors', the king himself went to Kent to pass judgement, 'and so punished the stubburne heddes'.[113] Like Cade's credulous troops, they agreed to disband with promises that the king would receive their demands, a freely elected parliament meet to discuss them, and all be pardoned for their part in the uprising. They hoped in treating with Norfolk that his influence with the king would replace Cromwell's. Norfolk, who probably shared this hope, wrote to Henry before the meeting to 'take in gode part what so ever promes I shall make unto the rebells for sewerly I shall observe no part thereoff'.[114] Their loyalty to the Crown made them an easy prey to delaying tactics. No answer came for several weeks, causing agitation in the north, which supplied Henry with a motive to revoke his pardon. From the documents, 178 were executed.

The executions needed a defender, for they were not well received by public opinion. Morison's answers to the Pilgrims were printed the same autumn as his *Apomaxis* by Berthelet.[115] There were also private contributions to the doctrine of obedience. William Calverley, a Yorkshire gentleman who took sides with the Pilgrims, was sent to the Tower, where he wrote a verse *Dyalogue bitwene the playntife and the Defendaunt*, dedicated to Henry VIII. It may have won him his liberty, for he was released months later.[116] Like More's *Dialogue of Comfort* and Boethius's *Consolatio*, it takes place in jail, where the plaintiff blames his misery on Fortune and is shown by the defendant, Reason, that he fully deserves this punishment. All men guilty of murder, robbery, or dissension use the same excuse, 'It is nat fortune that causeth their yll chaunce | But them/selues for lacke of good gouernance',[117] anticipating Edmund's mockery of those who blame their faults on adverse planets: 'I should have been that I am had the maidenliest star in the firmament twinkled on my bastardizing'. Having recalled the sad fates of

112 Mary Bateson, 'The Pilgrimage of Grace and Aske's Examination', *English Historical Review*, 5.18 (1890), 563–64.

113 *Hall's Chronicle*, p. 222. *Holinshed's Chronicles*, III, p. 227.

114 In Fletcher, *Tudor Rebellions*, p. 23.

115 The Pilgrim's petitions, the king's answer, and Morison's pamphlets are all reproduced in *Humanist Scholarship and Public Order*, ed. by Berkowitz.

116 Janice Liedl, 'The Penitent Pilgrim: William Calverley and the Pilgrimage of Grace', *The Sixteenth Century Journal*, 25.3 (1994), 586–87.

117 William Calverley, *Dyalogue* (London: Thomas Godfray, 1535), fol. B i. r.

Sardanapalus and Icarus, Reason praises the best of all living knights, King Henry himself, who gave 'Res publica to us his subiectes | With reuerent fere & loue obeying his precepts'.[118]

Royal Attainders

The Tudors' adherence to fair rule of law was at best intermittent, as in the 'very special case' of Thomas More. Elton is so set on demonstrating More was tried and convicted lawfully, however atrociously, that where crucial evidence is missing, he thinks that probably 'More for once took the hypothetical manner of argument just that little bit too far', making it possible to persuade the jury he had in fact spoken treason.[119] The trial marked 'a turning-point in English constitutional history' by establishing Parliament's omnicompetence.[120] This is not how it appeared at the time. From various accounts, it was a farce, with More made 'from a State pleader a stage player'. The chancellor stood in the dock where he had formerly been supreme judge, giving many proofs of a clear conscience, 'All which not withstanding, the Jury found him guilty.'[121] More summed up the proceedings in one last killing pun: the matter was 'tryed by a quest of xii men, a iury as I remembre they call it, or elles a periury'.[122]

Far fewer pains were taken to save appearances at Anne Boleyn's trial. She was indicted three months after a miscarriage which must have proved to Henry that God did not like this marriage any better than the first. Her trial jury was presided by the ubiquitous Lord High Steward, her uncle Norfolk. Circumstantial evidence of her adultery, incest, and other horrifying misdeeds was produced before the juries; no witness was heard nor dissenting voice at the verdict. Those accused of sinning with Anne were all found guilty of high treason and executed. The whole procedure took four days, and she was beheaded on the fifth, 19 May 1536. Hall's report dispatches her in two paragraphs, while her final speech absolves Henry from any hint of tyranny: no king is more merciful or gentle, 'accordyng to the lawe and by the lawe I am iudged to dye, and therefore I wyll speake nothyng against it'.[123] Henry's jealous suspicions, like Othello's, were first aroused by a dropped handkerchief that one of her gallants picked up to wipe his face.[124] Cranmer wrote with many circumvolutions to tell the king his high opinion of the queen, his belief 'that she should not be culpable', his wish that she may declare herself innocent, and his vow to hate her if she is guilty.[125] Having gone

---

118 *King Lear*, I.ii.131–33. Calverley, *Dyalogue*, fols B iv. v–C i. v.

119 Elton, *Policy and Police*, p. 417.

120 Derrett, 'The Trial of Sir Thomas More', pp. 449, 451.

121 Roper, *The Lyfe of Sir Thomas Moore*, p. 92.

122 Letter to Alice Arlington, More, *The Correspondence*, no. 206, p. 523.

123 *Hall's Chronicle*, p. 819.

124 Burnet, *The History of the Reformation of the Church of England*, I, bk III, p. 306.

125 Letter reproduced by Burnet, *The History of the Reformation*, I, bk III, pp. 310–12.

so far, indeed much farther than any of Anne's former friends, he undid his earlier work by pronouncing her marriage null. The ground of annulment this time was her sister's alleged precontract with the king, and on 30 May, the brand new bridegroom was wedded to Jane Seymour. In June Parliament adjudged the king's two first marriages unlawful. A new Act of Succession cancelling the earlier ones gave Henry full power in case of lack of heirs to 'give, dispose, appoint' as he thought best 'the imperial crown of this realm'.

Henry's reign 'marks the heyday of attainder by statute', with a 'frantic climax' in 1539 and 1540.[126] The instrument of Cromwell's destruction was the machinery he had set up, especially the extension of treason laws. 'No man ought to be condemned without answer', Edward Coke would write in discussing his case.[127] Attainders in the past usually followed some sort of judicial procedure and did not inevitably incur a death penalty, but after 1534, by a bill of attainder the person accused of serious crimes like treason, felony, or misprision was declared guilty without benefit of a trial, a measure especially devised to dispatch the Nun of Kent and her followers.[128] The measure took the form of a petition from both Houses, begging the king to punish the offenders, as if the whole public were clamouring for their blood from a too merciful prince.

Hall gives Cromwell even shorter shrift than Anne. The articles of his attainder appear in the Record, but are 'too long to be rehearsed here'. The readings of the attainder passed with the clerk's mention, *nemine discrepante* (no one disagreeing).[129] Probably because, as the judges would answer Coke, 'it was a dangerous question'.[130] Again, Cranmer bravely if not boldly wrote to Henry, saying he found it hard to believe that such a good servant could be a traitor, but if he was, then all he deserved was hatred. In his dying speech Cromwell like Anne declares he is justly condemned by the law, for he has lived a sinner, but he dies in the faith of the holy Church, with a prayer for the king.[131] His real fault, which Hall never mentions, was the king's disastrous marriage with Anne of Cleves, designed to win the alliance of the north German princes against the emperor. Henry married Catherine Howard, his fifth wife, on the day of Cromwell's execution.

Both Cromwell's fall and Henry's marriage into an eminent Catholic family raised hopes abroad that England might yet return to the bosom of Rome. That Henry had no such plans was soon made clear by the pursuit of his independent policy. The Howards' influence was doomed to be short-lived anyway. An Act of Attainder was passed by Parliament in January 1542, ruling that any unchaste woman marrying the king shall be guilty of high treason. The twenty-year-old Catherine was indicted for misprision with some twelve members of her

---

126 Lehmberg, 'Parliamentary Attainder', pp. 675, 685, 690.

127 Coke, *The Fourth Part of the Institutes*, pp. 36–37.

128 Lehmberg, 'Parliamentary Attainder', p. 684.

129 Lords' Journal, I, 145–46, in Lehmberg, 'Parliamentary Attainder', p. 694.

130 Coke, *The Fourth Part of the Institutes*, p. 37.

131 *Hall's Chronicle*, p. 839.

household, and on 11 February she was beheaded for her 'said abominable and detestable treasons'.[132] Henry's last Parliament met to attaint two more of the Howard family, Norfolk and his son the Earl of Surrey, whose fall was procured by their foe Edward Seymour. Surrey was found guilty by a jury and executed before the attainder. The bill was passed on 27 January 1547. Norfolk should have been beheaded on the twenty-eighth, had not the king died that night.

The day after Cromwell's execution, three of his clients were burnt at Smithfield, and three papists hanged for denying the royal supremacy.[133] The Act of the Six Articles in 1539, nicknamed 'the bloody whip with six strings', made heresy a felony at common law. With this new weapon, the secular arm equitably burnt Protestants and hanged Catholics. The empire, and Cromwell's programme of unifying it under State control, were now achieved. The realm after them was ruled by its own law and regulated by statutes. Parliament continued the king's best ally after Cromwell's fall, even releasing him from his debts, and enjoining creditors who had been refunded since 1542 to give the money back. In exchange for their good will they were confirmed in their privileges. The Commons gained some control of their assembly and kept records in what became the *Commons' Journals* in 1547. The idea had been growing since More's first petition that they should be allowed free speech. In 1542 the Speaker, Sir Thomas Moyle, requested the liberty for every member of the house freely to speak his mind, which the king granted, though he maintained the rule that they must send delegates if they wished to approach him.[134] When one of them was delivered from arrest without any writ, Henry ratified their authority by solemnly declaring 'that we at no time stand so highly in our estate royal as in the time of Parliament, wherein we as head and you as members are conjoined'.[135] The news of Henry's death was received with tears in the House.

132 1542. 33 Henry VIII. c. 21. 3 S. R. 857.
133 Mackie, *The Earlier Tudors*, p. 427.
134 *Journals of the House of Lords*, I, *1509–1577* (London: HMSO, 1802), p. 167.
135 *Holinshed's Chronicles*, III, p. 824. *Journals of the House of Lords*, I, p. 196.

CHAPTER 6

Fortune's Wheels

Common Prayers

> King Henry unhorsed the Pope: but king Edward toke awaye sadle, trappers and al.
>
> *Foxe, Actes and Monuments, Bk* IV

The dramatic turns of Fortune's wheel continued under Henry's successors. Stephen Gardiner, who led the conservative party, had fallen into disgrace some time before the king's death, leaving hardly any opposition to the reforming Seymours' seizure of power. Edward's minority and his wolfish uncles were a well-rehearsed theme: 'Woe to thee, O land, when thy king is a child'.[1] There was not much time nor inclination for play in the austere boy who ascended the throne, too wise too early. Like so many minors before — Richard II, Henry VI, Edward V — he had a surfeit of protectors. His political guides and guardians were his maternal uncles, Edward Seymour, who made himself Duke of Somerset, and Thomas, Lord High Admiral. John Dudley, the low-born son of the attainted Edmund, was created Earl of Warwick. The Parliament summoned by Somerset in November, almost a year after Henry's death, was duly convinced to regularize their positions. Except in matters of taxation, Parliament was generally compliant.

Somerset the 'good duke' made himself quite popular at first. His reforming council was well organized, his Star Chamber fairly lenient, he tried to contain enclosures, and he established a court of requests in his own house to deal with poor people's causes. His first Parliament repealed the acts against the new treasons created under Henry VIII and abrogated the legislation against heresy. But his poor administrative skills failed to deal with the social unrest in various parts of the realm through the summer of 1549. In Cornwall, where the enforcement of the English language in church caused great anger, the misinformed Protector allowed it to gather momentum before taking repressive measures. Kett's rebellion in Norfolk against enclosures further weakened his authority, while strengthening the position of his rival Warwick who finally defeated the rebels' army. In October, the Protector and his liberal views were accused of having encouraged a 'liberty' that degenerated into disorder. He was sent to spend a few months in the Tower. Warwick, now created Duke of Northumberland, took over the sole guidance

1 Ecclesiastes 10. 16, echoed by Richard III's London citizens, *Richard III*, II.iii.13.

of the young king. Two years later, Somerset was condemned for felony and executed.

A Discourse of the Commonweal of this Realm of England, published in 1581 under the title *A Compendious or briefe examination of certayne ordinary complaints*, reflects the state of affairs after the summer's rebellions. It is unusual in its detailed account of popular miseries. The dialogue, featuring a Knight and a Doctor in debate about the current economic hardships, is supported by a cast of choric figures — Merchant, Husbandman, Capper — who confirm that 'it was never merry with poor craftsmen since gentlemen became graziers',[2] yet show no hint of upsetting the social hierarchy and respectfully listen to their betters' opinions, even when those get excessively wordy.[3] The Doctor exposes current fallacies and explains the interconnections of finance and agriculture to his grateful audience: 'We felt the harme, but we wist not what was the cause therof', says the Husbandman. One of the causes of dearth is the import of expensive foreign trifles; another, the enclosure of common arable lands; another, the decaying of towns and villages; and last, the division of religious opinions. The chief cause, source of all the others, is the debasement of coinage, which raises the price of foreign goods. Before any plan of economic redress, the king must call in all the bad money in the realm: the worse groat will always chase away the better one, the Doctor explains, anticipating Gresham's law. But laws will not be enough if men are unreformed: they need material encouragements. The pillars of a healthy commonwealth, 'reward and pain', in other words profits and penalties, replace the old pious allegories of good governance.[4]

Cranmer's Faith

On Fletcher's analysis, it was a complex combination of rumours and fears over Church goods, new taxes, and the liturgy of the new prayer book that caused the uprising in Cornwall. Kett's manifesto, a similar mixture of agrarian grievances, social conservatism, and anxieties over the clergy's competence, 'looked forward to the popular protestantism of Elizabeth's reign'.[5] Among various propagandist answers to the Cornishmen's grievances was a long article by Archbishop Cranmer, who marvelled they would rather repeat Latin words like pies and parrots than understand what they prayed for in English, or observe rituals close to Christmas games rather than a service based on Scripture.[6]

---

2 Smith, *A Discourse of the Commonweal*, ed. by Dewar, First Dialogue, p. 20.

3 Elizabeth Lamond attributed it to John Hales: 'Authorship' in *A Discourse of the Common Weal of this Realm of England*, ed. by Elizabeth Lamond (New York: B. Franklin, 1971), pp. xxv–xxviii. Mary Dewar, 'The Authorship of *The Discourse of the Commonweal*', *Economic History Review*, 19.2 (1966), 388–400, thinks it is more probably Thomas Smith.

4 Smith, *A Discourse of the Commonweal*, Second Dialogue, p. 60.

5 Fletcher, *Tudor Rebellions*, p. 66.

6 In Jasper Ridley, *Thomas Cranmer* (Oxford: Clarendon Press, 1962), p. 293.

Cranmer had been for the past ten years a devoted servant of the Crown. It was while following the emperor around Germany with the hopeless mission of bringing him round to Henry's views that he first met continental reformers like Andreas Osiander, 'the first prominent Lutheran theologian to adopt the constitutional theory of resistance' put forward in 1529 by Hessian jurists, and developed by Martin Bucer.[7] Having married Osiander's niece Margarete, Cranmer brought her back with him to England when he was recalled to succeed William Warham as archbishop of Canterbury. With his blessing, Henry was married and unmarried as fast as he changed wives. Almost as fast: Anne Boleyn's execution had to be postponed forty-eight hours so Cranmer could have time to declare void her marriage and hear her last confession. It was the tireless archbishop who informed the king of Catherine Howard's infidelity. A group of conservative prebendaries led by Gardiner tried to get him convicted of heresy and ousted from office in 1543, but Henry had the good grace to rescue him by the gift of his own ring. Shakespeare's *Henry VIII* places the event earlier, before the birth of Elizabeth, to whom Cranmer is chosen godfather as a public sign of royal favour.

Cranmer's own religious beliefs when he took the see of Canterbury were not firmly set, on a par with the doctrinal fluctuations of the State. His Ten Articles of 1536, officially establishing *Ecclesia Anglicana,* were clearly a compromise: they recognized only three of the seven sacraments, but allowed images, worship of saints and the Virgin, the belief in purgatory, and prayers for the dead. Two Lutheran missions from the continent failed to convince Henry to complete the reform of his realm. The Six Articles' return to orthodoxy, which reinforced clerical celibacy, drove Cranmer to send his wife and children away to safety on the continent. The King's Book of 1543, entitled *The Necessary Doctrine and Erudition for Any Christian Man,* re-established Catholic doctrine except the pope's supremacy.

The ambiguous position of England on the religious map of Europe persisted to the end of Henry's reign. Both Cranmer and Gardiner stood by his death bed. Gardiner sang his requiem and a Mass invoking the Blessed Virgin. After his master's death Cranmer began to preach more radical views on Mass and the Eucharist and moved ever closer to the continental reformers, driving the country along with him. The bishops who resisted the changes were sent to think again in jail for a while. It was out of concern for the education of an often incompetent or illiterate clergy that Cranmer composed *Certain Sermons or Homilies Appointed to be Read in Churches,* a collection to which he contributed at least four himself. Several held distinctly Protestant views, focusing on justification by faith, which may explain why, although they were ready for print in 1543, they only appeared four years later, at the onset of Edward's reign.[8] John Ponet's visitation of 1551 still exposed an abysmal state of ignorance in parishes: over half of the clergymen

7 Skinner, *The Foundation of Modern Political Thought,* II, pp. 204–05.

8 The twelve homilies were first published in 1547. A second volume appeared in 1562, mostly written by John Jewel, and augmented in 1571 to twenty-one homilies.

questioned could not recite the Ten Commandments; some could not even repeat the Lord's Prayer. All preachers were ordered to confine their preachings to the official Homilies. Some of those were clean government propaganda: 'An Exhortation Concerning good Order, and obedience to Rulers and Magistrates' refutes all egalitarian principles with threats that, should degree be upset, 'no man shall keepe his wife, children, and possession in quietnesse, all things shall bee common, and there must needes follow all mischiefe, and utter destruction both of soules, bodies, goodes, and common wealthes'.[9] At the next session, Parliament gave the clergy the right to marry. At the next again, acts were passed prescribing the removal of images and superstitious books.

In 1549, Parliament adopted the new prayer book after much arguing and revising. The debates on the Eucharist had again divided conservatives and reformers. As for Cranmer, he publicly declared he no longer believed in the real presence. His original version borrowed heavily from German sources, especially Martin Bucer and Peter Martyr, whom he invited to England, but concessions were made on both sides. The result of this compromise was the Book of Common Prayer, which replaced the old Latin books of liturgy, now made illegal. Although Bucer thought it did not make much advance towards reformation, it triggered off the western uprisings. In the more radical version of 1552, the Eucharist was reduced to a symbol and the prayers for the dead suppressed.

The first edition was the moment chosen by John Hooper, freshly back from his exile in Zurich, to start the vestment controversy. Again, pamphlets were hurled at each other by contending parties, as to whether the king should be obeyed in things indifferent, *adiaphora*, not necessary to the faith. In a Latin letter of October 1550, Hooper made his point *Contra usum vestium* with biblical and historical precedents, though he eventually gave in under pressures to conform, and preached in episcopal garments before the king after his ordination. The vestments rubric was omitted in the revised prayer book of 1552, but the controversy continued among the Marian exiles and returned with them to England after Mary's demise, to develop into a major crisis under Elizabeth (see below in this chapter, '"Something Tawdry": The Political Pageant').

A codification of Church law had been promised at each banning of heretical books. When the Parliament of 1550 called for a revision of canon law, Cranmer and a committee of clergymen and lawyers produced a comprehensive *Reformatio legum ecclesiasticarum*.[10] The committee included William Fleetwood, Thomas Norton, John Foxe, Sir Thomas Smith, and Christopher Yelverton, who all indulged at some point in writing dialogues, poems, or plays, evidence enough that there was no deep hostility then between religious reform and theatre, quite the opposite, as we shall see (below, in Chapter 7). This code was never published under Edward VI, and finally rejected when Cranmer's son-in-law, Norton, presented

---

9 *Certaine Sermons or Homilies*, ed. by Rickley and Stroup, pp. 69–70. Cf. *Troilus and Cressida*, I.iii.104–10.

10 MacCulloch, *Thomas Cranmer*, pp. 500–533.

it before the Elizabethan Parliament: the peers could accept changes in doctrine but not a reformation of discipline. The second prayer book having established the liturgy of the Anglican Church, there remained to fix its doctrine. The Forty-Two Articles marked the height of the Calvinist influence: they expressed Cranmer's firm belief that Scripture validated the Church of England and endorsed justification by faith. Of the seven sacraments, only baptism and communion remained. The Thirty-Sixth Article provided a place in the hierarchy of power for the civil magistrate, who 'is ordained and allowed of God'. Edward's death a few weeks later prevented their enforcement, but they would form the basis of Elizabeth's Thirty-Nine Articles. It also left his archbishop exposed to Mary's resentful wrath.

Family Plots

The rise and fall pattern initiated by Henry VIII's queens and counsellors found accelerated momentum under Edward, bringing to the scaffold all his ambitious guardians. Violence first broke out within the family: as in so many tragedies past and future, from *Thebais* to *Gorboduc* to *Richard III*, brothers (in this case, the Seymours) fought each other to extinction. Thomas was arrested for having attempted to marry his niece Elizabeth, seize control of the young king, and usurp the throne, 'following the example of Richard III', and condemned by Act of Attainder. The Parliament Journals show that his brother was present throughout the proceedings: Somerset vowed to have used all the means to avoid this extremity, 'But were it son or brother, he must prefer his majesty's safety to them, for he weighed his allegiance more than his blood',[11] noble words that Shakespeare's Duke Humphrey and Gaunt would use to define a conservative hierarchy of duties. Gaunt puts the law before fatherly love when his son is banned, and recalls this natural order before it is disrupted:

> You urged me as a judge; but I had rather
> You would have bid me argue like a father.
> O, had it been a stranger, not my child,
> To smooth his fault I should have been more mild.
>
> *(Richard II, I.iii.237–40)*

Though some marvelled to see the Protector thus agree to his brother's death, the peers unanimously assented, well used by now to the attainder routine. All that was needed to send the admiral to the scaffold was the king's signature on the act which, on the evidence of his own journals, Edward gave without undue emotion. Somerset's 'extreme hatred' for his brother caused a severe drop in his popularity

11 'Articles of High Treason and other Misdemeanours against the King's Majesty and his Crown, objected to Thomas Seymour', in *Cobbett's State Trials*, pp. 492, 504. Cf. Humphrey in 2 *Henry VI*, Gaunt in *Richard II*.

and helped bring about his own fall. Foxe for one read it as divine punishment: his unbrotherly behaviour 'provoked the chastisement of Gods scourge and rodde'.[12] Edward had even fewer qualms in signing away his other uncle less than three years later, despite the indignant popular protest that accompanied the Protector up to the moment of his beheading. The fate of the 'Good Duke' and his 'proud Duchess' would be obliquely reflected by the falls of 'Good Duke Humphrey' and his proud wife in *The Mirror for Magistrates*, as in *Henry VI*.[13]

When the death penalty for heresy was reintroduced by his new guardian John Dudley, again Edward saw nothing wrong with this. But the newly created Duke of Northumberland would not long enjoy his victory, nor save the realm from falling back into popish error. His fatal end, like Seymour's, would be paralleled with the usurpation of Richard III, and evoked in nine of the *Mirror*'s 'Tragedies'.[14] George Ferrers, once a close friend of both Seymour brothers, recasts them in his 'Tragedie of Edmund Duke of Somerset' as innocent victim and remorseful culprit, whom a cruel villain (Dudley) set at odds with his lies.[15] Like his model, Ferrers's Somerset puts duty above brotherly ties, claiming that 'Constant I was in my Prynces quarrell'.[16] Enmity between brothers would be a running theme from *Gorboduc* to the end of the Shakespeare canon (see below, 'Political Tragedy' in Chapter 8).

In Scott Lucas's view, the authors of the *Mirror* being 'committed to the ends of the evangelical government of King Edward VI', each would suffer in the reign of Mary.[17] Edward's own end initiated yet another tale of terror and pity, yet another sequence of manipulative legislation: the rise and fall of the nine days' queen, Jane Grey, Henry VIII's grandniece, whose royal blood and youth would not save her from the axe. Edward's 'Devise for the succession', excluding both his sisters from the line, simply ignored Henry's Third Succession Act passed ten years earlier. Jane assumed the throne on 10 July 1553. When Mary rode into London on the nineteenth, Jane's proclamation was revoked by Parliament, and she was promptly sent to prison in the Tower with her husband Guildford Dudley. From other quarters of the Tower, Norfolk and Stephen Gardiner were immediately released, in time for Gardiner to crown the new queen. Various proclamations in the course of the summer restored the Catholic bishops and put preaching under license of Gardiner, but did not succeed in silencing Protestant preachers. In September Latimer and Cranmer were sent to the Tower for expressing seditious views.

---

12 See Foxe's *Actes and Monuments* on the hatred between the brothers, Bk IV (1563 edn), pp. 936, 940.

13 Lily B. Campbell, *Shakespeare's 'Histories': Mirrors of Elizabethan Policy* (London: Huntington Library, 1947), pp. 109–10.

14 On the parallels, see Campbell, *Shakespeare's 'Histories'*, pp. 326–30.

15 On the *Mirror*'s topicality, see Scott C. Lucas, 'The Consolation of Tragedy: *A Mirror for Magistrates* and the Fall of the 'Good Duke' of Somerset', *Studies in Philology*, 100.1 (2003), 44–70.

16 Baldwin and others, *The Mirror for Magistrates*, ed. by Campbell, p. 401. For a modernized and annotated edition, see Baldwin and others, *A Mirror for Magistrates*, ed. by Lucas.

17 Lucas, *'A Mirror for Magistrates' and the Politics of the English Reformation*, p. 36.

Mary's next move was to restore the authority of the pope. Parliament met on 5 October to repeal the religious laws of her brother and revive the old Heresy Acts. The Statute of Repeal Act returned the realm where Henry VIII had left it, to the Six Articles of 1539. Parliament obeyed Mary's wishes, except for two points on which they proved adamant: the supremacy, and the restitution of Church lands. In 1555, when she took the decision to revert the revenues of tenths and first fruits to the Church, her councillors maintained she had no right to give away the inheritance of her successor, an argument that Ponet pursued in his *Shorte Treatise of Politike Power,* along the lines developed by Terrevermeille: the king does not possess the kingdom; he cannot alienate it nor the right of his successor.

The lawyers who were told to execute Edward's will had replied it would be treason, but surrendered in the end. Among those pressed by Northumberland, only one, Sir James Hales, a justice of the Common Pleas, had refused to sign the 'Devise'. This did not save him from prison when he asserted that the previous legislation remained in force until repealed. It was the same Hales, John's cousin, whose suspicious death in 1554 would bring in a verdict of *felo de se* and inspire the gravediggers' comments on Ophelia's drowning.[18] Foxe reports he was tried and discharged, 'But neuer quiet in conscience till he had drowned him selfe in a riuer halfe a mile from his house in Kente'.[19] Of Edward's former councillors, at first Northumberland alone was executed, though all had shared in the plot to evict Mary. Jane's fate was sealed by her father's part in Wyatt's Protestant rebellion. There was no need of a new trial to establish her and Dudley's complicity since they stood already attainted by the earlier one. Both were sentenced to death and beheaded. Jane's younger sisters, Catherine and Mary, would survive to harass their cousin Elizabeth with further claims.

As for the new queen, she did not heed Gardiner's advice nor the Commons' petition that she marry an Englishman. The feelings expressed then easily matched those that Stubbs would pour forth in *The Gaping Gulf* when her sister Elizabeth would likewise consider a foreign marriage. Mary's chosen husband, Felipe II, was to be styled 'King of England' in all official documents, and England be ruled by their joint authority. However, the treaty maintained English laws and customs, and provided that Felipe would lose any hold on the realm if Mary died childless. It also guaranteed that England would not be drawn into any Spanish wars, a clause that proved meaningless in practice. The fact that Mary's husband was the son of Carlos V meant that England's diplomacy would have to be thoroughly reshaped. The Burgundian ascendancy of the Habsburg emperor was

18 Carolyn Sale, 'The "Amending Hand": *Hales v. Petit, Eyston v. Studd,* and Equitable Action in *Hamlet*', in Jordan and Cunningham, eds, *The Law in Shakespeare*, pp. 188–207, sanguinely sees Hamlet's alignment with women, his 'figurative divestiture', as compensating for 'the various forms of misogyny that have informed English jurisprudence'.

19 Foxe, *Actes and Monuments*, Bk v, p. 905. Plowden, 'Hales v. Petit, Common Pleas, 1562', in *The Commentaries, or Reports*, p. 253. See Philips, *Shakespeare and the Lawyers*, pp. 77–79. *Cobbett's State Trials*, p. 713, no. 46.

one more thread in the complex knot of Tudor relations with Spain. In her last speech before Parliament, discussing her foreign policy, Elizabeth recalls that she dissuaded 'theas malcontentes' of the Netherlands from revolting when they offered her their State, in memory of 'that old leage that had lasted long betwene the race of Burgundy and my progenitors'.[20] Mary was but pursuing her grandfather's policy of Spanish marriages, although in her case the match presented far more interest for the other party. When the widowed Felipe considered remarriage with Elizabeth despite their religious differences, he obviously thought it still worth his while.

Marian Tyrannicides

Bleed, bleed, poor country!
Great tyranny, lay thou thy basis sure,
For goodness dare not check thee. Wear thou thy wrongs.

Macbeth, *IV.iii*

Months after Mary's accession, seven reforming bishops were removed. Some of Cranmer's foreign friends had already fled abroad. They were soon followed by other eminent divines, several of whom would return later to help establish the Anglican Church, and by laymen who would man Elizabeth's council or her Parliament. Thomas Smith, appointed first Regius Professor of Civil Law at Cambridge under Henry VIII, remained in England but lost all his offices. In Strasbourg, Peter Martyr reunited with a group of English exiles before he went on to occupy a chair of Hebrew at Zurich. John Jewel, after first recanting under Mary, fled to Frankfurt where less radical Protestants were gathered around Richard Cox, and sided with them against John Knox's party in their disputes over the prayer book. Those who were satisfied with Edward's second prayer book sought to defeat and expel those who wanted it made purer. Knox's declaration of war against 'the monstrous regiment of women', a masterpiece of ill-timing, appeared just as Elizabeth was about to succeed his worst monster.

Other Marian exiles were busy revising their theories to accommodate the political change. Morison in *An Invective against the Great and Detestable Vice, Treason* had once argued that no one under any circumstance must ever 'think to pull down a prince whom God has chosen to rule over his people'.[21] Earlier propagandists of unconditional obedience must now frame new doctrines,[22] and would have to change them again when they returned home to organize Elizabeth's Church. According to Bucer's theory of constitutional resistance, God had given mandate not just to one but to all legitimate magistrates ordained

20 19 December 1601, *Proceedings*, III, p. 280.
21 London, 1539, sig. A, 5b, in Skinner, *The Foundation of Modern Political Thought*, II, p. 106.
22 See Skinner, *The Foundation of Modern Political Thought*, II, ch. 7, pp. 210–38.

for special duties: 'whenever a superior magistrate persecutes his subjects, then by the law of nature, by divine law and by the true religion and worship of God, the inferior magistrate ought by God's mandate to resist him'.[23] Théodore de Bèze (Beza) and other writers including Knox praised the example set by Magdeburg.[24] According to the *Vindiciae contra tyrannos* attributed to Philippe Duplessis Mornay, a future character in Marlowe's *Massacre*, if a king breaks the mutual contract with his people, he becomes a tyrant and can lawfully be resisted, under the guidance of magistrates.[25] Should one resist, obey a wicked ruler like Macbeth, help to the throne the lesser tyrant that Malcolm promises to be, or live in exile? Macduff is saved from an impossible choice when told that Malcolm's self-accusations were only designed to test him. But as Peter Herman brilliantly argues, in Shakespeare's play the ethical dilemma remains unresolved. The dramatist 'neither fully endorses nor fully subverts any political ideology'; he reflects the escalating conflict between rival theories: James I's absolutist claims and the traditions of English liberty.[26] But James was no bloody tyrant. The conflict had escalated and climaxed long before his accession.

In the wake of the Marian exiles, we find John Ponet, formerly chaplain to Cranmer and a pupil of Thomas Smith at Cambridge. His translation of Ochino's *Trageodie* in 1549 had brought him to the attention of Somerset, who made him bishop of Winchester when Gardiner was deprived of his see in 1551. Ponet lost it after Mary's accession, supported Wyatt's rebellion, and fled to the continent. He is generally credited with a sustained attack against the divine right of kings, although the first actual occurrence of the phrase comes much later, in Hooker's *Laws of Ecclesiastical Polity*.[27] In *A Shorte Treatise of Politike Power*, written in Frankfurt, Ponet vents his anger against the evil counsellors whom he holds responsible for the failure of the Protestant cause, especially some of his former friends, who switched their allegiance to Mary through lust for power and wealth.

Exploring biblical precedents to justify disobedience to evil authorities, Ponet goes further than most continental theorists in arguing that individual resistance to tyrannical rulers is legitimate.[28] It is only because men's reason is corrupted by the Fall that they need rulers, he begins, like 'oxen, sheep, goats and other unreasonable creatures' unable to rule themselves. The only perfect ruler is God.

---

23 *The Confession and Apology of the Pastors and other Ministers of the Church at Magdeburg*, 1550, in Skinner, *The Foundation of Modern Political Thought*, II, p. 208.

24 Especially the division in England between theories of absolute obedience and legitimate disobedience; see Turchetti, *Tyrannie et tyrannicide*, pp. 391–409.

25 Printed in Basel, 1579, under the pseudonym Stephanus Junius Brutus. Excerpts were published in 1689 under the title *A Defence of Liberty against Tyrants* (London: Richard Baldwin).

26 Peter C. Herman, '*Macbeth*: Absolutism, the Ancient Constitution, and the Aporia of Politics', in Jordan and Cunningham, eds, *The Law in Shakespeare*, pp. 208–32.

27 Hooker, *Of the Laws of Ecclesiastical Polity*, ed. by McGrade, Bk VIII, Ch. 2.6, vol. II. I owe this precision to my dear departed friend, Mick Hattaway.

28 See Barrett L. Beer, 'John Ponet's Short Treatise of Politike Power Reassessed', *The Sixteenth Century Journal*, 21.3 (1990), 37–84.

His rule is the law of nature, set forth in the Decalogue, and brought down by Christ to two commandments: love God, love thy neighbour. Like many earlier jurists, Ponet held that monarchy was subordinate to law. Just as the ancients had found means to check abuses of authority, 'So in all Christian realms and dominions God ordained means, that the heads, the princes and governors, should not oppress the poor people according to their lusts, and make their wills their law':[29] in Germany a diet, in France and England, parliaments.

In exceptional situations, it is right for private men to resist malefactors, even rulers. The worst sort are those who betray their country to foreigners, a pointed blow at the queen's Spanish marriage. All who abuse their authority deserve to be 'deposed and removed out of their places and offices, by the body or state of the realm or commonwealth' (Ch. 6). To this the Bible and European history show many precedents, as does England, with the deposition upon 'just causes' of Edward II and Richard II. 'It is lawful to kill a tyrant', Ponet hammers with each new chapter, an argument Norton would repeat against Mary Stuart. Yet who should take the responsibility for such a momentous act remains unsettled. The people must pray God to deliver them from evil, but are nowhere explicitly licensed to remove it themselves. Even with this caution Ponet was still the most radical of English exiles. Only the Scotsman Knox was louder in urging the deposition of Mary Tudor. English magistrates were more akin to the repenting ghosts portrayed in the *Mirror*, little inclined to reforming the State by open rebellion against the crowned monarch, even if they agreed with Knox that the presence of the crown on Mary's head was as unseemly as a saddle on the back of an unruly cow.[30]

Ponet had another axe to grind. In 1556, he published *An Apologie Fully Answering by Scripture and ancient doctors a blasphemous book*, Gardiner's pamphlet on clerical marriage, which Edward VI had legalized, and Mary hastened to suppress. Not only had Ponet married without waiting for the ban to be removed by Parliament, but his wife was priorly contracted to a Nottingham butcher, who claimed damages for bigamy.[31] Queen Elizabeth, who was reputed to abhor clerical marriage quite as much as her half-sister, was in no hurry to reinstate it. Shortly before her accession Ochino published a highly controversial *Dialogue of Polygamy* (1558), arguing that since most animals are not monogamous, why should men be? This, oddly enough, did not apply to women. It would evince an answer from Beza, and many after him, down to Milton's assertion 'that polygamy is allowed by the law of God'.[32] Before those divines, Chaucer's Wife of Bath had

---

29 Ponet, *A Short Treatise on Political Power*, ed. by Poole, ch. 1, <https://constitution.org/1-Constitution/cmt/ponet/polpower.htm>.

30 Knox, *The First Blast of the Trumpet*, ed. by Mason, pp. 1–7.

31 See Eric Josef Carlson, 'Clerical Marriage and the English Reformation', *Journal of British Studies*, 31.1 (1992), 12.

32 Milton, *De Doctrina Christiana*, ed. by Charles R. Sumner (Cambridge: Cambridge University Press, 1825), ch. x, p. 243.

defended the validity of multiple marriages — in succession — from the woman's side. Rabelais' Panurge, before Beatrice and Benedick, wondered whether one should marry at all. 'Marriage is destiny', the chroniclers wrote, when the comedy of marriage occupied the high political ground and tied up the fate of the realm with the success of an alliance, making the divide between public and private affairs intangible. The cohort of sexuality, betrayal, and inheritance attendant on matrimony made it excellent material for the theatre, and perilous matter for moralists who held drama under suspicion. Clerical marriage meant for Catholics the loss of any claim to sacred authority. Even Protestants deplored the general contempt for clergymen in England: their preachings 'are scoffed at, even of the vile and contemptible players'.[33]

Ponet's views offer an exhaustive catalogue of contemporary prejudices, creeds, loves, and old rancours. The final admonition to repent quotes a number of recent celestial signs — monstrous births, comets, blazing stars, eclipses — that express God's wrath. All the people's miseries are the rewards of sin. The prophets' threat 'is not holy water of the court, bare words of course, as the princes of the world use'.[34] The restitution of the cursed popish Mass has brought famine 'by the direct plague of God', and raised prices to unbearable heights: 'A pound of cheese at four pounds, two eggs a penny, a quart of wheat, sixty-three shillings.' All true English hearts must remember the conquest made by the ambitious Duke of Normandy, 'upon how small a title he entered, and how tyrannously he used himself', how he 'made his own lusts his laws, and put them in his own Norman tongue', so that 'he might catch the poor Englishmen, when it pleased him: and would have the laws to be pleaded and all things to be done in French'. The detested idiom, law French, would remain in practice until the eighteenth century, despite repeated attempts to ban it from the courts (see below, 'Won in Translation' in Chapter 7).

Heretics on Trial

In Mary's reign, Wyatt's rebellion seems to have crystallized the hostility of many who were reported to 'much mislike the comming of the Spaniards into this realm'.[35] Protestant writers thought it was punished with unusual severity, although the repression was far more lenient than, say, in 1536. Not quite a hundred were executed, nearly half of them in London.[36] The Tower was so

33 Thomas Cooper, *An Admonition to the People of England, 1589*, ed. by Edward Arber (Birmingham: Unwin Brothers, 1882), quoted in Knapp, *Shakespeare's Tribe*, p. 7.

34 Ponet, 'An Exhortation, Or Rather, A Warning, To The Lords And Commoners Of England'. Cf. *Lear*, III.ii.10–11, 'O nuncle, court holy-water in a dry house is better than this rain-water out o' door'.

35 *Holinshed's Chronicles*, IV, p. 42. *Cobbett's State Trials*, no. 52, pp. 861–902. Jardine, *Criminal Trials*, I, p. 71.

36 Fletcher, *Tudor Rebellions*, pp. 75–76.

crowded, Bishop Ridley wrote, that he had to share a cell with Cranmer, Latimer, and Bradford. Princess Elizabeth was there as well, on suspicion of complicity, but soon released for lack of evidence against her. Wyatt had pleaded guilty at his trial, but cleared her of any part in the design. The story that the people dipped their handkerchiefs in his blood as relics is thought to have inspired the bloody handkerchief held out by Shakespeare's Margaret to the vanquished Duke of York. The most significant feature of this failed rebellion, in Fletcher's view, is that the gentry learnt to channel their opposition through Parliament, where they succeeded in frustrating Mary's plan to disinherit Elizabeth by statute.

A 'Strange Acquittal'

Crack the lawyer's voice,
That he may never more false title plead,
Nor sound his quillets shrilly.

Timon of Athens, IV.iii

Among the more eminent suspects, Sir Nicholas Throckmorton was the first to stand trial at Guildhall on 17 April 1554. Thanks to his pugnacious defence, he got himself acquitted, an unusual feat for State offenders.[37] Lorna Hutson observes a tendency among Foucault's disciples to underestimate the evaluation of evidence at ordinary jury trials for felony, caused by the lack of transcripts, and its impact on the 'diffusion of certain habits of thought and practice through the culture', especially in the theatre.[38] Yet Throckmorton's extraordinary case provides a remarkable document on the judicial system, as well as a telling instance of the authorities' attachment to strict legality.[39] The 'boulting out of the truth' so praised by Sir Thomas Smith and by Hutson was not yet a major concern at State trials.[40] Paradoxically this acquittal measures the distance between the high standards set by theoreticians who kept repeating through the ages that the English king was under the law, and the degree of submissiveness to the Crown that lawyers had learnt to accept as a fatality, a behaviour obliquely exposed by George Ferrers in 'The fall of Robert Tresilian chiefe Iustice of Englande, and other his felowes, for misconstruyng the lawes, and expounding them to serue the Princes affections'.[41] The 'thyrst for gold' and 'vayne promocion' of Richard II's

---

37 The editor of *Cobbett's State Trials*, p. 407, no. 32, finds only one other acquittal for the period, Lord Dacres'.

38 Hutson, *The Invention of Suspicion*, p. 73.

39 *Holinshed's Chronicles*, IV, pp. 31–55. John Stow's *Annales, or a general Chronicle of England* (London: A.M, 1631), p. 626. Patterson, *Reading Holinshed's Chronicle*, pp. 160–61.

40 Smith, *A Discourse of the Commonweal*, p. 13. Hutson, *The Invention of Suspicion*, pp. 77–78.

41 Patterson's suggestion in *The Trial of Nicholas Throckmorton*, p. 30. Tragedie 1 of the *Mirror*. Lucas, 'The Trial of Sir Nicholas Throckmorton', in *'A Mirror for Magistrates' and the Politics of the English*

corrupt judges made them 'forget the fayth of our profession, | When serjeantes we were sworne to serue the common lawe.'[42]

The usual practice in court was to read the evidence to the jury, mostly written depositions and examinations by members of the Privy Council, carefully edited by Counsel for the Crown. There is no record of *viva voce* examinations of witnesses before the reigns of Edward VI and Mary, but the legal expert John Langbein has shown that the judges' refusal at Nicholas Throckmorton's and John Udall's trials to have their witnesses heard was illegal.[43] Throckmorton loudly marvelled at this absence when confronted with the confession of Sir James Crofts, who was present in court that very day: 'how comes it to pass that he is not brought face to face to justify this matter, and has not been all this while? Will you know the truth?' One witness was eventually heard in his case, more to confound the prisoner than as a legal right of his. His own witness for the defence, John Fitzwilliams, 'was not suffered to speak.'[44] The practice of cross-examination, sparingly introduced about then, was still unusual enough in 1616 for Francis Bacon to explain his course at the Overbury trial: examinations taken on oath will be read in the presence of the witnesses so they can 'justify or deny what they hear read, and diminish or add to their examinations', and be questioned by the jury of peers.[45]

The records show Throckmorton deftly taking to pieces the prosecution's case: the charges rest only on false and unproven testimonies. Here he quotes statutes of Edward VI, ruling that none shall be convicted for treason or misprision unless 'accused by two sufficient and lawful witnesses', or by his own willing confession, without violence.[46] He reminds them of the command 'from the Queen's own mouth', 'to administer the law and justice impartially':

> You seem to give and offer me the law, but in very deed I have only the form and image of the law; nevertheless, since I cannot have the statutes read openly in the book, I will with your leave guess at them as well as I can.

The book of statutes is raised to the height of a legal Gospel. Throckmorton stands on the truth of its written words, though he states he never studied the law. Yet he seems to remember it very well, Chief Justice Bromley remarks: 'I think, Throckmorton, you need not to see the statutes, for you have them pretty perfectly.'[47]

Reformation Politics, p. 184, n. 19, points out that Ferrers and Throckmorton had both enjoyed the patronage of Thomas Seymour and served in King Edward's two Parliaments.

42 Ferrers, 'Tragedie 1', Stanza 10, which echoes Throckmorton's own words at his trial, Lucas comments in *'A Mirror for Magistrates' and the Politics of the English Reformation*, n. 23.

43 Langbein, *Origins of Adversary Criminal Trial*, pp. 52–56.

44 Jardine, *Criminal Trials*, I, pp. 75, 87.

45 *Cobbett's State Trials*, II, p. 978.

46 Statutes 1. Ed.6, c. 13, s. 22, 5. & 6 Ed.6, c. 11, s. 12. Jardine, 'Throckmorton', in *Criminal Trials*, I, pp. 92, 80.

47 Jardine, 'Throckmorton', pp. 92, 93.

Throckmorton claims that what he knows he learnt 'of you, Master Serjeant, and others my masters of the law, in the Parliament-House'. There he heard his judges and the queen's learned counsel 'grievously inveigh against the cruel and bloody laws of Henry VIII, and some laws made in the late King's time'. Throckmorton's objection to their 'grievous racking' stresses the practice of torture, which lawyers mostly disapproved of but still compounded. Such judgements, he accuses, are repugnant to the law on their own principles, and the opinions of their learned predecessors.[48] What is at stake in the long debate with his own judges is the notion of treason by words. The prisoner admits that he did speak against the Spanish marriage; what he denies is that those words had any treasonable object or performative power. The prosecution have not a single 'open act' to hold against him.

Edward's laws still ruled the kingdom, since the statutes repealing them had not yet been passed, but the verdict of 'not guilty' was not easily accepted. Having warned the jury that 'the business concerns the Queen's Highness, and also yourselves. Take good heed what you do', Bromley ordered the lieutenant of the Tower to take his prisoner back with him 'for there are other things to be laid to his charge'. The Queen's Counsel requested that the men of the jury, 'who have strangely acquitted the prisoner of the treasons laid to his charge' be bound in a recognizance of five hundred pounds a piece, while the court committed them to prison.[49] Four were released after confessing their offence; the other eight were kept until October when they appeared before the Star Chamber, were heavily fined, and sent back to jail till December.

The acquittal may have appeared strange for other reasons. Throckmorton and his political friends must have taken an active part in the uprising, Jardine notes, for they were promoted to high office immediately upon Elizabeth's accession. Sir Nicholas would continue a long career of ambivalent plotting and narrow escapes. His part in Norfolk's conspiracy finally caused his disgrace, but he was soon released from prison to end his days in quiet, while his daughter Bess kept her place at court. Bess Throckmorton's maternal grandfather Nicholas Carew had not been so lucky: involved in Cromwell's plots against Anne Boleyn, he saw his former friend turn against him and was eventually executed for his alleged part in the Exeter conspiracy. Tudor families, however fortunate or highly connected, well knew that none of their members at any time was safe from Fortune's, or government's, blows. On the other hand, the fall of one did not compromise the others' chances to regain new heights.

---

48 Jardine, 'Throckmorton', pp. 95, 96, 98, 103, 101, 104. Jardine, *A Reading on the Use of Torture*, pp. 6–10, stresses that Fortescue, *De Laudibus*, cap. 22, Coke, *Third Part of the Institutes: Concerning High Treason*, p. 35, and Smith, *Commonwealth of England*, Bk II, cap. 27, all assert it is against the law of England to torture.

49 Jardine, 'Throckmorton', pp. 107–08.

Tragic Dialogues

> It is an heretic that makes the fire,
> Not she which burns in't.
>
> *The Winter's Tale, II.iii*

Some eight hundred rich Protestants left the realm shortly after Mary's accession. Those who remained to die at the stake were an estimated three hundred. Cranmer did not flee like many of his flock but stood his ground, and was sent to the Tower. There, at the end of his flexible career, he turned into a last minute resistant. His exit, as would the Jesuit Edmund Campion's, was preceded by one of those spectacular debates *pro et contra* designed to advertise the court's objective hearing of rival doctrines. The issue was a foregone conclusion, as Cranmer like Campion would soon realize, but in each case the contestants fought to the last, for the sake of proclaiming their faith. In retrospect it is difficult to assess which were more haunting to witnesses, the final speech or the blood of the martyrs. They bled on both sides: Edward VI's divines showed no more pity for Anabaptists than Henry or his daughter Mary for Protestants. Calvin, whose first published work was a commentary on Seneca's *De clementia*, now had no qualms about sending blasphemers to the scaffold.[50] Knox, in defending Calvin's will to see Michel Servet executed, makes a subtle distinction between conscience and conscience: 'We say, the man is not persecuted for his conscience, that, declining from God, blaspheming his Majesty, and contemning his religion, obstinately defendeth erroneous and false doctrine.'[51] On the basis of this distinction, Mary is a hateful monster. His *First Blast of the Trumpet* violently denounces the persecutions of reformers, as does Foxe's *Book of Martyrs*. There is no similarly vindictive portrait of Elizabeth in the contemporary monuments of Catholic recusants. Most of them, including Campion, would plead to the last their loyalty to the queen and Crown.

In Cranmer's case, a charge of heresy, the queen and the bishops had concluded before what should become of him, Foxe writes, 'yet it pleased them that the matter should be debated with arguments, that under some honest shew of disputation the murder of the man might be covered'.[52] Disputations were part of yearly rituals for students, like moots at the Inns of Court. On announcing the first one of Mary's reign, Hugh Weston, dean of Westminster, promised it would be lawful 'for all men freely to speake their conscience in these matters'.[53]

---

50 Calvin, *Commentaire du 'Traité de la Clémence'*, ed. by Ferrand and Quiviger.

51 Knox, *The Execution of Servetus for Blasphemy, Heresy and Obstinate Anabaptism Defended*, <https://www.truecovenanter.com/anti_toleration/knox_execution_of_servetus_defended.html>. Calvin wrote his own *Defensio Orthodoxae Fidei de sacra Trinitate*, ed. by Kleinstuber.

52 Foxe, *Actes and Monuments*, Bk XI, p. 2085 [2046], in 'Disputations, from a copy of the Report and Narration of the proceedings by one popish witness'. *Cobbett's State Trials*, p. 771.

53 Foxe, *Actes and Monuments*, 'Acte of the first day', 18 October 1553, Bk X, p. 1609 [1547].

Cranmer, Ridley, and Latimer were to be heard by learned doctors of Oxford and Cambridge 'so as their erroneous opinions, being by the worde of God justly and truly convinced, the residew of our subjects may be therby the better established in the true catholike fayth'.[54] So much for the openness of the debate.

As to its fairness, it seems that the reformers were constantly interrupted by the loud 'brawling' of the audience.[55] The well-disordered show combined farce with tragedy. Ridley records he would not have thought it possible for learned men 'so disorderly and vainly to behave themselves, more like to stage players in Interludes, to set forth a Pageant, then to be grave divines in Scholes to dispute'.[56] Time was spent in contumelious taunts, 'more than tolerable, even in stage-plays, and that in the English tongue, to get the people's favour withal'.[57] The university doctors appointed Dr Cuthbert Scot to dispute against the reformers, with the young John Jewel acting as one of the four notaries. The theme was the real presence in the sacrament. An ironic reversal, for some of these doctors had taken part years earlier in a public disputation at Cambridge on the same theme, transubstantiation, presided by Ridley.[58] Others had done time in Edward's prisons and subscribed to Ridley's catechism, Dr Weston reminds him, 'when you were a Byshop in your ruffe'. Ridley was one of the commissioners responsible for the deprivation of Gardiner and Bonner.

The debates, 'sometimes in Latin, sometimes in English', Foxe reports, lasted several days. At one of Cranmer's answers, that Christ is present but sacramentally in the Eucharist, 'the Prolocutor stretching forth his hand, set on the rude people to cry out at hym, fylling all the schole wyth hissyng, clapping of handes, and noyse'. The long perorations are punctuated by frequent 'I deny your major' and '*Ergo* you are deceived', or stichomythic exchanges:

> *Cranmer*. He hath communicated to us his flesh by hys nativitie.
> *Weston*. We have communicated to him our flesh when he was borne.
> *Cranmer*. Nay, he communicated to us his flesh when he was borne.

Predictably, the three men were declared heretics and committed to the sheriffs of Oxford. On 20 April 1554, a sentence of death at the stake was pronounced against them, to the general cry of 'Vicit veritas', truth has won. Foxe ironically concludes:

> And thus was ended thys most glorious disputation of the most holy fathers, sacrificers, Doctours, and Maisters, which fought most manfully (as ye may

---

54 Queen's letter to the Mayor and Aldermen of Oxford, in Foxe, *Actes and Monuments* (1563), Bk v, p. 1067.

55 On the disputation, see Henry J. Todd, *The Life of Archbishop Cranmer* (London: Rivington, 1831), II, pp. 392–99. MacCulloch, *Thomas Cranmer*, pp. 563–68.

56 Ridley's Report in Foxe, *Actes and Monuments*, Bk x, p. 1670 [1632]. Reprinted from Coverdale's Letters of the Martyrs, in Ridley, *The Works*, ed. by Christmas, p. 303.

57 Ridley, *The Works*, pp. 103–16, 117–48. Reported in Foxe, *Actes and Monuments*, Bk x, p. 1670 [1632].

58 Ridley, *The Works*, pp. 171–79.

> see) for their God and goods, for their fayth and felicitie, for their countrey and kitchin, for their beautie and bellie, with triumphant applauses and fauour of the whole Vniuersitie.[59]

The sentence being void in law until the old legislation was restored, a new commission was sent from Rome to try them on 12 September 1555 in the church of Saint Mary. The stage is carefully set. On a 'solemn scaffold' ten feet high, Dr James Brookes, bishop of Gloucester, represents the pope's person, seated between doctors of civil law, above other doctors and scribes, plus a 'rabblement of other like'.[60] Cranmer, dressed in the black gown and hood of a doctor in divinity, bows low and removes his cap to the doctors, then puts it back on to face the bishop, for he has sworn never to consent to the authority of the bishop of Rome in England.[61] When reminded of his oath at his consecration, he takes on the role of the accuser: 'you for your part my Lorde, are periured, for now ye sit iudge for the Pope, and yet ye did receaue your Byshopricke of the king'. Brookes's defence is an admission of guilt: 'You were the cause that I dyd forsake the Pope'. Cranmer reminds him that the universities concluded after long debate that Henry ought to be supreme head. Brookes closes this part of the proceedings with a lame, 'We come to examine you, and you, me thinke, examine us.'[62]

A lively dialogue follows on the observance of unlawful oaths. Accused of having twice reneged on his sworn obedience to Rome to cover an adultery, Cranmer asserts he had cleared himself of perjury by a prior protestation. About communion, he grants that his opinion has changed after conversations with Ridley and other doctors. On the supremacy, he admits that yes, Nero too was head of the Church, like Henry. Dr Martin's conclusion, 'Then hee that beheaded the heades of the Church and crucified the Apostles, was head of Christes Church', is left unanswered.[63] All this, Foxe reminds his readers, is the biased account of a popish notary. Other reports show Cranmer had much more to say, which Foxe proves by giving him a lengthy oration on English laws.

Throckmorton had slipped through a time gap between Edward's still standing legislation and Mary's revival of the old heresy laws, but there was no such loophole left for Cranmer. His trial, effected under papal jurisdiction, must await Rome's verdict.[64] The commission set up in February 1556, upon receipt of the pope's letters, was the occasion of another public show. Cranmer was first 'invested in all maner of robes of a Byshop and Archbyshop as he is at his installyng', except that these were made 'of canuas and old cloutes, with a miter & Palle of the same sute done vpon him in mockery', and the ceremony of

59 Foxe, *Actes and Monuments*, Bk x, pp. 1653 [1615], 1636 [1598], 1640 [1602], 1670 [1632].

60 *Cobbett's State Trials*, I, p. 772.

61 Foxe's Preface, 'The Order and Manner of the Examination of Dr Ridley', in Ridley's *Works*, p. 257.

62 Foxe, *Actes and Monuments*, Bk xi, pp. 2086 [2047]–2090 [2051].

63 Foxe, *Actes and Monuments*, Bk xi, pp. 2092 [2053].

64 'A Letter of Dr Cranmer to a Lawyer for the drawing out of his Appeal', in *Cobbett's State Trials*, pp. 833–35.

degradation began. His hair was clipped, any memory of anointment scraped off the skin of his fingers, his gown pulled off and replaced by an evil-favoured one, a 'pageant of degradation'.[65]

After nearly three years in prison, the archbishop at last gave in. His recantation was gladly received by the queen but did not alter her purpose to have him executed. On 21 March, a multitude was present: 'There was a stage set vp ouer agaynst the Pulpit', upon which Cranmer stood like an emblem of Fortune, 'a sorrowful spectacle to all Christian eyes'. The change of costume, from 'fresh ornaments' to 'vile and ragged apparell', completed the lesson on mutability. In his sermon, the celebrant, Dr Henry Cole, recalled the victims of his own party: 'it seemed meete, according to the law of equality, that as the death of the Duke of Northumberland of late, made euen with Thomas More Chauncellour that dyed for the church, so there shoulde be one that should make euen with Fisher of Rochester'. But 'there were other iust and weightye causes' to his execution, the orator hurries on, which the queen and council thought not meet to be opened to the common people.

When told he must 'now performe that you promised not long ago', Cranmer exhorted the audience to obey God, the king and queen, 'knowyng that they be Gods ministers, appointed by God to rule and gouerne you'. Having caught the public's ear and the officials' goodwill with this preamble, he solemnly denied what he had written contrary to the truth to save his life.[66] All stood amazed, the doctors who had so looked forward to their great victory 'began to let downe their eares, to rage, fret and fume', then 'Cranmer beyng pulled downe from the stage, was led to the fire'. Thus by his last testimony he fully deserved to be numbered among Christ's martyrs, 'much more worthy the name of S. Thomas of Caunterbury then he whom the Pope falsly before dyd Canonise'.[67] The parallel, like the nationalist theme, is not fortuitous: Cranmer's stance is the exact reverse of Becket's. His main quarrel with Rome, detailed in letters to the queen, is that the pope 'commaundeth to blot out of our bookes, all lawes and customes being repugnant to hys lawes'. If his authority is lawful, then all Her Grace's laws and customs are naught, all her judges are heretics. Had these points been fully opened in Parliament when it was reinstated, the queen, her councillors, the nobility, and the Commons would never have consented 'to receiue agayne such a forrayne authority'. No true subject could keep his allegiance to the Crown while submitting to such a 'preiudiciall and iniurious' power.[68]

Cranmer's persecutors had once sworn to reject the pope, whom Cranmer had once sworn to obey. Gardiner, for one, had composed a spirited argument in favour of the royal supremacy against 'the false pretended power of the bishop

---

65 Foxe, *Actes and Monuments*, Bk XI, pp. 2098 [2059]–2100 [2061].

66 MacCulloch, *Thomas Cranmer*, pp. 600–605. *Cobbett's State Trials*, pp. 767–862. John Strype's account of his recantation and death, in *Cobbett's State Trials*, pp. 853–62.

67 Foxe, *Actes and Monuments*, Bk XI, pp. 2102 [2063]–2105 [2066].

68 Foxe, *Actes and Monuments*, Bk XI, pp. 2106 [2067]–2107 [2068].

of Rome' in *De vera obedientia*.[69] Only Reginald Pole could boast a clean record of unswerving loyalty to Catholicism. Mutual accusations of perjury all had sufficient grounds to foreclose easy ways out of the dilemma. The successive turns of history's wheel made all claims to righteousness, loyalty, or legitimacy, all set norms dubious, at best relative, and anchored in time. Mary could not call back yesterday; even her Catholic subjects were reluctant to abandon the realm's hard-won independence from foreign yokes. The tensions of conflicting duties, the irretrievable loss of unity would be sounded in depth by the Elizabethan playwrights. Those whose political awareness was as keen as Shakespeare looked to the theatre as the last pleading stage for all dissenters, perhaps the only alternative to martyrdom.

'Something Tawdry': The Political Pageant

> The scenic apparatus of divine worship is now under agitation, as if the Christian religion could not exist without something tawdry.
>
> *John Jewel, Letter to Peter Martyr*

The political drama of the Elizabethan settlement begins with John Foxe, whose *Actes and Monuments* first staged the struggle between the Protestant House of Commons on the side of the queen, and the House of Lords united with the Marian bishops against her reforms. This scenario, in Norman Jones's summing up, was enriched by a roll call of great English historians, until John Neale advanced the view that the queen herself was on the side of the conservatives. All she wanted was the supremacy, but she was made to accept the 1552 Book of Common Prayer and an Act of Uniformity that made neither party happy.[70] Neale's theory of a Puritan choir who discovered their strength when united in Parliament was in its turn challenged by Elton. John Knox, who did see the need for a politically united Puritan party, wrote to the exiles suggesting that they of sound doctrine hold fast together, but his views on the 'monstrous regiment' of women made him unwelcome in England after Elizabeth's accession.[71] Yet even if the Puritan choir is a figment of Neale's imagination, there were enough solitary voices to rock the House with increasingly radical demands for free speech (see below, Chapter 9).

Communication via theatrical devices was a main concern of all parties from the earliest days of the new reign, with again complex intersections of law, politics, and theatre in the public arena. A Mantuan resident, Il Schifanoia (Don Aloisio

69 Gardiner, *The Oration of True Obedience*, in *Obedience in Church and State*, p. 93.

70 Jones, *Faith by Statute*, pp. 1–4, suggests a *via media* between Neale and Elton.

71 M. M. Knappen, *Tudor Puritanism: A Chapter in the History of Idealism* (Chicago: Chicago University Press, 1965), p. 164.

Schivenoglia) describes in a letter of 23 January 1559 the pageantry that celebrated the coronation of Elizabeth.[72] On the same day, Richard Tottel printed *The Quenes majesties passage through the citie of London to westminster the daye before her coronacion*, a command of the Corporation of London compiled by Richard Mulcaster.[73] It shows her paying close attention to each pageant and its symbols, which stress the virtues she must cultivate to secure her position on the throne: Pure Religion, Love of Subjects, Wisdom, and Justice. In '*The seat of worthie governance*' at Cornhill, a figure 'representing the Quenes highnes sate in this seate crowned with an Imperiall crowne'.[74] Her noble heart appeared first in her rejection of empty popish rites. This idealized performance was a politically pointed show, reflecting neither her religious doctrine, nor the ambiguities surrounding the actual coronation, nor the real place where good government stood. In the final pageant, Elizabeth was represented wearing the crimson Parliament robes, the first of its kind in entry processions. A Protestant imperial Queen-in-Parliament.

The Inns writers were not far behind in dispensing counsel through plays and translations, as we shall see (Chapter 8). In *Gorboduc*, of course, but also through feminine figures like Hecuba or Jocasta, whom Jessica Winston thinks designed as mirrors to 'represent the insubstantiality of a woman's royal power'. In her reading of *Troas*, published in 1559, Jasper Heywood uses the character of Hecuba to figure Elizabeth's precarious authority, 'perhaps to urge humility and compassion in the new queen', reminding her of the reversals of fortune she herself had known.[75] If that was his intent, then he came remarkably close to religious advisers like Bishop Jewel or Archbishop Grindal who sternly reminded her in private letters or openly in Parliament that she was but a mortal creature and advised her against vanity.

There are more records on the Elizabethan parliaments than on her predecessors', and also far more legislating: comments at her last session call to memory the beginning of her reign, 'when we had nothinge neere soe manye penall and entrappinge lawes as we nowe have'.[76] This High Court of Parliament is 'the greatest and comaunder of all other courtes', Sir Edward Hoby claims. Parliament men show vigilant care to chastise infringements of its privileges, increasingly aware that they speak for the whole nation. At a meeting of both Houses, Robert Cecil reminds Lord Buckhurst (formerly Thomas Sackville, co-author of *Gorboduc*) that 'we be all members of one bodye, and as we cannot be without your lordshippes, soe you cannot be without us': they are all 'coadiuteinge members of one united bodye, the Howse of Parleamente'.[77] In his journal, young Townshend of Lincoln's

---

72 Il Schifanoia to the Castellan of Mantua, *Calendar of State Papers, Venice*, ed. by Browne and Bentinck, pp. 11–19.

73 In *Elizabethan Backgrounds*, ed. by Kinney, pp. 13–39. On Mulcaster's authorship, see Anglo, *Spectacle, Pageantry, and Early Tudor Policy*, p. 346, n. 4.

74 *The Quene's Majestie's passage*, in *Elizabethan Backgrounds*, p. 22.

75 Winston, *Lawyers at Play*, p. 163.

76 Richard Symnell, 5 December 1601, *Proceedings*, III, p. 436.

77 Tenth Parliament, *Proceedings*, III, pp. 346, 465–66.

Inn reports his own speech to the House: 'every man here uppon his conscience', all shut up together in a chamber, they are 'the grand jurye men of this lande, bound to deale bothe trulye and playnelie'. After this grand opening, he applies their Speaker's image of the popish league to more practical matters, the abuses of prowling solicitors 'whoe sett dissention betwixt man and man, like a snake cutt in peeces, craule together to joyne themselves agayne to styrre up even spirrittes of contention'.[78] A vision shared by Shakespeare's young king:

> Civil dissension is a viperous worm,
> That gnaws the bowels of the commonwealth.
>
> (*1 Henry VI, III.i.72–73*)

Townshend then presents a bill to repress the multitudes of contentious minds. The representative ideal will move stage and Parliament orators throughout the reign, we shall see. But helping the commonwealth begins at one's home, or Inn.

Religious Turnovers

Elizabeth's conservatism may have gone no farther than a taste for crucifixes and colourful vestments. Whether inherited from Anne Boleyn or taught by her stepmother Katherine Parr, the doctrine of her youth inclined to Protestantism, or so her supporters thought. To Bishop Jewel, she is 'earnest in the cause of true religion', but cannot be induced to effect a thorough change 'without the sanction of the law', lest she appear to be acting 'in compliance with the impulse of a furious multitude'.[79] Richard Goodrich, of Gray's Inn, whom she consulted on the religious issue at her accession, had been attorney on the Court of Augmentations after the dissolution of monasteries. Along with theology, the control of Church lands must have been high on the list of anxieties raised by the prospect of a new religious turnover. However sincere the queen's religion, her first concerns were practical.

A pressing aim was to recover the revenues that Mary had given to the Church. Goodrich's 'Divers Points of Religion Contrary to the Church of Rome' quote Bracton, to argue that the pope had never exercised any power in England without the king's permission, and the precedent of King John.[80] The anonymous 'Device for Alteration of Religion', written in December 1558, is set like a school exercise, in the form of questions and answers. It advises severity with the papist clergy, whose submission must be secured 'as well by parliament, as by the just laws of England, in the praemunire'. A group of learned divines should meet to revise the prayer book and take care that only a few people be hurt by it, before submitting

78 8 November 1601, *Proceedings*, III, p. 334.
79 *The Zurich Letters*, ed. by Robinson, I, pp. 17–18.
80 His 'Divers Points' are in *Calendar of State Papers, Domestic*, I, no. 68.

it to Parliament.[81] No radical change must be allowed to endanger England's uncertain future.

The speech for the Crown was delivered by Nicholas Bacon, of Gray's Inn like Secretary William Cecil and his strong arm Francis Walsingham. As Lord Keeper of the Great Seal, Bacon presided over the House of Lords. With Cecil, he helped secure the see of Canterbury for their friend Matthew Parker, a former fellow of their Cambridge days.[82] This 'trinity' devoted to the middle way would be the pillars of the Elizabethan Church and State. *Mediocria Firma*, moderate things endure, was the Senecan motto painted on a wall of Bacon's home: here Patrick Collinson stresses the importance for Bacon's formation of his exposure to the rhetorical tradition of Cambridge and Gray's Inn. This may well be how Neville, the translator of *Oedipus*, became secretary to the archbishop, and Norton, co-author of *Gorboduc*, man of business to Cecil. Neither young man gave further signs of an interest in drama, which had fulfilled its purpose by procuring their advancement.

The lists show a large range of religious beliefs in the 1559 House of Commons, especially among its lawyer members, whose opinions could also vary with circumstance. Reformers like Walter Haddon, of Gray's Inn, who had conformed under Mary, returned to their earlier faith. An active Protestant, Thomas Copley of Inner Temple, later converted to Catholicism. Some who preferred the Catholic Mass but disliked the pope's authority took the oath of supremacy to remain in office. Some hoped to recover lands given to the bishops. There were a few zealots on both sides, and a majority, even among the dozen identifiable Marian exiles, of moderates. This voice count discards any notion of an organized radical opposition to the queen's wishes.[83] However, John Jewel complained that they had none 'on our side' in the Upper House, where the bishops 'reign as sole monarchs in the midst of ignorant and weak men, and easily overreach our little party'.[84] The anonymous 'lewd Pasquil' of 1566 shows that the dissenting voices of the 'little party' had gathered force by then and were growing audible.

The Puritans at that stage were not the first target of religious conformity. The threat most feared in the early days of the reign was papistry. Jewel was right in noting little support for his party among the Lords. In the first Parliament, Viscount Montague's speech against supremacy recalled, again, the dangerous precedent of King John, and reminded his fellow peers that the eyes of all Christendom were bent upon them: 'be not noted thus often to chaunge your faithe and religion, and with the prynce to burye your faithe'.[85] After 'very great altercations and disputes' in the Upper House, most of the reforms agreed to in Commons were removed, leaving only the royal supremacy. Meanwhile,

81 BL, Cotton MS Julius F. 6, fols 167–69, in Jones, *Faith by Statute*, pp. 23–26.

82 On the network of government men, see Hudson, *The Cambridge Connection*, pp. 38–60.

83 Jones, *Faith by Statute*, pp. 63–75.

84 Jewel, Letter of 20 March 1559, in *The Zurich Letters*, I, p. 9.

85 *Proceedings*, I, p. 11.

according to our Mantuan diplomat, the court preachers in the presence of Her Majesty and the people were 'doing their utmost to convert the latter, seeking to prove by their false arguments that the Pope has no authority' in England, and the act for restoring to the queen the benefices, tenths, and ecclesiastical pensions confiscated by Henry VIII was passed.[86]

A return match for the Oxford disputations was staged at Westminster to give the Catholic bishops a chance to express themselves and have their doctrinal errors exposed.[87] All but one on the reform side were Marian exiles. Again, the end of this show was pre-written: the bishops would 'have no ground of complaint that they are put down only by power and authority of law', John Jewel wrote to Peter Martyr.[88] He who had served as notary in the Oxford dispute must have found food for meditation in the ironies of fate. Eight Catholics and eight Protestants met on Good Friday, 31 March 1559, under the supervision of Nicholas Bacon, to dispute of three propositions: that it was against the word of God to use 'a tongue unknown to the people' in common prayer and sacraments; that every Church had a right to change ceremonies and rites; that nothing proved there was a sacrifice in the Mass. After a bitter quarrel over procedure the meeting was adjourned, which helped the government advertise the obstruction of the Catholics.[89] Two bishops were arrested a few hours later on a charge of disobedience to the common authority. The other six were fined for contempt of the queen's order and forbidden to leave London.[90] After more committeeing and amending in the Upper House, the revised bill for supremacy made Elizabeth Supreme Governor on 29 April, and in May, Marian bishops who refused to take the oath were deprived of their see. Cecil had told the Commons that she was unwilling out of humility to accept the headship: the title, she vowed, belonged to Christ alone. However she was quite as determined to maintain the full royal prerogative it entailed.

'Jackanapes': A Change of Costumes

> Though honesty be no puritan, yet it will do no hurt; it will wear the surplice of humility over the black gown of a big heart.
>
> *All's Well That Ends Well, I.iii*

The royal prerogative, or so the queen thought, included the choice of ornaments as *adiaphora*, neither ordered nor forbidden by Scripture. Unnecessary to

86 Il Schifanoia, *Calendar of State Papers, Venice*, p. 46.

87 G. W. Jenkins, 'Whoresome Knaves and Illustrious Subjects at the 1559 Westminster Disputation: The Intent and End of an Ecclesio-political Exercise', *Anglican and Episcopal History*, 75 (2006), 315–39.

88 *The Zurich Letters*, I, p. 10.

89 The original government report is reproduced in *Holinshed's Chronicles*, IV, pp. 180–83.

90 MacCaffrey, *Queen Elizabeth and the Making of Policy*, p. 56.

salvation they may have been, but she did not plan to let the more radical Protestants eradicate what they considered superstitious popish rags. Now, it was hoped, the Act of Uniformity giving her the exclusive right to alter ornaments, rites, and ceremonies would put a stop to iconoclasm. The matter of surplices in particular raised such fierce quarrels among parishioners that religious authorities abroad like Bullinger preached moderation to the recalcitrant clergymen who refused to wear them.[91] A rather embarrassed Beza enjoined them to obey the queen, and beware of Satan.[92] Some were deposed but continued to preach regardless. Priests under Mary had stood watching the fires of Smithfield in their surplices. On the other hand, the black robe smacked of Geneva. The term 'Puritan' applied to non-conformists began to circulate around 1564.[93] The 'first Puritan manifesto' was Robert Crowley's *A brief discourse against the outwarde apparell and ministring garmentes of the popishe churche*, in 1566.[94]

Count Feria soon informed his master Felipe II that Elizabeth did not seem well-disposed in matters of religion.[95] She had walked out of the church when the bishop of Carlisle, Owen Oglethorpe, elevated the Host for adoration. Yet the following month, he reported that 'she would appear to continue in the religion professed by her sister'.[96] Whatever her own beliefs, she was reluctant to force consciences and would veto three successive bills designed to enforce yearly communion. Attendance at church could legitimately be imposed, 'for that by religion onely a man is knowne and discerned from brute beastes, and this is to be iudged by the outward shewe; but the conscience of man is internall, invisible, and not in the power of the greatest monarch in the worlde'.[97] Norton retorted 'that not onely the externall and outward shewe is to be sought, but the very secrettes of the harte in God's cause', and the good seed sifted from the cockle. The touchstone to discover 'who be those rebellious calves whom the bull hath begotten, must be the receiving of the communion', with punning stress on mendacious bulls.[98]

The main issue, of course, was not yearly obligation but the nature of the Eucharist.[99] Transubstantiation, argued over since Berengar's days, stood at the heart of the controversies. Article 28 would finally reject it as 'repugnant to the

---

91 Bullinger, Letter of 1 May 1566, Zurich, in Burnet, *The History of the Reformation of the Church of England*, III, pp. 427–35.

92 He would rather not give an opinion, says his letter of 24 October 1567, in Strype, *Historical and Biographical Works*, IV, pp. 507–16.

93 Cottret, *Histoire de l'Angleterre*, p. 223.

94 Patrick Collinson, Arnold Hunt, and Alexandra Walsham, 'Religious Publishing in England, 1557–1640', in Barnard and McKenzie, eds, *The Cambridge History of the Book in Britain*, IV, p. 39.

95 'Letter to Philip, King of Spain, 14 November 1558', in *Camden Miscellany*, vol. XXVIII, Camden Society, 4th Ser., 29 (London: Royal Historical Society, 1984), p. 13.

96 Feria, Christmas 1558, in appendix of *Documents Illustrative of English Church History*, pp. 62–63, 66.

97 April 1571, *Proceedings*, I, p. 240.

98 *Proceedings*, I, p. 241.

99 Alford, *The Early Elizabethan Polity*, pp. 24–26.

plain words of Scripture', and a cause of superstition. After some wavering, Cranmer had reached a compromise with the notion of spiritual presence: Christians receive Christ's body and blood in a heavenly manner; the wicked consume only the elements. When the bill on Uniformity came up for its third reading in the Upper House, Cuthbert Scot, who had presided over the Oxford disputation, tied up the debate over the real presence with costume: to worship Christ in heaven but not in the sacrament is like saying 'that when the Emperour sytteth under the clothe of his estate princly appareled he is to be honorede, but if he come abrode in a frise cote he is not to be honoured', yet he is all one emperor.[100] Perception of this unity will sound less assured by the time Shakespeare's Henry V tours the battlefields of Agincourt meditating on 'idle ceremony'.

Discussing the bill before the Lords, Dr John Feckenham, abbot of Westminster, deplores the 'sodden mutacion' since the reign of Queen Mary: the people defy authority, spoil churches, pluck down altars, and hang up the knave of clubs in the place of the sacrament. Like Gardiner he unites sermons and plays in one reproof: 'by the onlye preachers and scaffold players of this new religion, all thinges are chaunged and turned upsidowne'. The reformers all quarrel about the variety of their own doctrines, not one might be found 'that did longue agre with hymselfe'. Take Cranmer, for instance: 'How contrarie was he unto hymselfe in this matter', writing one book that asserted Christ's real presence in the Eucharist then another denying it.[101] Henry VIII used to act with the consent of Parliament, the Spanish ambassador recalls, but 'now not a single ecclesiastic has agreed to what the Queen has done'.[102] The charge that the doctrines of predestination and salvation by faith alone were incentives to disobedience must have given them pause. Why behave well if it holds no guarantee of heaven?

Prophecy, or its near equivalent, preaching, was another matter that caused the queen's distaste. There was far too much of it in churches, she would inform Grindal. All that was required of clergymen was the reading on Sundays of prewritten homilies.[103] The latent fear was that free discussion of the Scriptures would allow laymen an equality of speech with ecclesiastics. At the onset of the reign, varying doctrines, debates *pro et contra*, free speech, theatrical eloquence, disorder were all tied up in public opinion and associated with the Protestant camp. But the more radical of those would soon discard drama and its trappings, along with the over cautious *via media* (see below, Chapter 7). Jewel deplored a lack of alacrity among his friends, and worried about their quest 'after a *golden*, or as it rather seems to me a *leaden* mediocrity'.[104]

Costume, to Tyndale, made the Mass a grotesque show where the celebrant

---

100 27/8 April 1559, *Proceedings*, I, p. 24.
101 27/8 April 1559, *Proceedings*, I, pp. 28, 30, 31.
102 *Calendar of State Papers, Spain*, I, pp. 67–68.
103 See Collinson, *Godly People*, pp. 371–98.
104 *The Zurich Letters*, I, p. 23.

> disguiseth himself with a great part of the passion of Christ, and playeth out the rest under silence, with signs and proffers, with nodding, becking and mowing, as it were jackanapes, when neither he himself, neither any man else wotteth what he meaneth.

The bishops' 'sandals, gloves, mitres, and all the whole pomp of their disguisings' were so many 'false signs in which Paul prophesied they should come', all of them paid for by naïve worshippers.[105] The delicate matter of vestments was not restricted to religious dress. A 'long bill of apparel, as well for temporal men as spiritual', was prepared by the council's orders for the session of 1566 and 'caused a lot of trouble'.[106] The real issue was ostentation and waste of cloth, much of it foreign. Another 'Bill for Reformation of Excess in Apparel, that Her Majesty by proclamation may appoint what kind of apparel was right for every degree' was presented on 10–13 March 1576, and failed again. The nether House did not think a proclamation 'should take the force of law', as it would set a dangerous precedent for future times, when princes might not be as gracious as good Queen Elizabeth.[107]

The other issue that occupied the Commons for weeks was the recovery of Church lands, on which many had claims prior to Mary's reign. Bishop Bonner, for one, pleaded he had been deprived by Edward VI in favour of Ridley before Mary's letters patent restored him. The Commons considered he had been lawfully deprived 'for his contumacy', but the Lords gave him enough support to defeat the bill. One of the trickiest cases was the Winchester lands. A warrant given by Queen Mary to Bishop White had cancelled all the deeds of his predecessor Bishop Ponet in favour of King Edward, creating another dangerous precedent. If records could be destroyed and nullified, the possessions of all men 'may come to such dowte and question' that no one could know for certain who was the lawful owner.[108] Take from Time his charters, York would argue in *Richard II*, and what will remain of monarchy, 'For how art thou a king | But by fair sequence and succession?'

On the other hand, if grants could be invalidated at the beginning of each new reign, there could be no security of tenure. In this case, time's charters were treated with due regard. Where the Marian bishop had obtained his rights by confiscation from a deprived predecessor, the claimant won. If he came without such prehistory he lost.[109] Compared with the struggles over supremacy and uniformity, the bills on ecclesiastical property passed without much obstacle but a great deal of negotiating. They were very popular for, as Il Schifanoia points out, many had an interest in them: the queen is to have the revenues, but 'all make demands on her, some for a piece of land, some for a garden, some for a house,

105 Tyndale, *Obedience of a Christian Man* (1528), ed. by Russell, I, pp, 260, 285.
106 Elton, *The Parliament of England*, p. 271.
107 *Proceedings*, I, p. 454.
108 House of Lords Records Office, Original Acts, 1 Eliz. I no. 34, in Jones, *Faith by Statute*, p. 106.
109 Jones, *Faith by Statute*, p. 112.

and some for the fee simple of estates for their residence'. Nor can she refuse: the Crown is so poor that she has nothing else to give.[110] The queen and her subjects, Norman Jones ironically concludes, 'spent half a Parliament seeking to restore the true religion and the other half casting lots for the spoils of the church'.[111]

Wedding Bells, Prompt Books, and Lighted Candles

> Thrice blessed they, that master so their blood,
> To undergo such maiden pilgrimage:
> But earthlier happy is the rose distill'd,
> Than that which, withering on the virgin thorn,
> Grows, lives, and dies, in single blessedness.
>
> *A Midsummer Night's Dream, I.i*

Along with the continuing tragedies of Fortune and Revenge, a comedy of marriage would much exercise Elizabeth's Commons, and spin itself out until it became obvious that the Tudor dynasty would die with her. All seven parliamentary sessions from 1559 to 1581 produced some reference to the marriage and succession issue, as did supporting dialogues and plays. Elizabeth was past her twenty-fifth birthday when she ascended the throne. Her councillors wasted no time in telling her she must choose a husband who would take the charges of power from her feeble hands, and concentrate on providing an heir to the realm. Her attack of smallpox in 1562 made it the major concern of the second Parliament. A group of twenty-four members led by the ever active Norton met with the councillors to draw articles for the queen's marriage, and were politely rejected.[112] The Lords represented to her all the perils of an unsettled succession.[113] The monarch is *lex animata*. If she dies, the law dies with her. The Dean of Saint Paul's lent them support with a sermon 'strongly reminiscent of Gorboduc characters', expressing concern for her health and fears of religious war.[114] The question of who would succeed her 'hung over the drama of her reign from its first major work, *Gorboduc, or Ferrex and Porrex*, to *Hamlet*, one of its last'. The character of Fortinbras, who appears only in Shakespeare's version of the story, 'complicates succession issues radically by translating what had been an intra-family revenge plot into one of regime change'. Fortinbras, heir of Norway and Denmark, will unite the two realms at the end of the play, as they actually

110 *Calendar of State Papers, Venice*, p. 73.
111 Jones, *Faith by Statute*, p. 168.
112 *Journal of the House of Commons*, I, p. 63.
113 Petition of 1 February 1563, *Proceedings*, I, p. 61.
114 Alford, *The Early Elizabethan Polity*, p. 104, of Alexander Nowell's sermon on 11 January 1563.

were at the time, under one king who happened to be James VI's brother-in-law, Christian IV.[115]

The Inns made theatrical history, interweaving drama, law, and politics, when two of their members composed the first Elizabethan tragedy, *Gorboduc,* to urge a settlement of the succession by Parliament, stigmatize foreign threats, and promote their patron Dudley, Earl of Leicester, as the most suitable spouse for the queen. Nicholas Guildenstern, Eric of Sweden's ambassador, had arrived in England that summer to prepare his king's visit and been treated to a grand if not unanimous welcome:[116] Leicester's friends, the mayor and the aldermen of London refused to attend the ceremonies organized in the Swede's honour by the Privy Council. The earl then was high on the list of candidates,[117] so high, and so tainted by ugly rumours, that Cecil compiled a list of reasons against this marriage.[118] Incidentally, Mr Secretary disagreed with the view that the law died with the prince. An undated draft bill of his archives, 'ment for the succession but not passed', makes provisions for an interregnum: if need be a 'council of estate' would govern until Parliament could declare a successor.[119]

The Commons' traditional petitions for liberty became inextricably tied up with the marriage issue. Elizabeth vowed she was determined to marry, in her own good time, but would not be constrained, 'For yt ys monstruous that the ffeete sholde dyrecte the hed.'[120] The requests that she marry and/or name a successor, reminders that she was mortal, grew more frenzied with each passing year, until the departure of her last suitor, François d'Alençon, now Duke of Anjou, in 1582. She was then fifty-one. Whether she had seriously considered marrying him or not, the violent popular opposition to this alliance was no doubt an obstacle: 'Our people ought to congratulate and to applaud', she wrote him, but 'the public exercise of the Roman religion sticks so much in their hearts, that I shall never consent to your coming among such malcontents'.[121] Before it found its way to the stage, attached to atrabilious characters, the term Malcontents applied to the French aristocratic party who had joined the Huguenot Monarchomachs behind Alençon against his royal elder brother after the Saint Bartholomew massacre.

Having a single woman rule the realm was bad enough, but surrendering the sceptre to a foreigner was far worse. The level of xenophobic insults reached

115 Dutton, *Shakespeare, Court Dramatist*, pp. 232, 233–34, part of his argument that Q2 dates from an 'augmented' court revision for the Revels season of 1603/1604, coinciding with 'This innovation', i.e. new regime.

116 Walker, *The Politics of Performance*, pp. 208–10.

117 Doran, *Monarchy and Matrimony*, pp. 55–56. Marie Axton, 'Robert Dudley and the Inner Temple Revels', *Historical Journal*, 13.3 (1970), 365–78.

118 Alford, *The Early Elizabethan Polity*, p. 30. The death of Leicester's wife was rumoured to be murder.

119 On this clause, see Alford, *The Early Elizabethan Polity*, pp. 110–12.

120 Queen's speech to a delegation of both Houses, 5 November 1566, *Proceedings*, I, p. 148.

121 Elizabeth, letter of January 1580 to Alençon: 'je ne consentiray jamais que vous veniez en telle compagnie de malcontents', *Calendar of the Manuscripts of the Marquis of Salisbury, Part II 1572–1582*, (London: Eyre and Spottiswoode, 1899), p. 299, translated in *Stubbs's 'Gaping Gulf'*, p. xviii.

heights with the venomous pamphlet of John Stubbs, of Lincoln's Inn: the thought of their dear queen led blindfold as a poor lamb to the slaughter by this 'serpentine attempt' was enough to make him 'shake to speak', but not to write ninety pages of abuse against France and the French. Monsieur's train 'are the scum of the King's Court, which is the scum of all France, which is the scum of Europe'. Recalling Richard II's marriage, Stubbs asserts that 'the French match it was which within one year brought the King to dishonourable captivity, death, and deposing'. If Elizabeth had a son, and died in childbirth, as was very likely, this infant would be in the position of poor Henry VI, inheriting 'two overgreat scepters to play withal' and losing both.[122] Stubbs, his printer, and his publisher had their right hands cut off in punishment. James Dalton and Robert Monson of Lincoln's Inn were imprisoned for having voiced their opposition to the match. In 1581, Norton would be sent to the Tower, and remain there till the end of Anjou's visit, 'for his overmuch and undutiful speaking' touching Monsieur's cause.[123]

Within months of Elizabeth's accession Jewel already complained they had 'as yet heard nothing concerning the queen's marriage, an event which we all desire most earnestly', and betrayed some impatience about 'this woman, excellent as she is', who showed such wariness in establishing the reformed faith. Still, 'many alterations in religion are effected in parliament, in spite of the opposition and gainsaying and disturbance of the bishops'.[124] He was personally much involved in the bitter parliamentary struggle over the revision of the prayer book. The result, quite a conservative one compared with the Book of Geneva, was a compromise that staunch reformers like Edwin Sandys found mutilating.[125] Under the guidance of Archbishop Parker, the fundamentals of Anglican doctrine were fully expressed in the Thirty-Nine Articles finalized in 1571. But the more radical Presbyterians were not prepared to accept the authority of either prayer book or bishops. The following June, two reformed clergymen, John Field and Thomas Wilcox, published an *Admonition to Parliament for the Reformation of Church Discipline*, which brought forth an *Answere* from Bishop Whitgift, and in turn Thomas Cartwright's *Replye to an answere*. Field and Wilcox were imprisoned for a year; Cartwright fled to the continent. A year later his disciple Walter Travers published *A full and plaine declaration of ecclesiasticall discipline*. Bishop Sandys recommended that they be banned from the City, but they stayed. Field became lecturer at St Mary's Aldermary. As lecturer of Temple Church, Travers would expound his views against the milder Richard Hooker.[126]

The queen herself was the butt of harsh complaints from Protestants who found her reforms insufficient. She did her best to keep the settlement as

122 *Stubbs's 'Gaping Gulf'*, pp. 4, 44, 53–54.
123 Graves, *Thomas Norton*, p. 390.
124 Jewel, letter VI to Peter Martyr, 14 April 1559, *The Zurich Letters*, I, p. 18.
125 In *Correspondence of Matthew Parker, 1535–1575*, ed. by John Bruce (Cambridge: Cambridge University Press, 1853), p. 66.
126 See Collinson, *The Elizabethan Puritan Movement* [1967] (London: Routledge, 2020).

conservative as could be. Poor William Byrd would never be able to hear his polyphonic Masses performed in public and was repeatedly fined for recusancy, yet he lived fairly peacefully under her protection, retaining his post in the Chapel Royal.[127] Elizabeth kept candles and a silver crucifix in her private chapel, but sharply dismissed the candle-bearers of Westminster Abbey who came to meet her at the opening of her first Parliament: 'Away with these torches, we have light enough'.[128] She would have allowed them in public places and insisted on clerical robes, but her newly appointed bishops raised loud protests against popish ceremony.[129] Brutal accusations were expressed, heralding the maimed rites of Ophelia's burial by a dour clergyman who would not bow to princes:

> Her death was doubtful,
> And but that great command o'ersways the order,
> She should in ground unsanctified been lodg'd
> Till the last trumpet. For charitable prayers,
> Shards, flints, and pebbles should be thrown on her.
>
> *(Hamlet, V.i.208–12)*

Under Henry VIII, a set of royal injunctions had ordered wardens to destroy idolatrous images and extinguish all lights from churches, except those used for practical purposes. Protector Somerset went one step further by ordering the destruction of all shrines to which offerings were made or candles burned. From then on, 'there would be no more lights and images, no more pilgrimages and processions, no guild plays and no ringing for the dead, no maypoles or Masses or holy water, no birch at midsummer and no roses at Corpus Christi'.[130] Since there was no Purgatory to pray about, no hope of an intermediate place between Heaven and Hell, propitiating rites were unnecessary. Chantries, where prayers were offered for the dead, were abolished in 1545, the blessing of candles at Candlemas and three other religious ceremonies in 1548. Between the first and the second Edwardian prayer book, all links between the living and the dead were broken, Greenblatt observes: the priest no longer addressed the dead person, but those standing by his grave. 'I commend thy soul to God' was replaced by 'We therefore commit his body to the ground'.[131] Four years later, Mary restored lights in the churches. The Elizabethan settlement countered the Counter-Reformation with a statute returning more or less to the state of affairs as Edward VI had left it.

The impact of these measures, and the number of committed Protestants, were minimal, some argue, compared with the extent of popular conservatism.

---

127 Byrd was suspended for a while when suspected of complicity in the Throckmorton plot.

128 Thomas M. Lindsay, *A History of the Reformation* (New York: Scribner's, 1907), II, p. 390.

129 Rosamund Oates, 'John Jewel and the English National Church: The Dilemmas of an Erastian Reformer', *English Historical Review*, 122.498 (2007), 1083–84.

130 Ackroyd, *The Life of Thomas More*, p. 372.

131 Greenblatt, *Hamlet in Purgatory*, pp. 244–45.

But how, if Catholicism was so deeply entrenched, did the reformist authorities manage to wipe it out so rapidly? Fierce centralist control is Eamon Duffy's answer.[132] Law courts were an efficient tool of vigilance, with twice-yearly circuits of the shires. This did not prevent constant complaints that Parliament's good laws were but idly enforced.[133] In his closing speech of 1576, the Lord Keeper Bacon compares magistrates with the gardener who prepares good tools to prune superfluous branches, then leaves them in boxes: 'is it not as strang, trowe yee, to make lawes to reforme men's manners and to pruine away the ill braunches and members of the common wealth and then to lay upp those lawes in faire bookes or boxes without executeing of them?'.[134] *Richard II*'s gardeners will perform the exact lesson before their weeping queen.

'An Axe or an Acte': The Execution of Justice

> Go thou, and like an executioner,
> Cut off the heads of too fast growing sprays,
> That look too lofty in our commonwealth.
>
> *Richard II, III.iv*

Cardinal Pole had left eight bishoprics vacant when he died, on the same day as Mary. Bishop White was arrested after the queen's funeral. The most ardent Catholics of her council were dismissed, to be replaced by friends and relatives of Elizabeth, or of William Cecil, who seems to have begun work as her secretary even before her accession.[135] Like many other servants of Edward VI, Cecil had lost his position under Mary, conformed without regaining it, and returned to government at her demise. Five new peers of Protestant sympathies were created. When Parliament met, 'ther lacked no industry on the papistes syde', Foxe records, to hold fast to the established doctrine, but 'suche was the prouidence of God at that tyme, that for lacke of the other byshops, whom the Lord had taken away by death a litle before, the residue that ther wer left, could do the lesse'.[136] It appears from the pages dedicated to 'The terrible end of persecutours' that Foxe's God was kept busy at the time: 'Henry 2. the French King' who was 'sore set against the poore protestants' was 'stricken meruelously by the hand of God'.[137] The new lay peers who sat in the Upper House in March 1559 helped Providence tip a delicate balance in favour of the supremacy.

---

132 Duffy, *The Stripping of the Altars*, ch. 11.
133 8 May 1559, *Proceedings*, I, p. 50.
134 *Proceedings*, I, p. 464.
135 Read, *Mr Secretary Cecil*, p. 122.
136 Foxe, *Actes and Monuments* (1563 edition), Bk v, p. 1812 [1727].
137 In July 1559. Foxe, *Actes and Monuments*, Bk xii, marginal note, p. 2351 [2311].

From Elizabeth's second Parliament onwards, anxiety for survival of the Anglican settlement inspired repeated demands to stiffen penalties against recusants. The Act for Assurance of the Queen's Power in 1563 made it treason to refuse the oath of supremacy, raising vain protests from more than a third of the Commons, led by an Inner Temple student, Robert Atkinson:[138] those who would enforce it were the same who called Mary's bishops 'blood suckers', and 'now desire to establish that as a law which they thought then so far unlawfull'.[139] A few scapegoats were fined heavily and repeatedly, to project an impression of competent authority.[140] Actually the government was ill-equipped to act: the Court of High Commission, a hybrid of lay and Church officials created to enforce the Act of Supremacy, was impotent for large-scale problems. The only real safety was through Walsingham's and Cecil's spy system: it proved spectacularly ruthless, and victorious in the long run, unarming its fifth columnists with their 'discovery' of the Babington Plot and the impeachment of Mary, Queen of Scots as an accomplice.[141]

The act also secured the loyalty of future Commons by prescribing that every member must take the oath before he was allowed to sit in the House. Papists were also officially barred from practising in court. If Catholicism was not a complete bar to the profession, it could still hinder a career. Egerton of Lincoln's Inn, listed a recusant in 1569, made poor progress until he conformed, and then became prominent in enforcing anti-Catholic penal laws.[142] He was one of those who assisted the prosecution at Edmund Campion's trial. The presiding judge, Chief Justice Wray, was considered in his day a Catholic at heart, performing a hateful task.[143] When Wray noticed the lawyer Plowden in the crowd, he asked him to leave, and Plowden obliged. Still, the legal profession remained largely immune. Atkinson was expelled for papistry from the Inner Temple, yet he remained Recorder of Oxford, a notoriously Puritan town, to the end of his life, an instance among many of the religious ambiguities of the age. In the same period, despite his refusal to take the oath, Plowden was treasurer of the Middle Temple and had the queen for client. Catholic lawyers, who used their skills to 'walk a fine line between their consciences and their careers',[144] enjoyed a degree of tolerance which, to the more radical, amounted to laxity. On the eve of the Civil War, the poet Milton would accuse lawyers of having hindered the establishment of the

138 See the speech, misdated, by Robert Atkinson, MP for Appleby, in *Proceedings*, I, p. 96.

139 January 1563, *Proceedings*, I, pp. 96–98. Here it is Elton, *The Parliament of England*, p. 161 n. 35, who misreads Neale (*Elizabeth I and her Parliaments*, I, p. 125), accusing him of 'unsupported guesswork'.

140 MacCaffrey, *Queen Elizabeth and the Making of Policy*, pp. 141–44.

141 Douglas, '"Jesuites ghostly wayes"', pp. 41–61.

142 *Records of the Honorable Society of Lincoln's Inn*, ed. by Baildon, I, pp. 372, 381. *Acts of the Privy Council*, ed. by Dasent, VIII, p. 160.

143 Simpson, *Edmund Campion*, p. 398.

144 Jones, *The English Reformation*, p. 127.

Elizabethan Church, through 'the great Places and Offices executed by Papists, the Judges, the Lawyers, the Justices of the Peace for the most part Popish'.[145]

Historians of the Inns generally agree that they were a nest of papists, a chief destination of the Jesuit missionaries, and a community so tightly knit that all attempts to enforce conformity were deflected. This view was largely shared at the time by the Privy Councillors. Parmiter's close study of recusancy shows that the government's suspicions were justified, yet the Inns were treated with extraordinary leniency.[146] Why? The usual answer is that the Privy Council were baffled by the lack of cooperation from the Inns' governors, that the professional solidarity and the old tradition of liberties were stronger than religious feelings. As Jessica Winston puts it, 'one's identity as an inns-of-court man could override other differences'.[147] To O'Sullivan, 'the coercion of conscience was repugnant to the genius of the Common Law'.[148] This attractive idea is not quite supported by the evidence. It is hard to believe that Cecil Lord Burghley or Walsingham would be so easily defeated by a bunch of old brother lawyers. The cause of their delicacy must be sought elsewhere.

What occurred in the 1580s between the court and the Inns of Court looks like a gentlemen's tacit agreement. The Elizabethan government could not afford to antagonize the legal body by harassing Inns members but made it clear to them where their best interests lay. The legal profession had no other martyrs of More's eminence. Recusants were left to work on, taking regular if slower steps up the ladder of honours. The government needed lawyers to conduct trials, draw reasons *pro et contra*, counter libellous books, and eliminate potential threats to the safety of the realm. Thomas More of Lincoln's Inn may have been an admired icon, his colleagues under Elizabeth may have had a tolerant eye for their fellow members' waywardness, yet they did not rise as a body to denounce injustice, illegal procedures, or the process of treason by words. Being but men before the almighty machine of State security, not cut out for martyrdom, they thought it wiser to keep their silence.

The Inns under Scrutiny: Norton the Scolde

A succession of anti-Catholic laws devised increasingly harsh penalties for recusants, but the Inns applied them with only tepid energy. In the 1580s, their 'liberties' covered other behaviour than unruly seasonal rituals: the goods they received from the Continent were priests, books, and subversive ideas. Their location outside the city, the nearby fields and woods, furnished convenient meeting places. The privileges granted them led the clerk of the Privy Council,

145 Milton, *Of Reformation Touching Church Discipline*, p. 15.
146 Parmiter, *Elizabethan Popish Recusancy*, pp. 19–30.
147 Winston, *Lawyers at Play*, p. 36.
148 Richard O'Sullivan, *Edmund Plowden, 1518–1585* (Cambridge: Cambridge University Press, 1952), p. 11. Parmiter, *Edmund Plowden*, pp. 42–43.

William Waad, to send 'articles' to Chief Justice Popham in June 1592, betraying his anxiety about the Inns 'wher now by the exemption they have more recusantes and badd persons harbored there then heretofore have been'.[149]

Despite their suspected papistry, the Inns were also a nursery for Parliament, with steadily rising figures of membership, from just over a quarter of all MPs in 1563 to over a third in 1584, which explains the government's interest in their doings. The Inns were equally interested in the government's politics. In October 1566, days after the opening of Parliament, a moot at Lincoln's Inn rejecting the claims of Mary Stuart led to the imprisonment of the Reader, William Thornton:[150] three of the men about to emerge as insurgent MPs, James Dalton, William Lambarde, and Robert Monson, were alumni of that Inn.[151] Law students sneaked into Commons, and debates of the bills continued in classrooms. Elizabeth herself complained 'that she hard how Parlyment matters was the common table talk at ordinaryes, which was a thing against the dignitie of the Howse'.[152] In April 1571, a bill for the burgesses was read and committed, 'the same beinge apoynted to be dyscoursed at the Temple the Saterday folowinge'.[153] The same month, two young Inner Templars who sneaked into the House were expelled.[154] In 1576, one Charles Johnson of Inner Temple was found out 'having sit in the parliament howse one houer and a halfe being none of the same'. Here the Recorder recalls precedents under Richard II and Henry VI when all acts had to be revoked, because 'others besides those of the Howse had ioyned in the making of the lawes'.[155]

Among the Inns members, many complained of laxity in enforcing government instructions. Norton was constantly pressing for stricter measures, asking for a new oath, not just of allegiance but of religious conformity, to be sworn by all officials serving the City 'in function of law'. He devised an elaborate system of vigil to purge the educational system from 'lurking' papists: butlers of respective Inns were to take the names of all the absentees at church, while benchers must advance none to the bar, bench, or other place of preferment but those known to be sound in religion. Even when jailed in the Tower, he kept suggesting measures to improve universities, public schools, Inns of Court and Chancery. 'Norton the scolde', as he was labelled in the *Pasquil*, rode his hobby horses to the end, Graves notes: 'He did not evolve, mellow or shift his priorities with advancing age, and the cast of his life's drama were theatrical stereotypes', his perpetual heroine and heroes, the queen and her councillors, versus villains, 'papistical traitors' all.[156]

---

149 Lansd. MS 72, no. 41, at fol. 118^{v}, quoted in Parmiter, *Elizabethan Popish Recusancy*, p. 30.

150 Cecil, *A Collection of State Papers*, ed. by Haynes and Murdin, II, p. 762. Baker, *Readers and Readings*, p. 126.

151 Levine, *The Early Elizabethan Succession Question*, p. 170.

152 *Annymous Journal*, March 1585, *Proceedings*, II, p. 118.

153 Hooker's Journal, *Proceedings*, I, p. 247.

154 5 April 1571, Thomas Clarke and Anthony Bull, *Proceedings*, I, pp. 200, 478.

155 13 February 1576, *Proceedings*, I, p. 478.

156 Graves, *Thomas Norton*, p. 61.

When missionary priests arrived from Douai, Burghley advised Walsingham to enlist the energetic lawyer among those appointed to examine them.[157] Norton was also employed as licenser of the press, to give or withhold the *imprimatur*. This task involved him in searches to hunt down seditious books or incriminating papers.

To Greg Walker, Norton was never the incendiary Puritan portrayed by Neale, just one strongly committed to the Protestant cause, while unfailingly upholding the queen's supremacy.[158] Incendiary he sounds, though, judging by his virulent speeches in Parliament. His first personal contact with tragedy had come early in his career, when he served as Somerset's secretary and witnessed what he described to Calvin as a great man's fall 'from the pinnacle of prosperity'.[159] The next was the death at the stake of his father-in-law, Cranmer. He had further opportunity to study the theme when Walsingham commissioned him to write a summary of English political history since 1066, with special stress on the consequences of rebellions in each prince's time. The first phase of Norton's grand design led to the division under Gorboduc; the last showed the forces of his good queen and the true faith fighting the powers of darkness. The rise of the Welsh house of Tudor, retraced with strong lyrical accents, shows a fine mixture of British stock and Jacob's seed 'from whence such a rosse is descendid. Manie a marche Leeke may she weare and many a Christmas harpe may sounde to hir prayse and every true manes harte say Amen'.[160] Captain Fluellen would hardly do better.

Norton's second nickname, 'the rack-master', was earned through less innocuous enthusiasm by his examinations of priests. The co-author of *Gorboduc* did not believe that the 'sweet violence' of tragedy so praised by Sidney would suffice to clean ulcers in the body politic: his fear of Catholic infiltration drew him to recommend all the weapons of dictatorial regimes, including torture.[161] Though forbidden by common law, as Fortescue had proudly stressed,[162] torture often served when needed. The notorious pursuivant Richard Topcliffe, who had a torture chamber installed in his living quarters at Bridewell, worked under the direction of the queen's Privy Council.[163] Elizabeth openly claimed her royal prerogative to use torture for the safety of the realm, upon warrant from her

157 Graves, *Thomas Norton*, p. 249. See Parsons's account of 'Norton the Rackemaister' in *An Epistle on the Persecution of Catholickes in Englande* (Douai, *c.* 1582).

158 Walker, *The Politics of Performance*, p. 198.

159 In a letter to Calvin, who had inquired about Somerset's fate in 1552, *Original Letters*, ed. by Robinson, I, p. 339.

160 'Norton of the v periodes of 500 yeares', quoted in Graves, *Thomas Norton*, p. 227.

161 As in the case of John Felton, for circulating bulls, *Cobbett's State Trials*, pp. 1085–88.

162 Fortescue, *In Praise of the Laws of England*, ch. 21, accuses John Tiptoft, then constable of the Tower, of having introduced 'the law of Padua', meaning illegal torture, in the realm.

163 On his activities, see Dympna Callaghan and Chris R. Kyle, 'The Wilde Side of Justice in Early Modern England and *Titus Andronicus*', in *The Law in Shakespeare*, ed. by Jordan and Cunningham, pp. 38–57.

Privy Council, while several of her legal counsel, including Edward Coke and Francis Bacon, were involved in the torture of suspected traitors.[164] The Ridolfi plot to invade England, spurred by the pope's bull *Regnans in Excelsis,* seemed justification enough for extreme measures. Its collapse led to a severe military repression in the north. On a list of seven hundred conspirators, only those prisoners who took the oath of supremacy saved their lives. Yet Cecil complained that the Catholic sympathies of judges and lawyers in civil and common law were matters of 'evident knolledg'.[165]

In the aftermath of the bull, Parliament's first concern was not the general purge Norton desired, but the pretenders to the crown who were openly encouraged by the pope's invitation to depose Elizabeth, ushering in the next tragic show of the reign. Buchanan had argued for the right of a people to depose an evil tyrant, even kill him if need be, though he did not recommend it: 'non ad rem suspiciendam exhortor'.[166] In the 1571 debates over the new Treason Act, Norton urged the right of Parliament to settle the succession, and bar any claim from Mary Stuart — again urging the remedies *Gorboduc* had spelt out a decade earlier. The following year, Norton came forward again with a great speech, recorded in the diaries of both Houses, arguing that Norfolk must be executed, as should be Mary Stuart. A committee of the two Houses then proceeded with him to set down reasons moving the conscience to act thus, while 'the civilians drewe reasons pro et contra'.[167] The duke being very popular, his trial was carefully organized, and public opinion well ploughed. The whole sequence reads like a blueprint for the dispatch of Hastings in *Richard III*: the Lord Mayor with a select group of aldermen were summoned to the Star Chamber, where the councillors informed them of great treasons against the queen and government, and went on to the Guildhall, along with a great multitude of citizens, where they were treated to an oration by the recorder Fleetwood. Norfolk was executed in June. In a dying speech he confessed his faults, denied being a papist, and expressed his gratefulness to the sovereign, with hopes she would be good to his orphans.[168] The hopes no doubt explain the confession.

In the same session, Parliament attempted to reduce religious laxity in all sensitive areas, including the Inns, which were repeatedly denounced for harbouring papists. The bishops had proposed a bill on the authority to compel attendance at church.[169] It was vetoed by the queen, but the bishops kept a suspicious eye on the Inns: weeks later, Archbishop Parker complained to Cecil that the Inns 'do now of late grow again very disordered in over bold speeches and doings

---

164 See Heath, *Torture and English Law*, pp. 119–20, 134. Guy, *Tudor England*, p. 318, records fifty-three cases of legal torture under Elizabeth.

165 In a 1569 memorandum headed 'Perills' by Cecil, in Parmiter, *Elizabethan Popish Recusancy*, p. 3.

166 Buchanan, *De jure regni apud Scotos, dialogus*, in *Rerum Scoticarum Historia* (Aberdeen: Chalmers, 1762), § 88, p. 46.

167 *Proceedings*, I, pp. 331–32.

168 *Proceedings*, I, p. 312. *Richard III*, III.v–vi.

169 Elton, *The Parliament of England*, pp. 200–206.

touching religion'.[170] Matters came to a head with the arrival of the first missionary priests from Douai in 1574. In 1577 the government launched a national census, ordering the bishops to make lists of recusants in their dioceses, with the value of their lands and goods. Similar instructions were given to the vice-chancellors of Oxford and Cambridge. A month later, the council realized they had omitted the Inns — visibly not their main concern — and required Lord Keeper Bacon and Lord Chief Justice Wray to inquire of religious conformity in every Inn of Court or Chancery, for they were thought 'greatlie infected with poperie'. The inquiry cannot have been very thorough: the time allowed was too short for any rigorous investigation, and through either that or deliberate negligence, notorious recusants were omitted. Cecil's own Inn, then reported most 'infected and corrupted', was singled out in 1585 by the Privy Council for further enquiry: a large search was made there, since 'some seminarie popish priests have bene heretofore harboured in Graies Inn' to say Mass and pervert young gentlemen.[171] Apart from this pointed search, the government took no direct hand in the affairs of the Inns after 1577, and the benchers were again left to ensure conformity as they saw fit. From the surviving records, they did little.

Bloody Questions: Campion's Brag

The earls who led the northern rebellion asked for support from Pope Pius V, but they had already fled the country when the answer came, in March 1570: the bull *Regnans in Excelsis* deposed Queen Elizabeth as a heretic and threatened excommunication for English subjects who continued to attend church services. A man from Norfolk, John Felton, collected copies of the bull in Calais, fixed one to the gates of the Bishop of London's palace, and gave one to his friend William Mellowes, of Lincoln's Inn, where the incriminating paper was discovered. Mellowes having confessed on the rack, Felton was arrested on 26 May 1570, tortured, and executed for treason in August.[172] The same year, George Buchanan wrote his *De jure regni apud Scotos*, legitimating the rebellion of Mary Stuart's subjects, who had acted in agreement with the laws of Scotland and the law of nature.

In England, the year of the national census, 1577, marks another turning point, with the trial of Cuthbert Mayne, recently ordained at Douai, who had come to catechise Cornwall. He was tried under the new Treason Act of 1571 on five counts, the first being that he had brought in a 'faculty' or *bulla* from the Roman see containing the absolution of the Queen's rebellious subjects. Though 'plain proofs were wanting', Justice Manwood admitted to the jury, there were 'strong presumptions' enough against him. Thus firmly directed, the jury pronounced

170 In a letter of June 1571, quoted by Parmiter, *Elizabethan Popish Recusancy*, p. 17.

171 PRO, SP 12/192/46, Catholic Record Society (R) 9, 166–73, in Parmiter, *Elizabethan Popish Recusancy*, p. 43.

172 *Cobbett's State Trials*, pp. 1085–88. Jardine, *A Reading on the Use of Torture*, p. 78.

Mayne guilty of high treason on all five counts, according to statutes of Elizabeth's reign, and sentenced him accordingly. One of the judges, Sir John Jeffries, not satisfied with the proceedings, referred the matter to the Privy Council. They submitted the case to the whole Bench of Judges, who inclined to Jeffries's view. Nevertheless the council ordered the execution to be carried out 'as a terror to the Papists'.[173] Mayne was the first seminary priest convicted for bringing in a 'faculty', the first of 123 priests executed under Elizabeth's reign, over half of whom were sentenced before 1590.[174] English recusants under arrest had to struggle as best they could with the 'bloody question': whether the pope had authority to depose the sovereign, and whom would they obey in case of an invasion? Many prisoners declined to answer on the grounds that it was a matter of divinity, and beyond their competence.

The English colleges abroad were only the visible part of Catholic activities on the continent. As early as 1572, William Allen was one of thirteen Englishmen who signed a petition to the new pope Gregory XIII to interest him in the pitiful state of England, stressing that if occasion arose, many who had deserted Rome would easily be moved to return.[175] As the years passed, Allen grew increasingly urgent in pressing Felipe II to launch his 'great Enterprise'. He and Robert Parsons sent several memoranda to pope and king up to March 1587, when they elected the Spanish line to the succession of the English crown and again urged the invasion.[176] Catechising the Inns does not seem to have stood high in Allen's agenda. He does write that it is of primary importance that the young men in this 'famous curriculum of English civil law' be rightly instructed, but its main interest was as a useful shelter, 'for nowhere do men lie hid more safely than in London'.[177] The government must have shared Allen's view that they were making excellent headway there, for mentions of secret meetings at the Inns are scattered throughout the papers of Cecil and the councillors.

As for the threat the Inns represented, Wilfrid Prest notes a huge gap between their public image and reality: after the 1570s papists among Inns members were never more than a small impotent minority, and the missionaries' main impact was psychological.[178] But then psychology is a decisive factor in matters of public opinion. With due respect to Prest, the 'psychological impact' of the Jesuits' mission seems huge. Robert Parsons and Edmund Campion landed in June. In mid-July, a royal proclamation was issued against traitors and the hunt began. A letter of December from the council gave instructions to make a public example of missionaries, while Norton was required to examine several of the accused.[179]

173 Butler, *Lives of the Saints*, ed. by Thomas, p. 228.

174 Allen, *A briefe Historie of the Martyrdom of* XII *reverend priests*, pp. 104–10.

175 *Letters of William Allen and Richard Barret*, ed. by Renold, p. 275.

176 Allen, *Letters and Memorials*, ed. by Knox, pp. 222–86.

177 'Allen to Father Everard Mercurian on the Conversion of England', in *Miscellanea VII*, Catholic Record Society Publications (London: Aberdeen University Press, 1911), IX, pp. 63–65.

178 Prest, *The Inns of Court*, pp. 182–86.

179 As attorney general, solicitor general, and lieutenant of the Tower. Graves, *Thomas Norton*, p. 249.

Those months marked the peak of anti-Catholic legislation in a Parliament specifically recalled for the purpose. A succession of bills and committees eventually produced the 'Act to retain the Queen's Majesty's subjects in their due obedience'. Fines against recusants were heavily upgraded and assorted with jail sentences. Harbouring priests was also made illegal.[180] The 'Act against seditious words and rumours' repealed and replaced the Marian statute of 1554–1555, now found insufficiently severe. It included 'any prophesying, calculation or other unlawful act' seeking to know how many more years Her Majesty might live. A second offence made it felony, punishable by death.

Despite numerous motions and royal proclamations, the missionaries were giving new impetus to the flood of 'corrupt and wicked books that came from beyond the sea'. On 15 March 1581, Allen informed his correspondent in Rome that 'the Fathers and Priests are doing admirable work, and write the necessary books with incredible grace and speed, and print them in London itself'. Some books printed at one Mr Brookes's house near London had 'Doway' on their title-page, but an expert like Norton was able to detect that 'the print is done in England'. He wanted to know where Parsons's were printed and aimed to rack it out of Father Briant. Campion's *Rationes decem*, ten reasons not to adhere to the Anglican Church, were printed in June 1581 near Henley, and four hundred copies found their way to every seat in Saint Mary's church, Oxford, before a graduation ceremony. This feat made Campion's capture a priority. He was caught on 15 July. A month later the council wrote to the vice-chancellor of Oxford, directing him to weed out popery from the colleges.[181]

Campion's *Challenge to the Privy Council*, soon renamed *Campion's Brag* by his enemies, was also creating a stir. It was a triple challenge, addressed to the lords of the council, to the doctors and masters of the universities, and thirdly to the lawyers spiritual and temporal, 'wherein I will justify the said faith by the common wisdom of the laws standing yet in force and practice'.[182] The 'yet in force' must have sounded ominous. Bishop Aylmer was charged by the government with the task of replying to Campion's book. A series of duelling pamphlets followed.[183] In answer to Campion's challenge, Aylmer ordered a public conference on 31 August in the chapel of the Tower. The place was full, its two sides fitted up as for a tournament. With piles of books at hand, the first team of disputants, Alexander Nowell, dean of Saint Paul's, and William Day, dean of Windsor, faced a lonely opponent. To Campion's complaint that he was unprepared, Nowell retorted that the matter of the disputation would be taken from the first page of his bragging

180 Elton, *The Parliament of England*, pp. 185–88.

181 Simpson, *Edmund Campion*, pp. 285–87, 345–47.

182 'Campion's Brag', point 5, in Simpson, *Edmund Campion*, p. 226.

183 Two confutations of *Campion's Brag*, and Parsons's retort in Robert Parsons, *Defence of the censure, gyven upon two bookes of william Charke and Meredith Hanmer mynysters, whiche they wrote against M. Edmond Campian preest* (Rouen: Fr. Parson's Press, 1582; repr. in microfilm, Ann Arbor: UMI Research Press, 1952).

book. At the second conference, Campion protested again that it was not this kind of disputation he requested, but one under equal conditions before the universities. Two more were held in September, Norton acting as notary at the last.[184] Campion was indicted, not for heresy but for having conspired to raise a sedition in the realm and dethrone the queen. On 1 December he was executed at Tyburn with two fellow priests, Sherwin and Briant.

With Campion's death, a fresh batch of books denounced this act of tyranny. Only one of those, William Allen's *A briefe Historie of the Martyrdom of xii reverend priests* (1582), dealt with the trials from the legal point of view, probably because few exiles came from the Inns of Court. Most of them were Oxford men.[185] Allen, a leading figure of the Counter-Reformation, persisted with *An Admonition to the Nobility and People of England and Ireland* (1588) to justify the planned invasion of England by the Spanish Armada. His three major reasons why the queen lacks 'right' to the throne all have relevance to Shakespeare's *King John*, Jeffrey Knapp notes: she is an excommunicate, a bastard, and she never received the pope's approbation. Yet John's stirring defence of royal supremacy in the play does not exonerate him, for no one denies Arthur is the rightful heir, the international candidate who correlates legitimacy and Christian charity.[186] Knapp could have pursued his parallel further by casting Mary Stuart in the part of rightful heir and international candidate, two points hotly discussed then in Parliament and Inns moots.

Cecil was alerted by William Parry, writing from Venice in March 1583, to the fact that persecutions of Catholics caused much talk on the continent and did great damage to England's reputation.[187] Norton's boast that he had stretched Briant a foot longer than God had made him was also a byword, of which he complained bitterly.[188] Such was the weight of public opinion that master and servant felt compelled to react. Cecil's uncouth *Execution of Justice in England* appeared in December 1583, and Norton's *Declaration of the fauourable dealing of her Maiesties Commissioners appointed for the Examination of certaine Traitours and of tortures unjustly reported to be done upon them for matters of religion* was appended to its second edition the following January. Translations of both works in Latin, French, Italian, Dutch, appeared that year, some of them printed in London.[189]

---

184 *A true report of the disputation or rather private conference had in the Tower of London with Ed. Campion Jesuite, the last of August 1581* (London: C. Barker, 1583).

185 Clancy, *Papist Pamphleteers*, p. 119.

186 Knapp, *Shakespeare's Tribe*, pp. 95–98, never mentions Mary Stuart. His point is to disprove a nationalist reading of John's schism.

187 British Library, Lansdowne MS, vol. XXXVII, no. 32, in Clancy, *Papist Pamphleteers*, p. 130.

188 PRO, SP 12/152/72. The story of his boast, told by Parsons in the *Defence of the censure*, is acknowledged by Norton in a letter to Walsingham, Simpson, *Edmund Campion*, p. 286.

189 *Iustitia Britannica: per quam liquet perspicue, aliquot in eo regno perditos ciues [...]* (Londini: excudebat Thomas Vautroullerius, 1584); *L'execution de iustice faicte en Angleterre [...]* Descrite premierement en Anglois, puis traduite en langue Françoise, en faueur de autres nations & personnes, qui ont

Cecil's *Execution of Justice* claims that the proceedings were perfectly lawful, for the missionaries were advance agents on a military errand: they had justly suffered death, not by any new laws as slanderous libellers would have it appear, but 'namely by the laws of Parliament made in King Edward the Third's time'.[190] Since the pope took the sword by stirring Her Majesty's subjects to rebellion, she used her lawful authority to subdue and punish rebels, as any prince would.[191] Those who used mere words, 'your unarmed scholars and priests' were as guilty as any other malefactors, guilty of thought crime: 'their titles nor their apparel hath made them traitors, but their traitorous secret motions and practices; their persons have not made the war, but their directions and counsels have set up the rebellions'. Six questions have been put to them, apt to try the truth or falsehood of seditious persons, that 'these lewd unarmed traitors, I say, would nowhise answer directly hereto'. Their mission was to pour poison and to bring names, powers, and dwellings into a muster roll to aid a foreign invasion. 'Those actions, not their cakes of wax or relics have made them traitors.'[192]

Norton's *Declaration* completes this fine piece of eloquence by stating that torture was applied very gently and only to those who would not give plain answers: Campion 'was never so racked but that he was presently able to walk and to write'. And Briant was not starved, as slanderous reports claim; he refused to ask for food in writing as he was told. No prisoner was put to the rack 'but where it was first known and evidently probable by former detections, confessions and otherwise that the party so racked or tortured was guilty and did know and could deliver truth of the things wherewith he was charged'.[193] Admittedly, his fellow Templar Francis Throckmorton was racked, 'and somewhat pinched, although not much: for at the end of three daies following, he had recovered himselfe'. It was his last flourish, as a priest would joyfully report to the rector of the English College in Rome: 'Finally Norton himself, who in the Tower had afflicted so many with the tortures of the rack, came to die and endure the tortures of hell.'[194]

So far, the Privy Council had acted on reliable information but little or no evidence, which made their plea of legality dubious. Campion had committed no treasonable offence. No impartial judge would have found the priests guilty, since a charge as potential traitor had little standing in English courts.[195] The government's difficulty, which Allen seizes upon, was to find a link between faith and political treason. Cuthbert Mayne's case, back in 1577, or even earlier, Thomas

---

l'vsage d'icelle (Vautroullier, 1584); *Atto della Giustitia d'Inghilterra [...]* (London: Appresso G. Wolfio, 1584); *D'executie van Iustitie totñ christelicke vrede in Engelandt ghedaens [...]* (Middelburgh: R. Schilders, 1584).... On the revisions of these episodes in Holinshed's 1587 'Continuation' of the *Chronicles*, and their European legacy, see Kilroy, *Edmund Campion*, pp. 375–85.

190 25 Edw. III, st. 5, c. 2, 1351.

191 Cecil, *The Execution of Justice*, ed. by Kingdon, pp. 30, 33.

192 Cecil, *The Execution of Justice*, pp. 36–39.

193 Norton, *Declaration*, in *The Execution of Justice*, pp. 46, 48.

194 Barret to Alfonso Agazzari, 16 April 1584, *Letters of William Allen and Richard Barret*, p. 93.

195 Cecil, *The Execution of Justice*, Introduction, p. xxxi.

More's were two instances of illegal proceedings. In both cases, the authorities had trouble framing the indictment and used false witnesses. More was convicted by a law passed but months before his execution, the Treason Act of 1535 (27 Hen. 8. c. 2). In Mayne's case, a recent statute (13 Eliz.I, c. 2) made it high treason to bring from Rome pictures or writings of any kind, even a traveller's letter of credit. How could bringing in a bull from Rome be treason in the days of Edward III, Allen asks in *A True, Sincere, and Modest Defence of English Catholics That Suffer for their Faith both at Home and Abroad; against a False, Seditious, and Slanderous Libel.* Despite Cecil's claims, the Marian executions were perfectly legal; they applied old laws of the realm and of all Christendom, which Elizabeth's first Parliament has repealed: 'Therefore you can neither adjudge of our doctrine as of heresy nor of us as of heretics. Nor have you any law left whereby to execute us.'[196]

There was no denying the strength of Allen's point. Thanks to Walsingham's spies, Cecil knew that some papist plot was underfoot but had no evidence that could be produced in court till after Campion's death. Then in September 1584, a Scottish Jesuit, William Creighton, was captured, failed to swallow the plan of the 'English enterprise' he was carrying, and confessed.[197] At long last the Council now possessed some hard proof of treasonous plots, enough to take the next step, the trial of Mary Stuart that Norton had so persistently urged, though he did not live to see the success of his crusade.

Killing the Queen: 'It Lawfully Maie Be Done'

Not all the water in the rough rude sea
Can wash the balm off from an anointed king.

Richard II, III.ii

The government's need to show a clean front dominated proceedings up to and after the death of Mary Stuart. All in the cast, the two queens foremost, were acutely aware that they stood on the world's stage. The theatrical element, enhanced by the halo surrounding royal persons, stands out vividly and governs its other dominant feature, the will to observe the terms of the law. Even Henry VIII, the *radix peccati* as Allen calls him, had always claimed to respect the authority of common law. Like Henry's team, the Elizabethan think tank and Parliament explored several tracks before they took the awful step of cutting an anointed head. First Mary was to be judged and condemned for her crimes, adultery and murder. The inquiry set up to decide whether she should be tried for contriving the death of her second husband, Darnley, had rendered a conclusion of not proven: the authenticity of the notorious casket letters meant to incriminate her is

---

196 Allen, *Defence of English Catholics* in Cecil, *The Execution of Justice*, p. 94.

197 On this 'ridiculous story', as historians term it, see T. G. Law, 'Father William Crichton, S. J.', *English Historical Review*, 8.32 (1893), 697–703. Allen, *Letters and Memorials*, pp. 425, 432.

still strongly questioned.[198] The next was to bar her from the succession: though next of blood to Her Majesty, Mary is a stranger, Sadler argues, and 'the nature of English men hath alwaies so moche detested the regiment of straungiers that they have made lawes to barre all tytles which any straungier may clayme of inheritaunce within the realme'.[199] These objections would be raised again by vehement Commons, when her son James I's attempt to unite his two realms would cause renewed anxieties over national identity and inheritance (see below, Chapter 9).

Mary Stuart appeared to many doubly alien, part Scot and more than half French, supported by the hated de Guise family. In 1566 the moot at Lincoln's Inn had rejected her claims on the grounds that she was a foreigner.[200] At that point, Edmund Plowden was approached for a learned opinion and wrote a treatise developing his doctrine of the King's two bodies.[201] In his argument it is their conjunction that produces the special qualities of kingship. Any disability of the natural body is removed once it is conjoined to the body politic.[202] The obverse suggests that the natural body is of itself powerless, a division of person and dignity to be exposed with tears by Shakespeare's Richard II. The common law rule against alien inheritance, for one, has no application to the crown, which is passed by succession, not by inheritance or descent, Plowden goes on, although the successor is in general determined by proximity of blood: this is applicable wherever the next of blood was born, any foreign country 'out of the lineage of England', which Scotland is not. The Queen of Scots could not be regarded as an alien. A while later Plowden went further with 'A briffe Declaracion of the invaliditie of the last will of the late kyng of famous memory king Henry the viijth': as the law then stood, Henry had no power to dispose of the crown; it was Parliament that empowered him to do so.[203] If Henry's will were followed, the kingdom would have been 'gayned by estoppel, and not by truth'.[204] Estoppel, a principle derived from French law, 'non concedit venire contra factum proprium', forbade self-contradiction.

Requests for the head of the Scottish queen came fast and early. Two bills were devised in the Parliament summoned in May 1572 after the Ridolfi plot, one for the execution of Mary as a traitor, the other to bar her from the succession.

198 They were part of the dossier Buchanan sent to Cecil in June 1568, *A Detection of the doings of Marie Queen of Scots, touching the murder of her husband, and her conspiracy, and pretended marriage [...]*, Guy, *Queen of Scots*, pp. 386–419, 453.

199 *Proceedings*, I, pp. 87, 89. The speech, undated, is included by Hartley in the debates of 1563.

200 Cecil, *A Collection of State Papers*, II, p. 762.

201 Plowden, 'A Treatise on Mary, Queen of Scots, 1566', in *Early Modern Catholicism*, ed. by Miola, pp. 55–57.

202 Plowden, 'Case of the Duchy of Lancaster at Serjeant's Inn', Michaelmas Term, 4 Eliz., in *The Commentaries, or Reports*, pt II, pp. 212–13. See Parmiter, *Edmund Plowden*, pp. 76–78.

203 See Axton, 'The Influence of Edmund Plowden's Succession Treatise'. Both *Treatise* and *Tract* are in the same manuscript, quoted in Parmiter, *Edmund Plowden*, pp. 90–92.

204 Plowden's treatise on the succession, BL, Harley MS 849.

The first one won near unanimous support. On 12 November a petition of both Lords and Commons argued that her death was permissible and even required in justice. The joint committee had agreed on a division of labour: the bishops were to deal with reasons of conscience, the laymen with reasons of polity, the lawyers with the legal pros and cons.[205] Three separate journals have survived, which together conjure up a vivid picture of the arguments. To Norton, 'Though many heades be ill, yet it is good to cut them of so fast as maie be.'[206] In war an enemy prince may be killed by a commoner: 'If a king invade this realme the meanest souldier by lawe of armes may kill him: why not in cause of iustice?' Let them remember 'the battell of Agincourte' where 'uppon a new assault in case of necessitie, and for avoiding a greater daunger, by commaundement the prisoners were killed'.[207] Unlike Shakespeare's squeamish modern audiences, the Commons visibly approve Henry V's ruthlessness. In the Upper House, the good bishops insist that leniency would be criminal. They find six sound reasons, and many biblical precedents, to eliminate the Scottish queen. If in Deuteronomy God willed his magistrates to spare neither brother nor sister, son, daughter, wife, or friend who sought to seduce his people from true worship, 'how muche lesse is an ennemye, a traytor and an adulterer to be spared'.[208] The Commons are more rhapsodical still, and freer with pagan references: let not Her Majesty's ears be charmed by the sirens' poisoned sounds of mercy.[209] Norton clamours that 'the execution of the Scottish Queen is of necessitie', and promises that 'it lawfully maie be done'.[210]

Paul Wentworth neatly sums up the dilemma with his question, 'whither wee should call for an axe or an acte'. In Norton's dramatic terms, peril is at hand: 'The Scottish Queen, which is termed the sonne risinge, is but a comet, which doth pronosticate the overthrowe of this realme.' Thomas Hussey of the Middle Temple recalls the contention of York and Lancaster, 'betweene two kings as this is betweene two queenes'. Once he was named heir apparent, York could not wait to seize the crown. Such will be 'the sequell of the Queene of Scots'. Snagge insists: 'Henry the iiijth thought himselfe never in safety while Richard the Second had his head upon his shoulders.'[211] Norton, paving the way to the stage Richard, evokes 'the fear that is conceaved of twoe sonnes in one fyrmament, and of the one riseng and the other setteng',[212] a fear vividly recalled on stage when two claimants for the crown waving white and red roses propose to tear England apart.

205 *Proceedings*, I, pp. 331–32, 342, 364.
206 *Proceedings*, I, p. 325. *Richard II*, III.iv. On factional lines, see Adams, *Leicester and the Court*, ch. 5.
207 *Proceedings*, I, p. 353.
208 26 ? May 1572, *Proceedings*, I, pp. 277, 280, 282. Cottret, *Histoire de l'Angleterre*, p. 225.
209 *Proceedings*, I, pp. 294, 376.
210 15 May 1572, *Proceedings*, I, p. 326.
211 *Proceedings*, I, pp. 376, 325, 374, 375.
212 17 November 1586, *Proceedings*, II, p. 264. *Richard II*, IV.i.262–64.

A tense *pro et contra* argument follows. Arthur Hall pleads for leniency, warning them they may yet have to kiss Mary's feet one day, but is scarcely heard.[213] The other lonely voice for the defence is Francis Alford's, a civil lawyer, who deals with the trickiest point, 'Her I take to be a queene still *in esse*, although she be deposed by her subiectes: a queene I meane in England, not of England'. She is as vile a creature as ever was on earth, yet it cannot stand with the honour of England, 'for the avoyding of forreine slaunder, either to condemne her unheard or to towche her in life for that she never knewe of'.[214] His opponents fire back. In England, Mary is but a private person and will be treated as such in the highest place of judgement in the realm.[215] She is no longer a queen by her own fault. Even if she were of equal rank, treason submitted her to Her Majesty's jurisdiction. Both Houses have already agreed in their petition that law is powerless against such peril, for 'desperation feareth no laws'.[216] Many who would not risk anything for mean matters will adventure deep for a kingdom. Anyone lending her support must be punished by death. At this point the fate of Norfolk is sealed. Since Her Majesty will not deal with their first bill 'against the monstrous and huge dragon, and masse of the earth, the Queene of Skottes', conscience urges them to move 'the execution of the roaring lion, I meane the Duke of Norfolk'.[217] Peter Wentworth, Snagge, Norton, and others of the budding 'choir' all move the House for a petition to have him executed. To make assurance doubly sure against mutability, a final clause in the bill promises those who have spoken or acted against Mary that they will not be called to account, should she ever succeed to the throne.[218] The bill to remove Mary from the succession was passed by Commons on 24 June without any dissenting voice, and two days later by the Lords.

Norton had wanted an addition to the bill for preservation of the Queen's Majesty, stipulating that whoever has or will claim Elizabeth's crown must be declared a traitor, and barred from the succession, for once entered, ambition will never be satisfied. Not all agreed that reference to past faults was acceptable in law, yet felt it justified, for plotting treason begins long before the act: 'such a mischeefe as to overthrow a crowne is not in a day compassed', therefore 'what hereafter is thought or ment to bee executed is already begone, compassed and devised'.[219] The thought travelled on. When discussion of the bill against Mary was resumed in June after the duke's beheading, the Recorder Fleetwood declared himself 'amazed' with a sentence of Tully: 'Yf breach of lawes a man should

---

213 15 May 1572, *Proceedings*, I, p. 273.
214 *Proceedings*, I, p. 316.
215 *Proceedings*, I, p. 335.
216 Text of the petition in BL, Cotton MS Titus F. I, fols 172–86, in Neale, *Elizabeth I and her Parliaments*, I, pp. 269–73.
217 *Proceedings*, I, p. 312.
218 The Commons' amendments to the Lords' bill are quoted by Neale, *Elizabeth I and her Parliaments*, I, pp. 282–83.
219 April 1571, *Proceedings*, I, p. 214.

undertake, then breake them boldly for kingdome's sake. Causes of kingdomes cannot be pleaded by way of estopell.'[220] This was a direct quote from Nicholas Grimald's 1556 translation of *De officiis*, where Cicero observes that Caesar

> had alwaies in his mouthe Euripides greke verses of the Phenissians: which I will expresse, as well as I can: perchaunce without their grace, but yet so as the meaning may be conceiued.
>
> If breach of lawes, a man shall vndertake:
> He must them boldely breake, for kingdoms sake:
> In eche thing els, looke you regarde the right.
>
> Hainous was that Eteocles, or rather Euripides: who excepted only this, which was most detestable.[221]

If anyone calls this an honest ambition he must be mad, Cicero goes on, 'for he alloweth the ouerthrow of law, and libertie', treating both law and liberty as one common aspiration of the Roman people.[222] In Gascoigne and Kinwelmarsh's Englishing of *Phoenissae* (see below, Chapter 8), a shameless Eteocles declares that

> If lawe of right may any way be broke,
> 'Desire of rule within a climbing brest
> To breake a vow may beare the buckler best.'
>
> (*Jocasta*, II.i.391–93)

'For a kingdom any law may be broken', Tilley's aphorism went. The same creed is voiced by Edward in *Henry VI* when he urges his father York to seize the crown: 'I would break a thousand oaths to reign one year'.[223]

Upstaging the Execution: 'Ye Make Laws at your Pleasure'

> They love not poison that do poison need,
> Nor do I thee; though I did wish him dead,
> I hate the murderer.
>
> *Richard II*, V.vi

New evidence concerning Mary Stuart has recently emerged from various archive collections of the Bibliothèque nationale de France: fifty-four letters in cipher written from 1578 to 1584 by Mary to the French ambassador in London, Michel de Castelnau, via her 'voye secrette', a confidential channel of correspondence

220 9 June 1572, *Proceedings*, I, p. 398.
221 Cicero, *Thre Bokes of Duties*, ed. by O'Gorman, Bk III, XXI, 1140–49, p. 176.
222 Cicero, *Thre Bokes of Duties*, XXI, 1151, p. 176.
223 Tilley, *Dictionary of the Proverbs in England*, K90. 3 *Henry VI*, I.ii.16–17.

alongside 'la voye de Walsingham', the official one. They confirm that she hoped to be re-established to the Scottish throne with her son, detected bad faith in the negotiations with the Privy Council, and paid close attention to their triangular diplomatic games and to the Anjou marriage project. The discovery of the Throckmorton plot made her suspect that a spy at Castlenau's embassy was leaking information to Walsingham and deplore the arrest of Francis Throckmorton, who was a trusted courier under the alias of 'Sieur de la Tour'.[224]

In the midst of momentous debates over Mary's fate, on 11 June, 1572, both Houses adjourned to make room for the ratification of the Treaty of Blois uniting France and England against Spain and the reception of the French ambassador Montmorency who brought Duke François' offer of marriage to Elizabeth. Two months later, the Saint Bartholomew massacre ended any hopes of a joyous conclusion to their idyll. The next years saw the outbreak of the Dutch rebellion against Spain and the diplomatic exchanges with its leader, Willem of Orange. François joined the Protestant rebels and was named Protector of the liberties of the United Provinces, despite his unpopularity with the Dutch. In 1578, the marriage negotiations were revived. Walsingham was opposed to a union with a Catholic, now heir to the French crown, but Mary, who had hoped it would convert Elizabeth to Catholicism, actively supported it. In the correspondence unearthed at the BnF, she repeatedly warns Castelnau of the factions at work against the Anjou marriage, asking him to inform the queen of their doings.[225] After Anjou's failed attack on Antwerp, which inspired parallels with the Saint Bartholomew massacre, Elizabeth ended their engagement, was again offered the crown of the Netherlands, and again refused it. The murder of Willem in July 1584 added more urgency still to the search for a suitable heir to the English crown. Suitable, that is, Protestant and designated by Parliament. In October, Cecil and Walsingham drew up a Bond of Association designed to ensure it, in sheer disregard of hereditary rights.[226] Members of this covenant swore to defend Elizabeth and, should she come to harm, spare no pretended successor for whom the attempt was made, nor his heirs. Not only a license to kill, Guy notes, but to kill any innocent beneficiary on suspicion of intent.[227] When required to put Mary on trial, Elizabeth let it be understood that she would prefer the association to fulfil their promise, but no Piers Exton rose to execute her undeclared wish.

Anthony Babington, of Lincoln's Inn, had abandoned the bar to join a circle dedicated to the protection of Jesuits. Walsingham, who was informed of his every move, used him to implicate the Scottish queen in a plot to murder Elizabeth.

---

224 George Lasry, Norbert Biermann, and Satoshi Tomokiyo, 'Deciphering Mary Stuart's Lost Letters from 1578–1584', *Cryptologia*, 47.2 (2023), 101–202, report the methods used to decipher them and their content.

225 François, Duke of Alençon, became Duke of Anjou and was received as Monsieur at the French court after the accession to the throne of his elder brother Henri III.

226 Text of the Association Bond in *Cobbett's State Trials*, I, pp. 1161–62.

227 Guy, *Queen of Scots*, pp. 460–61.

In a letter of July 1586, Babington informed Mary of the plan for her delivery, which she approved in her reply, though leaving the matter of the assassination to his own judgement. Once the plot had properly thickened, young Babington and his associates were caught. The first seven, including him, were drawn and quartered in Lincoln's Inn fields. The barbarity of the demonstration, no doubt designed to warn off young law aspirants, was such that even the well-seasoned Londoners protested, and the queen ordered the remaining culprits be properly hanged before their disembowelment. A meeting of the Star Chamber having ruled that Mary must be tried to answer charges, a Commission of the Council travelled to Fotheringay Castle.

Mary first denied the court's competence to try a queen. Let her enemies be warned that 'the theatre of the whole world is wider than the kingdom of England'.[228] Although she was ready to answer before a free and open Parliament, this meeting was but 'to give some shew and color of a just and legal proceeding'. Her cousin's letters made it plain that she was 'already fore-judged to be guilty of the crime'. A selection of commissioners learned in civil and canon law threatened to proceed in her absence: 'Ye make laws at your pleasure', she accused them, laws to which she need not submit, as in the past the English had refused to submit to the Law Salique.[229] At her trial, on 14–15 October, Mary pleaded the right of a prisoner to seek liberty and her wish to support the Catholic cause, but denied any attempt against Elizabeth. She claimed that the casket letters were forgeries, accusing Walsingham of treachery. He protested that his mind was free from all malice: as a private person he had done nothing dishonest and as a public one nothing 'unworthy my place',[230] a fine Machiavellian distinction bordering on reason of State.[231] The assembly was prorogued to 25 October at the Star Chamber.

A document of 17 November 1586, 'Considerations for Queen's Safety', points out that when Roman emperors suspected treachery, for better safety of the empire *designabant sucessorem*, one whom they joined in government with them.[232] This, Elizabeth had begun to do with veiled promises to James VI that he would inherit if he abstain from interfering with his mother's trial. In the Parliament summoned for mid-October, the demands for Mary's head were forcefully rehearsed. To Job Throckmorton, mercy is fine until it may bring justice in contempt and commonwealth in danger. See the results of the queen's leniency in 1572, when she vetoed their bill.[233] Mercy to Mary would be death to thousands of Her Majesty's loving subjects, the Speaker argues, rushing through his table of affinities: she is only a remote cousin, 'But we be sonnes and children of this land,

228 See for instance the detailed report in *Cobbett's State Trials*, I, no. 64, pp. 1161–1228.
229 *Cobbett's State Trials*, I, pp. 1169–72.
230 *Cobbett's State Trials*, I, pp. 1171, 1182.
231 See J. H. Pollen, *Mary Queen of Scots* (Edinburgh: Scottish History Society, 1922), pp. 18–46.
232 *Proceedings*, II, pp. 264–65.
233 Throckmorton's speech against Mary, *Proceedings*, II, p. 230.

wherof you be not onlye the naturall mother but also, the weddyd spouse.'[234] The Chancellor of the Exchequer Mildmay reminds MPs of the threats to property they suffered under Mary Tudor. The invaders would give all to foreigners. Let rebellious Catholics remember 'that ambitious princes do love the treason, but not the traytor'.[235]

The queen's answer denies any wish to trap her cousin, adding a pastoral note to her oration, as would the stage Henry VI in witnessing the destruction of his realm: if only they had been as two milk maids, with pails under their arms, with no more dependency upon them! She entrusted the proceedings to the greatest men in the country, though she might as justly have tried her by ancient laws: 'But yow lawiers are so nice and so precise in sifting and scanning every word and letter, that many times yow stand more upon forme then matter, upon syllabs then the sense of the lawe.' She does not want it said that she consented to have the executioner's hand imbrued in the blood of her kinswoman, however guilty. As to their petition for speedy justice, it is not her way to give speedy answers without due consideration, 'for wee princes I tell you are set on stages, in the sight and veiw of al the worlde duly observed. Th'eyes of many behold our actions, a spott is sone spied in our garments, a blemish quickly noted in our doinges'.[236]

The theatrical import of the show was in the minds of all concerned. Mary Stuart 'was determined to turn her execution into a stage for her vindication as martyr to the Roman Catholic Church'.[237] Elizabeth was equally determined to make it a sad accident. Her unlucky secretary, Davison, was accused of having misinterpreted her order. In Camden's report, this good and simple man

> was brought upon the Court stage, of purpose (as most men thought) to act for a time this person in this tragedy; and soone after, this person being taken away, as if hee had failed in the last acte, hee was thrust downe from the stage and, not without pitty of many, shutt up a long time in prison.[238]

Elizabeth's reluctance was well founded: an official execution under the terms of the Act for the Queen's Safety would justify regicide as a legal precedent and abandon to Parliament part of the royal prerogative. Her warrant was an invitation to dispatch Mary, of the *nolite timere bonum est* type that killed Edward II, not a royal command for a public execution. But neither Robert Beale who delivered the order to Fotheringay nor the recipient, Paulet, would comply: 'they disliked that course as dishonourable and dangerous', and thus 'thought it convenient to have it done according to law, in such sort as they might justify their doings by

---

234 'Reasons against Mary Queen of Scots', *Proceedings*, II, p. 241.
235 3 November 1586, *Proceedings*, II, p. 226.
236 *Proceedings*, II, pp. 251–52, 270. 3 *Henry VI*, II.v.21–22.
237 Lewis, *The Trial of Mary Queen of Scots*, p. 41.
238 Camden, *Annales Rerum Gestarum Angliae*, ed. by Sutton, Anno Domini 1587, § 27.

law', although 'Her Majesty would fain have had it so, alleging the Association.'[239] By choosing a public execution instead of the hoped for murder, Elizabeth's councillors gave Mary Stuart an opportunity for one last flamboyant show, advertising the sacrilege her kinswoman had so dreaded to commit. The road to popular sovereignty now stood open.

The reactions abroad were as shocked as could be expected. Opinion was well used to the violent deaths of kings: here it was the publicity and authority of the act that offended most, the arrogance of passing judgement on an anointed prince. The Armada sailed in May 1588. Copies of Pope Sixtus V's declaration renewing the excommunication and deposition of Elizabeth and Allen's rousing *Admonition* to the Catholics to execute this sentence against 'a Bastard, conceived and borne by incestuous adultery' were loaded on the ships, to be circulated after the invasion. The papal declaration guaranteed that the purpose of the enterprise was not to change laws, nor 'bereave of liberty or lively hoode any man (other then rebels and obstinate persons) or make mutation in anythinge', except what was necessary to restore the Catholic religion. All controversies arising from 'the deprivation of this woman' would be determined according to justice and Christian equity. Besides her late cruelty against the most gracious Queen of Scots, she had usurped the crown, 'contrary to the auncyent acorde made between the See Apostolike and the realme of England, upon reconciliation of the same after the death of S. *Thomas of Canterbury*', that none would be king or queen thereof without the pope's consent.[240] The controversial saint had recently resurfaced in Norton's diatribe against benefit of clergy as 'that rebell Bushopp Beckett', the holy man who could not brook to be rebuked by a temporal judge.[241]

Elizabeth's legendary reply was delivered in shining silver armour from the army camp at Tilbury. Since there is no eye-witness account of this event, one likes to imagine that some young still unknown poet wrote her speech while meditating a harangue for Britomart or Henry V. Though a weak and feeble woman, she is resolved, 'in the midst and heat of the battle, to live and die amongst you all': 'I myself will take up arms, I myself will be your general, judge, and rewarder of every one of your virtues in the field.'[242] The intended rape of the Faerie Queene and her magic realm was defeated by this cross-gendered 'band of brothers'. The Spanish fleet sank, inspiring tales of Eliza's victorious chastity, magnified by painters and poets. More prosaically, the war did not end there. The Parliaments of 1593 and 1597 are filled with denunciations of the Spanish

---

239 Beale's report of 'The Order and Manner of the Execution of Mary Queen of Scots, Feb. 8, 1587', in Guy, *Queen of Scots*, p. 481.

240 Sixtus V, *A Declaration of the Sentence and Deposition of Elizabeth* (Antwerp, 1588), <https://quod.lib.umich.edu/e/eebo/A12273.0001.001?view=toc>. Allen, *An Admonition to the nobility and people of England and Ireland.*

241 Anonymous Journal, 1572, in *Proceedings*, I, p. 224.

242 9 [19] August 1588, in Susan Frye, 'The Myth of Elizabeth at Tilbury', *Sixteenth Century Journal*, 23.1 (1992), 98. Joel Hurstfield, *Elizabeth I and the Unity of England* (New York: Macmillan, 1960), pp. 156–57, printed the speech as verse, as if written by Shakespeare.

king's and the pope's treacheries, all other sects being considered minor evils in comparison with the 'Romishe crue', their 'bloudy hands, and most cruell hartes'.[243]

In Paris, Mary's de Guise kinsmen rode the wave of resentment that followed her death to seize power, indirectly leading to the assassination of Henri III. Later searches of the Jesuit college brought to light a writing by Father Jean Guignard, who deplored that Henri de Navarre had been spared during the Saint Bartholomew massacre: had France but let blood then from the basilic vein,[244] they would not have fallen into the hot fever they were suffering now. Other hated sovereigns who deserved the same fate included Elizabeth the 'she-wolf of England'.[245] Guignard was hanged on Place de Grève for having attempted by his seditious books to establish it was permissible to kill King Henri IV.[246] The Jesuits were expelled from the realm by an order of the Parlement de Paris, but Guignard's spirit survived: after several failed attempts, Henri IV was murdered in 1610.

In England, thrift again prevailed: Buchanan's 'virulent' *Detection of the Douings of Marie*, published shortly after her abdication, was reprinted to justify Puritan rebellion against her grandson.[247] Dryden, a strong supporter of Oliver Cromwell, would be mocked for having 'praised his opening of the basilic vein'.[248] Cromwell himself, whose early biographers claimed he had trained at Lincoln's Inn,[249] came from a long line of Inns members. There is no record of him in the archives, but his son Richard, who succeeded him as Lord Protector, was registered there in 1647, two years before the execution of Charles I. Having declared war against King Charles in 1642, Parliament had him judged and executed 'in the King's name',[250] to the lasting horror of France, who would wait another century and a half to take the jump. When Louis XVI was publicly tried by the Convention nationale, a Scottish traveller attests that while the deputies voted in a house filled to capacity, pedlars sold copies of the *Procès de Charles Ier* to the crowds massed outside:

---

243 Speaker Yelverton's speech, 27 October 1597, *Proceedings*, III, p. 192.

244 A large vessel of the forearm used for blood-letting, 'royal' because long considered primordial.

245 *Chronologie novenaire de Palma Cayet* (1608), in *Nouvelle Collection des Mémoires pour servir à l'histoire de France*, ed. by J.-F. Michaud and J.-J. F. Poujoulat (Paris, 1838), XII, pp. 625–26.

246 'Extrait des Registres de Parlement', 7 janvier 1594, *Mémoires de la Ligue concernant les événements les plus remarquables depuis 1576* (Amsterdam : Arkstée &Merkus, 1758), VI, p. 236.

247 See E. J. Lewis, 'The Reputations of Mary Queen of Scots', *Études écossaises*, no. 10 (2005), 41–55.

248 Thomas Shadwell, *The Medal of John Bayes, A Satire against Folly and Knavery*, 1682.

249 The Rev. Mark Noble for one, in *Memoirs of the Protectoral House of Cromwell* (London, 1787). On the reliability of 'these poor Books', see Thomas Carlyle's scathing 'Of the Biographies of Oliver', in *Oliver Cromwell's Letters and Speeches, with Elucidations* (London: Chapman and Hall, 1850), I, ch. II, pp. 12–17.

250 Kantorowicz, *The King's Two Bodies*, p. 23. See also Rolls, *The Theory of the King's Two Bodies in the Age of Shakespeare*.

> The Trial of Charles the First of England, translated into French from the State Trials, is to be found of late on all the booksellers' tables around the hall of the Convention. An abridgment of the same is cried by the hawkers of pamphlets in the Palais Royal and the various entries to the National Assembly: the conversation is now greatly turned to that subject, and to the expected process of Lewis XVI.[251]

The verdict 'Guilty' was nearly unanimous, but the death sentence won by only a short majority. Of the regicides, about half were lawyers.

To kill or not to kill Caesar? Tyrannicide had long been a matter for *pro et contra* arguments when Shakespeare wrote *Julius Caesar*. Recent illustrations were then in everyone's mind: the murders of Henri III and Willem of Orange, the failed Babington plot. The slogan of Brutus's friends, not 'law and liberty' but 'Death or Liberty!', is hammered throughout the play, culminating when Cassius intreats Brutus to spare his valuable self and kill their oppressor instead. The conspirators all swear they would rather die than bear Caesar's rule, which is equated with slavery. But on second thought, Caesar's death would be a surer way to freedom. Tyrants are created by cowards who fear for their lives. And thus the original choice of death or liberty morphs into suicide or tyrannicide.[252]

This thought process found unexpected heirs among the initiators of the French Revolution: those who created the words 'Terreur' and 'terroriste' were a group of lawyers, looking for judicial precedents to the execution of a king. Saint-Just, for one, fully agreed with Cassius when he wrote 'to His Fellow Assemblymen': 'O God, must Brutus languish forgotten, far from Rome! My resolution is made, however. If Brutus does not kill the others he will kill himself.'[253] When threatened with the fate of Caesar,[254] Robespierre bitterly complained: 'What difference does it make that Brutus killed the tyrant? Tyranny still lives in the hearts and Rome no longer exists but in Rome.'[255] In 1812, a reviewer of Kemble's production of *Julius Caesar* would recall the execution of King Louis, when 'the assassins of France used to cover their atrocities under the name of Brutus'.[256] Because of its ambivalence, the play often did and still does serve to reflect mutability in the political arena, with Caesar and Brutus repeatedly exchanging places in the sympathies of audiences. Given the proper context, its topicality need hardly be stressed. *Julius Caesar* is often revived against a background of political

---

251 Moore, *A Journal during a residence in France*, October 31, 1792, II, p. 276.

252 Goy-Blanquet, 'Shakespeare's Unholy Martyrs'.

253 Geoffrey Bruun's translation in *Saint-Just: Apostle of Terror* (Hamden, CT: Archon Books, 1966), pp. 22–23. In his speech of 13 November 1792 he argued that all citizens have the same right over the king that Brutus had over Caesar, *Débats de la Convention nationale*, 5 vols (Paris: Baudouin Frères, 1828), I, p. 379.

254 *Papiers inédits trouvés chez Robespierre, Saint-Just, Payan, etc.: Supprimés ou omis par Courtois* (Paris: Beaudoin Frères, 1828), no. 58, p. 152.

255 Maximilien de Robespierre, Discours du 17 pluviôse an II (15 February 1794), in *Œuvres de Robespierre*, ed. by J. Vermorel (Paris: F. Cournol, 1866), p. 300.

256 *Bell's Weekly Messenger*, unsigned review, 8 March 1812, no. 831, 77.

assassination, as in answer to a common need for meditation and catharsis after the loss of a charismatic leader. Or it can operate the other way round, when hated despots are wishfully executed in the guise of Caesars made up to look like them.[257]

To Colin Burrow, the play creates 'an antiquity of ghosts, spirits, blood, pollution, sacrifices, portents and murders',[258] but is this Roman world so far removed from the Plantagenet England staged in the Henriad? More significantly, the antique setting of *Julius Caesar* provided an escape from Elizabethan theocentric monarchy and its ruling moral precepts to a world of ambivalence. Dante had consigned Brutus to the last circle of hell for his treachery. Shakespeare changed the tide of popularity when he drew on Plutarch, more favourable to Brutus than Suetonius who was the source of most contemporary Caesar plays, making him the 'ethical light' of his play.[259] Shakespeare never says if Brutus was right or wrong. He explores the depths of heroic martyrdom with impressive lucidity, ages ahead of contemporary thought on assassination. There is evidence enough of Caesar's ambition, but all proof of his potential tyranny is killed in the egg, the 'serpent's egg'. The signs given by the gods are unreadable, open to opposite interpretations. Only after the deed will the weight of public opinion, carefully manipulated, decide the proper name to give it. Brutus puts it to the mob that their act was a sacrifice, that he himself killed a beloved friend for the good of his country. By labelling the conspirators 'butchers', Antony works up the crowd to a righteous anger, and himself to the triumvirate. With Octavius he 'pricks' the 'traitors' designed for target killing, which include Cicero, wins the war, and thus the power to impose his version of the murder to be recorded for posterity. Brutus's handicap, like other idealists', is that he has no ulterior aim, ambition, or programme: the deed is its own end, since he will not accept the crowd's spontaneous offer to take Caesar's place, a tragic misunderstanding of his motives.

Brutus, before Hamlet, hoped by one clean sweep to eliminate corruption and restore the health of the body politic. Both characters begin to lose their integrity in the demands of plotting murder. Yet neither believes in the crude symmetries entertained by heroes of revenge tragedies, or by their own companions. When Cassius complains that like a Colossus, Caesar fills the world, leaving no room for any one else, he echoes the feelings of the First Tribune whose republicanism aims at general levelling, bringing the Colossus down to his petty height. But Brutus means to substitute to this inhuman cosmic order one guided by free men's will, a social ethics based on contract. Such an ideal may have appeared within reach, and yet was straightaway made impossible by Rome's refusal to subscribe to this contract. The *pro et contra* debate in the forum on political assassination denies any legitimacy to Brutus's stillborn righteous order. The play tells the story of his

---

257 Goy-Blanquet, 'Dance of Death, or Bread and Circuses?'.

258 Burrow, *Shakespeare and Classical Antiquity*, p. 224.

259 *Julius Caesar*, ed. by Arthur Humphreys (Oxford: Oxford's World Classics, 1984), Introduction, p. 67.

failure, Marienstras points out, but the fact that ethics was defeated by politics does not cancel the value of his attempt.[260]

By giving the political assassination a pagan setting, in a system of government that had no continuity in the present, Shakespeare could pursue his reflection on history beyond the limits set by the absolutes of Christian faith and sacred monarchy. In Plutarch's *Lives*, the dramatic issue is a choice between civil war or tyrannical government. The historian bows to historical necessity, convinced that the expanse of Roman dominion and the division between Pompey's and Caesar's parties made the empire an unavoidable conclusion. An increasing number of Romans thought 'that there was no other help to remedy the trouble of the common wealth, but by the authority of one man only that should commaund them all'.[261] Brutus is doomed, for he cannot be that man; his commitment to liberty, his very virtues make it impossible for him to be Caesar. The problem that exercises Elizabeth's Parliament, killing the serpent's egg, is the one that confronts Brutus. The dialectics of death or liberty and its sacrificial resolution, Caesar's murder on presumption of tyranny, drive the conspirators from self-offering to ritual murder, admission of guilt, and republican suicide, an act condemned in the Justinian *Digest* as felony to oneself. Brutus's death, more than Caesar's, is the sacrifice required by political necessity, which makes the victim both guilty and innocent, and the world tragic that has no time or place for Brutus's honour.

---

260 Marienstras, *Shakespeare et le désordre du monde*, ch. 17.

261 'Life of Caesar', in Plutarch, *Lives*, trans. by North, v, p. 30.

Part III

The Conscience of England

Freedom of Speech

CHAPTER 7

The Languages of Law

Long before the dramatic falls of the Tudor reigns, law and legal issues had furnished the stage with both matter and form. One of the oldest features of law in Europe was its dramatization: a poetic language seemed more appropriate to the solemnity of law than prosaic everyday speech. Contracts, transfers of property, alliances were sealed with symbolic gestures. Trials began with elaborate oaths, often set in alliterative verse form, which must be recited word perfect.[1] 'So long as law is unwritten, it must be dramatized and acted', Maitland asserts.[2] In England, and to a lesser degree in France, this particular feature would long outlive the age of unwritten law. Its expounding was primarily an oral tradition: 'Common lawyers shared with their Druidical ancestors an inherent suspicion of the written word.'[3] The opinion of French jurists, expressed in a manifesto of 1312 against ordinances, was that 'England is not governed by written laws but by ancient laws and customs used and approved in the time of the king's forebears: and where these are in any point deficient the king and his prelates, earls and barons, on the complaints of the people (*ad querimoniam vulgi*) are bound to amend them.'[4] Pier delle Vigne, chancellor to Emperor Friedrich II, Geoffrey Chaucer, justice of the peace, Thomas Norton and Thomas Sackville, the Inns of Court authors of *Gorboduc*, obviously did not think of poetry-writing as a separate activity, distinct from their legal occupations. Whether expressed through educative dialogue, legal treatises, or poems, justice must be every thinker's concern.

The Legal Nursery

My conscience hath a thousand several tongues,
And every tongue brings in a several tale,
And every tale condemns me for a villain:
Perjury, in the high'st degree,
Murder, stern murder, in the dir'st degree,

1 Berman, *Law and Revolution*, pp. 58–59.

2 Maitland, 'Early English Law, 600 AD–1066', in Maitland and Montague, *A Sketch of English Legal History*, p. 18.

3 Raffield, *Shakespeare's Imaginary Constitution*, p. 45.

4 *Annales Londonienses 1194–1330*, ed. by William Stubbs, in *Chronicles of Edward I and Edward II*, (Cambridge: Cambridge University Press, 2012), I, pp. 211–15.

All several sins, all us'd in each degree,
Throng to th'bar, crying all, 'Guilty, Guilty'.

Richard III, V.iii

Shakespeare's poetry is deservedly famous as a major source of the English language. He is both the inventor of innumerable neologisms and the alchemist who transmuted centuries of commonplaces, figures of speech, moral aphorisms, and rhetorical patterns. The rhetorical handbooks popular at the time are but one of his and many Elizabethan orators' sources. Discussing the various *genera* of rhetorical utterance, Quentin Skinner finds Shakespeare principally concerned with judicial modes of address.[5] His political rhetoric often parrots or parodies the judicial one, blending the sounds and furies of his age in a chamber of echoes, reordering the common babble into meaningful dialectics and telling images. Taking its cue from the tradition of good counsel, as in a forum or a tribunal, the theatre summoned on stage the conflicting voices of the realm.

Arguments pro et contra

The method of argument *in utramque partem* had behind it a long history of moral and philosophical education, perfecting the method of the dialogue in dialectics that allowed a progressive unveiling of the truth. Inspired by memories of Plato, Cicero, Lucian, Boethius, the medieval preachers and pamphleteers made generous use of the dialogue in their exempla. The Platonic model itself had its foundations in the *mime*, a genre cultivated by the Sicilian poets Sophron and Epicharmus, half a century before Plato copied their works. Theatre was banned by the laws of *The Republic* along with the imitations of the actor, *hupocrites*, but allowed in its narrative form, to sing in praise of noble heroic deeds. Boethius explicitly brought Fortuna and its dramatic reversals in his dialogue with Philosophy. His combined virtues as statesman, scholar, philosopher, and stoic hero made him a perfect embodiment of the tragic fall, earning him a place in Boccaccio's *De Casibus*, and a sculpted effigy in Laon cathedral, holding the wheel of Fortune. Boethius had Charlemagne's minister of education, Alcuin, as a commentator, and among his translators, King Alfred, Jean de Meung, Chaucer, Elizabeth I. Next to him in popularity, Lucian of Samosate, author of *Dialogue of the Gods* and *Dialogue of the Dead*, was one of Erasmus's and More's favourite writers.

A similar alliance of didacticism and literature prevailed among Friedrich II's lyrical poets in Palermo, many of whom were notaries or jurists, like Giacomo da Lentini or Pier delle Vigne, but none showed a dominant interest in the theatre: they were all sonnet-bound, and their debates restricted to themes of love, inspired from troubadour poetry. However, the Provençal *cours d'amour* held at Alienor of Aquitaine and Henry II Plantagenet's courts included dramatic trial

5 Skinner, *Forensic Shakespeare*, ch. 2.

scenes, a distant model to the Prince of Purpoole in the Christmas revels at Gray's Inn.[6] But the fiercest jousts went on elsewhere. The schools that were just then developing opened the stage of their polemics to wider themes, larger audiences, and less courtly behaviours. Blows could be exchanged as well as arguments in the public disputations around matters of faith and ethics. Masters did not hesitate to excommunicate the theses of heretical pupils.

Medieval debates on law and justice were transnational, and easily recognizable as the first distant sources of dramatic debates on stage or lectern. The theme of Abélard's 'Dialogue of a Philosopher with a Jew and a Christian', which confronts new reasoning with both Ancient and New Law, ran all around the Mediterranean.[7] The creation of a Dominican *studium arabicum* in Tunis, shortly before Saint Louis's crusade, by Ramon de Peñafort, who studied law at Bologna, encouraged the model of *disputatio* between Christians and Muslims initiated by twelfth-century treatises. In *Disciplina Clericalis*, an Arab father transmits knowledge and moral advice to his son via a collection of oriental tales that found their way to the *Gesta Romanorum*, *Roman de Renart*, medieval fabliaux, and Caxton's edition of Aesop's fables. Translated as *Discipline de Clergie ou Chastoiement d'un pere a un fils*, it inspired the *Enseignements de Monseigneur Saint Louis a son Fils*, the ethical and political testament of Louis IX to his son Philippe III, two areas that the dialogue form could serve equally well. James VI was following old precedents when he wrote the *Basilikon Doron or, His Maiesties Instructions to his Dearest Sonne, Henry the Prince*. So did Shakespeare with the Countess of Rossillion's virtuous advice to her departing son, its parody through Polonius's unvirtuous ersatz, or Shylock's stance for Ancient Law against unmerciful Portia's plea for Christian Mercy.

As we saw above, a long line of pedagogues from Alcuin onwards cast their teachings in dialogue mode. There is usually little drama in the master-and-student form of exchange or its variant, the dialogue between father and son, marked as they are by a clear imbalance between the debating characters: the son/disciple is usually restricted to naïve questions, answered at great length with learned examples by the father/master, and if they happen to disagree on any point, the issue is a foregone conclusion. The form visibly found favour among jurists, many of whom adopted it in their writings. Although the imbalance persists in the works of later lawyers, Bracton, Fortescue, Saint-German, or More, it is nuanced by the *pro et contra* mode which demands that the writer espouse each view in turn. In school exercises, apprentices were taught to plead both sides of a controversy with equal energy and competence. Sir Thomas Smith perfectly sums up the common opinion inherited from Cicero's *De inventione* when he explains what motivated his choice of the dialogue mode for his *Discourse of the*

6 See Paul Hyams, 'Henry II and Ganelon', *Syracuse Scholar*, 4.1 (1986), 23–25.

7 Abélard, *Conférences*, ed. and trans. by Gandillac. Peter Abélard, *Collationes*, trans. by John Marenbon (Oxford: Oxford University Press, 2001).

Common Weal: 'that kind of reasoning seems to me best for boulting out of the truth which is used by way of dialogue or colloquy, where reasons be made to and fro, as well for the matter intended as against it'.[8]

Mock Kings and Trials

The earliest known shift from trial court or classroom to stage was made by law students in Paris. When French kings inhabited the Palais, the whole law personnel were known as *clercs de la Basoche*, slang for *Basilica*, the palace. Like the Inns', the origin of their association is obscure. It was granted special privileges in 1303 by Philippe le Bel, and became a separate guild of lawyers in 1344. Each year, the assembly of clerks, calling themselves a *parlement*, solemnly elected their *roi de la Basoche*, a mock king who had his own court, officers, and armouries and received visits from the real king at Pré aux Clercs.[9] Their seasonal ceremonies were accompanied with shows: Carnival, planting the May, *montre d'été*. On Mardi Gras, Shrove Tuesday, they pleaded imaginary cases known as *causes grasses*. The *Arrêts d'Amour* of Martial d'Auvergne, a set of love judgements before a *cour d'amour*, are probably echoes of such mock trials. Among their privileges was the right to perform religious plays, a right which they used and abused between political moralities, *soties*, or *charivaris*. Successive decrees by the Parlement de Paris show that prohibitions were poorly observed. From the records, at least on three occasions the authors of these entertainments went to jail: the 'joueurs de farce' reported in the *Journal d'un Bourgeois de Paris*; Henri Baude, who played a part in the Praguerie of 1440; and the court poet François Habert, a former *basochien*.[10] One of Baude's satirical pieces is the 'Testament of a Mule' who bore eminent court characters and went down the scale to the lowest clerk as it aged. Habert's 'Fable du Lyon, du Loup et de l'asne' has the Wolf plead before the Lion King in decasyllables: as king he can do what he likes and ignore laws, no one will dare contradict him.[11]

Some renowned authors wrote plays and scripts for the Basoche, from Guillaume Coquillard and Pierre Gringore to Clément Marot. Gringore or Gringoire, a clerk of the Basoche, is often considered an unconditional supporter of monarchy, possibly paid by Louis XII to write satires against Pope Jules II, pieces designed to justify the French forays into Italy.[12] But his plays are strongly critical

---

8 Smith, *A Discourse of the Commonweal*, p. 13.

9 Fabre, *Études historiques sur les clercs de la Basoche*.

10 Bouhaïk-Gironès, *Les clercs de la Basoche*, pp. 143–52.

11 Baude, 'Le Testament de la Mule Barbeau', in Jules Quicherat, *Les Vers de Maître Henri Baude, Poète du XVe siècle* (Paris: Aubry, 1856), pp. 19–25. François Habert, 'Fable moralle du Lyon, du Loup et de l'asne', in *Le premier livre des emblemes, Composé par Guillaume Gueroult* (Lyon: Balthazar Arnoullet, 1550), pp. 40–44.

12 Gringore, *Sottie contre le Pape Jules II*, in *Recueil général des sotties*, ed. by Émile Picot (Paris: Firmin Didot, 1904), II, no. 11, pp. 132–73.

of government ministers, through the use of yet another significant feature, the recurrent character of *Bon Conseil*, who champions justice and warns the king against the evils of flattery. The same Gringore designed the Parisian entry of Louis XII's bride, the first Mary Tudor, Henry VIII's younger sister, in 1514. At the heart of the pageant, on place du Châtelet, the king appeared seated on the lower level of the scaffolding, with Justice above him brandishing her sword. It was from a wish to keep in tune with popular opinions that Louis XII 'allowed freedom of expression in the theaters', wishing that 'actors might freely represent the injustices being committed in his court and his entire kingdom; he did this thinking that he would learn and know many things from these performances that otherwise would be impossible for him to know'.[13]

The glorification of 'good counsel' was not long tolerated after him. Throughout the fifteenth century, the *basochiens* were repeatedly forbidden to perform publicly or otherwise by Parlement, and the whole administration of theatre regulated by *intendants des Menus Plaisirs*, under strict control of the First Gentlemen of the King's Chamber. The part of French Basoche in theatrical performances might have followed trends that developed in England at the Inns, had they not been nipped in the bud as a result of their political involvement and plain speaking. If they provided models for the young Inns, their revels were sooner ended. François Ier found their plays too impertinent for his taste and forbade all public performances. A few decades later, his grandson Henri III transferred all the privileges of the *roi de la Basoche* to his own chancellor, and suppressed the title. By 1600 the number of performances had dwindled into near silence, and the theatre of the *basochiens* 'quickly perished for lack of the freedom that was essential to it'.[14]

Drama caused anxiety to English rulers long before it grew suspect in jaundiced Puritans' eyes. It soon appeared, as it had in France, that theatre was a double-edged instrument. Louis XII had employed Gringore's Parisian company to mock the papacy, but they became an embarrassment with their attacks on other authorities, leading to severe restrictions on plays and playwrights. Similarly when England broke with Rome, it was thought that popular Robin Hood plays led to 'lewdness and ribaldry': they must be replaced by plays demonstrating the pope's wickedness and teaching obedience to the king.[15] In 1537 the Duke of Suffolk heard rumours about a May Day play 'of a king how he should rule his realm', in which the actor playing Husbandry 'said many things against gentlemen, much more than was in the book of the play'. He warned the justices to watch

13 Translated in Jody L. H. McQuillan, 'Dangerous Dialogues: The Sottie as a Threat to Authority', in *Bakhtin and Medieval Voices*, ed. by Thomas J. Farrell (Gainesville: University Press of Florida, 1995), p. 71.

14 Harvey, *The Theatre of the Basoche*, p. 232.

15 See G. Parfitt, 'Early Robin Hood Plays: Two Fragments and a Bibliography in Popular Theatre', *Renaissance and Modern Studies*, 22 (1978), 5–12.

out, especially 'at games or plays where any number of idle persons shall meet'.[16] Henry VIII's royal proclamations continued at regular intervals, limiting the performance of interludes and plays in October 1544, and on 8 July 1546 requiring printers to identify themselves, their authors, and dates of publishing.[17] His three children would each take censorship further. A proclamation, the first known of its kind, was made under King Edward on 6 August 1549 for the 'inhibicion of Plaiers', prohibiting all interludes and plays in English from 9 August to 30 November, because for the most part such interludes 'contain matter tendyng to sedicion, and contempnyng of sundery good orders & lawe', daily causing 'muche disquiet, diuision, tumultes & vprores in this realme'.[18] The next major step was taken under Mary, when she authorized the creation of the Stationers' Company and gave them the power to destroy all unlicensed printing. Elizabethan plays would be ruled by two authorities, the master of the revels and the Archbishop of Canterbury.

Protestant Playwrights

> Your bait of falsehood takes this carp of truth.
>
> *Hamlet, II.i*

Lorna Hutson makes a strong case for the influence of Gascoigne's *Supposes* on *The Comedy of Errors* and assumes, as I do, 'quite a lot of continuity in terms of political-didactic interests between the Inns of Court drama of the 1560s and 1570s and the popular dramaturgy of the 1570s and 1580s'. The learned circles of the universities and Inns of Court adapted 'the elements of intrigue and forensic argument that drove the dramatic action of Roman New Comedy' to the requirements of 'a civic humanist plot of the magisterial detection and examination of abuses'.[19] The importance of Terence and Plautus in the curricula of Tudor schools and universities, the reworking of their models by the early playwrights to reflect issues and concerns of daily life, their forensic rhetoric and investigative plots having been amply studied already,[20] I will concentrate here on strands more directly connected with the dramatic turns of policy reviewed above.

The Reformation did not straightaway change the course of English drama. The Coventry Corpus Christi Pageants, for instance, continued until their final suppression in 1579. The early Protestants in England had no objection to plays and players. Some of the spectacular items gracing their productions could easily

---

16 *Letters and Papers, Henry VIII*, XII.1, p. 1212.

17 *Tudor Royal Proclamations*, I, no. 186, pp. 270–06, I, no. 240, pp. 341–42, I, no. 272, pp. 373–76.

18 *Proclamations of King Edward VI* (London: Grafton, 1550), no. 240.

19 Hutson, *The Invention of Suspicion*, p. 217.

20 By Lorna Hutson, Barbara Shapiro, Alan Nelson, Adele Scafuro, Joel Altman, Subha Mukherji, among other scholars.

out-Herod Herod. Luther and Melanchthon shared a taste for Roman comedy. Even Calvin mentions once the 'pleasant spectacle' that may be enjoyed in the theatre, though pleasure disappears in the French version of 1560, where 'theatralis plausus in iucundo aliquo spectaculo' is replaced by 'comme un cry du peuple en un théâtre'.[21] And of course he would condemn the transvestism of European drama, 'for such disguisings are but inticements of baudry', and 'the suffring hereof is the opening of a gap to all whoredom', words that would repeatedly serve in civic campaigns to close those areas of perdition.[22] He mistrusted its 'lying fictions',[23] but his followers were more tolerant. Beza, who had studied law at Orleans, was an occasional playwright, author of the first French tragedy, *Abraham sacrifiant,* which draws its inspiration from Greek theatre and medieval mysteries, and of a satire against the *chambre ardente,* an inquisitorial court of exception created in 1535 to track heresy.[24] In *Abraham sacrifiant,* dramatic scenes alternate with sung passages in verse, and Satan appears dressed as a monk to face the patriarch. Beza's argument praises the magic of a theatre that can show his immortal hero 'au vif représenté' (represented live) and do service to Protestant faith.[25] After its creation at the University of Lausanne, it was given a reading at the court of Jeanne d'Albret, Henri de Navarre's mother, who read the part of Sarah herself. In 1577, Arthur Golding made a translation of it entitled *A Tragedie of Abraham's Sacrifice,* his only known contribution to drama.

If the British Protestants received humanism from Italy and France, their religious philosophy and its theatrical expression originally came from Germany. The early reformers were part of the humanist community, readers and translators of the classics, who were invited in English universities and intellectual circles, especially under the reign of Edward VI, when England stood as a stronghold against the Counter-Reformation. In Russ Leo's argumentation, the history of Protestant tragedy begins in the Lutheran universities, continues with Lodovico Castelvetro, a founding father of neoclassical theatre, and culminates with Milton. The Inns of Court playwrights get but scant notice, while the anti-theatrical writings of the 'rabid Puritan' John Rainolds are revisited for their 'positive vision of tragedy', a vision 'consonant with Aristotle's *Poetics*'. Shakespeare receives a modicum of attention thanks to *Hamlet,* which shows an understanding of what is at stake in Rainolds's tragic vision, along with a distrust of histrionic performance and spectacle.[26] Rainolds took an active part in the Oxford debates over the

21 Calvin, *Institutio Christianae religionis,* lib. III, cap. IX, 2 (Geneva: Robertus Stephanus, 1559), p. 255. *Institution de la religion chrétienne,* ed. by Frank Baumgartner (Geneva: Beroud, 1888), p. 329. See Heller, *Penitent Brothellers,* pp. 17–19.

22 Calvin, sermon of 3 January 1556 on Deuteronomy 22. 5.

23 In 1546 he concurred with the Genevan Council in suppressing 'a drama of Hercules'. Bouwsma, *John Calvin,* p. 179.

24 So called because held in a room lit with candles, but taken to mean the prisoners burnt at the stake, especially in the reign of Henri II, when it proved most cruel to the Huguenots.

25 Beza, *Abraham sacrifiant,* ed. by Cameron and others.

26 Leo, *Tragedy as Philosophy,* ch. 3.

vulgarities and falsehoods of stage-plays,[27] of which Shakespeare was well aware, Leo argues, and in the war against the public players. So was Stephen Gosson, who may have been his student at Corpus Christi College (see below, Chapter 8), while his works deeply impressed the equally militant William Prynne. Leo makes an interesting case for the identification of Polonius's servant, the *mendax* Reynaldo, with Rainolds, although it is mostly Polonius who airs his views about contemporary theatre. Of course, 'from the outset Hamlet recognizes spectacle and stage-playing as integral to tragedy and absolutely crucial to discovery', thus reversing Rainolds's claims.[28] The dumb show fails to move Claudius, but this does not mean that it fails to catch his conscience and thus proves inefficient, as Leo asserts. Claudius is a seasoned politician who, thanks to the dumb show, knows very well where *The Murder of Gonzago* is heading, and interrupts it when the 'nephew to the king' clearly states Hamlet's intention to kill him. Not guilt but legitimate indignation is what the court can read in his reaction.

Castelvetro, who authored the first Italian translation of Melanchthon's *Loci Communes Theologici*, recruited Aristotle's *Poetics* to serve Reformation ends, which drew him to defend 'spectacle and stage-playing in their capacity to accommodate tragedy's philosophical insights' and help audiences to a higher understanding.[29] Erasmus had found tools for his theological and philological studies in antique works and translated tragedies, which Melanchthon used in his own course on Euripides at Wittenberg, demonstrating the relevance of the tragic canon to theology and philosophy. His student Vitus Winshemius translated all Sophocles' tragedies, integrating Melanchthon's lectures and his own reflections on the nature of tyranny in his printed edition, dedicated to Edward VI (1546). To Micha Lazarus, the theological lessons that he 'coaxes out of the plays range from straightforward sententiae to the harder knots of Reformation thought.' They provided material for the Protestant resistance theory, 'locating in Sophocles the hard ethical and political questions that pressed on nascent Protestant states and individuals'.[30]

In their wake, Martin Bucer's *De regno Christi* (1551), also dedicated to King Edward, draws a list of measures to advance the Reformation with *honesti ludi*, honest pastimes crucial to the civil education of youth, including plays if they can be exploited to reform the desires and passions of mankind. The Scriptures offer a rich material for tragedies, more appropriate to his project of pious education than the 'godless fables and stories of the pagans'.[31] Even comedies can contribute, when they express the 'consolations of God' in everyday life like the comic

---

27 John Rainolds, William Gager, and Alberico Gentili, *The Overthrow of Stage-plays* (1599), in Pollard, ed., *Shakespeare's Theater*, ch. 12.

28 Leo, *Tragedy as Philosophy*, p. 158.

29 Leo, *Tragedy as Philosophy*, pp. 3–5 and ch. 2.

30 Lazarus, 'Tragedy at Wittenberg', pp. 39, 40.

31 Bucer, *De regno Christi*, ed. by Wendel, ch. LIV, p. 257. A French translation was printed in Geneva in 1552.

episodes of Jacob's story. After rejecting the emperor's religious policy, Bucer was invited to England and made Regius Professor of Divinity at Cambridge, where he died two years later. His widow sold his library to Cranmer and to King Edward, whose early death put an end to Bucer's reforming programme. Some of Cranmer's papers were collected by Matthew Parker, former master of Corpus Christi College, who kept them hidden under Mary's reign. Only in 1577 would Bucer's *Scripta Anglicana* be published in Basel.[32]

As Russ Leo points out, a number of reforming playwrights had already turned to tragedy to address theological questions, resolve the contradictions between fate and free will that were at stake in the Arminian Controversy over predestination, and reconcile *hamartia* with divine justice in a Christian perspective. Scriptural tragedy 'became an important medium of exchange between England and the Continent' in the 1540s.[33] Bucer himself was influenced by the *dramata sacra* of Thomas Kirchmeyer (Naogeorgus), John Bale, George Buchanan, and other British reformers. Morison, Cromwell's favourite apologist, recommended the writing of plays as an efficient tool of propaganda that would expose 'lively before the peoples eies the abhomynation and wickednes of the bisshop of Rome, monkes, freers, nonnes, and suche like', and show them 'thobedience that your subiectes by goddes and mans lawes owe unto your magestie'. This mode is particularly apt because 'Into the commen people thynges sooner enter by the eies then by the eares: remembryng more better that they see then that they here.'[34] Taking Morison's advice, Cromwell gave his patronage to Protestant playwrights. Among his protégés was John Bale, who could be depended upon to spread new ideas. In Bale's earliest play, *A Comedy Concerning Three Laws*, first published in 1538, natural, Mosaic, and Christian laws each speak in turn to define their place in history from the origin to the end of time, and conclude with a celebration of Henry VIII, Edward VI, and the dowager Queen Katherine Parr.[35]

King John's stance against papacy inspired three distinct Tudor plays, Bale's *Kynge Johan*, Peele's *Troublesome Raigne*, and Shakespeare's *King John*, each reflecting the political situation at the time of their writing, all three reacting to one cause, Joshua Phillips claims, monasticism, which granted monks immunity and exception from the common law.[36] If Bale's and Peele's plays do 'provide a legal rationale for the dissolution of the monasteries', Shakespeare's never even mentions the word 'monastery'. It is rather stretching facts to assert that the Angers citizen stands for religious immunity when he declares his loyalty to 'he

---

32 See Jean Rott, 'Le sort des papiers et de la bibliothèque de Bucer en Angleterre', *Revue d'Histoire et de Philosophie religieuse*, 46.4 (1966), 346–67.

33 Lazarus, 'Tragedy at Wittenberg', p. 60.

34 *A Perswasion to the Kyng that the laws of the realme shulde be in Latin*, in Sydney Anglo, 'An Early Tudor Programme for Plays and Other Demonstrations against the Pope', *Journal of the Warburg and Courtauld Institutes*, 20 (1957), 176–79.

35 Bale, *Three Laws*, in *The Complete Plays*, ed. by Happé, vol. II.

36 Joshua Phillips, 'Immunity and Monasticism: Bale to Shakespeare', in Hutson, ed., *The Oxford Handbook of Law and Literature*, ch. 15.

that proves the king' when both John and Philip claim possession of his town. Besides, Shakespeare does not support the accusation made in Bale's and Peele's versions, that John was poisoned by a monk, but plays it down as just a rumour, the only occurrence of the word 'monk' in his text.

The same year that Cromwell authorized Coverdale's Bible,[37] *Kynge Johan* was performed at Christmastime in Archbishop Cranmer's house, then went touring all England with its undisguised messages:

> This noble Kynge Johan, as a faythfull Moses
> Withstode proude Pharao for his poore Israel.
> But the English people remained in the bondage of Rome,
> Tyll that duke Josue, whych was our late Kynge Henrye,
> Clerely brought us out in to the lande of mylke and honye.[38]

Under Cromwell's patronage, Bale had formed a company of actors to perform plays in support of the new religion, and composed four pieces in 1538 for their repertory. His original two-part *Kynge Johan*, probably written by the autumn of 1536, was revised into one piece suitable for a stage production. If for no other merit, it deserves a place in the history of drama as the first morality play to historicize Deadly Sins: Sedition is Stephen Langton, Private Wealth Cardinal Pandulph, Dissimulation Simon of Swynsett (Swinstead, the monk who murdered John), and Usurped Power of course the Pope, who league themselves against the Widow England after driving out her husband, God. Her champion, John, dies in fighting them, but Imperial Majesty, Henry VIII, enters to restore the kingdom, while Nobility, Clergy, and Civil Order, exhorted by Veritas, promise to exile the Pope and defend Majesty. The final words of Veritas are borrowed from Tyndale's *Obedience of a Christian Man*.

John Bale, in his crusade to bring down the pope, wrote twenty-four scriptural plays, and an English translation of Kirchmeyer's *Pammachius* that did not survive.[39] His books were banned after Cromwell's fall, but a few Protestant plays still appeared in their wake. The staging of *Pammachius*, a play dedicated to Luther and Cranmer, in Spring 1545 at Christ's College, Cambridge, raised a controversy echoed in the correspondence between Gardiner, chancellor of the university, and his vice-chancellor Matthew Parker.[40] To Cuthbert Scot, it was 'thorough out poisoned' and should not be performed, but the organizers having replied that their aim was 'but to rebuke the popes vsurped powr', they went unpunished. The crowning of Pammachius by Satan, one of its high points, mimics the papal

---

37 Michael Coverdale's translation was partly absorbed and replaced in English churches by the Matthew Bible, which includes the beginning of Tyndale's Old and New Testaments.

38 Bale, *King Johan*, ed. by Pafford, p. 52, ll. 1097–1103. On Bale's touring company, see Gurr, *The Shakespearian Playing Companies*, p. 35.

39 Blatt, *The Plays of John Bale*, pp. 20–24.

40 Kirchmeyer, *Pammachius*, trans. by Love. See Leo's analysis of its tragic structure in *Tragedy as Philosophy*, pp. 53–58.

coronation, while Satan's banquet parodies the Lord's Supper with an episode of cannibalism.[41] Christ, entering at Act IV, comments that there are scarcely seven thousand people left in the world who are not followers of the Roman beast. Gardiner berated Parker and the university administrators for having allowed the performance, which had occasioned riotous behaviour from the students, but with little effect. It took place the year after Gardiner's failed attempt to have Cranmer impeached on heresy charges, an episode later staged in Shakespeare and Fletcher's *Henry VIII*. Both Foxe's *Christus Triumphans* and Nicholas Udall's *Ezechias* drew on Kirchmeyer's iconoclastic dramaturgy.[42]

It was the advent of commercial companies, in the late 1570s, that fuelled the Puritans' antitheatrical prejudices. Until then, most plays since Cromwell's time were written or translated by reformists, mostly Inns or university alumni. Bale, Udall, Baldwin, Ferrers all provided dramatic entertainments at the court of Edward VI. Roger Ascham, Elizabeth's tutor, undertook to translate Sophocles' *Philoctetes*. The stern Buchanan translated Euripides' *Medea* and *Alcestis* in Latin, authored tragedies himself, and wrote some *pompae*, short pieces for performance at the court of young Mary Stuart.[43] While a master at Bordeaux, he wrote two Latin tragedies for his pupils, one of which, *Jephthes*, was printed in 1554. Thus, to Gardiner's complaint against some 'very pernicious, sedicious & slaundrous' books, Foxe could retort that 'thys insensible Asse', as he calls the bishop in a side note, 'wrangleth much agaynst Preachers, Printers, & Players. And no maruell why: For he seeth these three thyngs to be set vp of God, as a triple bulwarke agaynst the triple crown of the Pope, to bring him down, as God be praysed, they haue done meetely well already.'[44]

Tragedy, still understood as defined by Chaucer — a story in verse, of falls from high places — was treated by early modern polemicists as interchangeable with dialogue. While in England, financially supported by Edward VI, Bernardino Ochino had written a Latin *Tragedie or Dialoge of the unjuste usurped primacie of the Bishop of Rome*, published in 1549 in John Ponet's translation. It shows Lucifer calling together a council of fiends to check the spread of Christ's kingdom and setting up the pope as Antichrist, a scene thought to have inspired Milton. They are about to succeed when Henry VIII and his son enter, with England's 'Christian protectour', Somerset, to overthrow them. Tragicomic depictions of Christ's Passion could combine sadness, horror, and blissful joy at his resurrection. When Shakespeare's rude mechanicals performed their 'very tragical mirth', they may have been parodying Nicholas Grimald, who defined his *Christus Redivivus*

41 Paul W. White, 'The Pammachius Affair at Christ's College, Cambridge, in 1545', in Happé and Hüsken, eds, *Interludes and Early Modern Society*, pp. 266–87.

42 *Christus Triumphans* was staged at Trinity in 1561–1562, and *Ezechias* before Elizabeth in 1564.

43 Buchanan's Latin translations of Euripides' *Medea* and *Alcestis*: Buchanan, *Tragedies*, ed. by Sharratt and Walsh.

44 Foxe, *Actes and Monuments*, Bk IX, p. 1562 [1562]. The note on the 'insensible Asse' appears in the 1563 edition, Bk IV, 801.

(1543) as a 'comoedia tragica'. Foxe too wrote Latin plays on biblical subjects during his exile.[45] His 'comoedia apocalyptica', *Christus Triumphans*, expresses a widely spread feeling among Protestants that Mary's persecutions were the final assault of Antichrist, proof that the end of time was near. *Titus et Gesippus*, drawn from Boccaccio's tale after due cleaning of all its immoral elements, anticipates *The Comedy of Errors* with a Plautian pair of friends who, thanks to the endeavours of their slaves Phormo, Syrus, and Dromo, end up marrying each other's brides. Thus 'Foxe explored the meaning, form, and purchase of tragedy' before he narrated the 'tragedies' of Jan Hus and eminent reformers like Ridley or Latimer.[46] As news of the persecutions in England arrived on the continent, he began to collect material for a *Book of Martyrs* that would update the history of the English Lollards undertaken in Edward's reign. The first English edition of his *Actes and Monuments of the Christian Church*, dedicated to Elizabeth, was published by John Day in 1563, followed in 1570 by a new version double its size. Its vision of English Protestants as God's elect people would cause indignant retorts from the Catholic camp who declared it packed with lies and errors. It would also provide abundant source material to Elizabethan and Jacobean playwrights.

Shortly after the accession of Elizabeth, Il Schifanoia would complain that many frivolous and foolish people 'daily invent plays in derision of the Catholic faith, of the Church, of the clergy, and of the religion', and that 'by placards posted at the corners of the streets, they invite people to the taverns, to see these representations, taking money from their audience'. It seems Elizabeth patronized similar modes of entertainment: before his account of the coronation, the Mantuan describes a masque performed at court in her presence on Twelfth Night, a mummery of 'crows in the habits of Cardinals, of asses habited as Bishops, and of wolves representing Abbots', and masquerades of friars in the streets of London. These may have grown out of control, for a royal proclamation banned such shows: straight after the arrest of the Catholic bishops in April 1559,

> forbidding in future the performance in the hostels and taverns of certain plays and games on holidays, which used to be held in abuse and derision of the Catholic religion, of the mass, of the Saints, and finally of God.

He still hopes that things may yet return to their former state, and a happy marriage be concluded between England and Spain, but his next news is that 'The title of "Supreme Head of the Church" passed through the two Houses'.[47] The tradition of anti-papal plays would continue later through the city comedies of Dekker or

45 John Foxe, *Two Latin Comedies by John Foxe the Martyrologist: Titus et Gesippus. Christus Triumphans*, ed. and trans. by John Hazel Smith (Ithaca, NY: Cornell University Press, 1973). Escobedo, *Nationalism and Historical Loss*, p. 91.

46 Leo, *Tragedy as Philosophy*, p. 63.

47 Letters of 6 February 1559 to Ottaviano Vivaldino, and of 23 January and 11 April 1559 to the Castellan of Mantua, *Calendar of State Papers, Venice*, pp. 27, 11, 65. On the court masque, see Orgel, *The Illusion of Power*; Knowles, *Politics and Political Culture in the Court Masque*.

Middleton. *A Game at Chesse* proved worthy of its predecessors, satirizing the Spanish ambassador so openly that Middleton was prosecuted, ending there his dramatic career, and the Globe shut down during the prosecution.[48]

Won in Translation

Drama, through dialogues and debating jousts, had always featured prominently in the Inns' formative exercises. University performances until the late sixteenth century were usually in Latin, whereas the Inns performed plays in English. The community of writers and translators that developed there in the 1560s found it an ideal way of advertising themselves to prospective patrons: 'As with many of the writings at the Inns in this decade, the translations of Seneca helped to foster connections, as well as political expression.'[49] The works of Inns members show 'the natural bias of law students looking to the state services for their future' as well as genuine concern for the immediate future of the realm.[50]

In the first half of Elizabeth's reign, the Inns of Court virtually monopolized translations classic and modern. From roughly 1550 to 1575, Finkelpearl asserts, and Jessica Winston confirms, they formed the literary centre of England, through a group of serious young men intent on making the Reformation in England humanistic and its government secure. Those seemingly 'drab' authors helped 'to create the cultural platform on which the towering achievements of the following generation could take place'.[51] It gave the Inns a special character: 'critical, independent, aesthetically innovative, and politically concerned'.[52] This cultural vitality, largely the result of the humanists' insistence on classical education, produced an exceptional body of both translations and original writings. In his Preface to *Thyestes*, Heywood is visited by the ghost of Seneca, who wants him to translate more of his work, as we shall see (in Chapter 8), but he modestly directs his visitor to the Inns of Court where 'finest witts doe swarme'. Of the eight young men he cites as deserving praise for their works of poetry and translation — North, Sackville, Norton, Yelverton, Thomas Blundeville, William Bavand, Barnabe Googe, and Baldwin — six were Inns members.[53] So were Neville, Studley, and Gascoigne.[54]

---

48 See Edward M. Wilson and Olga Turner, 'The Spanish Protest against *A Game at Chesse*', *Modern Language Review*, 44 (1949), 480, and Gary Taylor's Introduction to *Thomas Middleton and Early Modern Textual Culture: A Companion to the Collected Works* (Oxford: Oxford University Press, 2007), p. 712.

49 Winston, 'Seneca in Early Elizabethan England', p. 34.

50 H. B. Charlton, *The Senecan Tradition in Renaissance Tragedy* (Manchester: Manchester University Press, 1946), p. 163.

51 Winston, *Lawyers at Play*, p. 121.

52 Finkelpearl, *John Marston of the Middle Temple*, p. 25.

53 *Jasper Heywood and his Translations of Seneca*, ed. by de Vocht.

54 Conley, *The First English Translators of the Classics*, p. 133.

Linguistic Independence

> I am so good a proficient in one quarter of an hour that I can drink with any tinker in his own language during my life.
>
> *1 Henry IV, II.iv*

The nationalist spirit so audible in Tudor England had focused for over a century on a sensitive area: language. Aristocratic England still spoke French when Henry V imposed the use of English in peace negotiations, a fact that no Tudor chronicler mentions. Only Shakespeare seems aware that the Englishing of Europe began about then. His French Princess vows she 'cannot speak your England', yet her remarkable foresight, or his shrewd historical hindsight, leads her to practise it before the battle has even started, and by the end of the play she must be turned into 'the better Englishwoman'.[55]

The division of Christendom, in destroying Latin hegemony, made a new Babel of Europe and saw the flourishing of treatises in defence of national languages. A centuries-long controversy over the *questione della lingua* opposed those who favoured Latin to supporters of various Italian dialects, whose very diversity reflected the chaotic political state of Italy. Petrarch and Boccaccio contributed to the establishment of Florentine as the best literary language, but still considered it second to the nobility of Latin, whereas Dante's *De vulgari eloquentia* had argued that between *grammatica* and the language infants learn from their nurse, 'the more noble is the vernacular', because it is what the first man spoke, 'as soon, indeed, as God's creative power had been breathed into him'.[56] Political agendas would further stress this nobility. Long before François Ier's Ordinance of Villers-Cotterêts in 1539, Saint Louis had begun the establishment of French as the *langue nationale* and prided himself on speaking *le langage de France*. Thanks to Joinville we even hear his voice rasping over the word *r-r-rendre*, to give back, the first French king recorded in the vulgar tongue, Le Goff notes.[57] Charles V (1364–1380) would continue his good work by strengthening the domination of the 'royal vernacular',[58] the *francien* spoken in Île-de-France, over other dialects. His ambitious programme of translating Latin works deemed essential for monarchy received praise from his eminent biographer Christine de Pizan.[59] This strategy calculated to unify the kingdom through a common language was also a means

55 *Henry V*, V.ii.102–03, 118. See Goy-Blanquet, 'Translating Europe into Your England'.

56 Dante, *De Vulgari Eloquentia*, ed. and trans. by Botterill, Bk I, i, p. 3, and I, v, p. 11.

57 Joinville, *Histoire de Saint Louis*, ed. by de Wailly, p. 13: 'rendre écorchait la gorge par les r qui y sont, lesquels signifient les rateaux du diable'. Le Goff, *Saint Louis*, in *Héros du Moyen Âge*, pp. 688–89, 817.

58 Lori J. Walters, 'The Royal Vernacular: Poet and Patron in Christine de Pizan's *Charles V* and the *Sept psaumes allégorisés*', in *The Vernacular Spirit: Essays on Medieval Religious Literature*, ed. by R. Blumenfeld-Kosinski and others (New York: St Martin's/Palgrave, 2002), pp. 205–66.

59 Christine de Pizan, *Le Livre des fais et bonnes meurs du sage roy Charles V*, ed. by Solente.

of establishing French as a medium of *translatio studii* 'through a material identification with royal power'.[60]

With similar objectives, Henry V (1413–1422) promoted the use of written English in royal bureaucracy. He was the first to impose the vernacular language in official documents, as Shakespeare's wild Prince Hal records when he learns tavern English. In this regard he was taking up where his noble ancestors had left off. In the past, Edward I and Edward III had rallied support for their wars with threats that the French king wanted to destroy the English realm and its language. In 1362, the king's speech at the opening of Parliament was given in English, and in the following months a Statute of Pleading directed — in Anglo-Norman French — that pleas in all courts of justice should be pleaded and judged in English, because French was 'trope desconnue en ledit realme' (largely unknown in the said realm).[61] This measure, coming shortly after the Treaty of Brétigny, may have been an answer to popular requests, when the Lord Mayor and aldermen of London had ordered the use of English in the sheriffs' court of the city.[62] The same year, Langland wrote *Piers Plowman*, the first literary masterpiece in modern English. Two decades later John Trevisa, in a note to his translation of Higden's *Polychronicon*, writes that 'in alle the gramere scoles of Engelond, children leveth Frensche and construeth and learneth English'. The disadvantage is that, now, they 'conneth na more Frensche than can hir lift heele'.[63] And Fortescue, in the chapter explaining 'why the laws of England are not taught in the Universities', testifies to the progress of English pleading after the statute, although French was not abolished, for reasons of accuracy.[64] Despite successive attempts to rule law French out of law courts, the use of English would not be made obligatory until George II.

The question of languages was a standing argument between the two countries. From his first diplomatic exchanges, Henry V had straightaway opposed the use of French, on the grounds that neither he, his council, nor his envoys could properly write or understand it, till it was agreed that all documents would be translated into Latin and English.[65] His other prerequisite when he first made his claim for the terms defined at Brétigny, as Edward III's grandson, was the

60 Copeland, *Rhetoric, Hermeneutics, and Translation*, p. 135. On Charles V's translation programme, see C. R. Sherman, *Imaging Aristotle: Verbal and Visual Representation in Fourteenth-Century France* (Berkeley: University of California Press, 1995), pp. 6–9.

61 W. M. Ormrod, 'The Use of English: Language, Law, and Political Culture in Fourteenth-Century England', *Speculum*, 78.3 (2003), 750–87.

62 In 1356. Ormrod, 'The Use of English', p. 752.

63 *Polychronicon Ranulfi Higden; together with the English translations of John Trevisa*, ed. by Churchill Babington (London: Longman, 1869), II, Bk I, ch. LIX, p. 161. See Ronald Waldron, 'John Trevisa and the Use of English', *Proceedings of the British Academy*, 74 (1988), 171–202; Waldron, 'Trevisa's Original Prefaces on Translation: A Critical Edition', in *Medieval English Studies Presented to George Kane*, ed. by Edward Kennedy and others (Wolleboro, NH: Brewer, 1988), pp. 285–99.

64 Fortescue, *In Praise of the Laws*, p. 66.

65 François Ganshof, *Histoire des Relations internationales*, ed. by Gaston Zeller (Paris: Hachette, 1953), II, pp. 250–53.

hand of his cousin Catherine, two points also well made in Shakespeare's lessons to the Princess. As for Prince Hal's familiarity with the language of tapsters, it may have been inspired by the gratitude of the London Brewers' Guild to Henry V who in his letters and personal affairs 'for the better understanding of his people, hath, with a diligent mind, procured the common idiom (setting aside others) to be commended by the exercise of writing'.[66] After a close study of the royal correspondence, Malcolm Richardson notes about the Brewers' prose that 'this type of London English is closer to Henry's language than any other early fifteenth-century English thus far printed'. The description of his writing style could apply equally well to the simplicity of speech Shakespeare's Henry affects in his courtship: 'not a word is wasted, nor is an inflated, bombastic phrase to be found anywhere; here is the unadorned, sometimes rough, but still identifiable English plain style in its early form'.[67] Both the historical and the stage characters show themselves fully aware of its propaganda value. The phrase 'the King's English' appears only once in the canon, Margaret Tudeau-Clayton points out, in the Folio version of *The Merry Wives of Windsor* (I.iv), as distinct from 'our English' and 'our English tongue', which 'expose to ironic interrogation the exclusionary ideology and specific exclusion it is used to serve'. Ironically indeed, since it is uttered by the Hostess of the tavern, the illiterate Mistress Quickly, who accuses Dr Caius of abusing 'God's patience and the King's English', while displaying a creative variety of the vernacular herself. If the phrase was inserted some time after 1603 in a version that somehow found its way to the Folio, possibly as a discreet form of resistance to James's appropriation of this ideology to bolster his authority, it 'must have carried particular resonances for the company renamed, after 1603, "the King's Men"'.[68] Its first recorded occurrence, according to the EEBO database, is in Wilson's *Arte of Rhetorique*, against the use of 'outlandishe' words, especially Latinate, French, and Italian forms, which other militant Tudor writers will reject.

Like his grandfather Edward III, the historical Henry V tied up conquest with the independence of language. Both their military triumphs could be largely credited to the yeomen archers who defeated the heavy cavalry charges of their betters. The two weapons, native English and arrows, were intimately allied in the 'Poems of Scorn' of the Hundred Years' War.[69] In 1417, the year of his second invasion of France, Henry V's official correspondence suddenly and almost entirely stopped being written in French. Many government documents and business letters from then on were in English. But Henry's rulings had little effect on English lawyers

66 *A Book of London English*, ed. by R. W. Chambers and M. Daunt (Oxford: Clarendon Press, 1931), p. 16.

67 Malcolm Richardson, 'Henry V, the English Chancery, and Chancery English', *Speculum*, 55.4 (1980), 738, 731.

68 Margaret Tudeau-Clayton, '"The King's English" "Our English"? Shakespeare and Linguistic Ownership', in Halsey and Vine, eds, *Shakespeare and Authority*, pp. 114, 130.

69 See R. H. Robbins, 'A Middle English Diatribe against Philip of Burgundy', *Philologus*, 39.1 (1955), 131–46, and *Historical Poems*, ed. by Robbins, pp. 34–39.

who blithely continued to read, write, and plead in law French. This remnant of the Norman idiom, used by lawyers in court and school exercises, was increasingly closed to outsiders. No wonder if Shakespeare's rebels accuse them of speaking like foreigners. One of the popular charges against lawyers was their use of an opaque foreign idiom, a prejudice echoed in Jack Cade's demagogic pun: Lord Saye 'can speak French, and therefore he is a traitor', for he 'speaks with the tongue of an enemy'.[70]

Protests were presented to Henry VIII against the continued use of law French, 'as therby ys testyfied our subjectyon to the Normannys'.[71] Foreign laws and languages had helped the Conqueror's barony take possession of the land. What does it mean, Bradin Cormack wonders in studying 'the embarrassment of Norman French', that the principal marker of a nation's legal autonomy 'should be a language that speaks so powerfully of accommodation and assimilation and even a prior hybridity'? Henry V's conquering war is to Cormack but an episode in a reiterative pattern, a history of invasion and counter-invasion extending from the Norman Conquest, and including the long history of English losses on the Continent.[72] Actually, the slanging match between Pistol and Fluellen goes even further back in the British memory with allusions to Cadwallader, the last British king of Geoffrey's *Historia*, whose people were chased to Wales by the invading Saxons and became *Welsh*, strangers in their own land, and to the Trojans, the first settlers from whom the British kings claimed descent.[73]

In *The Lawiers Logike*, Abraham Fraunce refers to the language of English common law as to 'that Hotchpot French, stufft up with such variety of borrowed words, wherein our law is written'.[74] If the Inns stood at the hub of the Tudor translation workshop, it was originally for practical reasons. To Ian Lancashire, 'The Inns of Court faced two linguistic challenges under the early Tudors, first to put their law French and Latin into order, and secondly to translate legal terms into English.'[75] Law French had become so hermetic to non-professionals that lexicons explaining each notion had to be devised when, early in his reign, Henry VII ordered the publication of statutes in English, a decision followed by his son's project to have the complete body of statutes translated.[76] In the preface to his 1519 translation of medieval statutes, John Rastell explains that William's

---

70 Starkey, *A Dialogue between Reginald Pole and Thomas Lupset*, ed. by Burton, p. 82. *2 Henry VI*, IV.ii.154–60.

71 In Kathleen Lambley, *The Teaching and Cultivation of the French Language in England during Tudor and Stuart Times* (Manchester: Manchester University Press, 1920), p. 22.

72 Cormack, *A Power to Do Justice*, pp. 180–83.

73 See Goy-Blanquet, '"This Realm Is an Empire"'.

74 Fraunce, 'To the Learned Lawyers of England, especially the Gentlemen of Grays Inne', in *The Lawiers Logike*, Prefatory Epistle, facsimile.

75 Lancashire, 'Law and Early Modern English Lexicons', p. 9.

76 See above, 'Clashes of Jurisdictions' in Chapter 1. John H. Baker, 'John Rastell and the Terms of the Law', in *Collected Papers on English Legal History* (Cambridge: Cambridge University Press, 2013), I, V, 119–31.

Norman counsellors had judged the native language too rude for their laws, but Henry VII, 'worthye to be called the seconde Solomon', found it marvellously amended: where English was lacking in vocabulary, learned men have lately translated 'many noble works into our English tongue', making 'our vulgar tongue so amplified and sufficient of itself to expound many laws or ordinances'.[77]

A Middle Templar turned printer, Rastell specialized in printing legal works and stage plays, some of which he wrote himself, like the *Interlude of the Four Elements*.[78] At the time he published his lexicon, around 1525, he had a little theatre built on his home grounds. His *Expositiones terminorum legum anglorum*, compiled around 1525, providing parallel texts in English and French, gave to young beginners in the study of law one of the earliest dictionaries. His efforts in the long term promoted the use of English for legal purposes, Baker thinks, especially in the 1530s when he printed George Ferrers's full translation of the medieval statutes, but for the time being the glossary served only to emphasize the continued primacy of law French.[79] English then was practically unknown in France, where it was considered barbarous and useless, an attitude that may have nourished many an English writer's xenophobia.

Biblical and Secular English

> You taught me language, and my profit on't
> Is, I know how to curse: the red plague rid you
> For learning me your language.
>
> *The Tempest, I.ii*

Prejudice still ruled when John Florio wrote in his *Firste Fruites* that 'English is a language that wyl do you good in England, but passe Dover it is woorth nothing'.[80] The humanists' common language remained Latin, the lawyers' an obsolete version of French, yet English was slowly gaining ground, and prestige. Richard Pynson, royal printer since Henry VII and expert at printing law texts, published the first collection of Chaucer's *Tales*. William Thynne's fuller *Chaucer's Works* appeared in 1532, sponsored by the king. This edition and the next, ten years later, included various medieval works that served to reconstruct Chaucer as a proto-Protestant, leading Foxe in his *Actes and Monuments* to declare him 'a right Wickleuian'.[81] Thomas Hoccleve had saluted him in *The Regiment of Princes* as 'the first fyndere of our faire language', a claim repeatedly stressed in later campaigns

77 Rastell, *The Abbreviacion of Statutis translated out of French into English*, p. A1^{r-v}.
78 On the typographic conventions used in printing plays, see Peters, *Theatre of the Book*, pp. 19–27.
79 Baker, *The Oxford History of the Laws of England*, VI, p. 26.
80 *Florio his firste fruites which yeelde familiar speech, merie prouerbes, wittie sentences, and golden sayings. Also a perfect induction to the Italian, and English tongues* (1578), dedicated to Leicester, p. 50.
81 Foxe, *Actes and Monuments*, Bk VII, marginal note to p. 1004.

against the courtly muses of the continent by many who chose to ignore the part they had played in shaping Chaucer's Middle English.

One of the reforms begun under Henry VIII's reign allowed the introduction of English into the church offices. A decree of June 1544 prescribed to 'set forthe certayne prayers and suffrages in our natyve Englyshe tongue'. The first authorized vernacular service, a processional Exhortation and Litany, was published that year, and later included in the Book of Common Prayer.[82] The law and the Scriptures should be 'written in the common tongue', in order to be understood by all, Starkey declared in his *Dialogue between Pole and Lupset*. Originally, Erasmus's aim in publishing a Greek New Testament with a Latin translation was to clean the original text of its many accretions and errors for scholars, not to make it more easily available to all readers. Several of his friends, More first, did not think it wise to put these texts into untaught hands, a point that would open the great divide between humanists. One of them, Martin van Dorp, wrote to him that 'it cannot but be harmful, Erasmus, for a crowd of people will discuss the integrity of the Holy Scriptures, and many of them will even wonder if, perhaps, there might not be some erroneous things in them'.[83] Many Catholics were hostile to the 'new learning', and even if Erasmus led the way, the work of translating was in great part done later by Protestant erudites, under the reign of Elizabeth. Carey Conley finds eleven translations from the classics in Edward's reign, four in Mary's, and sixty in the years 1558–1572, half of whose authors were Inns members.[84]

Cranmer, who crossed paths at Cambridge with Tyndale and Miles Coverdale, had convinced the king of the need to commission an authorized English version from Coverdale. Richard Grafton began the printing of the Great Bible in Paris until his presses were seized, and completed it in London with Cromwell's patronage. Large sections of the Old Testament were translations from the Vulgate rather than from the Greek or Hebrew texts. When Henry ordered a revision, Cranmer was given a list composed by his adversary Gardiner of some hundred words that needed retranslation, while the task of revising was entrusted to the universities.

Concerning secular texts, Erasmus and More both thought of translation primarily as a useful exercise to master Latin and Greek, rather than a means of offering foreign masterpieces to less learned readers. The urge to enrich the English language would appear later and take on a more political turn. The early humanists felt they were participating in a great *translatio studii*. Paris claimed the succession of Athens and Rome, and expected *translatio imperii* to follow, with some competition from other European capitals. Polydore Vergil had described a shift of learning to the north, for in the reign of Henry VII 'polished letters, both Latin and Greek, were excluded, uprooted, and banished from Italy by its

82 It is partly Cranmer's own writing, mixed with borrowings from the Sarum processional, the Lutheran litany, and the Greek orthodox litany. Original text at <http://justus.anglican.org/resources>.

83 Letter by Dorp, 1514, L. 305. Erasmus's letter 843 of 1518 to Martin Lipse.

84 Conley, *The First English Translators of the Classics*.

criminal wars, and made their way over the Alps, flowing throughout all Germany, France, England, and Scotland'.[85] All the Tudor monarchs were showered with well-meaning translations from Plutarch, whose educational treatise was incorporated whole into John Lyly's *Euphues*. Some of these translations, especially from the Greek, were often done with the help of extant Latin or French versions, as would North's *Lives* from Plutarch and Amyot.

The Inns followed the fashion set by the more eminent humanists among them. Accomplishments and languages were necessary for high employments at court or in diplomacy. During his years at the Inner Temple, Robert Ashley would study Spanish, Italian, Dutch, and French. Ascham would act as secretary to Morison and follow him in his missions as ambassador to Emperor Carlos. Some of these well-travelled young men were torn between love of the classics and love of the nation. Thomas Phaer explains that his purpose in translating the *Aeneid* is 'the defence of my countreys language'. Hoby in the preface to *The Book of the Courtier* declares each learned man should engage in a piece of translation, 'that we alone of the worlde maye not bee styll counted barbarous in oure tunge, as in time out of minde we have been in our maners'.[86] Even Sidney the classicist claims in his *Defence of poesie* that English is now equal to any tongue.

Against Imported Cloth

Remuneration! O, that's the Latin word for three farthings!

Love's Labours Lost, III.i

As has been amply demonstrated by recent scholarship, the Elizabethan Inns members had read the classics, and some at least among the reputedly insular supporters of the common law were familiar with the works of Jean Bodin, Pierre de la Ramée, François Hotman. Ancient English constitutionalism shows some similarities with Hotman's *Francogallia*, Christopher Brooks observes, though he does admit to a dose of 'legal and political chauvinism which can be traced back at least as far as Fortescue'.[87] This evolution of feelings towards chauvinism appears nowhere more clearly than in the works of Roger Ascham, one of the earliest supporters of the native idiom, or of George Gascoigne. Ascham was trained in the house of a barrister, Sir Humphry Wingfield, Speaker of the House of Commons in 1533, and initiated there to archery before he went to study the classics at Cambridge under John Cheke. His dedication of *Toxophilus* (1545) to Henry VIII claims he would have found it easier to use Latin or Greek, but he chose to write 'this English matter in the English tongue for Englishmen'. The essay, a dialogue between an archer and a rhetorician, compares the precision of their two

85 Vergil, *Anglica Historia*, ed. by Sutton, XXVI. 51.
86 Phaer, Postface to *The Eneidos of Virgill*, p. 81. Hoby, 'Epistle', in Castiglione, *The Courtyer*, p. 7.
87 Brooks, *Lawyers, Litigation*, pp. 206–08, 223.

arts and stresses the importance of the longbow in English history, crowned by the victories of the Hundred Years' War. *The Scholemaster*, begun in 1563 at the request of Sir Richard Sackville, then governor of Inner Temple, is an essay 'on the right order of teaching'. Like Erasmus and More, Ascham was an adept of double translation, 'a plaine and perfite way of teachyng children to understand, write and speake in Latin tong'. The book he particularly recommended to this end was 'Sturmius' Select Letters of Cicero'. His disgust with all other foreign goods leads him to proclaim England the new seat of classicism:

> Now, let Italian, and Latin itself, Spanishe, French, Douch, and Englishe bring forth their lerning, and recite their Authors, Cicero onelie excepted, and one or two moe in Latin, they be all patched cloutes and ragges, in comparison of faire wouen broade clothes.

Where earlier writers copy Italian fashions, Ascham, who had briefly visited Italy ten years before, advises parents against sending their sons there. Italy is no longer fit to teach anything. Venice, once the humanists' model republic, is now '*Circes* Court,' a nest of vices. Rome used to be the best breeder of worthy men, but 'though the place remayne, yet the olde and present maners, do differ as farre, as blacke and white, as vertue and vice'.[88]

Ascham's textile metaphor would have a long line of chauvinistic followers. With the threats of papist invasion, the strain grows to intense xenophobia. Gascoigne, of Gray's Inn, who had gathered his *Hundreth Sundrie Flowres* 'partely by Translation in the fyne outlandish Gardins of Euripides, Ovid, Petrarke, Ariosto, and others, and partly by invention out of our owne fruitfull orchardes in England', ended by repudiating his youthful flirtation with foreign styles:

> What be they? women? Masking in men's weeds?
> With Dutchkin doublets, and with jerkins jagg'd?
> With Spanish spangs, and ruffs fet out of France,
> With high-copp'd hats, and feathers flaunt-a-flaunt?[89]

Robert Greene pursues the theme with *A Quippe for an Upstart Courtier*, a 'quaint dispute' between two pairs of breeches, home cloth and Italian velvet, 'Wherein is plainly set down the disorders in all estates and trades'. Cloth-breeches belongs 'to the old ancient yeomanry' with a pedigree going back to Noah's sons. Velvet is 'sprung from the ancient Romans'. Like Rosalind in Arden, Velvet is accused of having defiled his own nest with vices; like Malvolio 'There be some that seek honour', and 'Others there be whom honour itself seeks'. A jury of craftsmen and gentlemen unsurprisingly declare Cloth-breeches 'most worthy to be rightly resident and have seisin in frank tenement here in England', whereas the upstart Velvet-breeches, brought into the country by newfangleness, is 'a raiser of rents,

---

88 Ascham, *The Scholemaster* (1570), Gutenberg e-book, #1844, pp. 213, 226, 223.
89 Gascoigne, *The Steele Glass*, ll. 1160–63.

and an enemy in the commonwealth.'[90] In a more courteous mood, Rosalind will dismiss Jaques with a 'Farewell, Monsieur Traveller. Look you lisp, and wear strange suits; disable all the benefits of your own country [...] or I will scarce think you have swam in a gondola.'[91] Greene's chatty breeches find numerous echoes in Shakespeare's opalescent doublets, cheveril gloves, and turncoats.

Various writers rejected another item of imported goods: foreign words. Wilson lists them in *Arte of Rhetorique* for 'this should first be learned, that wee never affect any straunge ynkehorne termes, but to speake as is commonly received', and quotes a letter purportedly written by a Lincolnshire man to the Lord Chancellor, so filled with obscure words that no ordinary reader could understand it. John Cheke declared English must be kept 'unmixt and unmangeled with borowing of other tonges' and replaced former Latinized words by old Saxon compounds, like *resurrection* by *uprising*.[92] Ralph Lever devised his own brand of Newspeak in his *Arte of Reason*, coining words like *yeasay* and *naysay* to avoid *affirmation* and *negation*.[93] One of Gascoigne's late works, an essay on prosody, makes Chaucer his reference, not the Latin poets. He recommends avoiding polysyllables, for 'the most auncient English wordes are of one sillable, so that the more monasyllables that you use, the truer Englishman you shall seeme, and the lesse you shall smell of the Inkehorne.'[94]

On the other hand, some imports could be claimed as legitimate conquests. Mulcaster's *Elementarie* (1582) stresses the example of Cicero who 'transported' Greek culture to Rome: he advocates this 'enfranchisement' of foreign words, provided they will be obedient of English rules, 'as the stranger denisons be to the lawes of our cuntrie.'[95] What he does not say is that most of his suggestions are adapted from Du Bellay's *Deffence et illustration de la langue françoyse*. The theme of conquest, which Cormack sees as integral to the self-fashioning of British national identity, and its attendant anxieties are explicitly voiced by various translators. In the tense climate of the Armada years, the national theme takes on new warlike accents. Samuel Daniel prefaces Sylvester's translation of Du Bartas with the image of an English vessel ravaging the French coasts, to 'take that wealth wherein they gloried most, | And make it ours by such a gallant prey'. His poem goes on less aggressively to stress mutual interest in 'The glory of the worke, that we may boast | Much to have wonne, and others nothing lost,' since the treasure

90 In Greene, *The Life and Complete Works*, vol. XI, XXIX, pp. 205–94. Modern spelling transcript copyright ©2003 Nina Green All Rights Reserved, <http://www.oxford-shakespeare.com/>, pp. 12–13, 16, 36.

91 *As You Like It*, IV.i.16–18. And *Twelfth Night*, II.iv.78.

92 See the bibliography of Hans H. Hock and Brian D. Joseph, *Language History, Language Change, and Langage Relationship: An Introduction to Historical and Comparative Linguistics* (Berlin: De Gruyter, 1996). The first attested use of 'inkhorn term' dates from 1543.

93 Ralph Lever, *The arte of reason, rightly termed, witcraft teaching a perfect way to argue and dispute* (London, 1573; repr. Ann Arbor: EEBO, 2004), Bk II, ch. 11, 'Of a yeasay, and a naysay'.

94 Gascoigne, *Certayne Notes of Instruction in English Verse*, ed. by Arber, p. 35.

95 Mulcaster, *The Elementarie*, p. 155.

is made 'by thy taking greater than before'. Decades later, Philemon Holland, who won the nickname of 'Translator Generall in his Age', introduced his translation of Pliny as an endeavour 'by all means to triumph now over the Romans in subduing their literature under the dent of the English pen, in requitall of the conquest some time over this Island, atchieved by the edge of their sword'.[96] At the end of the Elizabethan era, Camden would praise the virtues of English like so many chips on the shoulder, for the native language of the realm was now 'as fluent as the Latine, as courteous as the Spanish, as court-like as the French, and as amorous as the Italian'.[97] The antiquary Richard Carew, of Middle Temple, closed the century with *An Epistle concerning the Excellencies of the English Tongue*.

A determined wish to be free from foreign influences led to a revision of the history of sources. Thus English law must antedate Norman Conquest and Roman law; common law must exist before and above canon law. And yet the chronicles were themselves translations of old Latin annals or of foreign works. Edward Hall's is largely a translation of Vergil's *Anglica Historia*, augmented with extracts from Burgundian chroniclers, or from Robert Gaguin whom the London chronicler Fabyan so reviled and looted. Lodovico Dolce's name disappeared for centuries from Gascoigne's so-called translation of Euripides' *Phoenissae*. Like *Jocasta*, John Wilkinson's version of Aristotle's *Ethics* came from the Italian. Adlington's of Apuleius's *Golden Ass*, Nicolls's Thucydides, Arthur Broke's *Romeus and Juliet*, Fenton's Bandello were all done from French versions, a fact seldom advertised by publishers then and now. Editors still tend to forget that some of Spenser's early poems are translations from *Les Antiquités*, although Spenser himself made no mystery of the fact and paid tribute to Du Bellay's work as 'the first garland of free Poesie | That *France* brought forth'.[98]

In other areas, political or religious, ideology created links that stimulated various apologists. Henry VIII's team had shown the way with their *Collectanea*. Continental theories and doctrines circulated in Latin and French, or in translation. The jurist François Hotman's views on succession, his criticism of the Salic law, his plea for a return to the primitive Church as a weapon against corrupt Roman tyranny found a large audience at the time in England, and would serve again against the Stuarts.[99] An adventurous life of exile took Hotman all around Europe, acting as Calvin's secretary, teaching law and humanities between two diplomatic missions for Protestant princes, until his appointment as councillor of State to Henri de Navarre.[100] When invited to Oxford by Queen Elizabeth, he caused much resentment by decrying the work of Littleton, which he found 'absurde'.[101]

---

96 'The Preface to the Reader', in Pliny the Elder, *The Historie of the World*, trans. by Holland, pp. ii–vii.

97 Camden, *Remaines*, p. 20.

98 Envoy to *Rome*. Spenser's translations for Jan van der Noot's *Theatre for Worldlings* (1569).

99 On Hotman's influence, see Pocock, 'The French Prelude to Modern Historiography', in *The Ancient Constitution and the Feudal Law*, pp. 21–28.

100 See Goy-Blanquet, '"Ces petits livres en français de Messieurs les Hotman"'.

101 He found the book 'incondite, absurde et inconcinne scriptum', and concluded 'stultitiam in eo libro cum malitia et calumniandi studio certare', quoted in Maitland, *English Law and the Renaissance*, p. 59.

His *Francogallia*, written in 1573, one year after the Saint Bartholomew massacre, was more influential: a charge against French absolutist ambitions, it defended the right for a people to rebel if their government did not respect the contract binding them reciprocally.[102] The massacre itself gave rise to numerous other treatises denouncing tyranny, while Protestant writers did their best to make the protests of their continental brothers available in English. Not content with Ovid, Golding translated Beza's *Tragedie*, Duplessis Mornay's *Trewnesse of the Christian Religion*, Calvin's *Treatise concerning offenses*, and a biography by Hotman of Admiral de Coligny who was killed in the massacre. Salluste du Bartas was taken over by Sylvester. Pierre de la Ramée's thesis attacking Aristotle met strong opposition from the Anti-Ramists, but his adversarial translation of Cicero's *Orator* and his educational programme attracted supporters all around Europe. They were all notorious enough in England to appear in the cast of Marlowe's fiercely chauvinistic *Massacre at Paris*.[103]

While at Inner Temple, Thomas Norton made the first English translation of Calvin's *Institutio*, which was published the same year as *Gorboduc*. In his preface to a re-edition of *Institutes of the Christian Religion*, he sums up the translator's dilemma: either follow the words and give the translation greater hardness than the original tongue, or freely render into English what he thinks the meaning must be, and risk error. Eventually, he 'rested upon this determination, to follow the words so near as the phrase of the English tongue would suffer me', and so performed his purpose, 'that if the English book were printed in such paper and letter as the Latin is, it should not exceed the Latin in quantity',[104] an economy all translators of drama would have to keep in mind. It was in the *Institutes* that he first used blank verse, to translate the passages of Virgil's *Aeneid* that Calvin had quoted in the original. In the world of dramatic production, to which we shall now turn, Heywood's dedicatory Epistle to his translation of Seneca's *Hercules Furens* claimed that the play was 'so faithfully translated into English metre' that he had attempted to translate not just verse by verse but also 'word for word wyth the latyn', as a learning aid for young scholars,[105] possibly to compete with several contemporary Parisian editions, Emily Mayne suggests. As evidence of his claim, the play was printed in facing-page parallel texts, an unusual practice at the time, so that the English served 'as a gloss to the Latin text as much as a translation'.[106]

---

102 Hotman, *Francogallia*, ed. by Giesey and Salmon. Kelley, *François Hotman*.

103 See *Constitutionalism and Resistance*, ed. by Franklin.

104 Norton, 'The Translator to the Reader', Preface to fourth edition, 1582.

105 Epistle, in *Jasper Heywood and his Translations of Seneca*, ed. by de Vocht, pp. 199–201.

106 Mayne, 'Presenting Seneca in Print', pp. 841, 842.

CHAPTER 8

Theatres of Law

Some of the Inns members would abjure their juvenile taste for foreign fashions but nonetheless provide a route for the motifs of classical tragedy into the commercial theatre. A playwright like Thomas Kyd, educated at Merchant Taylors' School, could both write the highly popular *Spanish Tragedie* and translate Robert Garnier's *Cornélie*. Garnier, a lawyer of the Parlement de Paris and counsellor of King Henri II, authored the first French neoclassical tragedies, a genre that Sidney's erudite circle hoped to accommodate in England. The no less extensive debt of English Renaissance drama to the 'forensic discourse' and judicial narrative of New Comedy has been abundantly discussed in recent scholarship.[1] It appears clearly in Gascoigne's *Supposes*, performed at the Gray's Inn Christmas revels of 1566, or in the *Arcadia* of Philip Sidney, who was admitted to Gray's Inn in 1567. From them, Hutson argues, Shakespeare absorbed 'an awareness of the underlying legal or forensic quality of *narratio* and of its mimetic uses in drama'.[2] This was only part of the food he absorbed at the Inns, from other sources tapped by Inns members. Gascoigne's *Supposes* lent material to *The Comedy of Errors*, staged at Gray's Inn in 1594; *Jocasta* finds echoes in the histories; and his last play, *The Glasse of Government*, inspired George Whetstone's *Promos and Cassandra*, which Shakespeare would draw on in *Measure for Measure*.

Dramatic Justice

When the bad bleeds, then is the tragedy good.

The Revenger's Tragedy, III.v

One of the major channels from literature to the stage was historiography. Tudor writers had admired Ariosto and Castiglione, but when things Italian became synonymous with perfidy in popular opinion, they looked for substitute material in tales from the English past. The chronicler Edward Hall of Gray's Inn, another of Henry VIII's devoted servants, did not suffer the harsh fate of Cromwell or Cranmer, yet he fully understood and lamented in his magnum opus the reversals that brought down ambitious statesmen from their high places. Their spectacular

1 On these debts, see Scafuro, *The Forensic Stage*. Erne, *Beyond the Spanish Tragedy*.
2 Hutson, *The Invention of Suspicion*, p. 131, and n. 74.

falls play a major part in shaping his notion of history: 'thus Lady Fortune daily turneth her whiele, and mightie Mars, often varieth his countenaunce', for 'suche is worldly vnstablenes, and so waueryng is false flattering fortune'.[3]

Hagiographic Chronicle

Hall's Christian divinity is as impenetrable as the Greek oracle, as whimsical as Fate: 'But se the chaunce, what so euer man intendeth God sodainly reuerseth, what princes will, God wil not, what we thinke stable, God sodainely maketh mutable'. Divine will and Fortune's caprice bravely mix in Hall's lessons, as do his metaphors: if fortune once shone on Edward IV, 'yet now she might turne her saile on the otherside, causyng him to tast eger vineger as she before had giuen hym to drynke dilicate Ypocrace'.[4] Hall endlessly wavers between Providential and Machiavellian views of history, superstition and scepticism, pious and practical recipes to steer the ship of the common weal. The only constant in his political philosophy is a preference for the regime in power, and a hatred of rebels who threaten its stability. The only deposition he approves is that of Richard III, which enabled the Tudor rose to grow on the ruins of the civil war.

Hall 'sees history as a stage on which a moral drama is enacted', the scholar Wolfgang Iser perceptively notes, a repeated *agon* of good versus evil. Its aim is to provide guidelines in a world indifferent to man's needs: 'Norms like the rise and fall pattern, the alternation of good and bad rulers are not structures of history, but endeavours to come to grips with it'.[5] To Hall, history is still a collection of heroic deeds. His chronicle is designed as a monument of 'memory by litterature', erected against 'Oblivion the cancard enemie to Fame'. Poetic licence, invention of speeches for historical characters, and frequent torsions of the truth are all legitimate weapons in this desperate fight against devouring time. Hall's aim is not to interpret God's mind, but to understand, and at all costs eradicate, the factors of unrest. It is to him a great pity that York's brood was not exterminated when the opportunity arose, since it would have spared the country a civil war, 'But the necessitie of destinie, can not by any mans deuise, be either letted or interrupted'.[6]

From a lawyer committed to common law, this sounds close to heresy. But then Hall generally showed a greater zeal for reform than for rule of law. He sat as burgess for Much Wenlock in the Reformation Parliament of 1529, where he faced the new-made chancellor, Thomas More. They were summoned, he explains, to revise laws that were 'insufficient and out of date'. A reformist from

3 *Hall's Chronicle*, p. 173.
4 *Hall's Chronicle*, pp. 45, 298.
5 Iser, *Staging Politics*, pp. 37, 67.
6 *Hall's Chronicle*, Dedication to Edward the Sixth, p. v, p. 226.

the first, Hall had no quarrel with this programme.[7] He showed no qualms either when, obeying the royal command to remove all images of Becket from churches and chapels, he supervised the destruction at Gray's Inn of a 'gloriously painted' window representing the Canterbury saint.[8] When Henry VIII's policy veered back to Catholic doctrine with the Act of the Six Articles, Hall the ever loyal Henrician made a speech in Commons supporting this bill, although it was wholly at odds with his own beliefs. He does admit that the whip with six strings, as it was called, 'brought many honest simple persons to their deaths', and blames the conservative Bishop Gardiner who used it to execute reformers, but omits the fact that he himself was selected for a commission established to enforce the articles in London, a point recorded in Foxe's *Book of Martyrs*.[9]

When passion moves him, Hall's ponderous rhetoric gives way to vivid images and characters. His tone varies with his sources, gossipy when he draws on Fabyan, somberly proleptic after Vergil, venomous about Joan of Arc's fiends, yet scornful like Commynes of superstitious sign readers: 'thus as mennes immaginacions ranne, their toungues clacked'.[10] The haunting picture of Margaret of Anjou's last years, 'more lyke a death then a lyfe, languishyng and mornyng in continuall sorowe', consumed by the thought that she and her husband were 'both ouerlyuer of their progeny, and also of their kyngdome', may well have inspired the ghostly widow of *Richard III*. The union of the rival families, the keystone of Hall's politics, is proclaimed at the end of Shakespeare's first Henriad by the victorious Richmond, the official Tudor voice, as if to bring the whole sequence into conformity with the authorized version of history. *Richard III* finally acts out Hall's obsessive image of the civil war, brother against brother, inflicting mortal wounds on their native country: 'Wherefore, let euery indifferent persone, serche Histories, rede Chronicles, looke on aucthores, aswell holy as prophane', they shall find no worse enemy 'as is roted malice, inwarde grudge, and dissimuled hatred'.[11]

The union of the two noble and illustre famelies of Lancastre and Yorke was posthumously published in 1548, and again in 1550, augmented with tables. Queen Mary's proclamation added 'the book commonly called Hall's chronicle' to a long list of works to be destroyed, for its favourable view of Henry VIII's divorce. Both editions included More's *History of Richard III*, which Grafton had already absorbed into his 1543 *Continuation of Hardyng's Chronicle*. More's nephew, William Rastell, took the opportunity of the banning under Mary's reign to restore their 'garbled' text to its original condition, and published the English

---

7 Margaret McGlynn, 'Edward Hall and the Reformation: The View from Gray's Inn', paper presented at 'The Intellectual and Cultural World of the Early Modern Inns of Court' Conference at the Courtauld Institute, 14–16 September 2006.

8 Dugdale, *The History and Antiquity of the Inns*, p. 284.

9 Foxe, *Actes and Monuments*, Bk VIII, p. 1414.

10 *Hall's Chronicle* pp. 286–87. Commynes, *The Memoirs*, ed. by Kinser, trans. by Cazeaux, I, Book IV, ch. X, 283.

11 *Hall's Chronicle*, pp. 297, 320, 338.

History in 1557.[12] Even the Protestant Roger Ascham thought More's *History* so good that 'if the rest of our story of England were so done, we might well compare with *Fraunce, Italy,* or *Germany* in that behalfe', but he had only mockeries for Hall's 'indenture English', inkhornisms, and superfluous additions of idle words.[13] Among other features, Hall is heavily prejudiced, vociferously anti-French, anti-clerical, anti-feminist, and he shares Fabyan's dislike of all foreigners, who ruin the trade in London. With all its faults, *The union* would still prove highly popular, far more than Vergil's superior *Anglica Historia,* and in turn inspire the works of Foxe, Holinshed, Stow, and others. It would also feed his fellow lawyers' *Mirror for Magistrates* and Shakespeare's first histories.

Poetic History

It must be Hall's harpings on Fortune that brought him to mind, along with Seneca's ghosts, when a group of Inns members undertook to continue Lydgate's *Fall of Princes* with examples drawn from English history. *A Mirror for Magistrates* marked a milestone on the way to Elizabethan drama with a chain of narrative 'Tragedies' borrowed from Hall. Like his chronicle, their verse history began with the reign of Richard II and covered the Wars of the Roses. Italy still stood in the background: Lydgate's work, commissioned by the Lord Protector Humphrey of Gloucester, was adapted from Boccaccio via the French translation of Laurent de Premierfait. The printer, John Wayland, aimed to continue 'where as Bochas lefte, vnto this presente time, chiefly of suche as Fortune has dalyed with here in this ylande'.[14] His plan was to publish *A Memorial of suche Princes* along with a reprint of Lydgate, but the edition of the *Memorial* in 1554 was 'hyndered by the Lord Chauncellor', Gardiner.[15] The book is Marian, not Elizabethan, Scott Lucas insists in his self-labelled 'revolutionary analysis': the period of its composition was 'that of the wrenching divisions and upheavals of Queen Mary's early reign', and these are 'texts of political admonition, protest, and even opposition'. They should be read not as abstract universal sixteenth-century political and philosophical ideas, but as 'retrospectively topical exempla to lead readers to consolatory understandings of the past, righteousness and unfulfilled promise of the Edwardian period'. Far from being 'abstract musings on enduring problems of governance, as *Mirror* scholars traditionally have characterized them, these works are in fact engaged acts of political intervention', attempts to 'alter the political behavior of Marian England's highest officers', for fear they would 'lead the country to

12 See Goy-Blanquet, 'Positions of the Texts', in *Shakespeare's Early History Plays*, pp. 209–15.

13 Ascham, *Report of the Affaires and State of Germany*, in *English Works*, ed. by Wright, p. 126.

14 'Baldwin to the Reader', in Baldwin and others, *The Mirror for Magistrates*, ed. by Campbell, p. 66.

15 According to Baldwin. See Scott C. Lucas, 'The Suppressed Edition and the Creation of the "Orthodox" Mirror for Magistrates', *Renaissance Papers*, 1994, 31–54.

injustice, tyranny, and even civil war'.[16] Some of the tragedies champion the imperialistic foreign policies of Henry VIII and Somerset, their expansionist designs on Scotland and France.[17]

Part I of the *Memorial* appeared in the year of Elizabeth's accession, retitled *A Mirror for Magistrates*. Six editions of new stories followed the original nineteen 'Tragedies'. Sackville's 'Induction' appeared with Part II in 1563. The next instalment, ten years later, went back to the falls of British kings *From the comming of Brute to the incarnation of our saviour and redemer Jesu Christe*. The edition of 1587 united the parts and filled the gaps left.[18] Closest in time to the writing of *Henry VI*, it includes thirty-four 'Tragedies' on the period treated by Hall. The heroes of this poeticized history of England's woes return as the protagonists of Shakespeare's historical sequence. Saluted as the ideal humanist synthesis, the *Mirror* provided inspiration to a long list of poems and plays. Sidney gave it a place in his *Defence of poesie* between Chaucer and the Earl of Surrey's lyrics, accounting it 'meetly furnished of bewtiful partes', a few lines above his critical review of *Gorboduc*.[19]

In his preface to *Thyestes*, Heywood invites Seneca to visit the Inns where he will find talented translators, and ends his list of 'Minervaes men' with 'Baldwyns worthie name | Whose Myrrour dothe of Magistrates procclayme eternall fame'.[20] The dedication of the *Mirror* 'To the nobilitie and all other in office' stresses their responsibility to the public, for 'Ye be all Gods, as many as have in your charge any ministracion of Iustice'. But recent scholarship tends to see the volume as something more than a manual of good behaviour, possibly an act of resistance against the increasing number of proclamations and statutes designed to restrict political expression. The first story in the *Mirror* tells how 'Robert Tresilian chiefe Justice of Englande, and other his felowes' were punished in the reign of Richard II 'for misconstruying the lawes' and bending them to please the Prince:

> If sum in latter dayes, had called unto mynde
> The fatall fall of us for wresting of the ryght,
> The statutes of this lande they should not have defynde
> So wylfully and wyttingly agaynst the sentence quyte.

Tresilian confesses how even the plainest words 'We turned by construction like a welchmans hose', 'wurkyng lawe lyke waxe', until Richard's transgressions grew

16 Lucas, *'A Mirror for Magistrates' and the Politics of the English Reformation*, pp. 5, 9, 14, 175, detects specific echoes of Mary's reign in the tragedies.

17 Lucas, *'A Mirror for Magistrates' and the Politics of the English Reformation*, p. 16, and ch. 4.

18 On its evolution from counsel book to propaganda, see Paul Budra, 'The *Mirror for Magistrates* and the Politics of Readership', *Studies in English Literature*, 32.1 (1992), 1–13.

19 Sidney, *The defence of poesie*, ed. by Ponsonby, p. 152.

20 Heywood, Preface to his translation of *Thyestes* (London: Th. Berthelet, 1560). Baldwin and Ferrers between them are credited with fifteen of the original nineteen tragedies. The others were the work of Phaer, Chaloner, and Churchyard.

so outrageous that the nobility and commons in Parliament undertook to remove evil counsellors like himself from the king's circle.[21] Almost a justification of rebellion.

Unlike *Seneca His Tenne Tragedies*, discussed below, the 'Tragedies' of the *Mirror* were undoubtedly the product of a collective design. To Lucas it is the work of a 'group of like-minded evangelical authors', eager to remedy the failure of Edward Seymour's religious and political reforms with suitable advice to obey the law and listen to independent counsellors. Like so many earlier advisors, they too were convinced 'that the well-being of the commonwealth depends on the ability of poets to admonish their governors'.[22] Each 'Tragedie' begins with a prose introduction, asking Baldwin to warn princes and magistrates against the vices that caused these falls. Each 'hero' speaks as if soliloquizing on a stage. The prose frame 'makes the *Mirror* appear as the record of a collaborative conversation about the governance of the commonwealth', reflecting the varied political positions of its authors, a conversation that would include an increasingly large audience in the following decades, 'fostering discussions about the leadership of the state'.[23]

The *Mirror*'s Dame Fortune, a combination of God's will and Fate, draws her main features from Boethius, who is often represented in medieval iconography standing by the side of her wheel. 'What other thinges bywaylen the cringes of Tragedies. but only the dedes of fortune. that with an vnwar stroke ouerturneth the realmes of grete nobley', Boethius asks in Chaucer's Englishing of his *Consolatio*.[24] To his cries against inconstant Fortune, Philosophy objects that Fortune is deceitful only as an actor is, and constant in her fickleness: men whom she has wheeled to the top should not complain when her wheel continues to turn. Having translated Boethius and Boccaccio, Chaucer lays down the basics of English tragedy in the Monk's Prologue of his *Canterbury Tales*:

Tragedie is to seyn a certeyn storie,
As olde books maken us memorie,
Of hym that stood in greet prosperitee
And is yfallen out of heigh degree
Into myserie, and endeth wrecchedly.

(*ll.* 1973–77)

The Monk then narrates seventeen stories drawn mostly from biblical and ancient history, with incursions into the recent history of Italy. As victim of a barbarous tyrant, Boethius featured in Boccaccio's *de casibus* tales, and Lydgate includes him among the tragic figures of his *Fall of Princes* when he continues the translation in

21 *The Mirror for Magistrates*, ll. 141–44, p. 80, ll. 75, 85, p. 77.

22 Lucas, *'A Mirror for Magistrates' and the Politics of the English Reformation*, p. 16.

23 Winston, *Lawyers at Play*, pp. 141, 144, sees it as part of a larger conversation 'about the possibility for social mobility within the state'.

24 *Chaucer's Translation of Boethius' 'De Consolatione Philosophiae'*, ed. by Morris.

rhymed iambic pentameters. His Prologue traces the tradition to Seneca, whose death at Nero's hands is reported in the Monk's Tale:

> Senek in Rome, thoruh his hih prudence
> Wrot tragedies of great moralitie.[25]

The *Mirror*'s 'Tragedies' are told by the ghosts of fallen statesmen returned from Hades, one of their many Senecan features, each of whom visits the narrator Baldwin 'to bewail unto me his grievous chances, heavy destinies and woefull misfortunes'. Unlike Boccaccio's tales which depict accidents of fortune, most of their woes are the deserved punishment of some grievous fault, though several of them accuse Fortune of their downfall. Like Hall, they waver between Fate and Providence, never quite solving the contradictions between those two agents.[26] The 'Tragedies' do not depict *hamartia* but the inevitability of divine retribution on those who betray their office: 'For here as in a loking glass you shall see (if any vice be in you) how the like hath been punished heretofore'.[27] The censorious Sidney still had no more time for *hamartia* than they did when he praised

> the high and excellent Tragedie that openeth the greatest woundes, and sheweth forth the Ulcers that are covered with tissue; that maketh Kings fear to be Tyrants, and Tyrants manifest their tyrannicall humours; that, with stirring the affects of Admiration and Comiseration, teacheth the uncertaintie of this world, and upon how weak foundations guilden roofes are builded.[28]

Within a year of its appearance, the *Mirror* had achieved status as a monument of tragedy. The quality of its poetry was at best uneven, yet its broad patterns paved the way from chronicle to dramatic form: its arbitrary ordering of episodes, introduction of causal links between discrete events, and elimination of all matters not essential to the purpose anticipated several dramatic requirements. Out of the complex, uncertain, amoral, raw matter of history emerges a clear pedagogic concatenation of deeds, a skeleton to which the playwrights would freely add flesh.[29] Its influence is patent when Heywood pads Seneca with choruses explaining to governors that Hecuba 'A mirrour is, to teache you what you are'.[30] No doubt drawn in their turn by the popularity of *Troas*, two of the *Mirror*'s authors breached the gap between didactic literature and its staged representations with the first Elizabethan tragedy, *Gorboduc*, while audiences of *Hamlet* would still weep 'for Hecuba'.

---

25 Lydgate, *The Fall of Princes*, ed. by Bergen, Bk I, ll. 253–54.

26 See Allyna E. Ward, '"Fortune Laughs and Proudly Hovers": Fortune and Providence in the Tudor Tradition', *Yearbook of English Studies*, 39 (2009), 39–57.

27 Baldwin's Dedication, in *A Mirror for Magistrates*, ed. by Lucas, p. 4.

28 Sidney, *The defence of poesie*, p. 85.

29 On the Inns' poetry, drama, and translation in the 1560s, see Winston's exhaustive bibliography in 'Minerva's Men', and '*Translatio Studii*', *Lawyers at Play*, chs 2 and 4.

30 Heywood, *The Sixt Tragedie. Entituled Troas*, in *Seneca His Tenne Tragedies*, vol. II. His translation of *Troas* had three printings between 1559 and 1562.

The education of princes that so exercised Henry VIII's humanist courtiers was very much in the air again under the reigns of his children. The Inns' tragedies hold up oblique mirrors to the past the better to castigate permanent political sins committed against the common weal and help magistrates cure vices. Gower had already used the method in his *Speculum Meditandis* or *Mirour de l'Omme*. These mirrors are part of the long didactic tradition in which the Inns students had been raised. Their object is not to explain the course of history but to stop the movement of Fortune's wheel, which is bound to take over if men give in to their weaknesses.[31] How pointedly topical the *Mirror*'s reflections were is hard to assess, for the parallels were so intemporal that they might seem to reflect both past and future: if the fall of Protector Somerset was perhaps mirrored in the tragedy of Good Duke Humphrey, destroyed through enmity between brothers and jealousy between their wives, half a century later Elizabeth would still fear to recognize herself in the fate of Richard II, 'for his evyll governance deposed from his seat'.[32]

Abuses and Excuses

> Dwell I but in the suburbs
> Of your good pleasure? If it be no more,
> Portia is Brutus' harlot, not his wife.
>
> *Julius Caesar, II.i*

In December 1574, the clash of competing notions of liberty appeared in an Act of Common Council decreeing that 'no playe, Commodye, Tragidye, enterlude, nor publycke shewe shalbe openlye played or shewed within the liberties of the Cittie'.[33] While Parliament debated about free speech, James Burbage and his brother-in-law John Brayne were building a new venue for rhetorical jousts in Shoreditch, on the site of an Augustinian priory, Holywell. On 13 April 1576, Giles Allen leased a portion of the ground for twenty-one years to Burbage, there to erect a building for the performance of plays. The Theatre opened in the autumn of 1576, to harbour the acting company of Robert Dudley, Earl of Leicester, whose patronage they had secured when the act of 1572 made travelling players vagrants. Having obtained the first royal patent granted to a company, they were authorized by the queen to play comedies, tragedies, stage plays, and interludes 'as well for the recreation of our loving subjects as for our pleasure and solace when we shall think good to see them', in the liberties of all her cities 'throughout our realm of England'.[34] Leicester's Men had performed at court in

---

31 See Iser, *Staging Politics*, pp. 40–43, on the *Mirror*'s main difference from historical narratives.

32 George Ferrers, Tragedy 5, in *The Mirror for Magistrates*, p. 111.

33 In Chambers, *The Elizabethan Stage*, IV, p. 274.

34 Royal Patent, 10 May 1574, repr. in *English Professional Theatre, 1530–1660*, ed. by Glynne Wickham and others (Cambridge: Cambridge University Press, 2000), p. 206.

the Christmas seasons of 1574 and 1575, and in the summer at Kenilworth, twelve miles from Stratford. The earliest reference to their building appears in an order of the Privy Council, dated 1 August 1577, against those who play without the liberties of the City, 'as *the theater* and such like'.[35] The erection of the Theatre and the Curtain in 1576 and 1577 in liberties escaping the jurisdiction of the town authorities, outside the City's boundaries, instantly spurred tracts and sermons denouncing the immorality of the theatres, the plagues they brought on London, and the shockingly huge gains of players who attracted more audience than the pulpit.

After an order of 28 July 1597 by the Privy Council, at the end of Allen's lease, the Theatre was taken down in December 1598 and its boards secretly carried to Southwark to build the Globe.[36] Another disused monastery, Blackfriars, would later provide Burbage's sons, Richard and Cuthbert, with an indoor theatre. It stood on a free precinct, outside the authority of the Lord Mayor, but the residents were alert to the move: 'now all players being banished by the Lord Mayor from plaing within the Cittie by reason of the great inconveniences and ill rule that followeth them, they now thincke to plant them selves in the liberties'. They petitioned the Privy Council to protect them from 'the great pestring and filling up of the same precinct' by 'all manner of vagrant and lewde persons', and prevented them from performing there for eleven years.[37]

That drama stood in low esteem even among those who enjoyed it appears plainly in its listing by Inns members among pleasures of 'no account', or Lady Mary Herbert's invitation to her son to visit Wilton with the enticing news that 'we have the man Shakespeare with us', at the height of the man's career.[38] Stephen Gosson's *School of Abuse*, dedicated to Sidney, described the theatre as 'a generall market of bawdrie'.[39] Gosson was himself an actor before he became a schoolmaster, and the author of at least three plays: one of them a comedy in the Italian style, 'a cast of Italian devices called *The comedie of Captaine Mario*'; *Catalines Conspiracy* which was performed at the Theatre; and 'a moral' entitled *Praise at Parting*.[40] He had been 'drawn like a novice to these abuses', he confessed to the reader, but abandoned any such folly before he turned twenty-five: 'I have sinned, and I am sorry for my fault'.[41] Perhaps John Northbrooke's earlier 'Treatise wherein Dicing, Dauncing, Vaine Playes or Enterluds &c. are reproved' (1577) incited him to mend his ways. Sidney did not directly answer Gosson's unsolicited tribute, but his *Apologie for Poetrie* gives a side kick to poet-haters and to 'all that

---

35 *Acts of the Privy Council*, 1575–1577, IX, p. 388.

36 *Acts of the Privy Council*, n.s., XXVII, p. 314.

37 Petition of November 1596, in Gurr, *The Shakespeare Company*, appendix 2.5, pp. 248–49.

38 Samuel Schoenbaum, *William Shakespeare: A Documentary Life* (Oxford: Oxford University Press, 1975), p. 126.

39 Gosson, *The Schoole of Abuse*, ed. by Arber, p. 26.

40 Gosson, *The Schoole of Abuse*, p. vi.

41 Gosson, *The Schoole of Abuse*, pp. 19, 30.

kind of people who seek a praise by dispraising others, that they do prodigally spend a great many wandering words in quips and scoffs'.[42]

Why Gosson chose to dedicate his *Schoole* to Sidney, and 'was for hys labor scorned',[43] is not clear from his dedicatory epistle. Perhaps because Sidney made no mystery of the poor esteem in which he held the English stage, *Gorboduc* excepted by a thin margin, and thus made Gosson hope to find in him a kindred spirit: 'A good physition, when the disease cannot be cured within, thrusteth the corruption out in the face, and delivereth his patient to the chirurgion' — Sidney, presumably.[44] Lodge in his 'Defence of Poetry, Music and Stage-Playes' (1579) accused Gosson of using 'divinity to cover your knavery', yet admitted there was room for improvement in the theatre and gave his own proleptically medical view of the stage: poets use pagan gods and metaphors to draw men to wisdom by way of pleasure, 'for seeing the world in those days was unperfect, it was necessary that they, like good phisitions, should so frame their potions that they might be appliable to the queasy stomachs of their wearish patients'.[45] Nashe will pursue the same line of defence in *Pierce Pennilesse*, arguing that the theatre is the best place for idle men, as it keeps them from worse occupations and sharpens their wits by teaching them the history of their country: ten thousands wept to see brave Talbot, the terror of the French, triumph again on stage — a triumph apparently more memorable than his final defeat.

According to Gosson's *Ephemerides of Phialo*, the players vainly asked several members of the universities to answer his pamphlet, until they found 'one in London to write certaine *Honest Excuses*, for so they tearm it, to their dishonest abuses which I revealed'.[46] Gosson retaliated with *Plays confuted in Five Actions* (1582), in which he called Lodge, his contemporary at Oxford, 'a vagrant person, visited by the heavy hand of God', and received support from Philip Stubbes's *Anatomie of Abuses* (1583). Written as a dialogue, this pamphlet included a section 'Of Stage-plays and Interludes, with their wickedness' that stressed the devilish origin of plays, and in turn caused Nashe to retort with *The Anatomie of Absurditie*. Camps were now fairly set for battle. Puritans of Gosson's ilk had a complex relation to drama, probably a nostalgia for the heroic times when their Calvinistic forerunners used this medium to proclaim their faith, and did not

42 Philip Sidney, *An Apology for Poetry*, ed. by Shepherd, p. 121. First printed in 1595, it was renamed *A Defence of Poesie* in subsequent editions.

43 According to Spenser, in a letter of 15–16 October 1579 to Gabriel Harvey: Spenser, *The Poetical Works*, ed. by Smith and Selincourt, p. 635.

44 Gosson, *The Schoole of Abuse*, p. 4.

45 *A Reply to Gosson's School of Abuse*, in Pollard, ed., *Shakespeare's Theater*, p. 41. Lodge's work was published surreptitiously, having been refused a licence, in the late summer of 1579. Gosson refers to the attack written at the players' request as *Honest Excuses*, which John Dover Wilson argues was its original title, 'The Missing Title of Thomas Lodge's Reply to Gosson's School of Abuse', *Modern Language Review*, 3.2 (1968), 166–68.

46 Gosson, 'An Apologie of the Schoole of Abuse', in *The ephemerides of Phialo* (London: Thomas Dawson, 1579) p. 90.

gladly relinquish it to unworthy money-makers. That they feared to be robbed of their monopoly of the public spoken word is audible when, according to Northbrooke, people shame not to say openly 'that playes are as good as sermons, and that they learne as much or more at a playe, than they doe at God's worde preached'.[47]

This specific rivalry combined with another offence, the abuse of Sunday by the practice of idle sports. One of Gosson's supporters and a friend of Gascoigne, George Whetstone, in his 'Touchstone for the Time' denounced 'the use of stage-plays on the Sabbath-day, and the abuse of them at all times', but he too was a self-confessed dramatist, having committed *The right, excellent and famous Historye of Promos and Cassandra,* a two-part play drawn from a story in Giraldi Cinthio's *Ecatommiti.* Its preface is addressed to William Fleetwood, of the Middle Temple, then Recorder of London. The anonymous author of *A second and third blast of retrait from plaies and Theatres* (1580) sponsored by the City of London, introduced himself as a repented actor. According to his tract, the root of the evil was the support given to players by the nobility, a point already made by Gosson. If Anthony Munday was indeed the author of the *Blast,* as some critics think, the Puritan party must have quite cynically used his brief conversion for their propaganda. William Rankin published a very abusive *Mirrour of Monsters,* then went on to write plays for Henslowe and the Rose Theatre.[48] Considering the intensity of polemical and philosophical debate around the theatre, it is no wonder, as Tanya Pollard observes, that the contemporary stage repertoire should be so self-reflexive: inset plays like Hamlet's 'Mousetrap' are everywhere in Renaissance drama.[49]

A disaster at the Paris Garden in January 1583 offered the occasion of a concerted attack against pleasure grounds and entertainments. The scaffolds over-charged with spectators fell during a Sunday performance, John Dee notes, 'Many being killed thereby, more hart, and all amased. The godly expownd it as a due plage of God for the wickednes ther usid, and the Sabath day so profanely spent.'[50] The Lord Mayor of London, Sir Thomas Blank, wrote the following day to inform Burghley of 'this greate mysshappe' which gave 'greate occasion to acknowledge the hande of god for suche abuse of the sabboth daie', and begged his lordship 'to give order for redrese of suche contempt of gods' service'. Within a week John Field, part author of the first *Admonition to Parliament,* produced his *Godly Exhortation by occasion of the late Judgment of God shewed at Paris Garden,* listing all such items of terrible judgements passed on players and their audiences. In an earlier letter, Field had pressed his protector Leicester not to give his hand in behalf of wicked men 'as of late you did to the great greife of all the godly': let

47 Northbrooke, *A Treatise Against Dicing,* p. 93.

48 On this exchange of abusive pamphlets, see Gosson, *The Schoole of Abuse,* pp. vii–xi.

49 Pollard, ed., *Shakespeare's Theater,* p. xviii.

50 *The Private Diary of Dr John Dee,* ed. by James O. Halliwell (London: Camden Society, 1842), 1583, Jan. 13th, p. 18.

him join forces with the City and all those who cried out against 'those impure interludes and playes'. Fleetwood, in his record of the proceedings in the City wrote on Sunday, 14 January 1582–1583 that 'Upon the same daie the violaters of the Saboth were punished by God's providence at Paris Garden'.[51] The Privy Council issued an order against performances on Sundays. On 10 March 1583, two months after the Paris Garden catastrophe, Edmund Tilney was required by Mr Secretary to choose out a company of twelve players for Her Majesty, which effectively stopped the City's attempts to suppress them altogether.

The City having temporarily lost its assault on the theatre, the debate continued in the universities, where academic plays were better tolerated, unlike 'common plays' used as a means of livelihood which raised a large measure of scorn. When Elizabeth visited Cambridge in 1564, students and masters were warned they were expected to entertain her with all manner of scholarly exercises, disputations, orations, verses, in Latin, Greek, and English, and playing of comedies and tragedies. On her visit to Oxford, two years later, the bill of festivities included a comedy, *Marcus Germinus*, Richard Edwards's *Palamon and Arcyte*, drawn from 'the Knight's tale' that will inspire *Two Noble Kinsmen*, and a Latin tragedy, *Progne*, drawn from Ovid's *Metamorphoses*, a source shared with *Titus Andronicus*. There was such a crowd of spectators come to see *Palamon* that part of a wall collapsed, killing and maiming several, but this accident does not seem to have spoilt the feast nor raised fears of God's wrath.

One of the more prominent Senecan authors, William Gager, doctor of civil law, won a place on Francis Meres's list among the chief dramatists of the day.[52] One of his Latin tragedies, *Meleager*, was performed in front of Leicester and his kinsman Sidney in 1584, no doubt rejoicing Sidney's heart by its strict observance of the unities. As for his comedies, they did not scruple to lampoon well-known figures like the three Harvey brothers, or the town authorities, a practice that would reach a height with the famous *Parnassus Trilogy*. In one of these, 'sweet Mr Shakespeare' is comically worshipped by the silly would-be patron of letters Gullio. But the St John's dramatists did not appreciate the competition of unscholarly successful rivals any more than London wits. The 'upstart crow' was accused of believing himself the only Shake-scene in a country, when in fact universities, Inns of Court, and public playwrights all beautified themselves with the same feathers: Ovid and Seneca, English chroniclers, Italian poets and storytellers,

---

51 Field, letter of 25 November 1581 to thank Leicester for having obtained his release from jail. 'A Godly Exhortation', 13 January 1583. See J. Payne Collier, *The History of English Dramatic Poetry to the Time of Shakespeare* (London: John Murray, 1831), I, pp. 253–54, and the Lord Mayor's endeavours to suppress the Theatre and the Curtain, I, pp. 258–60. Fleetwood's 'account to Burghley of the Parliamentary debates of November 1584, *Proceedings*, II, pp. 65–66.

52 On the contention between William Gager of Christ Church, and the theologian John Rainolds of Corpus Christi, see F. S. Boas, *University Drama in the Tudor Age* (Oxford: Clarendon Press, 1914), ch. 10.

while the French neo-classics seem an acquired taste restricted to Sidney's select circle. Among their common obsessions, political stability stood predominant, though the ways recommended to secure it vary.

Political Tragedy

Erasmus had owned himself not entirely satisfied with his improved edition of Seneca's works and invited young scholars to continue the effort. Taking him at his word, Calvin's first publication, at the end of his legal studies in Orleans, was a commentary on Seneca's *De clementia*, with a foreword warning readers that he would occasionally correct Erasmus on various points the revered scholar had missed. Why he chose Seneca, and why this particular text, he does not say. It has often been thought that it was designed to urge François Ier to show clemency to the Protestants, just as Seneca had implored Nero's benevolence for his subjects. But not a word, not a learned note in the volume confirms this, François Wendel points out. Besides, as we saw above about Servet, Calvin's distaste for violent persecutions did not long overlive his own conversion. Seneca was popular among the Christian humanists who saw in Stoicism an apt counterweight to Epicurean hedonistic doctrines. Calvin's expressed wish was to contribute in rehabilitating Seneca, not so much as a Stoic, a belief he did not wholly adhere to, but as a philosopher and stylist. He possibly also wished to establish himself as a humanist scholar, using the methods of Valla, Erasmus, and Guillaume Budé, which he would later apply to his exegesis of the Scriptures.[53] The commentary did earn him a place among renowned European humanists, while his championing of Seneca would find eager followers at the Inns, coinciding with the English translation of his *Institutio* by Cranmer's son-in-law, Thomas Norton, barrister of the Inner Temple.

Bleeding Seneca

> English Seneca read by candlelight yields many good sentences [...] and if you entreat him fair in a frosty morning, he will afford you whole *Hamlets*.
>
> *Thomas Nashe, Preface to Menaphon*

The works of Inns members are in every sense educational exercises in ethics, politics, law, and diplomacy. Where necessary, they do not hesitate to expound their views with unwarranted additions to their translations, or adapt the original to stress moral teachings. Heywood embellishes Seneca's *Troas* with a wrathful ghost of Achilles, summoned from the Underworld to vociferate some ninety original lines demanding the sacrifice of Polyxena. Choruses are given extra lines

53 Wendel, *Calvin*, ch. 1.

to stress premonitions and perils. Heroic deeds, human sufferings, the weight of power, the torments of hell also receive their shares of additional stanzas. These expansions require the old fourteener, redolent with alliteration, to do them justice:

> O Kyng of Dytis dungeon darke, and grysly ghosts of hell,
> That in the deepe and dredfull denns, of blackest Tartare dwell.[54]

Thus the effects of Medea's charms must have sent refined thrills of horror down the lawyers' spines:

> A mowsie, rowsie, rusty route with cancred Scales Iclad
> From musty, fusty, dusty dens where lurked long they had,
> Doe craull.
>
> (*Medea, The Fourth Acte, ll. 683–85*)

The translators of the *Tenne Tragedies*, like most early Elizabethan playwrights, did not attempt to imitate Seneca's prosodic variety. Norton, we saw, had already experimented with blank verse, when translating Calvin's *Institutio*, for his quotations from the *Aeneid*. Where *Thyestes* alternated rhyming lines of ten and fourteen syllables, *Gorboduc* uses unrelieved pentameter throughout.[55] As to the matter itself, the playwrights' main dilemma is to combine Senecan vengeance, cruel fortune, and blind fate with divine justice. Here again, occasional twists and additions give the last word to Christian judges.

The Senecan plays show unresolved tensions between capricious fortune and vengeful retribution: kings 'are but dust', subject to 'waveryng welth', yet they suffer the penalty of their own faults. This contradiction, which still raises many academic questions,[56] did not yet greatly trouble readers of Boethius: there was a cyclical regularity, a strong moral law, a superior Providence, behind Fortune's apparent vagaries. Doubts about the providential order of the world would mature with the years into major tragedy, at some distance from the Inns. When two of the young men named in his Preface moved on towards the stage, Heywood had just left England and become a Jesuit priest. Norton and Sackville's *Gorboduc*, 'clyming to the height of Seneca his style' in Sidney's tribute, copies his five-act structure, chorus, and political meditations. So will its follower, *Gismond of Salerne*, authored by five gentlemen of the Inner Temple.

An advocate and a teacher of rhetoric, Seneca was a rich source of *sententiae* to both playwrights and political orators (see below, Chapter 9), one that 'could

---

54 Heywood's original soliloquy (1560) for *Thyestes: The seconde tragedie of Seneca*, The Fifth Acte, The fourth Sceane, Added to the Tragedy by the Translatour.

55 In *Thyestes*, the decasyllable is reserved to the Chorus; the other characters speak in fourteeners. Their lines being too long for the page, Berthelet printed them as two lines of eight and six.

56 Winston, 'Seneca in Early Elizabethan England', p. 49, for one, who quotes Frederick Kiefer and Bruce Smith on this point.

be mined for purple patches and fine phrases'. Perhaps they sounded archaic when Nashe mocked his adapters,[57] but his experience did not. The Roman dramatist had witnessed all the horrors he depicted: 'Exile, murder, incest, the threat of poverty and a hideous death, and all the savagery of fortune were the very texture of his career.'[58] He had managed to survive four successive emperors (Augustus, Tiberius, Caligula, Claudius) before dying victim to the tyranny of the fifth.[59] A new generation of ambitious young Inns men was ready to revive the humanist hopes of taking part in the government of the realm. Where could they find better informed, more resilient lessons on the mutability of court life? A successful lawyer himself, Seneca had combined playwriting with his role of counsellor, though a very evil one in the eye of the Protestant bishop John Ponet:

> Nero the Emperor was of nature very modest, gentle, and merciful, and the first five years of his reign he behaved himself with virtue. After other counselors and masters, then Seneca crept into his favor, who told him that he might do what he lusted for. He was soon persuaded of the same. And to show some proof that he had well carried away their advise, he killed his mother Agrippina.

This proved fatal to both men, for in the end Nero 'killed his master Seneca' and 'never left his cruelty until the people found occasion and opportunity to utter their hatred, and slew him'.[60] The philosopher plays a brief role as Nero's mentor in *Octavia*, long erroneously attributed to him. His advice, that a monarch should be obeyed out of love rather than fear, is not heeded, and would be reversed by Machiavelli. But the plot offers interesting parallels with recent events in England, and obliquely proves the counsellor right, when Nero's decision to divorce Octavia and marry Poppea causes a popular riot.

Whether designed as advice to Nero, or urges to unthrone him, Seneca's plays had political relevance in his own days, earning him respect throughout the medieval tradition as a 'moralist philosopher'.[61] With a little mending they could be translated into the present turmoils of Tudor monarchy, and act as 'glasses of governance', encouraging Inns members in their will to act as advisors, while developing literary styles that would move from the Inns to the Elizabethan stage. To Linda Woodbridge, translating his plays demonstrated 'serious commitment to political resistance in an era of religious regression and censorship'.[62] In his dedication to Thomas Heneage, treasurer of the queen's chamber, Thomas Newton rejects the accusations of 'some squeymish Areopagites' that these tragedies tend to praise ambition and cruelty: Seneca stands high in 'the Catalogue of

57 Burrow, *Shakespeare and Classical Antiquity*, p. 177.

58 C. J. Herington, 'Senecan Tragedy', *Arion*, 5 (1966), 430.

59 Winston, 'Seneca in Early Elizabethan England', p. 37.

60 Ponet, *A Short Treatise on Political Power*, ch. 2.

61 See Pastore-Stocchi, 'Un Chapitre d'histoire littéraire', pp. 11–36.

62 Woodbridge, *English Revenge Drama*, p. 131.

Heathen wryters' with philosophical sentences that beat down 'sinne, loose lyfe, dissolute dealyng, and unbrydled sensuality', as well as 'cloaked dissimulation & odious treachery.'[63] The *Tenne* translations, by five different writers, seven of which had already been printed, may display 'a wide variety of motivations, formats and intentions', as does Newton's own translation of *Thebais*, self-promotion as a serious scholar, didactic purposes or other, 'rather than a project, ideal or actual, between all the authors'. The presentation and bibliographical apparatus of the *Tenne Tragedies* suggest that Newton intended the volume 'to serve as an English equivalent to collected continental editions of Seneca's tragedies'.[64] Rather than representing the culmination of interest in 'Elizabethan Seneca', Emily Mayne concludes, Newton's *Tenne Tragedies* may have created it. In Burrow's opinion, confirmed by Nashe's irony, their style must have seemed old-fashioned to the new generation of playwrights: Heywood probably thought his own *Troas* a modish modern affair, but throughout the translation, 'he echoes the neo-medieval idiom of *The Mirror for Magistrates*'. Shakespeare would have his work cut out when aiming to renovate Old English Seneca. There is no doubt in Burrow's mind that Seneca's influence on his plays was deep and continuous. *Hippolytus* especially 'stayed with him throughout his career'.[65]

At that point, the repertoire of the Elizabethan theatre still borrows heavily from the continent. Unsurprisingly, the models of Senecan and neoclassical plays came at first from Italy, via Giraldi Cinthio and Lodovico Dolce, then at a later stage from France, through the influence on Sidney's circle of the dramatist Robert Garnier. The use of dramatic blank verse and dumb shows also had Italian precedents. The Italian playwrights had established *endecasillabi sciolti*, unrhymed verse, on the tragic stage since 1515, with Trissino's *Sofonisba*.[66] They were also pioneers in the use of *intermedii*, which Cinthio and Dolce defended against the purists as moments of recreation for the spectators, while admitting there was no classical authority for them. There are no details known on the 1549 performance of Dolce's *Giocasta*, but it was revived in 1570 at the Academy of Viterbo with spectacular *intermedii*. 'There can be little doubt', the Victorian scholar Cunliffe recognizes 'that we owe to the Italian *intermedii* the English dumb shows, which are of the same general character and serve the same purpose.' Dumb shows may have arisen from native pageants, he admits, yet the coincidence with *intermedii* is too marked to be ignored.[67]

63 Newton's Original Dedication to Sir Thomas Henneage of *Seneca His Tenne Tragedies*.

64 Mayne, 'Presenting Seneca in Print', pp. 827, 837.

65 Burrow, *Shakespeare and Classical Antiquity*, pp. 172, 182. He detects the influence of Seneca in several of Shakespeare's plays besides *Titus* and *Hamlet*, in *Richard III*, *Lear*, and *Macbeth*, pp. 185–201.

66 See Michel Paoli, 'Alberti, Trissino, Algarotti: Le vers blanc italien entre modèle antique et génie du toscan', in *Invisibilité du vers blanc*, ed. by Jacques Darras, In'hui, 55 (Brussels: Le Cri, 2000), pp. 16–25.

67 John W. Cunliffe, *Early English Classical Tragedies* (Oxford: Clarendon Press, 1912), p. xl.

The interest in Seneca was not restricted to England. As Jean Jacquot shows in his overview of European Renaissance drama, the vogue of Seneca varied from one country to the next.[68] It is worth noting that the Roman playwright entered the Italian and the French stages through the works of lawyers. The first Senecan tragedy, 'indeed the first tragedy of Western theatre',[69] was the work of a Paduan notary, Albertino Mussato, in 1315: by order of the Commune his *Ecerinide*, modelled on *Thyestes* to stigmatize the tyranny of Ezzelino III, was read publicly every year as a political antidote.[70] Mussato's treatise on *Evidentia Tragediarum Senece* takes its definition of tragedy from Boethius, 'Testante Boetio', but shows no interest for the stage.[71] Seneca was the friend and philosopher to whom Petrarca addressed the letters of his old age. It was Boccaccio who began to invent a distinct *Seneca tragicus*, who must be the son, or the brother, of the philosopher, *Seneca moralis*.[72] The first recorded Latin performance of Seneca was *Hippolytus* in Rome in 1471. Antonio Cammelli's *Filostrato e Panfila* (1499), drawn from the *Decameron*, is introduced by the ghost of Seneca, who returns from the realm of shadows to present the plot. In France, Robert Garnier, the king's advocate general at the Parlement de Paris, who had studied law in Toulouse, drew his formal models from Seneca, basing his plots on famous historical or mythical events. Pierre Corneille, also a former student of law, drew his *Médée* from Seneca and Euripides, with changes designed to attenuate Medea's guilt. Seneca's violence would soon be rejected as unseemly by the strict adepts of decorum, yet Racine's *Phèdre* was still indebted to him.

In England, years after the *Tenne Tragedies*, the Inns gave Seneca a new life that had no equivalent on the continent. *The Misfortunes of Arthur* (1588), a joint effort by Thomas Hugues and seven other gentlemen of Gray's Inn, based on Geoffrey of Monmouth's *History*, relates Arthur's war against Rome and the usurpation of his incestuous son Mordred. With again a fine mix of Christian and pagan fatality, Guenevora 'through despaire purposyng diversley, sometimes to kill her husband, sometimes to kill her selfe, at last resolved to enter into religion'.[73] Considered the best Senecan tragedy of the period, it marked the height of Seneca's influence.

---

68 Jean Jacquot, 'Sénèque, la Renaissance et nous', in Jacquot, ed., *Les Tragédies de Sénèque et le théâtre de la Renaissance*, p. 279.

69 Pastore-Stocchi, 'Un Chapitre d'histoire littéraire', p. 25.

70 See the commentaries of the grammarians Guizzardo and Castellano in Albertino Mussato, *Ecerinis*, ed. by Luigi Padrin (Bologna: Padrin, 1900), p. 109. Ezzelino III da Romano ruled Padua from 1236 to 1259.

71 Pastore-Stocchi, 'Un Chapitre d'histoire littéraire', p. 30.

72 On the variations concerning his identity and authorship of some of the ten plays collected in Newton's edition, see Mayne, 'Presenting Seneca in Print', pp. 824–25.

73 'The Argument of the Tragedie', in Hugues and others, *The Misfortunes of Arthur*, ed. by Collier, p. 10. Bacon, Yelverton, and John Lancaster devised the masques.

'Astreas Servants'

With Muses still we entercourse allowe,
T'enrich our state with all there forreine fraight.

The Misfortunes of Arthur, Prologue, ll. 95–96

The early playwrights' most urgent concern was not metaphysical. Elizabeth herself was well aware of the lawyers' wish to guide her political steps with Senecan exempla. The enmity between brothers that launches the action of *Thyestes* forms the core of *Gorboduc*, and of many ensuing plays, from *Jocasta* to *As You Like It*, *Hamlet*, or *The Tempest*. The preceding century with its rivalries at the heart of the Plantagenet family had plentifully shown their deadly effects. Now the theme was again relevant, with the potential threat of rival claimants to the succession: Mary, Queen of Scots supported by the Catholics, and Catherine Grey, the Protestants' candidate. If there was any point of agreement between counsellors, it was that Elizabeth should promptly marry and entrust the reins of power to her husband. But the choice of a suitable one was another source of discord. *Gorboduc* does not provide a solution to the 'succession crisis', Dermot Cavanagh argues, but is 'an attempt to *embody* it, to rehearse the dilemmas, even the disorientation, characteristic of a time that presented grave and difficult choices'. Its practice of controversy, so prevalent at the Inns, offers an exemplary demonstration of 'how history elicits conflicting rather than unitary understanding'.[74]

Gorboduc, or *The Tragidie of Ferrex and Porrex*, as it was originally called, was part of the Christmas revels of 1561–1562 at Inner Temple, and followed by a performance at court in January. The diary of Henry Machyn confirms that the revels lasted several days, and that 'mony of the conselle was ther'.[75] On both occasions, the play went with a masque of Beauty and Desire, variously entitled *Pallaphilos* or *Pallas, Perseus and Andromeda*, a tale of chivalric wooing crowned by a marriage in the temple of Pallas. Reporting the revels, Gerard Legh praises the Inns in Fortescue fashion as 'a place priviliged by the most excellent princes' where they are sure to find 'the store of gentlemen of the whole realm, that repair thither to learn to rule, and obey by law, to yield their fleece to their prince and commonwealth'.[76] The gentlemen did yield their fleece to their patron, Robert Dudley, Earl of Leicester, and served the commonwealth as they thought best, by recommending him as the wisest choice of husband to their queen. There is definite hostility in the play to the foreign pretender, Fergus, Duke of Albany, who might be a combination of the 'northern' threats offered by both Mary Stuart and

74 Cavanagh, *Language and Politics*, p. 45.

75 Machyn, *A London Provisioner's Chronicle*, 27 December 1561, fol. 144v, stored in the library of Robert Cotton. Modernized electronic scholarly edition by Richard Bailey, Marylin Miller, and Colette Moore, <https://quod.lib.umich.edu/m/machyn/>.

76 Legh, *Accedens of Armorie*, fol. 119b. Axton, *The Queen's Two Bodies*, pp. 39–48, reconstructs the masque from his account.

Eric of Sweden. The subject of matrimony was highly topical in and out of Parliament. In 1560, Thomas Smith 'drew out an ingenious book, consisting of divers orations for or against the Queen's marriage'. Francis Walsingham introduces the topic when, during a walk in Smith's garden, they hear the rumour 'of the King of Sweden Ericus's coming hither'. Walsingham considers that the speculations of philosophers and rhetoricians will only unsettle simple men, and that anyone favouring a foreign marriage must be some mongrel with a dose of outlandish blood, but evinces a sharp retort from Smith: 'Ye judge very fast, before ye know the man or have perused his reasons.'[77] Here we have the very gist of the *pro et contra* argument, on stage as in court, which the dialogue then proceeds to illustrate. Agamus, or Spitewed, thinks the Queen should remain single. Philoxenes, Love-alien, favours marriage to a foreigner. Axenius, Homefriend, recommends that she marry at home with an English nobleman. Norton and Sackville share Smith's interest in fluctuating political circumstances, Cavanagh argues, and the need to weigh events carefully before deciding on a course of action.[78] Thomas More, we saw above, had given a similar warning to any would-be counsellor who came on stage 'in the garb of a philosopher'.

An eyewitness of the court performance of *Gorboduc* was particularly struck by the dumb shows. In the second one, the king must choose between a gold cup filled with poison or a transparent glass filled with wine which he rejects and crushes underfoot, suggesting 'that men refused the certen and toocke the uncertein, wherby was ment that yt was better for the Quene to marye with the L[ord] R[obert] known than with the K[ing] of Sweden', her two notable suitors at the time.[79] This interpretation differs considerably from the printed argument, where the dumb show is taken as a warning against flattery. Stranger still are this witness's remarks about the third dumb show, that 'many thinges were handled of mariage, and that the matter was to be debated in parliament', for the text as we know it does not discuss matrimony, though it does advocate a parliamentary solution to the dynastic crisis.[80] It seems likely that the reporter had the whole show in mind. As Graves put it, 'the political significance of *Gorboduc* can only be understood in conjunction with the masque of *Pallas, Perseus and Andromeda*'.[81]

The Tragidie of Ferrex and Porrex was printed by John Day in 1570 'altogether as the same was showed on stage before the Queenes Maiestie'.[82] Seen in retrospect as the father of history plays, its most significant steps were the dramatization of an episode from the British chronicles, the insertion of dumb shows, and

77 Strype, *The Life of the Learned Sir Thomas Smith*, pp. 60–64, and the dialogue pp. 184–259.

78 Cavanagh, *Language and Politics*, p. 47.

79 'A Journall of Matters of State [...] From and Before the Death of King Edw. the 6th Untill the Yere 1562', found in the papers of Robert Beale. See Archer, *Religion, Politics and Society*, pp. 45–51, and the text of the 'Journall', pp. 52–122. The editors of the volume think the anonymous witness might be John Hales, who supported Catherine Grey's claim to the throne.

80 James and Walker, 'The Politics of *Gorboduc*', pp. 112–14.

81 Graves, *Thomas Norton*, p. 96.

82 Facsimile of the title page in *Five Elizabethan Tragedies*, ed. by McIlwraith, p. 71.

the use of blank verse. Seen on its own merits, the play has worse faults than those Sidney found damnable. Its didactic aim overwhelms all artistic considerations.[83] No interaction, no suspense is allowed to interfere with the political lessons, which the dumb shows and choruses stress redundantly, in case the audience failed to get the points argued at length by the characters. Altman's view, that the potential conflict between its several ideas is not a matter of concern, is an understatement.[84] The arguments usually fail to impress the protagonists, who stick to the course they had chosen before their counsellors have their verbose say. Act I scene i informs us that Gorboduc has decided to divide his kingdom between his sons and 'will endeavour to procure assent | Of all his council to his fond device', yet after listening without interruption to some 250 lines of contrary advice he sees no cause to change his mind, 'In one self purpose do I still abide.'[85] The Chorus then warns us that his children, like Phaeton, will set his realm on fire: this great king

> A mirror shall become to princes all,
> To learn to shun the cause of such a fall.
>
> *(Chor. I.ii.23–24)*

By the end of Act II, both sons have chosen to follow the path shown by their evil counsellors, the one they were determined to take anyway. At the onset of Act V, the royal family is wholly extinct. The void releases tyrannical ambitions and leaves standing no heir nor law that might have ruled the succession 'When is of parliament no hope at all'. Parliament should have been holden

> While yet the prince did live, whose name and power
> By lawful summons and authority
> Might make a parliament to be of force,
> And yet have set the state in quiet stay.
>
> *(V.ii.268–71)*

All the models of government discussed have failed. Though no solution to the dilemma is offered, the play ends with a vote of confidence in God's justice,

> For right will always live, and rise at length,
> But wrong can never take deep root to last.
>
> *(ll. 278–79)*

83 Paul White and Norman Jones, '*Gorboduc* and Royal Marriage Politics: An Elizabethan Playgoer's Report of the Premiere Performance', *English Literary Renaissance*, 26.1 (1996), 3–16. Axton, *The Queen's Two Bodies*, pp. 38–48. Graves, *Thomas Norton*, pp. 91–99.

84 Altman, *The Tudor Play of Mind*, p. 251.

85 Norton and Sackville, *Gorboduc*, I.i.49–50; I.ii.342.

The frontier between the early Elizabethan political and stage arenas was of the flimsiest. Norton the Scold sat in the first Parliament of Elizabeth. Shortly after the queen's illness, in January 1563, he was one of the commission appointed 'to drawe artycles of peticion for the Quenes mariage and Succession',[86] and as their spokesman it was he who read their petition to the House. Sackville his co-author was also elected to Parliament in 1559. The play has two alternative modes of succession fought out by the rival brothers, primogeniture or the king's testament, the two modes Henry VIII had mixed and confirmed in Parliament. Not all lawyers agreed that he had any right to do so. Robert Aske, the Pilgrims' lawyer, had firmly denied it. Now Plowden was of the same mind. William Rastell, judge of the Queen's Bench, fled the country the day before the court performance of *Gorboduc* rather than give an opinion, 'declaring as it is suspected, that there is no certain heir'.[87] Nor was the suggestion to settle the issue in Parliament unanimously well received. In James and Walker's view, the play persuasively presents several options to a partly sceptical audience, and a no less sceptical queen, urging a parliamentary solution as better than civil war, and marriage to Dudley as an even better option. This does not exclude more ambitious aims to establish permanent principles of government.[88] Stephen Alford is undoubtedly right in claiming for *Gorboduc* a more universal significance with a stress on the three elements of mixed monarchy: king, council, and parliament.[89]

In 1566 five gentlemen of Inner Temple each contributed an act to *Gismond of Salerne*. The incestuous King Tancred causes the death of his daughter and her lover, before committing suicide in the tomb of Gismond to lie with her through eternity. To Curtis Perry, the plot, borrowed from Boccaccio's *Decameron*, offers a general criticism of autocracy, possibly a reflection on Elizabeth's absolutist leanings and increasing use of her prerogative (see below, Chapter 9), but Jessica Winston finds 'little sense for most of *Gismond* that the actions of the characters are linked to the nation in any way'. In her assessment, the post-*Gorboduc* plays of Inns members withdraw from sustained political engagement, a sign of tension between individual and collective interests: they had to 'work through the prerogatives, boundaries, limits, and significance of the political community that they and their literary play had, perhaps only half-knowingly, helped to form'. Their writings aimed to 'influence the values and behaviour of their extended community, to define and elevate the status of magistrates, and to construct the Inns as a politically distinct space'.[90] A programme, *mutatis mutandis*, rising but one step above Fortescue's *Praise*.

The plot of *Ghismonda* had already inspired poems and narrations in Latin, Italian, French, and English, plus five Italian tragedies between 1508 and 1614.

86 *Journal of the House of Commons*, I, p. 63.
87 Rastell, *State Papers Spain*, no. 149, in James and Walker, 'The Politics of *Gorboduc*', pp. 116–17.
88 James and Walker, 'The Politics of *Gorboduc*', p. 119.
89 Alford, *The Early Elizabethan Polity*, pp. 100–102.
90 Winston, *Lawyers at Play*, pp. 210, 212, 216.

Later renamed *Tancred and Gismunda*, the Inns play combined Senecan ghosts and *sententiae* with another facet of Boccaccio's tales, romantic love, plus faint echoes of Dante's hell.[91] To these obvious sources, the Cambridge historians of literature add an undeclared one, Lodovico Dolce's *Didone*, widow Dido, another victim of passionate love. Their final judgement, though harsh, is not undeserved: 'When due deductions are made for what the authors borrowed from Boccaccio, Dolce and Seneca, not much remains to be credited to their own originality.' Even if it struck a new path by endeavouring to 'present a romantic subject with something of the gravity and dignity of classical tragedy', it is still 'a far cry' to Shakespeare's pair of star-crossed lovers.[92]

The originality is in the treatment, now addressed to law-abiding not too sympathetic citizens. Where Boccaccio's moving Ghismonda asserts her love in the face of social conventions and authority, the Inns gentlemen turned his heroine into a deplorable case of excess, for all to decipher 'their overthrow that master not their unruly affections', while the chorus holds up worthy examples like Penelope or Lucrece, better suited to the chaste tempers of 'our dames', as 'a mirror and a glass to womenkind'. British ghosts never tell Pluto such horrendous tales, for disordered passions are unknown 'in Britain land'. The play, five or six years after *Gorboduc*, again engages with the succession, warning Elizabeth against mistreatment of her heirs. In the preface to the revised edition of 1591, William Webbe, author of *A Discourse of English Poetrie*, declared it 'either in stateliness of show, depth of conceit, or true ornaments of poetical art, inferior to none of the best in that kind: no, were the Roman Seneca the censurer'.[93]

A Looking Glass for England

Sir, I lack advancement.

Hamlet, III.ii

Many Inns of Court members tried their hand at drama after Norton, gracing Elizabethan entertainments with verse, speeches, dialogues, and spectacular devices. Of his own generation, only Lodge saw his works performed in the public theatres that had opened on the fringes of the City to rival the Middle Temple Hall. In the autumn of 1563, his father Sir Thomas Lodge, Lord Mayor of London, was imprisoned in the Fleet for debt, 'to the great scandal and slander of the whole

91 See Scott, *Elizabethan Translations from the Italian*, pp. 150–51.

92 John W. Cunliffe, 'Early English Tragedy', in *The Cambridge History of English and American Literature*, ed. by A. W. Ward and A. R. Waller (New York: Putnam, 1907–1921), v.1, ch. iv, § 11–12.

93 *Tancred and Gismunda*, in *A Select Collection of Old English Plays*, vii, pp. 6, 49; Webbe, 'To His Friend R[obert] W[ilmot], in *A Select Collection of Old English Plays*, vii, p. 11. See Jane Kingsley-Smith, '*Gismond of Salerne*: An Elizabethan and Cupidean Tragedy', *Yearbook of English Studies*, 38.1–2 (2008), 199–215.

city', the chronicler Stow reports.[94] A merchant adventurer, he was one of the syndicate who backed the Gold Coast trade, fitting ships to Guinea for cargoes of gold dust, ivory, and slaves.[95] Perhaps too large a part of the Lord Mayor's wealth was at sea. A veritable Antonio, his biographer Sisson notes.[96] He never recovered from his first financial disaster and was kept in Chancery for years by an entanglement of lawsuits.

Sir Thomas may have hoped that one of his brood would learn enough law to keep him out of jail when he sent his son to Lincoln's. Young Thomas had an infinite variety of talents, and tried them all successively in hopes of reaching fortune or fame, but he never practised the law, though the title-pages of his works are proudly signed 'Thomas Lodge of Lincolns Inne, Gentleman'. The life of this gentleman reads like several Shakespearean characters rolled into one.[97] In 1591 he embarked with Sir Thomas Cavendish on a 'dismall and fatal voyage' to China and the Philippines that took him to the Straits of Magellan and to the Jesuits' library of Santos, Brazil, where he found the source of his novel *A Margarite of America*.[98] Storms, diseases, and losing fights forced them to turn back, Cavendish died, and a much depleted crew made it home. Lodge's ensuing literary efforts were as varied and unsuccessful as his adventures at sea. The twelve works published between 1584 and 1596 have twelve different dedicatees, none of whom, visibly, gave him substantial support.[99] After some time spent among the poets of London, when he was esteemed the best for satire among English men, he went to study medicine in Avignon, 'and was as much cried up to his last for physic, as he was in his younger days for his poetical fancy'.[100]

Apart from his role in the quarrels over drama, Lodge is best remembered, unfairly enough, for his connections with Shakespeariana. In *Wits miserie, and the Worlds madnesse* (1596), Hate-Virtue evokes a stage ghost 'which cried so miserably at ye theator, like an oisterwife, *Hamlet revenge*'.[101] Reciprocally, *Wits miserie* is alluded to in *A Midsummer Night's Dream*, when 'One sees more devils than vast hell can hold.' And *As You Like It*, as is well known, draws its plot from *Rosalynde*. Lodge's modern editor describes his romance as 'one huge narrative isocolon': in his view, this 'rhetorical figure which balances one element of the

---

94 Stow, *Three Fifteenth-Century Chronicles*, ed. by Gairdner, pp. 126–27.

95 See the poem 'The first voyage of Robert Baker to Guinie', one of the factors, printed in the first edition of Hakluyt's *Principall navigations, voyages and discoveries* (London: George Bishop, 1589), p. 134. And the relation of the voyage in vol. XI, *Africa*, p. 167. W. Walton Claridge, *A History of the Gold Coast and Ashanti: From the Earliest Times to the Commencement of the Twentieth Century* (London: John Murray, 1915), pp. 73–75.

96 Charles J. Sisson, *Thomas Lodge and Other Elizabethans* (London: Routledge, 1966), pp. 19–22.

97 Paradise, *Thomas Lodge*, p. 17. Cuvelier, *Thomas Lodge, témoin de son temps*, pp. 50–54.

98 Letter of Dedication to Elizabeth Cooke, Lady Russell, 4 May 1596.

99 Cuvelier, *Thomas Lodge, témoin de son temps*, p. 119.

100 Wood, *Athenae Oxoniensis*, II, pp. 282–83. Philip Drew, 'Was Greene's "Young Juvenal" Nashe or Lodge?', *Studies in English Literature*, 7 (1967), 55–66.

101 See Harold Jenkins' Introduction to *Hamlet*, The Arden Shakespeare (London: Bloomsbury, 1990), pp. 82–83.

structure against another is not a Euphuistic tic for Lodge, but the way his mind works in the narrative as a whole as well as in the detail of its writing'.[102] Actually it is not just a rhetorical figure, but the *pro et contra* argument that all Inns students were taught to practise, and some carried over to the stage. If Lodge played a decisive part in the development of playwriting, it is as a link between these two worlds. And if young Shakespeare borrowed feathers from fellow playwrights, they must have been Lodge's more than Greene's.

Written in the years following the Throckmorton plot, while the trial of Mary Stuart was debated at the Inns and in Parliament,[103] Lodge's *Wounds of Civill War, lively set forth in the true Tragedies of Marius and Scilla* draws the same lesson from republican Rome as *Gorboduc* did forty years earlier from British legendary history.[104] The rivalries of Ferrex and Porrex, Jocasta's sons, Lancaster and York, Marius and Scilla all spell the same horror for their country: the enemy 'Laughs at these fond discensions I complain | While we in wrangling for a Generall | Forsake our friends (*Wounds*, I.i.12–14). Shakespeare's first Henriad had just refreshed memories with urgent calls to 'cease these jars'.

Lodge had well absorbed the humanists' diagnosis on Roman institutions. His Senators are important 'Pillers that beare and hold our Rule aloft'. Having heard the *pro et contra* arguments of Marius's and Scilla's supporters, they appoint Marius as general, but now Scilla enters 'with Captaines and Souldiers' to 'brave the Capitoll' as York does the Parliament in 3 *Henry VI*. Antony pleads in vain for amity and peace, and moans over the City's inevitable destruction 'through ciuill discords and domesticke broiles'. When another Senator tries to reason with him, Scilla orders his soldiers to 'arrest | The gray-beard and cut off his head in iest'. This head will decorate the Capitol, a fashion more specific to London Bridge. The tyrant then demands that the name of Tribune be banished out of town, which the Senators fearfully agree to. He sends to execution those who beg him to stop massacres, proscribes forty more, 'least they grow too proud', and has himself proclaimed Perpetual Lord Dictator.[105] News arrives then that the son of Marius has chosen to kill himself rather than endure tyranny or murder Roman citizens. What Hadfield dismisses as a 'futile gesture' operates a last and spectacular reversal,[106] by driving Scilla to meditate on fame and surrender his power to the Senate. Having resolved, Timon-like, to dwell in a country cave, he dies moments later. No one emerges as a successor, but audiences well knew that Rome must endure several more decades of civil broils until Augustus establishes a robust *pax romana*.

---

102 Lodge, *Rosalynd*, ed. by Brian Nellist (Keele: Ryburn Publishing, 1995), pp. 19–21.

103 15 May 1572, *Proceedings*, I, p. 326.

104 See Hadfield's analysis in *Shakespeare and Republicanism*, pp. 66–72.

105 Lodge, *The Wounds of Civill War* (London: John Danter, 1594), pp. 5, 7, 12, 17, 62, 65–66.

106 Hadfield, 'Thomas Lodge and Elizabethan Republicanism', Göteborg Universitet, December 2005, <https://gupea.ub.gu.se/bitstream/handle/2077/227/NJES_4_2_Hadfield.pdf>, pp. 96–98.

Hadfield's republic is not significantly different from mixed monarchy. The word 'republic' never occurs in Lodge's play, where Rome is sometimes called 'this monarchy', to bring it nearer to England, presumably, instead of the other way round. Rather than an act of faith in the virtues of republican institutions, *The Wounds of Civill War* shows a wholly impotent Senate turning to each victorious warrior as Fortune varies, confirming Plutarch's view that Rome was crying out for a strong man to take command of the State.[107] Lodge's republican Rome glitters with full Augustan splendour, 'Burnisht with gold and Iuorie pillors faire, | Shining with Iasper, Iet, and Ebonie'. Scilla, who is said to 'gape for monarchy', returns from Asia in a chariot drawn by slaves, with manacled kings, armies, prisoners of diverse nations, and sundry disguises, the mode of triumphant entry made fashionable by the Inns revels and Gascoigne's *Jocasta*. The exact date of the play being unknown, it is impossible to tell if Marlowe's *Tamburlaine* influenced Lodge or the reverse: both took a leaf from the Inns' style of grand pageantry.[108]

Lodge repeatedly begged his countrymen, and more particularly Londoners, to remain united when their City is under threat of losing what their predecessors have built. *A Larum for London, or the siedge of Antwerp*, which is attributed at least in part to him,[109] invites them to fear the fate of the Flemish town, recently destroyed in an episode known as 'the Spanish fury'. Gascoigne who had witnessed it denounced the conquerors as barbarous, but still criticized the wickedness of the money-grasping libertine citizens as perhaps 'a sufficient cause of God's so just a scourge and plague'.[110] Antwerp was Sodom and Gomorrah, struck by divine justice. To Gascoigne, they were also unfortunate, living in such a wealthy city close to an army in dire need of money.[111] But Lodge begins with a terrible warning of the Spaniards' cruelty: if the burgesses are unthrifty, the Spanish prove incredibly harsh, thirsting for gold, and they are the ones who explain the sack of Antwerp by God's wrath. The diplomatic context had changed. England was not at war with Spain when Gascoigne went to serve Willem of Orange. After Willem's assassination, England openly gave help to the Dutch rebels, and the following decades saw a rich production of anti-Spanish propaganda.

The hero of Lodge's play, a cynical old soldier, will not fight for Antwerp's liberty because the citizens have refused to pay him. This directly echoes orators in Parliament who warn the House that they endanger the kingdom's safety in refusing to spend enough for its defence, and anticipates the messenger in *1 Henry VI* who stresses the true cause of losses in France: 'No treachery, but want

107 Plutarch, *Lives*, v. 30.

108 Charles Whitworth, '*The Wounds of Civil War* and *Tamburlaine*: Lodge's Alleged Imitation', *Notes & Queries*, 22.6 (1975), 245–47, sets out to prove that, Lodge's play being inferior to Marlowe's, it was probably the first.

109 See Laurie Johnson, *The Tain of Hamlet* (Cambridge: Cambridge Scholars Publishing, 2014), pp. 113–16.

110 Lodge, *Alarum for London, together with 'The Spoyle of Antwerp', by George Gascoyne*, ed. by Simpson, p. 19.

111 See McKeown, *English Mercuries*, p. 89.

of men and money.' In the debate over subsidies, Sir John Fortescue observes that the Turk on conquering Constantinople found three hundred millions of gold there: 'Yf they, quoth he, had bestowed but 3 mylliones in deffence of their cittye, I could never had gotten yt.'[112] The last sessions of Elizabeth's reign are filled with demands that maimed soldiers be relieved by some minimal charity. The name of the hero, Stump, suggests he must be one of the wounded whom the State was so reluctant to thank appropriately. When he does join the fight, it is moved not so much by a belated sense of duty, but by a refusal to live under the rule of 'haughty Spaniards', and winning their admiration as the only brave fighter in this overfed town.

In *A Looking Glass for London and England,* written with Greene, it is King Rasni's arrogance that draws the divine wrath on him and on sinful Nineveh. The subplot features two young men in the clutches of a usurer, who seek justice in a law court until they realize that the judge is himself in the hands of his moneylender. London is likewise threatened with God's vengeance if the citizens will not avoid dissension. *An Alarum against Usurers* paints a scathing portrait of the legal system and its corruptions. The Epistle to 'my curteous friends, the Gentlemen of the Innes of Court' asks their support in a just cause, against usurers and caterpillars who 'spread their venim among some private Gentlemen of your profession.'[113] Again, the hero is a young profligate, this time a law student, who goes down the fatal spiral of gaming, debt, usury, law, prison, and poverty. The first abusers are the Merchants, who enrich themselves by others' misfortunes, and 'eate our English gentrie out of house and home'. They will cozen a youth, 'and feede his humoures, till they free him of his farmes'. To do this, they find some old soaking solicitor, furnish him with money and send him canvassing up and down St Paul's to catch some young novice. Having got new supply, the youth is pricked on to new sin, from broker to harlot to usurer.

Burton Paradise, who aims to show Lodge was not a dissolute waster, denies that the *Alarum* is autobiographical.[114] Yet Lodge's parents had threatened to disinherit him, making the father in *Alarum* sound like his to the life as he gives the young man a sound thrashing: everything went well at the university,

> but beeing by mee brought to the Innes of Court, a place of abode for our English gentrie, and the onely nurserie of true lerning, I finde thy nature quite altered, and where thou first shuldes have learnt law, thou art become lawless.

The son promises to amend. His fond parent sends him back to the Inns, 'exhorteth him to follow vertue, and intentively to long after learning'. No sooner out of view, the son returns to his broker Merchant and mistress Minx. He ends in jail, is released after signing papers to his kind creditor, and set to recruit gulls of his

112 Townshend's Journal, November 1601, *Proceedings,* III, p. 332.

113 Lodge, *An Alarum against Usurers,* in *Complete Works,* ed. by Gosse, I, p. 5.

114 Paradise, *Thomas Lodge,* p. 21. Cuvelier, *Thomas Lodge, témoin de son temps,* pp. 66–67, is of a contrary opinion.

own kind. Here Lodge takes pains to expose the technicalities of the whole trap: if English laws were as severe as Solon's in Athens, these caterpillars could be reined in, but in England, this vice is allowed to prosper.[115]

To conclude, Lodge addresses a warning to greedy usurers: they will be tortured by their conscience and end in everlasting fire. This is their last hope to be reclaimed. Whatever the reactions may have been to Lodge's tract, he was touching a sore point. In 1596, two brokers were convicted in the Star Chamber for 'cosening' young gentlemen, and Burghley warned parents against sending their sons to the Inns without appointing superintendents over them. A student at Oxford or Cambridge was kept in by his tutor, but coming to London and the Inns, surrounded as they were with theatres and all metropolitan temptations, he was 'crept from the cradle of learning to the court of liberty': at the turn of the century, the common literary stereotype of the law student was an idle dissolute young man with a preference for 'Shakespeare's plaies instead of my Lord Coke'.[116]

If there is constancy in Lodge's varied life, it is his determination to cure his country's miseries. It is hard to assess how much impact he had on public morality, but quite moving that having failed to succeed with his pen, he undertook to treat his countrymen's ailments. Having done his best to mend their ways, he died nursing the Londoners during an epidemic of the plague that killed thirty-five thousand in 1625. When all who could fled to safety, he remained in town with an official charge from the Court of Aldermen 'to be one of the Physicians for cure of those visited with the plague'.[117] On this recurrent calamity he had written a *Treatise*, dedicated to the Lord Mayor, being moved to do so by 'the duetie and love I owe to this Citie (wherein I was bred and brought up)'.[118]

Shades of Euripides

Among his many activities, Lodge had translated Seneca's *Josephus*, bolstering T. S. Eliot's opinion that 'no author exercised a wider or deeper influence upon the Elizabethan mind or upon the Elizabethan form of tragedy than did Seneca'. Having set down the law, Eliot gives as evidence the fact that Scaliger preferred him to Euripides. Seneca's plays have 'verbal' beauty rather than the 'beauty of thought and emotion' found in Greek tragedy, and are thus 'admirably adapted for declamation before an imperial highbrow audience of crude sensibility but considerable sophistication in the ingenuities of language'. This by implication must apply to Elizabeth's crude sophisticated imperial subjects. Their taste for Senecan violence could be traced to Italy: 'The French drama is from the beginning

115 Lodge, *An Alarum against Usurers*, in *Complete Works*, I, pp. 20, 25, 29–37.

116 Francis Lenton, *The Young Gallant's Whirligigg* (1629) p. 3, and *Characterismi* (1631), sig. F4, in Prest, *The Inns of Court*, pp. 136–42.

117 *The Repertories recording the proceedings of the London Court of Aldermen*, XXXIX, 274b, in Frank P. Wilson, *The Plague in Shakespeare's London* (Oxford: Clarendon Press, 1963), p. 22.

118 Lodge, *A Treatise of the Plague* (1603), Dedication, in *Complete Works*, IV, p. 3.

decorous and restrained. [...] The Italian is bloodthirsty in the extreme.'[119] In Eliot's wake, Rees for one proclaims that 'it was Seneca, not Aeschylus, Sophocles, or even Euripides, who provided the classical models for Renaissance and Elizabethan Tragedy'.[120] Not only among playwrights, but among early modern academics, 'Seneca let bloud line by line and page by page at length must needes die to our stage'.[121]

And yet at the back of Seneca stood Euripides. *Troades, the Trojan Women,* makes the basis of *Troas,* the first of Jasper Heywood's translations. Trinity College, Cambridge in the 1560s saw a *Hecuba* which was not *Troas,* Alan Nelson argues, but Erasmus's translation of *Troades.*[122] *Phoenissae* stands behind Seneca's *Thebais,* and behind Gascoigne's *Jocasta.* The first English translation of Euripides, Lady Jane Lumley's *Iphigeneia at Aulis,* never went to print in her days, and could thus long be safely ignored.[123] Thanks to Eliot, no doubt, little interest was wasted among twentieth-century scholars on the one 'Greek' play in English that Shakespeare undoubtedly knew, *Jocasta,* performed at Gray's Inn, and apt to teach him more about the dramatic *agon* than any Senecan plot. A Victorian scholar, John Mahaffy, one of the few who even mention *Jocasta,* dismisses it as 'a motley and incongruous piece': its chief literary interest is Eteocles' lines, which may have suggested Hotspur's speech in *1 Henry IV.* 'So far as I know,' the footnote goes, 'this is the only direct contact with, or rather direct obligation to, the Greek tragedy in Shakspeare'.[124] In 2004, Andrew Nuttall still considered the notion that 'Shakespeare was cut off from Greek poetry and drama' as 'probably a bleak truth that we should accept'.[125] But scholarship of the past decade 'has begun to redeem sixteenth-century England from its undeserved reputation as an isolated intellectual backwater',[126] Micha Lazarus shows — less to acknowledge a large debt to continental productions of the time than to reclaim British excellence in a field that British research had long deserted. The main point of many a recent

119 Eliot, Introduction to the 1927 reprint of Newton's *Seneca His Tenne Tragedies,* pp. v, vii, ix, xxvii, later entitled 'Seneca in Elizabethan Translation', in his *Elizabethan Dramatists,* pp. 11–32.

120 B. R. Rees, 'English Seneca: A Preamble', *Greece & Rome,* 2nd Ser., 16.2 (1969), 119.

121 Nashe, 'To the Gentlemen Students of both Universities', Preface to Robert Greene, *Menaphon* [1589], ed. by G. B. Harrison (Oxford: Blackwell, 1927).

122 *Records of Early English Drama,* ed. by Nelson, pp. 208, 968, 1214. On Greek tragedies available in Greek, Latin, and Italian, see Charlton, *The Senecan Tradition,* pp. 31–51. On Erasmus's translations of Euripides, see Virginie Leroux, 'Les premières traductions de l'*Iphigénie à Aulis* d'Euripide, d'Érasme à Thomas Sébillet', in 'Translating Dramatic Texts in Sixteenth-Century England and France', special issue, *Renaissance et Réforme,* 40.3 (2017), 243–63.

123 *Three Tragedies by Renaissance Women,* ed. by Purkiss. See Stephanie Hodgson-Wright, 'Jane Lumley's *Iphigeneia at Aulis: Multum in parvo,* or, Less Is More', in Cerasano and Wynne-Davies, eds, *Readings in Renaissance Women's Drama,* Part III, ch. 3.

124 Gascoigne, *Jocasta,* I.ii. John Mahaffy, *A History of Classical Greek Literature* (London: Longmans, 1880), I, pp. 365–66.

125 Andrew Nuttall, 'Action at a Distance: Shakespeare and the Greeks', in Martindale and Taylor, eds, *Shakespeare and the Classics,* pp. 207–22.

126 Lazarus, 'Greek Literacy', p. 434.

study like Tanya Pollard's is to establish that 'the English played a crucial role in new transnational conversations' over rediscovered classic texts.[127] A point that found little echo two decades ago when I discussed *Jocasta* at a conference on Shakespeare and European politics.[128]

I remarked at the time that it was hard to understand the lack of interest in Shakespeare studies for *Jocasta* and *Phoenissae*, which some Elizabethans at least, especially at the Inns of Court, found good enough to read, translate, perform, publish, and for the Greek theatre generally. No piece was more copied or quoted than the *Phoenissae*, Mahaffy claims, along with Erasmus's rendering of *Hecuba*, while T. W. Baldwin notes that it was part of Johann Sturm's curriculum in Strasbourg. Sturm and Erasmus, who provided models for grammar schools all over Europe, both lay great emphasis on the declamation and acting of plays. Melanchthon compared moving scenes like the conclusion of *Phoenissae* to the voice of God directing men to salvation. Euripides was on most school programmes and his extant tragedies were all available in Latin versions,[129] yet according to the Martindales, 'if Shakespeare read them he gained little from the experience'. Like most critics, they tend to dismiss Euripides on the ground that the Elizabethans much preferred Seneca.[130] 'In the background to Seneca are the tragedies of Euripides', John Jowett notes in reference to *Richard III*, but he doubts Shakespeare knew them.[131] Altman agrees with him that Seneca was the only tragic dramatist most Elizabethans knew. Even in *Jocasta*, lines drawn from *Phoenissae* 'are cast against a background that is Senecan rather than Euripidean'.[132]

Only in the last decade has the influence of the Greek theatre begun to attract serious studies.[133] Burrow's *Shakespeare and Classical Antiquity* has a section on *The Comedy of Errors* and its connection to the Inns, but never mentions *Jocasta* or *Phoenissae*. Hutson, who has amply shown that Roman New Comedy provided legal scenarios and characters that were lacking in Seneca, does not waste any time either on *Jocasta* or Euripides.[134] Russ Leo briefly mentions Gascoigne's and Kinwelmarsh's with other Elizabethan plays featuring dumb shows.[135] Pollard's *Greek Tragic Women* turns the tide with a chapter on 'Greek Plays in England', making *Jocasta* come second to Jane Lumley's *Iphigenia* with their mother-daughter dyad.

127 Pollard, *Greek Tragic Women*, p. 43.

128 Goy-Blanquet, 'Translating Europe into your England', from a paper given at the ESRA Conference in Utrecht, 2003.

129 *Euripidis tragici poete nobilissimi Hecuba et Iphigenia, Erasmo interprete.*

130 Martindale and Martindale, *Shakespeare and the Uses of Antiquity*, pp. 41–44. Kerrigan, *Revenge Tragedy*, has many references to Euripides, but none to *Jocasta*.

131 Shakespeare, *The Tragedy of King Richard III*, ed. by Jowett (Oxford: Oxford University Press, 2000), p. 23.

132 Altman, *The Tudor Play of Mind*, pp. 231, 261.

133 By Demetriou, Pollard, Lazarus, Leo, Martina Tarlinskaja, Marjorie Garber.... Carla Suthren's 2018 PhD dissertation, 'Shakespeare and the Renaissance Reception of Euripides', which detects the influence of *Alcestis* especially in *The Winter's Tale*, is to be a monograph, entitled *Tyrannous Passions.*

134 Hutson, *The Invention of Suspicion*, discussing *Supposes* at ch. 4, mentions *Jocasta* p. 189.

135 Leo, *Tragedy as Philosophy*, p. 162.

As for Shakespeare, she argues, his interest in Greek tragic women may have been spurred by working on *Titus Andronicus* with George Peele, a former Oxford student, who translated Euripides' *Iphigenia*. 'The play's references to Hecuba mark the start of Shakespeare's reflections on her ability to inspire tragic grief and rage in audiences.'[136] Her focus is on Euripides' emotional appeal and the early modern attraction to Greek suffering heroines rather than the political implications of the civil war, which plays a significant part in both *Jocasta* and *Titus*.

Jocasta was originally presented as 'A Tragedie written in Greeke by Euripides, translated and digested into Acte by George Gascoygne and Francis Kinwelmershe of Grayes Inne, and there by them presented, 1566.'[137] 'Digested' is the operative word, for in actual fact this *Jocasta* is an expanded rendering of Lodovico Dolce's Italian version of *Phoenissae* published in 1549.[138] Pollard is right when she asserts that it is not just a translation of Dolce's *Giocasta*, but it is definitely not a translation from the Greek, nor any closer than Dolce's to Euripides. Translating through a mediator, we saw earlier, was fairly common practice, though usually the helper would be mentioned on the title page.[139] Dolce was quite well known to the Elizabethans. He had studied with Castelvetro at Padua, the birthplace of neoclassical tragedy, where a number of young English aristocrats went to complete their education.[140] His *Didone* inspired the prologue of *Gismond of Salerne*, and some of his sonnets were translated by Lodge. No great scholar himself, Dolce did not translate his *Giocasta* from the Greek either, but adapted and expanded Collinus's Latin version of the play. The English *Jocasta* enjoyed a measure of success in its time, attested by several reprintings during the reign of Elizabeth.[141] Gabriel Harvey praised it in the margin of his own copy as 'An excellent Tragedie: full of many discreet, wise and deep considerations', in line with '*The Tragoedy of King Gorboduc*' and '*The Myrrour of Magistrates*'.

It is true that the neoclassical school did not greatly admire Euripides, for all the reasons that must have made him attractive to Shakespeare. He was apt to introduce comic elements in his plays and give active parts to low-born characters, features strongly disapproved of by the Italian theoreticians. Cinthio, for one, thought the Greek poet's works were marred by a natural diction unsuited to the dignity of tragedy, although he was quite tolerant of other irregularities like *intermedii*, and found strong pedantic arguments to justify violent deaths on

---

136 Pollard, *Greek Tragic Women*, pp. 61–68, 100. She adds to the sources of *Jocasta* Rudolfus Collinus's 1541 Latin translation, which actually is Dolce's main source.

137 Gascoigne, *Supposes; and Jocasta*, ed. by Cunliffe.

138 Dolce, *Giocasta*. See Ronnie H. Terpening, *Lodovico Dolce: Renaissance Man of Letters* (Toronto: University of Toronto Press, 1997).

139 North's *Lives* are unequivocally presented in the 1579 edition as 'Translated out of Greek into French by Iames Amyot [...] and out of French into English by Thomas North'. But Amyot's work was famous and widely read, where Dolce was a mere go-between.

140 See Woolfson, *Padua and the Tudors*.

141 *Jocasta* was published on its own in 1566, then as part of *A Hundreth Sundrie Flowres* in 1573, and included in the posthumous *The whole woorkes of George Gascoigne* (London: Abel Ieffes, 1587).

stage.[142] A recent French translator of *Phoenissae* still complains that the play suffers from an excess of characters, and of dead bodies: too many people run around, too many things happen, while its inconclusive end makes it 'a slightly mongrel play'.[143] The brothers' struggle for power, the result of both their father's curse and their own thirst for power, is overcast by the shadow of Oedipus, an 'airy ghost' (*aitherophanes*), who enters after the fight to hear the report of his wife's and sons' deaths, be sentenced to exile, and leave under the guidance of Antigone.

The English translators followed Dolce's plot quite faithfully, with the addition of an opening Argument, an Epilogue, and dumb shows before every act. The most striking of these shows offers a memorable emblem of civil war. At the opening of Act II, two coffins are brought on stage to the doleful sound of flutes by sixteen mourners, 'and after they had caried the coffins about the stage, there opened and appeared a grave, wherin they buried the coffins, and put fire to them, but the flames did sever and parte in twaine, signifying discord by the history of two brethren'. Gascoigne must have had some knowledge of Italian stage practices, for in the third dumb show, he uses the story of Curtius, one of the stock figures of Italian *intermedii*.[144] The most significant departure from the Italian source is in the verse technique. Where Dolce alternates *settenari* and *endecasillabi* to interpret the varying metres of Euripides, the English team alternate blank verse and rhyme royal, but keep a rigidly regular pentameter, even when it means elongating Dolce's heptasyllabic lines. The need to fill in the line is met with padding devices of the 'God wot' kind, or doubled vocatives, 'Beholde, O queene, beholde, O worthie queene'. The metrical demands often lead the translators very far from the naturalness of Dolce's (and Euripides') diction: 'Padre io debbo morir, non voi' becomes 'I father ought, so ought not you, to die' (III.ii.64).

The three versions each bring other lasting novelties, each making the same points with increasing length, for instance when Eteocles declares:

> If what to some seemes honest, good, and just,
> Could seeme even so in every doubtfull mind,
> No dark debate nor quarrel could arise:
> But looke! How many men so many mindes,
> And that, that one man judgeth good and just,
> Some other deemes as deepely to be wrong.[145]

Multiple viewpoints are the very matter of the play's *agon*. Stichomythia makes its first entrance here on the English stage. There is nothing in the ponderous exchanges of *Gorboduc* to compare with the slanging match between brothers:

---

142 Cinzio, *Discorsi*.
143 Victor-Henry Debidour, *Les Tragiques grecs: Théâtre complet* (Paris: Livre de Poche, 1999), p. 1461.
144 Gascoigne translated it from Valerius Maximus in *The Glasse of Government* (1575), p. 31.
145 *Jocasta*, III.i.350–55. Cf. *Phoenissae*, ll. 499–502. *Giocasta*, II.i.328–33.

Po. Punish, O gods, this wicked tyrant here.
Ete. Pray to the gods in Greece and not in Thebes.
Po. No savage beast so cruell nor unjust.
Ete. Not cruel to my countrie like to thee.
Po. Since from my right I am with wrong deprived.
Ete. Eke from thy life, if long thou tarie here.

(*II.i.558–63*)

Similarly deft is Antigone's moving plea for equity against State law, or Creon's dispute with Tiresias about divine justice:

Cre. Unjust is he condemnes the innocent.
Tyr. A fole is he accuseth heavens above.

(*III.i.213–14*)

As Allyna Ward shows, the women play a more significant role than is usual in Inns plays. Mother and daughter represent themselves as 'a weak old woman' and 'a silly simple mayd', yet both are endowed with a political wisdom far above their male counterparts'. Although they advocate peace and justice with sound political arguments and strong rhetoric, no one listens to their advice, they are dismissed and silenced, but to Ward, who reads Gascoigne as a proto-feminist, they reveal a cultural shift in thinking about women as able political participants.[146]

Nor does *Jocasta* lend itself to the kind of overt didacticism found in *Gorboduc*. It does abound in traditional lessons on the versatility of fortune, evil ambition, vain royal pomp, but these are challenged by less orthodox innuendoes. Thus, the characters' sufferings are not the deserved punishment for misdeeds, as in many so-called Elizabethan tragedies. There is much ground for Antigone's complaint at the end that 'Justice lyes on sleepe': ill stars and harsh, possibly malevolent, gods loom above. Where the translator of *Oedipus* interprets his hero's fate as 'a dreadfull Example of Gods horrible vengeaunce for sinne',[147] *Jocasta* shows a clearer understanding of *hamartia* than most Elizabethan characters outside Shakespeare's:

So deeply faulteth none, the which unwares
Doth fall into the crime he can not shunne.

(*I.i.134–35*)

Even if the play remains on the whole reasonably didactic, this line alone would suffice to show up Gascoigne as more of a dramatic poet than a lawyer.

---

146 Ward, *Women in Tudor Tragedy*, pp. 62–73.
147 'Preface to the Reader', in *Seneca His Tenne Tragedies*, p. 190.

Many features of the original *Phoenissae*, the very ones that lay it open to censorious criticism, made it intractable to Senecan reduction: its episodic structure, wealth of incidents, open conclusion, lack of a central hero, numerous characters, and distinct scepticism. Harvey aptly defined 'Euripidis Jocasta apud Gascoignum' as 'Quasi Synopsis Tragoediarum Omnium', a compendium of all the Theban tragedies, on the play's opening page.[148] If Shakespeare had access in his youth to half a dozen English tragedies at best, then this would have been the one closest to a model. *Jocasta* has many elements that would be refined in the histories, most prominently in *Henry VI*: fatal curses, revenge, ghosts, and stichomythia (all of which were Greek before they turned Senecan), oath breaking, prophecies and soothsayers, and strong feminine figures (Jocasta, like Queen Margaret, survives her husband's fall). The servant's speech on 'The glittering mace, the pompe of swarming traine' paid for by heavy cares ushers in Shakespeare's sleepless kings. Eteocles, decades before Edward of York, vows he would break a thousand oaths to reign one year. Creon and his son who compete to die for their country herald the Talbots. The other characters express equally patriotic feelings: they love the commonwealth, resent the violation of their homeland by foreign troops, and cannot bear to live in exile. Blood-drawing scenes alternate with tear-drawing scenes, as the protagonists move from violent anger to violent sorrow. The fratricidal war induces symmetries of construction, duels, normative images of a cosmos ruled by the regular division of day and night, the same lost world evoked by Henry VI's nostalgic dream of harmony in the midst of battle. *Jocasta* should definitely figure among the Inns' gifts to Shakespeare, along with Hall's chronicle, Senecan translations, and *A Mirror for Magistrates*.

---

148 See Tanya Demetriou's detailed study of this copy in 'How Gabriel Harvey Read Tragedy', *Renaissance Studies*, 9 March 2021, <https://onlinelibrary.wiley.com/doi/full/10.1111/rest.12720>.

CHAPTER 9

Lawyers in Parliament

Piece out our imperfections with your thoughts:
Into a thousand parts divide one man,
And make imaginary puissance.

Henry V, Prologue

The wish to guide the queen with good counsel was not restricted to the Inns' revels. The lessons delivered in the halls of the legal societies soon found a much larger auditorium in the House of Commons, where a growing number of lawyers took their seat and frequently peppered their speeches with dramatic references. There is grim irony in the fact that the Elizabethan theatre, born in a lawyers' auditorium, will thrive under the censorious eye of the town's legal authorities, and die a terminal death when the Puritan party in Parliament comes into power. Like a brief parenthesis, it takes its place in a centuries-long history of struggles over freedom of speech and national representation. There was an element of rivalry between the great stages of public speech, pulpit, Parliament, and theatre, sometimes a declared hostility to their trading of ideas and relative freedom of speech. The rare followers of Erasmus, a lover of the theatre who consistently urged reconciliation, could only lose against Calvinists who attached the word 'renegade' to any attempt at mediation.[1] Although regularly denounced as immoral, the commercial theatre in Elizabeth's days generally maintained high ethical standards with its oblique or outspoken lessons in the civil spirit.

'Shall Cassandra Bee Punished?' The Liberties of the House

Cry, Trojans, cry! A Helen and a woe!
Cry, cry! Troy burns, or else let Helen go.

Troilus and Cressida, II.ii

1 See for instance Hotman's correspondence with Théodore de Bèze and Jeanne d'Albret, in Kelley, *François Hotman*, p. 142.

We saw above how France and England, after following similar paths towards national independence, diverged in their definitions of monarchy, the *légistes* providing their sovereigns with the arguments of absolutism, the Estates General being efficiently neutralized, while the English jurists hammered that the king is under the law, bound to observe the statutes, customs, and ancient liberties of the realm agreed upon in Parliament. One major parliamentary issue would develop over the Speaker's opening petitions, which included 'libertye of speeche for the well debating of matters propounded'. Thomas More's modest request of 1523 did not include a right of initiative. From the records, Elizabeth's Commons were increasingly assuming it without her leave, declaring it their duty to voice the nation's remonstrances and emotions.[2] Yet despite a few precedents,[3] there would be no proper immunity nor free speech in Parliament until the Bill of Rights in 1689. Among early demonstrations of parliamentary independence was the Ferrers case of 1543. George Ferrers of Lincoln's Inn, MP for Plymouth, had stood surety for the debts of a friend who defaulted and was taken to the Counter, a debtors' prison. The angry Commons demanded his release and, on their own authority, imprisoned the two sheriffs who had haughtily refused to hear them.[4] Henry VIII confirmed the parliamentary privilege and immunity during a session, but to him those were derived from his own sovereignty:

> We be informed by our iudges that we at no time stand so highly in our estate royal as in the time of parlement, wherein we as head and you as members, are conioined and knit togither into one bodie politike so as whatsoever offence or iniurie (during that time) is offered to the meanest member of the House, is to be iudged as done against our person, and the whole court of parlement.[5]

Since this privilege extended to royal servants, MP or not, Ferrers would have enjoyed it anyway as a court official.[6] But the Commons interpreted the decision differently, as appears from their frequent allusions to the case. The Ferrers precedent was cited by William Fleetwood in his demand for 'the liberties of the House' on 20 February 1576, when the arrest of Arthur Hall's servant caused much indignation, and repeated whenever the Commons felt their privileges were thus infringed. At the time of Ferrers's case, Bishop Bonner and Parliament were fighting other liberties, with an act against 'printed bokes printed balades playes rymes songes and other fantasies' falsely instructing the people, 'speciallye the youthe', with untrue opinions.[7]

---

2 April 1571, *Proceedings*, I, p. 207.

3 *Rotuli Parliamentorum*, III, p. 434. *Tudor Constitutional Documents*, ed. by Tanner, pp. 555, 558–59.

4 See H. H. Leonard, 'Ferrers' Case: A Note', *Historical Research*, 42.106 (1969), 230–34.

5 *Hall's Chronicle*, p. 843. *Holinshed's Chronicles*, III, pp. 824–26.

6 He was appointed to the royal household in 1539. See Streitberger, *Court Revels*, p. 194.

7 34 Henry VIII, c. 1. *Statutes of the Realm*, III, pp. 894–97, in Anglo, *Spectacle, Pageantry, and Early Tudor Policy*, p. 271.

The traditional petitions included free access to Her Majesty for the Speaker, 'that noe indulgence be left to misreported informations'.[8] Enter rumour, painted full of tongues. It is one of the grievances listed on stage by Hotspur, who complains in *Henry IV* that they have been denied access to the king, and serves to excuse his turning rebel. This request, usually granted, more often worked the other way round in practice: the Speaker who had come to deliver the Commons' mind returned with messages from the monarch. When a 'faulse brother' reported to Elizabeth what had been said in Commons of the need for religious reform, she commanded that the Speaker, Serjeant Puckering, 'should presentlie attende hir pleasure beinge then at Grenewhich, which withe out the privitye of the House he did'. He returned with a commandment to tell them that 'as by hir allowance he was made the mouthe to the Lower House, she gave this caution that in no wise such matters shoulde be medled withall'. Her mouth, rather. A quailing John Croke who was sent for in the midst of the monopoly controversy (see below, 'Clean and Unclean Money' in this chapter) explained that his 'ffeare' on the occasion may have caused him to forget something in the delivery of her message.[9]

The Commons' legislative mission as the queen understood it is summed up in the Lord Keeper's speech of 1597: there are many laws already, some obsolete, some idle and vain, some too severe or too slack, some unclear. Where they find superfluity, let them prune and cut, where defect, supply, where ambiguity, explain. Speaker Yelverton's closing speech exposes the gist of the Tudor reforming policy: it is wiser to retain old laws than establish new ones, for innovation is often stained by inconstancy, and good laws are not enough if they are unobeyed. He begs for her Majesty's forgiveness if they have overstepped the liberty she has vouchsafed in the free debating of this great council. The bounty of her pardon is worth more than all the subsidy she receives. The infiniteness of her mercy is her most fitting diadem.[10]

'Brideles Colts': The Queen's Unruly Choir

> Dost thou think, because thou art virtuous, there shall be no more cakes and ale?
>
> *Twelfth Night, II.iii*

The threats to national security from the 1570s onwards had helped legitimate increasingly clamorous manifestations of free speech in Commons. With the Scottish queen out of the way, Parliament could turn to other business when they reconvened after her execution, and continued to assert a right of initiative,

8 Speaker Yelverton's speech, 1597, *Proceedings*, III, p. 193.
9 *Proceedings*, II, p. 182; III, p. 395.
10 *Proceedings*, III, pp. 186, 200–205.

consistently denied by the queen, on any subject touching the common weal. Anthony Cope, an Oxfordshire JP, who tried to suppress maypoles, morris dancing, and Whitsun ales in his county,[11] now offered a bill against the ecclesiastical government and suggested they replace the Book of Common Prayer with the Genevan prayer book. The Speaker, Sergeant John Puckering, tried to stop the reading of the bill, with a reminder that the queen would not have them discuss religion, but the House protested. Job Throckmorton rejoiced of the worthy act lately done at Fotheringay, 'the cuttinge of from the earth of that wreatched Athalia', but insisted that though it was good to execute that Guisian imp, it were ten times better to reform the house of God. O lamentable days and times, he goes on. Two worthy counsellors, Leicester and Sir Amyas Paulet, have been labelled Puritans by the late unlamented Babington. 'To bewayle the distresses of God's children, it is puritanisme. To finde faulte with corruptions of our Church, it is puritanisme', Throckmorton protests: 'the Lorde sende her Majestie stoare of such puritanes'.[12]

Throckmorton's defence of Puritanism, the first recorded in Parliament, unrolls a long list of dramatic references. Mutability is his theme. When Elizabeth is offered the crown of the Low Countries, he quotes Terence's *Eunuchus* to remind them that 'thease Alcion dayes of peace' will not last forever: 'the chawnge and whirling about of the affayres of the worlde will preache unto us the contrarye'. Philip of Macedon prayed his heathen gods to send him but moderate scourges, for well he knew that nothing continues long in one state on earth, that 'after the comedye of good happe is ended, then looke for the tragedye of mishap to followe'.[13] There is but 'a shew of freedome' in the House, Throckmorton complains, since they must not meddle with religion nor the succession, the very groundworks of all their happiness. Famous precedents of negligence, classical or recent, that will haunt the stage support his fears: 'Shall Cassandra bee punished for fearing the distruction of Troye? Shall Calphurnia be plagued for dreaming she saw her husbande all blouddy in the Senate?' Caesar, Lord Hastings, Coligny the Admiral of France before 'that brutishe Parisian slaughter', all ignored signs of peril. The Prince of Orange had several escapes before he was slain. These 'bee warninges to pull her Majestie by the slieve' and 'crye to her *Cave, Caesar* [...] For who doubtes but there is a scourge dew to us?'[14]

The grievance had been brewing from the onset of the reign, when Elizabeth listed the issues she did not wish to hear discussed in Parliament. When she forbade the Lower House to speak any more of the succession, Paul Wentworth,

11 In May 1589, Sheriff John Danvers denounced the 'bad proceedings' of 'Sir Anthony Cope and his Puritan allies', *Memorials of the Danvers Family*, ed. by Francis N. Macnamara (London: Hardy and Page, 1895), p. 522. Dean, *Law-Making and Society*, pp. 99–100.

12 'Job Throckmorton's speech on the Bill and Book', 27 February 1587, *Proceedings*, II, pp. 313–14.

13 'Job Throckmorton's speech on the Low Countries', 23 February 1587, *Proceedings*, II, pp. 282–83.

14 *Proceedings*, II, pp. 311–18. Cf. *Richard III*, *Julius Caesar*, *Massacre at Paris*, and 'halcyons' days' in *1 Henry VI*, I.ii.131.

Peter's elder brother, asked whether this restriction 'be a breache of the lybertie of the free speache of the Howse or not', whether the queen's councillors 'are of awthorytye suffycyent to bynde the Howse to scylence in that behalffe'.[15] Among their demands was the recognition of their competence for self-discipline and, beyond it, of Parliament's authority as a supreme law court.[16] They let it be known on occasion that they would grant subsidies in exchange for increased power. One MP, deploring that religion could not be freely discussed, thought the request of a grant a fit opportunity to advance it 'for that hir Majestie expectinge a benevolence from them woulde the sooner yealde to theire lawfull and necessarie petitions'. This caused a sharp retort via the Speaker, who condemned the whole House for aiming to broach any matter she had expressly forbidden.[17]

Through the debates, the Commons were reinterpreting the notion of King-in-Parliament in a way that significantly diminished the authority left to the king's person. They should be allowed to discuss all issues touching the commonwealth, they argued, and not be punished for plain speaking. The queen's marriage and succession were matters of State security. Let her remember dangerous precedents 'when the title of the Crowne was tossed in question betwene two royall howses of Lancaster and York', a civil war happily ended by her grandparents' wedding.[18] The Lords agree, for experience has shown that 'civile warres, effusion of Christian blood, and consequently ruyne of kyngdomes, do followe where realmes be left without a certeintie of succession'.[19] Imbued with a sense of their representative role, the Commons go a step further, with a claim to embody the nation. Thomas Snagge denies having said the Lords were but 'shadows', yet he insists that in Parliament the queen and noble men represent their own voices only, while 'the knightes and burgesses of the lower howse represented all the commynalty of the realme'.[20] Admittedly, the concept of initiative had been germinating for ages. The Elizabethan Parliament gave it a decisive push. Their chorus may or may not have been Puritan, and may or may not have coincided with 'Our choir', as it is labelled in 'A lewd pasquil', but it was decidedly rebellious, and not just a figment of Neale's imagination.[21]

At her first Parliament the queen graciously granted the traditional petitions, provided they did not forget their duties.[22] With each session, her reservations increase as the Commons ignore her commands. In 1566 she marvels before a delegation of both Houses 'that brideles colts do not knowe ther ridar's hand,

15 11 November 1566, *Proceedings*, I, p. 154.

16 *Proceedings*, I, p. 335.

17 Fitzwilliam's Journal, 1584, *Proceedings*, II, pp. 181–83.

18 Commons' petition, 28 January 1563, *Proceedings*, I, p. 91.

19 Lords' petition, 1 February 1563, *Proceedings*, I, pp. 59, 61.

20 1572, *Proceedings*, I, p. 403. See Neale, *Elizabeth I and her Parliaments*, I, p. 302.

21 To Elton, *The Parliament of England*, pp. 353–54, 'our choir' might be the committee appointed on 19 October 1566. He rudely adds, n. 7, that Neale, *Elizabeth I and her Parliaments*, I, p. 140, must have been dreaming his evidence for its composition.

22 Lord Keeper's speech, 25 January 1559, *Proceedings*, I, p. 43.

whome bit of kingely reine did never snafle yet', and points out 'Mr Bell with his complyses' who alleged that their country must perish unless the succession were ordered.[23] She has found in this assembly much dissimulation, 'yea 2 faces under one hoode (and the bodie rotten) beinge covered with 2 viseres, successyon and libertie'.[24]

Hartley cautiously detects in the records of 1581 possible 'evidence of a Puritan campaign to secure what had been started years before'.[25] Four years later, the royal speech promises retaliation to the handful of troublemakers who went so far beyond their duties as to forget their menial state. Elizabeth forgives the body of the House, but there are 'some perticular persons' among them whom she wants punished.[26] In 1587, the troublemakers are clearly identified when the queen bids the House waste no more time on 'the werysome sollicitations of those that commonly be called Puritans, wherewithall the late Parliaments have been exceedingly importuned'. Puritans have been at work for some time, in the estimation of Her Majesty, who may have grown paranoid before Neale, and spots their hand in the propositions of these 'new-fangled refiners' who labour to advance a new eldership, disturbing the Church and commonwealth. On the present issue, free speech, 'it may be doubted whether they or the Jesuites do offer more danger, or be more speedily to be repressed', for Jesuits poison hearts only in privy corners, while these men print and preach and openly teach opinions dangerous to the State. Though they claim to be at war with papists, they concur with the Jesuits in opening the door to the Spanish invasion that threatens the realm.[27] Her choice of a *via media* is firmly delineated: she will neither 'animate Romanists', known adversaries to her estate, 'nor tollerate new-fanglenesse', but means 'to guyde them both by God's holy trew rule.' Touching religion, she is supreme governor by their own decision, she would have them remember. The state of the Church is her responsibility.[28]

Archbishop Grindal is even more outspoken than this 'choir' in addressing his sovereign, whom he begs to offend with his good will. Since she sends questions touching the laws of the realm to her judges, she should similarly refer matters of religion to the head ministers of the Church: 'Remember, Madam, that you are a mortal creature', and must not look only 'upon the purple and princely array, wherewith ye are apparelled'. Although a mighty prince, she must 'remember that he which dwelleth in Heaven is mightier' and beware, after many years of blessed felicity, 'you do not impute the same to your own deserts or policy, but give God the glory'.[29] Thus would the stage Henry V crown his show of humility

23 5 November 1566, *Proceedings*, I, pp. 145–46.
24 Closing speech, 2 January 1567, *Proceedings*, I, p. 172.
25 16 January – 18 March 1581, *Proceedings*, I, p. 500.
26 29 March 1585, *Proceedings*, II, p. 191.
27 Speaker's Speech, 2 March 1587 (?), *Proceedings*, II, p. 332.
28 Queen's Closing speech, 29 March 1585, *Proceedings*, II, p. 32.
29 'Letter to Her Majesty on preaching and prophesying', 20 December 1576, in Strype, 'An Appendix of Original Papers', in *The History of Edmund Grindal*, Bk II, no. 9, pp. 570–73.

after Agincourt 'with this acknowledgment, | That God fought for us.' But the queen showed her virtuous archbishop less magnanimity than Prince Hal to the Chief Justice, and had him confined to his house, while Whitgift unofficially assumed the leadership in his absence. Grindal would not ask forgiveness, though he begged the Privy Council to be intercessors for Her Majesty's clemency. They remonstrated to her that a vacancy would restore the pride and practice of papists, 'And then King Richard the Second's men will flock to Court apace.'[30] After five years, and a petition by Convocation, she relented, but never took him back in favour.

At the close of the first Parliament, Lord Keeper Bacon had thanked the Commons for their good work: decisions were reached with well nigh a universal consent, after 'declaringe what might be saide *pro et contra* in all cases of doubte' so that 'when all was sayde and hearde on both partes', what stands most with honour of God and commonwealth might be safely agreed upon.[31] This ideal balance is extolled by Speaker Bell in his petition of 1572 for free speech, 'for except the obiections on every parte be hearde, answered and confuted, the councell cannot be perfected'.[32] But soon the queen's prerogative is seen to clash with 'the Libertie of the House'. Soon she complains that some have been presumptuous, questioning her authority and 'medling with matters neither perteining unto them nor within the capacitie of their understanding'.[33] She will not have the feet lead the head. To each part of the body its place, which Speaker Popham duly recites: a commonwealth with two heads or no head is a monster. It is composed of rustical members, its feet, and martial hands, the soldiers. The nobility are its eyes and ears, the council its heart.[34]

Before they actually severed the monarch's head from the body of the realm, the revisers of monarchy often paid heavy prices for the liberties taken. Elizabeth's notion of freedom is strictly defined by her Lord Keeper:

> For libertie of speech, Her Majestie commaundeth me to tell yow that to saye yea or no to bills, God forbid that any man should be restrained, or affrayde to answear according to his best likinge, with some shorte declaracion of his reason therin, and therin to have a free voyce; which is the verye trew libertie of the House, not as some suppose to speake there of all causes as him listeth, and to frame a forme of relligion, or a state of government as to their idle braynes shall seeme meetest. She sayth no king fitt for his state will suffer such absurdities.[35]

30 Sir Francis Knollys' letter to Secretary Wilson, 1577, in Strype, *The History of Edmund Grindal*, p. 354.
31 Closing speech, 8 May 1559, *Proceedings*, I, p. 47.
32 May 1572, *Proceedings*, I, p. 341.
33 Closing speech, 29 May 1571, *Proceedings*, I, p. 188.
34 March 1581, *Proceedings*, I, p. 525, one of many organic metaphors of the commonwealth.
35 February 1593, *Proceedings*, III, p. 22.

The Crown's first articulate definition of freedom of speech, in answer to the Speaker's petition of 1571, distinguishes matters of State, which Parliament has no right to initiate, royal prerogative, and commonwealth matters. At the next Parliament, these distinctions having been ignored, the Lord Keeper reminds them what they are exactly: 'the prince by his prerogative hath power to order causes otherwise then the lawe is, and to helpe the subiectes in a cause wherein hee hath noe other helpe in lawe, which seemes in reason as great a prerogative as may bee'.[36] But the royal commands are persistently unheeded. When Sir Humphrey Gilbert criticizes Bell's motion against a grant of licenses as derogatory of the prerogative, he is sharply reproved by Paul Wentworth who finds this speech injurious to the House and designed only 'to inculcate feare into those which should bee free'.[37]

The debates in successive Parliaments show a growing antagonism between opposite notions of counsel. Against the limits set to them the Commons vow they must in conscience speak, as peril drives them to put all fear aside.[38] Free debating is necessary to good counsel, but opinions are divided as to the extent of this freedom, and those allowed to enjoy it. On a great matter like Norfolk's fate, Fleetwood would have speech more liberally suffered within the House, though not without, and stiffly reminds Arthur Hall that 'words tollerable in this Howse are not sufferable at Blunte's table'.[39] 'Infinite the estimation of libertie' but 'Noe libertie to be graunted to licentiousness',[40] and of course no liberty for treacherous words.[41] Esdras 'sayd consciences may bee free, but not to disturbe the comon quiett'.[42] There may be corporational fights for the rights of lawyers and MPs, protests against peremptory messages from Lords or government 'prejudicial to the liberties of the House', but no room for 'unorthodox' ideas.

Mutual tolerance is no part of the Commons' agenda. To Job Throckmorton, the secrecy of a papist's thoughts is tantamount to the overthrow of Church and commonwealth, 'ffor under the wynges of this serpentine conscience is hatched the broode of all thease pestilent conspiracyes'.[43] Francis Alford, speaking for Mary Stuart's right to a defence, 'desireth that every man maie speake his conscience', to little effect.[44] From 1572 onwards the law invoked is predominantly martial. Objections for the rights of defence or against retroactive laws are brushed away. In vain does Goodyear plead against making treason a fault already committed: 'to call againe the tyme past, or to raise what is dead in any

36 Sir Nicholas Bacon's speech on Lord Cromwell's case, 1572, *Proceedings*, I, p. 265.
37 April 1571, *Proceedings*, I, pp. 224, 237.
38 15 May 1572, *Proceedings*, I, p. 352.
39 Recorder's speech, 18 May 1572, *Proceedings*, I, p. 360.
40 Fennor's and Snagge's speeches, 1572, *Proceedings*, I, p. 361.
41 12 April 1571, *Proceedings*, I, p. 213.
42 9 April 1571, *Proceedings*, I, p. 206.
43 Speech on the Bill and Book, 27 February 1587, *Proceedings*, II, p. 316.
44 15 May 1572, *Proceedings*, I, p. 326.

kynd, man may not, nor in reason is to bee presumed'.[45] Marsh wants them to consider treason in words. Edward Fenner applauds a motion to remove Norfolk, for justice is to be chosen over mercy.[46]

Inside the House, offensive behaviour could be forgiven, offensive words touching the honour of Parliament could not. Arthur Hall would be finally excluded for he 'had infamously sayd that our parliamentes were but of yesterday; they were assembled for graunting of subsidyes only'.[47] The case of William Strickland was quite another matter. He was called before the Privy Council in 1571 after exhibiting a bill for reformation of the Book of Common Prayer. His sequestration moved members to claim that the House was a competent court of justice for self-discipline. Since he was not now a private man 'but to supply the roome, person and place of a multitude especially chosen', they should not 'permitt him to bee detayned from us': whatever his offence, he should be sent for to the bar of the House, there to be heard and answer.[48] Yelverton added that all matters not treasonable or derogatory of the imperial crown were tolerable there 'where there was such fullnes of power as even the right of the crowne was to bee determined'. Men were here not for themselves but their country, and showed 'it was fitt princes to have their prerogative but yet the same to bee straytned within reasonable limittes'. Contrary to Jean Bodin's creed, the prince could not of herself make or break laws.[49]

'Sweet indeed is the name of libertye and the thing it selfe a value beyond all inestimable treasure', Peter Wentworth begins on 8 February 1576. Rumours of what Her Majesty likes or dislikes, messages brought to the House commanding or inhibiting, are 'very injurious unto the freedome of speech and consultacion'. May God send the queen 'a melting yeilding heart unto sound counsel', he pleads, quoting Bracton, for no estate can stand where the prince will not be governed by advice. When examined by a committee, he warns them that if they question him as councillors, he won't answer, for he is no private person. If as committees of the House, he will. If messages from Her Majesty be against the glory of God, the prince's safety, or the liberty of Parliament, he will not hold his peace. He openly called the Scottish queen the most notorious whore in the world and is not afraid to do so again. Nobody is perfect, Her Majesty herself has committed great faults in rejecting laws designed for her safety. Though he felt fear in composing this speech, his conscience dictated it: he will never confess it a fault to love Her Majesty and warn her of danger.[50] After a month in the Tower, Wentworth was brought to the bar of the House and treated to Mildmay's reproof: opinions may be delivered freely for debating, but liberty does not extend so that a man in

---

45 12 April 1571, *Proceedings*, I, p. 213.

46 16 May 1572, *Proceedings*, I, p. 355.

47 15 May 1572, 31 March 1593, *Proceedings*, I, pp. 326, 330; III, p. 153.

48 Carleton's speech, 16 April 1571, *Proceedings*, I, p. 247.

49 20 April 1571, *Proceedings*, I, pp. 238, 239.

50 8 February 1576, *Proceedings*, I, pp. 425–39, speech and committee, text from Inner Temple.

this House 'may speake what, and of whom he lyst'. Wentworth made humble submission upon his knees and was readmitted.[51]

The Commons as a body were equally wary of pressures: on receiving instructions from the Upper House that same week, they expressed displeasure at the Lords' attempt to tell them what to do. The Lords complained that 'the comon howse did not use that reverence towardes them as they ought to do', nor were they entitled to add or mend anything in a text that bore the queen's signature. To this the Commons signified reverence as far as was not prejudicial to the liberties of the House, which must be left to their posterity in the same freedom they received them. As for the queen's signature, they took it as only a recommendation. The bill went no farther.[52]

In the debates of March 1587 on the Bill and Book, Peter Wentworth returned unto the breach with eight questions on the liberties of Parliament, a list strongly reminiscent of his speech eleven years earlier. Instead of reading them one by one as he was asked to, Speaker Puckering pocketed up the questions, and 'Mr Wentworth was sent to the Tower'.[53] Four supporters of the Bill and Book soon joined him there.[54] The wheel of the State ship was fast veering from one set of treacherous rocks to the next. Having momentarily disposed of Wentworth, Puckering reported the queen's command to ignore the Puritans' solicitations. Again, spiritual interests were filled with material considerations: this bill would condemn three of the thirty-nine articles set out by law in 1562, Hatton pleaded, and take away *ius patronatus*, the right of inheritance unto ecclesiastical livings, first fruits, and tenths. This was an offence to the realm, 'to bringe into it a barbarous equalitie', as if it were unlawful for Her Majesty to confer honour where best deserved. Indeed, he concludes, 'I finde this platforme iniuriouse to her supremacye, to her strength, and to her person'.[55]

Licence and Licensing: Whitgift's ex officio *Oath*

> our decrees,
> Dead to infliction, to themselves are dead,
> And Liberty plucks Justice by the nose.
>
> *Measure for Measure, I.iv*

Free speech outside Parliament did not deserve consideration. Books and printed plays were submitted to an even more severe censorship than idle 'vagrants'. At his accession to the see of Canterbury, John Whitgift of Gray's Inn obtained

---

51 *Proceedings*, I, pp. 452–54.
52 *Proceedings*, I, pp. 458–60, and 492.
53 *Proceedings*, II, p. 322.
54 Cope, Lewknor, Hurleston, and Bainbridge.
55 *Proceedings*, II, p. 337. On Hatton's speech, see Dean, *Law-Making and Society*, p. 101.

increased powers over licensing for the Court of High Commission. In 1586 an edict of the Star Chamber empowered the archbishop to control all the printing apparatus of the realm. This came shortly after discussion of a bill to suppress 'lewd and ill books'. Not those slanderous to the State, for which statutes existed already, but 'unprofitable and idell pamphlettes, leud and wanton discourses of love, propha[n]e ballades, lying historyes, which all tend to the corruption of manners and expence of tyme which otherwise men would bestow in reading of the scripture'. Young Shakespeare then had just done his own reading of such lewd works. The ban must include Ovid's *De arte amandi*, which was taught in schools along with the Gospel, while women should be prevented from reading 'wanton Italian discorses and tales, which be nothing els but very scholmasters of wantones and uncleannes'.[56] The House rejected it, a defiance that earned them a sound berating from the Lord Chancellor.[57]

In the House of Lords' Journal, Whitgift's name begins to emerge in 1584, in debates relating to a petition of the Commons filled with grievances on the mismanagement of the Church.[58] Whitgift answers each article, 'some of which he mislikes', since they would free ministers from obedience, but does not satisfy the Commons. Their answers to the answer are rebuked by Speaker Puckering, for their manner of seeking redress, however grounded, shows intent to abridge the queen's authority as supreme head of the Church. Such matters are to be dealt with by the Upper House, 'for unto us beinge the lower and third House, and so the meanest, such matters did nothinge at all belonge'.[59] The proper way to lodge complaints is through the bishop of their diocese. At this point, the reporter observes, the House was greatly moved and wounded, for either they must offend their gracious sovereign, or else suffer the liberties of their House to be infringed. The way out of their dilemma was to present a bill for the better execution of a 1572 statute against disorders touching ministers of the Church. In the Upper House, the bill was 'greatly inveighed against by Dr Whitgift', but won support from Leicester. The Commons were satisfied with this, for they were not so much concerned with perfection of a law, the narrator asserts, 'as they ioyed in the passage thereof from theire House to the Lordes, whereby theire wounded libertie had nowe received healthe and saifetie'.[60] End of Act I, a draw.

Act II concentrates on *ex officio* proceedings, in the background of the Martin Marprelate tracts against episcopacy. After thirty years of paranoid obsession with the papist threat, the defeat of Spain had moved the political stress to the other side of England's anxieties. Through the voice of Christopher Hatton, on 4 February 1589, Elizabeth complains it is not enough that she must suffer at

56 'Speech on bill for ban on printing certain books', 10 February? 1585, *Proceedings*, II, pp. 40–43.

57 Neale, *Elizabeth I and her Parliaments*, II, pp. 95, 98. See Auchter, *Dictionary of Literary and Dramatic Censorship*, p. 231. *Protestant Nonconformist Texts*, ed. by Tudur Jones, document I.15, pp. 87–90.

58 *Proceedings*, II, pp. 161–69.

59 *Proceedings*, II, pp. 181–83.

60 *Proceedings*, II, pp. 183–86.

the hands of her Catholic enemies, now her own friends threaten her. The Lower House are again commanded not to meddle, 'excepte it be to bridle all those, whether papists or puritanes, which are therewithal discontented'. Five days later, Richard Bancroft, chaplain successively of Chancellor Hatton and Archbishop Whitgift, launches an attack at Paul's Cross against the Puritan false prophets, claiming episcopacy was established since the Apostles' time and bishops derive their authority from Christ.[61] The *Laws of Ecclesiastical Polity* would confirm it, aligning bishops with the apostles who were the first degree of Church hierarchy, a rank superior to mere priesthood.[62] But Sir Francis Knollys thought it treasonable talk, for if bishops held their authority *jure divino*, then the queen was not the only supreme governor. A new line of attack on the royal supremacy was developing, a new crack that the Stuarts would widen: their choice in accepting the divine right of bishops and joining the High Church party would 'bring about the alliance of Puritans and common lawyers against the claims of the Crown'.[63]

In the House, within days of Bancroft's sermon, Whitgift was accused of using *ex officio* proceedings and laws devised as anti-Catholic against the Protestants. Whitgift did not want lawyers to barge in: appeals to Parliament for breach of law would transform it into a *parlement*, making it 'a sette courte, as it is in Paris'.[64] The injustice of *ex officio* proceedings had been a strong point in the Supplication against the Ordinaries presented by the Commons to Henry VIII: it resulted in their abolition, Henry's daughter is now politely reminded. Among requests that she would graciously establish a Christian peaceable toleration as was used in the time of her brother, John Stubbs submits a humble supplication, complaining that honest ministers are proceeded against *ex officio*, not for contempt of her laws, nor any matter of faith, but of ceremony and order. He swears to crave no innovation, for he abhors seditious persons, heretics, and fantastical sectarians — a moderation wholly at odds with the tone of his earlier pamphlet against her marriage plans.

Cecil Lord Burghley had written to Whitgift in 1583 to criticize the Romish style of his articles: his executions *ex officio mero* were so curiously penned, so full of branches, 'that I think the *Inquisition of Spain* used not so many questions to comprehend and entrap their prey!'[65] In his reply, Whitgift explained that the oath was essential, because common law procedure was inadequate in collecting sufficient evidence to secure convictions. If witnesses were required, it would set a precedent for papists and all other sectarians who would expect the same favour, not to mention the expenses. Using an oath *ex officio*, that they would truthfully answer all questions, the Court of High Commission had succeeded in

61 Richard Bancroft, *Pretended Holy Discipline* (London: John Wolfe, 1593), p. 154.

62 Hooker, *Of the Laws of Ecclesiastical Polity*, Bk v, Ch. 78.1–12, II, pp. 292–300.

63 Allen, *A History of Political Thought*, p. 183.

64 *Proceedings*, II, p. 440.

65 Thomas Fuller, *The Church History of Britain from the Birth of Jesus Christ until the Year 1648* (London: John Williams, 1656), Bk IX, p. 151.

suspending over two hundred Puritan ministers. Those who refused to take the oath were guilty of contempt of court and could be imprisoned indefinitely. The presbyterian Thomas Cartwright, Stubbs's brother-in-law, was thus committed to the Fleet in 1591, from where he wrote an account of the proceedings to Burghley, arguing that the oath he was asked to take was contrary to the laws of God and of the land: in common law, not a self-incriminating oath but two or three witnesses were needed to establish the truth.[66] James Morice, of the Middle Temple, produced a treatise arguing this point with canons of the Church, which he too offered to Burghley but refused to publish 'lest any offence should be taken'.[67] When offered release against a recantation, Cartwright and his Puritan colleagues indignantly refused.[68] After various appeals, they were set free a few months later, though still deprived of their benefices.[69]

In February 1593, the same Morice presented two bills in Commons against unlawful oaths and unlawful imprisonments by bishops' courts, and denounced proceedings *ex officio mero*, with mention of his 'breefe treatise to admonishe our judges ecclesiasticall of this their errour': he invoked Magna Carta, Bracton, and all the statutes of the realm against the lawless practices of the bishops.[70] The heated discussion continued, with civilians and commoners throwing Becket or Foxe's martyrs at each other, till Secretary Robert Cecil called for a halt until the queen was consulted. Speaker Edward Coke reported on the following day that she marvelled at their boldness: as she had the authority to summon and dissolve the Parliament at her good pleasure, 'so had she likewise power to appoynt unto them what causes they were to treat of'.[71] Morice was brought before the Privy Council and told by Thomas Sackville, Lord Buckhurst, co-author of *Gorboduc*, that some little submission would do well. Being impenitent, he was suspended from his office and kept in confinement for two months.

All in all, seven members were imprisoned or sequestered during this Parliament, a record figure in Elizabeth's reign. These arrests did raise protests, but nothing to compare with the fiery indignation Strickland's had caused in 1571. On 10 March, a humble petition moving that Her Majesty be pleased to release the members restrained was opposed by all the councillors present, who thought it best not to press her. She would no doubt release them shortly, whereupon, the diarist notes, 'the motion cessed from further speach'. A strange silence. 'The dynamic of Elizabethan England was weakening and the period entering its silver

66 Cartwright, *Cartwrightiana*, ed. by Peel and Carlson, p. 35.

67 Rev. B. Brook, *Memoir of the Life and Writings of Thomas Cartwright* (London: John Snow, 1845), p. 382.

68 Cartwright, *Cartwrightiana*, pp. 309–16, 325–27.

69 See John Strype, *The Life and Acts of John Whitgift*, 4 vols (Oxford: Clarendon Press, 1822), I, p. 318. Hill, *Society and Puritanism*, pp. 295–98.

70 *Proceedings*, III, pp. 30–44. Morice's account, *Proceedings*, III, p. 39, and Anonymous Journal, *Proceedings*, III, 77.

71 Report of the Speaker's speech, *Proceedings*, III, 52.

age', Neale diagnoses.[72] Whitgift had succeeded momentarily in breaking the Puritan drive. The discussion over the oath *ex officio* would be resumed under James I, when Francis Bacon, Coke, and the Chief Justices would lay the adage that 'By the laws of England, no man is bound to accuse himself'.[73] They would recall the case of Cawdrey, a Rutlandshire minister who was deprived of his benefice in 1596 for having refused to wear a surplice, although Morice in his defence had pointed out the weaknesses of the charge.

While Cartwright and his friends were in custody, Peter Wentworth broached another issue with a *Pithie Exhortation to her Majesty for establishing her Successor to the Crown*. When the new Parliament met, in February 1593, he gathered a group of young lawyer MPs at Lincoln's Inn to discuss plans for a bill, news of which reached the authorities. When asked for a draft of his prepared speech, Wentworth refused, invoking the privilege of Parliament, and was sent to the Tower where he spent the remainder of his life. Imprisonment did not weaken his spirit. To the Jesuit Parsons's *Conference* in support of the Spanish Infanta, he replied with a *Discourse containing the Author's opinion of the true and lawful successor to her Majesty*, designating James VI, regardless of the fact he had loudly opposed the Scottish claim when Mary was alive. Where Parsons argues that Parliament has power to decide the succession in spite of hereditary right, Wentworth asserts that the authority of Parliament is restricted by justice and equity. Parsons invokes the precedent of Richard II, rightfully deposed by an act of Parliament. Wentworth declares that Henry IV was a usurper and quotes *Gorboduc*.

Wentworth's *Pithie Exhortation* and his *Discourse* were printed posthumously at Edinburgh in 1598.[74] The same year, James VI published his own views on divine right: kings had been entrusted with sovereignty by God before parliaments existed, 'And so it followes of necessitie, that the Kinges were the authors & makers of the lawes, and not the lawes of the Kings'. The king is 'therefore countable to that great GOD, who placed him as his lieutenant ouer them'.[75] He finds a legal basis to his claim that '*Monarchie* is the true paterne of Diuinitie' in Jean Bodin's recently published theory of the State, which asserts that 'in a popular estate nothing can bee greater than the whole body of the people themselues. But in a monarchie it is otherwise, where euerie one in particular, and all the people in generall, and (as it were) in one bodie, must sweare to the obseruation of the

72 Neale, *Elizabeth I and her Parliaments*, I, p. 297. *Proceedings*, III, p. 121.

73 M. H. Maguire, 'The Attack of the Common Lawyers on the Oath *ex officio*', in *Essays in History and Political Theory in Honour of C. H. McIlwain*, ed. by Carl Wittke (Cambridge, MA: Harvard University Press, 1937), pp. 222–26.

74 Peter Wentworth, *A pithie exhortation to her Maiestie for establishing her successor to the crowne* (Edinburgh: Robert Waldegrave, 1598); electronic repr. Early English Books Online, University of Michigan, 1999, <http://name.umdl.umich.edu/A14936.0001.001>.

75 James VI & I, *The True Lawe of free Monarchies*, pp. 57–82.

lawes, and their faithfull alleageance to one soueraigne monarch; who next vnto God (of whome he holdeth his scepter & power) is bound to no man'.[76]

Against Edward Coke's claims James will repeatedly assert his own ability to judge, his dislike of the 'Sophistrie or straines of wit that must interprete', and his preference for 'either clear Law, or solid reason': 'remember you are no makers of Law, but interpretours of Law', he will tell the Star Chamber.[77] At age seventeen, when advised by Walsingham to heed the counsel of his Parliament lest he end like Edward II, James had answered that he was 'an absolute king'.[78] If his *True Lawe* anticipates *Richard II*, it also echoes contemporary strains: James paid close attention to English new writing and repeatedly demanded sanctions against works he found derogatory to his dignity or injurious to his mother, like *The Faerie Queene*'s Duessa, arguing that Book v contained matter prejudicial to 'himself and his mother deceassed'.[79] The long latent opposition between absolutist and constitutional theories of monarchy was oozing towards the stage. Neale's Elizabethan twilight was the dawn of its sunniest theatrical age. Parliament had set the agenda to playwrights and young upstart crows for a decade of productions (see below, 'A Parliament of Voices' in Chapter 10). How laudative of monarchy is still a moot point. *Macbeth* is often read as paying homage to James I, but as Herman points out, the show of eight kings does not highlight an unbroken lineal descent, since it is Duncan's line which is restored at the end, not Banquo's. The promise to Banquo's heirs is made not by three 'creatures of an elder world' embodying the Fates, as in the sources of the play, but by three 'obviously Satanic hags': 'the switch from a positive to a negative origin effectively taints the entire line, and the ideologies propounded by that line'.[80]

Parliamentary Chroniclers: John Hooker's Constitutional Monarchy

> Away, burn all the records of the realm, my mouth shall be the parliament of England.
>
> *2 Henry VI, IV.vii*

It is an index of a developing interest for arguments about free speech that various attendants thought them worth recording in close detail. The first surviving unofficial accounts of parliamentary proceedings under Elizabeth go back to 1571. Among the journalists who recorded debates was John Hooker, better known to

76 Bodin, 'Of soueraingtie', *The six bookes of a common-weale*, Bk I, ch. VIII, 100.
77 James I's speech in the Star Chamber, 20 June 1616, in Kenyon, *The Stuart Constitution*, pp. 84–86.
78 Read, *Mr Secretary Walsingham*, II, pp. 213–18.
79 In the report of the English Ambassador Robert Bowes to Elizabeth. Goldberg, *James I and the Politics of Literature*, pp. 12–17.
80 Herman, '*Macbeth*', pp. 221–22, 218. The story of the weird sisters, invented by Hector Boece in his *Historia Gentis Scotorum* (1527), was incorporated by Francis Thynne into Holinshed's *Chronicles* (1577).

readers of Holinshed as Vowell, the antiquary, one of the team who produced the second edition of Holinshed's *Chronicles* in 1587. He is of interest here in both capacities. It is Hooker, MP for Exeter, who reports Richard III's visit to the nearby Castle of Rougemont and the prophecy evoked on stage by the last Plantagenet king, 'that when he came once to Richmond he should not long liue after: which fell out in the end to be true'.[81] With his patron Sir Peter Carew, who wanted to establish his title to lands in Ireland, Hooker was allowed to search the royal archives in the Tower. This is probably when he found and translated a manuscript of the medieval *Modus tenendi parliamentum*. He had it privately printed along with his own *Order and usage of keeping Parlement in England*, a pamphlet which Annabel Patterson reads as 'a modern redaction of the *Modus*'.[82] He did this, he explains, not just for Antiquity's sake, but 'also for a presedent to the good government in tholde yeeres'.[83] *Order and usage* was reprinted in the 1587 version of Holinshed, infusing it with the stuff and spirit of the *Modus*.[84]

Sir Thomas Smith in *De republica anglorum* had treated Parliament strictly in terms of its authority to legislate. But Hooker, also trained in civil law, made a list of great causes upon which the ruler must have the counsel of all estates. The right of initiative, so firmly denied by the queen just months before, is reclaimed in the *Order*: every member has not only a right of free speech on any matter proponed, but 'of him selfe to propone any matter for the commoditie of the Prince and of the common welth'. Good government gave a major role to the Commons, whose presence was necessary to the proceedings, whereas the king's person was not. Without them, the king cannot make laws, he insists. Like the first Holinshed, who found the idea in Polydore Vergil, he adds to the original *Modus* the notion that the separation in two Houses was designed so the lower members could speak more freely, out of sight from their betters.[85] This is how it became understood after Hooker, not from the *Modus* directly, but from the chroniclers' interpretation of the division. As Speaker of the House in 1593, at the onset of his oppositional career, Edward Coke quotes the *Modus* to show 'how we satt altogether' at the first, but actually he is following Holinshed's and Hooker's explanations on the origin of bicameralism: the Commons sitting in presence of the king and among the nobles 'found fault that they had not free liberty of speech'. On being asked why they wanted to sit apart, a knight 'answered stoutly that his Majestie and the lordes there every one being great persons represented but themselves, but his commons though they were inferiour men yet every one of them represented a thowsand men'.[86] A proud claim echoed in *Henry V*, with

81 *Holinshed's Chronicles*, III, p. 421. *Richard III*, IV.ii.

82 Patterson, *Reading Holinshed's Chronicle*, p. 126.

83 Preface to the Fitzwilliam edition of *Order and Usage*, p. 206, in Patterson, *Reading Holinshed's Chronicle*, p. 125.

84 See above, 'Model Parliaments' in Chapter 2, and Patterson, *Reading Holinshed's Chronicle*, pp. 124–27.

85 See Snow, *Parliament in Elizabethan England*, p. 153.

86 *Proceedings*, III, p. 160.

a 'mingled sense of modesty and pride', Jonathan Baldo notes: 'Into a thousand parts divide one man', for ''tis your thoughts that now must deck our kings'. The similitudes work both ways: if in Hooker's description the Lower House 'is made like a Theater',[87] the theatres 'bore at least a hint of Elizabethan Parliaments'.[88]

Before Hooker stepped in, Patterson contends, Holinshed had led the way to parliamentarism through 'a discontinuous story of ancient constitutionalism'. In the theory of its origins, drawn from Polydore Vergil, the chronicler found arguments to make consent rather than counsel the significant point of the medieval assemblies.[89] Actually, Holinshed may not be 'quintessentially monarchical', as John Watts claims, but he was definitely hostile to rebellion for any cause.[90] We saw Hall above, cautiously avoiding all but oblique criticism of Henry's religious policy, whatever his own Protestant heart may have felt. Hall the common lawyer had closed his eyes to any abuse of royal prerogative for the sake of stability, welcoming the prevention of all budding rebels and their brood. Holinshed, who copied large sections of Hall verbatim, was no less cautious. His main theme, like his predecessor's, is national unity. 'All rebels pretend reformation but indeed purpose destruction both of king and countrie', he notes about the Peasants' War of 1381. Both chroniclers are obsessed with the horrors of civil strife, both equally strong in condemning ambitious lords and giddy heads ready to march with them on the least excuse. The prejudice against the naturally rebellious lower classes is such that they seldom take pains to distinguish between the representative Commons of the Lower House and the rabble. Even the Commons' demands for justice seem to threaten ochlocracy. All that can be said in support of Holinshed's superior regard for Parliament is that he occasionally tones down some of Hall's scathing references to the 'mutable commons'.[91]

With Hooker's *Modus*, Harrison's addition 'Of the High Court of Parliament and Authority of the Same' to the second edition of Holinshed does sketch an image of constitutional monarchy. Though he claims to follow Smith's orthodox *De republica* step by step, Harrison differs from him on the power of Parliament, which he accounts the most high and absolute of the realm, 'for thereby kings and mightie princes have from time to time beene deposed from their thrones, lawes either enacted or abrogated', and 'corrupted religion either disanulled or reformed'.[92] The succeeding history of medieval parliaments confirmed that their radical views were drawn from 'tholde yeeres', from Boadicea the spokeswoman of 'ancient liberty' to George Ferrers whose fellow MPs in 1543 had set him free. A history culminating, of course, with the deposition of Richard II.

---

87 John Hooker, *Order and Usage*, in Snow, *Parliament in Elizabethan England*, p. 163.

88 See Baldo, '"Into a thousand parts"' p. 57.

89 Patterson, *Reading Holinshed's Chronicle*, ch. 6.

90 John Watts, 'Holinshed as History', report on Holinshed Workshop, Jesus College, Oxford, 5–7 January 2009, p. 3. See Watts, 'Monarchy', in *The Oxford Handbook of Holinshed's 'Chronicles'*, ed. by Paulina Kewes and others (Oxford: Oxford University Press, 2013), pp. 374–88.

91 Goy-Blanquet, *Shakespeare's Early History Plays*, pp. 117, 235–42.

92 *Holinshed's Chronicles*, I, p. 291.

Bolingbroke's victorious usurpation was tricky to deal with, when the orthodox Homilies invited subjects to read the chronicles as evidence that God never prospered any rebellion against their lawful prince. A list of illustrious families 'now cleane extinguished and gone' was there to drive the point home.[93] The Tudor chroniclers were palpably embarrassed by the fact that the case against Richard was fairly light, touching a king of undeniable legitimacy. Moved by the many who 'came flocking vnto him from euerie part', Bolingbroke found himself carried to a throne which he 'perchance neuer thought of or yet dreamed'. When he comes face to face with the king, and claims he wants only 'restitution of my person, my lands and heritage, through your fauourable licence', Richard lucidly answers, 'Déere cousin, I am readie to accomplish your will, so that you may inioy all that is yours, without exception.' To Holinshed, Richard had little choice: 'On the one part he knew his title just, true, and infallible [...]. On the other side, he saw the puissance of his adversaries, the sudden departure of them whom he most trusted, and all things turned upside down'.[94] In other words, a revolution.

How to legitimize the usurpation, when the whole kingdom had sworn faith to Richard, that was the problem then facing his Parliament, as we saw above. How to report it without offence is now Holinshed's, who takes refuge behind earlier records in an elaborate *mise en abyme*, a frame-within-the-frame construction. Bolingbroke's claim is reported through an official document, 'I Henrie of Lancaster claime the realme of England and the crowne', which is granted him straightaway. Parliament's thirty-three articles of accusation were summed up 'by maister Hall as followeth'. Hall had added to his predecessors' accounts a willing confession made by Richard of his faults, for which he expresses due remorse. Richard himself is never present in person. Hoping to save his life, he was persuaded in the Tower to resign voluntarily, 'as it should seeme by the copie of an instrument hereafter following'. This text is cast like a testimony, involving both a narrative plural, 'we', sixteen commissioners whose names follow, and a singular 'me the said earle', Northumberland, according to whom the king acknowledged his inability to govern, promising 'he would gladlie leaue of and renounce his right and title'.[95] To this effect, 'he desired to haue a bill drawne of the said resignation, that he might be perfect in the rehearsall thereof', and insisted on reading it himself, 'with glad countenance'. 'Rehearsal', 'rehearse' occur four times in the thirty-line account of the performance. Embedded in this testimony, a document in the first person, 'I Richard', frees his subjects from their allegiance and renounces all his titles. The witnesses then go with this 'voluntarie renunciation' to Westminster where it is endorsed by both Houses, and the Duke of Lancaster presents his title to the crown. His accession is signified to Richard, who gives up all his property to compensate for his errors, 'in hope to be in more

93 'An Homilie against disobedience and wilful rebellion', *Certaine Sermons or Homilies*, p. 301.

94 *Holinshed's Chronicles*, II, pp. 853–55.

95 'A copie of the instrument touching the declaration of the commissioners sent from the states in parlement, vnto king Richard', *Holinshed's Chronicles*, II, pp. 861–62.

suertie of life for the deliuerie thereof' but again, 'whatsoeuer was promised, he was deceiued therein'.[96] In this painstaking account, Holinshed significantly differs from his sources, Froissart who paints Richard in full majesty delivering the crown with his own hands to Bolingbroke, or Hall who further embellishes the ceremony with a remorseful confession of his faults. It is left to Shakespeare to subvert the uncrowning ritual: the play makes Richard the actor and director of this 'woeful pageant', thus pre-empting Henry's coronation, and sets it not in the secrecy of the Tower, but on the grand national stage of Parliament.[97]

After Holinshed, a large interest for Elizabethan parliaments appears in the numbers of reports and later copies made, especially of the 1593 and 1601 sessions.[98] With Hayward Townshend, of Lincoln's Inn, and Simonds D'Ewes of Middle Temple, a new turn is taken as they specialize in chronicling parliamentary affairs. In his brief diary of his first Parliament, 1597, Townshend dedicates much room to its accompanying rituals, opening and closing, morning prayer, collection of money for the poor, and to the speech of a fellow member from Lincoln's Inn. His freshman's eye also notices a 'rebellious corner' on the right-hand side of the House. At the next Parliament, Elizabeth's last, he shows a growing interest for the workings of this institution. He also reports an interest outside the House for matters debated, paying special attention to some speakers: Francis Bacon, Robert Cecil, Ralegh, and lawyers generally.[99] Townshend's work, 'pillaged' by Simonds D'Ewes,[100] edited and 'mangled' by D'Ewes's nephew Paul Bowes, provided the main source of information until T. E. Hartley published his sources. D'Ewes was more a copyist than a great antiquary. A member of the Long Parliament, where he sat with the more moderate Puritans, he is also emblematic of the familial divisions in England. Charles I had made him a baronet, but he sided with Parliament when the Civil War began, while his brother, lieutenant colonel in the royal army, was mortally wounded at the siege of Reading.

Ecclesiastical Polity: Richard Hooker's via media

> God for his Richard hath in heavenly pay
> A glorious angel.
>
> *Richard II, III.ii*

Debates over religious policy were no more confined to Parliament precincts than other political issues. When Parliament reconvened after Mary Stuart's execution, Richard Hooker must have had first-hand accounts from his uncle John, who then

96 *Holinshed's Chronicles*, II, pp. 855–65.
97 Goy-Blanquet, 'Richard II ou l'art de la mise en scène'.
98 On the issue of authorship, see Hartley's Introduction to *Proceedings*, III, pp. xviii–xxvi.
99 *Proceedings*, III, p. 253.
100 In A. F. Pollard, 'Hayward Townshend's Journals', *Historical Research*, 14.42 (1937), 149.

sat as member for Exeter, of the Presbyterian attacks against Whitgift and the discipline of the Church, the very theme of his own duel with Walter Travers a year before in Temple Church, when 'the pulpit spake pure Canterbury in the morning and Geneva in the afternoon until Travers was silenced', forbidden to preach by Whitgift in the spring of 1586.[101] Actually Richard Hooker was not pure Canterbury: it seems he was a compromise solution between Whitgift's determinedly anti-Puritan candidate and Cecil, who wanted Travers elevated.[102] He must have been appalled by some of their speeches and deeply stirred by their demand for freedom of expression.[103] *Of the Laws of Ecclesiastical Polity* is in part an answer to Travers's Presbyterian treatise of 1574, *A full and plaine declaration of ecclesiasticall discipline*. While laying down principles on governance of the Church, Hooker defended the position of Elizabeth as its supreme governor and of the episcopacy. His *via media* denied both the absolute authority of Scripture and the apostolic succession of bishops, which tended to place men outside human law.[104]

To Hooker, the authority of the Bible did not extend to matters of Church organization. Those belonged with *adiophara*, not damnable, not worth fighting or dying for: if the differences of a few ceremonies 'have kindled so much fire, or have caused it to flame so long' it was because the parties labouring for Reformation 'had somewhat more than this mark whereat to aim', that is, the suppression of episcopacy.[105] The purpose of Christ's revelation is the salvation of souls, not ecclesiastical polity. The government of Church and State is rooted in natural and positive law, not rules laid down immutably in the Bible. Where Lutheran or Calvinist doctrines made every man sovereign of his soul, Hooker unequivocally states that authority must be obeyed, even if wrong, in which case reason must strive to remedy the wrong. Let bishops remember that the force of custom rather than any heavenly law maintains them in their place, and use their authority with humility and moderation.[106]

What matters primarily to Hooker is the preservation of the best, or least bad, institution to foster Christian religion. Quoting Saint-German's *Doctor and Student* in his notes, he aims to suppress all bases for legitimate disobedience to the laws of the realm and present a coherent vision of royal ecclesiastical headship.[107] Hooker is the first to employ the phrase 'divine right' in connection with royal power: 'Unto kings by human right, honour by divine right, is due'.[108] This does not make him support absolutism, for he believes in an original political

---

101 Thomas Fuller, *The History of the Worthies of England* (London: John Fuller, 1662), p. 264.
102 Secor, *Richard Hooker*, pp. 137–38.
103 Secor, *Richard Hooker*, pp. 213–17.
104 Hooker, *Of the Laws of Ecclesiastical Polity*, p. xvi.
105 Hooker, *Of the Laws of Ecclesiastical Polity*, VI, I, i.
106 Hooker, *Of the Laws of Ecclesiastical Polity*, I, XVI, 5; VII, v, 8.
107 Eppley, *Defending Royal Supremacy*, pp. 141, 88, 224–25.
108 Hooker, *Of the Laws of Ecclesiastical Polity*, VIII, II, 6.

contract.[109] If the association of a people is intentional, it follows logically that consent is required to make the exercise of power by its head legitimate, an idea already present in Fortescue and other Bractonians. Yet he does not condone social upheavals of the kind stirred by Anabaptists, nor the 'manifold dangerous events' that a strict Presbyterian programme might cause.[110] Hooker is more original in his focusing on the role of Parliament, a construct which echoes decades of discourses in and outside Commons, the Inns, the pulpits, the stage: 'the parliament of England together with the convocation annexed therunto, is that wherupon the very essence of all government with the realm doth depend'. Elizabeth is supreme governor 'by the authority of this present parliament'. It is the monarch's prerogative to operate outside the law in key areas like Church government, but this authority is not supreme: 'the entire community giveth general order by law how all things publicly are to be done, and the king as head thereof, the highest authority over all, causeth according to the same law every particular to be framed and ordered thereby'.[111]

Hooker's theory of mixed monarchy would not go down well with Elizabeth's successors. Nor did Elizabeth agree to share power with the Lower House. In 1593, she told the Commons that knights and burgesses of the House were councillors 'but during the parliament', unlike the Privy Councillors who were permanent counsellors. The dogma of law's sovereignty was reasserted in the closing speech of her Speaker John Croke at her last Parliament: 'Lawes at the first were not written with any humane penne'; God engraved them with his own finger in the heart of man. When this light was darkened, when faith and truth fled away, 'God sent good kinges and princes his lieftenantes, the best and greatest guifte in this world geven from God to mortall men, to geve lawes to his people'.[112] Religion is the binding hand of a common weal, the orator goes on: 'ut lex divina iubet et vestra cogit'. There can be no worse fate than the horrors threatened by united Spain and Rome, whose envoys rail upon 'the handmaid of the living God', encouraging her liege subjects to deprive her of her kingdom. But he can 'turne there owne swordes which they have whett against the anointed of God into there owne bozomes, and send his angell to scatter and destroie them'.[113] Essex's rebellion, with its wishful revival of *Richard II*, is but two months away.

The Stuarts would redefine prerogative on continental lines, Bodin's especially, who held it to operate not alongside law but above it. The final step in the marriage of monarchy and Church, divine right, placed the monarch well on his way to absolutism, begging for a fall. The recusant Plowden's legal fiction was drawn to extremes when the body natural of King Charles was executed by

109 See Michael Brydon, *The Evolving Reputation of Richard Hooker: An Examination of Responses, 1600–1714* (Oxford: Oxford University Press, 2006), p. 67.

110 McGrade's Introduction to Hooker, *Of the Laws of Ecclesiastical Polity*, p. xxi, and Preface to ch. VIII.

111 Hooker, *Of the Laws of Ecclesiastical Polity*, VIII, VIII, 4.

112 19 December 1601, *Proceedings*, III, p. 263.

113 *Proceedings*, III, pp. 265–66.

decision of the king's body politic.[114] Both Houses made the point clear in their declaration to justify the raising of armies against their sovereign:

> it is acknowledged that the king is the fountain of justice and protection; but the acts of justice and protection are not exercised in his own person, nor depend upon his pleasure, but by his courts and by his ministers, who must do their duty therein though the king in his own person should forbid them. And therefore, if judgments should be given by them against the king's will and personal command, yet are they the king's judgments.[115]

It is Parliament's duty to preserve the peace and safety of the kingdom 'although his majesty, seduced by evil counsel, do in his own person oppose or interrupt the same'. Puritan slogans hammer the same point, vowing that they 'fight the king to defend the King'.[116] Having disposed of the natural body, the body politic goes one step further by abolishing kingship after the execution. Since experience has shown that the office is 'unnecessary, burdensome, and dangerous to the liberty, safety, and public interest of the people', Parliament ordains that it shall not henceforth be exercised by any one single person: 'a most happy way is made for this nation, if God see it good, to return to its just and ancient right of being governed by its own representatives'.[117] Two days later the House of Lords was declared equally 'useless and dangerous', and abolished without further ado. Those Lords who had behaved with honour and fidelity to the commonwealth would be admitted in Parliament if they got themselves elected.[118] William Prynne had recently declared that '*King, Lords and Commons*, by the Common law, make up but one intire *Corporation*'.[119] Now the Commons remained sole representatives of the King-in-Parliament. Unconcerned with the fact that some dramatists were equally critical of monarchy's abuses, they had also decided that theatre was unnecessary, and closed all houses.

Books VI and VIII of Hooker's *Laws* were published in 1648, before the fall of monarchy, when it was still thought they might contribute to a peaceful settlement, and Book VII just after the Restoration. The unfinished work was appealed to by all sides in the clashes between ecclesiastical and political powers in the years before and after the Civil War.[120] Cromwell's supporters aimed to transfer Hooker's view of the sovereign's supremacy onto the Lord Protector. Revisionism continued with the complete edition of 1662, when Archbishop Sheldon commissioned Izaak Walton to write a biography of Hooker. This fanciful

---

114 *Acts and Ordinances of the Interregnum*, 6 January 1649, ed. by Firth and Rait, I, 1253–55.

115 27 May 1642, *Journals of the Lords*, V, 85–88, in *Sources of English Constitutional History*, p. 488.

116 Kantorowicz, *The King's Two Bodies*, p. 18. See Ethyn Kirby, *William Prynne, a Study in Puritanism* (Cambridge, MA: Harvard University Press, 1931), p. 60.

117 *Acts and Ordinances of the Interregnum*, 17 March 1649, II, pp. 18–20.

118 *Acts and Ordinances of the Interregnum*, 19 March 1649, II, p. 24.

119 Prynne, *The Soveraigne Power of Parliaments*, p. 41.

120 Hooker, *Of the Laws of Ecclesiastical Polity*, p. xiv.

Life, which presented the last books as corrupt and mutilated by Puritan editors, with the complicity of Hooker's shrewish wife, was appended to every successive edition.[121]

Clean and Unclean Money

> Robes and furr'd gowns hide all. Plate sin with gold,
> And the strong lance of justice hurtless breaks;
> Arm it in rags, a Pigmy's straw doth pierce it.
>
> *King Lear, IV.vi*

Speaking for the last time in Elizabeth's reign, the Speaker declared that the three most important things in a commonwealth were first, religion, second, religion, third, religion. Actually her previous Parliament had dedicated most of its time to financial matters, and not much to religious affairs, apart from a bill to punish non-attendance at church on Sundays and have it enforced by justices of the peace. Here, the House was treated to a long disquisition by one Edward Glascock, of Gray's Inn, against justices of the peace in general, and the worst kind especially, the 'adulteratinge justice' who is virtuous, discreet, and wise, yet poor and needy: no poor man ought to be in authority, for 'the sweete sent of ryches and gayne takes awaye and confoundeth the true taste of justice and equitye'. Glascock dismisses those basket judges 'that ffor halfe a dozen of chickens will dispence with a dozen of penall statutes'. Despite some few protests on behalf of honest judges, a majority refused to have the author of these offensive words brought to the bar, perhaps implicitly acknowledging the truth of the accusation. The Lord Keeper ended his own speech with an admonition not to deserve unsavoury epithets, 'sueing justices whoe doe sucke and consume the welth and good of the common welth'.[122] Outside the House, their venality was a favourite target of satirists like John Day or Marston, or melancholy Jaques's picture of the justice 'in fair round belly with good capon lin'd'.

With the unbuckling of speech in Parliament, MPs made increasing protests against the use of royal prerogative to avoid common law jurisdiction. In the House itself, law meant politics and politics meant business.[123] The 1597 session was mostly concerned with economic and social issues. Times had changed, the old councillors were all dead or dying, and godliness no longer ruled in Parliament. Francis Bacon put money on a par with laws, 'the one being the

121 The inventiveness of Walton's work was exposed by C. J. Sisson, *The Judicious Marriage of Mr Hooker and the Birth of the Laws of Ecclesiastical Polity* (Cambridge: Cambridge University Press, 1940).

122 December 1601, *Proceedings*, III, pp. 484, 424–26, 492.

123 In Graves, 'The Common Lawyers and the Parliamentary Men-of-Business, 1584–1601', *Parliamentary History*, 8.2 (2008), 189–215.

sinews of peace, the other of war', both the main business of Parliament.[124] On 5 November 1597 he presented a motion against enclosures and their resulting depopulation, increase of poverty and vagrancy. Shall men live in a brutish land where sheep devour men? an unnamed orator asks.[125] Yes, is the unmincing answer of Henry Jackman, a cloth merchant educated at the Inns. Cloth feeds on sheep, not grain. His realistic philosophy did not quite prevail. With exemptions for half the counties of the realm, the bill passed. Eleven bills on poverty and vagrancy produced two acts, one 'for the relief of the poor', one 'for punishment of rogues, vagabonds and sturdy beggars', a neat division of worthy and unworthy poor. The false cripple's plea in *Henry VI*, 'Alas, sir, we did it for pure need', did not carry much weight with the best Elizabethan socialists. Robert Cecil's 'Notes for Parliament' diagnose the ills of society on a list that seems the reverse of Jack Cade's agenda: scarcity and high prices were caused by excessive consumption of bread too fine, beer too strong in too many ale houses. One suggestion to mend the situation was to close those houses of perdition one day a week.[126]

Bills against vagabonds since the 1530s had aimed to distinguish the 'impotent poor' who deserved help from the 'idle', 'vagrant', or 'sturdy beggars' who must be whipped back to their home parishes. The 1563 act made the parishes responsible for poor relief. In 1571, they were allowed to raise a tax of their own for charity. Dr Wilson, Master of the Requests, argued 'that poore of necessity wee must have, for soe Christ hath given untill his latter cominge'. But there is such looseness and lewdness in this realm that he would rather wish them imprisoned.[127] In between moves for the execution of Norfolk, the Commons discussed a revised bill for relief of the poor and punishment of vagabonds. Norton wished the minstrels excluded, the one trace of his partiality to art in his whole parliamentary career: over 'these wordes "minstrelles", whether they shoulde be conteined within the saide bill or not, great argument rose'. On the third reading, 'Much argument *pro et contra* was made aboute minstrels, and the bill commytted.'[128] In the end, 'players of interludes belonging to gentlemen' were excluded from the list, though a majority agreed that free minstrels should be counted as vagrants.

Another set of financial criminals exercised the wits of MPs. Despite its careful and lengthy wording, the Fraudulent Conveyances Act of 1571 against attempts to defraud creditors had proved insufficient and called for further measures, like allowing victims to appeal to the Star Chamber. The bill, when sent with approval of the Lords, raised an uproar in the Lower House as an encroachment on the common law courts. Fleetwood pleaded against the Star Chamber with

124 26 February 1593, *Proceedings*, III, p. 109.

125 *Proceedings*, III, p. 217. On this speech, probably a lawyer's, see *Proceedings*, III, p. 181.

126 2 *Henry VI*, I.ii.153; IV.ii.56–62. On measures for the poor, Elton, *The Parliament of England*, p. 267, redirects readers to E. M. Leonard, *The Early History of English Poor Relief* (Cambridge: Cambridge University Press, 1900), on which all later discussion rests.

127 April 1571, *Proceedings*, I, p. 219. Bill against vagabonds, April-May 1571, *Proceedings*, pp. 247-53.

128 20, 29, 30 May 1572, *Proceedings*, I, pp. 312, 367, 384.

etymological arguments: its name *stella* did not derive from a star, but a variety of reptile called *stellio*, and like a serpent it must be cut off. The bill, 'spoken to *pro et contra*', caused a division of the House and was not committed. While State affairs were debated, business continued in Commons. In the same session, December 1584, a bill to expel all Jesuits and seminary priests was followed by one granting 'Mr Walter Rawley' all land beyond sea and out of jurisdiction of any Christian king he should at his costs discover, reserving the fifth part of gold or silver ore for Her Majesty. Ralegh was also given authority to establish laws not repugnant to doctrine and to English laws in America.[129] Of a bill for general demurrers, that is, challenging the legal sufficiency of a claim, after a debate on lawyers' fees, Fleetwood, who had just complained that 'all our billes ar long billes, full of *tautologia* and *cakaphonia*, pend in barbarous English', declared it one of the best he ever heard in the House: 'The lawe is not made to gett us money, but to help men to their right'.[130]

Usury

> he was wont to call me usurer, let him look to his bond! he was wont to lend money for a Christian cur'sy, let him look to his bond!
>
> *The Merchant of Venice, III.i.*

Inextricably tied with financial issues in Parliament was the ethical problem of credit and its worse manifestation, usury. Everyone since Antiquity knows that usury is wrong, the argument *pro et contra* ran, but commercial conditions make it difficult to prohibit it altogether. Where usury was condemned by the medieval popes, its Elizabethan opponents identify it with popish idolatry. Yet the debate on usury outlines timid steps towards a secularization of the law. The matter was hotly discussed between theologians and politicians whose concerns were drawing steadily apart.

Abroad, usury had long divided intellectuals of all colours as well as the divines. Disputations on interest were held at Augsburg in 1514, in the Carmelite monastery patronized by the Fugger banking family, and the following year at Bologna, where the 'Italian solution' of a compromise between law and theology was devised.[131] Johann Eck in his *Tractatus de contractu quinque de centum* (1515) defended a rate of 5 per cent as harmless, if the loan was to further an honest business opportunity. The General Council of Trent admitted to a large practice

---

129 12 December, 14 December 1584, *Proceedings*, II, pp. 74–75. Confirmation of the queen's letters patent to Sir Walter Ralegh concerning Wingandaco, which he would rechristen Virginia at her behest, 29 March 1585, *Proceedings*, II, p. 104.

130 *Proceedings*, II, pp. 110, 114–16. On 29 May 1571 (*Proceedings*, I, p. 256), a bill against lawyers' excessive fees had already been passed.

131 Oberman, *Masters of the Reformation*, pp. 137–46.

of usury within its own walls, and forbade the clergy to gain any money in this manner. Most Lutherans, Eck's arch-enemy Luther first, and Melanchthon in his preface to the Goldberg Catechism of 1558, had denounced any taking of interest as theft and murder. But in a letter of 1545 on usury, Calvin criticized those who misinterpret the Scriptures to forbid the taking of interest. The walls and roof of a house are barren, yet it is legitimate to charge a fee for the use of them, he argued. Beza offers him a way out with his distinction of two Hebrew words, both translated as usury: *neshek* means 'to bite', 'eat away at its victims', and *tarbith* 'increase' or 'add', or 'gain'. The increase of wealth is by industry, which deserves a profit. When asked if it was permissible for ministers to make a profit from their money, he gave a qualified approval to their making 'a fair and honest return'.[132]

Henry VIII had fixed interest at a statutory maximum of 10 per cent, but under the stiff government of Edward VI a much harsher bill was passed forbidding any taking of interest, for 'usury is by the word of God utterly prohibited, as a vice most odious and detestable'. When the bill for reversing this statute came on the Parliament's agenda in 1571, the arguments drew on all the old and some recent authorities. There is nothing in law to punish it, yet no author, Christian or pagan, denies it is ill. Usury destroys all trades, by procuring greatest gain without hazard or venture. To Beza, it is the biting and oversharp dealing which is misliked, but Norton argues that all usury is biting. At that point, the reporter notes, arguments came to an end, the House rose and nothing was concluded.[133] Both Elizabethan and Jacobean Parliaments saved their conscience by pronouncing usury a crime while tolerating it in practice. 'Many have written witty invectives against usury', Bacon will conclude, quoting among other authorities More's *Utopia*, 'but few have spoken of usury usefully.' Lending at interest is based upon natural laws; it is vain to expect men will lend freely. To make sure 'that the tooth of usury be grinded, that it bite not too much' the rate must be kept below the price of land, and banks under vigilance.[134] Yet reasonable arguments recognizing loans with interest as a necessity could not stop militant preachers like Bishop Sandys who claimed that 'this biting Worme of Usury, that devouring wolfe hath consumed many [...]. This canker hath corrupted all England': it must be repressed by law, else the heavy hand of God will strike them all.[135]

Nicholas Sander's *Briefe treatise of usurie* quotes the Gospel, '*date mutuum, nihil inde sperantes*, giue to lone, hoaping for nothing out the lone it self, or in the respect thereof' and stresses that coins loaned out at interest 'be no where at al', for 'it is feyned, that the tenne crownes lye still in a certaine bancke, and there

132 This letter to Claude de Sachin was only published posthumously, by Beza. See Jean Calvin, *Calvin's Ecclesiastical Advice*, trans. by Mary Beaty and Benjamin W. Farley (Louisville, KY: John Knox Press, 1991), pp. 139–43.

133 *Proceedings*, I, pp. 231–36. See Jones, *God and the Moneylenders*.

134 Bacon, 'Of Usury', in *Essays*, ed. by Pitcher, pp. 183–86.

135 Quoted with the testimonies of 'six learned bishops' by John Blaxton in his treatise *The English Usurer, or Usury Condemned* (London: John Norton, 1634), sig. C2.

do begette litle ones'. The 'begetting' of little ones is precisely Shylock's impious boast when he claims to make his money breed as fast as ewes and rams. Antonio's answer, 'when did friendship take | A breed for barren metal of his friend?', echoes both Aristotle's designation of interest by *tokos* (offspring), and the bar against usury repeated at the Lateran council, *pecunia pecuniam non parit* (money must not beget money).[136] Searching the origin of the name Shylock, Gollancz thought it might be due to an erroneous association with 'Shallach', the biblical Hebrew for 'cormorant', which is a frequent synonym in Elizabethan English for 'usurer'.[137] In which case, Gordon McMullan suggests, the enigmatic insult hurled at Antonio, 'fawning publican', might be a misprint for 'pellican' and make him share with this bird, the model of Lear's 'pelican daughters', a reversible identity, both villain and victim. This would enhance the polarity between Shylock and Antonio, a kinship stressed by Portia when, posing as a doctor of law, she asks 'Which is the merchant here, and which the Jew?'.[138] If McMullan is right, it also highlights the fact that these two symmetrically opposed creditors make heavy demands on the feelings of Bassanio, both demands negotiated by Portia with dazzling legerdemain.

Since everyone in court accepts the legality of Shylock's bond, Portia 'is left appealing not from one jurisdiction to another, but rather to a higher realm above the reach of law', Quentin Skinner points out, and since Shylock rejects it, she abandons all concern for compassion, thereon conducting her case less on legal practices than on the precepts of Cicero's *De inventione*.[139] Shylock's cause is overturned by a contrary law designed to protect Christian citizens from harm. And yet above all it is the precept of Christ in Luke 6. 35, 'Lend, hoping for nothing again', that inspires the philosophy at Belmont. Lorna Hutson's brilliant discussion of *The Merchant* notes a significant departure from its source, *Il Pecorone*, with the introduction of the usurer's daughter, but does not discuss the second most significant move, the lottery of the caskets, drawn from *Gesta Romanorum*, wholly at odds with the businesslike spirit and values that rule Belmonte in the Italian novella.[140] Shakespeare follows Giovanni Fiorentino's story closely enough until its hero reaches Belmonte. There the tale is no longer one for children. Instead of a maid burdened with a dead father like Portia, Gianetto finds a widow who makes the law herself, and does not hesitate to bend it, when it comes to marriage. Her suitors must possess her to win her hand, but a sleeping potion disables them and

---

136 Sander, *A brief treatise of usurie* (Louvain: John Fowler, 1568), pp. 3 (from Luke 6. 35), 44–45. The anonymous *The Ruinate Fall of the Pope Usurie, Derived from the Pope Idolatrie*, similarly denounces the unnatural increase of money and the idolatrous religion that allows it. See Hawkes's exhaustive list of sources in *The Culture of Usury*.

137 Israel Gollancz, *A Book of Homage to Shakespeare* (Oxford: Oxford University Press, 1916), p. 172.

138 *The Merchant of Venice*, I.iii.128–29; I.iii.36; IV.i.169. Gordon McMullan, 'Cormorant Shylock', *Shakespeare Quarterly*, 71.3–4 (2022), 221–41.

139 Quentin Skinner, 'Why Shylock Loses his Case', in Hutson, ed., *The Oxford Handbook of English Law and Literature*, ch. 5, p. 99.

140 Hutson, *The Usurer's Daughter*, pp. 224–30.

allows her to seize all their goods as penalty for their failure. It appears that she is set on increasing her fortune rather than electing the most suitable partner, until she is cheated by her own servant who helps the hero win the prize on his third attempt.

In the *Gesta Romanorum* the law is set not by a dead nobleman but by a living emperor who wants to ascertain the virtue of the maid destined to marry his son. The mottos on the gold and silver vessels are fairly similar to those in the play: 'Who so chooseth me shall finde that he deserveth' and 'Who so chooseth me shall finde that his nature desireth' — in *The Merchant* men desire gold and at best deserve silver. The third one, on the leaden vessel, deserves pause: 'Who so chooseth me, shall finde that God hath disposed for him'; in the play the choice to 'risk and hazard' takes the place of God as supreme touchstone. It is by this golden standard that each behaviour is measured: Bassanio's bet on 'meagre lead, | Which rather threaten'st than dost promise aught', Launcelot Gobbo who gives up mean safety in Shylock's house for a poor gentleman's livery, Jessica who casts riches to the four winds, as if to buy her way into the Christian world by abjuring her father's thrift. It also explains Portia's strange insistence to make Bassanio give up his wedding ring, though she had made it clear what it meant — 'This house, these servants, and this same myself | Are yours, my lord's, I give them with this ring' — and apparently betray her. Bassanio's gift of this priceless ring to the young lawyer, at Antonio's request, could make him lose all again, but actually sets him free: it is the only time in the play when he does risk and hazard more than the wealth of his friends, thus repaying his debt to amity.

In mercantile Venice, money rules over love. The first to conflate human beings with coins, we saw, is Shylock. All the points where the play departs from the novella converge to stress a different order of values, especially in modes of accounting. Homonymy, paronomasia, antanaclasis, similes point to differences, never redundancies, when the same word is descanted with a succession of altered meanings. Words used for money and set rates overstep their usual boundaries, as in Portia's gift of herself and all her possessions, 'the full sum of me'. She explicitly confronts two modes of calculation when to 'stand high in your account' she wishes she 'might in virtues, beauties, livings, friends, | Exceed account'. Increase in her vocabulary is not monetary interest but the unlimited, freely given benefit of love.

A number of critics today are convinced that Portia breaks her father's rule to give Bassanio a hint, through the rhyming scheme of the song performed before his choice of a casket.[141] Not only would this require suitable gestures to make the audience aware of the hint, but it would thoroughly upset the balance of the play. 'Your father was ever virtuous, and holy men at their death have good inspirations', says Nerissa in defence of the 'Belmont lottery'. This virtuous father added a condition likely to deter the faint-hearted: he who chooses the wrong

141 See for instance Ost, *Shakespeare*.

casket must renounce marriage forever, whereas in the novella the loss incurred by the suitors was restricted to material goods. Whether we believe or not that Portia agrees to be guided by a dead man's wisdom, that Bassanio's thriftlessness makes him the ideal companion for a lady 'richly left', 'fair, and, fairer than that word, | Of wondrous virtues', the plot stresses that there can be no safe investment in love, no fixed rate of interest, all must be given without hope of return or benefit.

Mark Shell finds it odd that Antonio did not insure his ships, since marine insurance was a well-established practice in sixteenth-century Venice and London — though one that Ser Giovanni seems equally unaware of — and thinks it might be because to the merchant's nice conscience, this would be like taking or paying an interest, which he refuses on principle.[142] It is worth recalling here that early insurance contracts often took the form of sea loans *in mutuo gratis et amore*, that is, without interest.[143] Although there remain but faint traces of transcendence in *The Merchant*, and of the simple faith that guides the maid of *Gesta Romanorum*, by this light, there is little doubt that Antonio and Portia are on the right side of the Gospel, while Shylock's attempt to make money breed is doubly sacrilegious. The point here is not a celebration of ethically superior characters, but their superior bounty, or simply their ability to give, spend, and waste boundlessly, a theme to be explored at greater philosophical depth in *Timon of Athens*. Unlike the novella, the play confronts two opposite worlds, ruled by two different laws and systems of values, both inhabited by weak, fallible, sometimes cruel human beings who in the 'soft stillness of the night' believe they can hear 'the touches of sweet harmony'. To the naughty world where good deeds shine like lonely candles, the play offers a world elsewhere, rich and prodigal as their dreams, distant enough to inspire the nostalgia that permeates the opening scene: 'In sooth, I know not why I am so sad.'

Taxation

I have kept back their foes
While they have told their money, and let out
Their coin upon large interest; I myself,
Rich only in large hurts.

Timon of Athens, III.v

---

142 Mark Shell, *Money, Language, and Thought: Literary and Philosophic Economies from the Medieval to the Modern Era* (Berkeley: University of California Press, 1982), p. 54 n. 19. See Luke Wilson's comments in 'Drama and Marine Insurance', in Jordan and Cunningham, eds, *The Law in Shakespeare*, pp. 127–42.

143 Florence Edler de Roover, 'Early Examples of Marine Insurance', *Journal of Economic History*, 5.2 (1945), 180–85, notes it was common practice in the mid-fourteenth century, but the Genoese contracts reversed the earlier relation, since it was now the insurer who promised to repay a sum of money he had not actually received if a ship or cargo was lost.

In Elizabeth's first Parliament, Nicholas Bacon begins with a rhetorical question foregrounding Bassanio's: 'Doth not the wise merchant in every adventure of daunger give part to have the rest assured?'. The queen needs help to ensure their safety. Nothing is demanded, only what they of their own free will are content to offer. Their greatest gift is the general consent to grants, considering how in times past it was only done after vehement persuasions. *Bis dat qui cito dat* (he gives twice who gives quickly): the tone and the tag are set for future donations.[144] Of all thirteen sessions during Elizabeth's reign, all but one asked for money. The Crown's revenues increased less than inflation, making it impossible for her to 'live of her own' and forcing her to sell royal lands. At each opening, her Lord Keeper requests the Commons to give rapidly, without wasting time on idle questions, and closes the session with hearty thanks for their spontaneous generosity. Debates revolve around the number and extent of subsidies, each levy bringing in less money than the precedent, since many of her wealthier subjects are under-assessed or manage to escape altogether, a point the Commons are well aware of. In the last Parliament, when Ralegh suggests to spare the three-pound men, Secretary Herbert answers that if the meaner taxpayers were exempted, two thirds of the contribution would be lost. He voices crudely what has long been known and practised: make the poor pay, they are more numerous.

Traditionally, government was allowed to raise taxation for extraordinary circumstances only, foreign wars or security of the realm. With the papist threat over their heads, the Elizabethan Commons usually agree to make this special effort. The subsidy bill of 1563 begins with a warm recital of the queen's protection against foreign powers, which her Commons are glad to thank by their 'small gift'. Three years later, the Speaker reminds them that princely prerogatives do not allow the prince to take money 'or doe as he will at his own pleasure without ordere, but quietly to suffer their subiectes to enioy their owne without wrongfull suppressione'. Here he gives advisory praise: Her Majesty is not given to a tyranny contrary to her laws. Let her accept the subsidy with their good will, and joy at her inclination for marriage, the tacit incentive to their generosity.[145]

The requests offer good opportunities for State propaganda and self-eulogy. In 1571, the queen's need is motivated by the threat of Scottish invasions. But their money will not be misused for her pleasure or pomp, Nicholas Bacon promises. The 'gorgeous, sumptuous, superfluous buildinges of times past' have been turned into necessary ones, 'the chardgeable, glitteringe, glorious triumphes into delectable pastimes and shewes', all for the realm's good. Where many princes are able to dry up flowing fountains of any treasury, she is free from these quills, 'a phenixe, a blessed birde of this brood God hath blessed us with'.[146] Mildmay's speech for supply in 1576 reminds them that if war needs money, so does peace. As wise mariners in calm weather, they must provide against tempests. The coffers

144 *Proceedings*, I, pp. 38, 48.
145 *Proceedings*, I, p. 170. Probably a widely held view on prerogatives, Hartley comments, p. xxiv.
146 *Proceedings*, I, pp. 186–87.

are low, but Her Majesty will not use earlier evil methods, debasing of coinage, sale of land, borrowing upon interest. Five years later he raises the danger signal again. England, still a quiet haven, has become the chief sanctuary for afflicted members of the Church who flee the tyranny of Rome, while the pope with his malicious bulls sends swarming hither a number of popish priests and monkish Jesuits. Her Majesty stands fast, but her enemies have joined hands against her subjects, who must make provision of forces to answer violence. 'God has placed this kingdom in an island envirionned with the sea as with a naturall and strong wall'[147] — this royal throne of kings, this sceptred isle, and these four times dear souls.

Continental trade is another strong consideration for MPs. When Elizabeth is offered the crown of the Netherlands, a petition specifies that if she wishes to accept it at any time, they will yield a voluntary yearly contribution, for with the loss of that country, all commodities should be stopped, and instead of exporting their wool, 'we shold be suffocatyd in our owne ffatte'.[148] Ships and shipping occupied a high place in the parliamentary agenda: hardly any bills failed to pass. Their preambles expressed concerns for the merchant fleet, and the need to keep a sufficiency of trained seamen for security. Cecil made his longest surviving parliamentary speech to plead for a fish day in order to restore the navy and prevent the decay of port towns. There was little risk that fishermen would overgrow other states of men, he argued, for no great increase in fish eating was to be expected. Thus Wednesday became known as Cecil's fast.[149]

Occasionally a bolder member suggests that their demands should be satisfied in return. The connection between subsidy and succession was openly made in 1566 by the Spanish ambassador, De Silva, who reported rumours that if the queen would not marry or name a successor, Parliament would not vote her any supplies.[150] A month later, John Molyneux made the move 'for the Reviving of the Suit for Succession and to proceed with the Subsidy', a method later known as tacking.[151] Sir Ralph Sadler rejects the idea as unseemly: he wishes heartily to see the succession settled, but thinks it is not their business, and must not be mixed with the matter of the subsidy. They must proceed in the matter without condition.[152] If Elizabeth eventually abandoned the third instalment of the grant she originally asked for, it was perhaps, Alsop suggests, to restore harmony between monarch and subjects, the ideal of Tudor polity. The crucial issue was marriage, not money. Even if we accept his claim that the notion of no taxation

147 25 January 1581. *Proceedings*, I, pp. 502–06.
148 February 1587, *Proceedings*, II, p. 305.
149 January 1563, *Proceedings*, I, pp. 57, 103–06.
150 Letter of 14 September 1566, *Calendar of State Papers, Spain*, I, p. 580.
151 *Journal of the House of Commons*, 18 October 1566, I, p. 74.
152 *Proceedings*, I, p. 143.

without redress was foreign to sixteenth-century England, the notion was visibly in the air.[153] It would come out loudly voiced in the debate over monopolies.

Shakespeare's first Henriad begins with a sharp indictment of politicians at home who keep the army in France short of means: neither treachery nor evil stars are responsible for English reversals abroad, 'but want of men and money'. This sound diagnosis, confirmed by modern historians, is nowhere stated in Hall's chronicle, the main source of *Henry VI Part I*. Those Shakespearean critics who think the siege mentality had abated after the defeat of the Armada will find that it had not, at least not in Elizabeth's government or Commons. In 1593, the Spanish threat still calls for special fundraising: the King of Spain still plans to invade England; he is building new ships 'after the moulde and manner of the English navie', alluring Scotland to his side with money and pensions.[154] Her Majesty has spent much of her own money to ensure safety. The Lord Keeper recites the list of her predecessors who fought the pope's treacherous agents to recover their rights. The Chancellor of the Exchequer reminds them she has four kingdoms to maintain, England, France, Ireland, and Scotland, while Ralegh draws a fearful map of all Europe falling under control of the Spanish king. On 14 March, the preamble to the subsidy bill is read 'and some thinges in it dislyked, as this: the prostratinge our selves, our lyves, and landes at her Majestie's feete', to maintain the wars.[155] After some haggling as to who should pay, when, and how much, a triple subsidy is voted, to be paid over four years.

Along with these concerns, an anonymous plea is made for a foundation by act of Parliament in favour of maimed soldiers, who cry for relief in the streets and will soon curse those who have charity in their mouths but none in their hands: the risk, if they receive no better encouragement, is that men will hide when they are pressed. Cecil suggests taxation of all alehouses and inns. The usual distinctions resurface between 'three sortes of people: maymed soldiers; poore beggers old sick and impotent; and the stoute and vagabond roages'. A new bill puts the charge of maimed soldiers on the parishes where they were pressed: they must repair there with a certificate of their hurts and services delivered by the general mustermaster of England. An act is passed against overpopulation and overbuilding in London, 'a pesteringe of the City with poore, and a dispeopling of the contry, drawing so many to inhabit thereabout'. Successive orators speak for or against the extension of charity to aliens, who impoverish the country. To Finch's plea that 'they are strangers now. We must be strangers hereafter, therefore let us doe as we would be done to', Ralegh answers that Antwerp, where most of them come from, never allowed an English artisan to dwell there: they are all 'Dutchmen who pay no subsidy, that eat out our profit and supplant our nation'. Worse still, they are the people who maintain the King of Spain in his greatness.

153 Alsop, 'Reinterpreting the Elizabethan Commons', p. 225.
154 Puckering, 19 February 1593, *Proceedings*, III, pp. 16–17.
155 *Proceedings*, III, pp. 122–23.

He sees no charity, honour, nor profit in relieving these strangers.[156] Both the anonymous *Sir Thomas More*, which opens with a riot against Flemish craftsmen, and *The Merchant of Venice*, where Shylock falls under a law against aliens, were written in the mid-1590s. Few voices besides Finch's then rose in Parliament asking fellow members to

> Imagine that you see the wretched strangers,
> Their babies at their backs, and their poor luggage,
> Plodding to th'ports and coasts for transportation,
> And that you sit as kings in your desires,
> Authority quite silenc'd by your brawl.
>
> (*Sir Thomas More*, II.iii.74–78)

In October 1597, again, more money is needed if the queen is to continue her good work against the plots of 'the Devill, the Pope, the Spanish tirannie and the mischeevous designes of all her enimies'.[157] Fears about enclosures, depopulation, and other social ills are rehearsed in the draft of an impassioned speech, probably the work of a lawyer.[158] A question is raised touching monopolies, but Her Majesty's loving subjects are warned off her prerogative by the Lord Keeper.[159] The question will return with full blast in 1601. At her last Parliament, the Speaker rails against Spanish tyranny, the pope's ambition, the Irish rebels. Robert Cecil confirms with figures that Spanish armies everywhere threaten English safety and trade, making it vital to maintain troops in Ireland and the Low Countries. And now to serious matters. The queen needs £300,000 before Easter.[160]

Monopolies

> No, faith, lords and great men will not let me; if I had a monopoly out, they would have part on't.
>
> *King Lear*, I.iv

Elizabeth's grants of licences raised low-voiced but steady discontent in the Lower House.[161] The grumbling began, briefly, on 7 April 1571, when Robert Bell pointed out that the subsidy was hard to levy because the people were galled by two afflictions, licences and the abuse of promoters. According to Simonds

156 *Proceedings*, III, pp. 122, 155, 139–44. See McCluskey, *Representations of Flemish Immigrants*.
157 Lord Keeper's opening speech, 24 October 1597, *Proceedings*, III, p. 186.
158 *Proceedings*, III, p. 181.
159 *Proceedings*, III, pp. 232, 242.
160 Cecil, 7 November, Townshend's journal, *Proceedings*, III, p. 332. Other reports say £500,000.
161 See David Harris Sacks, 'The Countervailing of Benefits: Monopoly, Liberty, and Benevolence in Elizabethan England', in *Tudor Political Culture*, ed. by D. E. Hoak (Cambridge: Cambridge University Press, 1995), pp. 272–91.

D'Ewes, Her Majesty's request to avoid long speeches was specifically aimed at Bell's mention of licenses.[162] Privilege holders could appeal to the conciliar courts, Privy Council, or Star Chamber, against illegal competition. By a statute of Edward VI, designed to protect the declining prosperity of the Calais Staple, none but clothiers and staplers could buy wool from producers. All parliamentary efforts to break the monopoly, even after the loss of Calais, failed in seven sessions down to 1581: 'Clothiers, the middlemen, retained their hold on the raw material.'[163]

Thomas More was the first in his *Utopia* to employ the term 'monopoly': 'Suffer not thies ryche men to bye vp all, to ingrosse and forstalle, and with theyr monopolye to kepe the market alone as please them.'[164] 'Forestalling', buying outside the market, and 'engrossing', buying in large quantities to raise prices, were specifically forbidden by the Forestallers Act of Edward VI in 1552. Speculation, like usury, was generally considered illicit, but grants often served to reward royal service, failing other means. Licences could also be government measures to protect English trades, like Cecil's fish day to strengthen the merchant navy. The medieval system designed to advance industry changed significantly under the Tudors with the inclusion of monopoly clauses and patents on existing products.[165] Some of the earliest were given to printers, as on the continent: in 1518, an exclusive imperial privilege kept the Polyglot Bible waiting until Erasmus was ready to print his own New Testament.[166] In 1504 Henry VII appointed the first printer to the Crown, the Frenchman Guillaume Faques, later anglicized as William Fawkes, with the sole right to print government documents.[167] Some three hundred books were printed with privilege under his son's reign, approximately one-seventh of all the titles extant.[168] Apart from their advantages for the Crown in terms of censorship and public service, those privileges had a price. In 1534, Cambridge University received a royal charter for a perpetual right to print books approved, in exchange for taxes, tallages, and customs.[169] Under Elizabeth, an ordinance of the Star Chamber gave the Stationers' Company a monopoly over printing, and the right to enter any printer's shop to examine his operations.

Elizabeth made an even larger use of patents than her predecessors, to dispense favours or to increase her own revenues, granting monopolies over many

162 1 H. C. Jour. 83, 10 April 1571, in D'Ewes, *A Compleat Journal*, p. 159.

163 Elton, *The Parliament of England*, pp. 246–50.

164 Ralph Robynson's 1551 translation of More, *The Utopia*, ed. by Lupton, pp. 57–58, 'Refrenate coemptiones istas diuitum, ac uelut monopolii exercendi licentiam'.

165 L. R. Patterson, *Copyright in Historical Perspective* (Nashville: Vanderbilt University Press, 1968), p. 83.

166 Granted in 1516 for four years by Maximilian and Pope Leo X.

167 R. Deazley, 'Commentary on the Statute of Monopolies 1624', in *Primary Sources on Copyright (1450–1900)*, ed. by Bently and Kretschmer.

168 Clegg, *Press Censorship*, p. 9.

169 David McKitterick, *Printing and the Book Trade in Cambridge, 1534–1698* (Cambridge: Cambridge University Press, 1991).

home-made or imported goods. Parliament reflected a range of conflicting interests, expressed by innumerable privately promoted bills. One such bill that tried to prevent merchants from turning into landed gentlemen 'got the fate it deserved in a House full of merchants, lawyers and gentlemen anxious to keep the land market open'.[170] The evils denounced by More in 1516 were still untreated when the Commons of 1597 heard a motion by Francis Moore, of the Middle Temple, 'touching sundry enormities growing by Patents of Priviledge and Monopolies'.[171] Elizabeth answered their plea with a hope that her loving subjects would not take away her prerogative, which was 'the principall and head pearl in her crowne and dyadem', and a promise to examine all patents.[172] Some fifteen were repealed by her command, but the pressures of suitors continued.

Monopolies return to the forefront in the last Parliament of the reign, again raising voluble complaints in the House, with no Nortons or Fleetwoods present to stem the resentment, Graves notes.[173] Whatever they do by an act of Parliament, Francis Moore deplores, the queen will undo by her prerogative.[174] To a burgess for Warwick, the etymology of the word *monopoly* being *unus* and *civitas*, it means 'a restrainte of anythinge publicke in a cittye or common welth to a private use', so the user may be termed 'the whirlepoole of the prince's profittes'. A London lawyer complains that the main commodities 'are ingrossed into the handes of these bloodsuckers of the commonwealth'. Ralegh defends his own patent on tin with the plea that he has doubled the workmen's wages since he took control of the mines, and agrees to have it cancelled if all others are repealed. John Davies suggests they 'generouslye and bravelye like Parleament men' summon the monopolists, cancel their patents to their faces, and send them to the Tower till they have paid a good fine to the queen, 'at which all laughed'. They are called sharply to order by Secretary Robert Cecil, who declares that in all his career he has never seen the House in so great confusion: 'This is more ffitt ffor a grammar schoole then a courte of Parleamente'.[175]

The issue raised as much agitation outside, where 'a multitude of people' at the door asked for compassion of the House, 'they beeing spoyled, imprisoned and robbed by the monopolists', and demanded that a delegation be allowed in. Worse insubordination was going on inside, where the subsidy bill should have been read that day, 'but the Howse cryed it away and called for the report of the monopolies; and so the subsidy was defered'. At that point the queen entered lists. All abusers would be punished, all grievances redressed, the delay in remedying them had been caused by 'the late trobles (meaninge the earle of Essex' matters)'. Cecil then

170 Elton, *The Parliament of England*, p. 262.
171 D'Ewes, *A Compleat Journal*, 7 November 1597, pp. 551–66.
172 *Proceedings*, III, p. 242.
173 Graves, 'Managing Elizabethan Parliaments', in Dean and Jones, eds, *The Parliaments of Elizabethan England*, pp. 60–63.
174 9 February 1598, *Proceedings*, III, p. 242, and 20 November 1601, p. 376.
175 *Proceedings*, III, pp. 370–92.

announced she had magnanimously decided to grant the Commons their desire, and read the list of the monopolies to be revoked, not the whole, 'ffor the Queene meanes not to be swepte out of her prerogatyve'.[176] All were moved by this speech; one of the more rebellious orators wept. In variant versions, Elizabeth thanked the Lower House for having denounced 'the abusers of our liberalitie, the thrallers of our people, the wringers of the poore', and thus preserved her honour.[177] A clause warning subjects of the validity of the prerogative royal 'saved the principle from the wreck of the substance'.[178] As Thomas Macaulay puts it, the opposition had been silently gathering force for forty years and won its first victory.[179] Twelve monopolies were abolished, leaving intact a good many more.

Despite their moment of emotional communion, Townshend's journal of her last Parliament ends on a sad somber note: when the queen came out of the House 'very ffewe said "Glod bless your Majestie", etc. as in all assemblyes they were wonte; and when she came by the Speaker she onlye offerred him her hand to kysse, and went by'. As the crowd parted to make way for her she 'said not one word, but went presently thorough'.[180] Her fight ended ingloriously in 1602 with the famous *Darcy v. Allein* case, known as the 'Case of the monopolies', which established that the grant of such exclusive rights was improper. Coke, recently chosen attorney general over Bacon, appeared for the plaintiff.[181] The court determined that the queen's grant was invalid: Her Majesty had allowed it for the public good, but in this case she was deceived, for it served only private gain.[182] For the first time, sole control of a product was declared against public policy and therefore against common law. Coke in his speeches to Parliament admitted the usefulness of government interference in some cases, like protection against foreign trade, import or export of certain goods and of bullion, but he grew increasingly hostile to restraints on free trade, many of which he thought illegal. When James I revived monopolies, Coke alone among the judges stood against him and was dismissed from office. The historian David Hume would trace the origin of *laissez-faire* precepts to the controversy over monopolies, when the House of Commons attempted to 'give liberty to the trading part of the nation'. To him, 'The severe, though popular government of Elizabeth, had confined this

176 *Proceedings*, III, pp. 375–97.

177 There are several versions of this speech, see *Proceedings*, III, pp. 249–51. Neale, *Elizabeth I and her Parliaments*, II, pp. 392–93.

178 Neale, *Elizabeth I and her Parliaments*, II, p. 388.

179 Thomas Macaulay, *The History of England* (Leipzig, 1849), I, pp. 61–62.

180 *Proceedings*, III, p. 493.

181 'The Case of Monopolies', in Coke, *The Reports*, Pt XI, pp. 84b–88b. See Barbara Malament, 'The "Economic Liberalism" of Sir Edward Coke', *Yale Law Journal*, 76.7 (1967), 1321–58.

182 Sidney T. Miller, 'The Case of the Monopolies: Some of its Results and Suggestions', *Michigan Law Review*, 6.1 (1907), 1–24.

rising spirit within very narrow bounds'. With the advent of a prince less dreaded and beloved, 'symptoms immediately appeared of a more free and independent genius in the nation'.[183]

The Lawyer's Glasses of Governance

Like the social spectrum of the Inns societies, their members' religious views covered a large range, which no surveys or rules of conformity managed to suppress. Eminent Puritan divines were invited to preach at Temple, while a recusant like Plowden was able to continue as treasurer of his society and coexist with the fiery Norton, or the Erastian antiquary John Selden with the radical Puritan Nicholas Fuller, a 'graceless rogue' who would fight James's royal prerogative. Among known participants in pre-Civil War disturbances at the Inns, Prest notes three future regicides, a parliamentarian judge, and a recruiter MP, plus two royalist officers.[184]

Opulent Recusancy: Edmund Plowden's Reports

the case is alter'd.
When you disgrac'd me in my embassade,
Then I degraded you from being king.

3 Henry VI, IV.iii

The death of Queen Mary cancelled Plowden's fresh appointment as serjeant. Elizabeth would have made him chancellor, had he agreed to adopt the Anglican faith. He nobly refused, because his conscience would not allow it, though he had not scrupled to share the spoils of Reformation with his fellow lawyers, buying monastic property.[185] He pursued a successful practice with clients of both religions. Elizabeth consulted him on occasion as did her councillors, even the puritanically inclined Leicester. Having retained his post as chief steward of the South Parts of the Duchy of Lancaster, Plowden was one of the thirteen lawyers assembled at Serjeant's Inn by Elizabeth's command in 1561 to confer on law touching the duchy. The problem had long vexed the Tudor lawyers, who tried to conciliate the humanity of the king with the requirement of State and law that the Crown be impersonal and immortal. This case, the validity of a lease granted by Edward VI in his nonage, led Plowden to work on the few references in medieval

183 David Hume, *History of England: From Julius Caesar to the Revolution in 1688* (Philadelphia: M'Carty & Davis, 1836), II, p. 141.

184 Prest, *The Inns of Court*, p. 114.

185 On his conscience, see Jordan, 'Shakespeare's Law and Plowden's Authority', pp. 72–73.

law books suggesting a distinction between the natural and the political capacity of the king.[186]

It was probably Norfolk who sought his advice on the succession, when John Hales's tract against Mary Stuart's claim invoked common law on the inheritance of aliens.[187] Plowden rejected the argument, we saw, citing authorities both legal and historical. He did not want his treatise advertised, 'for you knowe right well that in dealing in tytles of kyngdomes there is mutche danger. and specially to the subjecte, and in these cases I thinke the surest waie is to be sylent'.[188] Yet he does not seem to have suffered retaliation when Norfolk disclosed its existence to the Privy Council. His doctrine of the two bodies was not so much to support Mary Stuart's claim, Hutson recently argued, but English claims of Scotland's historic vassalage, as part of 'an *insular nation*'. In kneeling before his Lord, the liegeman 'disableth himself of all strength', Plowden writes, thus transforming 'the symbolic rituals of feudal tenure into metaphors for the containment of Scotland within the sovereignty of English law and the English constitution'.[189] Twenty years after Plowden's death, his son prepared a copy of his *Treatise* for James I, when Parliament acknowledged in the first statute of the reign that the crown 'did, by inherent birthright and lawful and undoubted succession, descend and come to him as being lineally, justly and lawfully next and sole heir of the blood royal of this realm'.[190]

Among irregular offspring of Plowden's *Treatise*, one entitled *Leicester's Commonwealth* caused much stir at the time, attested by the official efforts to suppress it. Plowden's client Englefield, a leading spokesman for the English Catholics at the Spanish Court, wrote in a letter dated 27 February 1585 (Old Style) that 'the two books of justice and Leicester's life have raised the building'.[191] Three years later, a report informed Walsingham that a French translation entitled *Discours de la vie abominable [...] de my Lorde de Lecestre* had appeared in Paris. Sidney visibly did not know the identity of the author when he undertook to write a 'Defence of the Earl of Leicester'. Rumours imputed it to the Jesuit Parsons. Dwight Peck thinks it was probably written by Charles Arundell, in the cloud of intrigues surrounding the Anjou marriage project: it may have been the collective work of

186 Parmiter, *Edmund Plowden*, pp. 76–78.

187 See Marie Axton's discussion in 'The Influence of Edmund Plowden's Succession Treatise', p. 217.

188 Plowden's first prologue to his treatise, BL, Harley MS 849, fol. i, in Axton, 'The Influence of Edmund Plowden's Succession Treatise', p. 215.

189 Hutson, 'On the Knees of the Body Politic', pp. 28, 31, 42, quoting Plowden's *Treatise* on p. 114. She does not pursue the inquiry up to James's projected union of the crowns, but promises p. 51 n. 6 to develop it in her *Insular Imagining: The Elizabethan Erasure of Scotland* to be published by Cambridge University Press in September 2023.

190 Presentation copy for James VI, Bodleian MS Don.c.43. The British Library's longer version is Harley MS 849. Parmiter, *Edmund Plowden*, pp. 92–95.

191 Or in the New Style, 9 March 1586, the date often attached to this document. *Calendar of the State Papers Relating to Scotland*, vol. VII, *A.D. 1584–1585*, doc. 552, pp. 572–73. The 'two books of justice' presumably refer to Cecil's *Execution of Justice* and Allen's *Answer to the Libel of English Justice.*

pro-Anjou courtiers attached to the conservative Howard clan, who held Leicester for an opportunist upstart and resented his influence at court.[192]

Leicester's Commonwealth shows an innovative use of the dialogue form. To Peck who admires 'its artful blending of truth and fiction', the participants, a gentleman, a lawyer, and a young scholar, 'take on something of the personalities expected of characters from the stage'. In Richard Wilson's opinion, Plowden himself must have served as model for the 'ancient man that professed the law'. He speaks Plowden's arguments and shares his fear of being overheard.[193] The dialogue, which revolves on the issue of succession, supports the Stuart line, with legal and dynastic arguments based on Plowden's. The lawyer 'inclined to be a Papist, yet was it with such moderation and reservation of his duty towards his prince and country, and proceedings of the same, as he seemed always to give full satisfaction in this point to us that were of contrary opinion'.[194]

The piece makes a rare case for religious toleration. At the opening of the dialogue, the lawyer is reading Cecil's *Execution of Justice*. On being asked what might prevent Catholics from turning traitors if occasion arose, he answers that fear of servitude under foreign nations may restrain them. One of the best arguments in favour of Mary Stuart's succession was her willingness to allow her Scottish subjects liberty of conscience. Similar views were being developed by moderate Catholics on the continent, the French *politiques*, like Jean Bodin, who were associated with the Duke of Anjou and whom Arundell had frequented while in Paris. If some small degree of toleration were admitted, 'men would easily be brought, that have English bowels', to join in preserving their country from bloodshed and foreign oppression. The gentleman agrees and cites countries 'where a little bearing of th'one with th'other hath wrought them much ease'. Alas, England's powerful conspirators will not permit what would tend to the stability of their government.[195]

In discussing the uncertainty of the succession, they return to the vicissitudes of the past: since the Conquest, three lawful kings have come to harm by alienation of their subjects, the chief cause of their fall being too much favour towards wicked persons. In the case of Henry VI, a simple and holy man, the cause was Queen Margaret's favour to Suffolk, whose counsel made away with good Gloucester and created havoc just as Leicester does. The contention of the red rose and the white caused sixteen or seventeen fields to be fought in less than a century, from Richard II's reign 'when this controversy first began to bud up' till the thirteenth year of Henry VII. At that time, by cutting off the chief claimant of the House of Huntingdon, young Edward of Warwick, son of Clarence — whose

192 *Leicester's Commonwealth*, ed. by Peck.

193 An eighteenth-century bibliophile 'takes Serjeant Plowden to have been the author of it, viz. Leycester's Common Wealth', Thomas Hearne, *Reliquiae Hernianae: The Remains of Thomas Hearne*, ed. by Philip Bliss (London: J. R. Smith, 1869), vol. III, appendix III, p. 209.

194 *Leicester's Commonwealth*, p. 65.

195 *Leicester's Commonwealth*, pp. 183–85.

heir happens to be Leicester's candidate — 'the contention most happily was quenched and ended'. The lawyer then details at length the various branches of the family tree in a style worthy of Shakespeare's York, and similar confusions of Mortimers, to conclude that all have titles superior to Huntingdon's.[196]

Later editions of the pamphlet include anonymous copies of *Leicester's Ghost*, 'a metrical history of his life, written much after the manner of *The Mirror for Magistrates*',[197] warning King James to beware of favourites. The author, Thomas Rogers, was a young member of the Middle Temple whose thriftless ways left him prey to usurers and made him the model of Ben Jonson's gull Dapper in *The Alchemist*, again evidence of the flimsy boundaries between legal and theatrical concerns.[198] Leicester's ghost recalls the tragic decline of his family till 'sacred Cynthia' restored it and confesses his faults: he may have compacted a few deaths, though never without a good reason. His first wife he did mourn, but then 'What man so fond that would not lose a pearl | To find a diamond, leave brass for gold?'. In his hour of favour all bowed to him, all lawyers 'Did yield to me in matters of import, | Although sometime I did the law extort'.[199] Now the State is taken over by villains far worse than himself. 'Can equity dwell here, where conscience wants?' No, 'Divine Astraea up to heaven is fled, | And turned to Libra', a line from Ovid quoted in *Titus Andronicus*.[200] Rogers is also credited with twenty-one untitled stanzas on the conviction of Ralegh which echo a line from *Richard II*, 'Off goes his bonnet to an oyster-wench':

> Renowned Essex, as he past the streets,
> Would vaile his Bonnett to an Oyster wife,
> And with a kinde of humble Congie greete
> The vulger sorte that did admire his life.[201]

In paying homage to the recently executed Essex for his courtesy to the vulgar sort, the poem stigmatizes Ralegh's pride and recalls the performance of Shakespeare's play on the eve of Essex's failed rebellion.

The source of the notorious legal proverb, 'The case is altered, quoth Plowden', is reportedly his defence of a gentleman caught hearing Mass, in which having established that the service had been performed by a layman, Plowden declared, 'The case is altered: no priest, no mass', and won his client's acquittal. It was

196 *Leicester's Commonwealth*, pp. 144, 150, 153.

197 Hearne, *Reliquiae Hernianae*, ed. by Bliss, Appendix III, p. 206.

198 Franklin B. Williams Jr, 'Thomas Rogers as Ben Jonson's Dapper', *Year Book of English Studies*, 2 (1972), 73–77. Rogers was John Donne's uncle.

199 Rogers, *Leicester's Ghost* [1604], ed. by Franklin B. Williams Jr (Chicago: Chicago University Press, 1972).

200 'Terras Astrea reliquit', Ovid, *Metamorphoses*, I, 150. *Titus Andronicus*, IV.iii.4.

201 'Watt I wot well thy over weaning witt', 'Early Stuart Libels: An Edition of Poetry from Manuscript Sources', in *Early Modern Literary Studies Text Series I*, B4, ll. 55–58, p. 124, ed. on line by Alastair Bellany and Andrew McRae (2005), <https://www.earlystuartlibels.net/htdocs/early_jacobean_section/B4.html>.

obviously a common phrase, not necessarily restricted to the legal field. Burghley for one, recalls past tussles with the King of Spain, who took towns from them, 'But now the case is altered': he wants whole countries.[202] The phrase made its way to the stage, in Lodge and Greene's *A Looking Glass for London*, Dekker's *The Batchelars' Banquet*, and as the title of Ben Jonson's comedy, *The Case Is Altered*.

Plowden's *Commentaries or Reports*, published in 1571 by Richard Tottel, deal with specific points of law, some of which also drifted to the stage, like the *Hales v. Petit* case, whose metaphysical arguments on suicide are gleefully parodied in the grave-diggers' scene of *Hamlet*.[203] As Raffield notes, the reference to Plowden in the concluding lines of *Woodstock*, when the corrupt Chief Justice's servant announces he has searched the *Reports* in vain for precedents, shows their importance to the Elizabethan writers of political drama.[204] The relevance of Plowden's theory to *Richard II* has been amply discussed by Kantorowicz, although he did not know the succession treatise of 1566 where it is exposed at length, and quotes only the later *Reports*.[205] In the play, the king's claim to divine status in no way allows him to appropriate his subjects' goods, change the laws on inheritance, or farm the Crown lands. Between the interrupted trial by combat at the opening of the play, and Bolingbroke's expeditive trial of Richard's friends even before the king's deposition, divine majesty has expired. The extent of the revolution is stressed by two parallel scenes in Acts I and V, Gaunt's pleading for his son's release, York's pleading to have his son arrested: 'Forget to pity him, lest thy pity prove | A serpent that will sting thee to the heart.' Two sets of emblematic fathers and sons summed up the horror of the Civil War in *Henry VI*. In more realistic mode, the disruption of the York family — the mother urging the son to strike his father and run, the father offering his son's head to save his own — stands again for the whole damaged realm. The next play, *Henry IV Part I*, opens with complaints that the new king has illegally appropriated his allies' prisoners, boding ill for the future of justice in the realm.

Another point indirectly linking lawyer and playwright was the building of a new hall at Middle Temple, for which Plowden organized fundraising and the recruitment of able craftsmen. It harboured the Christmas revels of 1597, in which John Donne's anti-monopolist friend Richard Martin performed the part of Prince d'Amour, and more memorably still, Shakespeare's *Twelfth Night* at Candlemas, 1602. The performance would be reported in the diary of a law student, John Manningham, who compares the play to Plautus's *Menaechmi*, and

202 The Lord Treasurer's speech, February 1593, *Proceedings*, III, p. 24.

203 On Plowden's interpretation of the Hales case, see Sale, 'The "Amending Hand"', pp. 194, 197.

204 *Thomas of Woodstock*, ed. by Corbin and Sedge, V.vi.35–36. The last page of the manuscript, which would have revealed the nature of the case investigated, is missing. Raffield, *Shakespeare's Imaginary Constitution*, p. 89.

205 Raffield, *Shakespeare's Imaginary Constitution*, ch. 3, notes that Kantorowicz makes a selective use of quotations from Fortescue and Plowden. To Hutson, 'Not the King's Two Bodies', p. 167, Kantorowicz's reading of Plowden deserves to be remembered for his Aristotelian theory of equitable interpretation rather than for his famous metaphor.

to *The Comedy of Errors*, first performed at Gray's Inn in 1594, but finds it closest to the Italian *Inganni* (Deceits), thus confirming the dramatic connoisseurship of Inns members.[206]

As well as the legal knowledge and 'acquisitive intelligence' of Shakespeare, Andrew Zurcher argues, in the *Comedy* we see him 'inviting us to ponder, and adjudicate upon, the importance of the connection between causes, errors and ends — between literature, interpretation and law'. At the time, the tensions between the two royal courts of Westminster were such that Elizabeth established the Exchequer Chamber as a court of error to resolve their disputes in law. The political system that tried to regulate the Elizabethan social organization was the common law of contract, and this part of the law was changing rapidly at precisely the time that the *Comedy of Errors* was first performed: 'by 1596, Exchequer Chamber had begun reversing King's Bench judgments' on the recovery of debts and other financial damages. We saw above ('Clashes of Jurisdictions' in Chapter 1) that the play was part of revels dedicated to the Prince of Purpoole, which were troubled by a quarrel between Gray's Inn and the Inner Temple. The two pairs of twins mirror a quandary then facing common law judges: 'whether a contract and a contemporaneous promise to perform it could give rise simultaneously to two distinct forms of action to achieve the same end'.[207] Zurcher finds a striking analogy between the pattern of error and reform which structures the 1594 revels and the structures of error-return and consideration-completion of contracts in *The Comedy of Errors*. While the judges of the King's Bench and the Common Pleas sought, in the 1590s, to come to some agreement over the proper relationship between promises, evidence of promises, and contracts, the action of the play serves 'to undermine the epistemological stability of the causa in each case'.[208]

Guides to Navigation: Nicholas Bacon's Silver Prose

> Avoid sophisticall, captious and frivolous argumentes and quiddities, meeter for ostentation of witt then consultacion in weightie matters, comelyer for schollers then for counsellors, more beseeminge for schooles then for parliament howses.
>
> *Lord Keeper Bacon's opening speech to Parliament, 25 January 1559*

---

206 Manningham, *Diary*, ed. by Bruce, p. 18. There were three contemporary Italian plays featuring twins, the most popular being *Gl'Ingannati*, performed in Latin at Cambridge in 1595.

207 Baker, *The Legal Profession and the Common Law*, p. 397.

208 Andrew Zurcher, 'Consideration, Contract and the End of *The Comedy of Errors*', *Law and Humanities*, 1.2 (2007), 145–65. He notes (n. 3) that Thomas More's *Utopia* had anticipated the incompatibility of legal regulation with 'the unstable ironies, contradictions and irrationalities of literary imagination'.

Manningham closes his account of *Twelfth Night* with the trick played on Malvolio. The next entry in his diary is this *sententia* which smacks of Inns wisdom, '*Quae mala cum multis patimur laeviora putantur,* The griefe that we with many beare | we better may sustaine.'[209] The line is a slightly incorrect quote from *Zodiacus vitae*, a long moral treatise in Latin verse taught in Elizabethan schools, where Pier Angelo Manzolli (Palingenius) was accounted one of the 'Christian poets', with Prudentius and Erasmus. It was translated in 1565 by Barnabe Googe, dedicated to William Cecil, and it inspired Shakespeare's Seven Ages of Man. The hexameter is echoed in Edgar's meditation: 'Who alone suffers, suffers most i'th'mind.'[210]

The law student thus confirms that the Inns alumni were also connoisseurs in discourse, sharing not just legal material with drama, but its very language, its aphoristic and stylistic sources. Puttenham praised the rhetoric-filled public speeches of Sir Nicholas Bacon, 'from whose lips I have seen to proceed more grave and natural eloquence than from all the orators of Oxford and Cambridge.'[211] Nashe held 'Nicholas Bacon, Lord Keeper, and merry Sir Thomas More, for the chief pillars of our English speech', along with immortal Sir Philip Sidney.[212] He was but repeating the opinion of Du Bartas in *La Seconde Semaine* (1584), who gave praise to the four pillars of the English language: More, Bacon, Milord Sidney, and Queen Elizabeth. Collinson situates Bacon's rhetorical *via media* somewhere between Cicero and Seneca: 'Bacon cultivated the "pointed", silver, Senecan amble with its terse and strikingly antithetical figures of speech.'[213] Cicero was his wife's favourite. In a poem to her, he recalls how she made time short

> In reading pleasant things to me,
> Whereof profit we both did see,
> As witness can if they could speak
> Both your Tully and my Seneck.[214]

After studies at Cambridge and Gray's Inn, Nicholas Bacon and his friend Cecil had married two of the famed Cooke sisters, learned ladies both but not exactly models of tolerance. Anne Bacon had strong Puritan views and thought poorly of her husband's milder ones. While she urged ecclesiastical leaders to purge the Church from popery, he defended the religious settlement in Parliament against opponents and detractors, 'and in so doing scratched in the sand, as it were, the

---

209 Manningham, *Diary*, 11 February 1601, p. 18, quoting Barnabe Googe's translation. The correct line is 'Quae mala cum multis patimur leviora videntur.'

210 Manzolli, *The zodiake of life*, trans. by Googe, Liber v: Leo, l. 652. *King Lear*, III.vi.65a (Q1).

211 Puttenham, *The Arte of English Poesie*, ed. by Vickers, p. 223.

212 Nashe, *Pierce Pennilesse His Supplication to the Devil* (1592), in *Works*, ed. by Steane, p. 91.

213 Collinson, 'Sir Nicholas Bacon', pp. 257–59.

214 Nicholas Bacon, *The Recreations of his Age* (Oxford: Daniel, 1919).

line of the Anglican *via media*.'[215] Anne's fame was such that Beza dedicated his *Christian Meditation upon Eight Psalms* to her. The Spanish ambassador, Feria, painted her to his master as 'a tiresome prude'. On the home front, she was an obedient but critical wife, who grew increasingly cantankerous and miserly after her husband's death. She outlived him many years to make her sons' life a misery, if we believe Daphne du Maurier, though Francis recalls her as 'a very saint of God'.[216]

The style favoured by the Lord Keeper, 'the rhetoric which Sir Nicholas had learned at the Inns of Court',[217] was painted in *sententiae* on the walls of his home at Gorhambury.[218] He was following the precedent of Montaigne, to whose *Essais* Francis would reluctantly admit a debt. Montaigne had his library walls covered with inscriptions explaining why he chose to retire from the world, whereas Bacon draws from his the moral guidance he needs to steer the wheel of government.[219] To Elizabeth McCutcheon, his theatre of *sententiae* is 'a psychological survival kit', enabling a man in high office to survive the treacheries of a slippery world.[220] In this he could have no better guide than Seneca's warnings against the fate of Icarus: 'Those who avoid the middle path | will never run on a stable course.' Unlike the Lord Keeper's biographer Tittler, Collinson sees no deep impression made on him by Protestant doctrine, let alone Calvinism, and defines his piety as 'mere Christian', though he admits that the median position was moving left. Ideological simplicities belonged with the past. As international threats grew, Bacon must have died 'aware that the *via media* was unlikely to rest where he had drawn it'.[221]

Nicholas Bacon opened and closed all Elizabeth's Parliaments until his death. The writings on the wall often resurfaced in the Lord Keeper's speeches. His rules of action were incomparably simpler and more confident than Montaigne's, especially this cardinal precept he delivered in Commons: 'Gode's cause being sincerely weyed, considered and followed bringeth good successe in all affayres'.[222] His remedy for most evils is due execution of the law. Without execution laws are like torches unlit, rods without hands, unpruned garden, ship without rudder. Unscrupulous judges and neglectful ministers are the worst enemies of justice: 'such careles and slouthful men doe dayly courten and cloke these their faultes with the title of quietnes', living on other men's labours 'as drones doe among

215 Collinson, 'Sir Nicholas Bacon', p. 255.

216 Daphne du Maurier, *Golden Lads: A Study of Anthony Bacon, Francis and their Friends* (London: Gollancz, 1975), pp. 97–101, 124–35.

217 Collinson, 'Sir Nicholas Bacon', p. 269.

218 See Goy-Blanquet, 'Lord Keeper Bacon'.

219 See William N. West, 'Reading Rooms: Architecture and Agency in the Houses of Michel de Montaigne and Nicholas Bacon', *Comparative Literature*, 56.2 (2004), 111–29.

220 Bacon, *Great House Sententiae*, ed. by McCutcheon, p. 32.

221 Tittler, *Nicholas Bacon*, pp. 158–71. Collinson, 'Sir Nicholas Bacon', pp. 267–73.

222 *Proceedings*, I, p. 70.

bees'.[223] He deplores 'what an inconveniente thinge is it to haue a noble man bringe a matter into the Chauncerye, and the Courte shall haue power to doe iustice for him but not agaynste him. This is not *Jus equabile*'.[224] *Sententia* XXXIV captures the gist of it with 'Omne ius aequabile. Aliter ius non est.'

Bacon and his fellow Speakers all call for more solidarity, more virtue, and more money grants. It is a huge understatement to say that his intellectual circle were not interested in art for art's sake. There is not much music in Nicholas Bacon, and little lyricism, but a strong stress on rhetorical patterns, didactic repetition, and ponderous, painstaking chiasmic symmetry which owe more to the scales of justice than to the heavenly spheres. Part of the Lord Keeper's speeches is conventional routine:[225] make or amend laws where needed, vote subsidies to ensure the safety of the realm and its religion. The plea for subsidies, *bis dat qui cito dat*, returns with unsurprising regularity, and again in his son Francis's speech of 1617 upon taking his seat as Keeper of the Great Seal.[226] Nor does Nicholas hesitate to make a telling image speak several times. Ockham's principle of economy is another of his favourite quotes: *Frustra fit per plura quod potest fieri per pauciora* (it is futile to do with more what can be done with less). He must have kept notes, for the picture of the unscrupulous judge in 1559 is repeated almost verbatim at the closing of 1571. The same (inexact) quotation from Cicero illustrates his views on freedom eighteen years apart: *Acriores sunt morsus intermissae libertatis quam retentae* (the arrows of liberty are sharper when it is intermittent rather than permanently enjoyed).[227] A law tag, *Ultra posse non est esse, et vice versa* (what is beyond possibility cannot exist, and the reverse), serves in several speeches, and in the poem to his wife. As for the comparison of Queen Elizabeth with the phoenix, it must have been a tired bird, for at one point the reporter simply writes *rara avis in terris etc.*[228]

After 1571, as international tensions worsen, the Lord Keeper's tone grows increasingly martial: *gladius gladium juvaret* (the sword [temporal] should help the sword [spiritual]).[229] This keen formula, as old as Edward the Confessor, seems to be a family favourite, which father and son descant, *juvabit, juvaret, juvat*.[230] Nicholas had deplored the final loss of Calais in high rhetorical mode, foreboding stage laments over Anjou and Maine. Now he warns the Lords there are too many Frenchmen in England: they must consider 'how to be ridd of that noysome multitude, howe to have fewe French men or none at all. The way is

223 8 May 1559, *Proceedings*, I, p. 50.
224 Undated speech, in Bacon, *Great House Sententiae*, p. 89 n. 52. *Sententia* XXXIV, De ivre, p. 88.
225 *Proceedings*, I, pp. 50, 70, 86, 190, 127, 130–31, 135–36, 168–69, 174, 195, 525.
226 *Proceedings*, I, pp. 48, 189, 466.
227 *Proceedings*, I, pp. 83, 182. The exact quote is 'acriores autem morsus intermissae libertatis, quam retentae'.
228 *Proceedings*, I, pp. 187, 197. The phrase is used by Juvenal, *Satires* VI, 165.
229 Opening speech, 2 April 1571, *Proceedings*, I, p. 182.
230 Nicholas uses it in 1563, 1571, and again in 1572. 'Jurisdiction of the Council of the Marches', in Bacon, *The Works*, ed. by Spedding and others, VII, p. 589.

offred by this bill'.[231] Bacon prided himself on his plain speaking and could be offensively blunt, as his brother-in-law Cecil complained: 'though I lack the wit, the great wealth, the credit that you easilier get then I can, I will never, howsoever you use to nip me with speeches, that you love *plain dealing*, which words I often mark, lack any portion of truth, plainness or honesty that you have'.[232]

Seneca's *sententiae* increase tension by creating the most concise form of argument possible, Altman observes.[233] The Lord Keeper and his queen were always telling the Commons to avoid long speeches, the quicker to return home. The alleged Renaissance love for *multum in parvo* did not rule in England, not in Parliament at least, making the reporters repeatedly deplore 'muche talk and to no purpose'.[234] *Sententia* XXXV seems to echo Elizabeth's and her Chancellor's frustrations: 'Let the law be brief; let it order, not discuss'. She hated meddlers; his duty was to keep them to the point: 'Trifling digressions from matters proponed, idle and long discourses her Majestie misliketh and condemneth'.[235] Sir Nicholas was well aware that brevity is the soul of wit; his *sententiae* prove it in condensing Cicero and making concise Seneca even briefer. Yet in Parliament he often sounds like Polonius, with traces of his other education, the school of law. A sentence in his first closing speech, 'remembering also your great studyes, endeavors and diligences for the opening and declaring what might be said *pro et contra* in all cases of doubt [...] when all was sayde and hearde on both partes' is half a page long.[236] Sometimes a wordy paragraph ends with a 'But now to the matter'. The queen once rose in the middle of Bacon's peroration.[237] Her own speeches cultivate ambiguity, not to say equivocation, while he takes pains to make himself clear.

What the *sententiae*, *The Mirror for Magistrates*, and *Gorboduc* have in common apart from Seneca is their aim to provide 'glasses of governance'. Bacon with his long-winded oratory, his prickly sermons, and the trim epigrams that occasionally break the stately flow of his discourse does deserve Ben Jonson's praise as a pioneer of Elizabethan eloquence or McCutcheon's as the missing link in the history of English prose. Indeed the Lord Keeper's *sententiae*, his public speeches, and the exchanges in Parliament as a whole provide an even more significant link in the history of drama. Nicholas Bacon's style, his strong moral and political commitment, the Bacon couple themselves, and their conciliation of opposites in a model Protestant marriage will find ultimate expression on the Elizabethan stage.

---

231 BL, MS Add. 33271, fol. 15^{v}, quoted in Collinson, 'Sir Nicholas Bacon', p. 262.
232 July 1563, in Read, *Mr Secretary Cecil*, pp. 281–83.
233 Altman, *The Tudor Play of Mind*, p. 244.
234 April 1571, *Proceedings*, I, pp. 202, 367.
235 1572, *Proceedings*, I, pp. 341–42.
236 8 May 1559, *Proceedings*, I, p. 47.
237 She interrupts him on several occasions, *Proceedings*, I, pp. 418, 466, 467.

Philosophical Toys: Francis Bacon's Trials

> The word is late, but the thing is ancient; for Seneca's epistles to Lucilius, if you mark them well, are but essays, that is, dispersed meditations.
>
> *Essays, Dedication to Prince Henry*

The panelled room where Francis grew up is, to his editor John Pitcher, a Tudor allegory of the mind's perplexity: the wall sentences must have been his earliest read.[238] Despite his ambition to attain high places, Sir Nicholas's son owes his lasting reputation more to his philosophical writings than to his own progress in either political or legal arena. According to a critic's assessment, 'he made magisterial contributions to almost every significant aspect of seventeenth-century culture, from science to law, from rhetoric to myth'.[239] His education, begun by the Gorhambury walls and his learned parents, far exceeded common law. At Trinity College, Cambridge, he was under the tutelage of the then master John Whitgift. One of his tutors at Paulet's house was the son of the famous jurist François Hotman, Jean, who had studied law at Valence. However Francis did not think 'the ordinary practice of the law, not serving the Queen in place, will be admitted for a good account of the poor talent which God hath given me',[240] and strove to show that his abilities exceeded a mere lawyer's. His career under Elizabeth was quite short, and quite undistinguished. Under King James, it ended in disgrace and dismissal.

Several of Bacon's early literary pieces dramatize the choice between a contemplative and an active life, which meet in the idea that knowledge is power.[241] In a letter to his uncle Burghley he describes himself as having vast contemplative ends, and moderate civil ones, for he has taken all knowledge to be his province.[242] The essay 'Of Masques and Triumphs' comes piquantly enough between 'Of Ambition', which spells out the kind of aspiration that can be useful in the service of the State, and 'Of nature in Men' which advises Stoicism but intermittently, for no victory over nature can long be won. Masques are toys, he warns, but 'since princes will have such things, it is better they should be graced with elegancy than daubed with cost'. Thus he proceeds to give technical advice on the props, lighting, and colours most likely to please. Antimasques can feature

238 Bacon, *Essays*, ed. by Pitcher, p. 29.

239 Theodore K. Rabb, 'Have You No Sense of Decency, Sir Francis?', *New York Times*, 15 August 1999. On the range of his work, see Perez Zagorin, *Francis Bacon* (Princeton, NJ: Princeton University Press, 1998). Jardine and Stewart, *Hostage to Fortune*.

240 Bacon, Letter of 21 March 1594/95 to Lord Burghley, in Parker Woodward, *Sir Francis Bacon: Poet, Philosopher, Satesman, Lawyer, Wit* (London: Grafton & Co., 1920), p. 64.

241 Bacon, 'Confession of Faith', *Religious Writings*, in *The Letters and the Life*, ed. by Spedding and others, VII, pp. 217–62. See Geoffrey Bullough, 'Bacon and the Defence of Learning', in Vickers, ed., *Essential Articles for the Study of Francis Bacon*, pp. 109–11.

242 Bacon, in a letter of 1592, *The Letters and the Life*, I, ch. 5, p. 109.

a large variety of strange creatures, including 'statuas moving, and the like', as one statue will in *The Winter's Tale*. The glories of triumphs are the chariots carrying the challengers, when they are drawn by strange beasts, lions, bears, camels. 'But enough of these toys'.[243]

However dismissive of such trifles, Bacon regularly shared in the Inns' entertainments. At Essex's request, he wrote speeches for a device offered on the anniversary of the queen's accession, 17 November 1595: in this transparent piece of adulation by proxy, a worthy knight named Erophilus is pressed to forsake love and dedicate himself to meditation, war, or matters of State, but finds the course of his life best in serving his mistress.[244] Even if messages as strongly put as *Gorboduc*'s were no longer in fashion, masques still had some relevance to the political context. Bacon, who is thought to have argued for the execution of Mary in the Parliament of 1586, devised the dumb shows of the Senecan *Misfortunes of Arthur*, performed one year later. While Reader at Gray's, he was asked to organize a production of all four Inns, which failed, he writes apologetically to Burghley: yet his Lordship is not to worry, Gray's Inn is well furnished of gallant gentlemen who will not let this occasion 'pass without some demonstration of affection from the Inns of Court'.[245] Affection may not have been the only note struck. The *Gesta Grayorum* included *The Masque of Proteus*, composed by the poets Thomas Campion, who had lent a hand to *The Misfortunes*, and Francis Davison, the son of Elizabeth's ill-fated secretary. As for Bacon's agenda, suggestions of his great designs to restore the dominion of knowledge first appear in the *Gesta* whose counsellors' speeches are ascribed to him.[246] One of those, Spedding notes, forms a first draft of 'Solomon's House' in *The New Atlantis*, laying the ground of modern empiricism.[247]

Bacon first entered Parliament at the age of twenty-three in a by-election of 1581 but made little mark on his first two Parliaments, where his half-brothers also sat.[248] He became more audible in 1593, when the diarists record his vision of Parliament — 'in this court representatively all men are present' — his preference for lay to clerical justice, and a long convoluted speech on the clerkship of the Star Chamber, the reversion of which he had obtained through Cecil.[249] His most marking contribution at that session touched the subsidy: it should be granted willingly, but not by agreement with the Lords as they asked, for the Commons contributed more, yet 'the thankes wilbe theires and blame ours, they being the

243 Bacon, *Essays*, pp. 175–76.

244 See Brian Vickers, 'The Authenticity of Bacon's Earliest Writings', *Studies in Philology*, 94.2 (1997), 248–96.

245 Bacon, *The Letters and the Life*, II, ch. 10, p. 370.

246 'Gesta Grayorum, 1594', in Nichols, *The Progresses of Queen Elizabeth*, III, pp. 309–18, 288–95.

247 Bacon, *The Letters and the Life*, I, ch. 9, pp. 342–43.

248 One speech is attributed to him, *Proceedings*, II, pp. 291, 298. Other mentions of 'Bacon' (*Proceedings*, II, pp. 126, 388, 399) could mean either him or his half-brothers, Edward and Nathaniel.

249 *Proceedings*, III, pp. 132–34.

first movers'.[250] His advice won a majority in Commons. Not content with that first minor victory, he opposed a tax he considered too heavy, arguing that the gentlemen would have to sell their plate and the farmers their brass pots before this could be paid.[251] His support of seemingly radical platforms pleased the House but did him little good with the court party. The office of attorney general he hoped to gain was given to his rival Coke.[252] It was in this capacity that Coke interrogated Augustine Phillips about their performance of *Richard II* on the eve of the Essex rebellion.[253]

By 1601 Bacon had learnt his political lesson and supported the queen's request for four subsidies. At that session, where his cousin Robert Cecil pointedly requested that all pay the subsidy even if it meant selling their pots and pans, Bacon concluded 'yt was *dulcis tractus pari jugo*, and therfore the poore, as well as the riche, not to be exempted'. This brought him under his friend Ralegh's fire: 'call yow this *paris iugum* when a poore man paye as muche as the riche', 'when our estates that be xxx^{li} or 40^{li} in the Queene's bookes, it is not the hundreth parte of our wealthe?'[254] They fall at odds again over the statute of tillage, which Bacon defends for it is not the policy of the State to enrich a few pasturers, while Ralegh thinks the best course is to leave every man free, 'which is the desier of a true Englishman'. Cecil sides with Bacon, for 'exceptinge Sir Thomas Moore's *Utopia*, or some suche ffayned common welth, yow shall never ffinde but the plowghman is cheiflye provided ffor'. To debar tillage would be to give scope to the depopulators: 'undoe this statute and yow indaunger manye thowsandes'.[255] In that case, Bacon won the argument.

Apart from supporting the royal prerogative in the attack against monopolies, Bacon's most prominent service to Elizabeth was the prosecution of his friend Essex, putting the queen's service and the good of his country before private friendship, he explained.[256] It was through Essex that he had been able to approach her and become her legal counsel. In this capacity, his 'Maxims of the law' advocated a complete restructuring of the English law code. He had defended such a project in Parliament with references to ancient Rome, and more festively via the speeches he wrote for *Gesta Grayorum*. His lectures as Reader at Gray's Inn on the Statute of Uses further discuss law reform, which he consistently advised throughout his career, as he would advise reform of the methods and instruments of learning.

At Elizabeth's last Parliament, young Townshend paid special attention to Bacon's eloquence, perhaps because Bacon lent special attention to his, advising

---

250 2 March, *Proceedings*, III, p. 92.

251 *Proceedings*, III, pp. 109–10.

252 Bacon, letter to Essex, 1594, in *The Letters and the Life*, I, ch. 8, p. 290.

253 Boyer, *Sir Edward Coke*, pp. 286–88.

254 8 November 1601, *Proceedings*, III, p. 338.

255 *Proceedings*, III, pp. 451–52.

256 Bacon, letter of 20 July 1600 to Essex, *The Letters and the Life*, II, ch. 8, p. 191. *Apology in Certain Imputations Concerning the Late Earl of Essex*, X, 141.

the patents committee 'to preferre the wyse and discreet speeche made by the young gentleman, even the youngest in this assemblye that last spake'.[257] Thus we read how Bacon denounced the indifference of the House, who left so many bills undiscussed. When relief of the poor is debated, he thinks it would be uncharitable to repeal charity: '"I speake" (quoth he) "Mr Speaker even out of the very stringes of my harte, which doth alter my ordinarye fforme of speeche, ffor I speake not nowe out of the ffervencye of my brayne," etc.'[258] As the queen's counsel, when his brain speaks, Bacon watches over the legality of their proceedings, ever ready to instruct his fellow members on quiddities. As an orator, when the heart takes over, our essayist often sounds sanctimonious and excessively wordy, for instance when he treats the House to a lecture on the various forms of monopoly, and wishes them all to remember he is doing his best to uphold the prerogative.[259]

Bacon, who defended the Anglo-Scottish union, fared somewhat better under James I than in the preceding reign and eventually rose above his father's position although, as Brian Vickers put it, 'he was still only a tool of James'.[260] This led him to argue in *A View of the Differences in Question betwixt the King's Bench and the Council in the Marches* (1607) that the king held some prerogatives not 'mediately from the law, but immediately from God, as he holdeth his Crown', quoting James's *True Lawe of free Monarchies* in support, warning opponents that they might well 'open a gap unto new Barons' wars'.[261] Were he but made attorney general he would 'recover that strength to the king's prerogative, which it hath had in times past', for that purpose required 'some man of courage and speech, and a grounded lawyer'.[262] A week after his cousin Cecil's death, he offered himself as a successor, and ideal mediator with Parliament, having always been 'a perfect and peremptory royalist'.[263] These absolutist accents he balanced, though, in stressing that the king's sovereignty and the liberty of Parliament are as the two principles of this estate: 'All kings, though they be gods on earth, yet, as he said, they are gods of earth, and frail as other men'. Bacon was lucid enough to advise careful handling of the Commons' sensibilities: 'Take away liberty of parliament, the griefs of the subject will bleed inwards: sharp and eager humours will not evaporate; and then they must exulcerate; and so may endanger the sovereignty itself.'[264] It was unlucky for both him and the Stuarts that Prince Henry, who lent a sympathetic ear to his endless plans for reform, died at an early age.

---

257 21 November, *Proceedings*, III, p. 382.
258 6 November 1601, *Proceedings*, III, pp. 320, 326, 441–42.
259 20 November 1601, *Proceedings*, III, p. 373.
260 Bacon, *The Major Works*, ed. by Vickers, p. xviii.
261 Bacon, *The Letters and the Life*, III, ch. 9, pp. 371–72.
262 Bacon, 'Reasons for the remove of Coke', *The Letters and the Life*, IV, ch. 10, p. 381.
263 Bacon, in the draft of a letter to King James, 31 May 1612. *The Letters and the Life*, IV, ch. 8, p. 280.
264 Bacon, 'A Speech of the King's Solicitor Persuading the House of Commons to Desist from Farther Question of Receiving the King's Messages', 1610, *The Letters and the Life*, IV, ch. 5, p. 177.

Bacon's status at last improved through his friendship with the new favourite George Villiers, future Duke of Buckingham, thanks to whom he was promoted to the positions he had so longed for. Among the cases he dealt with was the removal from the King's Bench of Edward Coke, who had opposed the king's causes. The Lord Chancellor Bacon had just reached the height of honours, being created Baron of Verulam in January 1621, when a charge of bribery ended his own career. He retired at Gorhambury and dedicated the rest of his life to research, still hoping to interest James in reforming the legal system with 'an offer of a digest to be made of the laws of England', which 'are as mixt as our language, compounded of British, Roman, Saxon, Danish, Norman customs' and thereby so much the richer, still hoping to remedy their defects and inconsistencies with the teachings of Roman law, as Justinian had done with his *Corpus juris civilis*.[265] He kept plying James and his son Charles with volume after volume of his works. His *History of Henry VII*, from sources collected by Selden, and a promised 'History of Henry VIII' failed to convince the monarch he should be recalled as counsellor. In the depth of adversity he identifies with his father's beloved philosopher: 'Seneca saith, *Tam otii debet constare ratio quam negotii*. I make his majesty oblation of both.'[266] Appropriately enough he died a martyr to science, of a cold he caught while testing how long a chicken could be preserved by stuffing it with snow.

Legal Wars: Edward Coke's Prosecutions

> Your subjects have inherited this freedom, that they should not be compelled to contribute to any tax, tallage, aid, or other like charge not set by common consent, in parliament.
>
> *Petition of Right, 1628*

Biographers still disagree about the exact cause of Bacon's downfall. It came shortly after his suggestion to revoke patents which he knew would be brought up in Parliament, especially a patent for gold and silver thread that mostly profited Buckingham and his brother. Grievances had been piling up about the buying and selling of offices, the taking of briberies at all levels, and the system of monopolies attacked in vain by three previous Parliaments. Since the favourite could not be directly targeted, the reformers, Coke and the Lord High Treasurer Lionel Cranfield chose to prosecute the next best target.[267] That he had accepted gifts from litigants, Bacon admitted, claiming they had not influenced his judgement.[268] King James, probably unwilling to face a confrontation on corruption in Parliament, left

265 Bacon, *The Letters and the Life*, VII, ch. 8, p. 361.
266 In the draft of a letter of thanks to James for his pardon, Bacon, *The Letters and the Life*, VII, ch. 8, p. 351.
267 On the corruption charges, see Bacon, *The Major Works*, Notes pp. 695–702.
268 Rees and Wakely, *Printing, Politics, and Culture*.

judgement to the House of Lords: having announced he would 'strike dead' the three patents that caused particular grievance, he abandoned Bacon to his fate. The prosecutors would not long enjoy their victory: Coke was dismissed from the Privy Council and sent to the Tower for almost a year; Cranfield was impeached for corruption, found guilty, and dismissed from all his offices. As Bacon wrote in 'Of Great Place', 'The standing is slippery'.

Bacon's taking of briberies was so common an offence that historians find it hard to believe it could really have caused his dismissal. James himself owned that if he were to punish all who did, he would soon have not a single subject left. His chancellor may have served as scapegoat in a conspiracy to dislodge the favourite, Buckingham.[269] Many wonder why exactly Bacon pleaded guilty, for nineteen of the twenty-eight charges have since been established as groundless: poor health, hope to gain indulgence, unless he had been blackmailed with threats to expose his sexual inclinations? Although he stigmatizes homosexuality as an 'unlawful threat' in *The New Atlantis,* and clears its inhabitants — 'As for masculine love, they have no touch of it' — John Aubrey asserts that 'He was a Pederast. His Ganimeds and Favourites tooke Bribes'.[270] Much of Aubrey's information is unreliable hearsay, but Simonds D'Ewes, a barrister at the time, implies there was some talk of bringing Bacon to trial for sodomy, as some thought he should 'have satisfied the law most severe against that horrible villainy with the price of his blood'.[271] A decade later, sodomites would be liable to a death penalty.

Whatever the true cause, the fact that Bacon had facing him his old enemy, Edward Coke, did not help.[272] The rivalry between them was ostensibly over appointments, but more deeply over definitions of the law. As Bacon famously writes in the *Essays,* 'Judges ought to remember that their office is *jus dicere,* and not *jus dare*: to interpret law, and not to make law, or give law.' The best law, he insists in *Advancement,* is that 'which gives least to the discretion of the judge',[273] though as chancellor he governed an equity court. The 'peremptory royalist' repaid the king's favour with near sycophantic support of monarchic right: let the judges 'be lions, but yet lions under the throne, being circumspect that they do not check or oppose any points of sovereignty'.[274] Coke, Chief Justice of the

---

269 Nieves Mathews, *Francis Bacon: The History of a Character Assassination* (New Haven: Yale University Press, 1996).

270 John Aubrey, *Brief Lives, Chiefly of Contemporaries* (Oxford: Clarendon Press, 1898), p. 71.

271 Simonds D'Ewes, *Extracts from the MS Journals* (London: J. Nichols, 1783), p. 25. For varied opinions, see Matthew Parris and Kevin Maguire, 'Francis Bacon — 1621', in *Great Parliamentary Scandals: Five Centuries of Calumny, Smear and Innuendo* (London: Chrysalis, 2004), pp. 8–9. Jardine and Stewart, *Hostage to Fortune*, p. 148. Charles R. Forker, '"Masculine Love," Renaissance Writing, and the "New Invention" of Homosexuality: An Addendum', *Journal of Homosexuality*, 31.3 (1996), 85–93.

272 'A true remembrance of the abuse I received of Mr Attorney General publicly in the Exchequer', Letter to Cecil, 29 April 1601, Bacon, *The Letters and the Life*, x, ch. 3, pp. 3–4.

273 Bacon, *The Advancement of Learning*, Aphorism VIII, in *The Works*, ed. by Spedding and others, IX, *Translations of the Philosophical Works*, p. 314.

274 Bacon, 'Of Judicature', in *Essays*, pp. 222–25.

King's Bench, lost his position when he tried to indict Lord Ellesmere and others for equity judgements in scorn of common law courts, but his zeal to restrict the royal prerogative of the Court of Chancery was such, Gary Watt argues, that in this case he failed to see 'the possibility of seeking more equitable justice in his own court'. James ruled in favour of Chancery, 'and thereby established the principle which maintains equity's preeminent status to the present day'.[275] Bacon notes in his 'Remembrances' that Coke had been told by James to 'reform his Reports, wherein there be many dangerous conceits of his own uttered for law', but Coke did not manage to redeem his fault: after three months' consideration, 'he had offered his majesty only five animadversions, being rather a scorn than a satisfaction to his majesty'.[276] Now armed with his adversary's weakness, Coke could proclaim that 'a corrupt judge is the grievance of grievances',[277] to the public shame of Sir Nicholas Bacon's son.

Coke, like Bacon, was involved in the case of the Post-Nati, Scottish subjects born after James's accession to the throne, when judges had to determine their rights to own property in England, and whether these depended on allegiance, place of birth, or *jus sanguinis*.[278] For once, both lawyers fought on the same side, though from different principles. The trial of Robert Calvin's case in 1608 had echoes in the class conflict of *Coriolanus* over the foundation and components of the body politic.[279] As in the days of Mary Stuart's claim, the question was debated in and out of court and Commons, where hysterical fears of a Scottish or of any foreign invasion again resounded. Beyond the specific point, the Post-Nati's rights of inheritance, the main issue was the status of aliens. A momentous one, Coke noted when he commented that 'this little plea is a great stranger to the laws of England' and claimed proudly that it was all settled through common law. Bacon won the case, his client, Calvin or Collevill, having been pronounced English and thus entitled to own property, but he was aware of its extending the borders of the island and creating precedents for new colonies.[280]

Parliament was more than willing to conquer new markets and new lands, but had no intention of welcoming strange populations on an equal basis. Coke argued that English rights and liberties must be restricted to acknowledged members of the national community. The four sections of his argument — allegiance, kingdoms, laws, aliens — all set on tracing the legal and symbolic border between

---

275 Watt, *Equity Stirring*, pp. 67–72.

276 Bacon, 'Remembrances of His Majesty's declaration touching the Lord Coke', 1616, *The Letters and the Life*, VI, ch. 2, p. 96.

277 'Coke, Sir Edward', in *The History of Parliament: The House of Commons, 1604–1629*, ed. by Andrew Thrush and John P. Ferris (Cambridge: Cambridge University Press, 2010).

278 *Cobbett's State Trials*, II, p. 609.

279 See Richard Marienstras, 'Notice de *Coriolan*', in *Tragédies*, II, *Œuvres complètes de Shakespeare*, ed. by Déprats and Venet.

280 Bacon, 'The Case of the Post-Nati of Scotland', *Arguments of Law*, in *Literary and Professional Works*, ed. by Spedding and others, pp. 641–79. Coke, 'Calvin's Case', in *The Reports*, Pt VII, pp. 1–28.

Englishmen and Others, offer a vivid print of the Jacobean world picture.[281] Othello, however valued as a military servant of Venice, remained an alien, at best a denizen, only a step above Shylock in the appreciation of the Venitian citizenry. In Coke's hierarchy of otherness, 'Every Alien is either a friend that is in league, &c. or an enemy that is in open war. &c. Every Alien enemy is either *pro tempore*, temporary for a time, or *perpetuus*, perpetual, or *specialiter permissus*, permitted especially. Every subject is either *natus*, born, or *datus*, given or made'. Temporary aliens may become friends, 'but a perpetual enemy (though there be no wars by fire and sword between them) cannot maintain any action, or get any thing within this Realm'.[282] Perpetual enemies usually meant enemies of Christ, the Jews and the Saracens.

The insularity of common law did not easily lend itself to either James's visions of empire or Britain's budding expansionism. To Brian Lockey, because they could see beyond the insular tradition of nativist common law, writers of romance fiction rather than English jurists eventually provided ways of thinking about expansionism in more advanced ethical and legal terms: their narratives constitute a founding moment in the history of English imperialism, when expansion defined as imperative the idiosyncratic 'ethics of conquest' that would play a role in both the rise of a British empire and its final dissolution.[283] Shakespeare's Cymbeline, educated at the court of Augustus, but under sway of a wife and stepson determined to revive ancient British laws, seems to embody these opposites, before he pays tribute to Roman law and culture.[284] As Colin Burrow perceptively notes, Jupiter's polyglot prophecy does not promise *imperium sine fine*. It is not Roman, but 'rather distinctly Romano-British', fusing together 'the prophetic style of the native British wizard Merlin with imperial overtones from the *Aeneid*'.[285] Shakespeare, again, contributes even further to the fusing: by grafting branches of a stately cedar to the old stock, Britain shall be 'fortunate and flourish in peace and plenty'. *Cymbeline* may be thought to offer a stage equivalent of Camden's desired union of 'the Britons and Romans, in so many ages, by a blessed and joyful mutual engrafting'.[286]

According to various historians, Pocock first, it was Coke of the Inner Temple and his generation who insisted on the insularity of English law, which they still felt was threatened, as in Wolsey's time, by the encroachments of Chancery.[287] Coke's major innovation was to elevate past decisions into rules, giving history

281 Marienstras, 'The Calvin Affair and the Status of Foreigners', in *New Perspectives on the Shakespearean World*, trans. by Lloyd from *Le Proche et le Lointain*, ch. 5.

282 Coke, *The Reports*, Pt VII, p. 17.

283 Lockey, *Law and Empire*, pp. 9, 11, 179.

284 Various critics detect echoes of the Post-Nati in the name and exile of Posthumus Leonatus, like Marcus, *Puzzling Shakespeare*, pp. 124–25; Cormack, *A Power to Do Justice*, pp. 243–53.

285 Burrow, *Shakespeare and Classical Antiquity*, p. 88.

286 Camden, *Britain*, trans. by Holland, p. 88.

287 Pocock, *The Ancient Constitution and the Feudal Law*. John L. Barton, 'Roman Law in England', in *Jus Romanum Medii Aevi* (Milan: Giuffré, 1971), pt V, 13a.

an importance it had not enjoyed earlier: 'For Elizabethan lawyers, reason, not history, was the guide.'[288] The fact of conquest, Roman or Norman, had been subject to endless revisionism. Sir John Fortescue, guided by his will to strengthen the myth of a common law born and bred on English soil, had ignored the Roman conquest, though he admitted the Norman invasion, which caused the use of law French in the English courts of justice.[289] In 1602, Edward Coke denied this and argued that William the Conqueror had transported 'the excellencie and equitie of the Lawes of England' back to Normandy.[290] To Bradin Cormack, *Henry V* and *Richard III* represent not the glory but the impermanence of conquest. We remember not an event, but a pattern, a history of invasion since the Normans and the long history of English losses on the Continent: 'Put simply, 1485 is 1066'.[291]

Coke's concern for the legal system drove him to declare the immemorial integrity of the common law despite the various invasions of Britain. He carried to extremes Fortescue's belief in the superiority of common law over any other legal system by making it superior to the king. This article of faith did not cause any major conflict with Elizabeth, though in the Case of the Monopolies, his stance went against her prerogative. As Speaker in 1593 he made some impression on the anonymous diarist, certainly a lawyer himself, who informs us that Speaker Coke did not tolerate whisperings or secret talk among members, 'only publique speeches are to be used', after which Coke unrolled the history of England and the old statutes to show that all kings of England since Henry III's time had ruled as supreme head within their own dominions.[292]

Coke had studied at Trinity from 1567 to 1570, in the thick of the Cambridge religious quarrels. Not a Puritan himself, though he had many friends among them, he retreated behind his official role and generally limited his utterances to legal information and precedents.[293] When Morice proposed his *ex officio* bills, Coke deferred the reading that fell to him as Speaker, arguing he could not readily understand them. The most memorable act of his career under Elizabeth was the first publication in 1600 of his *Reports*, which everyone praised including Bacon, even though he criticized the innovative character of 'some peremptory and extrajudicial resolutions'. Coke's best cases were not of a political nature but dealt with leasehold interests, payments of debts, bankruptcy, and other private matters. Along with a rich marriage, they helped him build a huge fortune.

The conflict of principles came to a head under James I, when Archbishop Bancroft begged the king to establish clear boundaries between ecclesiastical and common law courts. Coke retorted that the common law judges alone determined

---

288 Christopher Brooks and Kevin Sharpe, 'History, English Law and the Renaissance', *Past & Present*, 72.1 (1976), 136.

289 Fortescue, *In Praise of the Laws*, ch. 17, pp. 26–27, and ch. 48, p. 66.

290 Coke, *Le Tierce Part des Reportes* (London: Thomas Wight, 1602), fol. 190 E1^{r-v}, repr. in Coke, *The Reports*, Pt III, p. xxi.

291 Cormack, *A Power to Do Justice*, p. 204.

292 *Proceedings*, III, pp. 99, 65.

293 See Boyer, *Sir Edward Coke*, pp. 21–24.

the law of the realm and was angrily reminded that his sovereign was the supreme fountain of justice. After repeated checks from his Chief Justice in his high-handed attempts to rule the law, James eventually dismissed him for insubordination. This sanction, Coke's relentless fight for the independence of Parliament, his part in the Petition of Right made him the acknowledged champion of law and liberty against absolutism. As attorney general he prosecuted Essex, Southampton, Walter Ralegh whom he called 'a spider of hell', and the Gunpowder Plot conspirators. He revived the old impeachment method to bring down Bacon, but subverted it by leaving the king out of the King-in-Parliament procedure: by agreeing not to preside, James lost the power to control attacks against his ministers or defend their policy, and furnished Parliament with a powerful political weapon. The next major impeachment would be Buckingham's.

Coke's *Reports* and *Institutes of the Lawes of England* taught law to future generations of British and American students and helped shape constitutional government in both countries. They were a main source of Thomas Jefferson's *Summary View of the Rights of British America*. The same Jefferson would later diagnose that 'the difference between the Whig and Tory of England is that the Whig deduces his rights from the Anglo-Saxon source, and the Tory from the Norman', the English constitution being derived from 'its rightful root, the Anglo-Saxon', thus transporting the legend of ancient liberties across the Atlantic.[294] Only one volume of Coke's *Institutes* was published in his lifetime; the other three were suppressed by Charles I on the eve of the Civil War as dangerous political material. Charles had taken the measure of Coke's tongue when he invoked his sovereign power in answer to the Petition of Right: 'I know that prerogative is part of the law, but sovereign power is no parliamentary word.' Coke retaliated in his speech to Parliament: 'Take we heed what we yield unto. Magna Carta is such a fellow that he will have no sovereign.' Or so the story goes.[295]

---

294 Letter of 1824 to John Cartwright, in David N. Mayer, *The Constitutional Thought of Thomas Jefferson* (Charlottesville: Virginia University Press, 1994), p. 11. See Elise Marienstras, *Les mythes fondateurs de la nation américaine* (Paris: La Découverte, 1976), pp. 43–59.

295 According to *Commons Debates, 1628*, ed. by Johnson and others, III, p. 503, Coke's actual words may have been 'no saving', i.e. no clause in the Petition of Right to save the royal prerogative. The *Journal of the House of Commons* (I, p. 893) mentions on 8 May, 'Much Dispute about the putting-in of some words' in the Petition, and on 21 May (I, p. 902), Coke's report of the Lords' argument over 'The Saving, in Articuli super chartas, stronger than this', and 'the Words "sovereign Power" milder than "Prerogative"' which make an addition 'necessary for the King's Satisfaction'. See Goldsworthy, *The Sovereignty of Parliament*, p. 114, on his 'supposed statement'. Stephen D. Whyte, *Sir Edward Cooke and the Grievances of the Commonwealth* (Manchester: Manchester University Press, 1979), pp. 266–67.

CHAPTER 10

Kings Do but Play Us

The Tudors had well understood before James the uses of legal history. Antiquarian research received full approval of the Crown in 1533 when Henry VIII gave John Leland a commission authorizing him to examine the libraries of all the religious houses in England. Leland had spent two years studying in Paris, where his acquaintance with the scholars Budé and Lefèvre d'Etaples developed his taste for antiquities. With the assistance of his friend John Bale, Leland kept notebooks of his journeys, filled with information from charters and oral sources, and presented them to the king under the title *A New Year's Gift*, which established him as the father of English local history. Leland's *Assertio inclytissimi Arturii Regis Britanniae* (1544), a prose treatise on the historicity of King Arthur, was translated with additions by Richard Robinson in 1582 under the title *A Learned and True Assertion of the original Life, Actes and death of the most Noble, Valiant, and Renoumed Prince Arthure, King of great Brittaine*, and dedicated to Arthur, Lord Grey of Wilton, whom young Spenser was then serving as secretary.[1] Polydore Vergil, perhaps incensed by his contribution to the Arthurian myth, dismissed Leland scornfully as a 'vain glorious man' but these collections provided valuable material to Lambarde, Stow, Camden, Dugdale, and other British antiquarians. Lambarde of Lincoln's Inn, who would receive Elizabeth's confidence that she identified with Richard II, had recently been appointed Keeper of the Records of the Tower. In his report of their conversation, she asks him to elucidate various technical terms as she reads, before she tests him with an oblique allusion to the Essex rising. It is a volume of *Pandecta Rotulorium* that he has offered her, thus giving her 'an opportunity to reflect on the course of history, and her place in it'.[2] Lambarde had studied Old English with Laurence Nowell and published a collection of Anglo-Saxon laws, *Archaionomia*, from Nowell's transcript of *Leges Edwardi Confessoris*, a copy of which bears a signature attributed to Shakespeare.[3] His *Perambulation of Kent* (1570) constitutes the first item of county history with its study of topography, local families, ancient laws and customs, heraldry, using techniques learnt from his legal expertise with archives. From Holinshed

1 Charles Millican, 'Spenser and the Arthurian Legend', *Review of English Studies*, 6.22 (1930), 167–74.
2 Scott-Warren, 'Was Elizabeth I Richard II?', p. 226.
3 See Samuel Schoenbaum, *Shakespeare: Records and Images* (Oxford: Oxford University Press, 1981).

to Samuel Daniel, it is also the chroniclers' source for William the Conqueror's legendary encounter with the men of Kent and promise to preserve their ancient laws. Coke's library contained both *Archaionomia* and the *Perambulation*.[4]

Lawyers in Resistance

Two other eminent Inns alumni, John Selden and John Donne, both suffered and benefited from the autocratic methods of Elizabeth's successor. So too did Shakespeare, under the livery of the King's Men, who suddenly quit stage and court at the height of a successful career. King James had vainly asked Coke to revise his *Reports*. He likewise took exception to Selden's *Historie of Tithes* and forced him to withdraw it, for it might cause scandal in the Church. When ordered to make a public acknowledgement of his error, Selden stuck to his guns, disingenuously claiming in his defence that he had 'resolved wholly to leave the point of divine right of tythes' and keep himself 'wholly to the historical part', leaving tithes to theologians.[5] As for the Catholic John Donne, desperate under the pressure of adversity, he eventually obtained royal preferment by taking holy orders and entering the Church of England. The Newbattle portrait, 'That Picture of myne wch is taken in Shaddowes', shows a handsome youth defying all the sumptuary rules of the Inns: wide-brimmed hat, lace collar, embroidered shirt, sword, thin moustache all suggest 'a young gentleman who had yet to decide whether he would be a lawyer or a soldier, and ended up being a poet and a priest'.[6]

Liberty of Research: John Selden's Archaeological History

no Italian priest
Shall tithe or toll in our dominions.

King John, III.i

Selden of the Inner Temple properly belongs with James I's reign, but his research into the history of law, which brings to maturity centuries of legal quarrels, calls for a brief mention here. His *Historie of Tithes* (1616) reopened the age-old controversy over ecclesiastical jurisdiction by exposing as erroneous the notion that tithes had always existed through the law of nature and were due by *jus divinum*, as some clergymen still claimed: the first recorded attempt to create a legal right to tithes was made under Charlemagne and enforced in Europe by its

4 Holt, 'The Ancient Constitution in Medieval England', pp. 71–73.
5 Selden, 'Of my Purpose and End in writing the History of Tythes', in *Opera Omnia*, ed. by Wilkins, II, p. 1454. Toomer, 'Selden's "Historie of Tithes"', p. 349.
6 Germaine Greer, 'Out of the Shadows', *The Guardian*, 28 January 2006.

more domineering popes, a vast programme that culminated in the time of King John. The sale of tithes to private owners after the dissolution of monasteries caused innumerable lawsuits, one of them involving Shakespeare, who bought 'a moiety' of the Stratford tithes, and used the word in nine different plays, most significantly in *King John*, of course, and in *Lear* where Poor Tom 'is whipped from tithing to tithing'.[7]

Although the book had been duly licensed, Selden told his friend the astronomer Fabri de Peiresc, the Archbishop of Canterbury seized all the printed sheets that could be found while the press was still hot, but the manuscript was saved from his furious raid.[8] Several works attacking the *Historie* appeared from 1619 to 1621, dedicated to James, though Selden himself was 'fiercely' forbidden by the king to publish anything more on the subject.[9] The crowning irony, recorded in Selden's *Table Talk*, came under Oliver Cromwell when the clergy 'consulted in Oxford where they might find the best arguments for their tithes, setting aside the *jus divinum*; they were advised to my History of Tithes, a book so much cried down by them formerly'.[10]

Selden had several friends and patrons in the College of Antiquaries, though he does not seem to have been one of their members.[11] This discussion group was founded around 1586, coinciding with the publication of Camden's *Britannia*, by young men who met every Friday in the term to confer upon some questions of history and sup together.[12] The founding four, James Ley, Robert Cotton, Camden, and Spelman, were soon joined by a fifth, John Dodderidge, of the Middle Temple. By 1591 they were twenty-four, with a majority of lawyers and self-educated legal historians. Their programme, dedicated to research in English source material, was predominantly nationalistic, not to say parochial.[13] Cotton placed at their disposal his library of books, and the archaeological remains he had collected with Camden on their tour of the north. All documents show the College alive between 1590 and 1607. Its most active period was the decade 1594–1604, during which their numbers rose to thirty-nine, thirty-two of whom had been through the Inns. A majority exercised public or private legal professions, ten sat in Parliament, three were heralds. In 1601, one of their most fruitful years, four

---

7 Tucker Brooke, 'Shakespeare's Moiety of the Stratford Tithes', *Modern Language Notes*, 40.8 (1925), 462–69.

8 'Epistolae ad Viros Clarissimos', *Joannis Seldeni Jurisconsulti*, in Selden, *Opera Omnia*, II, pp. 1696–99, trans. by Toomer in 'Selden's "Historie of Tithes"', pp. 355–56.

9 *Vindiciae secundum integritatem existimationis suae*, § II, in Selden, *Opera Omnia*, II, pp. 1417–19.

10 Selden, *The Table Talk*, p. 179.

11 Selden's name appears, but is crossed out, in the only first-hand history of the College, by one of its founders, Henry Spelman, prefaced to his tract *The Original of the Four Terms of the Year* (1695).

12 Linda Van Norden, 'Sir Henry Spelman on the Chronology of the Elizabethan College of Antiquaries', *Huntington Library Quarterly*, 13 (1949–1950), 131–60. Richard J. Schoeck, 'The Elizabethan Society of Antiquaries and Men of Law', *Notes & Queries*, 199 (1954), 417–21.

13 See Hearne, *Curious Discourses*, ed. by Ayloffe.

tracts out of a total twenty-one dealt with some feature of the Inns.[14] Elizabeth was presented about 1602 with a petition to establish the College as a permanent 'Academye for the studye of Antiquity and History', which her death prevented. It argued the value of history in training noblemen for government service. Among the precedents quoted to demonstrate the uses of historical research was Henry VIII's success in freeing his realm from Rome.

What makes history useful makes it equally dangerous, controversial, and less than objective, they soon learned. Members of the government were prone to ask the College to write official papers in support of a case. Political tracts were beginning to take precedence over scholarship.[15] Disagreements among members truly began at a meeting on the origin of Parliament, when Dodderidge claimed an antiquity for the House of Commons before the Romans, whereas Camden after a thorough examination of the evidence could find no trace of an assembly of the three estates before the reign of King John.[16] Years later, Cotton would be severely criticized for having mistranslated 'grantz' as 'Commons' instead of 'grandees', from either a mistake or an eagerness to establish an early precedent for consultation of the Lower House.[17] The meetings stopped in 1607, although some members continued collaboration. An attempt was made to revive the College in 1614, 'But before our Meeting, we had notice that his Majesty took a little Mislike to our Society; not being inform'd, that we had resolv'd to decline all Matters of State. Yet hereupon we forbare to meet again, and so all our Labours lost.'[18]

Robert Cotton did not just open his vast library to Selden. He seems to have actively collaborated on the *Historie of Tithes*.[19] Both scholars soon realized they would need to investigate foreign sources to explain the origin of titles, offices, or institutions, including the common law. Discussing the antiquity of the Constable's office, Cotton insisted: 'if we curiously will looke into the roots of this question, we must travell out of our owne country'.[20] But he was not so brave when it came to turning a critical eye on the origin of the legendary Brutus or Arthur, and Camden himself dared not carry the scrutiny too far: 'For mine owne part, let Brutus be taken for the father and founder of the British nation; I will not be of contrarie minde'.[21] *Britannia* still included pictures of Arthur's burial cross. As for Selden, he mocked 'the too studious affectation of base and sterile antiquity', preferring 'the fruitful and precious part of it wch gives necessarie light to posteritie in matter of state, law, Historie and the understanding of good

14 Van Norden, 'Sir Henry Spelman', p. 148.
15 Hearne, *Curious Discourses*, II, pp. 165–67, and II, pp. 155–60.
16 Hearne, *Curious Discourses*, I, pp. 281–92, and I, pp. 303–06.
17 Sharpe, *Sir Robert Cotton*, p. 44.
18 Spelman, 'The Occasion', in Van Norden's transcript, 'Sir Henry Spelman', p. 135.
19 Toomer, 'Selden's "Historie of Tithes"', p. 351.
20 Hearne, *Curious Discourses*, II, p. 65. Sharpe, *Sir Robert Cotton*, p. 23. Linda Van Norden, 'Peiresc and the English Scholars', *Huntington Library Quarterly*, 1.4 (1949), 369–89.
21 Camden, *Britain*, p. 8.

aucthors'.[22] His works constantly returned to the history of laws that had been excluded or ignored by the 'unscholarly breed of lawyers at the Inns of Court', Goodrich notes.[23]

Unlike many of his fellow lawyers who focused on common law, or the antiquarians bent on British fossils, Selden exercised his curiosity over a field of research that extended from Europe to Asia, supported by his mastery of a dozen languages ancient and modern. His research, based on 'true Philologie' and comparative methods, drew on a large range of foreign scholars, Valla, Joseph Scaliger (on Jewish tithes), Hotman, Fabri de Peiresc, Grotius (on dominion of the sea). This helped him face issues his predecessors since Fortescue had tended to shirk, like the relation of common to Roman law, or the level of change created by the Norman Conquest. His method of historiography derived from the humanists': use documents as close as possible to events for primary sources, and submit materials to critical analysis. The most reliable sources, to him, were the Acts of the State, preserved in public records. By 1609, he had gathered a collection of sources on early English governance, published posthumously as *England's epinomis* (1681).

The *Historie of Tithes* had provided a glamorous background to the authority of mixed monarchy: William the Conqueror, his barons, and some men learned in the law joined in a parliament that confirmed 'the former Laws of the Kingdome'. Selden would later recognize a major change from Anglo-Saxon to Norman laws on tenure. Conquests, by Romans, Saxons, Danes, or Normans, 'bring alwaies some alteration'; a conqueror keeps some old customs and adds new ones, but the shape of the State remains, like a ship mended with new pieces: it may have none left of the original, yet 'is to be accounted the same still'.[24] This importance given to structure shows his faith in the mastermind that first designed it. His dissertation on *Fleta*, a treatise of English law written in the reign of Edward I, argues that Roman law did not become the law of the land because of 'the unconcealed aversion which our ancestors had to it' and 'the remarkable esteem in which the English or common law was held'.[25] After the collapse of the empire, it was preserved under the early Normans by the monks of Abingdon, which explains its use by Bracton and in *Fleta*, but it declined after them, to reappear in the twelfth century when 'the two Codes were introduced into England together in order that the most complete manuals of the Roman law extant in Latin might be available'.[26]

---

22 *The Historie of Tithes* (London: [n.pub.], 1618), Dedication 'To the Most Honord S[r] Robert Cotton of Connington'.

23 Goodrich, *Oedipus Lex*, p. 237. See also his 'Salem and Bizance: A Short History of the Two Laws', *Culture, Theory and Critique*, 30.1 (1994), 13–30.

24 Selden's notes 9, 19 discussing Fortescue's *De Laudibus* in an edition of 1616.

25 *Ioannis Seldeni ad Fletam dissertatio* [1647], ed. with parallel trans. by David Ogg (Cambridge: Cambridge University Press, 1925), p. 165.

26 Selden, *Ad Fletam dissertatio*, ed. and trans. by Ogg, p. 109.

Selden's vast erudition was solicited from all sides. In Parliament, where he was elected in 1624, he provided invaluable help with precedents for the actions of the House, and largely contributed to the procedure of impeachment against Buckingham. He caused a sensation when he announced that there was 'no law to prevent the printing of any book in England, only a decree of the Star Chamber', no law either requiring free men to be pressed into military service.[27] The House of Lords employed him as expert legal historian in a research on the privileges of the English baronage. He was recruited by Sir Edwin Sandys, Richard Hooker's former pupil, to draw a new charter for the Virginia Company. In June 1621, he, Southampton, and Sandys were arrested for hindering the king's aim in Parliament, when Sandys managed to push through a protectionist bill against Spanish tobacco.[28] They were released a month later, after protests from Commons.

A friend of Drayton and Ben Jonson, Selden wrote poetry, none of which has survived. Ben Jonson famously questioned him on 'the counterfeiting of sexes by apparell'. This involved not just cross-dressing, but the whole masculine casting of Elizabethan plays, which was banned on the basis of Deuteronomy 22. 5, 'The woman shall not wear that which pertaineth unto a man, neither shall a man put on a woman's garment: for all that do so are abomination unto the Lord thy God.' Selden's answer is often quoted as an instance of his wide range of competence: according to Maimonides, the verse condemned not the dressing up itself but the ancient idolatrous cult connected with it, men who worshipped Venus and women who worshipped Mars, in clothing opposite to their sex. The theatre's association with idolatry 'in those times of the infancie of Christianitie' must be considered through the glass of history to be properly understood.[29] Shakespeare's 'master-mistress of my passion', like Viola-Cesario or Rosalind-Ganymede, properly belongs with Selden's polymorphous deities and their bisexual priests and priestesses.[30]

Liberty of Conscience: John Donne's Conversions

> Poore intricated soul! Riddling, perplexed, labyrinthicall soule!
>
> *Sermon preached upon the day of Saint Paul's conversion, 1629*

John Donne's career, like Selden's, belongs to the Tudor era by a thin margin. The Inns' greatest poet could well have figured on their list of young prodigals,

---

27 David S. Berkowitz, *John Selden's Formative Years: Politics and Society in Early Seventeenth-Century England* (London: Associated University Presses, 1988), p. 212.

28 Theodore K. Rabb, *Jacobean Gentleman: Sir Edwin Sandys, 1561–1629* (Princeton, NJ: Princeton University Press, 1998), p. 261.

29 Jason Rosenblatt and Winfried Schleiner, 'John Selden's Letter to Ben Jonson on Cross-Dressing and Bisexual Gods', *English Literary Renaissance*, 29 (1999), 44–74.

30 Rosenblatt, *Renaissance England's Chief Rabbi*, pp. 72–73.

and of recusants. His mother was a descendant of the Heywoods and Rastells who composed More's circle, and after a spell at Thavies, he chose Lincoln's, his great relative's Inn. If he declined the office of Steward of Christmas while a student there, in 1593, it was perhaps from lack of funds, but more likely want of festive spirit.[31] His brother Henry had been arrested in May for having sheltered a Catholic priest, William Harrington, in his rooms at the Inns and died of jail fever in Newgate in December, after denouncing under torture the priest, who was drawn and quartered the following February. This is when Donne began to express doubts about the faith he had been raised in, and the prevailing religious factions, with bitter resentment at the waste. In his *Pseudo-Martyr* he writes that no family 'hath endured and suffered more in their persons and fortunes for obeying the teachers of Christian doctrine', whom he accuses of fostering martyrdom.[32] Yet he does not lean to the opposite side. 'Why Puritans Make Long Sermons', *Problem 15* of his *Paradoxes and Problems,* answers its own question with scathing irony:

> I have thought sometimes that out of conscience they allow large measures to coarse ware, and sometimes that usurping in that place a liberty to speak freely of kings and all, they think themselves kings then, and would reign as long as they could. But now I think they do it out of a zealous imagination that it is their duty to preach on till their auditory wake again.[33]

Like some of his Inns fellows, young Donne seemed interested in everything but the study of law. A contemporary remembers him as 'not dissolute, but very neat; a great visiter of Ladies, a great frequenter of Playes, a great writer of conceited Verses'.[34] At Lincoln's he became friends with the sons of the Lord Keeper Egerton, and with the poet Christopher Brooke, future leader of the 'Sireniacs', an Inns of Court club reputed, if it did exist, to meet regularly at the Mermaid tavern when Parliament was in session, to discuss writing and political issues.[35] To this period belong Donne's first Satires, most of the Elegies, some of the 'Songs and Sonnets', verse letters, and an 'Epithalamion made at Lincolnes Inn', a topical parody of Spenser's recently published *Epithalamion.*[36]

Appointed private secretary to Egerton, Donne sat in Elizabeth's last Parliament but ruined his chances of preferment by making a runaway match which so infuriated his father-in-law Sir George More that he was sent to jail at the Fleet: 'Dunne is undonne', Manningham wrote in his diary,[37] repeating the poet's

---

31 He had to pay the customary fine, 26s. 8d., for his refusal to act, Parmiter, *Edmund Plowden*, p. 45.

32 See Tom Cain, 'Elegy and Autobiography: '"The Bracelet" and the Death of Henry Donne', *John Donne Journal*, 23 (2004), 25–57.

33 Donne, *The Major Works*, ed. by Carey, p. 142.

34 Sir Richard Baker, *Chronicles*, first ed. 1643, Pt II, p. 156, in Bald, *John Donne*, p. 72.

35 To I. A. Shapiro, 'The Mermaid Club', *Modern Language Review*, 45 (1950), 6–17, it is a baseless fabrication.

36 Bald, *John Donne*, p. 77.

37 Manningham, *Diary*, p. 99.

own pun, 'John Donne, Ann Donne, Undone'.[38] While seeking employment, John wrote his treatise *Biathanatos* and various works courting patronage. *Biathanatos,* the first early modern defence of suicide, echoes More's imitation of Christ in *De tristitia.* Christ offered the great model of voluntary death when he chose to crucify himself for mankind. Donne confesses he has often felt the lure of suicide himself, an urge that sounds like a prose Hamlet's,

> that a brave scorn, or that a faint cowardliness beget it, whensoever any affliction assails me, methinks I have the keys of my prison in mine own hand, and no remedy presents itself so soon to my heart as mine own sword.[39]

Pseudo-Martyr, the only work Donne published as a lawyer, urges Catholics to take the oath of allegiance demanded of them in the aftermath of the Gunpowder Plot. This obligation revived the Elizabethan issue of divided allegiance, since the oath included a clause declaring 'heretical' the doctrine that the pope could depose 'illegitimate' sovereigns. Beyond its immediate relevance to James's recusant subjects, Donne's treatise takes part in a much wider controversy over papal authority that drew in German Calvinists, French Gallicans, and various Christian sovereigns between 1608 and 1614. Although this point is seldom mentioned, it is a systematic refutation of the Jesuit Robert Bellarmine's position,[40] the target of a previous attack by James in his *Triplici nodo triplex cuneus* ('A triple wedge for a triple knot'), basing his right to impose an oath on the divine character of royal authority.[41] Donne develops James's points, denouncing 'the Popes pretence to temporal jurisdiction', and recalls three conflicts in which popes eventually agreed to share authority with Catholic monarchs: the recent excommunication of the Venetian Senate, Spain's claim to the spiritual monarchy of Sicily, and Gregory VII's quarrel with the German emperor over investitures all ended in a sharing of power between spiritual and secular authorities.[42]

To his modern editor, Donne's arguments are those of a canonist, since canon law provided the basis of the popes' claims for dominion over secular rulers. Before him, in *The Fifth Part of the Reports,* Coke had defended James against canonical arguments for Christian kingship on historical grounds.[43] Donne, who

---

38 In a letter to his wife; see Thomas Docherty, *John Donne Undone* (London: Methuen, 1986), p. 3.

39 Donne, 'The Preface', in *Biathanatos,* ed. by Rudick and Battin, p. 39.

40 Tutino, *Empire of Souls,* ch. 4, does not include Donne among the 'few exceptions' who took on Bellarmine's work, although Donne repeatedly addresses Bellarmine in his treatise.

41 James I, *Triplici nodo triplex cuneus, Or an Apologie for the Oath of Allegiance against the two Breves of Pope Paulus Quintus, and the late letter of Cardinal Bellarmine* [1607] (Ann Arbor: University of Michigan Press, 2011). Bellarmine had replied to the *Basilikon Doron* with a *Hieratikon Doron,* part of Pope Clement's strategy of appeasement.

42 Donne, *Pseudo-Martyr,* ed. by Raspa, 'A Preface to The Priestes, and Iesuits, and to their Disciples in this Kingdome'; chapters V, X and XII.

43 Donne, *Pseudo-Martyr,* pp. xxx–xxxvi. Coke's 'Of the Kings Ecclesiastical Law', *The Fifth Part of the Reports* (1607), evinced from the Jesuit Parsons the same year *An Answere to the Fifth Part of the Reportes Lately set forth.*

refers to 'the most Reverend and learned Sir Edward Coke' in his Preface, runs through the centuries of disputes we saw above, including the Donation of Constantine, to show that the English king lawfully 'defends the liberties of the Church', as the nature of his office 'binds him to do, if he defend the Church of England from foraine usurpation'. In the conflict between Gregory VII and the emperors, Donne recalls, 'the defence of the liberties of the Church, was the title and pretence on both sides'.[44] In such quarrels, some popes resorted to malicious distortions of the Scriptures to vilify princes. Nothing in the terms of the oath is contrary to faith, Donne asserts, nor deserves a martyr's death, which in this case would amount to suicide, for he has found nowhere, in any records of the Church, a law that made it heresy to deny the bishops of Rome a power to depose princes.

Donne insists in the Preface that before binding his 'conscience to any locall Religion' he has 'survayed and digested the whole body of Divinity, controverted betweene ours and the Romane Church'. Among other human frailties he confesses 'my Indulgence to my freedome and libertie, as in all other indifferent things, so in my studies also, not to betroth or enthral my selfe to any one science'.[45] This alleged weakness is the strong point of his argument: the oath is a matter of civil obedience, which is prescribed by the Gospels, not the Jesuits' blind obedience nor the visions of Franciscan monks, but one guided by reason and nature. It does not affect private conscience, which must trace its own path, by the same lights. Donne's plea, *mutatis mutandis*, is the substance of Henry V's sermon to his soldiers on the eve of Agincourt: 'Every subject's duty is the King's, but every subject's soul is his own.'

Donne's family subsisted for fourteen years on the charity of his friends, until James I drove him to take holy orders. Donne turned down the first offer to enter the Church, saying his past life would cause scandal,[46] but James made it clear that this would be his only way of advancement. Donne was ordained in January 1615, made Royal Chaplain the same year, and in 1616, Reader in Divinity at Lincoln's Inn. Anne died in 1617, giving birth to their twelfth child. According to his earliest biographer, Izaak Walton, Donne thereafter 'became crucified to the world, and all those vanities, those imaginary pleasures, that are daily acted on that restless stage'.[47]

Donne's most famous Meditation, 'No man is an island',[48] was composed while he was Dean of St Paul's, a post he would occupy to the end, a few weeks before the completion of the painting for which he posed in a shroud. His fine oratory gifts now served in that other favourite area of public speech, the pulpit. In his 'Poem to Mr Tilman after he had taken orders', the 'shadowy figure' of the

---

44 Donne, *Pseudo-Martyr*, p. 143.
45 Donne, *Pseudo-Martyr*, pp. 12–13.
46 Walton, *The Lives*, p. 24, and Donne's answer to the offer, p. 26. Bald, *John Donne*, pp. 205–06.
47 Walton, *The Life of Dr John Donne* (1640), ed. by Irene C. Teas, Project Canterbury, 2001, <http://anglicanhistory.org/walton/donne.html>.
48 Donne, Meditation 17, in *Devotions upon Emergent Occasions*, p. 1624.

ordained man is 'the same materials, as before | Onely the stampe is changed.' Heaven and earth, 'Both these in thee, are in the Calling knit, | And make thee now a blest Hermaphrodite':[49] a man between two worlds, trying to reconcile their conflicting demands, like a distant nostalgic shadow of Shakespeare's poetic persona, 'the master mistress of my passion' torn between two loves, 'of comfort and despair'. A poet who used to love plays, Donne gave back to the pulpit its original mastery over the spoken word, in the service of *via media*. The theatre by then had come under complete control of the Crown and lost its stance as a Parliament of all England's citizens.

A Parliament of Voices

Even more than Elizabeth, James gave pride of place to the works of the best contemporary dramatists in his courtly ceremonies, yet he did not show much consideration to the first of them: 'the man' Shakespeare stood in livery with his company to decorate the signature of the peace treaty with Spain in 1604. His plays figured prominently on the list of entertainments at the winter wedding of Princess Elizabeth, but one of them was summarily dismissed on the eve of its performance in favour of 'greater pleasures', a masque.[50] Shakespeare's opinion of the courtly genre, as expressed in *Henry VIII* — 'Now this masque | Was cried incomparable; and th'ensuing night | Made it a fool and beggar' — might well explain why he suddenly stopped writing for the stage after this royal slight.[51]

Liberty of the Stage: Curvaceous Mirrors

> Therefore, brevity is the soul of wit,
> And tediousness the limbs and outward flourishes.
> I will be brief.
>
> *Hamlet, II.ii*

The place allowed in society to poets, repeatedly considered as lawless vagabonds in Elizabethan England, had been since Antiquity a standing cause of argument. 'My dear Homer, can you not mention a city to which you gave a better government?' Plato sneers. 'Does any city name you a good lawgiver and its benefactor?' His lawmakers' decisions are inspired by the gods who gave Crete and Sparta their

49 Helen Gardner's phrase, in Donne, *The Divine Poems*, ed. by Gardner, p. 127; Poem, p. 32, ll. 13–14, 52–54. See Alan Pritchard, 'Donne's Mr Tilman', *Review of English Studies*, 24.93 (1973), 38–42.

50 Chambers, *The Elizabethan Stage*, II, p. 213. Various critics, like Kernan, *Shakespeare, the King's Playwright*, p. 156, think the play may well have been his latest, *Henry VIII*.

51 *Henry VIII*, I.i.26–28. I tentatively reconstruct the conditions of his departure in a play, 'Farewell, King!', Shakespeare Anniversary, 21 April 2015, <http://shakespeareanniversary.org/2015/farewell-king/>.

laws. Poets are unnecessary: if they ask to come in with their tragedies, 'we will say to them, we also are poets according to our ability of the best and noblest tragedy; for our whole state is an imitation of the best and noblest life, which we affirm to be indeed the very truth of tragedy. You are poets and we are poets, your rivals and antagonists in the noblest of dramas, which true law and that only can carry out in act, as our hope is.' The maker of images can only imitate, he 'has no understanding of what is, but only of what appears'. Poets have never helped men to be virtuous, never been educators or guides. If they are allowed in, 'pleasure and pain will be kings in your city instead of law'.[52]

Was it this challenge that drove Aristotle to write the *Poetics* in support of the intellectual pleasure we draw from representations? Yet pain seems to dominate in his treatise 'On memory and anamnesis', where the search inherent in recollection seeks an image, or ghost, of the past, *phantasmatos*. The annoyance caused by the effort of recollecting is especially felt by melancholics who are most powerfully moved by *phantasmata*, and most unable to stop the flow of reminiscences.[53] This is where the theatre's anamnesis operates, making the invisible trace of the past, its image through metaphor, doubly present. Ricœur's 'promise' for the future hinges on the term 'recognition': 'whatever the conjunction between the notion of recognition and survival of the past, recognition, taken as a phenomenological data, remains a kind of wonder, "un petit miracle" as I like to say'. Of course, he goes on, history is deprived from the 'blessing' of recognition which provides to memory 'a kind of illumination'. But the theatre does enjoy this blessing: the 'petit miracle' is the culmination of Shakespeare's late romances. By expressing the will if not necessarily the ability to treat wounded memories, they show where to draw Ricœur's line between amnesty and amnesia: 'The answer to this question cannot be found at the political level, but in the will and the heart of private citizens. Thanks to the work of memory, completed by that of mourning, each of us has the duty not to forget, but to recall the past, as painful as it may be, under the guidance of a pacified memory.'[54]

Plato's distrust of poets was perhaps spurred by an intuition that the best of them would never have complete confidence in the laws of his city, and never commit themselves to upholding them. Even with Aeschylus, 'the most optimistic of tragic writers', the dismissal of antique bloodthirsty gods, the victory over the dark forces of the past seem 'not to be making a positive declaration with tranquil conviction but rather to be expressing a hope, making an appeal that remains full of anxiety even amid the joy of the final apotheosis'.[55] Having ruled that citizens should not exact vengeance themselves, the Areopagus cleanses Orestes of his

52 Plato, *The Republic*, IX, 601b, p. 293. Plato, *The Laws*, VII, 817b, p. 330.

53 Aristotle, 'De memoria et reminiscentia', ch. II, 453 a 15–19, in *Parva Naturalia*, trans. by Beare.

54 Ricœur, 'Memory, History, Oblivion', Fonds Ricœur, pp. 6, 9.

55 Jean-Pierre (and not Jean-Paul as Luke Wilson rechristens him) Vernant, 'The Historical Moment of Tragedy', in Vernant and Vidal-Naquet, *Myth and Tragedy*, p. 33.

matricide and reinserts him in the city as a legitimate murderer.[56] The questions raised remain open, or, to put it like Simon Goldhill, the problem of *dikè* in *Oresteia* 'is not solved but endlessly restated'.[57] The anxiety remains with Roman, medieval, and early modern poets who look for an almighty enlightened prince to establish universal peace and protect good letters. Liberty … *sub divo Augusto*.

Plutarch himself observed that Athens spent more on plays than on fighting for hegemony: the questioning is as old as Western theatre itself, so much so that the best Hellenists today still wonder why a city would pay so much money just to quarrel with its own values.[58] Democracy intensified rather than abated the ancient heroic emulation, Frédéric Picco notes, by guaranteeing the right of each party to an equal weight and value of speech in the law court.[59] Even Florence Dupont, who claims that the questions met by the poets were of aesthetic and ritual rather than of civic and historical nature, ends with the same focal point: the rulings of civic justice on crimes of blood.[60] The Elizabethans were no democrats, nor would they have severed aesthetic from ethical concerns. With these nuances, the conditions of what Vernant called 'the historical moment of tragedy' in Ancient Greece could apply equally well to Elizabethan England. The continuity with the present is seldom as manifest as it was during the Avignon festival of 1995, where Matthias Langhoff was presenting his *Gloucester Time-Matériau Shakespeare-Richard III*. When the news arrived in Avignon on 14 July that Srebrenica had fallen to the Serbs, Ariane Mnouchkine and Langhoff's actors launched a movement culminating with a hunger strike at the Cartoucherie, Mnouchkine's theatre. President Jacques Chirac visited them in August on his way to the international conference where he pleaded for a UN Rapid Reaction Force.[61] In discussing this unprecedented action of the theatre on the world stage, the drama critic of *Le Monde* evoked the origins of the theatre and its moral commitment to the duties of representation since Aeschylus's *Persians*: 'tell the truth under the guise of falsehood, prevent and heal the diseases of the community, raise each man to the dignity of speech'.[62] If it is seldom the case today, it definitely applied to Shakespeare's stage.

Elizabethan lawyers and playwrights are, like their classical forebears, beset with hopes and conflicting desires. They mostly agree on major political issues

---

56 See Dupont, *L'Insignifiance tragique*, chs 2 and 3.

57 Simon Goldhill, *Reading Greek Tragedy* (Cambridge: Cambridge University Press, 1986), p. 56, quoting Vernant.

58 'The Fame of the Athenians', 349a, Plutarch, *Moralia*, trans. by Babbitt, IV, p. 513. Pierre Vidal-Naquet, 'Le mythe à l'épreuve de la cité', in 'Les Tragiques grecs', ed. by Bernard Mezzadri, special issue, *Europe*, January–February 1999, 54.

59 Picco, *La Tragédie grecque*, pp. 15–16.

60 Dupont, *L'Insignifiance tragique*, pp. 15–16.

61 See 'Conflit Yougoslavie', the official reports and speeches of July/August 1995, <https://www.vie-publique.fr/ressources/mots-cles/conflit-yougoslavie?page=3>.

62 Olivier Schmitt, 'Treize personnages en quête d'histoire: L'objection de conscience culturelle', *Le Monde*, 3 January 1996.

— the model of good commonweal, ruled by law — and on a few ethical ones. They share civic concerns with the Puritan MPs, speak the same language, uphold the same vision of the body politic. They are also equally attuned to the reversals of fortune and the tragic falls that are daily events in court or government. Machiavelli's obsession to control the course of Fortune's wheel, and maintain the principality on an even keel, is largely reflected in their anxieties. Not Denmark but Ireland is 'out of joynt', 'out of Tune' in Cecil's worries when he complains of 'Oneyles boldnes'.[63] Their State is in turns represented as beehive, ship, garden, fortress, island entire of itself but exposed to envious enemies, subject to the stars above, to mutability, to the whims of an angry or jealous God. With the occasional exception of Shakespeare, they commune in a hatred of aliens, vagabonds, papists, usurers, and rebels. Like most Elizabethans they believe that human law, governed by reason, must conform with divine and natural law. Their model of government equates political order with divine order and hierarchy, degree.

These cast-iron certainties are put to the test on stage, where they begin slightly to shake: 'take away ordre from all thynges what shulde than remayne?', Elyot asked, answering with plain sincerity, nothing but chaos. In the mouth of Ulysses, the same pious speech raises suspicions. Only sycophants like he or Rosencrantz and Guildenstern fervently defend the current orthodoxy. Lord Keeper Bacon at the opening of Elizabeth's first Parliament observed that the corporal image of the body politic was old and common, but no less true. It is repeated with equal confidence throughout the reign,[64] or in a variant formula, 'lawe hath made this counsell the eyes, the eares, and the tongue of the prince and realme'.[65] Parliament preaches, and theatre records this ideal model as a norm held against its own representation of reality at the onset of civil wars caused by the 'viperous worm' of dissension.

The eulogy of Queen Elizabeth is an antiphon divided between her counsellors' praises and her own protests or lists of good deeds. Her many declarations of selfless motherly love clash brutally with her angered tones when, like Prospero at his fiercest, she reminds her Protestant Commons how they were delivered by her 'whilest yow were hanging on the bowgh redy to fall into the mudde, yea, to be drowned in the donge'.[66] She knows her duty; let them not forget theirs. In 1571, when fears of a papist conspiracy grow to extremes, Knollys reminds the Commons of her unwillingness to punish offences against the sovereign. Though the law be sharp, such is her mildness that if any have offended, 'for soe much as may concerne her person, surely hee thought it would not bee executed, and soe

63 William Cecil to Thomas Smith, 26 March 1566, British Library, Lansdowne MS 102, fol. 132^{v}, and 11 April, Harley MS 6990, fol. 72^{r}, in Alford, *The Early Elizabethan Polity*, p. 140.

64 Nicholas Bacon's speech enabling Gargraves, 25 January 1559, *Proceedings*, I, p. 40. Hartley, *Proceedings*, I, p. xxii, notes it appears *ad nauseam* in this collection.

65 Second Parliament, second session, 1566, *Proceedings*, I, p. 136.

66 Queen's answer to the Speaker, 28 January 1563, *Proceedings*, I, p. 95.

her clemency, tempered with authoritie, could never growe to crewelty'.[67] Rough papers for Henry V:

> Touching our person seek we no revenge,
> But we our kingdom's safety must so tender,
> Whose ruin you have sought, that to her laws
> We do deliver you.
>
> *(Henry V, II.ii.170–73)*

Elizabeth is as good as Prince Hal or Hamlet on the humility topos, claiming to be a poor rhetorician, ill at these numbers: 'For eloquence, yf you looke for any I shall deceave yow: for I am farre from hit.' All she will say is that if she had 'the most eloquent tongue in the world' and would express 'the care that I have allwaies had of your welfare, I shold not come nere yt'.[68] Yet she speaks most properly as a good sovereign should by dramatic standards, vowing to love her subjects, upholding religion and justice, laying her life for the good of her people, sleepless in her care of them, and acknowledging her weakness under the mantle of ceremony:

> I knowe the tytle of a kinge is a glorious tytle, but assuer your selfe that the shineinge glorye of princelye authoritye hath not soe dazeled the eyes of our understandinge but that we well knowe and remember that we alsoe are to yeild an accounte of our accions before the greate Judge.[69]

After this, her last speech to Parliament, the reporter notes that on Sunday, 13 December about noon, there was a great eclipse, which he illustrates by a drawing.[70]

In the reign of Elizabeth, Parliament increasingly becomes the lawyers' main stage. They are usually the ones who draw the bills, and they have learnt the rules of oratory at the Inns, where they have been trained to defend opposite sides with equal strength. Piqued by the scholarly dons who consider them barbarians, they also like to display their classical culture, dotting their speeches with literary or dramatic references. Some of these quotations are visibly references as common as today's popular TV shows, memorized in a pre-electronic collective cloud. Such displays, we saw, irritate the queen and her Lord Keeper who demand that they avoid any ostentation of wit. But then rhetoric is so ingrained in the orators' make-up that it follows them to the scaffold: the reporter of Norfolk's beheading observes that in his dying oration 'he him self devideth his speech into 3 partes'. Elizabeth quotes with irony their endless preachings: 'I knowe I am but mortall, which good lesson Mr Speaker in his third devision of a virtuous prince's

67 Debates around the bill for Preservation of the Queen's Majesty, *Proceedings*, I, p. 215.
68 Queen's closing speech, 15 March 1576, *Proceedings*, II, p. 474.
69 Tenth Parliament, 30 November 1601, *Proceedings*, III, pp. 413–14.
70 *Proceedings*, III, p. 477.

properties with reason late remembered'.[71] Oxymorons of the *crudelis misericordia* type, so well suited to the *pro et contra* frame, are great favourites. The much proclaimed ideal of simple, naked truth is seldom practised in political discourse.

Like the queen, many in Parliament find their fellow members too prosy, especially the reporters who have difficulty keeping up with their flows of eloquence. The author of the Anonymous Journal complains that 'Sir Frauncis Knolls made a longe needeles discourse concerninge the subsedy'. And again, that 'Doctor Lewen made a longe speach to little purpose'.[72] After Norton's proposal for an Act of Succession, Mr Cleere of Norfolk 'made hereuppon a staggeringe speech: his conclusion I did not conceive'. Speaker Yelverton of Gray's Inn discourses at length on the lawyer's lack of eloquence, of which he makes a virtue: 'I never enured my tongue with the sweete speache of perswadeing rhetoric; nor, never sought to attire my naked phrase with elegancie. The unpleasant, plaine, and painefull travell in the laws can hardly lend any leasure unto eloquence.' The Lower House is all at once a stage and a trial court, where he prefers to discover his defects now, 'be mine owne accuser, and bewraye mine owne wantes here, as it were in the theatre of the world'. Perhaps because he was hailed as a poet in a 'lewd pasquil' caricaturing the House, confirmed by his contributions to *Jocasta* and *The Misfortunes of Arthur*, Yelverton distances himself from Homer, and gives praise to the law makers, Solon, Lycurgus, Plato.[73] The xenophobic Sadler so wants to heighten the intensity of the late horrors in France that he repeats everything twice: 'the horrible and cruell murders and slaughters whiche have ben commytted and executed there upon those of the religion, the lyke whereof hathe never ben harde nor redde of, doth playnely shew and declare the dedely hatred and malice of the papistes ayenst the professours of Godde's ghospell and trew religion'. Norton, whose *Gorboduc* is recalled when they discuss succession, has a record of the longest speeches, but is no doubt given licence as reputedly a poet when he speaks 'in his accustomed manner of naturall eloquence'.[74]

Despite their inclination to verbosity and strict rhetorical protocols, many of these orators can coin a strong pithy phrase, a telling image, pungent invectives. Some of their best punchlines find their way to the Elizabethan dramatic repertory. Along with their turns of speech and commitment to the British common weal, Norton, Yelverton, Gascoigne passed on the iambic pentameter to the professional playwrights. These professionals reorganize and cut through the heavy rhetoric of political oratory, and make the lawyer-poets' stiff end-stopped pentameters run on over the edge of the line. Unlike parliamentarians, they must work within a time limit, set by the length of daylight. The dramatic dialogue trims

71 2 June 1572, *Proceedings*, I, pp. 332, 473.

72 April 1571, *Proceedings*, I, p. 202. 14 March 1593, *Proceedings*, III, p. 124.

73 1597, *Proceedings*, III, pp. 188, 197.

74 *Proceedings*, I, pp. 141–42, 213.

the unwieldy mass of oratory, creates perspectives, problematizes ideological statements, questions the moral attitudes preached by government officials or puritanical ministers, and confronts words with deeds.

The Poet as Legislator

> Say then to Caesar,
> Our ancestor was that Mulmutius which
> Ordain'd our laws, whose use the sword of Caesar
> Hath too much mangled, whose repair and franchise
> Shall, by the power we hold, be our good deed,
> Though Rome be therefore angry.
>
> *Cymbeline, III.i*

Elizabethan lawyers wrote, watched, and quoted plays: 'Elizabethan dramatists often used legal allusions in their plays, and some used them more frequently and more accurately than Shakespeare', whose legal knowledge could easily be acquired 'by common reading, conversation, and life experience in legal London'.[75] Not to mention his father's and his own lawsuits. Writing under the weight of ideology accumulated through centuries of discourse, Lodge, Marston, Massinger, Middleton, Ben Jonson depict weak or wicked characters who distort laws or prove unable to enforce them, but seldom question their validity. At their most critical, they work like Bacon to 'open the law upon doubts, and not to open doubts upon the law'.[76] Unlike fellow dramatists who speak for an ideal common law that they were taught to revere, Shakespeare shows at best mild reverence, and little taste for its quiddities.[77] Skinner has shown that he drew more on rhetorical sources than on legal texts, a fact often underestimated, which can lead to misinterpretations: thus, Skinner points out, it is not plain to a modern audience that Shylock alienates the court from the start because he speaks in scornful defiance of all the rules.[78]

Jurists still disagree as to whether Shakespeare had a legal training, or just lawyer friends who could correct any glaring mistakes, and possibly 'show him around the courts so he could soak up the atmosphere'.[79] The authors of *Shakespeare's Legal Language* express their view, 'derived from cumulative evidence, that on the contrary Shakespeare shows a quite precise and mainly serious interest in the capacity of legal language to convey matters of social, moral, and intellectual

---

75 Kornstein, *Kill All the Lawyers?*, pp. 232, xiii.
76 *Reading on the Statute of Uses*, in Bacon, *The Works*, VII, p. 396.
77 Clarkson and Warren compare the works of seventeen Elizabethan dramatists in *The Law of Property*.
78 Skinner, *Forensic Shakespeare*, pp. 142–48.
79 Kornstein, *Kill All the Lawyers?*, p. 236.

substance.'[80] If this is correct, his interest seems to have been less in law per se than in the dramatic potential of its protocols. Hamlet's charge on lawyers proves him well-versed in legal terminology, yet his creator did not feel bound by the exact legal meaning of a term if its metaphoric echoes could reverberate in the dramatic sphere. In Corrigan's opinion, the fact that Antonio will have 'in use' one half of Shylock's property won't mean much to a modern audience: 'The gist is clear enough: Antonio is winning, Shylock is losing.' But a casual playgoer of the 1590s 'would understand the lay law significance of the images presented', while the law would resonate brilliantly within the work for the few audience members who did fully appreciate the significance.[81] Caviary for the general, again. Similarly, the 'use of my house', however faint its link with the Statute of Uses, crystallizes in this one word the violent dispossessions of *King Lear*. Shakespeare's interest concentrates on the interaction of law and politics, in a shady area of decision where the playwright is the only legislator. His characters down to the fourth citizen in *Coriolanus* use the *pro et contra* mode of debate with admirable nuance: 'You have deserved nobly of your country, and you have not deserved nobly [...]. You have been a scourge to her enemies, you have been a rod to her friends; you have not indeed loved the common people.'

When tyranny is the playwright's theme, the first of its adjuncts is lawlessness. Tyranny is the only moral justification for civil disobedience, a principle rarely recommended, let alone put into practice by Tudor authors or lawyers. Seen through the works of modern historians and literary critics the Elizabethan mind appears filled with the horrors of medieval civil wars, yet strangely unaffected by the horrors of the Tudor reigns. Henry VIII's methods escape lightly in the dramatic production of the period. Through censorship, or because his victims supposedly died by due process of law? The play *Sir Thomas More* draws a hagiographic portrait of the martyred chancellor without voicing any complaint about the treatment dealt him.[82] Whatever the eponymous hero's virtues and talents, not a word of criticism is uttered against the king who sends him to the scaffold. Shakespeare's *Henry VIII* does not probe the royal character either, nor come anywhere nearer the State reason that will require the death of half the cast. Four trials of mostly innocent characters are staged in the gap between Elizabeth's joyful christening at the end of the play and the happy future promised to the survivors when she will inherit the throne, twenty-five years later, yet denunciations of tyranny remain untold.

Shakespeare's reflection on the violence of royal power follows an oblique course, first in his early histories, and grows to full maturity in the Roman plays. When all the protective ramparts of the State embodying Christian charity, justice, and military power fail successively, the first Henriad gives dramatic

80 Sokol and Sokol, *Shakespeare's Legal Language: A Dictionary*, p. 3.

81 Corrigan, *Playhouse Law*, pp. 191, 192.

82 See Jowett's Introduction to *Sir Thomas More* on the attribution to the notoriously anti-Catholic Anthony Munday as chief dramatist, and Shakespeare's part as 'Hand D'.

expression to the great dilemma of Christian monarchy: how to conciliate *Realpolitik* with the demands of the Gospel, how to govern efficiently while practising the virtues that spawned such disasters. In the decade following the execution of Mary, Queen of Scots, the second Henriad takes up the thread of the argument before the decisive murder of God's elect, the ensuing emergence of rival ambitions, and the reconstructed image of the Christian prince. Henry V, wise judge, son of the Church, victorious warrior, temporarily solves the dilemma: he puts to rest the monsters of the past by practising virtue in his private person, and strict execution of justice through the impersonal machinery of State, covering the division under a cloak of ceremony.

In the Roman plays, Shakespeare addresses more explicitly issues which had been forbidden or dealt with circumspectly in Parliament. *Julius Caesar* returns to the issue of political assassination with the murder of a charismatic leader, a king in all but name, who wants an heir, through questions that harrowed Elizabeth and her MPs when faced with demands for the Queen of Scots' execution, even with guarantees that it 'lawfully maie be done'. The displacement of the debate to pagan Rome emancipates it from the frame of theocentred monarchy, with deeply disturbing effects:[83] outside Christian law, there is no way of knowing before the deed if the killing of Caesar is right or wrong; all depends on its end result. 'Death or liberty', the conjurors vow, but their readiness to give up their life in the cause of freedom soon turns into a readiness to kill the source of oppression. Caesar's assassins claim they acted to save the republic, and offer this sacrifice like priests to the gods. Caesar's friends point them out as butchers to the fickle crowd. They win the debate, and the power to write the sequence of the story, several decades of civil war that will put a final end to the republican ideals. Young, cold, austere Octavius finally defeats Caesar's champion and the lascivious charms of the Nile in *Antony and Cleopatra*. According to Plutarch's *Lives*, the city torn between warring factions was crying out for an enlightened dictator. Augustus's imperial *pax romana* will inspire Friedrich II and a succession of medieval monarchs, while his befriending of poets will nourish the nostalgic dreams of Petrarch, Erasmus, and his friends in their search for an almighty father for their republic of good letters: a major paradox that humanists hope to solve by offering to advise rulers, even after Machiavelli has shown them the inside of a prince's mind. Chapter XVII of *Il Principe*, 'Cruelty and Mercifulness', discussing 'whether it is better to be loved than feared', concluded that since men love at their own will and fear at the will of the prince, 'a wise ruler should rely on what is under his own control, not under the control of others; he should contrive only to avoid incurring hatred'.[84] It will take the fall of Chancellor More to bring the lesson home.

---

83 Burrow, *Shakespeare and Classical Antiquity*, p. 214, has a different explanation: the apparent similarities between Holinshed's mixed constitution and Plutarch 'was probably why Shakespeare turned to Rome after he had completed his series of plays on Henry V'.

84 Machiavelli, *The Prince*, ed. by Skinner, p. 61.

The mobs who support Brutus, then Antony, and will eventually bring imperial rule upon themselves, are out in the streets again at the opening of *Coriolanus*, Shakespeare again working up against the flow of time. Heroic values have so lost their shine that today's audiences find it difficult to decide if the play must be read as a dirge for the hero, a manifesto against war, a plea for the scorned people, or an indictment of democracy. Plutarch situates his 'Life of Coriolanus' in 'that time, when the golden and unsoiled age remained yet whole in judgment at Rome'. Though he believes there was no other way but to empire, he regrets the days when the young republic was free from all corruption: 'It was but of late time, and long after this, that buying and selling fell out in election of officers, and that the voyces of the electours were bought for money.'[85]

No other play is more finely political, none has better claim to be a parliament of voices. For the first time in the Shakespeare canon, the people are made to speak distinctively as a body. It does not greatly matter that they are hardly less fickle and vile than their stage predecessors, that they first give their voices to Coriolanus, then take them back. They are manipulated by utterly despicable tribunes, and ready to murder the hero from the lowest motives. Nowhere else in the canon are their weaknesses so stringently denounced, their bad breath so fiercely rejected by a haughty nobility: the argument is not over the virtues of the people, but their exact place in the City. Coriolanus belongs with the heroic past of Rome, 'a thing | Made by some other deity than nature'. Nothing seems able to stop this war machine on its way to destruction: 'he moves like an engine, and the ground shrinks before his treading'. He single-handedly embodies Rome's virile virtues against a whole population of lesser stature, in the first class conflict of Roman history. Ironically enough, only his mother has a share of this virility that will be the death of him. His rejection of the populace is so radical that it excludes any form of commerce: 'he seeks their hate with greater devotion than they can render it him'. The symbolic price the people want for their voice, 'to ask it kindly', is unacceptable, for it would be owning himself of a kind with them. Do they want some recognition as individuals? — 'He's to make his requests by particulars; wherein every one of us has a single honour'. He calls them 'the beast | With many heads'. Do they weigh their responsibilities with great seriousness in wanting to show gratitude? His scorn turns them into an anonymous pack, howling to death in one voice: '*All*. Down with him, down with him!'

'So if he tell us his noble deeds, we must also tell him our noble acceptance of them', the Third Citizen offers. By allowing them moments of dignity, Shakespeare for once tones down his source's hostility to the vulgar. North, like a majority of Elizabethan writers, detests ochlocracy, and takes sides with the Patricians in his reinterpretation of Plutarch, through marginal notes like 'Coriolanus oration against the insolencie of the people', stressing 'Coriolanus noble endevour', where

85 Plutarch, *Lives*, trans. by North, II, pp. 159, 158.

Plutarch finds him 'chollericke and impacient', 'churlishe, uncivill'.[86] On stage, this 'incivility' is the key to his alienation in the debate on what makes the City: in his own eyes he is Rome, whose martial foundation can be read in the scars of his body. 'I banish you', he shouts, when the tribunes insist that 'the people are the city' and condemn him to exile. Menenius in pleading his cause only brings out the antinomy: 'when he speaks not like a citizen, | You find him like a soldier.'

The old fable of the stomach, identified with *fiscus*, is evoked in many a speech requesting subsidy from the Elizabethan Commons. In 1585, MP Digges had complained that the commonwealth was now a monstrous belly with starving limbs: London, the belly, or head of England, must let the hands and legs live by it. Twelve years later, Bacon sounds closer to Menenius in presenting an act 'which tendes to the comfforte of the stomacke of this realme, I meane the marchant, which yf it quayle or ffale into a consumption, the State cannot choose but shortlye be sicke of that disease'.[87] Shakespeare turns the commonplace into a superb piece of cynicism, when the starving poor request a share of the corn that fattens the Patrician belly. Yet the strength of the image, 'my incorporate friends', binds them together more surely than material considerations. Where they demand 'the superfluity' of the corn kept in store to relieve their misery, Coriolanus cruelly offers to clean up 'our musty superfluity' by sending them to the wars. In his view, their reluctance to fight for their city makes them ineligible to the title of 'citizen'. In North's Plutarch, he is certain that 'the prowde attempt of the communaltie, was to abolish lawe, and to bring all to confusion'. Amyot's 'populaires harangueurs', popular orators, are converted by North into 'two seditious tribunes'.[88] The stage Coriolanus feels it would be sheer madness to give the mob a role in political decisions, a view conforming to North's, who had probably not read, certainly did not endorse, Machiavelli's brilliant analysis of the Roman policy in the *Discorsi*. John Wolfe had printed Italian editions of *Il Principe* and the *Discorsi* in 1584, allegedly published in Palermo, while copies of manuscript translations circulated at the time in London.[89]

Though hardly a democrat, Machiavelli defends a thesis wholly at odds with his time's doxa: the quarrels between the nobility and the plebs, which Plutarch for one thought one of the main causes of the republic's decline, was to the Florentine 'the primary cause of Rome's retaining her freedom', for 'all legislation favourable to liberty is brought about by a clash between them'; good laws proceeded from those tumults which many so inconsiderately condemn. 'Hence, if tumults led to the creation of the tribunes, tumults deserve the highest praise.' Instead of suppressing all threats of popular unrest, a little disorder must be

86 On Shakespeare's variations from both North and Plutarch, see Goy-Blanquet, 'La Solitude de Coriolan'.

87 *Proceedings*, II, p. 112. December 1597, *Proceedings*, III, p. 439.

88 Plutarch, *Lives*, II, pp. 148, 157.

89 See Roe, *Shakespeare and Machiavelli*. Napoleone Orsini, 'Elizabethan Manuscript Translations of Machiavelli's *Prince*', *Journal of the Warburg Institute*, 1.2 (1937), 166–69.

tolerated as a necessary inconvenience, for it is the best safeguard of liberties. The people are the strong arm of a State, their only strength the fact that they are needed to fight wars. Force them into utter submission, and you will destroy their combativity: 'every city should provide ways and means whereby the ambitions of the populace may find an outlet, especially a city which proposes to avail itself of the populace in important undertakings'.[90] A republic needs 'some institution whereby the changeful humours which agitate it are afforded a proper outlet by way of the laws.' The people need judges before whom to indict the great. A point well made in the case of Coriolanus, against whom the popular indignation was so fierce that 'he would have been killed in the tumult if the tribunes had not cited him to appear in his own defence'. Such an institution provides 'an outlet for the malignant humours to which men are prone'. If any citizen feels there is a remedy at home against injustice, he will not feel tempted to call in outside forces from abroad.[91] All leaders of mutinies in Shakespeare's histories enter with invading troupes of foreigners, the first anxiety of Elizabethan England.

As Richard Marienstras points out, the central issue of the play is the institution of the tribunate, in a new definition of the civic body and the organs that compose it.[92] *Coriolanus*, written under James I, coincides with a virulent debate of 1606 in Commons on democratic representation, when minister Robert Cecil accused John Hare, MP for Horsham, of behaving like a 'Tribune of the people', while Edwin Sandys was known as 'the old Tribune of the House'.[93] The struggle that is building up through political and social conflicts opposes the monarch to his people, 'in other words to Parliament'. Marienstras pinpoints the main issue of the quarrel, the naturalization of the Scots, to which the Commons were radically opposed, fearing it would make them equal with the English nobility. What is at stake is the foundation of the body politic, its composition, and its maintenance.[94] There is little to choose in the play between the senators who defend the rich and the tribunes who use the plebeians to serve their ends, yet all the characters strike a true note at some point, weaving a complex network of political attitudes. Only Coriolanus's integrity stands intact. He is archaic, yet admirable in his refusal to compromise, his strict adherence to the ideal of *virtus*. When his vengeful spirit relents, 'the skies do ope': he acknowledges nature, and bows to the Roman *ethos*, Marienstras observes, thus permitting the safety of Rome. Neither party is victorious. At the price of the hero's death which is his greatest victory, over himself, all find a voice and a place at the end in reunited Rome.

Shakespeare's plays generally insist that no one, king included, is above the law, that those who ignore it never long enjoy the benefits of their trespasses. But he repeatedly introduces unknown or antiquated life-threatening laws even in his

---

90 Machiavelli, *The Discourses*, ed. by Crick, trans. by Walker, Book I.4, pp. 113–15.
91 Machiavelli, *The Discourses*, Book I.7, pp. 124–25, 127.
92 Marienstras, 'Notice de *Coriolan*', pp. 1553–99.
93 On the parallel with the tribunes of *Coriolanus*, see Kernan, *Shakespeare, the King's Playwright*, p. 143.
94 Marienstras, 'Autour de Coriolan', in *Shakespeare et le désordre du monde*, pp. 116–17.

comedies, new statutes that might become part of a new social reality, as they so often did under the Tudor reigns. Whatever the legal system staged, fancy or real, the judicial authority is vested in a princely figure who embodies the ruthlessness of the law. Henry V, Cymbeline, the Dukes of Ephesus, Athens, Venice, Illyria, or Vienna, all declare themselves bound by the law of the country: they must execute the law and those who fall under its sanction indiscriminately, be they confirmed traitors, criminals, or innocent victims of circumstance. All invoke a higher reason that 'Excludes all pity from our threat'ning looks.' Princes are not at liberty to prove merciful, Duke Solinus declares. They 'may pity, though not pardon':

> Now, trust me, were it not against our laws,
> Against my crown, my oath, my dignity,
> Which princes, would they, may not disannul,
> My soul would sue as advocate for thee.
>
> (*Comedy of Errors*, I.i.141–44)

When Solinus feels it 'to our honour's great disparagement' to help an innocent man escape death, he sounds uncannily close to Clarence's murderer, whose conscience makes him a coward: 'it is turn'd out of all towns and cities for a dangerous thing; and every man that means to live well, endeavours to trust to himself, and live without it.' And yet, in early modern England, this harsh rigour of the law could be tempered at local government level, and cases settled out of court. The duties of justices of the peace were both to keep the peace by preventive measures and to punish breaches. Without going to such preventive extremes as Edward Hall, justices had the power to 'bind' a possible lawbreaker by some equivalent of the modern bail. William Lambarde for one, discussing their office in *Eirenarcha*, explains that the conservation of peace is as important as the punishment of offenders. Yet he deplores that their creation by assignment of the king took the role of community peace-keeping away from the common people.[95] The laymen still had a significant say in judicial matters when acting as local officials or jurors.

Virginia Lee Strain detects an 'Assize-like structure' in *Measure for Measure*, which 'frames a process of local intelligence-gathering and public revelation that was specifically associated with Assize judges'. The interventions of Duke Vincentio and the Provost in the lives of subjects advance the reformation of local justice, whereas justice in *The Winter's Tale* 'is restored through the more careful observance of the boundaries between legal and political power'.[96] In his comic plots involving 'snaring statutes', she points out, Shakespeare turns the focus from the statute itself 'to the need for regulation within legal practice or for discretion in those who invoke or administer the law'. In his first device for the *Gesta Grayorum*, Francis Bacon 'links the Queen's virtue as a sovereign to the

95 Lambarde, *Eirenarcha*, ch. 5.
96 Strain, *Legal Reform in English Renaissance Literature*, p. 24, and chs 4, 5.

protection she provided subjects from excessive penalties and snaring statutes'.[97] Carolyn Sale enrols Arendt, Agamben, and Habermas to denounce the kind of judgement exercised in Vienna under 'the authorizing figure of force who can ensure its execution'. It is precisely of the kind approved by James I, based on a 'self-evident letter that needs no interpreter and no exercise of reason'. The citizens at the constitutional threshold of the city gates in Act V 'are given no formal opportunity by the Duke to say anything at all', but the audience of the play, witnessing the capriciousness of Vincentio's judgements, may well experience 'precisely what is suppressed in the dramatic fiction, the communicative power of citizens as a group', and wish to determine the legal order by which they live.

When she pleads for Angelo, therefore, Isabella's predicament is 'the predicament of the English people in relation to a sovereign antagonistic to their common law'.[98] But then isn't Angelo far more antagonistic to any kind of law than Vincentio? Do we really 'know' that he is innocent of a crime, as Strain would have us, when he did order Claudio's death? In the eyes of the Catholic Church, he would be guilty as charged, since Claudio escaped through no will of his. And why should King James be denied the right to judge by himself, like a true Protestant? Thanks to the Duke's preventive measures, Strain concedes, no crime is committed in *Measure for Measure*, and the concluding judgement allows all the culprits space for reform: 'The further away Vienna moves from the letter of the law, the closer it gets to early modern English legal culture.'[99] Still, even if, as she claims, such practices were extolled in public opinion as 'giving voice to the common law tradition', most common lawyers preferred the impersonal justice of a trial to the discretionary powers of local magistrates and equity courts (see above, 'A Display of Legalism' in Chapter 4).

Cymbeline again protests he cannot be merciful:

> I am sorry for thee:
> By thine own tongue thou art condemn'd, and must
> Endure our law: thou'rt dead.
>
> (*Cymbeline*, V.v.297–99)

Dead unless he resort to the prerogative so severely condemned by lawyers in Parliament. He and Duke Vincentio will do so in the end, but not before long intricate denouements have tutored the characters through the tragic potentials of each bend on the way to appeasement, when their prerogative to make all well

97 Strain, *Legal Reform in English Renaissance Literature*, pp. 70, 82.

98 Carolyn Sale, '*Measure for Measure* and the "Open Court" of the Theatre', in Curran, ed., *Shakespeare and Judgment*, pp. 125, 128, 129, 132. In the essay following hers, 'The Laws of *Measure for Measure*', Paul Yachnin confirms that by the end of the play, 'there is no source of authority or value outside ourselves to which we could surrender the task of judging' (p. 150).

99 Strain, 'Preventive Justice in *Measure for Measure*', in Curran, ed., *Shakespeare and Judgment*, pp. 30, 33, 37.

offers a welcome relief. Prospero the all-powerful justiciar uses violent weapons to create the fictitious harmony of a brave new world offered as a wedding present to his daughter Miranda. Up to the end of his career, 'the poet invites reconciliation, demands it almost, through the voice of Prospero, because we must live together, though life together is at a price'.[100]

More profoundly still than *The Tempest*, *Cymbeline* gives the sum of Shakespeare's humanist philosophy, with a denouement that rehearses all the tragic possibilities of earlier plays before it restores lost children to their parents and reunites broken couples. When Imogen wakes up near a corpse dressed in her husband's clothes, instead of doing a Juliet, Thisbe, or Cleopatra, she moves on to live and bring his murderer to justice. The worst villains of the play, Cymbeline's Queen and her uncouth son Cloten, happen to be the staunchest supporters of British independence and pig-headedness. Under their sway, Cymbeline is determined to revive ancient British laws, but his plan to repair the laws that 'our ancestor' Mulmutius had ordained is a lost cause. Their empty romantic dreams, Cloten's claim that 'Britain's a world by itself', the Queen's argument for 'the natural bravery of your isle' are obliquely answered two hundred lines later by Cymbeline's lost sons; to Belarius who presents them with an idealized view of their rustic world they object that it is 'a cell of ignorance', prison, pinching cave: 'We have seen nothing; | We are beastly'. The fact that Guiderius goes disguised under the name 'Polydore', its only occurrence in the canon, may be the payment of a personal debt to the first competent historian Shakespeare read, Polydore Vergil. The boys have no time for pastoral delights or archaic nostalgias: where Belarius sounds like Duke Senior in the forest of Arden, they do not wish to live happy secluded lives away from court; they are bored in their low-roofed cave and want action. With their support, Cymbeline rejects insularity and offers a civilized way out of the narrow lane where Posthumus Leonatus and his Welsh brothers have won the day, by freely paying tribute to the larger model of independence, Roman law and continental culture.[101]

---

100 Marienstras, *Shakespeare et le désordre du monde*, p. 120.
101 Marcus, *Puzzling Shakespeare*, pp. 124–25. Cormack, *A Power to Do Justice*, pp. 243–53.

'This Magnificent Theatre of Heaven and Earth'

> As you from crimes would pardon'd be,
> Let your indulgence set me free.
>
> *The Tempest*, V.i

Interaction seems a feeble word for the interweaving of drama, law, and politics in the tapestry of public discourse. Its design shows a multicultural history, dotted with tragic or hagiographic biographies at points when a human life conflates collective memory and feelings with personal destiny. This national history, long fed by communication with the rest of Europe, is loaded with old grievances: exchanges, emulation, and external sources are countered by a strong nationalistic bid for independent self-fashioning, for native home-made law and literature. A group of tutelary ghosts sits watching debates in Parliament: Lucius and Eleutherius, Edward the Confessor, Bracton, Chaucer, the authors of Magna Carta. Old myths of mixed polity and good counsel are constantly revived and revised to suit the bill discussed, new ones are forged to establish the immemorial origin of common law, the independent monarchy of England, the supremacy of Parliament. Old scarecrows — the divisions of York and Lancaster, of Ferrex and Porrex, King John's losing duel with popery — still have life in them but are held at bay by a phoenix, *rara avis etc.*, Queen Elizabeth.

Where Plato asserted that lawyers could emulate playwrights, we saw above, parliamentarians like William Hakewell of Lincoln's Inn present themselves as actors who play a variety of parts: 'We must laye downe the respectes of our owne [persons], and put on others' and their affections ffor whome wee speake, ffor they speake by us.' Indeed, he explains, 'Yf the matter which is spoken of touche the poore, then thincke me a poore man he that speakes; sometymes, he must be a lawyer, sometymes a paynter, sometymes a marchante, some tymes a meane artifycer.'[1] The chronicler John Hooker, like many of his contemporaries, visualizes Parliament as a stage: he compares the Lower House to a theatre, 'having foure rowes of seates one aboove an other round about the same',[2] a proposition Shakespeare would reverse by making the stage a Parliament. William Empson

1 *Proceedings*, III, p. 433.
2 Snow, *Parliament in Elizabethan England*, p. 163.

alluded to 'that hint of Parliament which is the dignity of the theatre', suggesting their common representative function.[3] It is unlikely that budding poets and playwrights, let alone a fifteen-year-old Shakespeare, sneaked into Commons to hear their speeches, or that they were invited in to read the Lord Keeper's walls in Gorhambury. What theatre exactly Hooker had in mind then, years before Burbage's was built, remains an enigma, but Lower House and Globe were equally aware of their representative function.

Parliament stands for the whole nation before king and government. The Commons' claim to represent the multitude is echoed in the theatre. Indeed, the Chorus of *Henry V*, telling audiences they must 'Into a thousand parts divide one man', seems to echo the Speaker's oration at the closing of the 1593 Parliament.[4] Coke apologizes for repeating what has been often said, but never too often: 'this sweet Councell of ours I would compare unto that sweete commonwealth of the little bees'. Quoting Virgil's first *Eclogue*, he develops the image of the well-ordered beehive that will eulogize Henry V's rule of iron: 'The litle bees have but one governor whom they all serve, he is their Kinge'. His warning could also pass for a Shakespearean line: 'But where the bee sucketh honey thence the spyder also draweth poyson'; such venomous men must be expelled like drones from the hive.[5] The Elizabethan theatre, this popular Parliament, has a much larger social spectrum than the elected one: Holinshed's report on Wat Tyler, 'that within foure daies all the lawes of England should come foorth of his mouth', reappears in Dick the Butcher's suggestion to Cade, 'that the laws of England may come out of your mouth' and Cade's hubristic claim.[6] 'Whie, Parleamente matters are ordinarye talke in the streetes', Robert Cecil will complain in the midst of the 1601 debate on subsidy.[7]

As the traditional petitions for free speech grow more precise with each session, the Elizabethan Parliament vibrates with the claims of orators who insist they do not speak as private men 'but to supply the roome, person and place of a multitude especially chosen': they represent the commonalty of the realm, their common wealth of ideas, beliefs, proverbs, phrases, which the theatre will give them back in a renewed mode of argumentation.[8] In speech after speech, pamphlet, sermon, or dialogue throughout the Tudor reigns, thoughts are permeated by a dramatic vision of the world, of life as a constant *agon*. The tensions of man's infinite appetites, imagination, intellectual faculties opposed to the brevity of his life and his weak body find their best expression in the old metaphor of *theatrum mundi*, his acts being seven ages. Even Calvin, notoriously not a friend of the stage,

---

3 William Empson, *Some Versions of Pastoral* [1935] (New York: New Directions, 1974), p. 198.

4 Baldo, '"Into a thousand parts"', convincingly argues that Shakespeare borrowed from and complicated a parliamentary model when aiming to represent the nation in *Henry V*.

5 Anonymous Journal, 10 April 1593, *Proceedings*, III, p. 171.

6 *Holinshed's Chronicles*, II, p. 740. *Jack Straw*, l. 519. 2 *Henry VI*, IV.ii.173, IV.vii.5–6, 12–13.

7 *Proceedings*, III, p. 398.

8 *Proceedings*, I, p. 238. Neale, *Elizabeth I and her Parliaments*, I, pp. 302–05.

depicts the Creation as 'this magnificent theatre of heaven and earth replenished with numberless wonders, the wise contemplation of which should have enabled us to know God'.[9] But the key lesson of the early modern universe, punctured by spectacular reversals and tragic falls, is mutability. All must remember 'the counsail of the popyngay, saiyng: when thou thynkest thy self in courte moste surest, then is it high tyme to get thee home to rest'.[10]

English monarchs know like Prince Hamlet that they stand exposed as on a stage, a most unstable one, closer to More's scaffold than to Henry VIII's canopied throne of majesty. Even the greatest king is 'but a walking shadow | That struts and frets his hour upon the stage, | And then is heard no more'. Elizabeth's answer to the petition against Mary Stuart, 'wee princes I tell you are set on stages, in the sight and veiw of al the worlde', will be repeated by Mary's son: 'Kings being publike persons, by reason of their office and authority, are as it were set (as it was said of old) vpon a publike stage, in the sight of all the people.'[11] Intriguingly enough, James originally used the word 'skaffold', which was altered to 'stage' in the second edition of *Basilikon Doron*.[12] Could he have shied at the memory of Mary's execution, or even feared for his son's future? 'Your life is nothing but a continual acting upon a stage', the Statesman is reminded in Bacon's device for Essex. 'But I will leave you to the scorn of that mistress, whom you undertake to govern; that is, to fortune'.[13]

A similar sense of drama highlights all the State trials of the century, the ritual disrobing of Archbishop Cranmer, the setting of the stage with costumes, cues, and props for public disputations. Like fair trial by jury, controversies are felt a necessary item of equitable treatment, one ostentatiously offered by Queen Mary to Jane Grey, Cranmer, Ridley, Latimer, by Queen Elizabeth to her Catholic bishops or to Edmund Campion. That the conclusion of State trials is prewritten, as in a play, raises very few protests. Even the victims of royal tyranny agree to play their part in a masquerade of repentance on the scaffold: Henry VIII's wives and councillors die with apologies, proclaiming their faithful love to the king. At a deeper level, as in today's measures against terrorism, a majority will agree with Henry V that 'we our kingdom's safety must so tender' that even a parody of law will serve.

Freedom of speech on stage is kept under control of censorship, as the authors of *Sir Thomas More* discover when they show riots against foreigners, or as Ben Jonson experiences when he dares represent the queen in *Every Man Out of his Humour*. In Commons, though limited by various factors, from the official orders of restraint to the members' own inhibitions, the demands for freedom

9 Calvin, *Institutes*, 1:93. See Heller, *Penitent Brothellers*, pp. 17–19, and above, 'Protestant Playwrights' in Chapter 7.

10 *Hall's Chronicle*, p. 209.

11 Elizabeth, *Proceedings*, II, p. 270. James, 'To the Reader', in *Basilikon Doron*, p. 5.

12 On this change, see Stephen Orgel, 'Making Greatness Familiar', *Genre*, 15 (1982), 45–47.

13 Bacon, *Essex's Device* (1595), in *The Works*, ed. by Spedding and others, VI, p. 31.

of speech persistently oppose and will eventually defeat royal supremacy. When the Catholic Francis Alford of the Inner Temple 'craveth fredome of speech without murmoringes or other kinde of interruption, and desireth that every man maie speake his conscience', a great discussion ensues, in which 'divers men spake diversly, some for the libertie of the House in free speech, some that the libertie must be used in reverent and seemly sort'.[14] Homilies hammer the lessons of unquestioning obedience, quite at odds with the Protestant will of self-government. In Edward Hall's eyes, the Prince could do no wrong: should he happen to transgress, it could only be by God's mysterious design, to punish his guilty people. When Job Throckmorton was rebuked by the vice chamberlain for speaking sharply of princes in his speech on Bill and Book, the reporter noted: 'The reverence to princes is dew to God. That wee are bownd t'obay good princes. God doth correct by ill princes. That wee should use great regard of princes in free speache', even regarding the King of France![15] How far England today has travelled from such reverence could be measured when leaks of a correspondence from former Prince Charles to several ministers on government policy 'provoked a backlash among politicians furious that an unelected royal was meddling in the affairs of democratic government'. Once he was King Charles III, the PM Liz Truss firmly 'objected' to his attending the climate summit, despite his long-term interest in environment, and he bowed to her wishes.[16]

In less than a century, the Elizabethan theatre experienced a full revolution, from its birth as mouthpiece of law students to its divorce from law and execution by lawyers in Parliament. Early Calvinists in England, we saw, showed no compunction about plays and players: Bale, Udall, Baldwin, Ferrers were all Protestants of Puritan tendencies. The tradition of anti-papist plays, which French kings had soon repressed, was superseded in England by 'frivolous' ungodly ones, while public opinion bracketed together 'printers, players, preachers' in one form of oratory against the pope. It cannot be wholly accident if the public theatre begins to flourish at the precise moment when debates on free speech, religion, and government lose their edge, while its decline coincides with Donne's golden sermons, and its closure when Parliament takes the lead of the country. From the lawgivers' standpoint, the Elizabethan theatre must appear a parenthesis in the English drama of law, a new 'historical moment' of tragedy. Protestant preachers and polemicists who had opened the new theatrical age were overtaken by professional writers when theatre became a commercial enterprise, a major factor in the evolution of drama. It was no longer, at least not primarily, a medium for the playwrights' religious or political creeds, but a way to make a living: hardly a

14 Anonymous Journal, 1572, *Proceedings*, I, p. 326.

15 Anonymous Journal, 26 February 1587, *Proceedings*, II, p. 390.

16 Rob Evans and Robert Booth, 'Prince Charles Faces Fresh Meddling Claim over Letters to Ministers', *The Guardian*, 16 December 2009. According to the *Sunday Times*, 1 October 2022, Liz Truss had 'ordered' King Charles to stay away from Cop27, a decision 'likely to fuel tensions between the new prime minister and the new monarch'.

legitimate one in men's eyes, since minstrels were little better than vagrants, at best servants tolerated for the entertainment of an idle nobility and court. Like the Tudors themselves, it was but an interlude which survived, maintained artificially by Stuart doctoring, until law recovered its main stage, the parliamentary arena, and shut down its parroty rival. The Civil War closed the parenthesis. Shakespeare's practical lessons in taming a shrew, the shrew's husband, their heavy fathers, and all Puritanical masters had gone unheeded.

Why theatre happened, and why it happened then in England under a form unique in Europe, we more or less know. The Reformation in suppressing the performance of medieval religious cycles had opened a gap which the first playwrights invested with biblical plays or histories borrowed from the national chronicles. The dramatists, who were brought up on the same classics as the lawyers, added to the common pool large readings from those contemporary foreign books that parliamentarians tried to ban. But Sidney's circle failed to impose continental norms on the young Elizabethan theatre, which developed conventions and a theatrical structure of its own. Its self-fashioning entailed a great deal of chauvinism. Indeed Shakespeare, for all his mockeries of snobbish travellers and French ridicules, is remarkably restrained compared with the furious onslaughts of Ascham, Greene, Marlowe, of stern lawyers like Hall, Gascoigne, Stubbs, or like Sadler who warns his fellow MPs that the nature of English men has always detested the regiment of strangers.

The Elizabethan doxa is unashamedly xenophobic, reaching heights of hysteria when it comes to the queen's possible succession by a foreigner, threats of invasion, fifth columnists. Three successive waves of xenophobia coalesce under the Tudors, gathering the old Anglo-Saxon shreds of the Norman Conquest, the poems of scorn of the Hundred Years' War, and the Reformation hatred of the 'Popish league' into a fierce rejection of all things foreign. Religious and legal fanatics in Parliament largely agreed that guilt begins with the intention. A majority accepted the principle of retroactive justice, convinced that sin pre-exists its manifestations. Many believed like Norton that plotting treason begins long before the act itself and justifies pre-emptive strikes.[17] But on stage Brutus's delicate conscience makes him doubt he has a right to kill the serpent's egg before Caesar has committed any act of tyranny. Hamlet does not feel entitled to kill his father's murderer without any clear proof he is guilty. The once-cynical Bastard of *King John* rejects the ruses of commodity.

When MP lawyers forcefully demand innocent heads to ensure safety, in all matters of justice and equity Shakespeare has perfect pitch, rethinking, modulating, and humanizing the letter of the law. In answer to Portia's speech on justice and mercy, the ruthless Jew speaks for an equally ruthless law, yet has some of the most moving lines on common humanity in the whole repertory. When Duke Vincentio confesses that he has been too slack in exercising his

---

17 April 1571, *Proceedings*, I, p. 214.

authority, that Claudio's restraint comes 'from too much liberty', he shares a concern often expressed in Commons that laws are useless if unenforced. Yet through the trials of *Measure for Measure*, the court of the elusive Duke learns the value of forgiveness, moving from a state of tolerance condemned as sinful laxity to an understanding of its true worth, when Isabella agrees to plead for the life of her wrongdoer instead of demanding revenge. Here, Jessica Apolloni reminds us in her review of its Italian source and judicial structure, Shakespeare takes his inspiration from Cinthio's *Ecatommiti*, while Duke Vincentio has a touch of the Machiavellian Prince, leaving unpopular measures to a delegate. In *Measure for Measure*, she argues, 'Shakespeare uses the apparatus of foreign Italian jurisprudence to expose the gap between communal and state justice in English legal experience', when 'the centralization of English authority made officials increasingly distant from community concerns'.[18] Whether or not Shakespeare needed Italian legal concepts to make this point, he thoroughly alters Cinthio's version by making Isabella, unlike Epitia, a wholly disinterested and magnanimous pleader. At a much higher level of debate, her plea, when she remonstrates to the Duke that thoughts, intents, are not actual crimes, goes against the grain of *ex officio* proceedings and bloody questions. She seems to anticipate King James's order of 14 July 1616 which names Mercy and Justice as 'the true Supporters of our Royal Throne'.[19]

The last plays offer reconciliation, at a price. In *Cymbeline*, it can only take place after an excruciating review of all its potentially violent endings, while Hermione's silence at the end of *The Winter's Tale* has much exercised the critics' perspicacity: Does she forgive Leontes as her embrace suggests, or does she pause as she recollects the victims of his murderous will? Can she forgive him for crimes against others than herself? Lupton asks, discussing Arendt's and Auden's opposite notions of forgiveness. In place of Hermione's speech, 'Shakespeare gives us her silence, an active silence or leeway that affords a range of interpretations to actors, directors and audiences, as well as readers and critics'.[20] To Curran, Prospero's epilogue in *The Tempest* establishes 'a community of judgment founded on shared responsibility and the collective freedom to craft a world'.[21] Even if Shakespeare knew small *jus* and less law, his plays' invitations to share his innate sense of justice and their appeals to the community's capacity of judgement are England's best claim to the title of law-abiding country.

Coda: When the Serious Organised Crime and Police Act of 2005 banned unauthorized demonstrations within a mile of Westminster, ancient themes resurfaced in the newspapers: 'In a thousand tiny — and not so tiny — cuts Labour threatens

18 Apolloni, 'Local Communities and Central Power', pp. 125–26. Machiavelli, *The Prince*, ch. 7.

19 See Gary Watt's view that Shakespeare may have influenced the language and imagery of the royal order, *Equity Stirring*, pp. 72–76, and the chapter on 'Shakespeare's Equity', pp. 195–225.

20 Lupton, 'Judging Forgiveness', p. 651.

21 Curran, 'Prospero's Plea', p. 168.

our rights and freedoms, the rule of law and the sovereignty of Parliament.'[22] The then prime minister, Tony Blair, read in his critics' attitude to liberty 'a refusal to understand the modern world'. Court processes were now inadequate, he argued: 'The question is not one of individual liberty versus the state but of which approach best guarantees most liberty for the largest number of people.'[23]

As I reached the end of these pages, the theatres were again closed by a plague pandemic, and the age-old slogan 'death or liberty' took on a renewed tragic note. Ricœur's 'primary condition of living together' has never been under such threat, nor the price of liberty ever reached such heights. On All Souls Day 2020, as the number of deaths around the world totals 1,234,087, 'Latest coronavirus lockdowns spark protests across Europe', *The Guardian* reports: 'We are here and we are loud because we are being robbed of our freedom', marchers were chanting in Brussels. The case altered to 'Death and Liberty' by antivax supporters, it rang like an ominous dirge at the wounded centre of Europe.[24] Two years later the tragic slogan 'death or liberty' found a new dimension in Ukraine, alternating atrocious scenes of destruction with wishfully prescriptive statements that 'Putin's war has reinvigorated the west's defence of liberty. That unity must not crack now'.[25]

22 Henry Porter, 'Only a Constitution Can Save Us from this Abuse of Power', *The Observer*, April 2, 2006.

23 Blair, 'I don't destroy liberties, I protect them': 'Latest Coronavirus', *The Observer*, February 26, 2006.

24 John Henley, 'Putin's War', *The Guardian*, 2 November 2020.

25 Andrew Rawnsley, *The Observer*, 12 February 2023.

Select Bibliography

Primary Sources

Abélard, Pierre, *Collationes (or Dialogus inter Philosophum, Iudaeum, et Christianum, I and II)*, trans. by John Marenbon (Oxford: Oxford University Press, 2001)

———, *Conférences. Dialogue d'un philosophe avec un juif et un chrétien. Connais-toi toi-même. Éthique*, ed. and trans. by Maurice Gandillac (Paris: Éditions du Cerf, 1993)

Acts and Ordinances of the Interregnum, 1642–1660, ed. by Charles H. Firth and Robert S. Rait (London: HMSO, 1911)

Acts of the Privy Council of England, ed. by John Roche Dasent (London: HMSO, 1890–1907)

Adam of Usk, *The Chronicle of Adam Usk, 1377–1421*, ed. by Christopher Given-Wilson (Oxford: Oxford University Press, 1997)

Allen, William, *An Admonition to the nobility and people of England and Ireland* [Antwerp: A. Conníncx, 1588] (New York: Scolar Press, 1971)

———, *A briefe Historie of the Martyrdom of* XII *reverend priests* [1582] (London: Burns & Oates, 1908)

———, *Letters and Memorials of Cardinal Allen*, ed. by Thomas F. Knox (London: David Nutt, 1882)

———, *Letters of William Allen and Richard Barret, 1572–1598*, ed. by P. Renold (London: Catholic Record Society, 1967)

———, *A True, Sincere, and Modest Defense of English Catholics*, in *The Execution of Justice*, ed. by Robert M. Kingdon (Ithaca, NY: Cornell University Press, 1965)

Ancient Laws and Institutes of England, ed. and trans. by Benjamin Thorpe (London: Eyre and Spottiswoode, 1840)

Anselm of Canterbury, *The Major Works*, ed. by Brian Davies and Gillian R. Evans (Oxford: Oxford University Press, 1998)

Aristotle, *The Nichomachean Ethics*, trans. by David Ross (Oxford: Oxford University Press, 2009)

———, *On the Generation of Animals*, trans. by Arthur Platt (Whitefish, MT: Kessinger Publishing, 2004)

———, *Parva Naturalia*, trans. by J. I. Beare and G. R. T. Ross, *The Works of Aristotle*, vol. III, ed. by W. D. Ross (Oxford: Clarendon Press, 1908)

Ascham, Roger, *English Works*, ed. by William A. Wright (Cambridge: Cambridge University Press, 2012)

———, *The Scholemaster* [1570] (New York: Da Capo Press, 1968)

Augustine, *The City of God*, trans. by Marcus Dods (New York: Modern Library, 1950)
Aylmer, John, *An Harborowe for Faithfull and Trewe Subiectes* (London: John Day, 1559)
Bacon, Francis, *Essays*, ed. by John Pitcher (London: Penguin Classics, 1985)
———, *History of the Reign of King Henry VII*, ed. by Rev. J. Rawson Lumby (Cambridge: Cambridge University Press, 1902)
———, *The Letters and the Life of Francis Bacon including all his Occasional Works*, ed. by James Spedding and others (London: Longmans, 1861–1874)
———, *Literary and Professional Works*, vol. VII of *Collected Works*, ed. by James Spedding and others (London: Longmans and Co., 1879)
———, *The Major Works*, ed. by Brian Vickers (Oxford: Oxford University Press, 2008)
———, *The Works of Francis Bacon*, ed. by James Spedding and others [1857–1874] (Cambridge: Cambridge University Press, 2011)
Bacon, Nicholas, *Sir Nicholas Bacon's Great House Sententiae*, ed. by Elizabeth McCutcheon, English Literary Renaissance Supplements, 3 (Amherst: University of Massachusetts, 1977)
———, Thomas Denton, and Robert Carey, 'Henry VIII's Royal Commission on the Inns of Court', ed. by Desmond Bland, *Journal of the Society of the Public Teachers of Law*, n.s., 10 (1968), 178–94
Baldwin, William, and others, *The Mirror for Magistrates*, ed. by Lily B. Campbell (Cambridge: Cambridge University Press, 1938)
———, *A Mirror for Magistrates*, ed. by Scott C. Lucas (Cambridge: Cambridge University Press, 2019)
Bale, John, *King Johan*, ed. by J. H. P. Pafford (Oxford: Oxford University Press, 1931)
———, *The Complete Plays of John Bale*, ed. by Peter Happé (Cambridge: Cambridge University Press, 1985–1986)
Bede, *Ecclesiastical History of the English Nation*, trans. by Lionel C. Jane (London: J. M. Dent, 1910)
Bernard de Clairvaux, *Life and Works of Saint Bernard*, ed. by John Mabillon, trans. by Samuel J. Heales (London: Burn & Oates, 1889)
———, *Saint Bernard On Consideration*, trans. by George Lewis (Oxford: Clarendon Press, 1908)
Beza [Théodore de Bèze], *Abraham sacrifiant* [1550], ed. by Keith Cameron and others (Geneva: Droz, 1967)
———, *A Tragedie of Abraham's sacrifice*, trans. by Arthur Golding (London: Thomas Vautrollier, 1577)
The Bible: Authorized King James Version, ed. by Robert Carroll and Stephen Prickett (Oxford: Oxford University Press, 1997)
Boccaccio, Giovanni, *Des cas et ruyne des nobles hommes et femmes reversez par fortune*, trans. by Laurent de Premierfait from *De casibus virorum illustrium* (Paris: Jean Du Pré, 1484)

Bodin, Jean, *The six bookes of a common-weale. Written by I. Bodin a famous lawyer, and a man of great experience in matters of state. Out of the French and Latine copies, done into English, by Richard Knolles. A Facsimile Reprint of the English Translation of 1606* (Cambridge, MA: Harvard University Press, 1962)

Boethius, *Chaucer's Translation of Boethius' 'De Consolatione Philosophiae'*, ed. by Richard Morris (Oxford: Oxford University Press, 1868)

Bracton, Henry de, *Bracton's Note Book: A Collection of Cases Decided in the King's Court during the Reign of Henry III*, ed. by F. W. Maitland [1887] (Cambridge: Cambridge University Press, 2010)

———, *On the Laws and Customs of England*, trans. by George Woodbine [1922], ed. by Samuel E. Thorne (Cambridge, MA: Harvard University Press, 1976)

Bucer, Martin, *De regno Christi*, in *Martini Buceri Opera Latina*, vol. xv.2, ed. by François Wendel (Paris: Presses Universitaires de France; Gütersloh: Bertelsmann, 1955)

Buchanan, George, *De jure regni apud Scotos, or A Dialogue, concerning the due Privilege of Government, in the Kingdom of Scotland* (Edinburgh: apud J. Rosseum, 1579)

———, *Tragedies, Jephtha and Baptistes*, ed. by Peter Sharratt and G. Walsh (Edinburgh: Scottish Academic Press, 1982)

Budé, Guillaume, *Traitté de la vènerie* [trans. from *De Philologia libri II*, 1532], ed. by Henri Chevreul (Paris: Auguste Aubry, 1861)

Butler, Alban, *Butler's Lives of the Saints*, ed. by Sarah F. Thomas (Tunbridge Wells: Burns & Oates, 1997)

Calendar of the Inner Temple Records, ed. by F. A. Inderwick (London: Royal Collection Trust, 1896–1898)

Calendar of the Middle Temple Records, trans. by C. T. Martin (London: Butterworth, 1903–1905)

Calendar of State Papers, Domestic, 1547–1649: Tudor and Stuart Government Papers, ed. by Robert Lemon and M. A. E. Green (London: Public Record Office, 1856–1872)

Calendar of State Papers Relating to Ireland, II, *1574–1585*, ed. by Hans Claude Hamilton (London: Longmans, Green & Dyer, 1860–1890)

Calendar of the State Papers Relating to Scotland, VII, *A.D. 1584–1585*, ed. by William K. Boyd (Edinburgh: H.M. General Register House, 1913)

Calendar of State Papers, Spain, ed. by Pascual de Gayangos (London: HMSO, 1879)

Calendar of State Papers, Venice, VII, *1558–1580*, ed. by Rawdon Browne and G. Cavendish Bentinck (London: HMSO, 1890)

Calvin, Jean, *Commentaire du 'Traité de la Clémence'*, ed. by Pierre Ferrand and Pierre-Yves Quiviger (Paris: Classiques Garnier, 2017)

———, *Defensio Orthodoxae Fidei de sacra Trinitate, contra prodigiosos errores Michaelis Serueti Hispani* [1554], ed. by Joy Kleinstuber, Latin with introduction and footnotes in English, vol. v of *Scripta didactica et polemica* (Geneva: Droz, 2009)

———, *Sermons de M. Jean Calvin sur le V. livre de Moyse nommé Deuteronome* (Geneva: Thomas Courteau, 1567)

Camden, William, *Annales Rerum Gestarum Angliae et Hiberniae Regnante Elizabetha* [1587, 1615, and 1625], hypertext critical edition by Dana F. Sutton (Berkeley: University of California Press, 2001)

———, *Britain, or, a Chorographicall Description of the most flourishing Kingdomes, England, Scotland, Ireland*, trans. by Philemon Holland (London: George Bishop, 1610)

———, *Remaines of a greater Worke, concerning Britaine, the inhabitants thereof, their Languages, Names, Surnames, Empreses, Wise Speeches, poesies and epitaphes* (London: Simon Waterson, 1605)

Campion, Edmund, *Campion's Brag, or Challenge to the Privy Council*, in Richard Simpson, *Edmund Campion, Jesuit Protomartyr* (London: Burns & Oates, 1907), pp. 225–28

Cartwright, Thomas, *Cartwrightiana*, ed. by Albert Peel and Leland H. Carlson (London: Allen and Unwin, 1951)

Castiglione, Baldassare, *The Courtyer of Count Baldessar Castilio*, trans. by Sir Walter Hoby [1561], ed. by Walter Raleigh (London: David Nutt, 1900)

Cecil, William, *A Collection of State Papers [...] left by William Cecil Lord Burghley*, ed. by Samuel Haynes and William Murdin (London: William Bowyer, 1740–1759)

———, *The Execution of Justice in England*, ed. by Robert M. Kingdon (Ithaca, NY: Cornell University Press, 1965)

Certaine Sermons or Homilies Appointed to be Read in Churches in the Time of Queen Elizabeth I (1547–1571), ed. by M. E. Rickley and T. B. Stroup (Gainesville, FL: Scolars Facsimiles, 1968)

Chartes des libertés anglaises (1100–1305): Collection de textes pour servir à l'étude et à l'enseignement de l'histoire, ed. by Charles Bémont (Paris: Picard, 1892)

Chaucer, Geoffrey, *The Canterbury Tales*, ed. by Larry D. Benson, The Riverside Chaucer (Oxford: Houghton-Mifflin, 1988), <https://chaucer.fas.harvard.edu/pages/text-and-translations>

———, *The Complete Works of Geoffrey Chaucer*, ed. by Walter W. Skeat (Oxford: Clarendon Press, 1961)

Christine de Pizan, *Le Livre de la Cité des dames* [1405], trans. by Thérèse Moreau and Eric Hicks (Paris: Stock, 2005)

———, *Le Livre des fais et bonnes meurs du sage roy Charles V*, ed. by S. Solente (Paris: Honoré Champion, 1936)

Chronicon Angliae ab anno domini 1328 usque anno 1388 monacho Santi Albani, ed. and trans. by Edward M. Thompson, Rolls Series, 64 (Nendeln: Krauss reprint, 1874)

Cicero, *Dialogues sur l'éloquence: De Oratore, Brutus, Orator*, trans. by Pierre L. Lezaud (Paris: Didot, 1866)

———, *Laelius or an Essay on Friendship*, trans. by William Melmoth (London: Dodsley, 1795)

———, *The Letters to Brutus*, trans. by Max Cary, Loeb Classical Library (Cambridge, MA: Harvard University Press, 1989)

———, *Marcus Tullius Ciceroes Thre Bokes of Duties, trans. Nicholas Grimald de De officiis*, ed. by Gerald O'Gorman (Plainsboro, NJ: Associated University Presses, 1990)

Cinzio, Giraldi, *Discorsi di M. Giovanbattista Giraldi Cinthio [...] intorno al comporre dei romanzi, delle comedie, e delle tragedie, e di altre maniere di poesie* [Venice, 1554] (Paris: BnF microfilm, 1995)

Cobbett's Complete Collection of State Trials and Proceedings for High Treasons and Other Crimes and Misdemeanors, ed. by William Cobbett and Thomas Howell, I, *1163–1600*; II, *1603–1627* (London: Hansard, 1809)

Coke, Edward, *The Institutes of the Laws of England: Containing the Exposition of Many Ancient and Other Statutes*, 4 vols (London: E. & R. Brooke, 1797)

———, *The Reports of Sir Edward Coke, Kt. in English, in Thirteen Parts, with References to All the Ancient and Modern Books of the Law* (London in the Savoy: Gosling, 1738); available online at <http://lawlibrary.wm.edu/wythepedia/index.php/Reports_of_Sir_Edward_Coke>

———, *The Selected Writings and Speeches of Sir Edward Coke*, ed. by Steve Sheppard (Indianapolis: Liberty Fund, 2003)

Collection of State Papers relating to affairs in the reign of Queen Elizabeth from 1571 to 1596, ed. by William Murdin (London: William Bowyer, 1759)

Commons Debates, 1628, ed. by Robert C. Johnson, Mary Freer Keeler, Maija Jansson Cole, and William B. Bidwell (New Haven: Yale University Press, 1977)

Commynes, Philippe de, *The Memoirs of Philippe de Commynes*, ed. by Samuel Kinser, trans. by Isabelle Cazeaux (Columbia: University Press of South Carolina, 1973)

Constitutionalism and Resistance in the Sixteenth Century: Three Treatises by Hotman, Beza, and Mornay, ed. by Julian H. Franklin (New York: Pegasus, 1969)

Corpus Juris Canonici, ed. by Emil Friedberg (Leipzig: B. Tauschnitz, 1879–1881; repr. Graz: Akademische Druck- u. Verlagsanstalt, 1959)

D'Ewes, Simonds, *A Compleat Journal of the Votes, Speeches and Debates, both of the House of Lords and House of Commons throughout the Whole Reign of Queen Elizabeth, of Glorious Memory* [1693] (Wilmington: Scholarly Resources, 1974)

Dante Alighieri, *Dante: De Vulgari Eloquentia*, ed. and trans. by Steven Botterill (Cambridge: Cambridge University Press, 1996)

———, *The Divine Comedy*, trans. by Henry Wadsworth Longfellow (Boston: Ticknor and Fields, 1867)

———, *La Monarchie*, édition bilingue, trans. by Michèle Gally [from *De monarchia*] (Paris: Belin, 1993)

Debating the Hundred Years War: Pour ce que plusieurs (La Loy Salique) and A Declaracion of the trew and dewe title of Henrie VIII, ed. by Craig Taylor (Cambridge: Cambridge University Press, 2007)

Disputatio inter clericum et militem [*c.* 1297], in *Somnium Viridarii*, ed. by Marion Schnerb-Lièvre (Paris: CNRS, 1993)

Documents Illustrative of English Church History, ed. and trans. by Henry Gee and William J. Hardy (London: Macmillan, 1896)

Dolce, Lodovico, *Giocasta, tragedia di M. Lodovico Dolce* (Vinegia: Figliuoli d'Aldo, Aldi filii, 1549)

Domesday Book: A Complete Translation, ed. by Ann Williams and Geoffrey H. Martin (London: Folio Society, 2003)

Donne, John, *Biathanatos* [1608], ed. by Michael Rudick and M. Battin (New York: Garland, 1982)

———, *The Divine Poems*, ed. by Helen Gardner (Oxford: Clarendon Press, 1959)

———, *The Major Works*, ed. by John Carey (Oxford: Oxford University Press, 1990)

———, *Pseudo-Martyr* [1610], ed. by Anthony Raspa (McGill: Queen's University Press, 1993)

Dudley, Edmund, *The Tree of Common Wealth* [1509] (Manchester: Charles Simms, 1859)

———, *The Tree of Commonwealth*, ed. by Janice Liedl (Sudbury, ON: Laurentian University, 2012)

Dugdale, William, *The History and Antiquity of the Four Inns of Court, of the Nine Inns of Chancery, from Origines Juridiciales, or Historical Memorials of the English Laws*, ed. by Timothy Cunningham (London, 1780)

Early Modern Catholicism: An Anthology of Primary Sources, ed. by Robert S. Miola (Oxford: Oxford University Press, 2007)

Elizabethan Backgrounds: Historical Documents of the Age of Elizabeth, ed. by Arthur F. Kinney (Hamden, CT: Archon Books, 1975)

Elyot, Thomas, *The Boke named the Gouernour* [1st edn, 1531], ed. by Henry H. Stephen Croft (London: Kegan Paul, 1883)

English Historical Documents, ed. by Harry Rothwell (London: Routledge, 1996)

Erasmus, Desiderius, *Collected Works of Erasmus*, ed. by Harry Vredeveld (Toronto: Toronto University Press, 1987)

———, *The Complaint of Peace* and *The Praise of Folly* in *The Essential Erasmus*, ed. and trans. by John P. Dolan (New York: New American Library, 1964)

———, *La Correspondance d'Érasme*, ed. by Aloïs Gerlo, 12 vols (Brussels: Presses académiques européennes, 1969–1984)

———, *The Education of a Christian Prince* (Cambridge: Cambridge University Press, 1997)

Étienne de Bourbon (Stephani de Borbone), *Tractatus de diversis materiis predicabilibus*, ed. by Jacques Berlioz and Jean-Luc Eichenlaub, Corpus Christianorum, Continuatio Medievalis, 124 (Turnhout: Brepols, 2002)

Euripides, *Euripidis tragici poete nobilissimi Hecuba et Iphigenia, Erasmo interprete* (Paris: Josse Bade, 1506)

Évrart de Trémaugon, *Le Songe du vergier* [1376], ed. by Marion Schnerb-Lièvre (Paris: CNRS, 1982)

Fish, Simon, *A Supplicacyon for the Beggars* [1529], ed. by F. J. Furnivall (London: EETS, 1871)

Fitz Nigel, Richard, *Dialogus de scaccario / The Course of the Exchequer*, ed. and trans. by Charles Johnson (Oxford: Clarendon Press, 1983)

Florio, John, *Florio his firste fruites which yeelde familiar speech, merie prouerbes, wittie sentences, and golden sayings. Also a perfect induction to the Italian, and English tongues* (London: Thomas Dawson, 1578)

Fortescue, John, *A Learned Commendation of the Politike Laws of England [...] newly translated into Englishe by Robert Mulcaster* [1567] (New York: Da Capo Press, 1969)

———, *On the Laws and Governance of England*, ed. by Shelley Lockwood (Cambridge: Cambridge University Press, 1997)

———, *The Works of Sir John Fortescue, Now first collected and arranged by Thomas Lord Clermont* (London: privately printed, 1869)

Foxe, John, *Actes and Monuments of Matters most Special and Memorable, happening in the Church* [1563–1583], The Acts and Monuments Online, Variorum Edition (Humanities Research Institute, University of Sheffield, 2011), <https://www.dhi.ac.uk/foxe/>

Fraunce, Abraham, *The Lawiers Logike* [1588], facsimile (Menston: Scolar Press, 1969)

The French Chronicle of London [1188–1274], ed. by Henry T. Riley (London: Trubner, 1863)

Froissart, Jehan, *Chronicles of England, France, Spain and the Adjoining Countries*, trans. by Lord Berners [1525], ed. by Thomas Johnes, 3rd edn (London: Longman and Co., 1808)

Gaguin, Robert, *Grandes chroniques, excellens faits et virtueux gestes des très illustres, très chrestiens, magnanimes et victorieux roys de France, Composees en latin par [...] Robert Gaguin [...] reduictes et translatees [...] en nostre vulgaire francoys* (Paris: Galliot du Pré, 1514)

Gardiner, Stephen, *Obedience in Church and State: Three Political Tracts by Stephen Gardiner*, ed. by Pierre Janelle (Cambridge: Cambridge University Press, 1930)

Garnier, Robert, *Théâtre complet*, ed. by J.-D. Beaudin (Paris: Champion, 1997–2004)

Gascoigne, George, *Certayne Notes of Instruction in English Verse* [1575], ed. by Edward Arber (London: English Reprints, 1869)

———, *Jocasta* [1566], in *A Hundreth Sundrie Flowers* [1573], ed. by G. W. Pigman III (Oxford: Clarendon Press, 2000)

———, *The spoyle of Antwerpe. Faithfully reported, by a true Englishman, who was present at the same* [1576] (Amsterdam: Theatrum Orbis Terrarum, 1969)

———, *The Steele Glass* [1576] (Amsterdam: Theatrum Orbis Terrarum, 1973)

———, *Supposes; and Jocasta: Two plays translated from the Italian the first by Geo. Gascoigne, the second by Geo. Gascoigne and F. Kinwelmersh* [1566], ed. by John W. Cunliffe (Boston: D. C. Heath & Co., 1906)

Gerald of Wales, *De Principis Instructione. Instruction for a Ruler*, ed. by Robert Bartlett (Oxford: Oxford University Press, 2018)

———, *The Historical Works of Giraldus Cambrensis*, trans. by Thomas Forester, rev. by Thomas Wright (London: George Bell, 1887)

Gerson, Jean Charlier de, *Œuvres complètes*, ed. by Palémon Glorieux, 10 vols (Paris: Desclée, 1960–1973)

Gesta Grayorum, or, the History of the High and Mighty Prince Henry Prince of Purpoole, Anno Domini, 1594, ed. by Desmond Bland (Liverpool: Liverpool University Press, 1968)

Gilles de Rome, *Le Livre du gouvernement des rois et des princes*, trans. [from *De regimine principum*, 1279] by Henri de Cauchy (Paris, Bibliothèque nationale de France, MS fr. 213)

Glanville, Ranulf de, *The Treatise on the Laws and Customs of the Realm of England commonly called Glanvill* [1187–1189], ed. by G. D. G. Hall (Oxford: Clarendon Press, 1993)

Gosson, Stephen, *The Schoole of Abuse, Conteining a Plesaunt Inuectiue against Poets, Pipers, Plaiers, Iesters, and Such Like Caterpillers of a Commonwelth* [1579], ed. by Edward Arber (London: Reprints for the Shakespeare Society, 1841)

Gower, John, *The Complete Works of John Gower, edited from the manuscripts*, ed. by George C. Macaulay (Oxford: Clarendon Press, 1899)

———, *The Major Latin Works of John Gower*, ed. by Eric W. Stockton (Seattle: Washington University Press, 1962)

———, *The Minor Latin Works with 'In Praise of Peace'*, ed. and trans. by R. F. Yeager (Kalamazoo: Medieval Institute Publications, 2005)

Greene, Robert, *The Life and Complete Works in Prose and Verse of Robert Greene*, ed. by Alexander B. Grosart (New York: Russell and Russell, 1964)

Hakluyt, Richard, *The Principal Navigations, Voyages, Traffiques and Discoveries of the English Nation* [1589], ed. by Edmund Goldsmid (Edinburgh: E. and G. Goldsmid, 1884–1890)

Hall, Edward, *Hall's Chronicle (Selection)* [1548], ed. by James D. Mardock, last modified 11 January 2019, <https://internetshakespeare.uvic.ca/doc/Hall_H5_M/complete/index.html>

———, *The union of the two noble and illustre famelies of Lancastre and Yorke*, facsimile of Grafton's 1550 edition (Menston: Scolar Press, 1970)

———, *The union of the two noble and illustre famelies of Lancastre and Yorke. Hall's Chronicle*, ed. by Henry Ellis (London: J. Johnson, 1809)

Harrison, William, *The Description of England* [1577], ed. by George Edelen (Ithaca, NY: Dover Publications, 1968)

Hearne, Thomas, *A Collection of Curious Discourses written by Eminent Antiquaries*, ed. by Joseph Ayloffe (London: Richardson, 1771)

Henry VIII, *Assertio Septem Sacramentorum, or Defence of the Seven Sacraments*, ed. by Rev. Louis O'Donovan (New York: Benziger, 1908)

[Henry VIII], *A Glasse of the Truthe*, in *Records of the Reformation: The Divorce*, II, *1527–1533*, ed. by Nicholas Pocock (Oxford: Clarendon Press, 1870), pp. 523–31

Heywood, Jasper, *Jasper Heywood and his Translations of Seneca: 'Troas', 'Thyestes' and 'Hercules Furens'*, ed. by H. de Vocht (Louvain: Uystpruyst, 1878)

Heywood, John, *The Play of the wether. A new and very mery enterlude of all maner wethers* (London: Rastell, 1533)

Heywood, Thomas, *An Apology for Actors* (London: Nicholas Okes, 1612)

Historical Poems of the xivth and xvth Centuries, ed. by R. H. Robbins (New York: Columbia University Press, 1959)

Holinshed, Raphael, *Holinshed's Chronicles* [1577, 1587], 2009, <https://english.nsms.ox.ac.uk/holinshed/>

———, *Holinshed's Chronicles of England, Scotland and Ireland*, ed. by Henry Ellis, III, *1399–1553* (London: J. Johnson, 1807–1808)

Hooker, Richard, *Of the Laws of Ecclesiastical Polity*, ed. by Arthur S. McGrade (Cambridge: Cambridge University Press, 1989)

Hotman, François, *Francogallia*, ed. by Ralph E. Giesey and J. H. M. Salmon (Cambridge: Cambridge University Press, 1972)

Hugues, Thomas, and others, *The Misfortunes of Arthur* [1588], ed. by J. Payne Collier (London: Septimus Prowett, 1828)

Humanist Scholarship and Public Order: Two Tracts Against the Pilgrimage of Grace, ed. by David S. Berkowitz (Washington: Folger Shakespeare Library, 1984)

Ingulf's Chronicle of the Abbey of Croyland with the Continuation of Peter of Blois, trans. by Henry T. Riley (London: Henry G. Bohn, 1854)

Jacques de Voragine, *The Golden Legend: Lives of the Saints*, trans. by William Caxton [1483], ed. by George V. O'Neill (Cambridge: Cambridge University Press, 1914)

James VI & I, *Basilikon Doron, or His Maiesties instructions to his dearest sonne Henry the Prince* (Edinburgh, 1599; London, 1603)

———, *The True Lawe of free Monarchies* [1598], in *Minor Prose Works of King James VI & I*, ed. by James Craigie (Edinburgh: Scottish Text Society 1982)

Jean de Terrevermeille, *Tractatus de jure futuri successoris legitimi in regiis hereditatibus*, ed. by François Hotman (Arras: E. Vignon, 1586)

Jean de Wawrin, *Anchiennes Chroniques d'Engleterre* (Paris, Bibliothèque nationale de France, MS fr. 81)

John of Salisbury, *Le Policratique de Jean de Salisbury* [1372], trans. by Denis Foulechat, ed. by Charles Brucker (Geneva: Droz, 1994)

———, *The Statesman's Book of John of Salisbury: Being the Fourth, Fifth and Sixth Books and Selections from the Seventh and Eighth Books of the 'Policraticus'*, trans. by John Dickinson (New York: Russell & Russell, 1963)

Joinville, Jean de, *Histoire de Saint Louis*, ed. by Natalis de Wailly (Paris: Hachette, 1865)

———, *Life of Saint Louis*, in *Chronicles of the Crusades: Joinville and Villehardouin*, trans. by Caroline Smith (London: Penguin Classics, 2008)

Jonson, Ben, *Every Man Out of his Humour*, ed. by Helen Ostovich (Manchester: Manchester University Press, 2001)

Journal of the House of Commons, I, *1547–1629* (London: His Majesty's Stationery Office, 1802), <https://www.british-history.ac.uk/commons-jrnl/vol1>

Juvénal des Ursins, Jean, *Écrits politiques de Jean Juvénal des Ursins*, ed. by Peter S. Lewis (Paris: Klincksieck, 1978)

Kirchmeyer (Naogeorgus), Thomas, *Pammachius* [1538], trans. by C. C. Love, University of Toronto, *Records of Early English Drama* Project, 1996, <https://ccltlp.artsci.utoronto.ca/pammach.html>

Knighton, Henry, *Henrici Knighton Chronicon*, ed. by Joseph R. Lumby (Cambridge: Cambridge University Press, 2013), <10.1017/CBO9781139383028.002>

Knox, John, *The First Blast of the Trumpet against the monstrous regiment of Women* [1558], in *On Rebellion*, ed. by Roger A. Mason (Cambridge: Cambridge University Press, 1994), pp. 3–47

Kyd, Thomas, *The Works of Thomas Kyd*, ed. by Frederick S. Boas (Cambridge: Cambridge University English Classics, 1901)

Lambarde, William, *Archaionomia, sive De priscis Anglorum legibus libri* (London: John Day, 1568)

———, *Eirenarcha: or of the office of the iustices of the peace* (London, 1582)

'The Lament of Edward II', ed. by T. M. Smallwood, *Modern Language Review*, 68.3 (1973), 521–29

Langland, William, *Piers Plowman: The C version*, trans. by George Economou (Philadelphia: Pennsylvania University Press, 1996)

The Laws of the Earliest English Kings, ed. and trans. by F. L. Attenborough (Cambridge: Cambridge University Press, 1922)

Leges Henrici Primi, ed. and trans. by L. J. Downer (Oxford: Clarendon Press, 1972)

Legh, Gerard, *Accedens of Armorie* (London: Richard Tottel, 1562)

Leicester's Commonwealth: The Copy of a Letter Written by a Master of Art of Cambridge (1584) and Related Documents, ed. by D. C. Peck (Athens: Ohio University Press, 1985)

Leis e custumes: Lois de Guillaume le Conquérant, ed. by John E. Matzke (Paris: Alphonse Picard, 1899)

Letters and Papers of Richard III and Henry VII, ed. by James Gairdner (London: Longman, 1861)

Letters and Papers, Foreign and Domestic, of the Reign of Henry VIII, ed. by J. S. Brewer, Robert H. Brodie, and James Gairdner (London: Longman, 1862–1910)

Liber augustalis: The Liber Augustalis or Constitutions of Melfi, trans. by J. M. Powell (New York: Macmillan, 1967)

The Life and Death of Jack Straw [1593], ed. by Kenneth Muir (Oxford: Malone Society, 1957)

Lloyd, Richard, *A briefe discourse of the most renowned actes, and right valiant conquests of those puisant Princes, called the Nine Worthies* (London: R. Warde, 1584)

Lodge, Thomas, *Alarum for London, or The Siedge of Antwerp, together with 'The Spoyle of Antwerp', by George Gascoyne*, ed. by R. Simpson (London: Longmans, 1872)

———, *Complete Works of Thomas Lodge*, ed. by Edmund Gosse (Glasgow: Hunterian Club, 1883; digitized in 2008)

Loi salique: Recueil contenant les différentes rédactions de cette loi, ed. by J-M. Pardessus (Paris: Imprimerie royale, 1843)

Luther, Martin, *A Commentary on St Paul's Epistle to the Galatians*, trans. by Erasmus Middleton (London: Harrison Trust, 1939)

Lydgate, John, *The Fall of Princes* [1431–1438], ed. by Henry Bergen (London: EETS, 1924)

Machiavelli, Niccolo, *The Discourses*, ed. by Bernard Crick, trans. by Leslie Walker (Harmondsworth: Penguin, 1970)

———, *The Prince*, ed. by Quentin Skinner, trans. by Russell Price (Cambridge: Cambridge University Press, 1988)

Machyn, Henry, *A London Provisioner's Chronicle, 1550–1563*, ed. by Richard W. Bailey, Marilyn Miller, and Colette Moore (Ann Arbor: University of Michigan Press, 2006), <https://quod.lib.umich.edu/m/machyn/>

Manningham, John, *Diary of John Manningham of the Middle Temple, 1602–1603*, ed. by John Bruce (New York: AMS Press, 1868)

Manwood, John, *Manwood's Treatise of the Forest Laws, Fifth edition, corrected and enlarged by William Elton of the Middle Temple* (Farmington Hills, MI: Cengage Gale, 2009)

Manzolli, Pietro Angelo, *The zodiake of life written by the godly and zealous poet Marcellus Palingenius Stellatus, newly translated into English verse by B. Googe* (London, 1565; New York: Scholars' Facsimiles, 1976)

Map, Walter, *Master Map's book De nugis curialis (Courtiers' Trifles)*, trans. by Frederick Tupper (London: Chatto & Windus, 1924)

Marlowe, Christopher, *The Complete Plays*, ed. by Frank Romany and Robert Lindsey (London: Penguin Classics, 2003)

Marsilius of Padua, *The Defence of Peace, lately translated out of laten into englysshe* by W. Marshall [from *Defensor Pacis*, 1324] (London: R. Wyer, 1536)

———, *The Defender of the Peace*, trans. by Annabel Brett (Cambridge: Cambridge University Press, 2005)

Marston, John, *The Fawne*, ed. by Gerald A. Smith (London: Arnold, 1965)

———, *The Selected Plays of John Marston*, ed. by Macdonald P. Jackson (Cambridge: Cambridge University Press, 1986)

Martial d'Auvergne, *Les Poésies de Martial de Paris, dit d'Auvergne, Procureur au Parlement* (Paris: Coustelier, 1724)

Matthew Paris, *Chronica Majora*, ed. by Henry Richards Luard (London: Longman, 1877)

Middleton, Thomas, *The Collected Works*, ed. by Gary Taylor (Oxford: Oxford University Press, 2010)

———, *Michaelmas Term* [1607], ed. by Richard Levin (London: Arnold, 1966)

Milton, John, *Of Reformation Touching Church Discipline in England, and the Causes that hitherto have hindred it* [1641], Thomason Tracts (Ann Arbor: University Microfilms International, 1999)

Moore, John, *A Journal during a residence in France, from the beginning of August 1792 [...] to the death of the late King of France* (London: Robinson, 1793)

More, Thomas, *The Complete Works of St Thomas More*, ed. by R. S. Sylvester and others, 15 vols (New Haven: Yale University Press, 1963–1993)

———, *The Correspondence of Sir Thomas More*, ed. by Elizabeth F. Rogers (Princeton, NJ: Princeton University Press, 1947)

———, *The English Works of Sir Thomas More*, ed. by W. E. Campbell (London: Eyre & Spottiswoode, 1927)

———, *Utopia*, trans. by Robert M. Adams (New York: Norton, 1975)

———, *The Utopia of Sir Thomas More, Latin & English texts*, ed. by J. H. Lupton, from the Latin edition of 1518 and Ralph Robinson's translation of 1551 (Oxford: Clarendon Press, 1895)

Morison, Richard, *Apomaxis calumniarum, convitiorumque, quibus Ioannes Cocleus [...] Henrici octavi serenissimi regis Angliae famam impetere* (London: Berthelet, 1537)

———, *An invective ayenst the great and detestable vice, treason* (London: Berthelet, 1539)

Mouskès, Philippe, *Chronique rimée des rois de France du siège de Troie à 1243*, ed. by F. de Reiffenberg (Brussels: M. Hayez, 1836)

Mulcaster, Richard, *The Elementarie* [1582] (Menston: Scolar Press, 1970)

Nashe, Thomas, *The Unfortunate Traveller and Other Works*, ed. by J. B. Steane (London: Penguin Classics, 1972)

Northbrooke, John, *A Treatise Against Dicing, Dancing, Plays, and Interludes* [1577], facsimile reprint of the 1843 Shakespeare Society edition ([New York]: Elibron Classics, 2005)

Norton, Thomas, *A declaration of the fauourable dealing of her Maiesties commissioners appointed for the examination of certain traitours and of tortures vniustly reported to be done vpon them for matters of religion* (London: Christopher Barker, 1583); repr. in *The Execution of Justice in England*, ed. by Robert M. Kingdon (Ithaca, NY: Cornell University Press, 1965)

———, *Oration, of Arsanes agaynst Philip the trecherous kyng of Macedone* (London: John Day, 1560)

———, 'The Translator to the Reader', Preface to Jean Calvin, *Institution of Christian Religion* (London, William Norton, 1582; repr. facs. Amsterdam: Da Capo Press, 1970)

Norton, Thomas, and Thomas Sackville, *Gorboduc, or The Tragidie of Ferrex and Porrex* (London: John Day, 1570); repr. in *Five Elizabethan Tragedies*, ed. by A. K. McIlwraith (Oxford: Oxford University Press, 1971), pp. 69–129

Olivier de la Marche, *Les Mémoires de messire Olivier de la Marche*, ed. by M. Petitot (Paris: Foucault, 1825)

Orderic Vitalis, *Historiae ecclesiasticae*, ed. by Auguste Le Prévost (Paris: Jules Renouard, 1855)

Original Letters Relative to the English Reformation, ed. by Hastings Robinson (Cambridge: Cambridge University Press, 1846–1847)

Parliament Rolls of Medieval England, 1275–1504, ed. by C. Given-Wilson, 16 vols (Woodbridge: Boydell, 2005); online at <http://www.british-history.ac.uk/no-series/parliament-rolls-medieval>

Parliamentary Texts of the Later Middle Ages, ed. by N. Pronay and J. Taylor (Oxford: Oxford University Press, 1980)

The Paston Letters, A.D. 1422–1509, ed. by James Gairdner, 6 vols (London: Chatto & Windus, 1904)

Paul of Tarsus, *The Writings of St Paul*, ed. by Wayne A. Meeks (New York: Norton, 1972)

Phaer, Thomas, *The Seven First Bookes of the Eneidos of Virgill* (London: John Kyngston, 1558)

Philippe de Mézières, *Le Songe du Vieil Pèlerin*, ed. by G. W. Coopland (Cambridge: Cambridge University Press, 1969)

Piccolomini, Aeneas Silvius (Pius II), *Opera quae extant omnia*, with maps from *Cosmographia Munster* (Basel: Henricus Petri, 1551)

Plato, *The Laws*, trans. by Benjamin Jowett (London: Penguin Classics, 2005)

———, *The Republic*, trans. by A. D. Lindsay (London: Dent, Everyman's Library, 1992)

Pliny the Elder, *The Historie of the World, commonly called, the Naturall Historie of C. Plinius Secundus*, trans. by Philemon Holland (London: Adam Islip, 1601)

Plowden, Edmund, *The Commentaries, or Reports of Edmund Plowden*, George Whyte Collection (London in the Savoy: C. Lintot and S. Richardson, 1761; repr. London: S. Brooke, 1816)

Plutarch, *Plutarch's Lives of the Noble Grecians and Romans*, trans. by Thomas North from Jacques Amyot, ed. by George Wyndham (London: Tudor Translations, 1895–1896)

———, *Plutarch's Moralia*, trans. by Frank C. Babbitt (London: William Heinemann, 1936)

———, *Les Vies des hommes illustres*, trans. by Jacques Amyot, ed. by Gérard Walter (Paris: Gallimard Pléiade, 1959)

Ponet, John, *A Short Treatise of Politike Power, and of the true obedience which subjects owe to kings and other civill governors, with an Exhortation to all true and natural English men. Compyled by D.J.P.B. R.W* [Doctor John Poynet Bishop of Rochester and Winchester] [Strasbourg, 1556, STC 20178], facsimile edn (Menston: Scolar Press, 1970)

———, *A Short Treatise on Political Power*, ed. from the 1556 edition by Patrick S. Poole, 1994, <https://constitution.org/1-Constitution/cmt/ponet/polpower.htm>

Primary Sources on Copyright (1450–1900), ed. by L. Bently and M. Kretschmer, 2008, <http://www.copyrighthistory.org>

Proceedings in the Parliaments of Elizabeth I, ed. by T. E. Hartley, 3 vols (London: Leicester University Press, 1981–1995)

Progymnasmata: Greek Textbooks of Prose Composition and Rhetoric, trans. by George A. Kennedy (Leiden: Brill, 2003)

Protestant Nonconformist Texts, I, *1550 to 1700*, ed. by R. Tudur Jones (Aldershot: Ashgate, 2007)

Prynne, William, *The Soveraigne Power of Parliaments and Kingdomes* (London: Michael Sparke Sen., 1643)

Puttenham, George, *The Arte of English Poesie* [1589], ed. by Brian Vickers (Oxford: Clarendon Press, 1999)

Rabelais, François, *Five Books of the Lives, Heroic Deeds and Sayings of Gargantua and his Son Pantagruel*, trans. by Thomas Urquhart [1653] (London: Fraser Press, 1970)

———, *Œuvres complètes*, ed. by Jacques Boulenger (Paris: Gallimard Pléiade, 1955)

Ralegh, Sir Walter, *The History of the World* [1614], vol. II of *The Works of Sir Walter Ralegh*, ed. by William Oldys and Thomas Birch (Oxford: Oxford University Press, 1829)

Rastell, John, *The Abbreviacion of Statutis translated out of French into English by John Rastell* (London, 1519)

———, *Three Rastell Plays*, ed. by Richard Axton (Cambridge: Brewer, 1979)

Readings and Moots at the Inns of Court in the Fifteenth Century, ed. by Samuel E. Thorne and John H. Baker (London: Selden Society, 1990)

Récits d'un Ménestrel de Reims, c. 1260, ed. by Natalis de Wailly (Paris: Renouard, 1876)

Records of Early English Drama, ed. by Alan H. Nelson (Toronto: University of Toronto Press, 1989)

Records of the Honorable Society of Lincoln's Inn: The Black Books, ed. by W. Paley Baildon, I, *1422–1586*; II, *1586–1660* (London, 1897), available at <https://archives.lincolnsinn.org.uk>

Recueil général des anciennes lois françaises depuis l'an 420 jusqu'à la révolution de 1789, ed. by F. A. Isambert and others (Paris: Belin-Leprieur, 1822–1833)

Ridley, Nicholas, *The Works of Nicholas Ridley*, ed. by Rev. Henry Christmas (Cambridge: Cambridge University Press, 1841)

Roger de Hoveden, *The Annals of Roger de Hoveden, Comprising the History of England and of other Countries of Europe from AD 732 to AD 1201*, trans. by Henry T. Riley (London: Bohn, 1853)

Roger de Wendover, *Chronica, sive Flores historiarum*, ed. by Henry O. Coxe (London: English Historical Society, 1841)

Roper, William, *The Lyfe of Sir Thomas Moore, knighte*, ed. by Elsie V. Hitchcock (Oxford: Oxford University Press, 1935)

Rotuli Parliamentorum ut et Petitiones et Placita, ed. by Rev. John Strachey (London, 1767–1777; digitized in 2013)

The Ruinate Fall of the Pope Usurie, Derived from the Pope Idolatrie; Reueled by a Saxon of Antiquite (London: Allde, 1580)

Saint-German, Christopher, *Doctor and Student* [1518], ed. by William Muchall (Union, NJ: Law Book Exchange, 1998)

Sander, Nicholas, *A Briefe Treatise of Usurie* (Louvain, 1568)

Selden, John, *Joannis Seldeni Jurisconsulti Opera Omnia tam edita quam inedita*, ed. by David Wilkins (London: Bowyer, 1726)

———, *The Table Talk of John Selden*, ed. by S. H. Reynolds (Oxford: Clarendon Press, 1892)

Select Cases before the King's Council in the Star Chamber Commonly Called the Court of Star Chamber, A.D. 1477–1509, ed. by Isaac S. Leadam (London, 1902; facsimile repr., Kessinger, 2010)

Select Charters and Other Illustrations of English Constitutional History, From the Earliest Times to the Reign of Edward the First, ed. by William Stubbs (Oxford: Clarendon Press, 1870)

A Select Collection of Old English Plays, ed. by Robert Dodsley (London: Reeves and Turner, 1874–1876)

Select Historical Documents of the Middle Ages, ed. and trans. by Ernest F. Henderson (London: G. Bell, 1896)

Select Pleas of the Forest, ed. by G. J. Turner (London: Selden Society, 1899)

Selected Letters of Pope Innocent III Concerning England, 1198–1216, ed. by C. R. Cheney and W. H. Semple (New York: Thomas Nelson, 1953)

Seneca, Lucius Annaeus, *Seneca His Tenne Tragedies*, ed. by Thomas Newton (London: Thomas Marsh, 1581; repr. London: Constable and Co., 1927)

Shakespeare, William, *The Arden Shakespeare: Third Series Complete Works*, ed. by Ann Thompson and others (London: Bloomsbury, 1995–2020)

———, *Œuvres complètes*, bilingual edition, ed. by Jean-Michel Déprats and Gisèle Venet, 8 vols (Paris: Gallimard Pléiade, 2002–2021)

Sidney, Philip, *An Apology for Poetry or 'The Defence of Poesy'*, ed. by George Shepherd (Manchester: Manchester University Press, 1973)

———, *The defence of poesie* (London: Ponsonby, 1595)

Sir Thomas More, ed. by John Jowett (London: Arden Third Series, Bloomsbury, 2011)

Smith, Thomas, *A Discourse of the Commonweal of this Realm of England*, ed. by Mary Dewar, Folger Shakespeare Library (Charlottesville: University Press of Virginia, 1969)

Sources of English Constitutional History: A Selection of Documents from A.D. *600 to the Present*, ed. and trans. by Carl Stephenson and Frederick G. Marcham (New York: Harper & Row, 1937)

Spelman, John, *The Reports of Sir John Spelman*, ed. by John H. Baker (London: Selden Society, 1977–1978)

Spenser, Edmund, *The Poetical Works of Edmund Spenser*, ed. by J. C. Smith and E. de Selincourt (Oxford: Oxford University Press, 1959)

———, *A View of the Present State of Ireland* [1596], in *Spenser's Prose Works*, ed. by Edwin Greenlaw and others (Baltimore: Johns Hopkins University Press, 1949)

Stapleton, Thomas, *The Life and Illustrious Martyrdom of Sir Thomas More* [Douai, 1588], trans. by Philip E. Hallett (London: Burns, Oates and Washburn, 1928)

Starkey, Thomas, *A Dialogue between Reginald Pole and Thomas Lupset*, ed. by K. Burton (London: Chatto & Windus, 1948)

Statutes of the Realm, Printed from Original Records and Authentic Manuscripts, vols I–IV (London: Dawsons of Pall Mall, 1810–1819)

Stow, John, *A Survey of London* [1598], ed. by William J. Thoms (London: Whittaker, 1842)

———, *Three Fifteenth-Century Chronicles, with Historical Memoranda by John Stowe*, ed. by James Gairdner (London: Camden Society, 1880)

Strype, John, *The History of the Life and Acts of Edmund Grindal*, vol. XXIII of *Historical and Biographical Works* (Oxford: Clarendon Press, 1821–1827)

———, *The Life of the Learned Sir Thomas Smith, Kt., D.C.L* (Oxford: Clarendon Press, 1820)

Stubbs, John, *John Stubbs's 'Gaping Gulf' with Letters and Relevant Documents*, ed. by Lloyd E. Berry (Charlottesville: University Press of Virginia, 1968)

Thomas Aquinas, *Du gouvernement royal, traduction du De regimine principum or De regno* by Claude Roguet and M. l'abbé Poupon (Paris: La Gazette française, 1926)

———, *Somme théologique*, trans. by Aimon-Marie Roguet (Paris: Éditions du Cerf, 1984)

———, *Summa theologiae*, trans. by Alfred J. Freddoso (Notre Dame, IN: University Press of Notre Dame, 2018)

Thomas of Woodstock, or King Richard the Second, Part One, ed. by Peter Corbin and Douglas Sedge (Manchester: Manchester University Press, 2002)

Three Parnassus Plays, ed. by James B. Leishman (London: Nicholson & Watson, 1949)

Three Revels from the Inns of Court, ed. by Desmond S. Bland (Amersham: Avebury, 1984)

Three Tragedies by Renaissance Women, ed. by Diane Purkiss (London: Penguin, 1998)

The Towneley Plays, ed. by Garrett J. Epp (Kalamazoo: Medieval Institute Publications, 2018)

Trevisa, John, *Trevisa's Dialogus inter Militem et Clericum, Sermon by fitzRalph and the Bygynnyng of the World*, ed. by Aaron J. Perry, EETS, 167 (London: EETS, 1925)

Tudor Constitutional Documents, A.D. 1485–1603, ed. by Joseph R. Tanner (Cambridge: Cambridge University Press, 1940)

Tudor Royal Proclamations, ed. by Paul L. Hughes and James F. Larkin (Montreal: McGill University Press, 1912)

Tyndale, William, *An Answer to Sir Thomas More's Dialogue* [1531], ed. by Henry Walter (Cambridge: Cambridge University Press, 1850)

———, *Obedience of a Christian Man* [1528], in *The Works of the English Reformers: William Tyndale and John Frith*, ed. by Thomas Russell (London: E. Palmer, 1831), pp. 163–379

Vacarius, *The Liber pauperum of Vacarius*, ed. Francis de Zulueta, Selden Society, 44 (London: Quaritch, 1927; repr. 1972)

Valla, Lorenzo, *The Declamation of Lou. Valla [...] against the untruly forged falsely believed donation given to Sylvester Pope of Rome by Constantyne* [1525], *On the Donation of Constantine*, trans. by G. W. Bowersock (Cambridge, MA: Harvard University Press, 2007)

Vergil, Polydore, *Anglica Historia* [1555], Hypertext critical edition by Dana F. Sutton (Berkeley: University of California Press, 2005)

———, *Three Books of Polydore Vergil's English History, Comprising the Reigns of Henry VI, Edward IV, and Richard III*, ed. by Henry Ellis (London: Camden Society, 1844)

Walsingham, Thomas, *The Saint Albans Chronicle: The Chronica Maiora of Thomas Walsingham*, ed. by John Taylor, Wendy R. Childs, and Leslie Watkiss, 2 vols (Oxford: Oxford University Press, 2003–2011)

Walton, Izaak, *The Lives of Dr John Donne, Sir Henry Wotton, Mr Richard Hooker, Mr George Herbert* (London: Tho. Newcomb, 1670)

A Warning for Fair Women [1599], ed. by A. F. Hopkinson (London: Sims and Co., 1893)

William of Ockham, *Breviloquium de potestate papae: A Short Discourse on Tyrannical Government*, ed. by Arthur S. McGrade, trans. by John Kilcullen (Cambridge: Cambridge University Press, 1992)

Wilson, Thomas, *The Arte of Rethorique, for the use of all suche as are studious of eloquence* (London: John Kingston, 1553)

Wood, Anthony A., *Athenae Oxoniensis: An Exact History of Writers and Bishops who have had their Education in the University of Oxford from 1500 to 1690* (London: Tho. Bennet, 1692)

Wycliff, John, *Wycliffe's Latin Treatise, Trialogus*, trans. by Stephen Lahey (Cambridge: Cambridge University Press, 2013)

——, *Tracts and Treatises of John de Wycliffe*, ed. by Rev. Robert Vaughan (London: Blackburn & Pardon, 1845)

The Zurich Letters, comprising the correspondence of several English bishops [...] with some of the Helvetian reformers, A.D. 1558–1579, ed. by H. Robinson (Cambridge: Parker Society, 1842)

Secondary Works

Abbot, Lewis W., *Law Reporting in England, 1485–1585* (London: Athlone Press, 1973)

Ackroyd, Peter, *The Life of Thomas More* (London: Chatto & Windus, 1998)

Adams, Simon, *Leicester and the Court: Essays on Elizabethan Politics* (Manchester: Manchester University Press, 2002)

Alford, Stephen, *The Early Elizabethan Polity: William Cecil and the British Succession Crisis, 1558–1569* (Cambridge: Cambridge University Press, 1998)

Allen, John W., *A History of Political Thought in the Sixteenth Century* [1928] (London: Routledge, 2010)

Alsop, J. D., 'Reinterpreting the Elizabethan Commons: The Parliamentary Session of 1566', *Journal of British Studies*, 29.3 (1990), 216–40

Altman, Joel, *The Tudor Play of Mind: Rhetorical Inquiry and the Development of Elizabethan Drama* (Berkeley: University of California Press, 1978)

Anderson, M. D., *Drama and Imagery in English Medieval Churches* (Cambridge: Cambridge University Press, 1963)

Anglo, Sydney, *Machiavelli, the First Century: Studies in Enthusiasm, Hostility, and Irrelevance* (Oxford: Oxford University Press, 2005)

——, *Spectacle, Pageantry, and Early Tudor Policy* (Oxford: Clarendon Press, 1969)

Apolloni, Jessica, 'Local Communities and Central Power in Shakespeare's Transnational Law', *Studies in Philology*, 114.1 (2017), 124–47

Archer, Ian W., ed., *Religion, Politics and Society in Sixteenth-Century England* (Cambridge: Cambridge University Press, 2003)

Archer, J. E., Elizabeth Goldring, and Sarah Knight, eds., *The Intellectual and Cultural World of the Early Modern Inns of Court* (Manchester: Manchester University Press, 2010)

Arlidge, Anthony, *Shakespeare and the Prince of Love: The Feast of Misrule in the Middle Temple* (London: Giles de la Mare, 2000)

Arnold, Oliver, *The Third Citizen: Shakespeare's Theater and the Early Modern House of Commons* (Baltimore: Johns Hopkins University Press, 2007)

Auchter, Dorothy, *Dictionary of Literary and Dramatic Censorship in Tudor and Stuart England* (Westport, CT: Greenwood Press, 2001)

Axton, Marie, 'The Influence of Edmund Plowden's Succession Treatise', *Huntington Library Quarterly*, 37.3 (1974), 209–26

——, *The Queen's Two Bodies: Drama and the Elizabethan Succession* (London: Royal Historical Society, 1977)

Baker, John H., *An Introduction to English Legal History* (London: Butterworths, 1979; 3rd edn, 1990)

———, *The Legal Profession and the Common Law* (London: Hambledon Press, 1986)

———, *The Oxford History of the Laws of England* (Oxford: Oxford University Press, 2003)

———, *Readers and Readings in the Inns of Court and Chancery* (London: Selden Society, 2000)

———, *The Third University of England: The Inns of Court and the Common-Law Tradition* (London: Selden Society, 1990)

Bald, R. C., *John Donne: A Life* (Oxford: Clarendon Press, 1970)

Baldo, Jonathan, '"Into a thousand parts": Representing the Nation in *Henry V*', *English Literary Renaissance*, 38.1 (2008), 55–82

Baldwin, John W., *Paris, 1200*, trans. by Béatrice Bonne (Paris: Aubier-Flammarion, 2006)

———, '*Studium et Regnum*: The Penetration of University Personnel into French and English Administration at the Turn of the Twelfth and Thirteenth Centuries', *Revue des études islamiques: L'Enseignement en Islam et en Occident au Moyen Âge*, 44 (1976), 199–215

Barbey, Jean, *La Fonction royale: Essence et légitimité d'après les 'Tractatus' de Jean de Terrevermeille* (Paris: Nouvelles Éditions Latines, 2003)

Barlow, Frank, *William Rufus* (Berkeley: University of California Press, 1983)

Barnard, John, and D. F. McKenzie, eds, *The Cambridge History of the Book in Britain*, IV, *1557–1695* (Cambridge: Cambridge University Press, 2002)

Barton, Anne, *The Shakespearean Forest* (Cambridge: Cambridge University Press, 2017)

Beaune, Colette, *Naissance de la nation France* (Paris: Gallimard, 1985)

Bellamy, J. G., *The Law of Treason in the Later Middle Ages* (Cambridge: Cambridge University Press, 1970)

Bellomo, Manlio, *The Common Legal Past of Europe, 1000–1800* (Washington, DC: Catholic University of America Press, 1995)

Berman, Harold J., 'The Background of the Western Legal Tradition in the Folklaw of the Peoples of Europe', *University of Chicago Law Review*, 45 (1977/1978), 553–97

———, *Law and Revolution: The Formation of the Western Legal Tradition* (Cambridge, MA: Harvard University Press, 1983)

Biet, Christian, 'Law, Literature, Theatre: The Fiction of Common Judgment', *Law and Humanities*, 5.1 (2011), 281–92

Blatt, Thora, *The Plays of John Bale: A Study of Ideas, Technique and Style* (Copenhagen: Gads Forlag, 1968)

Bloch, Marc, *The Royal Touch: Sacred Monarchy and Scrofula in England and France*, trans. by J. E. Anderson [from *Les Rois thaumaturges* (Paris: Gallimard, 1926)] (London: Routledge, 1973)

Boswell, Jackson Campbell, *Dante's Fame in England: References in Printed British Books, 1477–1640* (Plainsboro, NJ: Associated University Presses, 1999)

Bouhaïk-Gironès, Marie, *Les clercs de la Basoche et le théâtre politique (Paris, 1420–1550)* (Paris: Champion, 2007)

Boureau, Alain, *Histoires d'un historien, Kantorowicz*, postface to Ernst Kantorowicz, *Œuvres* (Paris: Quarto Gallimard, 2000), pp. 1223–1312

Bouwsma, William, *John Calvin: A Sixteenth-Century Portrait* (Oxford: Oxford University Press, 1988)

Boyer, Allen D., *Sir Edward Coke and the Elizabethan Age* (Stanford: Stanford University Press, 2003)

Brandreth, Benet, *Shakespearean Rhetoric: A Practical Guide for Actors, Directors, Students and Teachers* (London: Bloomsbury, 2021)

Brooks, Christopher, *Law, Politics and Society in Early Modern England* (Cambridge: Cambridge University Press, 2008)

———, *Lawyers, Litigation, and English Society since 1540* (London: Hambledon Press, 1998)

Burnet, Gilbert, *The History of the Reformation of the Church of England* (London: R. Priestley, 1820)

Burrow, Colin, *Shakespeare and Classical Antiquity* (Oxford: Oxford University Press, 2013)

Bush, Michael, *A Study of the Rebel Armies of October 1536* (Manchester: Manchester University Press, 1996)

Campbell, W. E., *Erasmus, Tyndale and More* (London: Eyre & Spottiswoode, 1949)

Carpi, Daniela, ed., *Practising Equity, Addressing Law: Equity in Law and Literature* (Heidelberg: Universitätsverlag Winter, 2008)

———, and François Ost, eds, *As You Law It: Negotiating Shakespeare* (Berlin: De Gruyter, 2018)

Cavanagh, Dermot, *Language and Politics in the Sixteenth-Century History Play* (London: Palgrave Macmillan, 2003)

Cerasano, S. P., ed., *Medieval and Renaissance Drama in England* (Plainsboro, NJ: Associated University Presses, 2017)

———, and Marion Wynne-Davies, eds, *Readings in Renaissance Women's Drama: Criticism, History, and Performance, 1594–1998* (London: Routledge, 1998)

Chambers, E. K., *The Elizabethan Stage*, 4 vols (Oxford: Clarendon Press, 1923)

Charrier, Sylvie, *Recherches sur l'œuvre latine en prose de Robert Gaguin, 1433–1501* (Paris: Honoré Champion, 1996)

Cheney, Christopher R., *From Becket to Langton: English Church Government, 1170–1213* (Manchester: Manchester University Press, 1956)

———, *Hubert Walter* (Edinburgh: Nelson, 1967)

———, *The Papacy and England, 12th–14th centuries* (London: Variorum Reprints, 1982)

Clancy, Thomas H., *Papist Pamphleteers, the Allen-Persons Party and the Political Thought of the Counter-Reformation in England, 1572–1615* (Chicago: Loyola University Press, 1964)

Clare, Janet E., *'Art made tongue-tied by authority': Elizabethan and Jacobean Dramatic Censorship* (Manchester: Manchester University Press, 1990)

Clarkson, Paul, and Clyde Warren, *The Law of Property in Shakespeare and Elizabethan Drama* (Baltimore: Johns Hopkins University Press, 1942)

Clegg, Cyndia S., *Press Censorship in Elizabethan England* (Cambridge: Cambridge University Press, 1997)

Collinson, Patrick, *Archbishop Grindal, 1519–1583: The Struggle for a Reformed Church* (Berkeley: University of California Press, 1979)

———, *Godly People: Essays in English Protestantism and Puritanism* (London: Hambledon Press, 1983)

———, 'The Monarchical Republic of Queen Elizabeth I', *Bulletin of the John Rylands Library*, 69.2 (1987), 394–424

———, 'Sir Nicholas Bacon and the Elizabethan *Via Media*', *Historical Journal*, 23.2 (1980), 255–73

Conley, Carey H., *The First English Translators of the Classics* (New Haven: Yale University Press, 1927)

Copeland, Rita, *Rhetoric, Hermeneutics, and Translation in the Middle Ages: Academic Traditions and Vernacular Texts* (Cambridge: Cambridge University Press, 1991)

Cormack, Bradin, *A Power to Do Justice: Jurisdiction, English Literature, and the Rise of the Common Law, 1509–1625* (Chicago: University of Chicago Press, 2008)

———, Martha Nussbaum, and Richard Strier, eds, *Shakespeare and the Law* (Chicago: University of Chicago Press, 2013)

Corrigan, Brian Jay, *Playhouse Law in Shakespeare's World* (Madison: Fairleigh Dickinson University Press, 2004)

Coss, R., and S. D. Lloyd, eds, *Thirteenth Century England*, vol. v (Woodbridge: Boydell & Brewer, 1995)

Cottret, Bernard, *Histoire de l'Angleterre* (Paris: Tallandier, 2007)

Crevier, Jean-Baptiste-Louis, *Histoire de l'Université de Paris, depuis son origine jusqu'en l'année 1600* (Paris: Desaint et Saillant, 1761)

Cunningham, Karen J., *Imaginary Betrayals: Subjectivity and the Discourses of Treason in Early Modern England* (Philadelphia: Pennsylvania University Press, 2002)

Curran, Kevin, ed., *Shakespeare and Judgment* (Edinburgh: Edinburgh University Press, 2017)

Cuvelier, Éliane, *Thomas Lodge, témoin de son temps* (Paris: Didier, 1984)

Darras, Jacques, ed., *Les Métamorphoses du Sonnet*, In'hui, 52–53 (Brussels: Le Cri, 1999)

Dawson, William F., *Christmas, its Origin and Associations, Together with its Historical Events and Festive Celebrations during Nineteen Centuries* (London: Elliot Stock, 1902)

Dean, David, *Law-Making and Society in Late Elizabethan England: The Parliament of England, 1584–1601* (Cambridge: Cambridge University Press, 2002)

———, and Norman L. Jones, eds, *The Parliaments of Elizabethan England* (Oxford: Blackwell, 1990)

Demetriou, Tania, and Tanya Pollard, eds, *Homer and Greek Tragedy in Early Modern England's Theatres* (Oxford: Oxford University Press, 2017)

Derrett, J. Duncan M., 'The Trial of Sir Thomas More', *English Historical Review*, 79.312 (1964), 449–77

Dillon, Janette, *Theatre, Court, and City, 1595–1610: Drama and Social Space in London* (Cambridge: Cambridge University Press, 2000)

Dodd, Gwilym, 'A Parliament Full of Rats? *Piers Plowman* and the Good Parliament of 1376', *Historical Research*, 79.203 (2006), 21–49

Dodds, Madeleine H., and Ruth Dodds, *The Pilgrimage of Grace, 1536–1537 and the Exeter Conspiracy, 1538*, 2 vols (Cambridge: Cambridge University Press, 1915)
Doran, Susan, *Monarchy and Matrimony: The Courtships of Elizabeth* (London: Routledge, 1996)
Douglas, David C., *The Norman Achievement, 1050–1100* (Berkeley: University of California Press, 1969)
———, *William the Conqueror* (New Haven: Yale University Press, 1999)
Douglas, Sarah K., '"Jesuites ghostly wayes": Catholic Political Policy and the Control of Catholic Recusancy during the Reign of Elizabeth I' (senior honors thesis, Ohio State University Press, 2007)
Duby, Georges, *Medieval Marriage: Two Models from Twelfth-Century France*, trans. by Elbory Forster (Baltimore: Johns Hopkins University Press, 1978)
Duffy, Eamon, *The Stripping of the Altars: Traditional Religion in England, 1400–1580* (New Haven: Yale University Press, 1992)
Dupont, Florence, *L'Insignifiance tragique: 'Les Choéphores' d'Eschyle, 'Électre' de Sophocle, 'Électre' d'Euripide* (Paris: Gallimard, 1999)
Durand-Le Guern, Isabelle, and Bertrand Ribémont, *Charlemagne, empereur et mythe d'Occident* (Paris: Klincksieck, 2009)
Dutton, Richard, *Shakespeare, Court Dramatist* (Oxford: Oxford University Press, 2016)
Eliot, T. S., *Elizabethan Dramatists* (London: Faber, 1963)
———, *Selected Essays* (London: Faber, 1999)
Elton, Geoffrey R., *The Parliament of England, 1559–1581* (Cambridge: Cambridge University Press, 1986)
———, *Policy and Police: The Enforcement of the Reformation in the Age of Thomas Cromwell* (Cambridge: Cambridge University Press, 1972)
———, *The Tudor Revolution in Government: Administrative Changes in the Reign of Henry VIII* (Cambridge: Cambridge University Press, 1953)
Elton, W. R., *Shakespeare's Troilus and Cressida and the Inns of Court Revels* (Aldershot: Ashgate, 2000)
Eppley, Daniel, *Defending Royal Supremacy and Discerning God's Will in Tudor England* (Aldershot: Ashgate, 2007)
Erne, Lukas, *Beyond the Spanish Tragedy: A Study of the Works of Thomas Kyd* (Manchester: Manchester University Press, 2001)
———, *Shakespeare and the Book Trade* (Cambridge: Cambridge University Press, 2013)
———, *Shakespeare as Literary Dramatist*, 2nd edn (Cambridge: Cambridge University Press, 2013)
Escobedo, Andrew, *Nationalism and Historical Loss in Renaissance England: Foxe, Dee, Spenser, Milton* (Ithaca, NY: Cornell University Press, 2004)
Evrigenis, Ioannis D., 'Sovereignty, Mercy, and Natural Law: King James VI/I and Jean Bodin', *History of European Ideas*, 49.8 (2019), 1073–88
Fabre, Adolphe, *Études historiques sur les clercs de la Basoche suivies des pièces justificatives* (Paris: Potier, 1856)

Feenstra, Robert, 'L'École de droit d'Orléans au treizième siècle et son rayonnement dans l'Europe médiévale', *Revue d'histoire des facultés de droit et de la science juridique*, 13 (1992), 23–42
Finkelpearl, Philip J., *John Marston of the Middle Temple: An Elizabethan Dramatist in his Social Setting* (Cambridge, MA: Harvard University Press, 1969)
Fletcher, Anthony, *Tudor Rebellions* (London: Longmans, 1973)
Fortier, Mark, *The Culture of Equity in Early Modern England* (Aldershot: Ashgate, 2005)
Fox, Alistair, and John H. Guy, eds, *Reassessing the Henrician Age: Humanism, Politics and Reform, 1500–1550* (Oxford: Blackwell, 1986)
Fryde, Natalie, *The Tyranny and Fall of Edward II* (Cambridge: Cambridge University Press, 1979)
Geng, Penelope, *Communal Justice in Shakespeare's England: Drama, Law, and Emotion* (Toronto: University of Toronto Press, 2021)
Giesey, Ralph E., *Le Rôle méconnu de la loi salique: La succession royale XIVe–XVIIe siècles* (Paris: Belles Lettres, 2007)
———, *The Royal Funeral Ceremony in Renaissance France* (Geneva: Droz, 1960)
Gilson, Étienne, *La Philosophie au Moyen Âge* (Paris: Payot, 1922)
———, *Reason and Revelation in the Middle Ages*, ed. by William J. Courtenay, Richards Lectures (New York, 1938; repr. Turnhout: Brepols, 2020)
Goldberg, Jonathan, *James I and the Politics of Literature* (Baltimore: Johns Hopkins University Press, 1983)
Goldsworthy, Jeffrey D., *The Sovereignty of Parliament: History and Philosophy* (Oxford: Oxford University Press, 1999)
Goodrich, Peter, *Oedipus Lex: Psychoanalysis, History, Law* (Berkeley: University of California Press, 1995)
Goy-Blanquet, Dominique, '"Ces petits livres en français de Messieurs les Hotman": Peacemaking in a/the European Family', in *Early Modern Diplomacy, Theatre and Soft Power: The Making of Peace*, ed. by Nathalie Rivère de Carles (London: Palgrave Macmillan, 2016), pp. 47–68
———, *Côté cour, côté justice: Shakespeare et l'invention du droit* (Paris: Didier, 2016)
———, 'Dance of Death, or Bread and Circuses? The Murders of Julius Caesar', in *The Roman Plays*, ed. by Sarah Hatchuel and Nathalie Vienne-Guerrin (Rouen: Publications de l'Université de Rouen, 2009), pp. 123–42
———, 'Images de la monarchie dans le théâtre historique de Shakespeare', in *Les Voies de la création théâtrale*, vol. VIII, ed. by Elie Königson (Paris: CNRS, 1980), pp. 93–138
———, 'La Solitude de Coriolan', *Études anglaises*, 59.4 (2006), 387–400
———, 'Lord Keeper Bacon and the Writing on the Wall', *Law and Humanities*, 4.2 (2010), 211–28
———, 'The More Part: Upstaging the Law', *Law and Humanities*, 3.2 (2009), 151–74
———, 'Richard II ou l'art de la mise en scène', in *Richard II de William Shakespeare, une œuvre en contexte*, ed. by I. Schwartz-Gastine (Caen: Cahiers MRSH, 2005), pp. 99–111

———, 'Shakespeare and Voltaire Set Fire to History', in *Joan of Arc: A Saint for All Reasons*, ed. by D. Goy-Blanquet (Aldershot: Ashgate, 2003), pp. 1–38

———, *Shakespeare's Early History Plays: From Chronicle to Stage* (Oxford: Oxford University Press, 2003)

———, 'Shakespeare's Unholy Martyrs: Lessons in Politics', in *Shakespeare and Rome*, ed. by Peter Holland, *Shakespeare Survey*, LXIX (Cambridge: Cambridge University Press, 2016), pp. 141–52

———, 'The Silences of Sir Thomas More', in *Publish and Perish: The Practice of Censorship in the British Isles in the Early Modern Period*, ed. by Isabelle Fernandes (Wilmington: Vernon Press, 2020), pp. 73–88

———, '"This Realm Is an Empire": Tales of Origins in Medieval and Early Modern France and England', in *Interweaving Myths in Shakespeare and his Contemporaries*, ed. by Janice Valls-Russell and others (Manchester: Manchester University Press, 2017), pp. 65–85

———, 'Titus Resartus: Warner, Stein, and Mesguich Have a Cut at *Titus Andronicus*', in *Foreign Shakespeare: Contemporary Performance*, ed. by Dennis Kennedy (Cambridge: Cambridge University Press, 1993), pp. 36–55

———, 'Translating Europe into your England', in *Shakespeare and European Politics*, ed. by Dirk Delabastita, Josef de Vos, and Paul Franssen (Plainsboro, NJ: Associated University Presses, 2008), pp. 286–303

Graves, Michael A. R., *Thomas Norton, the Parliament Man* (Oxford: Blackwell, 1994)

Greenblatt, Stephen, *Hamlet in Purgatory* (Princeton, NJ: Princeton University Press, 2013)

———, *Renaissance Self-Fashioning: From More to Shakespeare* (Chicago: University of Chicago Press, 2005)

———, *Shakespearean Negotiations: The Circulation of Social Energy in Renaissance England* (Berkeley: University of California Press, 1988)

Gunn, S. J., 'The Courtiers of Henry VII', *English Historical Review*, 108.426 (1993), 23–49

Gurr, Andrew, *The Shakespeare Company, 1594–1642* (Cambridge: Cambridge University Press, 2004)

———, *The Shakespearian Playing Companies* (Oxford: Oxford University Press, 1996)

Gurr, Andrew, and Farah Karim-Cooper, eds. *Moving Shakespeare Indoors: Performance and Repertoire in the Jacobean Playhouse* (Cambridge: Cambridge University Press, 2014)

Guy, John A., *Christopher St German on Chancery and Statute* (London: Selden Society, 1985)

———, 'Henry VIII and the *Praemunire* Manoeuvres of 1530–1531', *English Historical Review*, 97.384 (1982), 481–503

———, 'Law, Lawyers and the English Reformation', *History Today*, 35.11 (1985), 16–22

———, *Politics, Law and Counsel in Tudor and Early Stuart England* (Aldershot: Ashgate, 2000)

———, *The Public Career of Sir Thomas More* (New Haven: Yale University Press, 1980)

———, *Queen of Scots: The True Life of Mary Stuart* (New York: Mariner Books, 2005)

———, ed., *The Reign of Elizabeth I: Court and Culture in the Last Decade* (Cambridge: Cambridge University Press, 1995)

———, *Tudor England* (Oxford: Oxford University Press, 1988)

Guy, John A., and H. G. Beale, eds, *Law and Social Change in British History* (London: Royal Historical Society, 1984)

Hadfield, Andrew, *Shakespeare and Republicanism* (Cambridge: Cambridge University Press, 2005)

Halsey, Katie, and Angus Vine, eds, *Shakespeare and Authority: Citations, Conceptions and Constructions* (London: Palgrave Macmillan, 2018)

Happé, Peter, and Wim Hüsken, eds, *Interludes and Early Modern Society* (Amsterdam: Rodopi, 2007)

Harvey, Howard J., *The Theatre of the Basoche, the Contribution of the Law Societies to French Mediaeval Comedy* (Cambridge, MA: Harvard University Press, 1941)

Harvey, I. M. H., *Jack Cade's Rebellion of 1450* (Oxford: Oxford University Scholarship, 1991)

Haskins, Charles H., 'England and Sicily in the Twelfth Century', *English Historical Review*, 26.103 (1911), 433–47 (pts I–II); 26.104 (1911), 641–65 (pts III–IV)

Hawkes, David, *The Culture of Usury in Renaissance England* (London: Macmillan, 2010)

Heath, James, *Torture and English Law: An Administrative and Legal History from the Plantagenets to the Stuarts* (Westport, CT: Greenwood Press, 1982)

Heller, Herbert Jack, *Penitent Brothellers: Grace, Sexuality and Genre in Thomas Middleton's City Comedies* (Plainsboro, NJ: Associated University Presses, 2000)

Hill, Christopher, *Society and Puritanism in Pre-Revolutionary England* (New York: St Martin's Press, 1997)

Hogrefe, Pearl, *The Life and Times of Sir Thomas Elyot, Englishman* (Ames: Iowa State University Press, 1967)

Holdsworth, William S., *A History of English Law* (London: Methuen, 1924)

Hollister, C. Warren, and John W. Baldwin, 'The Rise of Administrative Kingship: Henry I and Philip Augustus', *American Historical Review*, 83 (1987), 867–905

Holt, J. C., 'The Ancient Constitution in Medieval England', in *The Roots of Liberty: Magna Carta, Ancient Constitution, and the Anglo-American Tradition of Rule of Law*, ed. by Ellis Sandoz (Indianapolis: Liberty Fund, 2008), pp. 32–76

Honoré, Tony, *Emperors and Lawyers: With a Palingenesia of Third-Century Imperial Rescripts, 193–305 AD* (Oxford: Clarendon Press, 1994)

Houben, Hubert, *Roger II of Sicily: A Ruler between East and West* (Cambridge: Cambridge University Press, 2002)

Houliston, Victor, *Catholic Resistance in Elizabethan England: Robert Persons's Jesuit Polemic, 1580–1610* (London: Routledge, 2016)

Hudson, Anne, '*Piers Plowman* and the Peasants' Revolt: A Problem Revisited', *Yearbook of Langland Studies*, 8 (1994), 85–106

Hudson, Winthrop C., *The Cambridge Connection and the Elizabethan Settlement of 1559* (Durham, NC: Duke University Press, 1980)

Hugo, François-Victor, 'La Patrie, I', in *Œuvres complètes de W. Shakespeare*, trans. by F.-V. Hugo, XI, *Introduction* (Paris: Pagnerre, 1872), pp. 7–81

Hunt, Alice, *The Drama of Coronation: Medieval Ceremony in Early Modern England* (Cambridge: Cambridge University Press, 2008)

Hutson, Lorna, *The Invention of Suspicion: Law and Mimesis in Shakespeare and Renaissance Drama* (Oxford: Oxford University Press, 2007)

———, 'On the Knees of the Body Politic', *Representations*, 152 (2020), 25–54

———, ed., *The Oxford Handbook of English Law and Literature, 1500–1700* (Oxford: Oxford University Press, 2017)

———, *The Usurer's Daughter: Male Friendships and Fictions of Women in Sixteenth-Century England* (London: Routledge, 1994)

Iser, Wolfgang, *Staging Politics: The Lasting Impact of Shakespeare's Histories* (New York: Columbia University Press, 1993)

Ives, Eric P., *The Common Lawyers of Pre-Reformation England: Thomas Kebell, a Case Study* (Cambridge: Cambridge University Press, 1983)

Jackson, Richard A., *Vive le Roi! A History of the French Coronation from Charles V to Charles X* (Chapel Hill: University Press of North Carolina, 1984)

Jacquot, Jean, ed., *Les Tragédies de Sénèque et le théâtre de la Renaissance* (Paris: CNRS, 1973)

James, Henry, and Greg Walker, 'The Politics of *Gorboduc*', *English Historical Review*, 110.435 (1995), 109–21

Jardine, David, *Criminal Trials* (London: Charles Knight, 1832)

———, *A Reading on the Use of Torture in the Criminal Law of England* (London: Baldwin & Craddock, 1837)

Jardine, Lisa, and Alan Stewart, *Hostage to Fortune: The Troubled Life of Francis Bacon* (New York: Hill & Wang, 1999)

Johnston, Alexandra, 'The Plays of the Religious Guilds of York: The Creed Play and the Pater Noster Play', *Speculum*, 50.1 (1975), 55–90

Jones, Norman L., *The English Reformation: Religion and Cultural Adaptation* (Oxford: Blackwell, 2002)

———, *Faith by Statute: Parliament and the Settlement of Religion, 1559* (London: Royal Historical Society, 1982)

———, *God and the Moneylenders: Usury and Law in Early Modern England* (Oxford: Blackwell, 1989)

Jordan, Constance, and Karen Cunningham, eds, *The Law in Shakespeare* (London: Palgrave Macmillan, 2007)

Julia, Dominique, ed., *Culture et Société dans l'Europe moderne et contemporaine* (Florence: Institut Universitaire Européen, 1992)

Kahn, Victoria, and Lorna Hutson, eds, *Rhetoric and Law in Early Modern Europe* (New Haven: Yale University Press, 2001)

Kantorowicz, Ernst H., *Frederick the Second, 1194–1250*, trans. by E. O. Lorimer [from *Kaiser Friedrich der Zweite* (Stuttgart: Klett-Cotta, 1927)] (London: Constable, 1957)

———, *The King's Two Bodies: A Study in Mediaeval Political Theology* (Princeton, NJ: Princeton University Press, 1957)

———, *'Laudes regiae': A Study in Medieval Acclamations and Liturgical Worship* (Berkeley: University of California Publishings in History, 1958)

———, 'Mysteries of State: An Absolutist Concept and its Late Mediaeval Origins', *Harvard Theological Review*, 48.1 (1955), 65–91

Kantorowicz, Hermann, *Studies in the Glossators of the Roman Law: Newly Discovered Writings of the Twelfth Century* (Cambridge: Cambridge University Press, 1938)

Karim-Cooper, Farah, ed., *Titus Andronicus: The State of Play* (London: Arden Shakespeare, 2019)

Kelley, Donald R., *François Hotman: A Revolutionary's Ordeal* (Princeton, NJ: Princeton University Press, 1983)

Kelly, Henry A., *Divine Providence in the England of Shakespeare's Histories* (Cambridge, MA: Harvard University Press, 1970)

———, 'Thomas More on Inquisitorial Due Process', *English Historical Review*, 123.503 (2008), 847–94

Kenyon, John P., *The Stuart Constitution, 1603–1688: Documents and Commentary* (Cambridge: Cambridge University Press, 1986)

Kernan, Alvin, *Shakespeare, the King's Playwright* (New Haven: Yale University Press, 1995)

Kerrigan, John, *Revenge Tragedy: Aeschylus to Armageddon* (Oxford: Clarendon Press, 1994)

Kezar, Dennis, ed., *Solon and Thespis: Law and Theater in the English Renaissance* (Notre Dame, IN: University of Notre Dame Press, 2007)

Kilcullen, John, 'Ockham and Infallibility', *Journal of Religious History*, 16 (1991), 387–409

———, 'Ockham's Political Writings', in *The Cambridge Companion to Ockham*, ed. by Paul Vincent Spade (Cambridge: Cambridge University Press, 1999), pp. 302–26

Kilroy, Gerard, *Edmund Campion, a Scholarly Life* (Farnham: Ashgate, 2015)

Knapp, Jeffrey, *Shakespeare's Tribe: Church, Nation and Theater in Renaissance England* (Chicago: University of Chicago Press, 2002)

Knowles, James, *Politics and Political Culture in the Court Masque* (London: Palgrave Macmillan, 2015)

König-Pralon, Catherine, *Avènement de l'aristotélisme en terre chrétienne* (Paris: Vrin, 2005)

Kornstein, Daniel, *Kill All the Lawyers? Shakespeare's Legal Appeal* (Princeton, NJ: Princeton University Press, 1994)

Krontiris, Tina, *Oppositional Voices: Women as Writers and Translators of Literature in the English Renaissance* (London: Routledge, 1992)

Krynen, Jacques, *L'Empire du roi: Idées et croyances politiques en France, XIIIe–XVe siècles* (Paris: Gallimard, 1993)

Kyle, Chris R., *Theater of State: Parliament and Political Culture in Early Stuart England* (Stanford: Stanford University Press, 2012)

Labarge, Margaret Wade, *Saint Louis: The Life of Louis IX of France* (London: Eyre & Spottiswoode, 1968)

Langbein, John H., *Origins of Adversary Criminal Trial* (Oxford: Oxford University Press, 2005)
Lapsley, Gaillard T., *Crown, Community and Parliament in the later Middle Ages* (Oxford: Blackwell, 1951)
Laynesmith, J. L., *The Last Medieval Queens: English Queenship 1445–1503* (Oxford: Oxford University Press, 2005)
Lazarus, Micha, 'Greek Literacy in Sixteenth-Century England', *Renaissance Studies*, 29.3 (2014), 433–58
———, 'Tragedy at Wittenberg: Sophocles in Renaissance Europe', *Renaissance Quarterly*, 73.1 (2020), 33–77
Le Goff, Jacques, *The Birth of Purgatory*, trans. by Arthur Goldhammer [from *La naissance du Purgatoire* (Paris: Gallimard, 1991)] (Chicago: University of Chicago Press, 1986)
———, *Héros du Moyen Âge, le Saint et le Roi* (Paris: Quarto Gallimard, 2004)
Lehmberg, Stanford E., 'Parliamentary Attainder in the Reign of Henry VIII', *Historical Journal*, 18.4 (1975), 675–702
———, *The Reformation Parliament, 1529–1536* (Cambridge: Cambridge University Press, 1970)
Leo, Russ, *Tragedy as Philosophy in the Reformation World* (Oxford: Oxford University Press, 2019)
Leroy-Ladurie, Emmanuel, *Le Carnaval de Romans* (Paris: Gallimard, 1977)
Levin, Carole, and John Watkins, *Shakespeare's Foreign Worlds: National and Transnational Identities in the Elizabethan Age* (Ithaca, NY: Cornell University Press, 2009)
Levine, Mortimer, *The Early Elizabethan Succession Question, 1558–1568* (Stanford: Stanford University Press, 1966)
Levy, F. J., *Tudor Historical Thought* (San Marino: The Huntington Library, 1967)
Lewis, Andrew W., *Royal Succession in Capetian France: Studies on Familial Order and the State* (Cambridge, MA: Harvard University Press, 1981)
Lewis, Elizabeth J., *The Trial of Mary Queen of Scots: A Brief History with Documents* (Boston: Bedford/St Martin's Press, 1999)
Lewis, Peter S., 'War Propaganda and Historiography in Fifteenth-Century France and England', *Transactions of the Royal Historical Society*, 5th Ser., 15 (1965), 1–21
Lieberman, F., 'Magister Vacarius', *English Historical Review*, 11.42 (1896), 305–14
Lines, David A., *The Dynamics of Learning in Early Modern Italy: Arts and Medicine at the University of Bologna* (Cambridge, MA: Harvard University Press, 2023)
Lines, David A., and Sabrina Ebbersmeyer, eds, *Rethinking Virtue, Reforming Society: New Directions in Renaissance Ethics, 1350–c. 1650* (Turnhout: Brepols, 2013)
Lobban, Michael, Joanne Begiato, and Adrian Green, eds, *Law, Lawyers and Litigants in Early Modern England: Essays in Memory of Christopher W. Brooks* (Cambridge: Cambridge University Press, 2019)
Lockey, Brian C., *Law and Empire in English Renaissance Literature* (Cambridge: Cambridge University Press, 2006)
Lombard-Jourdan, Anne, *Aux origines de Carnaval* (Paris: Odile Jacob, 2005)
Lucas, Scott C., *'A Mirror for Magistrates' and the Politics of the English Reformation* (Amherst: University Press of Massachusetts, 2009)

Lupton, Julia, *Citizen-Saints: Shakespeare and Political Theology* (Chicago: University of Chicago Press, 2005)

———, 'Judging Forgiveness: Hannah Arendt, W. H. Auden, and *The Winter's Tale*', *New Literary History*, 45 (2014), 641–63

———, *Thinking with Shakespeare: Essays on Politics and Life* (Chicago: University of Chicago Press, 2011)

Lyne, Raphael, *Shakespeare, Rhetoric and Cognition* (Cambridge: Cambridge University Press, 2011)

MacCaffrey, Wallace, *Queen Elizabeth and the Making of Policy, 1572–1588* (Princeton, NJ: Princeton University Press, 1981)

MacCulloch, Diarmaid, *Thomas Cranmer: A Life* (New Haven: Yale University Press, 1996)

Mack, Peter, *Elizabethan Rhetoric: Theory and Practice* (Cambridge: Cambridge University Press, 2002)

Mackie, James, *The Earlier Tudors, 1485–1558* (Oxford: Oxford University Press, 1994)

Maguin, Jean-Marie, *Shakespeare and the Rhetoric of Elocution: Thirteen Plays* (Montpellier: IRCL, Université Paul Valéry, 2017)

Maitland, Frederic W., *The Collected Papers of Frederic William Maitland*, ed. by H. A. L. Fisher (Cambridge: Cambridge University Press, 1911)

———, *English Law and the Renaissance* (Cambridge: Cambridge University Press, 1901)

———, *Equity, also the Forms of Action at Common Law* (Cambridge: Cambridge University Press, 1910)

Maitland, Frederic W., and F. C. Montague, *A Sketch of English Legal History* [1915] (Boston: Elibron Classics, 2001)

Marcus, Leah, *Puzzling Shakespeare: Local Readings and its Discontents* (Berkeley: University of California Press, 1988)

Marienstras, Richard, *New Perspectives on the Shakespearean World*, trans. by Janet Lloyd [from *Le Proche et le Lointain* (Paris: Éditions de Minuit, 1981)] (Cambridge: Cambridge University Press, 1985)

———, *Shakespeare et le désordre du monde*, ed. by D. Goy-Blanquet (Paris: Gallimard, 2012)

Martindale, Charles, and Michelle Martindale, *Shakespeare and the Uses of Antiquity: An Introductory Essay* (London: Routledge, 1990)

———, and A. B. Taylor, eds, *Shakespeare and the Classics* (Cambridge: Cambridge University Press, 2004)

Mayne, Emily, 'Presenting Seneca in Print: Elizabethan Translations and Thomas Newton's *Seneca His Tenne Tragedies*', *Review of English Studies*, 70.297 (2019), 823–46

McCluskey, Peter M., *Representations of Flemish Immigrants on the Early Modern Stage* (London: Routledge, 2019)

McDonald, Russ, *Shakespeare and the Arts of Language* (Oxford: Oxford University Press, 2001)

McEvoy, James J., *Robert Grosseteste* (Oxford: Oxford University Press, 2000)

McGlynn, Margaret, *The Royal Prerogative and the Learning of the Inns of Court* (Cambridge: Cambridge University Press, 2003)

McIlwain, Charles H., *Constitutionalism Ancient and Modern* (Ithaca, NY: Cornell University Press, 1947)
McKendrick, Ewan, *Contract Law: Text, Cases and Material* (Oxford: Oxford University Press, 2012)
McKenna, J. W., 'The Myth of Parliamentary Sovereignty in Late-Medieval England', *English Historical Review*, 94.372 (1979), 481–506
McKeown, Adam, *English Mercuries: Soldier Poets in the Age of Shakespeare* (Nashville, TN: Vanderbilt University Press, 2009)
Mellot, Jean-Dominique, ed., *Productions et usages de l'écrit juridique en France du Moyen Âge à nos jours* (Geneva: Droz, 2005)
Meserve, Margaret, *Empires of Islam in Renaissance Historical Thought* (Cambridge, MA: Harvard University Press, 2008)
Michelet, Jules, *History of the French Revolution*, trans. by C. Cocks (London: H. G. Bohn, 1847)
———, *La Sorcière: The Witch of the Middle Ages*, trans. by Lionel J. Trotter (London: Simpkin, Marshall and Co., 1863)
Miller-Blaise, Anne-Marie '"Bit[ing] the Law by the Nose": Shakespeare's Revisions of Fear and Punishment', *Shakespeare et la peur*, Actes de la Société Française Shakespeare on line (2018), <https://journals.openedition.org/shakespeare/4152>
Milsom, S. F. C., *The Legal Framework of English Feudalism* (Cambridge: Cambridge University Press, 1976)
Mukherji, Subha, *Law and Representation in Early Modern Drama* (Cambridge: Cambridge University Press, 2006)
Neale, John E., *Elizabeth I and her Parliaments*, I, *1559–1581*; II, *1584–1601* (London: Jonathan Cape, 1953–1957)
Nichols, John, *The Progresses and Public Progressions of Queen Elizabeth* (London: Nichols and Son, 1823)
Norbrook, David, *Writing the English Republic: Poetry, Rhetoric and Politics, 1627–1660* (Cambridge: Cambridge University Press, 2000)
Norland, Howard B., 'More's and Elyot's Perspectives and their Classical Antecedents', *Moreana*, 40.153–54 (2003), 120–42
Oberman, Heiko A., *Masters of the Reformation: The Emergence of a New Intellectual Climate in Europe* (Cambridge: Cambridge University Press, 1981)
O'Donovan, Joan Lockwood, *Theology of Law and Authority in the English Reformation* (Atlanta: Scholars Press, 1991)
Orgel, Stephen, *The Illusion of Power: Political Theater in the English Renaissance* (Berkeley: University of California Press, 1975)
Ormrod, W. Mark, *The Reign of Edward III: Crown and Political Society in England, 1327–1377* (Charleston: Tempus, 2004)
Ost, François, *Shakespeare: La Comédie de la Loi* (Paris: Michalon, 2012)
Outhwaite, Richard B., *The Rise and Fall of the Ecclesiastical Courts, 1500–1860* (Cambridge: Cambridge University Press, 2007)
Paradise, N. Burton, *Thomas Lodge: The History of an Elizabethan* (New Haven: Yale University Press, 1931)

Parmiter, Geoffrey de C., *Edmund Plowden: An Elizabethan Recusant Lawyer* (London: Catholic Record Society, 1987)

———, *Elizabethan Popish Recusancy in the Inns of Court* (London: Institute of Historical Research, 1976)

———, *The King's Great Matter: A Study of Anglo-Papal Relations 1527–1534* (London: Longmans, 1967)

Pastore-Stocchi, Manlio, 'Un Chapitre d'histoire littéraire aux XIVe et XVe siècles: "Seneca Poeta Tragicus"', in *Les Tragédies de Sénèque et le théâtre de la Renaissance*, ed. by Jean Jacquot (Paris: CNRS, 1973), pp. 11–36

Patterson, Annabel, *Reading Holinshed's Chronicle* (Chicago: University of Chicago Press, 1994)

———, *Shakespeare and the Popular Voice* (Oxford: Blackwell, 1989)

———, *The Trial of Nicholas Throckmorton* (Toronto: Centre for Reformation and Renaissance Studies, 1998)

Pennington, Kenneth, 'The "Big Bang": Roman Law in the Twelfth Century', *Rivista internazionale di diritto comune*, 18 (2007), 43–70

———, 'The Birth of the "Ius commune": King Roger II's Legislation', *Rivista internazionale di diritto comune*, 17 (2006), 1–40

———, 'Learned Law, Droit Savant, Geltes Recht: The Tyranny of a Concept', *Rivista internazionale di diritto comune*, 5 (1994), 197–209

———, *Popes, Canonists and Texts, 1150–1550* (Aldershot: Variorum, 1993)

Perry, Curtis, 'British Empire on the Eve of the Armada: Revisiting *The Misfortunes of Arthur*', *Studies in Philology*, 108.4 (2011), 508–37

———, *Shakespeare and Senecan Tragedy* (Cambridge: Cambridge University Press, 2020)

Peters, Julie Stone, *Theatre of the Book, 1480–1880: Print, Text and Performance in Europe* (Oxford: Oxford University Press, 2000)

Philips, O. Hood, *Shakespeare and the Lawyers* (London: Routledge, 2005)

Picco, Frédéric, *La Tragédie grecque: La scène et le tribunal* (Paris: Michalon, 1999)

Plucknett, Theodore F. T., *Early English Legal Literature* (Cambridge: Cambridge University Press, 1958)

———, *Studies in English Legal History* (London: Hambledon Press, 1983)

Pocock, G. A., *The Ancient Constitution and the Feudal Law* (Cambridge: Cambridge University Press, 1957)

Pollard, Tanya, *Greek Tragic Women on Shakespearean Stages* (Oxford: Oxford University Press, 2017)

———, ed., *Shakespeare's Theater: A Sourcebook* (Oxford: Blackwell, 2004)

Pollock, J. G. A. and F. W. Maitland, *The History of English Law before the Time of Edward I* (Cambridge: Cambridge University Press, 1898)

Poole, Austin Lane, *Domesday Book to Magna Carta, 1087–1216*, 2nd edn (Oxford: Oxford University Press, 1993)

Poole, Robert, *Time's Alteration: Calendar Reform in Early Modern England* (London: Routledge, 1998)

Post, Gaines, *Studies in Medieval Legal Thought: Public Law and the State, 1100–1322* (Princeton, NJ: Princeton University Press, 1964)
Potter, Robert, *The English Morality Play: Origins, History and Influence of a Dramatic Tradition* (London: Routledge, 1975)
Prest, Wilfrid, *The Inns of Court under Elizabeth I and the Early Stuarts, 1590–1640* (London: Longman, 1972)
———, *The Rise of the Barristers: A Social History of the English Bar, 1590–1640* (Oxford: Clarendon, 1986)
Prestwich, Michael, *Plantagenet England, 1225–1360* (Oxford: Oxford University Press, 2007)
Raffield, Paul, *The Art of Law in Shakespeare* (London: Bloomsbury, 2017)
———, *Images and Cultures of Law in Early Modern England: Justice and Political Power, 1558–1660* (Cambridge: Cambridge University Press, 2004)
———, *Shakespeare's Imaginary Constitution* (Oxford: Hart, 2010)
Rashdall, Hastings, *The Universities of Europe in the Middle Ages* [1895] (Cambridge: Cambridge University Press, 2010)
Read, Conyers, *Mr Secretary Cecil and Queen Elizabeth* (London: Jonathan Cape, 1965)
———, *Mr Secretary Walsingham and the Policy of Queen Elizabeth* (Oxford: Clarendon Press, 1925)
Rebhorn, Wayne A., *The Emperor of Men's Minds: Literature and the Renaissance Discourse of Rhetoric* (Ithaca, NY: Cornell University Press, 1995)
Reed, A. W., *Early Tudor Drama: Medwall, the Rastells, Heywood, and the More Circle* (London: Methuen, 1926)
Rees, Graham, and Maria Wakely, *Printing, Politics, and Culture: The King's Printers in the Reign of James I and VI* (Oxford: Oxford University Press, 2010)
Reynolds, Philip L., *Marriage in the Western Church: The Christianization of Marriage during the Patristic and Early Medieval Periods* (Leiden: Brill, 1994)
Richardson, Henry G., and George O. Sayles, *The English Parliament in the Middle Ages* (London: Hambledon Press, 1981)
———, *Law and Legislation: From Aethelbert to Magna Carta* (Edinburgh: Edinburgh University Press, 1966)
Ricœur, Paul, 'Memory, History, Oblivion', lecture delivered 8 March 2003, 'Haunting Memories? History in Europe after Authoritarianism' conference at the Central European University of Budapest. Fonds Ricœur, October 2010; first published in French in 'La pensée Ricœur', special issue, *Esprit*, March/April 2006)
———, *Memory, History, Forgetting*, trans. by Kathleen Blamey and David Pellauer [from *La Mémoire, l'histoire, l'oubli* (Paris: Seuil, 2000)] (Chicago: University of Chicago Press, 2004)
———, *The Rule of Metaphor: Multi-disciplinary Studies of the Creation of Meaning in Language*, trans. by R. Czerny, K. Mc Laughlin, and J. Costello, SJ [from *La métaphore vive* (Paris: Seuil, 1975)] (London: Routledge, 1986)
Roe, John, *Shakespeare and Machiavelli* (Cambridge: D. S. Brewer, 2002)

Rolls, Albert, *The Theory of the King's Two Bodies in the Age of Shakespeare: Selected Documents* (Lewiston, NY: Edwin Mellen Press, 2006)

Rosenblatt, Jason P., *Renaissance England's Chief Rabbi: John Selden* (Oxford: Oxford University Press, 2006)

Roskell, J. S., *The Commons and their Speakers in English Parliaments, 1376–1523* (Manchester: Manchester University Press, 1965)

Royer, Jean-Pierre, *L'Église et le royaume de France au XIVe siècle d'après le 'Songe du vergier' et la jurisprudence du Parlement* (Paris: Librairie générale de droit, 1969)

Santner, Eric L., *The Royal Remains: The People's Two Bodies or the Remains of Sovereignty* (Chicago: University of Chicago Press, 2011)

Saul, Nigel, *Richard II* (New Haven: Yale University Press, 1997)

Scafuro, Adele, *The Forensic Stage: Settling Disputes in Graeco-Roman New Comedy* (Cambridge: Cambridge University Press, 1997)

Schiavone, Aldo, *IUS: L'invention du droit en Occident*, trans. by Jean Bouffartigue and Geneviève Bouffartigue (Paris: Belin, 2008)

Schoeck, Richard J., 'Aspects of the Inns of Court', *Canadian Catholic Historical Association*, Report no. 32 (1965), 17–45

Scott, Mary A., *Elizabethan Translations from the Italian* (New York: Franklin, 1969)

Scott-Warren, Jason, 'Was Elizabeth I Richard II? The Authenticity of Lambarde's "Conversation"', *Review of English Studies*, 64.264 (2013), 208–30

Secor, Philip B., *Richard Hooker: Prophet of Anglicanism* (Tunbridge Wells: Burns & Oates, 1999)

Sharpe, Kevin, *Sir Robert Cotton, 1586–1631: History and Politics in Early Modern England* (Oxford: Oxford University Press, 2002)

Simpson, Richard, *Edmund Campion, Jesuit Protomartyr* (London: Burns & Oates, 1907)

Skinner, Quentin, *Forensic Shakespeare* (Oxford: Oxford University Press, 2014)

———, *The Foundation of Modern Political Thought* (Cambridge: Cambridge University Press, 1978)

Smalley, Beryl, *The Becket Conflict and the Schools* (Oxford: Blackwell, 1973)

Snow, Vernon, *Parliament in Elizabethan England: John Hooker's Order and Usage* (New Haven: Yale University Press, 1977)

Soetermeer, Frank, *Livres et juristes au Moyen Âge* (Goldbach: Keip Verlag, 1999)

Sokol, B. J., and Mary Sokol, *Shakespeare's Legal Language: A Dictionary* (London: The Athlone Press, 2004)

Soulier, Gérard, *L'Europe: Histoire, civilisation, institutions* (Paris: Armand Colin, 1994)

Southern, Richard W., 'Master Vacarius and the Beginning of an Academic English Tradition', in *Medieval Learning and Literature*, ed. by J. J. G. Alexander and M. T. Gibson (Oxford: Clarendon Press, 1976), pp. 257–86

Stern, Tiffany, *Documents of Performance in Early Modern England* (Cambridge: Cambridge University Press, 2009)

———, '"A Ruinous Monastery": The Second Blackfriars Playhouse as a Place of Nostalgia', in *Moving Shakespeare Indoors: Performance and Repertoire in the Jacobean Playhouse*, ed. by Andrew Gurr and Farah Karim-Cooper (Cambridge: Cambridge University Press, 2014), pp. 97–114

Stow, George B., 'Richard II in Thomas Walsingham's Chronicles', *Speculum*, 59.1 (1984), 68–102

Strain, Virginia Lee, *Legal Reform in English Renaissance Literature* (Edinburgh: Edinburgh University Press, 2018)

Streitberger, W. R., *Court Revels, 1485–1559* (Toronto: University of Toronto Press, 1994)

Sutherland, Donald W., *The Assize of Novel Disseizin* (Oxford: Clarendon Press, 1973)

Suthren, Carla, 'Shakespeare and the Renaissance Reception of Euripides' (PhD dissertation, University of York, 2018)

Taylor, Craig, 'Sir John Fortescue and the French Polemical Treatises of the Hundred Years War', *English Historical Review*, 114.455 (1999), 112–29

Taylor, John, and Wendy R. Childs, eds, *Politics and Crisis in Fourteenth-Century England* (Gloucester: Sutton, 1990)

Thierry, Augustin, *History of the Conquest of England by the Normans, its Causes, and its Consequences, in England, Scotland, Ireland, & on the Continent*, trans. by William Hazlitt (London: H. G. Bohn, 1856)

Thorne, Samuel E., *Essays in English Legal History* (London: Hambledon Press, 1985)

Tierney, Brian, *Foundations of the Conciliar Theory: The Contribution of the Medieval Canonists from Gratian to the Great Schism*, augmented edn (Leiden: Brill, 1998)

———, *Origins of Papal Infallibility, 1150–1350: A Study on the Concepts of Infallibility, Sovereignty and Tradition in the Middle Ages* (Leiden: Brill, 1972)

Tilley, M. P., *Dictionary of the Proverbs in England in the Sixteenth and Seventeenth Centuries* (Ann Arbor: University Press of Michigan, 1950)

Tittler, Robert, *Nicholas Bacon: The Making of a Tudor Statesman* (London: Jonathan Cape, 1976)

Toomer, G. J., 'Selden's "Historie of Tithes": Genesis, Publication, Aftermath', *Huntington Library Quarterly*, 65.3/4 (2002), 345–78

Turchetti, Mario, *Tyrannie et tyrannicide de l'Antiquité à nos jours* (Paris: Presses Universitaires de France, 2001)

Turner, Ralph V., *Judges, Administrators and the Common Law in Angevin England* (London: Hambledon Press, 1994)

Tutino, Stefania, *Empire of Souls: Robert Bellarmine and the Christian Commonwealth* (Oxford: Oxford University Press, 2010)

Ullmann, Walter, *Principles of Government and Politics in the Middle Ages* (London: Methuen, 1974)

———, 'This Realm of England Is an Empire', *Journal of Ecclesiastical History*, 30 (1979), 175–203

Valente, Clare, 'The Deposition and Abdication of Edward II', *English Historical Review*, 113.453 (1998), 852–81

Vaughan, Richard, *Matthew Paris* (Cambridge: Cambridge University Press, 1958)

Vernant, Jean-Pierre, and Pierre Vidal-Naquet, *Myth and Tragedy in Ancient Greece*, trans. by Janet Lloyd (New York: Zone Books, 1988)

Vickers, Brian, ed., *Essential Articles for the Study of Francis Bacon* (Hamden, CT: Archon Books, 1968)

———, *In Defence of Rhetoric* (Oxford: Clarendon Press, 1988)

Walker, Greg, *Plays of Persuasion: Drama and Politics at the Court of Henry VIII* (Cambridge: Cambridge University Press, 1991)

———, *The Politics of Performance in Early Renaissance Drama* (Cambridge: Cambridge University Press, 1998)

———, *Writing under Tyranny: English Literature and the Henrician Reformation* (Oxford: Oxford University Press, 2005)

Walker, Julia M., 'Reading the Tombs of Elizabeth I', *English Literary Renaissance*, 26.3 (1996), 510–30

Wallace-Hadrill, J. M., *Early Germanic Kingship in England and the Continent* (Oxford: Oxford University Press, 1971)

Ward, Allyna F., *Women in Tudor Tragedy: Feminizing Counsel and Representing Gender* (Madison, NJ: Fairleigh Dickinson University Press, 2013)

Ward, Ian, *Law and Literature: Possibilities and Perspectives* (Cambridge: Cambridge University Press, 1995)

———, *Shakespeare and the Legal Imagination* (Cambridge: Cambridge University Press, 1999)

Watson, Alan, *Legal Origins and Legal Change* (London: Hambledon Press, 1991)

Watt, Gary, *Equity Stirring: The Story of Justice Beyond Law* (Oxford: Hart, 2012)

———, *Shakespeare's Acts of Will: Law, Testament and Property* (London: Bloomsbury, 2016)

Weisberg, Richard, *Poethics: And Other Strategies of Law and Literature* (New York: Columbia University Press, 1992)

Wendel, François, *Calvin: Source et évolution de sa pensée religieuse* (Geneva: Labor et Fides, 1985)

Wilson, Luke, *Theatres of Intention: Drama and the Law in Early Modern England* (Stanford: Stanford University Press, 2000)

Winston, Jessica, *Lawyers at Play: Literature, Law, and Politics at the Early Modern Inns of Court, 1558–1581* (Oxford: Oxford University Press, 2016)

———, 'Literary Associations of the Middle Temple', in *Middle Temple History*, ed. by Richard Havery (Oxford: Hart, 2011), pp. 147–71

———, 'Seneca in Early Elizabethan England', *Renaissance Quarterly*, 59.1 (2006), 29–58

Withington, Phil, 'The Inns of Court, Renaissance and the Language of Modernity', in *Law, Lawyers and Litigants in Early Modern England: Essays in Memory of Christopher W. Brooks*, ed. by Michael Lobban, Joanne Begiato, and Adrian Green (Cambridge: Cambridge University Press, 2019), ch. 6, pp. 114–39

Wolffe, B. P., *The Royal Demesne in English History: The Crown Estates in the Governance of the Realm from the Conquest to 1509* (London: Allen & Unwin, 1971)

Wood, Andy, *The 1549 Rebellions and the Making of Early Modern England* (Cambridge: Cambridge University Press, 2007)

Wood, James, *The Broken Estate: Essays on Literature and Belief* (New York: Random House, 1999)

Woodbridge, Linda, *English Revenge Drama: Money, Resistance, Equality* (Cambridge: Cambridge University Press, 2010)

Woolfson, Jonathan, *Padua and the Tudors: English Students in Italy, 1485–1603* (Cambridge: James Clark and Co., 1999)
Young, Archibald, 'Christopher Saint-German's *Doctor and Student*: From Legal Debate to Religious Division', *Moreana*, 37.143–44 (2000), 39–76
Zane, John Maxcy, *The Story of Law* (New York: Ives Washburn, 1927)
Ziskind, Martha A., 'John Selden: Criticism and Affirmation of the Common Law Tradition', *American Journal of Legal History*, 19.1 (1975), 22–39
Zulueta, Francis de, and Peter Stein, *The Teaching of Roman Law in England around 1200* (London: Selden Society, 1990)
Zurcher, Andrew, *Shakespeare and Law* (London: Arden Shakespeare, 2010; repr. London: Bloomsbury, 2014)

Index of Acts, Statutes, and Treatises

Index of Plays, Poems, Dialogues, and Masques

(Plays by Shakespeare are listed at the end)

Shakespeare

General Index